# Ars Magica

## THE STORYTELLING GAME OF MYTHIC MAGIC

WIZARDS OF THE COAST

# Ars Magica™ Third Edition Credits

**Development:** Ken Cliffe

**Design:** Ken Cliffe, Mark Rein•Hagen, Jonathan Tweet

**Design Contribution:** Andrew Greenburg, Wes Harris, Lisa Stevens, Stewart Wieck

**Authors:** Shannon Appel, Sam Chupp, Ken Cliffe, Chistopher Earley, Sarah Link, Dave P. Martin, Mark Rein•Hagen, Carl Schurr, John Snead, Travis Lamar Williams

**Editing:** Ken Cliffe, Rob Hatch

**Cover Art:** David O. Miller

**Cover Design:** Richard Thomas

**Magic Hand-Signs:** Charles Wright

**Interior Art:** John Bridges, Jeff Echevarria, Eric Hotz, Chris McDonough, Darrell Midgette, David O. Miller, William O'Connor, Richard Thomas, Josh Timbrook, Bryon Wackwitz, Ken Widing

**Cartography:** Eric Hotz

**Production:** Sam Chupp, Leigh Ann Hilderbrand-Chupp, Chris McDonough, Josh Timbrook

**ArsMagica™** originally designed by Jonathan Tweet and Mark Rein•Hagen

Special Thanks to Lisa Stevens

**Playtesters:** Carl Schnurr, Sarah Link, John Snead, Shannon Appel, Robert G. Schroeder, Peter Hentges, Tim Carroll, Travis Lemar Williams, Craig Neumeier, Gene Alloway, Ian Barkley, Brad Bloom, Piers Brown, James Lynn, Mike Minnotte, Fred Parham, Paul Sherliker, Chistopher Earley, Dave P. Martin, John Porter, Phillippe Queinnec, Esther Reeves, Richard Tomasso, Chris Benson, Darryl Anderson, Shawn Pullman, Bert Dinger, Sterling Coleman, Cliff Smudricks, Bobby Dinger, Kevin Spillman

# Table of Contents

# DOUBLE, DOUBLE TOIL AND TROUBLE; FIRE BURN AND CAULDRON BUBBLE.

It was not Jeremy's fault that he possessed the gift. He was cursed with it, the fault of a long-dead mother who had ventured too far into the faerie forest. Ever since childhood he heard the voices. Everyone in his village dismissed his ramblings as the noise of madness. No one would believe that the spirits of the dead were calling to him.

But the voices in his head grew, and on All Hallow's Eve, the callings became so overwhelming he felt he would burst without their telling. Thus it was that the villagers were horrified by Jeremy's talk of things only long-dead loved ones could know, things only spirits could whisper, and fiery brands were taken up.

Outcast and a beggar on the streets of Toulouse, Jeremy was at first frightened by the dark cloaked strangers who found him and offered him asylum. Their home was a looming tower carved from unnatural rock, a monument of cold stone, a corrupt rocky finger thrust from the earth. Thus it was that Jeremy was initiated into the mysterious arts of sorcery.

But with time, there arose in Jeremy's mind one voice, a strangely compelling voice, that spoke louder than all the rest. It goaded him to deeds forbidden by his masters, and its will he could not resist. The voice seemed to come from within, from his looking glass image, from something terrible, something terrifying.

And he could smell brimstone. . .

# Introduction

In a dark, dismal world where nobles wage their petty wars, friars preach to forlorn flocks, and rogues scrounge for ill-gotten wealth, a mystical order of wizards dwells on the outskirts of medieval civilization, dedicated to arcane pursuits. As sages of great lore and unrivalled potency, these sorcerers face the perils of a grim, desperate world, perils that peasants dare not even speak of. Gathered together as the enigmatic Order of Hermes, these wizards struggle against internal intrigue and persecution from without by those who do not care to understand their art. Though magic pervades the world of Mythic Europe, only these few gifted individuals, after grueling years of apprenticeship, have mastered *ars magica*—the art of magic.

In **Ars Magica** you assume the role of such a person; you are a wizard. Far from a simple weaver of charms, you are an educated and dedicated practitioner of the magical arts. As a Magus you stand in stark contrast to the rest of medieval society. While the mundanes are ignorant, largely illiterate, bound to a decadent hierarchy, and fearful of what lies beyond their villages, you are learned, free from social restraint, and willing to explore the mysteries of the unknown.

Though you study incessantly, you occasionally venture forth from your tower to gather magical ingredients for enchantments, to obtain new knowledge, and to assist those who warrant your aid. On these journeys you are accompanied by your companions and henchmen who advise and guard you from the perils of the world. These expeditions are the heart of **Ars Magica**, and enabling you to tell the stories of these journeys is the purpose of this book.

## MAGIC

Magic is the essence of **Ars Magica**. Magic is everywhere, and its existence affects every detail of life, almost always in the most subtle of ways. Magic is a mysterious and mercurial force, not a precise science, that cannot easily be harnessed to the whims of mortals. Magic is the supernatural force, the invisible connection, that binds everything together. It is, according the Order of Hermes, the very fabric of reality itself. Magic is a way of thinking about reality that modern people no longer find appropriate or useful. Magic is the medium you command in your pursuit of transcendence.

On one level you, as a Magus, explore the subtle connections of magic to exploit them and use the power gained, just as modern man exploits scientific laws to create new technology. Your exploitation of magic is a direct, albeit dangerous, means to inhuman potence. The best wizards, however, are driven by a need completely different from the mere acquisition of power. They investigate magic to understand the universe, just as our best physicists search for a unified field theory to understand our universe. Indeed, Magi may be considered scientists of a sort, operating in a completely different paradigm from ours, and with a completely different set of natural laws from ours, but using the same techniques we do to classify and understand the environment in which they live. They study reality, and use their knowledge in order to manipulate it.

As a Magus, power and knowledge are the forces that motivate you. Which you pursue is left to your will. You may begin your vocation by searching for better ways to put magic to practical use. In so doing you gain power, as your discoveries give you an advantage over the surrounding world and other wizards. However, as Magi grow older, more arcane and diverse matters attract their interest, and may likewise entice you. It is thus that curiosity often overwhelms ambition, luring you from the path of ambition to one of obscure obsession or greater benevolence.

With the pursuit of magic, whether for reasons of power or enlightenment, there also inevitably emerges a lure from the safe boundaries of human society and understanding. Your magical pursuits may lead you into encounters with enigmatic faeries in their deep, oppressive forests, with deceitful demons forever seeking to drag your soul down to perdition, with fierce griffins lurking in barren wastelands, with looming giants in their mountain caves, and with mysterious magical pools which provide insights into the secrets of human existence. Once you devote yourself to magic and its rewards, you must face those who are also attuned to magic. They, like you, are travelers on the road of the arcane, and in sharing that road, all eventually converge.

# Covenants

Some wizards, paranoid that rivals might steal their hard-won lore, live alone and in secrecy. The vast majority, however, live together in small communities bound by vows of friendship and cooperation. Without these vows, no matter how tenuous, Magi could not pursue their art and would surely perish to the xenophobic hordes of Mythic Europe.

The Covenant is the housing of the Magi. A Covenant is a self-sufficient collegium of magical learning where wizards gather for protection and to share resources. It is usually located in some remote magical area far from civilization, where magical forces can be more easily controlled and gathered, and closed-minded mundanes distanced. While Covenants can be of any size, most have fewer than a dozen members. However, many others besides Magi call the Covenant home. And, in **Ars Magica**, the stories of these lesser Covenant inhabitants are as important as those of their mystical masters.

The folk who reside in the Covenant and serve the Magi include mercenary guards, grizzled cooks, itinerant scholars, haughty servants, nervous scribes, stolid artisans, crafty spies, and assorted adventurers and hang-abouts. The Covenant supports and protects these individuals. In return they serve the Covenant. It is the classic feudal arrangement: the servants and masters form a contract, and each must fulfill their side of the agreement if they wish for it to prosper. Though not members of the three feudal classes — those who work, pray and war — most covenfolk relate to Magi in the same manner they would a liege lord, and accord great loyalty to those whom they give their allegiance. Thus it is that Magi and their servants live together as a social group, almost like a family, and must work together for a

mutually satisfying existence in an otherwise fatalistic world.

# The Order of Hermes

Binding all Covenants and all Magi together is the Order of Hermes. This mystical order of wizards is the one thing that brings otherwise disparate Magi together. Whereas most Magi care little for the activities of their foreign brethren, the Order of Hermes unites all who belong to it. And, belonging to the Order of Hermes, you gain the opportunity to learn from your peers without threat of harm, for such unlawful feuding would result in immediate retribution from those who seek to preserve the peace. Yes, Magi are an individualistic lot, and spare little love for one another. But, they realize that their lives have the potential to be hundreds of years long and that those who could most easily cut that life short are other Magi. By living within the Order and avoiding mortal combat with one another, Magi insure their livelihood. As a Magus, you belong to the Order of Hermes, and, as a member of that Order, must obey its dictates under punishment of death.

Central to the Order of Hermes is its Code, which regulates the activities of Magi, both among their peers and in society at large. By obeying the Code to the letter your safe existence is veritable fact. The Code specifies what you may do and who you may associate with. Just as it states that you may not act against other Magi, it restricts your relations with mundanes, both common folk and those of the Church. By adhering to the Code's demands, your safety is assured – no Magus can act against you without reprisal, and no mortal force is made aware of your existence; the paranoia of mortals is not inflamed and does not burn you without the exposure of your flesh. So functions the Code of Hermes. Unfortunately, few Magi follow the strictures so closely, for greater magical potency can be garnered through actions against other Magi, and actions involving mundanes. Thus, many Magi risk their own lives, and the stability of the Order itself, for their own pursuits.

# Mythic Europe
## 1220 A.D.

GROUND SCALE (miles)

0    100    200    300    400

# CONFLICT

Yes, the defiance of the Code by Hermetic Magi brings conflict with the common folk of the world. The Order of Hermes is a threat to the hierarchy of mortal society since Magi bow to neither Baron nor Bishop; the nobility and clergy resent any challenge to their tenuous power. True, the Order is powerful enough to protect its members from most harassment, but the knight's courage and the priest's prayers have supernatural powers of their own. Thus, Magi rarely attack mundane foes in open warfare, and those that do are often forsaken by their brethren, left to mortal whim to protect the Order from reprisal that cannot be countered.

Given this relative balance of power, there has long been a shaky peace between Hermetic and mundane factions. And yet, fanatic voices within the Order and Church have long called for an end to the uneasy truce. Fortunately, cooler heads have prevailed and the fragile order of Mythic Europe has not been turned on its ear by a war that could rock the very foundation of reality. Whether this delicate calm will persist is another question, and as a Magus, you may help preserve or shatter the status quo.

# The Medieval World

In the distant days of old, long before the dawn of science, there existed a people of pride and pageantry, of glory and grace, of sour suspicion and dark savagery. They were our ancestors, either in blood or spirit, but they lived in a different world than ours. Where we see light they saw darkness. Where we see hope, they saw despair. Where we believe we understand the true nature of things, they knew only their own blindness.

These were the people of the medieval world, people who lived in what we now know as the Middle Ages, the Dark Ages, and as the age of Chivalry. They spoke of themselves through song and poetry, and the beauty of their art remains with

us still; it is hard to dismiss the majesty of the cathedrals. We have all heard tales of the bravery of Sir Lancelot, the ferocity of Faerie stags, and the foreboding power that true love, destiny and black magic had over people. The age's heroes were unlike any of ours – Sir Roland and Saint George were of a different breed than Rambo and the Terminator – but were heroes all the same, revered as Knights imbued with divine blessing. And, in these "dark times," people believed in the supernatural, the same supernatural that we dismiss in fairy tales, treating it as an integral part of life. Indeed, medieval folk believed in magic.

In **Ars Magica** we assume that the medieval person's beliefs and values were correct, and thus real. This means the supernatural flourishes across the land, and that faeries, sprites, unicorns, dragons, demons and wizards roam the world. Nay, rule the world.

In **Ars Magica**, the imagined is real, and the real is whatever we imagine it to be.

# MYTHIC EUROPE

**Ars Magica** is set in a mythical version of Thirteenth Century Europe. Though the rules can easily be modified for any fantasy setting, they are designed to bring out the flavor of the Middle Ages and are perhaps best used to that end. This setting is not simply historical; it is meant to evoke a certain flavor, a certain grandeur. The setting is Mythic Europe.

Mythic Europe, the world of **Ars Magica**, is the world the way medieval folk believe it to be. It is as magical as they imagine it, and as full of frightening possibilities. It is a mythic setting, and poetic justice is part of everyday life. As even lowly peasants deal with the supernatural by some means — hags' curses haunt them, charms and saints' relics protect them from the evil eye, and simple prayers hold at bay the invisible demons that stalk the night — they too have a part in determining what is real. Some leave food on boulders to appease forest spirits, and then go to church to pray for forgiveness. Everyone with nightmares of what dwells in the dark has a hand in making real what lurks there. Imagination is the key to reality. The world is alive with mythic significance.

The beliefs of medieval folk are actually the inspiration for their fears. The Church is the pinnacle of creation and value, so all that lies outside its dominion is considered dangerous, unpredictable, and profane. The dangers we fear, such as accidents, crime, and war, may be threatening to us, but they are also natural and their causes easily discernable. A medieval peasant, on the other hand, does not fear such things. To her, the ravages of war and disease are commonplace and accepted as facts of life. It is the unknown that she fears. She fears that which is mythic made real.

The medieval person's perception of the world has no basis in logic or scientific rigor. No, they see connections in reality that we do not believe exist. Intuitive, universal principles, rather than concepts of genes, germs, and gestation, are what guide the world to the medieval mind. In short, the medieval paradigm is fundamentally different from our own. It is a different reality. For instance, in Mythic Europe an inclination towards evil is inheritable, and the sins of parents can cause their children to be crippled. Likewise, filth causes disease because disease, like filth, is corruption. These concepts are not merely beliefs; in this game they are world truths.

# A Roleplaying Setting

Almost every fantasy roleplaying game is based on medieval Europe to one degree or another, some more successfully than others. Ofttimes the mixture of high fantasy and historical fact creates a world that doesn't make any sense, a world which could not exist by any stretch of the imagination. Even in regards to their own paradigms many fantasy worlds don't hold together — they aren't self-consistent.

**Ars Magica** overcomes this weakness by evoking the full richness of the medieval world. **Ars Magica** is set in Mythic Europe because that's the only way to create a truly realistic medieval setting for a fantasy game.

From the perspective of the common folk, Mythic Europe really is the way they think it is. They believe in magic, but for the most part they've never actually seen if performed. That doesn't mean it doesn't exist, though. Thus, by creating a game setting where fact and imagination are combined, you have a game where history and imagination are united. The balance of the two is for you to weigh. You may put emphasis on historical fact over fancy, or may invoke imagination over history. Admittedly, Mythic Europe as presented in this book is more historically flavored than it is historically accurate. That flavor is only a starting point, though, a point from which you may build a world to your own tastes.

Accepting the medieval world view is easier to do than it may seem. Just think back to your childhood (when you used to play make-believe with your friends) and remember the mystical way you looked at the world. You didn't know all the rules, but you could see connections between things that adults ignored. The world was a more interesting and entertaining place when arcane mysteries lurked all around you (yes, even under the bed), back before you "figured everything out." Mythic Europe is imbued with the same sort of mystery and

# Be Bloody, Bold, and Resolute

'Ey Lad, what're ye doin' there?  Stand up straight!  Yer on sentry duty, not leanin' against some bar swillin' ale.  Keep yer eyes out over that wall an' keep 'em wide.  Ye may be young an' think ye know all, but there's much to the world yer bright eyes haven't ne'er seen, an' these tired ol' eyes'a mine have seen too much of.

Ye have some lessons ye'd better learn soon, or ye'll never see the leaves turn on yonder tree.  I learned this the 'ard way, an' learned it meself.  I didn' have no one to watch o'er me.  So listens good.  If ye do ye too may fin' yerself bein' Sergeant one day.

There's a lot'a dangers out there, lad.  Ye may not see 'em from here, but there be beasties beyond those hills that'd age ye ta death with just a look.  I can't even begin ta describe some of 'em, and choose not ta remember others.  Right here they don' seem real.  That's cause most'a the foul beasties know and fear our masters, but when we goes out into that world it's different.  There be monsters that can't tell a wizard from a farmer, and see both as bein' just as tasty.  That's when ye have to step in.  Tis yer job to stop that thin', and ye'd better do it well or ye'll be the first to fall.

Yea, there be much more to the world than we see here.  There's all a what they call Europe out there.  Tis full'a all kinds of folk and queer things.  The masters may have powers, but there's others out there wit powers of their own.  They's the ones we have to fear most, cause they's not afraid of us the way some beasties is.  They's prepared to march on our gates and kill us all.  I's not jus' talkin' bout some'a the more righteous churchmen.  I's talkin' bout the servants'a the Evil One hisself, an the outsiders, the ones that don' belong to our masters' Order.

Yea, there be death out there, e'en if we can't see it, it be there.  So keep alert an keep afraid an' ye may have a chance against the world.  If ye ask me, I'll admit it.  I's afraid.

romance as childhood. You will find it a most vivid and engaging world in which to exist, for however brief a time.

# Some Basic Concepts

If you've played other fantasy games, **Ars Magica** may seem closely related to them in theme, but it bears some major differences that you should be aware of. **Ars Magica** is played differently from other games, and makes a number of unique assumptions. By understanding some of the game's conceptual foundations, you can learn the rules and understand the setting much more easily.

The following is an explanation of some of the assumptions that **Ars Magica** makes. You may be surprised by some of them, but keep in mind that as radical as things may seem, everything works.

• **The Wizard: Ars Magica** is based on the pursuits of wizards (or Magi); they are the focus of the Saga (campaign). Every player has a Magus character. Magi are motivated not only to increase their own power and prestige through increasing mastery of the lore of magic, but to build their Covenant into a lasting institution.

• **Character Types:** There are three basic character types. They are not so much "character classes" as they are fundamentally different ways to play the game. By allowing wizards to be as powerful as they are in legend, we reject the assumption that all characters should balanced in power. Magi are clearly the strongest characters, and are by far more powerful than "magic-users" found in other games. The two other character types are the Grog and the Companion. Though they aren't as powerful as wizards all play an equal role in the story.

The Companion is any sort of exceptional person who is friendly or works with the Covenant. Companions provide Magi with the benefits of their superior abilities and knowledges, usually abilities and knowledges acquired in mundane areas where Magi have no time or inclination to tread.

The Grog is a warrior and guard and is largely played as a henchman, a character shared by the players. Grogs are the characters you create to flesh out the inhabitants of the Covenant. They should not be underrated, though, for Grogs are instrumental to the Magi's defense at home and abroad. Without Grog defenders, Magi could not survive to work their magicks.

• **Storytelling: Ars Magica** is a storytelling game as well as a roleplaying game. We call it a storytelling game because the stories you tell are as important as the power your character achieves. In fact, it is the story which is paramount, and the story with which you should be concerned, not accomplishments. It is for this reason we call the game referee the Storyguide.

• **Troupe-Style Play:** The game's rules are based on the concept of a Troupe, a group of friends who tell stories together and share responsibilities in order to have a good time. Though not vital to the way the rules work, different people can take the job of Storyguide for different tales.

• **Switching Roles:** Players switch roles between stories; a player may have both a Magus character and a Companion, playing whichever one best fits a story, but never playing both at once. The Grogs are commonly held by all the players and can be played by anyone, usually while playing another character. This switching helps make each story unique, as different combinations of characters result in fresh possibilities for interaction.

• **Wealth:** In the Middle Ages, wealth is tied to relatively inflexible factors such as status, family and privilege, rather than to bank accounts (which didn't even exist). Magi value raw *vis*, the essence of magic trapped in physical form, far more than they value gold or land.

• **Use of Latin:** To add to the arcane flavor of the setting we make frequent use of Latin as it relates to the art of magic. The names of the 15 magical Arts, for example, are in Latin. If you cringe at the thought of learning a number of foreign words, just use their English equivalents.

• **The Saga:** A typical **Ars Magica** Saga lasts for a great many game years because it is based on the lives of Magi who increase their powers through long periods of study and extend their natural lives with magical potions. We assume that stories (adventures) are the exciting, but infrequent, events that punctuate long months of quieter pursuits. The Laboratory Chapter describes the various tasks Magi can pursue in their sanctums: inventing spells, training apprentices, bonding Familiars, and enchanting magical items.

# THREE STYLES OF PLAY

There are three basic ways in which you can run an **Ars Magica** Saga, each of which involves different techniques and styles, and requires various levels of interest from the players. We ourselves have tried each of these three styles and, though we enjoy them all, favor one in particular. However, each Troupe is different so feel free to develop whatever style suits you best.

• **Mythic Europe**: Though this is the fall-back standard assumed throughout the rules, you shouldn't feel bound to play in a historical setting (particularly if you don't like history). However there are some definite advantages to setting your Saga somewhere in Mythic Europe. First of all, it makes the world seem more real than a purely fictitious setting. Second, history is so rich with fact and legend that the setting provides all sorts of ideas for stories and exotic locales. Finally, it is a familiar setting, which makes it easier for players to understand and visualize, just as their characters might. Besides, this is the world all our supplements will be based in. Since we've done a lot of hard work (historical research is tough), the Mythic Europe setting means less work for you.

• **Alternate World**: You can use the medieval setting described in this game, but you don't have to set it in Mythic Europe. Rather, you can use a world that is a close approximation of Mythic Europe, but with some major (albeit subtle) differences. This is a good option for those who can't quite get themselves to believe in an alternate history of Europe in which magic plays a part.

You should play the game as you normally would, with Magi, Companions and Grogs living together in a Covenant. Only the outside world changes. One of the earliest Sagas we ever played was set in Mythic America, an alternate world in which the Romans discovered and colonized the New World and the Order of Hermes went along with them.

• **High Fantasy**: Essentially, you use the game rules to create a Saga of your own design, in a world where magic plays an influential role in the affairs of the commoner. This is a high fantasy world as classical or bizarre as you like; the world is not medieval by any stretch of the imagination. Your world should be as self-consistent as possible, and realistic despite its fantastic roots. You can't really do that if you base it on historical precedent. You can even set the Saga in your version of Arcadia, Faerieland, which is about as high fantasy as you can get.

Generally, every player has one character in a high fantasy setting, and there might be only one Storyguide — characters tend to be more powerful in a high fantasy world, and only one person often knows all the world's secrets. You can allow Companions to have more Virtues and Flaws than usual (give them five free purchase points), thus making them more equal to Magi. Grogs in this world become simple henchmen, and purely an optional device. You can even abandon the concept of Covenants and use the traditional "adventuring party" motif to explain why the characters journey together. Magi in such a party do not have much time to study, and probably no laboratories, so raw vis and other magical treasures take on greater significance. At some point the characters might even want to set up a "home base." For such you can use modified Covenant rules.

# YOUR MYTHIC JOURNEY

As you read this book, treat it as if you are a young Magus. Until now you have only known your master's laboratory, and are now on a journey that introduces you to the vast and enigmatic worlds of magic and medieval society. It is not an easy journey, but is easily worth the effort, for what you learn now stands you in good stead later on. Open the pages of this tome carefully, for you are about to delve into a world of arcane mystery and unparalleled wonder.

"You dare come to me now, petty noble! Seeking my services, after all your denouncements of my magical arts and power?"

"Humbly mage, I do all that you say. The times have turned. The dark prophesies are fulfilled. Though I am King, Lord of all men, and alone chosen by God, I beseech the aid of your authority. Sire, I beg the services of the ancient arts which you have mastered."

# THE ART OF MAGIC

# Ars Magica Systems

Every game has to have rules, even storytelling games. Rules are what help make a game a game. Some games have only a few rules while others have a great many. Regardless of the complexity of their rules, all games are defined by them. **Ars Magica** is no exception.

The basic rule systems of **Ars Magica** are simple to use, and versatile enough to apply in nearly any situation. The same systems are used throughout the game, so you don't have to learn a new set of rules for every game mechanic. What follows is the basic structure of **Ars Magica**; the rest of the book contains only permutations of these rules.

Make sure you thoroughly understand these basic rules. You needn't master them in one reading. In fact, it's suggested that you simply skim the rules on your initial reading. Precise details make more sense after you have a wider understanding of how the game works. Though the basic rules may seem somewhat odd and exotic, especially in comparison to what you might be used to, you'll find that they really aren't that complicated. Just concentrate on learning these basics and everything else will come naturally.

## Game Rounds

Most bold actions in **Ars Magica** are performed in units of time called Rounds. The exception to this is when you merely need to make a single roll in the middle of a

## Die Roll Summary

On a simple die, a "1" means 1, and a "0" means 10.

On a stress die, a "1" means roll again and double, and a "0" means 0 and that you must roll for a Botch.

session of roleplaying. Whenever a situation arises when characters make multiple, simultaneous actions, Rounds of time are measured. In each Round players declare their actions in turn, and each character gets to do one thing, having the chance to make one roll. The order characters act in is determined by their quickness and wits. Alternatively, players can declare actions by going clockwise around the group's circle. Each character's action is announced, and that action is attempted by making a roll.

A Round can be any length of time, and varies widely from circumstance to circumstance. However, a Round is rarely longer than a minute – otherwise there is no use for them – and rarely shorter than three seconds. For the purposes of fast-paced action, such as combat, assume a Round to be three to 12 seconds. Rounds are of longer duration during times of more relaxed pacing, as when characters walk through a city marketplace. The purpose of Rounds is to help you, the Storyguide, regulate the game when things get stressful — they are a game mechanic used to help you organize events, so forget about them when they get in your way. You should never use Rounds when roleplaying; just let the players have fun at their own pace. But, if you are roleplaying with one only player, interrupt things every once in a while to give other players a chance to do something.

Whenever you do go into Round mode, counting down seconds and calling for actions, speed things up. Be impatient and don't tolerate any sort of stalling. Players have to make up their minds quickly. Basically, each player gets the chance to announce one action, and then you go on to the next player. If a player can't decide what action her character takes, go onto the next player. That indecisive character spends a Round waffling between acts, but can try something else next Round. Clamping down on players like this might make them angry, but the storytelling technique is true to the mood of the game, and insures that players are more decisive in the future.

## Ease Factor Chart

| | |
|----|----|
| 3 | Very Easy |
| 6 | Not too hard |
| 9 | Difficult |
| 12 | Very difficult |
| 15 | Extremely difficult |

# THE DIE ROLLS

Ars Magica is based solely on the rolls of ten-sided dice (d10s). Such limited use of dice gets them out of your way when you are prepared to roleplay or improvise events.

There are two different types of die rolls in Ars Magica, one for casual circumstances and one for stressful ones. Get a good idea of what each roll does, for they are found throughout the game. The chart provided gives you a quick reference. Remember that in most cases, a higher roll is better for the character concerned.

## Simple Roll

The die is rolled and read normally, with the zero counting as ten. Thus, there is an even spread over the 1 to 10 range. This roll is made in simple circumstances, when the variability of possible results is low.

## Stress Roll

The 0 on the die counts as a 0, not a 10, and when you roll a 0, you usually roll again to see if you Botch. A Botch means a horrible failure results (Botches are explained later). On the other hand, when a 1 is rolled, you may pick up the die and roll it again, doubling whatever number comes up. (Once you have started doubling on a specific roll, the 0 counts as a 10.) If a second 1 comes up, the die is rolled again and the result is quadrupled. A third 1 calls for yet another roll, multiplying the result by 8, and so on. The highest roll we've ever seen is 144, after four consecutive 1s.

Stress rolls are used when a character is in a stressful situation, and could either perform above normal ability or fail miserably. People under stress are scared and therefore give it all they've got, but are likely to make disastrous mistakes as well. Whenever you are in dangerous circumstances, assume that you make stress rolls. (Stress rolls can also be called for in highly unusual circumstances, even outside of stress.)

## Using Die Rolls

One of the primary tasks of the Storyguide is to determine how attempts to do something are resolved — how rolls are made. Rolls are important to the game, but should not be abused. Otherwise, players will get bored of simply tossing the dice. The solution is to avoid having players roll for everything they do. Try to find other means of resolving situations. For instance, instead of having everyone make Perception rolls to determine if they see something, simply say that all characters who have a positive Perception score spot what's to be seen. Alternatively, you can set a minimum trait rating that must be met to successfully perform an action. For example, following a faint trail through the woods might require a Track score of 3+, no matter how high a character's Perception score is. You may simply decree that if Track skill is high enough, the character with the skill can follow the trail (at least until she reaches a really tricky spot, where a higher Track score may be necessary in order to continue). In general, you should have players make rolls when rolls add to the tension or realism of the plot, and should otherwise avoid them. Remember, die rolls are tools which only serve you if you use them well.

If you decide that a roll is appropriate to a scene, you must determine what variety the roll is. You identify a roll by naming it after the trait it has the greatest similarity or application to. For instance, if a character is attempting to trick someone into giving him a bribe by saying he is a city official, the character's action involves guile, so he makes a Guile roll. As Guile is an Ability in the rules, the roll applies to the Ability the character has. If there is no Ability in the rules that applies to an attempted action, simply make up an Ability and have the player make the roll anyway. For almost all rolls, you take the score of the Ability that applies to the action, add the score of whatever Characteristic is appropriate (usually listed in the Ability description, but left to your discretion), and add the sum to the roll of a ten-sided die (d10).

The Characteristic (e.g., Strength, Communication, Perception) chosen to go with the Ability of your roll depends on how the Ability is used. Many Abilities have standard Characteristics that are almost always used with them. For instance, it is hard to imagine a situation in which the Intelligence Characteristic is not combined with the Scribe Ability to translate the foreign language of a book. The Characteristics that can be applied with other Abilities are more ambiguous, and may be determined by the nature of the scene in which the Ability is used. For example, if you are trying to lie, you use Guile (Ability) + Communication (Characteristic). But, if you are trying to detect someone else's lie, you apply Guile and Perception to your roll, as you are using your senses and judgment to recognize a lie, rather than your glib tongue to tell one.

Ability and Characteristic scores are the most common modifiers of die rolls for actions attempted. However, other factors can modify rolls, such as your Personality Traits, Passions, and scene conditions. These factors are fully discussed in their respective sections, later in this book.

Calling for a roll to perform an action is fine, but the Storyguide must designate what result is needed to determine success in the roll and thus the action. The value that rolls are made against is called the Ease Factor. When a character uses an Ability against a static force, such as when picking a lock, you assign an Ease Factor that the player's roll must equal or exceed. The difficulty of the task determines the difficulty of the roll; a complex lock calls for a high Ease Factor, and a simple lock calls for a low Ease Factor. When a task is directly opposed to another character's actions, such as when one character chases another, your rolls are compared to each another's. Since you're trying the same thing (e.g., both running at top speed), your rolls have the same Ability and Characteristic modifiers, and the high roller wins. If the the two of you are trying different but opposed tasks (e.g., one character is lying, the other trying to see through the lie), your rolls may have different Ability and Characteristic modifiers (e.g., Guile + Communication versus Guile + Perception). He who gets the higher roll defeats the other — the lie is successful or is recognized. Ease Factors can also be standards that are always applied to a given situation. For example, Fatigue rolls (an essential part of the game) are almost always made against an Ease Factor of 6. In fact, the value of 6 may be taken as a catch-all difficulty rating for any task. It represents roughly even odds of success for an average person (which makes the roll somewhat easier for the players' characters as the characters are certainly above average). If you're not sure of an Ease Factor to apply, use the value of six. The *Ease Factor Chart* provides some Ease Factor ranges.

Once the die is rolled and the result determined, you must determine the result in story terms. This means justifying the result of a roll in terms of the plot. Since you, the Storyguide, are the only one who knows the events of the plot, accounting for rolls in terms of the story is your responsibility.

As Storyguide you need not tell players ahead of time the circumstances behind a roll, its modifiers, or the results of success or failure. Those are factors only you need know, based on your knowledge of the story and events yet to come. While it is more fair for you to decide the effects of a roll ahead of time, including the results of Botches and exceptional rolls, doing so for every single action slows the game down. Instead, you may fabricate the results of a roll without having given it much advance thought (in fact, that's standard in roleplaying games). On the average, though, you have a general idea of what can happen with a given roll, and may make a final decision once the dice are rolled. A player can ask what kind of Ease Factor a certain activity requires, and you can tell them if so inclined. However, you can refuse to answer, instead requiring an estimation roll from the player to see if the character can figure the difficulty out. For example, the player can ask, "Just how hard does it look to jump this chasm?" The player makes an Athletics Ability roll, modified by Intelligence, to determine how well the character estimates the difficulty. If the roll is successful, you can tell the player the correct, or general, Ease Factor of the roll. If the estimation roll fails, you can give a false Ease Factor and surprise the character when her "successful" action attempt fails. (Toward this end, it's often wise for the Storyguide to make estimation rolls on behalf of characters, so the player's aren't always sure their guesses are right.) If players complain about not knowing the circumstances behind a roll, you can remind them that the Fates are far less forgiving than the mortal world, and that you control the Fates.

When a character attempts an action, even though he has no score in the appropriate Ability, there are three possible results. For Talent Abilities, roll normally, but it's assumed that you have a score of 0, and you must make three additional Botch rolls if you roll a zero. For Skill Abilities, you receive a -3 penalty to the roll, as well as three extra Botch rolls. For Knowledge Abilities, you cannot even make a roll if you lack the appropriate Ability — if you don't know the subject, you simply cannot make an attempt to know anything about it. The only exception to this Knowledge rule is if, during your life, you learn something that is common knowledge, like who Pope Constantine was. In this case, you might get a roll to see if you recognize the name, even if you don't have a Church Lore Ability score. Like everything else in this game, it's entirely up to the Storyguide and players to interpret possible knowledge and lack of knowledge. Use and

## Characters' Glossary

### Words Actually Used by Characters

These words are used by characters in Mythic Europe, so feel free to use them when talking in character. Some characters, naturally, may be unfamiliar with the more esoteric terms.

**apprentice:** Someone working for a Magus and, in exchange, learning the art of magic. (There are also apprentices in mundane professions.)

*Certámen:* A magical, non-lethal duel between Magi.

**the Church:** The hierarchical religious institution central to medieval society.

**the Code of the Order of Hermes:** The code of conduct that all apprentices must swear to obey before becoming Magi; it limits destructive competition between Magi and guides Magi's conduct with common folk.

*consors* :(pl. *consortis* — partner) A non-Magus who works closely with a Covenant and probably lives there; many Companions are *consortis*, but not all.

**Covenant:** A durable group of associated and ostensibly allied Magi, or their headquarters. The peasant folk ignorantly call these groups "covens."

*custos:* Select Grogs who are the favorites of Magi. These Grogs often receive special treatment by the Magi, but earn their keep, usually by protecting Magi abroad, where dangers are most intense. Not all Grogs are *custos*, though many aspire to be.

**demon:** An infernal, deceptive, magical creature bent on the corruption of humanity, in order to collect souls.

**diabolist:** One who worships the Prince of Darkness and is given destructive power by Him. Diabolists are common enemies of the Church and the Order of Hermes.

**Dominion:** The area under the holy influence of the Church; Magical, Infernal, and Faerie powers all function at reduced ability within the Dominion.

**faerie:** A supernatural being of the wilderness, usually human-shaped.

**Formulaic magic:** Magic by use of standard gestures and words that almost always brings about the same specific effect each time.

**Grog:** A henchman hired by Magi to serve them as a bodyguard and warrior. Sometimes less martial covenfolk are ranked amongst the Grogs, people like cooks and servants who also go on journeys and play important roles at the Covenant. Naturally, the latter folk are not often recognized as peers by "official" Grogs. "Grog" is a popular slang.

**Hermetic:** Of or relating to the Order of Hermes.

**infernal:** Coming from or related to Hell or devils.

**Magus:** ([MAHgoose], pl. Magi [MAHgee] — wizard) One trained in the magical arts of the Order of Hermes; non-Hermetic users of magic are called warlocks and witches, but not Magi.

**mundanes:** The common, non-supernatural people of Mythic Europe. This group includes nobles, but does not include clergy, who are aligned with the supernatural power of the Church.

**Order of Hermes:** The Magi's organization that regulates their behavior and protects them from threats, including each other.

**pace:** A yard, more or less.

*Parma Magica:* ([PARmah MAHgikah], pl. *Parmae Magicae* [PARm-eye MAHgik-eye — magic shield) A spell-like ceremony that protects a Magus from magic, usually activated continuously by Magi.

**pawn:** A unit of raw *vis*, equal to one point in game terms.

**raw vis:** Magical energy in physical form, highly prized by Magi.

**sigil:** The unique side effect or quality of a Magus's magic, or the physical symbol representing a Magus's membership in the Order of Hermes.

**spell:** A use of magic to achieve a desired supernatural effect; can be memorized or invented on the spot.

**Spontaneous magic:** Use of magical skills without a Formulaic spell; the result is variable.

**turb:** A group of Grogs, used as you would use a "pride" of lions or a "murder" of crows; from the Latin *turba*, meaning gang, turmoil or confusion.

**vis:** ([wees] — power) Magical force directed by Magi with their spells; the word from which the word "Vim" is derived.

## Players' Glossary *Game Terms (Not Used by Characters)*

When speaking in character do not use these terms. These terms are strictly intended to help players communicate the rules and do not necessarily refer to anything tangible in Mythic Europe.

**Botch:** a disastrous failure, indicated by the roll of a second 0 after a first is rolled during a stress roll.

**Companion:** A skilled person who aids Magi but is not necessarily in their pay.

**Ease Factor:** A number that you must match or exceed with your die roll for your attempted action to succeed.

**Fast-Cast spell:** A hasty and dangerous Spontaneous spell.

**Level:** A number rating the strength of a spell or similar power.

**Magic Resistance:** The passive, magical capacity to resist the effects of other magic.

**Natural Resistance:** Resisting a spell's effects through natural means, such as one's physical or mental fortitude (only possible against certain spells).

**Saga:** A campaign made up of a number of different stories involving the same Covenant.

**score:** A single independent number, such as a Characteristic; it can be used as a die modifier by itself or combined with other scores to produce a total.

**simple roll:** a die roll in which 0 is considered 10 and 1s do not call for doubled re-rolls.

**Soak:** In the Action Combat System, a total to reduce or withstand damage. In the Dueling Combat System, a roll to do the same.

**Specialty:** The area of a trait for which a character has a special aptitude (+1 or more on appropriate rolls).

**stat:** (or trait) Any number relevant to game mechanics, including Characteristics, Soak score, and magic Art scores.

**story:** A tale created by the Troupe; an adventure.

**Storyguide:** The person who sets up and leads the story, assuming the roles of all characters not assumed by the players, and determining all events beyond the control of the players' characters.

**stress roll:** A die roll in which 0 counts as zero and 1s call for a doubled re-roll.

**total:** A number derived from a selection of scores and used as a die modifier.

**Troupe:** A group of gamers, particularly one in which the players assume different roles at different times.

abuse this game system as best suits your needs. Your rule interpretations define the world almost as much as your actions do.

## Botches

As explained in the die roll descriptions, above, it is possible to sink below an ordinary failure to a truly dismal showing. Whenever you roll a zero while making a stress roll, you must roll the die again. A second 0 means you have Botched; you have done something horribly wrong. Since you are rolling the second die just to see if you get another zero, any other numbers rolled are disregarded.

In particularly tricky situations, you may have to roll more than one Botch die, and the number of zeros rolled indicates the extremity of your failure. For instance, if you are battling in a crowded, cluttered campsite in the woods at night, you have plenty of roots to trip on and tents to run into. Rolling two extra Botch dice, in addition to the normal one, every time you roll a zero is appropriate.

Sometimes the rules detail circumstances under which extra Botch rolls are required, but more often, the Storyguide decides on the number made. Remember that extra Botch dice are dependent on a task being tricky, not dangerous. You have to make more Botch rolls while juggling five balls than while juggling three knives. Though a Botch with the knives is more dangerous, it is less likely.

## Complications

The simplicity of the basic rolls for success and failure described above are useful, but they might not have enough flair for your purposes. The expansion rules that follow have been designed because not everyone has the same tastes. While some people might like combat, others might prefer in-depth roleplaying, while yet others might like a lot of political intrigue. The basic rules systems provide enough to run a full game of **Ars Magica**. These additional rules are provided only so that you can add more depth and detail to the game in the places where you want it. There are, however, many possible elaborations you can make on the basic rules, so you can improvise to your heart's content and make up whatever complications that suit you. Provided here are some ways to manipulate the basic rolls in order to simulate various circumstances. These complications might give you an idea or two on how to further modify the rules yourself.

Buffers are used when a draw between contestants is likely, at least for a given roll. For instance, two characters playing chess roll a die and add Intelligence + Chess skill, the higher winning the game. But, if you win simply by outrolling your opponent, draws occur less than one-tenth of the time, which is not accurate for the situation. For a greater chance to draw, use a buffer, a number by which you must exceed your opponent's roll in order to

win. If you have to beat your opponent's roll by two points instead of just one, the chances of a draw increase greatly. If you have to beat your opponent's roll by eight, draws are almost inevitable between well-matched adversaries.

**Multipliers** represent the relative value of different strengths and weaknesses in a given endeavor. For instance, if you are trying to get someone to befriend you, you roll a die and add Presence + Charm Ability. You have only a moment to make a good first impression, so the Storyguide says you should add double your Presence but only half your Charm. That's because you don't have time to win the person over, and the first impression is more important. But, if you have a week to work on the other character, the Storyguide tells you to add double your Charm but halve your Presence. In this circumstance, you have plenty of time to lay on the charm, and the first impression isn't that important any more. Thus, even if you and another character have the same Presence + Charm total, one might be better at first impressions (the one with higher Presence score).

Multipliers also reduce the element of chance in your rolls by making the scores you add to the roll larger or smaller relative to the die roll. For example, in a weight lifting contest between you and another person, the two of you might add 5 times your Strength scores to your die rolls. Thus, just two points of difference in your scores becomes an overwhelming +10 difference on the rolls. So, a difference in Strength becomes much more important than the mere chance of the die. Remember, multiplying a score before adding it to a die is not always a bonus. If your Dexterity Characteristic is -3, multiplying it is a tremendous burden to your roll.

**Accumulated points** represent your progress over a series of rolls. When using accumulated points, you get one point for every point by which you exceed the Ease Factor of a given roll. You succeed at the action as a whole by accumulating enough points. Suppose, for instance, that you have been captured by diabolists who intend to sacrifice you at Black Mass in three days. You decide to use your Pretend Ability to convince them to set you free so you can join them, when you actually want to escape. You roll a die and add your Communication + Pretend scores. You can make one roll per day against an Ease Factor of 8. If you accumulate 10 points, you convince your captors to free you. Note that you can succeed with just one roll if you roll 18+.

**Carryover advantage** is similar to accumulated points, but the points by which you exceed the Ease Factor are added to your next die roll. Suppose that you and an enemy are struggling in unarmed combat (see *Brawling* in the Combat Chapter) on a natural stone bridge spanning a giant chasm. Each of you is trying to hurl the other over the edge. You each add Dexterity and Brawl to opposing die rolls to strike each other. The roll has a buffer of 5, so it is difficult to hurl your opponent over in one roll, but any points by which you exceed your opponent's roll in one Round are added to your roll the next Round. So, even if you can't throw your foe over the edge in one Round, a good roll indicates that you have gained the upper hand and that you find it easier to do so next Round.

The **roleplaying modifier** adds or subtracts 1 or 2 (or on occasion even more) to rolls for exceptional roleplaying or actions. If you describe your character's actions or roleplay them out unusually well or particularly poorly, you get a bonus for good ideas and a penalty for bad ones — at the Storyguide's discretion. For instance, suppose you are trying to intimidate a baron into leaving you and your comrades alone. If you, as a player, cannot think up a good strategy to follow, the Storyguide can impose a penalty to your intimidation roll. But, if you think up an excellent strategy, you get a bonus. Furthermore, if you roleplay out what you say in a vivid, entertaining way, the bonus may be even higher. The roleplaying modifier assures that players cannot rely solely on die rolls to get them through.

## Our Best Advice

As you read **Ars Magica**, keep in mind that the only hard and fast rule is that there are no hard and fast rules. What follows are essentially several thousand suggestions, and these suggestions are now yours to use, abuse, neglect, or reject as you see fit.

We have created a game which limits you, the roleplayer, in myriad ways. It is now up to you to transcend those limits, to make this game truly fit your needs.

True fantasy cannot result solely from game rules; the delight that results from roleplaying in a magical world only comes through a generous dose of imagination and a taste for the fantastic.

# Characters
## chapter two

his Chapter offers you guidelines and ideas about how to create characters in **Ars Magica**, the people around and about whom your Saga is told and your game is played. In creating a character you must envision a person to enact in the game's stories. That character vision is then translated into numbers to be used with the game's mechanics. Though numbers and mechanics are important to playing your character, they are not the soul of your character. The soul of a character lies in the detail and personality invested in him; a character is only as interesting and entertaining as you make him. Thus, in this Chapter we strive to help you develop the most well-rounded, unique character possible.

While creating a character requires an initial investment of time, it prepares you for a lifetime of roleplaying. It takes anywhere from five minutes to an hour to create a character. The more time is invested, the more developed and thoughtful your character is.

## Two Creation Systems

**Ars Magica** offers two character creation systems, basic and advanced. Each system has its advantages and drawbacks, and you should use whichever best suits your needs and tastes. Each system allows for characters of equal power, though the advanced system poses more risk in the final character created, as there is more room for her to have several failings or flaws — she's made more

human. Beginning players are advised to use the basic system. It quickly teaches the fundamentals of the game, but doesn't overwhelm you with all the rules that can be incorporated into play. It's advised that you use the advanced system when you have learned and are comfortable with the game system (this is particularly true for players of Magus characters).

Both character creation systems offer great latitude in determining who you are. By choosing Characteristics, Virtues and Flaws, Abilities, Personality Traits and Reputation, you decide what your character is like. However, it is your responsibility to create a character that suits the Saga being told, the Covenant to which all characters belong, and the Troupe to which you belong. Backstabbing Grogs, maniacal Companions, and demented Magi do not suit and are not allowed in most Sagas, Covenants or Troupes. After all, Ars Magica is designed to help you tell stories, so you are advised to create characters who can live and work together — characters who together may weave fabulous tales of romance and adventure.

And, always keep in mind that the most important element of character creation goes beyond the numbers. True, it's important that as you create your character you get all the right numbers written down — you can't play the game without them. However, as your character becomes more concrete, it's imperative that you get a precise idea of who he is. Constructing a complete character is really what the systems provided here are about. The numbers are only a device, not an end in themselves. For a complete explanation of the statistics that define your character, see the Traits Chapter.

# Types of Characters

There are three different types of characters in **Ars Magica**: Magi, Companions, and Grogs. They are not character classes, such as you might find in other games, but are three variations on how you play the game, each with its unique role in the Saga, each with a varying degree of power, and each with a different place in the story. Each also has slightly different rules for character generation, though the basic concepts are all the same.

Each player creates a Magus, a Companion, and one or more Grogs. In the Troupe style play that **Ars Magica** is based on (see the Storytelling Chapter for details), you switch playing your Magus and Companion with each new story. Your Grogs, on the other hand, are usually played with each story. Grogs tend to be needed in considerable numbers, so a group of them — a turb — is kept in retainer by Magi and Companions who are abroad. Sometimes you may simply play Grogs in a story, a role that may superficially seem subservient, but one that offers remarkable potential for roleplaying and entertainment.

## Magi

Magi (wizards) are the true focus of **Ars Magica**. The game is designed to emulate all the spell casting possibilities we see in films and novels, possibilities that are often given short shrift in most roleplaying games. Magi therefore have immense magical might, even at the beginning of the game, which makes them more powerful than other character types. That is, they aren't depreciated in the interest of an artificial concept such as "character balance."

However, with great power comes great responsibility. The magical potential of Magi makes them very demanding characters to play, particularly when others look to Magi for salvation from a particularly dire threat. Magi are also the leaders of their Covenants, so when you go abroad with an entourage, others look to you for fateful decisions. If you are not decisive and practical, you may have a revolt on your hands. Furthermore, Magi tend to be deficient in social and basic everyday skills that are necessary to survive. Thus, where Magi seem superior to other character types, they actually rely heavily on Companions and Grogs in dealings with the world. That dependency is what ultimately makes Magi, Companions and Grogs equal.

In creating a Magus you need to concentrate on acquiring magically oriented Abilities, Virtues, and Flaws in order to facilitate spell casting power. Without a range of magical abilities you not only weaken yourself as an initiate Magus, but curtail your potential for future development. This acquisition of magical abilities also leaves you deficient in worldly capabilities. And, rather ironically, your magical skills only compound your inability to deal with the physical and social world; your Gift of magic affects those around you. All rolls you make (i.e., Communication and Presence) that involve interaction with normal people suffer a -3 modifier. Animals are also ill at ease with you and rolls to handle or deal with them suffer the same penalty. The Gift is precious, but not without its price.

You must also select a Magical House for your Magus, which is the particular lineage of Magi from which you and your master descend. The Mythic Europe Chapter describes all thirteen Houses. See p.41 for Vocations that you can use to create Magi quickly, based on the magical Houses they belong to.

## Companions

A few exceptional and highly skilled people are also associated with the Covenant. They are called Companions. Some work for the Covenant and live there, acquiring the rank of *consors*. Others are friends of the Magi and visit only occasionally. Companions provide any skills that the Magi, in their pursuit of magic, have not had time to learn, and provide a connection between the esoteric Covenant and the mundane world around it — Magi do not often mix well with society. Companions can include scholars, foresters, sages, healers, thieves, spies and leaders of Grogs — any profession that you come up with and the Storyguide approves.

When creating your Companion, be sure to explain why you have come to work for the Magi and their Covenant. Medieval society often drives men and women to a Covenant. In the outside world gender, nationality, religion, poverty, disease and the happenstance of birth endanger life, curtail its freedoms, or restrict its happiness. In a Covenant, women, Moors, and Pagans are welcomed, given autonomy, and treated with the respect they're denied elsewhere. Some work for Magi to gain knowledge available at the Covenant, while others have more lucrative goals: the acquisition of wealth and power.

Other people have backgrounds or talents that make life in mundane society difficult. You might join the Covenant based on the Virtues and Flaws that you choose to describe your character; these are things that make you exceptional. These traits may make you an outcast elsewhere. At least the Magi respect your talents and put them, and you, to constructive use. If you have a powerful mystic ability (chosen as a Virtue or Flaw) people can tell that you are somehow "different," and, like the Magi, you suffer -3 to rolls that involve winning the trust and affection of normal people.

See p. 36 for Vocations that you can use to create Companions quickly.

## Grogs

Grogs are made by all players, and played by everyone. It is common to have one or more Grogs who are played in each story, alongside the Magus or Companion whom you are also enacting. Grogs are the henchmen of the Covenant, and can be guards, servants, messengers, cooks, carpenters or individuals of any other mundane profession. Essentially, Grogs include all the people who help keep the Covenant going, but are not characters central to the Saga.

Think of grogs as the vibrant lower-class characters common to many Shakespearean plays — characters whose lives are often insignificant compared to those of the major characters, but whose lives and actions often reflect upon or even direct the basic themes and plot of the play. Yes, Grogs are peripheral characters, but they're still a lot of fun to roleplay, just as Shakespeare's servants and guttersnipes are so enjoyable to watch.

When you create your Covenant you need to create many Grogs in order to flesh out its inhabitants. Some Grogs are actively played story after story, while others exist simply as background characters. Such background characters only become fully developed and roleplayed by players when and if they enter a story. Eventually, after the Saga has continued for some time, each Grog undoubtedly has a complete and individual identity. By having so many characters in your Saga, you run the risk of burdening yourself with too many characters, but the effort makes for a fulfilling Saga, alive with a wealth of vibrant personalities.

Playing a Grog can be difficult for inexperienced players, who see their limited role in the group as a limit to their roleplaying potential. The strength of the Grog's character lies in her personality. Play it up as much as possible; roleplay the extremes. Part of this characterization comes from Grogs' way of life. They live hard, menial lives, so often complain about their fate. And just as they work and live hard, they play hard — drinking is a favorite pastime for all medieval folk. Keep in mind that Grogs tend to be the intellectual inferiors of the Covenant and thus make for excellent foils and "straight-men."

The term "Grog" is a slang term first used by the guards at the Covenant of Doissetep. The name has spread throughout much of the Order, mainly because Grogs themselves use it. Grogs have other names, sometimes used by other people. Elite Grogs are called *custos*, the name Magi have for warriors and servants who journey with and protect them. More common Grogs simply perform mundane duties at the Covenant, rarely straying from its walls.

See p. 31 for Vocations that you can use to create Grogs quickly.

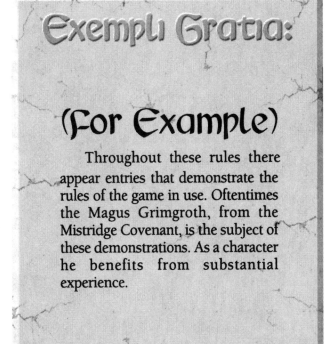

# Exempli Gratia:

## (For Example)

Throughout these rules there appear entries that demonstrate the rules of the game in use. Oftentimes the Magus Grimgroth, from the Mistridge Covenant, is the subject of these demonstrations. As a character he benefits from substantial experience.

# Basic Character Creation

The basic character creation system is not simply intended to be an easy means to learn Ars **Magica**. It is a legitimate creation system that you may use throughout your play of the game. While it is somewhat less open-ended than the advanced system, it does provide a broad overview of the potential characters available, and they are easily modified.

It's important to note at this point that the traits and qualities your character has are described in the Traits Chapter. That section gives meaning to the scores your basic character has. This, the Characters Chapter, only introduces those concepts.

The basic character creation process is simple. Pick a Vocation (listed below) appropriate to the type of character you are playing, be it Magus, Companion or Grog. All the information you need to play is provided. All you may want to do is add some Specialties (described later), and explain your capabilities in terms of your background. In many cases even this is done for you. As soon as you

understand the capacities of your chosen Vocation you are ready to play.

However, if you please, you can modify the Vocation to make the character uniquely yours. Picking an interesting Vocation is simple enough. They are in some ways like character archetypes, examples of what a medieval or magical person might be like. Modifying the character is equally simple; it's a matter of changing some of the details of the character. For instance, you can change the character's sex, decide she is from a different background, or decide her personality is radically different from that described.

You can also change your character by switching around your traits (i.e., Characteristics, Virtues and Flaws, Passions, Personality Traits, Abilities, and Reputations). There are some rules to changing traits, though. You can switch around your trait scores as much as you like, as long as you switch them around within their appropriate categories. Thus, you can switch around your Strength and Perception scores because both are Characteristics. You can switch your Brawl and Hermes Lore scores because both are Abilities. However, you cannot switch the scores of your Strength and Brawl; one is a Characteristics and one is an Ability.

If you want a new trait not listed for your Vocation, you can acquire it by exchanging a trait you do have. As above, the new trait and that replaced must be of the same category. The score of your new trait is the same as that of the trait which is replaced. Of course, you can change the new trait's score by switching it with that of another trait you still possess. In the case of Virtues and Flaws, you can only acquire a new one if its score is the same as that of a Virtue or Flaw you are discarding the new one's place. Flaws can only be traded for Flaws, and Virtues for Virtues.

Magi can even switch around their Art scores (but you have to be careful as that can affect what spells you are allowed to take). See the Magic Chapter to learn how Arts operate.

Why would you want to use a Vocation, rather than create your character from scratch? Mostly for expedience and convenience. Vocations make for fast character creation. They also give you a distinct concept for your character, which you might lack when starting the process from scratch (especially if you don't fully understanding the rules or setting yet). Vocations guide you through character creation and help you understand how the game works as you learn about your basic character. Finally, Vocations are invaluable for Storyguides who must create several characters for each story. If you are telling a story that involves a Forester, for example, all you need do is give a quick personality to the stats provided below and you have an instant Storyguide character.

# VOCATIONS

Vocations provide a set of Characteristics, Abilities, and specific privileges that are common or particular to a certain profession or lifelong devotion. In choosing a "Vocation character," you receive a template that provides the basics for the kind of character you want.

Remember that most of these Vocations are generic in nature; they're designed to suit any Saga's setting. The best way to tailor them to your specific Saga is to choose Characteristic and Ability Specialties that relate to your setting. For example, if you are a Forester and live in a Covenant in the Pyrenees, your Tracking Ability is probably Specialized for mountains, not lowlands.

Players are welcome to create new Vocations and make them available to the rest of the Troupe. Of course, we will list many more in our supplements to the game. The possible variety of Vocations is endless, and the ways in which they can be adjusted is close to infinite.

Note: Vocations approach the Advanced Character Creation rules, but are first intended to help you understand game basics.

## Grog Vocations

## SHIELD GROG

| Intelligence | -2 | Presence | -3 |
| Perception | 0 | Communication | -2 |
| Strength | +2 | Dexterity | 0 |
| Stamina | +4 | Quickness | +1 |

**Age:** 22

**Virtues & Flaws:** Well-Known +1, Superior Armaments +2, Mute -2, Simple-Minded -1

**Abilities:** Brawl 2, Alertness 2, Dodge 3, Folk Ken 2, Drinking 3, Weapon Skill (attack) 3, Weapon Skill (parry) 3, Shield Parry 4, Scan 1, Athletics 1

**Confidence:** 3

**Reputation:** Unshakeable (combat) 2

**Personality Traits:** Devoted +3, Brave +1

**Weapons & Armor:** Tower Shield, Battle Axe, Chain Hauberk

**Encumbrance:** 6

You are considered one of the most trusted and loyal *custos* in the Covenant, and are entrusted with the life of a Magus. You travel with and constantly remain close to your charge, whom you are sworn to protect — you are expected to sacrifice yourself if necessary. The idea is to protect the Magus from attack long enough for her to get off a spell. As the Magus relies so heavily on you for protection in battle, you and she have developed a bond born of need; social status is quickly overlooked when one's life is at stake. Because of this relationship, you have the Magus's understanding, and may receive special treatment.

*"Tis not so much that I like my guardian. I certainly don't like the way she smells at times, but I confess that I'd trust none other when my life is in jeopardy and only one may stand on my behalf."* — Magus defending her close relationship with her shield Grog.

# STABLE HAND

| | | | |
|---|---|---|---|
| Intelligence | 0 | Presence | -1 |
| Perception | -4 | Communication | 0 |
| Strength | +3 | Dexterity | +1 |
| Stamina | +1 | Quickness | 0 |

**Age:** 16

**Virtues & Flaws:** Light Sleeper +1, Compulsion (spying) -1

**Abilities:** Speak Own Language 4, Brawl 1, Athletics 2, Folk Ken 2, Animal Handling 4, Ride 3, Drinking 2, Weapon Skill (attack) 2, Weapon Skill (parry) 1, Search 2

**Confidence:** 3

**Reputation:** None

**Personality Traits:** Curious +1, Brave -2

**Weapons & Armor:** Club

**Encumbrance:** 0

You probably began as a stable boy, the task foisted upon you at a young age to keep you out from underfoot. However, as you grew you learned to appreciate the job; it provides you with a roof, a luxuriously soft bed, and companions who appreciate your efforts and don't talk back. You're not *custos*, but the warriors of the Covenant usually treat you well for they value the work you perform.

*"I have a good position here at the Covenant, and I owe them a lot, They took me in when I was but a lad, this is the only home I know. Mayhaps I will advance to become* custos *someday."*

# SCOUT

| | | | |
|---|---|---|---|
| Intelligence | -1 | Presence | -3 |
| Perception | +3 | Communication | +1 |
| Strength | -2 | Dexterity | +1 |
| Stamina | -1 | Quickness | +2 |

**Age:** 20

**Virtues & Flaws:** Keen Vision +1, Hired Sword -1

**Abilities:** Speak Own Language 4, Brawl 2, Scan 4, Dodge 2, Folk Ken 2, Track 3, Drinking 1, Estimate 2, Missile Weapon Skill (attack) 2,    Weapon Skill (attack) 3, Weapon Skill (parry) 2.

**Confidence:** 3

**Reputation:** Blessed Senses 1

**Personality Traits:** Brave +3, Independent +3

**Weapons & Armor:** Self Bow, Short Sword, Ring Mail Cuirass

**Encumbrance:** 3

You are invaluable to your traveling companions because they rely on you to pick the safest route through harsh terrain, and expect you to spot the enemy before they spot you. You also need to be able to estimate the threat posed by an enemy and have to communicate that threat to your superiors. If you do your job well, you receive the thanks of all your companions, and may get first dibs on any spoils.

*"It isn't so much a matter of sneaking around as it is being aware of what's around you. Tis a dangerous place to be, though, being out in front. You need quick legs, to be sure."*

# COOK

| | | | |
|---|---|---|---|
| Intelligence | 0 | Presence | -2 |
| Perception | -3 | Communication | +4 |
| Strength | 0 | Dexterity | +3 |
| Stamina | -2 | Quickness | 0 |

**Age:** 22

**Virtues & Flaws:** Piercing Gaze +2, Orphan -1, Poor Memory -1

**Abilities:** Speak Own Language 4, Brawl 3, Search 2, Dodge 3, Folk Ken 2, Drinking 3, Cook 3, Intimidation 3, Weapon Skill 2, Weapon Parry 2, Stealth 2

**Confidence:** 3

**Reputation:** Intimidating 1

**Personality Traits:** Brave +1, Gruff +3

**Weapons & Armor:** Butcher's Knife (treat as short sword), Leather Cuirass

**Encumbrance:** 1

Your talents may not always be appreciated, but covenfolk quickly praise your name when times are hard and good food is their only solace after a grueling day's work. However, when supplies are short, a stern demeanor is required to deal with troublesome bellyachers. Sometimes your talents are even called for on the road, when a turb and the odd Magus go on a journey. On the road, morale can rest solely on a hot meal, so Magi look to you to keep the others happy.

*"Slop! You call my food pig slop! I ought to cut you up and put you in the pot, only you're too scrawny to make naught but dog gissle — which is all you'll be eating tonight!"*

# TURB SERGEANT

| | | | |
|---|---|---|---|
| Intelligence | 0 | Presence | +3 |
| Perception | -2 | Communication | +1 |
| Strength | +2 | Dexterity | +1 |
| Stamina | -2 | Quickness | -3 |

**Age:** 30

**Virtues & Flaws:** Self-Confident +2, Good Armaments +1, Tainted with Evil -2, Bad Reputation -1

**Abilities:** Speak Own Language 4, Brawl 3, Alertness 3, Dodge 3, Leadership 3, Drinking 2, Chirurgy 3, Intimidation 3, Weapon Skill (attacks) 3, Shield Parry 3, Legend Lore 2, Ride 2, Diplomacy 2, Athletics 1

**Confidence:** 5

**Reputation:** Violent 2

**Personality Traits:** Devoted +3, Reliable +2

**Weapons & Armor:** Mace, Round Shield, Chain Mail Hauberk

**Encumbrance:** 3

There are only a handful among the Grogs with your status. You are responsible for several turbs. That authority affords you considerable respect from underlings and superiors alike; you sleep in your own quarters, eat good food, and are often recruited for missions abroad. Your job also involves a lot of responsibility. You must ensure that your Grogs perform their duties, that they stay alert on guard, and that they stay sober on duty. Ultimately, you are responsible for the actions of your troops, so are punished and rewarded as they are.

*"It's not the recruits who cause the trouble — they're usually too frightened to speak — it's always the oldtimers who stir up things. They think they know what's best, certainly more so than the Magi, and won't listen to sense. I have to pound it into them sometimes."*

# POINT GUARD

| | | | |
|---|---|---|---|
| Intelligence | -4 | Presence | 0 |
| Perception | 0 | Communication | -3 |
| Strength | +5 | Dexterity | +1 |
| Stamina | +1 | Quickness | 0 |

**Age:** 18

**Virtues & Flaws:** Berserk +1, Superior Armaments +2, Common Fear -2, Simple-Minded -1

**Abilities:** Speak Own Language 4, Brawl 3, Alertness 2, Dodge 2, Folk Ken 2, Drinking 3, Weapon Skill (attack) 4, Shield Parry 3

**Confidence:** 3

**Reputation:** Fearless 2

**Personality Traits:** Brave +3, Crude +1, Abusive +2, Angry +2

**Weapons & Armor:** Bastard Sword, Knight Shield, Chain Mail Hauberk

**Encumbrance:** 1

You're the bruiser of your turb. You are *custos*, and everyone knows it. When a fight is anticipated, you lead the way, hacking through any barriers that stand between you and the your allies' foe. If that means assaulting a castle's front gate, so be it. At least you're outfitted with heavy armor, and your fellow Grogs admire you, but certainly don't want to be you.

*"I'm the meanest. I'm the nastiest. I'm the toughest Grog in the turb."*

# BEGGAR

| | | | |
|---|---|---|---|
| Intelligence | 0 | Presence | -5 |
| Perception | +1 | Communication | +3 |
| Strength | -2 | Dexterity | 0 |
| Stamina | +2 | Quickness | +1 |

**Age:** 26

**Virtues & Flaws:** Clear Thinker +1, Cursed -1

**Abilities:** Speak Own Language 4, Brawl 4, Alertness 2, Dodge 3, Pretend 3, Stealth 4, Drinking 2, Weapon Skill (attack) 2, Folk Ken 3, Search 3

**Confidence:** 3

**Reputation:** None

**Personality Traits:** Reliable -3, Brave -3, Crafty +2

**Weapons & Armor:** Club

**Encumbrance:** 0

You came to the Covenant with the intent to beg from its inhabitants. You lived outside its walls with some of your associates but soon found you could slip into the Covenant to steal what you wanted — no one seemed to notice. Before long one of the Magi came out and invited you to stay, "to pay for what you had taken," she said. What choice did you have? Now you live with the turb, but still find it difficult to do an honest day's work. You've perfected the art of looking busy.

*"Yes, my Lord, I'm working as hard as I can. Yes, my Lord, I'll work faster. My Lord, you wouldn't happen to have a spare bite on you?"*

# ARCHER

| | | | |
|---|---|---|---|
| Intelligence | -1 | Presence | 0 |
| Perception | +4 | Communication | -4 |
| Strength | +1 | Dexterity | +1 |
| Stamina | -2 | Quickness | +1 |

**Age:** 17

**Virtues & Flaws:** Knack (bows) +2, Keen Vision +1, Sense of Doom -3

**Abilities:** Speak Own Language 4, Brawl 1, Scan 2, Climb 2, Dodge 2, Folk Ken 2, Drinking 2, Missile Weapon Skill (attack) 4, Weapon Skill (attack) 2, Weapon Skill (parry) 3.

**Confidence:** 3

**Reputation:** None

**Personality Traits:** Brave -1, Perverted +2

**Weapons & Armor:** Self Bow, Dagger, Hard Leather

**Encumbrance:** 0

You are *custos*, and when the turb goes into action you are often positioned to the rear of any conflict, where you may shoot at the enemy. Your traveling companions look to you for backup and expect you to be vigilant for surprise attacks that they cannot look for, being locked in combat. You can also be called upon to kill a target, like the leader of a group of bandits, before melee commences. If your eye fails you, you commit your friends to a battle in which you lack the advantage.

*"I got 'em. . . just hold still."*

# MANSERVANT/HANDMAIDEN

| | | | |
|---|---|---|---|
| Intelligence | +3 | Presence | +1 |
| Perception | +1 | Communication | +1 |
| Strength | -2 | Dexterity | -3 |
| Stamina | -2 | Quickness | +1 |

**Age:** 18

**Virtues & Flaws:** Free Expression +1, Ambidextrous +1, Over-Confident -2

**Abilities:** Speak Own Language 4, Brawl 1, Dodge 3, Folk Ken 2, Charm 3, Drinking 2, Intrigue 3, Chirurgy 2, Weapon Skill (attack) 1, Weapon Skill (parry) 1, Guile 3, Etiquette 1

**Confidence:** 3

**Reputation:** None

**Personality Traits:** Devoted +3, Brave -2, Greedy +1

**Weapons & Armor:** Club

**Encumbrance:** 0

You are the personal servant of one of the more important inhabitants of the Covenant. That could make you a knight's page, a Magus's butler, or a Lady's Reeve. Though your position is ostensibly subservient, you live well, receiving food, shelter, and a warm bed. However, if your master is prone to travel, you find yourself on the road as well, and constantly in danger. A silent observer of the upper classes, you've picked up many of their secrets and can use them for your own ends.

*"I endeavor to make my master's life as comfortable as possible, and in so far as I am able to perform my duties, I am well rewarded. My task is to also insure that my master is divested from the unpleasantness of those around him."*

## SENTRY

| | | | |
|---|---|---|---|
| Intelligence | 0 | Presence | -3 |
| Perception | +5 | Communication | -1 |
| Strength | +1 | Dexterity | -2 |
| Stamina | +1 | Quickness | -1 |

**Age**: 18

**Virtues & Flaws**: Well-Traveled +1, Weak-Willed -1

**Abilities**: Speak Own Language 4, Brawl 2, Scan 4, Alertness 2, Dodge 2, Folk Ken 2, Drinking 3, Weapon Skill (attack) 2, Weapon Skill (parry) 2, Shield Parry 2

**Confidence**: 3

**Reputation**: None

**Personality Traits**: Brave +1, Determined +1

**Weapons & Armor**: Short Sword, Round Shield, Scale Mail Cuirass

**Encumbrance**: 2

Whether by dint of punishment, recognition of your perceptive eye, or your own ability to resist sleep, you constantly find yourself on guard duty. At the Covenant that means patrolling the fortress walls, or standing outside a locked door. Abroad, that means watching over your traveling companions while they sleep. You've learned to appreciate sentry duty. It leaves you time to yourself and it's taught you independence. Though you may not be *custos* yet, you may soon rise to that rank when you save some slumbering Magus's hide.

*"Sleep, now that's something you yearn for. After the fifth bell rings and your eyelids grow heavy, you grow jealous of those who sleep. But, I am always watchful despite my weariness. Our enemies are too numerous to ignore. The Covenant will not fall on my account, of that you can be sure."*

# Companion Vocations

## TROUBADOUR

| | | | |
|---|---|---|---|
| Intelligence | +2 | Presence | +1 |
| Perception | -1 | Communication | +3 |
| Strength | -3 | Dexterity | +1 |
| Stamina | -1 | Quickness | -2 |

**Age**: 27

**Virtues & Flaws**: Exceptional Talent (Enchanting Music) +2, Jack-Of-All-Trades +3, Famous +2, Haunted -2, Cursed -4, Black Sheep -1

**Abilities**: Speak Own Language 5, Dodge 1, Charisma 3, Folk Ken 3, Sing 4, Play 3, Legend Lore 3, Weapon Skill (attack) 2, Weapon Skill (parry) 2, Enchanting Music 3, Charm 3, Acting 1

**Confidence**: 3

**Reputation**: Adulterous 2, Good Storyteller 4

**Personality Traits**: Charming +3, Lusty +1, Poetic +2

**Weapons & Armor**: Short Sword

**Encumbrance**: 0

You are a minstrel, an actor-musician-comedian. Though you might have wandered the land at one time, you've since settled at the Covenant. The people there appreciate your music and pay you well — be it coin, food or ale — for a song. Even the rather aloof Magi seem to enjoy the occasional tune. You can also embellish your repertoire at the Covenant. There are plenty of legends to learn of there, and you can sometimes partake in their making.

*"Ah, can you spare a bit of wine for this poor parched throat? Thank ye."*

# KNIGHT

| Intelligence | -1 | Presence | 0 |
|---|---|---|---|
| Perception | -3 | Communication | -1 |
| Strength | +3 | Dexterity | +1 |
| Stamina | +3 | Quickness | -2 |

**Age:** 22

**Virtues & Flaws:** Knight +3, Honor Passion +2, Strong Willed +1, Higher Purpose +1, Demon Plagued -4, Oath of Fealty -1, Dark Secret -1, Lost Love -1

**Abilities:** Speak Own Language 5, Athletics 2, Dodge 3, Brawl 2, Ride 4, Intimidation 2, Intrigue 1, Weapon Skill (attack) 3, Shield Parry 3, Weapon Skill (lance attack) 3

**Confidence:** 3

**Reputation:** Tormented 1

**Personality Traits:** Brave +2, Melancholy +3

**Weapons & Armor:** Morning Star, Lance, Chain Mail Full Armor, Knight's Shield

**Encumbrance:** 5

You are a warrior with a vow to serve a higher power. That power could be your lord, and in turn your king, or you may pay homage to a Magus, a Covenant or the Order of Hermes itself. Maybe the Covenant has protected you and your people in the past and now you repay the debt. As a knight you are able to move through all social circles, both magical and mundane. Magi therefore value you as a medium between them and worldly powers. You are also essential to the Covenant's defense, to which you may apply your armor, many arms, and steed.

*"Hail, stranger. I mark the crest upon thy shield as that of Duke Leopold. Perhaps thou didst not know, but I am protector of these lands, and long have I held a fiery grudge against Duke Leopold. . . "*

# MERCHANT

| Intelligence | +2 | Presence | 0 |
|---|---|---|---|
| Perception | +3 | Communication | +2 |
| Strength | 0 | Dexterity | -2 |
| Stamina | -2 | Quickness | -3 |

**Age:** 28

**Virtues & Flaws:** Patron +2, Protector +3, Social Contacts +1, Well-Traveled +1, Obligation -1, Social Handicap -1, Noncombatant -3, Clumsy -2

**Abilities:** Speak Own Language 5, Alertness 2, Guile 3, Pretend 2, Charm 2, Ride 1, Intimidation 3, Evaluate 4, Diplomacy 3, Folk Ken 4, Charisma 3, Scan 1, Search 1

**Confidence:** 3

**Reputation:** Shifty 3

**Personality Traits:** Practical +1, Trustworthy -2, Brave -2

**Weapons & Armor:** None

**Encumbrance:** 0

You are a seller of wares, and may be itinerant to the Covenant. As such you travel the lands acquiring provisions and necessities for your Covenant. When not abroad you at least maintain lines of communication with your contacts, customers, and suppliers. If you don't the Magi may terminate your services. Then what would you do for profit? Traveling Magi often take you on the road to deal with mundanes and their "petty business tricks."

*"Yea, I've been to Iberia — a turbulent place with the invasions of those accursed Moors, and of course, the antics of your Flambeau brethren. In fact, I've done some decent trade with the Crusaders there. Why do you ask?"*

# Hermit

| | | | |
|---|---|---|---|
| Intelligence | +2 | Presence | 0 |
| Perception | +2 | Communication | +2 |
| Strength | -3 | Dexterity | +1 |
| Stamina | -3 | Quickness | -1 |

**Age:** 33

**Virtues & Flaws:** Educated +1, Exceptional Talent (Sense Holiness & Unholiness) +1, Exceptional Talent (Second Sight) +1, Destiny +4, Disfigured -1, Magic Susceptibility -1, Cursed -4, Fragile Constitution -1

**Abilities:** Speak Own Language 5, Sense Holiness & Unholiness 4, Folk Ken 1, Pretend 3, Survival 3, Meditation 2, Chirurgy 2, Area Lore 3, Occult Lore 3, Second Sight 2, Church Knowledge 3, Scribe (Latin) 4, Humanities 3

**Confidence:** 3

**Reputation:** Blessed 1

**Personality Traits:** Calm +2, Introspective +3, Helpful -1

**Weapons & Armor:** None        **Encumbrance:** 0

You once belonged to society, but ostracized yourself or were exiled to solitary life, maybe for religious reasons. You've learned much about humankind, the world, and the supernatural in your lonely life. It seems a shame not to share your insight, but ordinary people just don't understand you. At least the Magi listen to what you have to say, and they treat you with respect; their lives have been devoted to solitary contemplation much like yours. Though you may not live in the Covenant, you're not too far away.

*"There's much to be learned from the isolated life. The secrets of the world are opened to you when the distraction of mortality is out of your ears. I have learned much in my solitude, maybe more than a man should know."*

# Forester

| | | | |
|---|---|---|---|
| Intelligence | -2 | Presence | -2 |
| Perception | +2 | Communication | -3 |
| Strength | +3 | Dexterity | +1 |
| Stamina | +2 | Quickness | -1 |

**Age:** 25

**Virtues & Flaws:** Ways of the Woods +4, Large +2, Sharp Ears +1, Soft-Hearted -1, Sensitive -1, Compulsion -1, Hatred -1, Enemies -1, Poor Equipment -1, Infamous Family -1

**Abilities:** Speak Own Language 5, Alertness 2, Dodge 3, Area Lore 3, Survival 2, Track 3, Chirurgy 2, Weapon Skill (attack) 2, Missile Weapon Skill (attack) 3, Animal Handling 4, Faerie Lore 2, Scan 1

**Confidence:** 3

**Reputation:** Uncorruptable 3

**Personality Traits:** Gentle +2, Violent +2, Brave +1

**Weapons & Armor:** Quarter Staff, Self Bow, Fur Cuirass  **Encumbrance:** 0

You patrol the forests of a lord or the King himself, or maybe you protect lands deeded to a Covenant's Magi. Either way, you are your own keeper, though you must be ever vigilant for poachers, for if you don't protect the reserved game, you could lose your hand in place of a poacher's. You are of value to the Covenant because you know the lands you keep, and can help Magi find things they seek there. In return the Covenant offers companionship, for most commoners fear you — they don't want to be recognized by you.

*"In this part of the wood you have to watch your step. There's a nasty little faerie hereabouts. I've never seen him, but I've heard him to be sure, and he's always looking to snag me up with branches and roots. I figure, I don't bother him so why should be bother me, but for some reason he's got his dander up."*

# BANDIT

| | | | |
|---|---|---|---|
| Intelligence | 0 | Presence | -4 |
| Perception | +2 | Communication | -1 |
| Strength | -1 | Dexterity | +3 |
| Stamina | -1 | Quickness | +2 |

**Age:** 19

**Virtues & Flaws:** Rebel Passion +3, Reckless +1, Good Armaments +1, Gang Leader +2, Outlaw -4, Criminal Brand -1, Driving Goal -1, Enemies -1

**Abilities:** Speak Own Language 5, Alertness 3, Dodge 2, Climb 1, Pretend 2, Stealth 4, Pick Locks 3, Weapon Skill (attack) 2, Weapon Skill (parry) 3

**Confidence:** 3

**Reputation:** Outlaw 4

**Personality Traits:** Self-Concerned +2, Compulsive +2, Devoted -1

**Weapons & Armor:** Broad Sword, Quilted Cuirass

**Encumbrance:** 1

You are crafty and slippery by nature. You probably acquire most of your money in town, but hire your services out to the Magi when they need a job done. If there's frequent work to be found at the Covenant you may live there full-time, relying on the Magi for protection against the law — you have to do some entrepreneurial work, after all. When Magi go abroad you often accompany them, to acquire information and the occasional trinket.

*"Bon jour, mes ami. I'm afraid I will have to take your possessions. I am a helpful man and they seem such a burden to you. Keep your hands where I can see them. I know who you folk are. If I see even the slightest flash of your magic I'll. . ."*

# TURB CAPTAIN

| | | | |
|---|---|---|---|
| Intelligence | +1 | Presence | +2 |
| Perception | -2 | Communication | +1 |
| Strength | +1 | Dexterity | -3 |
| Stamina | +2 | Quickness | -2 |

**Age:** 30

**Virtues & Flaws:** Leadership +3, Superior Armaments +1, Educated +1, Light Touch +2, Missing Hand -2, Obsessed -1, Fury -3, Weakness -1

**Abilities:** Speak Own Language 5, Scribe Own Language 4, Dodge 3, Alertness 2, Brawl 3, Ride 3, Intimidation 3, Leadership 3, Weapon Skill (attack) 3, Weapon Skill (parry) 3, Drinking 2

**Confidence:** 3

**Reputation:** Demon Tainted 1

**Personality Traits:** Brave +3, Rational -1, Excitable +2

**Weapons & Armor:** War Maul, Full Chain Mail

**Encumbrance:** 6

You are in command of all the Covenant's Grogs, and rose from the ranks through your exemplary service. Though you still move among the Grogs, you now spend much of your time doing paperwork, either filing information about your troops or requisitioning supplies. The Magi turn to you to assemble a turb for journeys, and rely on your expertise to choose skilled, dependable Grogs. With such power you are able to escape the doldrum of your position by assigning yourself to traveling parties.

*"You there, what are you doing from your post? Why, when I was down in the ranks I never strayed from my duty. With Heaven as my witness, you Grogs are getting more and more lax with each passing day!"*

## FRIAR

| Intelligence | +2 | Presence | +1 |
| Perception | +1 | Communication | +3 |
| Strength | -3 | Dexterity | -3 |
| Stamina | 0 | Quickness | -1 |

**Age:** 27

**Virtues & Flaws:** Clergy +3, Educated +1, True Faith +3, Meddler -1, Delusion -1, Poor Eyesight -1, Vow -4

**Abilities:** Speak Own Language 5, Speak (Latin) 3, Scribe (Latin) 4, Church Lore 4, Occult Lore 2, Church Knowledge 4, Chirurgy 2, Folk Ken 2, Scribe (own language) 3, Swim 2

**Faith:** 3

**Reputation:** Meddler 1

**Personality Traits:** Humble +2, Inquisitive +3, Brave +1

**Weapons & Armor:** None

**Encumbrance:** 0

You are a clergyman who has taken a vow of poverty, and you dedicate your life to the common people. You work with the Magi because you know they are, or can be, good people. You also don't see any harm in trying to convert them to Christianity, and are careful that they don't take the Church for granted. Above all that, the Covenant offers you an opportunity to see the world and invites you to do things your vows fail to prohibit.

*"Good morning, my son. Maybe you can tell me something. I had retired to my chambers last night, and was devoted to prayer, when I heard a terrible crash and shouting from the floor above. That wouldn't happen to be your laboratory above my chambers, would it?"*

## LADY

| Intelligence | +2 | Presence | 0 |
| Perception | +2 | Communication | +2 |
| Strength | -2 | Dexterity | -2 |
| Stamina | -3 | Quickness | +1 |

**Age:** 16

**Virtues & Flaws:** Educated +1, Temporal Influence +2, Gossip +2, Indentured Servant +2, Noncombatant -3, Sensitive -1, Bad Reputation -1, Curse of Venus -2

**Abilities:** Speak Own Language 5, Charm 3, Pretend 2, Ride 2, Diplomacy 2, Intrigue 3, Intimidation 2, Scribe Latin 1, Speak Latin 2, Humanities 2, Etiquette 1

**Confidence:** 3

**Reputation:** Brat 2

**Personality Traits:** Precocious +2, Bitchy +2, Demanding +2

**Weapons & Armor:** None

**Encumbrance:** 0

You are educated, trained in social skills, able to get the best out of social situations, and of high enough rank to do as you wish. Courtly life occupies your time, but bores you. Out of curiosity and a desire for adventure, you associate with the Covenant. However, you try to keep that association secret for it could mean social alienation back at court.

*"What do you mean you won't carry my bags! I have the Baron's ear! When he hears of this he will have your head!"*

## TORTURER

| Intelligence | -1 | Presence | -3 |
| Perception | 0 | Communication | -2 |
| Strength | +3 | Dexterity | +1 |
| Stamina | +3 | Quickness | -1 |

**Age:** 24

**Virtues & Flaws:** Reserves of Strength +2, Ghostly Warder +4, Ambidextrous +1, Terrors -2, Deep Sleeper -1, Hunchback -2, Infamous -2

**Abilities:** Speak Own Language 5, Athletics 2, Dodge 2, Brawl 4, Intimidation 4, Drinking 3, Weapon Skill (attack) 3, Weapon Skill (parry) 3, Chirurgy 2, Bargain 1

**Confidence:** 3

**Reputation:** Merciless 4

**Personality Traits:** Angry +2, Impressionable +1, Brave -1

**Weapons & Armor:** Short Sword, Leather Cuirass

**Encumbrance:** 0

At one time you may have worked for a lord, or still do and occasionally lend your services to the Covenant. You may not love your work, but you have to admit it's a living. The Magi may not advertise your employment, but can't deny that your methods get results. At least in working for the Covenant you hope your abilities are being used toward some good. The Magi sometimes invite you on special missions in which they expect difficulty getting information.

*"This won't hurt for but a moment."*

## Magus Vocations

Magus Vocations are based on Houses, the means by which those in the Order of Hermes separate themselves from one another. Normally a Magus joins the House of her master, though this is not always the case. Each House has a unique outlook on life, specialized magics, and an organizational structure of some sort. One Vocation is provided for each House, so you are as much choosing a House as you are a character. Each House is described in the Mythic Europe Chapter.

## MAGUS OF BONISAGUS

| Intelligence | +4 | Presence | 0 |
| Perception | 0 | Communication | +3 |
| Strength | -1 | Dexterity | -2 |
| Stamina | -3 | Quickness | -1 |

**Age:** 20

**Virtues & Flaws:** Cautious Sorcery(Vim) +3, Inventive Genius +1, Book-Learner +1, Strong Writer +1, Hermetic Prestige +1, Magical Affinity (Vim) +3, Major Magic Deficiency (Ignem) -3, Fragile Constitution -1, Driving Goal (Study Magic) -1, Social Handicap (among Magi; only speaks of magic & magical things) -1, The Blatant Gift -1, Sense of Doom -3

**Abilities:** Speak Own Language 4, Speak (Latin) 5, Scribe (Latin) 3, Magic Theory 5, Hermes Lore 2, Hermes History 3, *Parma Magica* 3, Craft (Lab Equipment) 2, Meditation 2, Magical Affinity (Vim) 2, Finesse 2, Penetration 1, Legend Lore 1

**Confidence:** 3 **Reputation:** Inventive +3

**Personality Traits:** Obsessive +3, Expressive -2

**Weapons & Armor:** None **Encumbrance:** 0

**Techniques & Forms:** Creo 7, Intéllego 7, Muto 0, Perdo 0, Rego 7, Animál 0, Aquam 0, Auram 0, Córporem 0, Herbam 0, Ignem 0, Imágonem 4, Mentem 7, Terram 0, Vim 7

**Spells:** *Invisible Eye Revealed* (Intéllego Vim 20), *Return of Mental Lucidity* (Creo Mentem 20), *Ring of Warding Against Spirits* (Rego Mentem 20), *Scales of the Magical Weight* (Intéllego Vim 15), *Sense the Nature of* Vis (Intéllego Vim 10), *Shell of False Determinations* (Creo Vim 15), *Wizard's Boost* (Rego Vim 25), *Wizard's Communion* (Rego Vim 20), *Wizard's Subtle Touch* (Intéllego Vim 5)

## BONISAGUS MAGUS CONTINUED

A follower of Bonisagus, you are the epitome of what the Flambeau Magi call, "lab rats." Obsessed with your art and related topics, you eat, drink, sleep and breathe magic, barely pausing to sleep. Accordingly, you suffer from perpetual minor ailments and discomforts, and occasionally have to be forced to rest by the Covenant's healer. Your deficiency in Ignem causes you to be somewhat prejudiced against the baser "elemental" Forms, so your studies tend to range into the more esoteric Imágonem, Vim, and Mentem.

*"Yes, yes, quite true, quite true, but look at it this way. . ."*

# MAGUS OF BJORNAER

| | | | |
|---|---|---|---|
| Intelligence | +1 | Presence | -2 |
| Perception | -2 | Communication | -3 |
| Strength | +2 | Dexterity | +2* |
| Stamina | +2 | Quickness | +2 |

\* Two points of Flaws used to buy positive Characteristics

**Age:** 24

**Virtues & Flaws:** Heart-Beast (Wolf) +2, Will Over Form +2, The Hidden Shape +2, Passion (Valor) +1, Self-Confident +1, The Blatant Gift -1, Discredited Lineage (*Parents* may have aided House Diedne at one time) -2, Uncommon Fear (hunters' traps) -1, Social Handicap (among Magi; no tact or etiquette) -1, Susceptible to Faerie Power -4, Minor Magic Deficiency (Ignem) -1

**Abilities:** Speak Own Language 4, Speak (Latin) 5, Scribe (Latin) 3, Magic Theory 5, Hermes Lore 2, Hermes History 2, *Parma Magica* 2, Athletics 1, Climb 1, Dodge 2, Brawl 1, Swim 1, Survival 2, Track 2, (Area) Lore 2, Weapon Skill (attack) 2, Weapon Skill (parry) 2, *Certámen* 1, Will Over Form 1

**Confidence:** 4    **Reputation:** Foolhardy 1

**Personality Traits:** Wolf +3, Brutal +2, Charming -3, Angry +1

**Weapons & Armor:** Quarter Staff, Fur Hauberk

**Encumbrance:** 0

**Techniques and Forms:** Creo 4, Intéllego 7, Muto 7, Perdo 0, Rego 0, Animál 7, Aquam 0, Auram 0, Córporem 7, Herbam 0, Ignem 0, Imágonem 0, Mentem 0, Terram 0, Vim 7

**Spells:** *Tongue of the Beast* (Intéllego Animal 20), *Tongue of the Bird* (Intéllego Animal 20), *Tongue of the Fish* (Intéllego Animal 20), *Soothe the Pains of the Beast* (Creo Animál 20), *Opening the Tome of the Animal's Mind* (Intéllego Animál 25), *Form of the Avenging Beast* (Muto Animál 20), *Perceive the Magical Scent* (Intéllego Vim 20), *Change the Nature of* Vis (Muto Vim 5)

A member of the animalistic, shapechanging Bjornaer House, you are often mistaken by covenfolk and other Magi for *custos* given your physique. This, coupled with your complete lack of tact, and the fact that the Magus you apprenticed under may have aided members of House Diedne, has given you a nasty reputation in the Order. No matter. Your Bjornaer brethren and your animal companions are the only company you need. You are short-tempered, gruff, and have no use for most two-legs. The only way a human can gain your respect is to show a genuine concern for the forest and its inhabitants. As an apprentice you were once caught in a hunter's trap, have since developed a great fear for such things, and even grow angry when near those who trap for a living.

*"I do not care a fig about the state of mortal affairs. It is toward my brothers and sisters of the forest that I reserve my compassion. Their company is the only brand of civilization I can endure."*

# MAGUS OF JERBITON

| | | | |
|---|---|---|---|
| Intelligence | +3 | Presence | +1 |
| Perception | -1 | Communication | +1 |
| Strength | -2 | Dexterity | -2 |
| Stamina | +2 | Quickness | -2 |

**Age:** 22

**Virtues & Flaws:** Hermetic Prestige +1, Free Expression +1, Well-Traveled +1, Piercing Gaze +2, The Gentle Gift +1, Silent Magic +4, No Familiar -2, Noncombatant -3, Delusion -1, Compulsion (intrigue) -1, Enemies -1, Personal Hatred -1, Weakness (art & beauty) -1

**Abilities:** Speak Own Language 4, Speak (Latin) 5, Scribe (Latin) 3, Magic Theory 5, Hermes Lore 2, Hermes History 2, *Parma Magica* 2, Charisma 1, Folk Ken 1, Diplomacy 1, Leadership 1, Intrigue 3, Church Lore 3, Penetration 3

Confidence: 3          Reputation: Hermetic Prestige 3

Personality Traits: Calculating +2, Impetuous -3, Cunning +2

Weapons & Armor: None          Encumbrance: 0

Techniques and Forms: Creo 0, Intéllego 10, Muto 0, Perdo 0, Rego 10, Animál 0, Aquam 0, Auram 0, Córporem 0, Herbam 0, Ignem 0, Imágonem 2, Mentem 8, Terram 0, Vim 1

Spells: *Perception of the Conflicting Motives* (Intéllego Mentem 15), *Frosty Breath of the Spoken Lie* (Intéllego Mentem 20), *Posing the Silent Question* (Intéllego Mentem 25), *Peering into the Mortal Mind* (Intéllego Mentem 30), *Aura of Rightful Authority* (Rego Mentem 20), *Scent of Peaceful Slumber* (Rego Mentem 20), *The Ear for Distant Voices* (Intéllego Imágonem 20)

Cool and calculating, you consider yourself the Order's last chance to relate to the mundane world, and thus its last chance to avoid destruction. Of course, your devotion to this goal is largely based on personal gain. You cannot resist complicating any situation through intrigue, and often switch loyalties between factions before finally siding with that which best serves your purposes. Your command of the language, weakness for all things beautiful (especially pre-Christian Celtic art), and gentle Gift make you quite popular among members of your House, who like you despite your reputed hatred for a high-ranking House official. Throughout the years you have found yourself at odds with many people, some of whom have not willingly accepted defeat at your hands.

*"I am of the aristocracy within the only democratic society the world has seen since the days of ancient Athens. My noblesse, however, is not determined by my blood, but by my responsibilities."*

# MAGUS OF CRIAMON

| Intelligence | +3 | Presence | -3 |
|---|---|---|---|
| Perception | +3 | Communication | 0 |
| Strength | -2 | Dexterity | -1 |
| Stamina | +1 | Quickness | -1 |

Age: 32

Virtues & Flaws: Independent Magic +2, Extra Arts +1, Life-linked Spontaneous Magic +3, Charmed Life +4, The Blatant Gift (your magic inflicts itself on the world around you) -1, Incomprehensible -2, Magic Addiction -3, Twilight Points -1, Disfigured -1, Cursed -2

Abilities: Speak Own Language 4, Speak (Latin) 5, Scribe (Latin) 3, Magic Theory 5, Hermes Lore 2, Hermes History 2, Finesse 3, *Certámen* 1, *Parma Magica* 4, Concentration 2, Meditation 3, Occult Lore 2, Enigmatic Wisdom 3

Confidence: 3          Reputation: Weird +2

Personality Traits: Distracted +3, Energetic +1

Weapons & Armor: None          Encumbrance: 0

Techniques and Forms: Creo 4, Intéllego 9, Muto 4, Perdo 0, Rego 0, Animál 0, Aquam 0, Auram 0, Córporem 2, Herbam 0, Ignem 0, Imágonem 10, Mentem 8, Terram 0, Vim 1

Spells: *Illusion of the Altered Image* (Muto Imágonem 10), *Notes of a Delightful Sound* (Muto Imágonem 10), *Phantasm of the Talking Head* (Creo Imágonem 10), *Phantasmal Fire* (Creo Imágonem 15), *Weight of a Thousand Hells* (Creo Mentem 25), *Peering into the Mortal Mind* (Intéllego Mentem 30), *The Inexorable Search* (Intéllego Córporem 20), *Perceive the Magical Scent* (Intéllego Vim 20), *The Invisible Eye Revealed* (Intéllego Vim 10)

A follower of Criamon, you are more interested in thoughts and perceptions than you are the physical world. Your thoughts are incomprehensible to most people, including other Magi, so your magical writings tend to be understandable only by other Criamon Magi (and even then, it is doubtful they truly understand them). Your addiction to magic is a result of magic's constant use to stimulate your mind, and the spells you usually cast to get your "rush" are of the Creo Imágonem variety. Because your life is linked to these magics, it is extremely dangerous for you to lose control. Thus, to most Magi you are a *Pilum of Fire* waiting to explode, while other Criamon Magi seem to acknowledge the wisdom gained through

## CRIAMON MAGUS CONTINUED

your experimentations. You are constantly looking for new Creo or Muto Imágonem spells to stimulate the senses and mind. Your Enigmatic Wisdom Ability gives you improved chances of surviving Twilight, and of understanding other Criamon Magi.

*"Armed soldiers approach? Pity, I was hoping for a learned man who might help me resolve this puzzle: 'The bird that wears the mountain.'"*

# MAGUS OF MERCERE

| | | | |
|---|---|---|---|
| Intelligence | -1 | Presence | +1 |
| Perception | +2 | Communication | +2 |
| Strength | -3 | Dexterity | -3 |
| Stamina | +2 | Quickness | 0 |

**Age:** 32

**Virtues & Flaws:** Passion (Honor) +1, Well-Traveled +1, Magical Animal Companion (raven) +2, Redcap +3, Highly Skilled +3, Curse (it rains on you more than anyone else) -1, Meddler -1, Favor -1, Common Fear -2, Enemies -1, Social Handicap (abrupt) -1, Vow (reliability) -3

**Abilities:** Speak Own Language 5, Folk Ken 2, Etiquette 1, (Area) Lore 2, Church Lore 1, Faerie Lore 1, Speak Latin 4, Alertness 1, Chirurgy 1, Ride 2, Brawl 3, Survival 3, Track 1, Animal Handling 2, Stealth 3, Weapon Skill (attack) 2, Weapon Skill (parry) 2

**Confidence:** 3

**Reputation:** None

**Personality Traits:** Sincere +2, Restive +1, Lazy -2

**Weapons & Armor:** Quarter Staff, Quilted Cuirass

**Encumbrance:** 0

**Techniques and Forms:** None

**Spells:** None

**Potions:** *Chirurgeon's Healing Touch* (3 doses), *The Beast Remade* (2 doses).

**Enchantments:** Headband of *Thoughts Within Babble* (Intéllego Mentem 25)

Necklace of *Veil of Invisibility* (Muto Imágonem 30)

Ring of *Posing the Silent Question* (Intéllego Mentem 20)

Glass of *Sight of the Active Magics* (Intéllego Vim)

Ring of *Parma Magica* (3)

Wooden Bowl of *The Oat's Gifts* (Creo Herbam 20) — With a little water added this bowl creates enough hot boiled oats for one meal. Functions thrice per day and can keep you alive during lean times.

## RAVEN COMPANION:

| | | | |
|---|---|---|---|
| Intelligence | 0 | Presence | -3 |
| Perception | +1 | Communication | -3 |
| Strength | -4 | Dexterity | +3 |
| Stamina | 0 | Quickness | +3 |

**Magical Abilities:** Premonitions 3

Second Sight 2

Read Lips 2

*Parma Magica* 1.

Has a permanent *Speech of the Unbroken Silence* (Creo Mentem 25) cast on it.

**Magic Might:** 10; body is worth 2 Animál vis.

As a Magus of House Mercere, you have no Gift. You are a messenger, scout, and guide for the Order, a Redcap, so you've learned to live and work alone. You long to retire and spend your time hobnobbing with other Magi, exchanging stories of the road. However, while you work, you are totally devoted to your job. Nothing stays your swift delivery of the vital messages, which you carry from Covenant to Covenant. Your raven companion has proven extremely useful in warning you of potentially dangerous situations, although you sometimes wonder how she knows what she knows. You have learned not to carry on long, involved conversations with your raven in front of mundanes. You have also learned to blend in with villagers and commoners in your area, as long as you don't interact with them. You like to meddle in the affairs of others, but are quite abrupt with non-Magi, ostracizing yourself in mundane social situations.

*"The road is both a valued ally and deadly adversary. You must understand the road's needs and supplicate them to arrive at your destination. Understanding the path you travel is like understanding the course of your life. If you are well prepared, you get where you want to go."*

# MAGUS OF FLAMBEAU

| | | | |
|---|---|---|---|
| Intelligence | +1 | Presence | -3 |
| Perception | +3 | Communication | -4 |
| Strength | 0 | Dexterity | +1 |
| Stamina | +2 | Quickness | 0 |

**Age:** 20

**Virtues & Flaws:** Passion (Rage) +3, Fast-Caster +2, Self-Confident +1, Continuous Spontaneous Magic +4, Driving Goal (protecting the Order) -1, Enemies (Tremere Magi who bullied you during apprenticeship) -1, Social Handicap (among Magi) -1, Infamous -2, Sensitive (to insults against House Flambeau) -1, Weak Writer -1, Poor Reader -3

**Abilities:** Speak Own Language 4, Speak (Latin) 5, Scribe (Latin) 3, Magic Theory 5, Hermes Lore 2, Hermes History 2, *Parma Magica* 3, Survival 1, *Certámen* 2, Alertness 1, Scan 1, Search 1, Track 2, Weapon Skill (attack) 1, Weapon Skill (parry) 1, Penetration 2, Finesse (Targeting) 1, Concentration 1

**Confidence:** 4     **Reputation:** Mad 4

**Personality Traits:** Violent +3, Vindictive +3, Destructive +3

**Weapons & Armor:** Hand Axe    **Encumbrance:** 0

**Techniques and Forms:** Creo 10, Intéllego 0, Muto 0, Perdo 8, Rego 0, Animál 0, Aquam 0, Auram 0, Córporem 2, Herbam 0, Ignem 10, Imágonem 0, Mentem 0, Terram 0, Vim 1

**Spells:** *Flash of the Scarlet Flames* (Creo Ignem 15), *Pilum of Fire* (Creo Ignem 20), *Arc of Fiery Ribbons* (Creo Ignem 25), *Conjuration of the Indubitable Cold* (Perdo Ignem 20), *Well Without Light* (Perdo Ignem 25), *Grip of the Choking Hand* (Perdo Córporem 10), *Dust to Dust* (Perdo Córporem 15), *Wind of Mundane Silence* (Perdo Vim 20)

You have a hard time understanding the high-borne ideas that Magi, like those who follow Bonisagus, study. However, you know one thing and one thing well: fire. You know its hunger, and its dance—you love fire, love it like life itself. There is no more exhilarating a feeling than that of opening yourself to the energies of Ignem and flinging them skyward, except perhaps the immensely satisfying explosion that usually follows. Although some might accuse you of being too enthusiastic in the Wizard's March, you know in your heart you are loyal to the Order. You brook no insult to it, especially House Flambeau. You hate spending too much time with mortals, simply because the Order gets upset when you singe them. You like to hunt rogue wizards, it's true, but much of your free time is spent studying Ignem *vis* and other sources of fire-magic, to improve your understanding of the Hungry Power. Your temper is short and your spontaneous command of Ignem is great. Most Magi give you a wide berth. *"Destruction is more an art than most might think, for only by destroying the old can you make room for the new, and only by destroying the new can you preserve the old."*

# MAGUS OF TYTALUS

| | | | |
|---|---|---|---|
| Intelligence | +3 | Presence | -3 |
| Perception | 0 | Communication | -3 |
| Strength | 0 | Dexterity | +1 |
| Stamina | +3 | Quickness | -1 |

**Age:** 30

**Virtues & Flaws:** Magical Affinity (Rego) +4, Tough +1, Light Sleeper +1, Versatile Sleeper +1, Enduring Magic +3, Tormenting Master -1, Disgusted by Magic -3, Disfigured (awful scars on neck, back, and left cheek) -1, Demon Plagued -4, Orphan -1

**Abilities:** Speak Own Language 4, Speak (Latin) 5, Scribe (Latin) 3, Magic Theory 5, Hermes Lore 2, Hermes History 2, *Parma Magica* 3, Survival 1, Guile 1, Leadership 1, Brawl 1, Ride 1, Stealth 1, Chirurgy 2, *Certámen* 3, Alertness 2, Athletics 2, Magic Affinity (Rego) 3

**Confidence:** 3     **Reputation:** Squeamish (Order of Hermes) 2

**Personality Traits:** Determined +2, Timid +1

**Weapons & Armor:** None     **Encumbrance:** 0

**Techniques and Forms:** Creo 5, Intéllego 5, Muto 5, Perdo 5, Rego 6, Animál 2, Aquam 2, Auram 2, Córporem 5, Herbam 1, Ignem 3, Imágonem 4, Mentem 4, Terram 2, Vim 5

**Spells:** *Disenchant* (Perdo Vim 20), *Wind of Mundane Silence* (Perdo Vim 20), *Circular Ward Against Demons* (Rego Vim 20), *Demon's Eternal Oblivion* (Perdo Vim 20), *Lay to Rest the Haunting Spirit* (Perdo Mentem 20), *Coerce the Spirits of the Night* (Rego Mentem 20), *Scent of Peaceful Slumber* (Rego Mentem 20), *Despair of the Quivering Manacles* (Rego Córporem 10)

## TYTALUS MAGUS CONTINUED

You grew up on the street. Your birth is shrouded in mystery; it's said your mother, your only parent, was impregnated by a demon. She died giving birth to you, and you were forced into all manner of human indecencies to survive. Finally, your master-to-be found you, choosing you as one who knew the burdens of pain, survival, and conflict.

Life in your master's Covenant was only marginally better than that on the street. You had scant, regular meals, clean clothes, and a place to sleep, but you were in more danger than ever before. Your master would often enter your room at night to cast painful magics on you, or flog you, or to dump you out in the cold. You learned to sleep lightly, and took to hiding and sleeping during the day. Everything your master taught you about magic made parallels between it and pain, evil, and darkness. Now, in order to avoid "the shakes," you must wash your hands thoroughly after casting each spell. It sounds strange, but this simple mundane ritual calms you.

Given your loathing of your power, you are determined to turn it to good, and have devoted your life to the destruction of spirits and demons, who were often sent to torment you in your sleep. Your master still calls you by your apprentice name and believes you somehow rigged your Apprentice's Gauntlet during your initiation as a Magus. Now, you spend much of your time studying magic, hoping to one day find a spell which is "clean" and good, which will break through your fear of the arcane.

As a Tytalus Magus, you judge yourself not by your knowledge but by who you can dominate, control, and establish power over. The more people, particularly Magi, you can dominate the better you feel. For this reason you have studied a wide range of Arts so that you may defeat other Magi in *Certámen*, being flexible and fast in magical duels.

*"I still hear the demons' voices at night, calling out my name, intent on stealing my soul. They no longer frighten me as they did, for now I have power to use against them. Now the demons have reason to be frightened of me, just as my accursed master will one day."*

# MAGUS OF QUAESITOR

| | | | |
|---|---|---|---|
| Intelligence | +2 | Presence | +2 |
| Perception | +2 | Communication | +1 |
| Strength | -2 | Dexterity | -2 |
| Stamina | -2 | Quickness | -1 |

**Age:** 32

**Virtues & Flaws:** Exceptional Talent (Empathy) +1, Magical Affinity (truth) +1, Quaesitor +1, Extra Arts +1, Highly Skilled +3, Fast Learner +3, Deep Sleeper -1, Fragile Constitution -1, Obligation (duty to the House) -1, Uncommon Fear (sleeping in the open) -1, Curse of Venus -2, Poor Memory -1, Dark Secret -1, Tainted with Evil -2

**Abilities:** Speak Own Language 4, Speak (Latin) 5, Scribe (Latin) 3, Magic Theory 5, Hermes Lore 2, Hermes History 2, *Parma Magica* 2, Magical Affinity (truth) 4, (Area) Lore 1, Alertness 1, Hermetic Law 3, Church Knowledge 1, Concentration 2, Diplomacy 3, Empathy 4, Humanities 1, Intimidation 1, Intrigue 2, Leadership 2, Meditation 2, Scan 1, Search 1, Storytelling 1

**Confidence:** 3      **Reputation:** Malleable +1

**Personality Traits:** Secretive +3, Deceptive +2

**Weapons & Armor:** None      **Encumbrance:** 0

**Techniques and Forms:** Creo 1, Intéllego 10, Muto 0, Perdo 0, Rego 2, Animál 0, Aquam 0, Auram 0, Córporem 8, Herbam 0, Ignem 0, Imágonem 0, Mentem 10, Terram 0, Vim 4

**Spells:**

*Sight of the True Form* (Intéllego Córporem 10), *Whispers Through The Black Gate* (Intéllego Córporem 15), *The Inexorable Search* (Intéllego Córporem 20), *Despair of the Quivering Manacles* (Rego Córporem 10), *Peering Into The Mortal Mind* (Intéllego Mentem 30), *Sense of the Lingering Magic* (Intéllego Vim 30) — Affinity allows you to cast this spell when investigating crimes, *Panic of the Trembling Heart* (Creo Mentem 15), *Return of Mental Lucidity* (Creo Mentem 20)

You are Quaesitor. Your specialty within the House is the investigation of crimes against the Code of Hermes. You are specifically prohibited from participation in Tribunals because of your empathic talent, which prevents you from being objective. On the other hand, the talent makes you an excellent investigator. You make it a habit to appear unassuming and weak. Your particular phobias and sensitivities reinforce this idea, though, so your demeanor is not so different from your nature as you believe. Still, your demeanor enables you to enter a situation and learn as much as you can about it before revealing yourself as Quaesitor.

*"I am glad you have finally played your hand, my fine, fiery friend. I have been waiting for you to admit your crime, and return to its scene. Know that you have met your end, for I am Quaesitor, not the doddering fool you supposed me. And, for the crimes you have committed against the Order of Hermes, I shall have you Renounced from the Order, may the powers that be have mercy on your soul."*

# MAGUS OF TREMERE

| | | | |
|---|---|---|---|
| Intelligence | +3 | Presence | -4 |
| Perception | +3 | Communication | 0 |
| Strength | 0 | Dexterity | 0 |
| Stamina | +1 | Quickness | -3 |

**Age:** 25

**Virtues & Flaws**: Mastered Skill (*Certámen*) +4, Extra Arts +2, Self-Confident +1, Independent Magic +2, Good Armaments +1, No Sigil -1, *Vis* Obligation (former master) -1, No Familiar -2, Sense of Doom -3, Favors (official of House Tytalus) -1, Vow -2

**Abilities**: Speak Own Language 4, Speak (Latin) 5, Scribe (Latin) 3, Magic Theory 5, Hermes Lore 2, Hermes History 2, *Parma Magica* 2, *Certámen* 1, Concentration 1, Meditation 1, Games of Skill (chess) 3, Weapon Skill (attack) 2, Weapon Skill (parry) 2, Survival 1, Pick Locks 1, Stealth 1, Guile 1, Finesse 1, Penetration 2, Athletics 1, Intrigue 1

**Confidence**: 4      **Reputation**: Dangerous (Order of Hermes) 3

**Personality Traits**: Competitive +3, Good Loser -2, Fair -2

**Weapons & Armor**: Broad Sword, Ring Mail Cuirass      **Encumbrance**: 2

**Techniques and Forms**: Creo 7, Intéllego 7, Muto 7, Perdo 7, Rego 7, Animál 0, Aquam 0, Auram 0, Córporem 4, Herbam 0, Ignem 4, Imágonem 0, Mentem 0, Terram 0, Vim 4

**Spells**: *Incantation of the Milky Eyes* (Perdo Córporem 20), *Hornet Fire* (Muto Ignem 15), *Stone of the Hundred Shards* (Creo Terram 15), *Invisible Hand of the Thief* (Rego Terram 15), *Wizard's Boost* (Muto Vim 20), *The Sorcerer's Fork* (Muto Vim 20), *Shroud Magic* (Muto Vim 15), *Disenchant* (Perdo Vim 10), *Wind of Mundane Silence* (Perdo Vim 20)

As a Tremere Magus, you spent your apprenticeship in constant struggle. Nothing you learned was given to you freely — each bit of magical knowledge you have today was won through contest with your master. Then, one day, your master achieved the ultimate victory. He showed you your dark future, and made you aware of how you will one day meet your doom. You now live with the knowledge that, no matter what you do, you will eventually meet your fate. However, you continue to fight, for you have decided to bring down an impressive number of Magi before the day of your destruction. You even consider forcing others to share your fate, taking them down with you. Your innate talent for *Certámen* may one day make you great in House Tremere, if you survive that long.

*"I may not be long for this world, but before I am gone all the Order of Hermes will know my name and shudder at its sound. I shall be the ultimate champion, never to be rivaled."*

# MAGUS OF VERDITIUS

| | | | |
|---|---|---|---|
| Intelligence | +2 | Presence | -2 |
| Perception | +2 | Communication | -1 |
| Strength | -1 | Dexterity | +3 |
| Stamina | 0 | Quickness | -3 |

**Age:** 29

**Virtues & Flaws**: Magic Item (Staff of the Dragon's Scale — staff with the following spell powers: *Wings of the Soaring Wind* (Rego Auram 25), *Pilum of Fire* (Creo Ignem 20), and *The Seven League Stride* (Rego Córporem 35) +8, Inventive Genius +1, Personal *Vis* +1, Verditius Magic -1, Reclusive -1, Obligation (make items for Verditius Magi) -1, Compulsion (creation) -1, Slow Caster -3, Painful Magic -3

**Abilities**: Speak Own Language 4, Speak (Latin) 5, Scribe (Latin) 3, Magic Theory 5, Hermes Lore 2, Hermes History 2, *Parma Magica* 3, Verditius Magic 4, Craft (smithing) 3, Craft (woodwork) 1, Evaluate (metals and ores) 2, Bargain 3

**Confidence**: 3

**Reputation**: Prolific Creator 1

**Personality Traits**: Selfish +1, Arrogant +3, Self-Assured -1

**Weapons & Armor**: None

**Encumbrance**: 0

**Techniques and Forms**: Creo 5, Intéllego 5, Muto 5, Perdo 5, Rego 5, Animál 2, Aquam 3, Auram 1, Córporem 2, Herbam 2, Ignem 4, Imágonem 5, Mentem 2, Terram 4, Vim 6

**Spells**: *Stone of the Hundred Shards* (Creo Terram 15), *Phantasm Fire* (Creo Imágonem 15),

## VERDITIUS MAGUS CONTINUED

*Image of the Past State* (Intéllego Imágonem 15), *The Ear For Distant Voices* (Intéllego Imágonem 20), *Conjuration of Indubitable Cold* (Perdo Ignem 20), *Leap of the Fire* (Rego Ignem 15), *Sense the Nature of* Vis (Intéllego Vim 10), *Scales of the Magical Weight* (Intéllego Vim 15), *Disenchant* (Perdo Vim 20), *Wizard's Subtle Touch* (Intéllego Vim 5)

As a Verditius Magus you can only work Formulaic and Ritual magic if you have a Spell Focus appropriate to your spell. The Focus gives you no extra powers as it does for other Magi. However, you have transcended above that weakness by being a master of enchantment. In fact, your masterpiece, the Staff of the Dragon's Scale, is proof of your magical prowess. Who cares that you used up almost all your Covenant's vis to create it? Who cares that you had to raid the vis stores of another Covenant? Your creation was all that mattered, and you'd do it again, if the other Magi in your Covenant would only let you near the labs.

*"The Magi I've met from other Houses are always so staid and serious. They never appreciate a truly great act of craftsmanship and creation. Indeed, they wouldn't get a joke if it came up and bit them. That's why I animated the statue of the lion."*

# MAGUS EX MISCELLANEA

| | | | | |
|---|---|---|---|---|
| Intelligence | +3 | Presence | 0 |
| Perception | 0 | Communication | -4 |
| Strength | 0 | Dexterity | 0 |
| Stamina | +4 | Quickness | -3 |

**Age:** 34

**Virtues & Flaws:** Cyclic Magic (lunar) +5, Life-Linked Spontaneous Magic +3, Exceptional Talent (Weather Sense) +1, Magical Affinity (healing) +1, Unstructured Caster -6, Discredited Lineage -2, The Blatant Gift -1, Hedge Wizard -1

**Abilities:** Speak Own Language 4, Speak (Latin) 5, Scribe (Latin) 3, Magic Theory 5, Hermes Lore 2, Hermes History 2, *Parma Magica* 2, Sing 2, Play Drums 2, Chirurgy 4, Magical Affinity (healing) 2, Meditation 2, Concentration 3, Weather Sense 3

**Confidence:** 3     **Reputation:** Hedge Wizard 2, Witch 1

**Personality Traits:** Unpredictable +2, Rational -2, Verbose +1

**Weapons & Armor:** None     **Encumbrance:** 0

**Techniques and Forms:** Creo 10, Intéllego 4, Muto 0, Perdo 4, Rego 0, Animál 4, Aquam 0, Auram 0, Córporem 10, Herbam 4, Ignem 0, Imágonem 0, Mentem 0, Terram 0, Vim 0

**Spells:** *The Severed Limb Made Whole* (Creo Córporem 30), *The Chirurgeon's Healing Touch* (Creo Córporem 20), *Restoration of the Defiled Body* (Creo Córporem 25), *The Falcon's Hood* (Perdo Animál 20), *Image of the Beast* (Intéllego Animál 5), *Hunt for the Wild Herb* (Intéllego Herbam 15), *Weaver's Trap of Webs* (Creo Animál 20), *Gentle Touch of the Purified Body* (Creo Córporem 15)

Members of the much vaunted Order of Hermes tend to perceive their art as superior to all other magical forms, and frown upon practitioners of other arts. Ex Miscellanea is the House with the most tenuous membership in the Order for its members are not really Hermetic wizards. They originate from their own traditions and join the Order for fear of persecution; if you can't beat 'em, join 'em. However, some Ex Miscellanea Magi secretly defy the Order in an effort to restore the old ways of magic. You suspect your master is one of those people, as the Magi you know treat you worse than they do mundanes, and often mutter under their breath about your "witch of a *Parens*." Let them scoff. You don't need their arrogance, and your magic is capable of standing on its own, or so you hope.

*"Do not allow yourself the vanity of believing you are among the Gods who walk the earth. You and I are mortals, just like all the rest."*

# MAGUS OF MERINITA

| | | | | |
|---|---|---|---|---|
| Intelligence | +2 | Presence | +2 |
| Perception | -2 | Communication | +2 |
| Strength | -2 | Dexterity | -2 |
| Stamina | -1 | Quickness | +1 |

**Age:** 21

**Virtues & Flaws:** Faerie Blood +2, Extra Arts +3, Aptitude with Elements +4, Faerie Magic +1, Unpredictable Magic -4, Susceptible to Divine Power -4, Common Fear (fire) -2

**Abilities:** Speak Own Language 4, Speak (Latin) 5, Scribe (Latin) 3, Magic Theory 5, Hermes Lore 2, Hermes History 2, *Parma Magica* 2, Faerie Lore 3, (Area) Lore 2, Faerie Magic 3, Charm 2, Athletics 1, Dodge 1, Alertness 1

**Confidence:** 3

**Reputation:** None

**Personality Traits:** Wild +3, Calm -3, Jovial +2

**Weapons & Armor:** None

**Encumbrance:** 0

**Techniques and Forms:** Creo 4, Intéllego 3, Muto 7, Perdo 0, Rego 4, Animál 6, Aquam 7, Auram 7, Córporem 0, Herbam 6, Ignem 0, Imágonem 0, Mentem 7, Terram 0, Vim 0

**Spells:** *Clouds of Thunderous Might* (Muto Auram 20), *Disguise of the Transformed Image* (Muto Imágonem 15), *Notes of a Delightful Sound* (Muto Imágonem 15), *Wings of the Soaring Wind* (Rego Auram 25), *Talons of the Winds* (Muto Auram 20), *Deluge of Rushing and Dashing* (Creo Aquam 20), *Cloak of Winter* (Muto Aquam 30), *Unseen Arm* (Rego Terram 5)

Your pursuit of magical understanding is designed solely for one purpose: to better understand the faerie world. Born from the descendents of the Seelie Court itself, your very spirit yearns to join that world hidden behind the forest wall. The faerie nature is your own, making you privy to faerie motivations and intentions where others are left dumbfounded by the enigmatic beings. If you were to die. you would want to perish in the heart of a faerie forest where your spirit may unite with those of your kin.

*"Do you hear that tune? There it is again! I hear the most delightful little song coming from over that hill. What? That's where the gateway you spoke of stands? Well let us go then. I feel my family expects me!"*

## MAGUS OF HOUSE DIEDNE

You cannot play a Magus of House Diedne. Its members were wiped out and driven into hiding hundreds of years ago. The Order of Hermes no longer acknowledges the House's existence.

# Advanced Character Creation

The advanced process of character creation involves many steps. Initially you must form a rough idea of what your character is like, imagining a character concept to guide you. From that image you acquire Characteristics, purchase Virtues and Flaws, and finally select Personality Traits that apply to and develop the initial character image you have.

Once the process is complete, your character may become more than what you initially visualized, or even something completely different, but more to your liking than your initial concept. Often times you may find characters begin with only the seed of an idea and grow spontaneously on their own.

The following is an outline of the rules involved in advanced character creation.

STEP ONE: CONCEPTUALIZATION
STEP TWO: CHARACTERISTICS
STEP THREE: VIRTUES AND FLAWS
STEP FOUR: ABILITIES
STEP FIVE: MAGICAL STUDIES (MAGI ONLY)
STEP SIX: FINISHING TOUCHES
STEP SEVEN: FINAL CHARACTERIZATION

## STEP ONE: CONCEPTUALIZATION

The first step toward character creation requires that you conceptualize the person you wish to play. This initial concept is important because it's the foundation upon which you acquire all Characteristics, Virtues, Flaws and Abilities, and select all Reputations and Personality Traits. Without a concept to base trait selection on, your character is a chaotic mass of scores with no real identity, and identity is important. After all, you have to roleplay this character, so you want a firm grasp of who she is.

Also keep in mind that your character should be unique from others played by the Troupe; try not to crowd a niche occupied by another character. If there is already a Magus with a talent for Auram spells in the group, you probably don't need another. The Covenant benefits from diversity, and the Troupe would better appreciate a character with traits and talents not already in play.

You need to decide who and what your character is. What is your background, age, and gender?

Your character concept should start on a broad basis. You must first decide whether your character is a Grog, Companion or Magus. That decided, you can decide what nature you have. For instance, if you are a Grog are you a stable boy, a cook, or a guard? If you're a Companion are you a knight, a merchant or a friar? If you're a Magus what kind of spells do you see yourself wielding? Your nature is important for it determines your skills and traits, not to mention your identity.

Next, you need to decide your gender, age, name, and background. Many of these qualities may be determined by the nature you've chosen for your Grog, Companion or Magus.

You are free to choose any age you desire, but there are some things you need be aware of. First of all, the older you are, the closer you are to suffering the effects of age. In fact, if you are over 35 you may have to make Aging rolls before the start of the game. These pregame rolls do not mean your character dies before being played, but poor rolls might result in the effects of Decrepitude (see p.355 for more details). Once your age is determined, you can figure out date of birth based based on the year the Saga begins. That way, even if your character is out of play for several game-years, you can determine her age when she resumes play.

# STEP TWO: CHARACTERISTICS

The next step is to determine what your Characteristics are. How strong are you? How fast are your reflexes? How good are you at making a speech? Questions such as these are answered by your Characteristic scores.

Each Characteristic has a number associated with it, describing your native aptitude in that area. These numbers are used as modifiers on most dice rolls, helping decide when you succeed and when you fail an action. A zero is average for any Characteristic, while positive numbers indicate higher than average aptitude and negative numbers indicate lower than average aptitude. Scores of -5 to +5 describe the normal range of Characteristics, with -3 being pretty bad, and +3 being pretty darn good.

## Rolling Characteristics

Grimgroth rolls the dice four times for his Characteristics and gets the following results:

6 minus 6 = 0

7 minus 4 = +3

2 minus 3 = -1

1 minus 3 = -2

He wants a high score in Intelligence so he can be a competent Magus and a good Presence score to support the character concept. He assigns the rolls thus:

| | | |
|---|---|---|
| -1 on Intelligence/Perception | Intelligence -1 | Perception 0 |
| 0 on Strength/Stamina | Strength 0 | Stamina 0 |
| +3 on Presence/Communication | Presence +2 | Communication +1 |
| -2 on Dexterity/Quickness | Dexterity -1 | Quickness -1 |

He takes a low Intelligence score because he intends to take a Virtue to get a higher score, and that decision lets him keep an average Perception score instead of a low one to make up for a high Intelligence.

There are two different ways to go about generating your Characteristics: by rolling dice, or purchasing points. Generally, a Troupe selects one method or another for all characters, though some may allow players to pick whatever method they want for each separate character.

Purchasing your Characteristics gives you more control over who your character is, but creates a more static character than you get through rolling — chance is eliminated. Rolling, on the other hand, is dangerous since you run the risk of getting many low Characteristic scores. However, playing a character with a wide range of scores is a roleplaying challenge, more so than a character with a range of average scores. A wide range of scores may even encourage you to roleplay all the more, and may therefore heighten your appreciation of the Saga.

### Rolling Method

Rolling for your Characteristics is straightforward. You and another player each make a Simple roll (that is, you each roll a ten-sided die). You want the highest result possible, and you want the other player's roll to be as low as possible. Once you have the results, subtract the other player's roll from your own. Record the result and repeat the process three more times. When finished, you will have four numbers ranging from -9 to +9.

Now assign one of the pairs to each of the four pairs of Characteristics: Intelligence and Perception, Strength and Stamina, Communication and Presence, and Dexterity and Quickness. Divide the number assigned to each pair in any way you like, but insure that neither Characteristic has a value of less than -5 or more than +5. Thus, if you get a score of +3 to assign, you can take a +5 Strength and a -2 Stamina (which adds up to +3).

## Purchase Method

Each character gets up to 7 points to spend on positive scores in the eight Characteristics: Intelligence, Perception, Strength, Stamina, Presence, Communication, Dexterity, and Quickness. Each point spent buys a point in a single Characteristic, so if you spend 3 points on Strength, you have a +3 Strength. You cannot have a Characteristic score of 6; +5 is as high as they go (unless you acquire a Virtue that states otherwise).

However, you must take at least as many negative Characteristic points as you do positive. In effect, each positive point "buys" a negative Characteristic point. Thus, if you buy a +3 Strength, you have 3 negative points that must be spent elsewhere. These points can be spent on a single Characteristic, or divided among several. You cannot have a Characteristic score of -6; -5 is as low as they go.

The negative points you accumulate from positive Characteristics do not necessarily have to be spent on negative Characteristic scores. Your negative points can be used to purchase Flaws (see *Step Three*, below) on a point by point basis (i.e., you have to spend negative points equal to the Flaw's rating). However, your positive Characteristic points cannot be use to purchase Virtues, unless you have the permission of the Troupe. In any case, you should never use more than 3 Characteristic points to buy Flaws.

Similarly, when you choose Flaws, the positive points you receive in return (that are normally spent on Virtues) can be spent on Characteristics, making your Characteristic scores more positive. You can never spend more than three points earned from Flaws on positive Characteristics. See *Virtues and Flaws*, below, for more details.

A score of 0 is average for any Characteristic. If you don't spend any positive or negative points on a Characteristic, you are considered average in it (with a score of 0).

Whether rolled for or purchased, Characteristics may also have Specialties as chosen by you. A Specialty is an area pertaining to a Characteristic in which you are particularly adept. For a complete description of Specialties, see below, p.58.

# Step Three: Virtues and Flaws

Now that you have formed an idea of who your character is, you can become much more specific in your definition by purchasing Virtues and Flaws that further develop your concept. Virtues and Flaws are the exceptional attributes of a person, the things that make you special and truly unique. These ratings and qualifiers are inherent to you and are generally immutable; they can not

### Maximum Number of Flaw Points

| | |
|---|---|
| Magus | 10 points |
| Companion | 7 points |
| Grog | 3 points |

It's also suggested, though not mandatory, that Magi take half their total Virtue and Flaw points (or as close to half as you can get) from the Hermetic Flaw lists, as provided on p.67. Thus, if you have a total of 20 Virtue and Flaw points (10 of each), a total of 10 of those points can be spent on Hermetic Virtues and Flaws. The allocation of these points between Hermetic Virtues and Flaws need not be even.

be acquired through experience or training, but are an intrinsic part of your being.

Virtues are each assigned a positive value, and Flaws are each assigned a negative value. If you want to buy a Virtue, you first need to buy a Flaw of equal or greater absolute value.

Each Virtue has a positive rating, and a number of points equal to that rating is required to purchase the Virtue. For example, to purchase the Virtue Free Expression (rated 1), you must first have at least 1 Flaw point

# Exempli Gratia:
## Virtues and Flaws

Isabel chooses her Virtues and Flaws, which go a long way toward defining her character. First, she needs a strong concept of her character. She decides she is a former nun with visionary ability. Her Virtues and Flaws are based on this background. To begin with, she takes an above average Characteristic pair to get rid of some bad rolls, and then picks the Virtues and Flaws that fully characterize her.

| Virtues | Rating |
| --- | --- |
| Good Characteristic: Presence | +1 |
| Strong Personality | +1 |
| Exceptional Talent: Visions | +2 |
| Educated | +1 |
| Knack (+2) for arguing, debating | +1 |
| Clear Thinker | +1 |

| Flaws | |
| --- | --- |
| Sensitive to Frivolity | -1 |
| Social Handicap: unable to enjoy self socially | -1 |
| Weakness: for being treated with respect | -1 |
| Uncommon Fear: being helpless | -1 |
| Poor Eyesight | -1 |
| Small Frame | -2 |

Grimgroth's Virtues and Flaws are mostly concerned with his magical capabilities (as is appropriate for Magi):

| Virtues | Rating |
| --- | --- |
| Superior Characteristic: Intelligence | +2 |
| Affinity with Winds | +2 |
| Special Magical Ability: When angered he gains a forceful, formidable demeanor, giving him a +2 on appropriate Presence rolls | +1 |
| Gentle Gift | +1 |
| Self-Confident | +1 |

| Flaws | |
| --- | --- |
| Warped magic: spells accompanied by winds & keening whistle | -1 |
| Deleterious Circumstances (uncommon & minor): -5 when the sky is mostly clear of clouds | -1 |
| Restriction (rare): Magic does not work within earshot of music | -1 |
| Major Magic Deficiency: Terram | -3 |
| Cursed: Those close to him turn against him if he expects their loyalty selfishly | -1 |

Note: Grimgroth is entitled to ten Virtue and ten Flaw points, but does not take them all. As his Virtue and Flaw totals still balance out, this is fine.

(you must have bought a Flaw with a score of -1, or lower). As the Virtue Guardian Angel is rated 5, it costs 5 Flaw points.

The only way to get Virtues is to take Flaws. You may take as many Flaws as you like up to a certain amount, depending on whether you are a Magus, Companion or Grog. See the Flaw point chart.

For every Flaw you accept, you are granted its score in points to be spent on Virtues. These points can be spent on any Virtues you please. They may be spent on several Virtues with low scores, or on a few Virtues with high scores.

Rather than spend the points you acquire from Flaws on Virtues, you can spend them on your Characteristics, making Characteristics more positive. This is possible as negative Characteristic points can be spent on Flaws (as described under *Step Two*, above). However, you can only spend these points on Characteristics if you purchased

your Characteristic scores; you can't do it if you rolled your Characteristic scores.

Take note that for every Virtue you purchase, your character becomes weaker in some way due to the Flaws you must take. Your character becomes both stronger and weaker at the same time — TINSTAAFL (there is no such thing as a free lunch). This trade insures that no character becomes superhuman, and reminds you of your mortality.

Once play begins your Characteristics, Virtues, and Flaws cannot change, unless the Storyguide decides that drastic story events warrant some sort of modification.

# STEP FOUR: ABILITIES

Abilities are what you know. They reflect the learned skills and knowledges that you have acquired over the years, before play begins. You gain Abilities by spending

# Abilities List

| TALENTS | SKILLS | KNOWLEDGES |
|---|---|---|

## TALENTS

**Arcane Talents**
Finesse
Penetration

**Awareness Talents**
Alertness
Scan
Search

**Exceptional Talents**
Alchemy
Animal Ken
Contortions
Direction Sense
Divination
Dousing
Empathy
Enchanting Music
Entrancement
Healer
Herbalism
Hex
Magic Sensitivity
Mimicry
Perfect Balance
Premonitions
Read Lips
Second Sight
Sense Holiness & Unholiness
Visions
Weather Sense

**Physical Talents**
Athletics
Climb
Dodge

**Social Talents**
Charisma
Charm
Guile
Folk Ken
Pretend
Subterfuge

## SKILLS

**Arcane Skills**
*Certámen*
*Parma Magica*

**Forester Skills**
Animal Handling
Survival
Track

**Mental Skills**
Concentration
Debate
Meditation

**Performance Skills**
Acting
Storytelling
Jongleur
Sing
Play (Specific Instrument)

**Physical Skills**
Brawl
Ride
Swim

**Rogue Skills**
Disguise
Forgery
Legerdemain
Pick Locks
Stealth

**Social Skills**
Bargain
Diplomacy
Drinking
Etiquette
Intimidation
Intrigue
Leadership

**Weapon Skills**
(see description)

**Work Skills**
Boating
Chirurgy
Craft (Specify)
Evaluate (Specific Items)
Wagoneering

## KNOWLEDGES

**Arcane Knowledges**
Enigmatic Wisdom
Hermes History
Hermetic Law
Hermes Lore
Magic Theory

**Casual Knowledges**
(Area) Lore
Church Lore
Faerie Lore
Fantastic Beast Lore
Legend Lore
Occult Lore
Speak (Specific Language)

**Formal Knowledges**
Church Knowledge
Humanities
Medicine
Scribe (Specific Alphabet)

| Experience Point Table | |
|---|---|
| Level | Cost |
| 1st .................... 1pt | |
| 2nd .................... 3pts | |
| 3rd .................... 6pts | |
| 4th .................... 10pts | |
| 5th .................... 15pts | |
| 6th .................... 21pts | |
| 7th .................... 28pts | |

Experience Points, which represent the amount of learning and practical experience you have had in your life. Abilities have a direct bearing on your career as a Covenant member and adventurer, and are used frequently to help determine what you can and cannot do.

All characters get a starting number of Experience Points equal to twice their age, except Magi who get points equal to their age — a reflection of time devoted to spell mastery over worldly skill and experience. Obviously, the older you are, the more Experience Points you have. However, the older you are the sooner the affects of age set in. If you're over 35 at the start of the game you may have to make an Aging roll (see p.354). The "Death" result is replaced with the penalty of a Decrepitude Point.

**All characters gain Experience Points as determined by their age; Grogs and Companions take double their age in points, while Magi take only their age**

The Abilities you may choose from are described and listed in the Traits Chapter. Abilities are purchased on a step system (see the chart below). For example, if you want a score of 3 in an Ability, you must spend 6 of your starting Experience Points. A score of 3 suggests competence in an Ability. A score of 5 suggests mastery of an Ability.

**The costs for an Ability vary, depending on what level you wish to raise it to.**

Some Abilities are automatically possessed by each type of character — Grog, Companion, and Magus — with pre-assigned values. They are free. If you want to purchase a higher rating in a Basic Ability, you must purchase that score. You must spend an number of Experience Points equal to the cost difference between your current level and the level you want. For example, if you have a Basic Ability score of 1 in Brawl and want a

### Basic Ability Table

**Grog:** Speak Own Language 4, Brawl 1

**Companion:** Speak Own Language 5

**Magus:** Speak Own Language 4, Speak Latin 5, Scribe Latin 3, Magic Theory 5, Hermes Lore 2, Hermes History 2, *Parma Magica* 2

# Exempli Gratia:
## Choosing Abilities

Isabel is 26 years old, so as a Companion has 52 Experience Points with which to purchase Abilities. Most of her Abilities come from her background as a woman of wealth and her years as a nun, but she is practical enough to have gotten some training with sword and shield. The Specialties she chooses represent the sources of her Abilities, her temperament, and other aspects of her personality and personal history.

| Ability | Score | Cost |
|---|---|---|
| Speak Provençal (upper class diction) | 5 | 0 |
| Visions (love and lovers) | 5 | 15 |
| Concentration (attention to detail) | 2 | 3 |
| Scribe Latin (copying) | 3 | 6 |
| Church Knowledge (monastic orders) | 3 | 6 |
| Diplomacy (with clergy) | 2 | 3 |
| Church Lore (corruption) | 1 | 1 |
| Occult Lore (demons) | 2 | 3 |
| Meditation (praying the rosary) | 2 | 3 |
| Sing (hymns) | 1 | 1 |
| Dance (formally) | 1 | 1 |
| Guile (lying to underlings) | 1 | 1 |
| Short Sword Attack (standing ground) | 2 | 3 |
| Shield Parry (standing ground) | 3 | 6 |
| Total | | 52 |

score of 3, you must spend 5 Experience Points — a score of 1 costs 1 point, while of score of 3 costs 6 (6 -1 = 5). Furthermore, if you want a lower score in a Basic Ability, you free up the number of Experience points that are spent in getting the higher, standard score. These extra points can be used to purchase or increase other Abilities. You may want to lower the Basic Abilities listed if their scores do not suit your character concept.

## Choosing Abilities

When choosing Abilities keep in mind several guidelines based on your character and the story setting. First of all, make sure you have all the Abilities that make sense for your identity. Be sure to consider Abilities related to your profession, background and culture. Also have the linguistic proficiency necessary to communicate with other characters.

Certain Abilities are restricted. If your background keeps you from having a certain weapon, you can't have an Ability for using it. Also, some categories of Abilities (Arcane Skills, Exceptional Talents, Arcane Knowledges, and Formal Knowledges) are restricted. You require a particular Virtue to have them or must be a Magus.

Grogs should choose the Abilities they need to be good warriors, guards (custos), and servants. A few good weapon scores and some other useful skills, such as Scan, Survival or Chirurgy, make a competent Grog. Grogs' Specialties (see below) often relate to the role they have in the turb.

Companions often have many unusual skills, and are usually adept in one area of expertise, such as thievery. Companions should therefore have many varied Abilities related to their background. Specialties pose an excellent opportunity to fine-tune your Companion's background or personality.

Magi should choose necessary magical Abilities, such as Finesse, Concentration, and Penetration, as these can be as important as spells themselves in determining your capacities.

If you need an Ability that is important to your character but is not described in the Traits Chapter, invent it yourself. When considering what Abilities an average person has, take half the person's age in Experience Points and invest them in various mundane Abilities, like Brewing and Wagoneering.

Also note that Abilities have Specialties that you may assign. Specialties are areas in which you are particularly adept at an Ability. For a description of Specialities, see below, p. 58.

# STEP FIVE: MAGICAL TRAINING (MAGI ONLY)

As a Magus your exceptional powers are your magical ones. Your fifteen years of apprenticeship have taught you the use of the magical Arts and many spells. You get to choose what you learned from your magical training. Choosing your magical powers wisely is only possible if you understand the magic rules. Before creating a Magus character, you should familiarize yourself with the Magic, Spells and Laboratory Chapters.

## Magical Arts

Each Magus has a rating in each of the fifteen magical Forms and Techniques, as explained in the Magic Chapter. You have 150 points with which to purchase scores in these Arts. These scores are purchased with the same Experience system used with Characteristics and Abilities. (Note: with particular Virtues and Flaws more or less

### Magical Arts Experience Point Table

| Level | Cost |
|---|---|
| 1st | 1pt |
| 2nd | 3pts |
| 3rd | 6pts |
| 4th | 10pts |
| 5th | 15pts |
| 6th | 21pts |
| 7th | 28pts |
| 8th | 36pts |
| 9th | 45pts |
| 10th | 55pts |
| 11th | 66pts |
| 12th | 78pts |
| 13th | 91pts |
| 14th | 105pts |
| 15th | 120pts |
| 16th | 136pts |
| 17th | 153pts |
| 18th | 171pts |
| 19th | 190pts |
| 20th | 210pts |

### Common Art Scores

Purchasing Art scores can be complicated, there being so many different combinations possible. There are, however, some common ways to buy your Art points. For your convenience they are listed below.

**Specialist:** 16, 4, 2, 1 (this provides preeminent proficiency in a single Art, but at the expense of all the others)

**Dual Art:** 12, 11, 3 (as a Form/Technique combination, this is unbeatable, potentially offering 35th Level spell use)

**Concentrated:** 10, 10, 8, 2, 1 (if you allocate 10 to a Form and a Technique, you can easily get a 30th Level spell)

**Widely Adept:** 7, 7, 7, 7, 7, 4 (a temperate balance)

**Generalist:** 6, 5, 5, 5, 5, 5, 5, 4, 4, 3, 2, 2, 2, 2, 1 (you have a score in every Art)

Art points can be bought.)

A Magus character has 150 Experience Points to spend on the magic Arts. The costs for each score varies, depending on how high a score is.

Remember that, in purchasing Art scores, your Form scores count toward Magic Resistance (discussed in the Magic Chapter), so you may want higher scores in Forms that can protect you (e.g., Córporem). Vim is also important for many magical activities. Furthermore, at the beginning of play it's wise to invest more points in one Form or Technique that you plan to be particularly good with. Other, lower, Arts can be improved quickly during play.

## Spells

You can pick spells whose Levels add up to 150. Only those spells that are within 10 points of your Technique + Form + Intelligence total can be chosen; others are too difficult for you to learn. This limit applies only when selecting spells as a beginning character. It does not apply during play.

**Each Magus can take up to 150 Levels of spells. But you can take only those spells that are within 10 points of your Technique + Form + Intelligence total for that spell.**

When choosing spells, be sure to have the basics. A good, quick offensive spell often comes in handy. Don't waste time with low-Level spells that you can simulate with Spontaneous magic, unless you want to be able to

## Exempli Gratia:
### Choosing Spells

Grimgroth selects his beginning spells. First, he wants to learn *Clouds of Rain and Thunder*, a Level 25 Creo Auram spell. His Creo + Auram + Intelligence total is 19. Since that's within 10 of the Level of the spell, he may take the spell. He also needs a practical offensive spell, so he takes *Broom of the Winds*. It's only Level 15, so taking it is no problem for a Magus with control over the winds. Grimgroth then looks at *Whispers Through the Black Gate*. His Intéllego + Córporem + Intelligence total is 12, so a Level 15 spell is no problem, but he sees that it has a Mentem Requisite (see the Magic Chapter for details). That means his Córporem score functions as if it is no higher than his Mentem score, which is 3. His total therefore becomes 3 + 2 + 3 = 8, so he can still know the spell but it isn't easy to cast. He also considers *Charge of the Angry Winds* (CrAu 30). His total is only 19, not within the 10 point range, so he cannot normally take the spell (unless he has a Hermetic Virtue that applies, like one that gives him bonuses with wind spells).

cast those spells without speaking or using your hands.

# STEP SIX:
# FINISHING TOUCHES

At this point in character creation you should know what your character is capable of—what his strengths and weaknesses are. Now you have to flesh out your character's personality. Character personality in **Ars Magica** has a direct bearing on the game and its mechanics.

# CONFIDENCE

Each character begins the game with 3 Confidence Points, unless you have a Virtue that allows you more, or a Flaw that says you possess less. Confidence is a measure of how much self-esteem and willpower you have. The points may be spent in stressful situations into which you invest all your power and being. That being the case,

Confidence is often spent in conjunction with your nature. If you make a point of proving yourself to the Grog Sergeant, you're likely to spend a Confidence Point toward that end. On the other hand, if you're rolling to see if you clean the stables well (yawn), you probably don't bother with the effort and concentration of Confidence. Confidence Points can also be spent with your Passions, if you've chosen those Virtues, which are intrinsic to your identity.

# REPUTATION

Unless you take a Reputation as a Virtue or Flaw, you don't have one at the beginning of the game. However, a Reputation can be gained over the course of the Saga, and your character's particular Reputation can have a great effect on how others respond to him. (The Traits Chapter describes Reputations fully; see p.101.)

A Reputation is rated from 1 to 10, though 5 is usually the practical maximum. Your Reputation's score indicates how strong your Reputation is, as well as how widespread it is (that is to say, how many people know about you from hearsay). That score is also applied as a modifier to rolls that involve interaction with other people. Reputation is not applied to rolls involving interaction with other characters (players). Indeed, rolls should never be made between players' characters; roleplaying should be used.

If you have a Reputation at the beginning of the game, gained through a Virtue or Flaw, you may choose its nature. A Reputation gained during play is decided upon by the Storyguide based on story events. The following are some possible Reputations: Reliable, Independent, Famous, Honorable, Glorious, Renown, Forgiving, Demon Spawned, Cowardly, Anxious, Voyager, Heroic, Fair-minded, Tough, Saintly, Chivalrous, Witty, and Dishonest. The Traits Chapter lists more Reputations to choose from. Grogs often have an initial Reputation of Glory. A Companion has an initial Reputation of your choosing. Magi often have initial Reputations of Renown, which is their fame in the Order of Hermes and sometimes beyond.

Note that Reputations have Specialties (see below), which function just like other Specialties. Reputation Specialties specify the area in which your character is famous or infamous. A Specialty of Glorious might be knight *killer* or *fearless*. A Specialty of a Magus's Renown might be *alchemy* or *Seeker*. The choice of Reputation Specialty is left to you based on your character's identity.

# PERSONALITY TRAITS

Personality Traits are a way for you to more precisely define your character's identity. These traits allow you to indicate what inclinations and predilections, such as Gullible, your character has. You can have as many

Personality Traits as you like, assigning each a value from -3 to +3 (scores up to +5 and down to -5 can be had with special Virtues and Flaws). A list of suggestions for Personality Traits is found in the Traits Chapter (p.106). Of course, you may make up your own.

Keep in mind that, if you take a Passion as a Virtue or Flaw, the Personality Traits you have do not function when your Passion is activated. These concepts are fully explained in the Traits Chapter, under *Passions* (p.73) and *Personality Traits* (p.106).

## Specialities

Once you've acquired all your Characteristics, Abilities, Reputations and Passions (which are Virtues and Flaws), and have established your Personality Traits, you may choose Specialties. Specialties apply to Characteristics, Abilities, and Passions, and, when you develop them, Reputations. They are areas that you are particularly skilled or adept at in the case of Characteristics and Abilities. They are areas in which you are particularly driven in the case of Passions. And, they are areas you are particularly known for in the case of Reputations. Specialties should be chosen based on your character's personality and nature.

A Specialty is a phrase or one-word qualifier. With Characteristics and Reputations they are adjectives and with Abilities and Passions they are nouns. (Note that in the case of Characteristics, Specialties are only chosen for positive and negative scores, not for those of 0.) They help you visualize your character, making your Characteristics and other scores tangible in the real world, as well as in the dice rolling world. Generally, a Specialty functions to offer a +1 modifier to any roll that involves the Specialty. For example, if your Strength Specialty is *strong grip*, you gain +1 in Strength rolls to hold onto an item. However, for negative Characteristics, a Specialty means you suffer a -1 modifier to rolls when that Specialty applies. For example, if your Strength Specialty is *weak grip*, you suffer a -1 modifier to Strength rolls to hold onto things.

See the Characteristics, Abilities, and Reputations sections of the Traits Chapter for listings of Specialties. For Passion Specialties, see the Virtue and Flaw listings in the Traits Chapter.

# EQUIPMENT

You must decide what possessions you have, especially what you carry with you during a story. Most important are your weapons and armor, but you should also decide what incidental equipment you have. The Covenant often provides mundane supplies, but you

---

| Magical Arts List |
|---|

Note that the Art descriptions below are only simple. More complete descriptions are provided in the Magic Chapter, p.167.

### Techniques

Techniques are means by which to affect the world around you through magic.

**Creo:** The ability to create things from your imagination. If the object is not natural to the world, like oil that doesn't burn, it cannot be made to exist permanently.

**Intéllego:** The ability to perceive into the truth of the world, making you aware of facts and presences that others ignore.

**Muto:** The ability to change and alter the shape and composition of something.

**Perdo:** The ability to harm and destroy objects at will.

**Rego:** The ability to manipulate and control the world around you, forcing it to comply to your will.

### Forms

Forms are the elements of the world that you may affect through magic.

**Animál:** The animal kingdom. Spells that affect animals can influence their bodies and minds.

**Aquam:** The realm of water. This includes everything from humidity, to ponds, to rivers, to oceans, including ice.

**Auram:** The realm of air. Not only can you influence air itself, but you can make it fresh or corrupt it with the stench of decay.

**Córporem:** The human body. Spells that affect the human body cannot affect the mind.

**Herbam:** The realm of plants. As plants grow virtually everywhere, those with mastery over plants are a force to be reckoned with.

**Ignem:** The element of fire itself. This is one of the most dangerous and destructive Forms, though it can also be used to restore and preserve. Dealing in fire, Ignem also deals with heat and cold.

**Imágonem:** The realm of perception and imagination. Control of imagination can literally change the reality that others perceive.

**Mentem:** The realm of the human mind. Control of the mind means power for no physical armor can protect one's capacity to think.

**Terram:** The element of earth. There are many incarnations of earth, including glass, gems, and metal.

**Vim:** The power of magic itself. Those who control Vim are equipped to deal with demons and the very manifestations of magic.

## The Houses of Hermes

The following is a brief outline of the thirteen magical Houses of Hermes. These introductions are provided here to help you better conceptualize your character. The Mythic Europe Chapter provides more complete details on the different Houses.

**House Bonisagus:** Named after the founder of Hermetic theory, this House is at the roots of known magic, so its members receive considerable respect. Magi of Bonisagus commonly further the theoretical traditions of magic, while others further the political traditions of the Order.

**House Tytalus:** In their neverending search for conflict, the leaders of House Tytalus went too far in the 10th Century and were corrupted by demons. They were executed for diabolism, and the House has been mistrusted and in disgrace ever since.

**House Jerbiton:** This House is interested in the mundane world and assumes the duty of keeping Magi on good terms with the nobility and Church. Jerbiton Magi fear that members of the Order have dissociated themselves too far from the mundane world, losing their humanity.

**House Criamon:** This very secretive House is known for its obscure philosophy, its disdain for simple power, and its members' habit of marking their faces and bodies with arcane symbols.

**House Bjornaer:** This House is only marginally respected in the Order because its founder was from a Germanic rather than Roman magical tradition. The Bjornaer Magi's fascination with beasts and the animal side of human nature makes other Magi wary of them.

**House Verditius:** These Magi specialize in the making of magical devices, and have achieved power by making themselves valuable to Magi of other Houses. Verditius Magi like to pretend that they have less magical power than they really do.

**House Flambeau:** These aggressive and ferocious Magi often cause trouble within the Order, and are known for raising the ire of mundanes, whom Flambeau tend to despise. Flambeau Magi specialize in fiery and destructive spells.

**House Merinita:** This House is focused on the world of faeries, and its members tend to be just as strange as their obsession. These Magi have little to do with other Houses, except to defend faeries from the assaults of other Magi.

**House of Quaesitoris:** This tiny house investigates wrongdoings and passes sentence on those who break the Code of Hermes. They invite Magi of other Houses to become Quaesitoris (judges), though those Magi retain membership in their original Houses.

**House Ex Miscellanea:** Though originally founded as a rival order by a renegade from the Order of Hermes, this organization was eventually accepted into the Order of Hermes as a House of its own. The House accepts wizards of all kinds, many only nominally Hermetic, and many belonging to forms of magic akin to hedge magic.

**House Tremere:** This has proved to be a sensible House, providing strength and courage when needed, and refraining from actions when Hermetic peace is better served. Tremere Magi emphasize the importance of judgement, strategy, and planning.

**House Mercere:** The founder of this House lost his magic powers and assumed a non-magical role valuable to the Order: carrying messages. His followers have become the Redcaps, Hermetic messengers who are largely considered Magi of the Order.

**House Diedne:** This was a House of Magi from druidic tradition who were wiped out in the 11th Century by the combined forces of Flambeau and Tremere (under the approval of Quaesitoris). You cannot play a Magus of this House, though some say followers of its traditions are still hidden away.

should keep track of your personal items, such as fine clothes and writing equipment.

**Grogs'** equipment is based on the resources of the Covenant. When the Troupe designs its Covenant, you decide how well-equipped the Grogs are. You must stay within these limits when equipping your characters. Grogs are restricted to standard armaments unless your Troupe has designed an exceptional Covenant that has particularly well-armed Grogs or very poorly armed Grogs.

**Companions'** equipment depends on background. If you have no Virtues or Flaws that determine otherwise, you can only have inexpensive and standard arms and armor. If you are dependent on the Covenant, you are as well-equipped as the Grogs.

**Magi** have special considerations in choosing their equipment. As a Magus you are assured fair and respectful treatment, even by the enemy. If you dress as a Magus, with magical symbols on your cloak, people usually recognize your status and pay you proper respect. They also note everything you do, so traveling without being noticed is difficult. If you dress in finery, as a wealthy person might, you are afforded some respect, but people may still attempt to assault or harass you, having no idea of the danger they put themselves in. If you dress as a commoner, expect no special treatment. If you wear armor, enemies may mistake you for a warrior and attempt to best you in combat. Besides that, armor weighs you down and quickly tires you, and weariness is an important consideration for any Magus.

### Encumbrance

Your Encumbrance is a measure of how loaded down you are. It is a score that acts as a penalty on all rolls that require free, fast movement, including spell casting and nearly all Quickness rolls.

Total the Load values (listed in the Combat Chapter) for your weapons and armor to determine your total Load factor. If you carry other heavy things, the Storyguide can rule that they count as Load as well, and may estimate their Load value. If your Strength is 0 or negative, your Load total is used as your Encumbrance score. If your Strength is positive, subtract it from your Load total to get your Encumbrance score (minimum of 0). Drop all fractions.

# STEP SEVEN: FURTHER CHARACTERIZATION

## Appearance

Your character's appearance makes your traits visible to other characters. Turn the relevant traits of your character, such as ethnic origin, Characteristics (particularly Presence), background, Virtues and Flaws, and

Personality Traits into aspects of your appearance. High Intelligence, for example, can manifest itself as a clear, piercing gaze. A noble background can mean that you wear stylish and expensive clothes. A light-hearted disposition can mean you are usually smiling. By following this advice you make your character's traits more tangible and interesting. After all, it's better roleplaying to say, "You always see me with a sneer of disdain on my face," than to say, "You can tell I'm very disdainful."

## Size

Unless you have a Virtue or Flaw that states otherwise, your Size is 0, which is average for an adult human. See the Traits Chapter, p.109, for more information on Size and its effects on your character's scores.

## Quirks

You may also give your character quirks, interesting personal details that add depth and charm to your character. Simply write a short paragraph or two about the strange and unique things that define your character. A quirk can be a twisted sense of humor, a fondness for animals, or a habit of grunting yes to a question.

## Personal History

When you create your personal history, determine your connection to your family, the area where you grew up and what it's like, and any old enemies or friends that you still have. In particular, specify how you became linked to the Covenant, and why you maintain relations with it.

If you're not familiar with the Mythic Europe setting of the game, don't feel intimidated in creating your personal history. You can work on your character's history with those more versed in the world, or you can designate a section of the world as your responsibility and have your character originate from there. The latter option leaves you a moderate amount of freedom in determining your history. In general, don't worry. This is a game, not a history class. Do what feels right and have fun.

# LOOKING AHEAD

Once your character is finally complete, it's ready to participate in your Troupe's stories. In the process of creating your character you've probably prepared yourself to roleplay her as well. Part of the process of character creation is an attachment that develops between your character and you, enabling you to roleplay her realistically and creatively. Nurture your empathy for your character as you roleplay her; if you are at all different from her, roleplaying may not be easy.

The process of character creation does not end with the beginning of the Saga. Your character never stops growing, changing, developing and maturing. As the Saga progresses, make up new Personality Traits, quirks and history details. Furthermore, use your Experience Points (see the Saga Chapter) to wisely develop your Abilities, build your character's self-confidence, and add more detail. Most importantly, think of ways the personality of your character changes over time and with different events. Have an idea of how your character might change and then guide her growth in that direction. Let your character determine her own fate, though; don't "force" her to follow your early concepts.

Novelists often speak of characters in their books coming to life, refusing to be manipulated or directed by the writer. This type of character stands out from the page and says, "Leave me alone. I'm real," and then does exactly as she feels, regardless of the author's original intent. We roleplayers can learn a lot from this experience, for it speaks of what makes a truly good character.

If your character ever bores you, it's probably because you haven't developed and changed her enough over time. Ideally, your character grows more and more real as the Saga progresses, just as characters become more believable the more involved you become in a novel. Toward that end, make your character as complete and entertaining as possible throughout the length of the Saga, not just at its beginning.

# Exempli Gratia: Character Creation

Ken and a group of friends are starting up an **Ars Magica** Saga, and Ken must create his Magus character for the game. The steps he goes through can help you better understand the character creation process.

**Step One:** The first thing to do is come up with a concept. Ken decides to play a female character, specifically a Magus specializing in Terram spells. He wants her to be as resilient as stone, and feels she should have an intuitive understanding of the earth. She also has a sense for the future, and wants to forge herself a place in that future.

Based on this concept, Ken decides on the name Salistra, *filius* of Mostrensa, and decides that she belongs to House Tremere. Salistra is right out of apprenticeship, being 23 years old. As the Saga begins in 1197, Salistra was born in 1174. As she is young, Aging rolls are not necessary.

**Step Two:** Ken decides to purchase rather than roll Characteristics. He has seven positive points to work with, but decides right off the top that he wants at least two more, acquired from negative Flaw points taken later (i.e., two Virtue points are sacrificed to spend on Characteristics). Ken decides not to spend any negative Characteristic points on Flaws. Taking all seven positive Characteristic points, Ken must also use seven negative Characteristic points (though the two points gained from Flaws do not have to be accounted for with negative Characteristic points). The nine positive and seven negative points are allocated as follows, with Characteristic Specialties included:

> Intelligence (level-headed) +2
> Perception (visionary) +2
> Presence (unassuming) -2
> Communication (bland expression) -1
> Strength (rounded shoulders) -2 + 1 = -1
> Stamina (enduring) +1
> Dexterity (steady hand) +2
> Quickness (slow reflexes) -2 + 1 = -1

**Step Three:** The next thing to do is choose Virtues and Flaws. This is where Ken can begin in earnest to develop the strange bond his character has with the earth. Virtues and Flaws should also be take that reflect the House — Tremere — to which Salistra belongs.

Magus characters get ten Flaw points, which grants ten Virtue points. Ken plans to use them all. The rules suggest that Magus characters spend half their points on Hermetic Virtues and Flaws, but Ken wants a wider range of traits than that option allows. And, as two points normally spent on Virtues were spent on positive Characteristics, Salistra can only have eight points of Virtues.

Flaws Taken:

**No Sigil -1:** Being of House Tremere, Salistra's Sigil (the symbol of her membership in the Order of Hermes) is held by her master. She cannot vote at Tribunals (large meetings of Magi).

**Sensitive to Disrespect -1:** Belonging to Tremere, Salistra is used to being treated with respect and is offended when treated otherwise.

**Sense of Doom -3:** Salistra has had a vision of her demise, in which she is buried alive, or somehow becomes part of the earth. The vision, understandably, makes her fatalistic.

**Deleterious Circumstances (Uncommon & Severe) -2:** Magic rolls are halved when not standing on the ground or on stone.

**Major Magic Deficiency (Rare) -3:** Magical totals involving Auram are halved.

Virtues Taken:

**Knack with *Certámen* +2:** +4 to *Certámen* rolls.

**Self-Confident +2:** two extra Confidence Points are gained.

**Latent Mystical Ability +2:** Salistra doesn't realize it, but she can communicate with the earth, and has been talked to by the earth before, giving her strange visions.

**Exceptional Talent +2:** Visions, derived from *Latent Mystical Ability*.

The remaining two points were spent on positive Characteristics.

**Step Four:** Now that Ken has chosen Virtues and Flaws, he knows what restricted Abilities his Virtues allow him to take. He can also take Abilities that round out Salistra's magical capacities, and bond with the earth.

Since Salistra is a Magus, she gets as many Experience Points to spend on Abilities as she has years of age: 23. The following Abilities and their scores are free to a Magus character. Specialties are added.

Speak Own Language (Provençal) 4
Speak (Latin) 5
Scribe (Latin) 3
Magic Theory (enchanting items) 5
Hermes Lore (rules on mundanes) 2
Hermes History (Houses) 2
*Parma Magica* (Rego) 2

The following Abilities are purchased:

*Certámen* (Terram) 2 — costs 3 Experience Points

Visions (future) 2 — costs 3 points

Finesse (steadiness) 2 — costs 3 points

Penetration (Rego) 3 — costs 6 points

Church Knowledge (standing on Order of Hermes) 1 — costs 1 point

Concentration (long periods) 2 — costs 3 points

Meditation (calming) 1 — costs 1 point

Track (hard earth) 2 — costs 3 points

**Step Five:** As a Magus, Salistra must have scores in the fifteen Arts, and knows starting Formulaic spells which are part of her magical repertoire. She receives 150 Experience Points with which to purchase Art scores. She buys the following scores:

| Art | Score | Cost |
| --- | --- | --- |
| Creo | 2 | 3 |
| Intéllego | 6 | 21 |
| Muto | 4 | 10 |
| Perdo | 3 | 6 |
| Rego | 7 | 28 |
| Animál | 2 | 3 |

| | | |
| --- | --- | --- |
| Aquam | 0 | 0 |
| Auram | 0 | 0 |
| Córporem | 2 | 3 |
| Herbam | 3 | 6 |
| Ignem | 4 | 10 |
| Imágonem | 0 | 0 |
| Mentem | 0 | 0 |
| Terram | 9 | 45 |
| Vim | 5 | 15 |

Salistra also gets 150 points to spend on spell Levels. The Levels of the spells she chooses must be within ten points of her appropriate Technique + Art + Intelligence total. She selects the following spells, opting for higher Level spells in anticipation of duplicating lower ones with Spontaneous magic.

*Ward Against Faeries of the Mountains* (ReTe Gen, learned at Level 15)

*The Earth Split Asunder* (ReTe 25)

*Eye of the Treacherous Terrain* (InTe 15)

*Hands of the Grasping Earth* (MuTe 15)

*Circular Ward Against Demons* (ReVi Gen, learned at Level 20) — she fears her visions are demon-inspired

*Hornet Fire* (MuIg 15)

*The Invisible Eye Revealed* (InVi 15)

*Awaken the Sleeping Corpse* (ReCo 20)

*Decay Fur and Hide* (PeAn 10) — only ten Levels are left to spend, so a low Level spell is chosen

**Step Six:** Now that Salistra is developed in the more essential game terms, her scores and details of lesser importance — her finishing touches — in the game must be determined. Some of these details go far in determining Salistra's identity, making her enjoyable to roleplay.

Normal characters begin with three Confidence Points, but as Salistra has the *Self-Confidence* Virtue (+2), she adds two points to Confidence, giving her five points.

Since Salistra is a beginning character, and has no Virtues or Flaws that state otherwise, she has no Reputation, but can certainly gain one once the Saga begins.

As for Personality Traits, Ken decides that Salistra is headstrong and cold to others, being absorbed by her own world and her fears of her mysterious destiny. As a member of House Tremere, she also has some Traits appropriate to her upbringing. Without a Virtue that states otherwise, Salistra cannot have Personality Traits in excess of +3 or -3. Ken gives Salistra the following Traits:

Stubborn +2

Impressionable -2

Fatalistic +3

Understanding -1

Brave +2

Respectful +1

As for equipment, Salistra travels light. She wears only a plain, dark robe that suggests nothing of her magical power. She carries no weapons, lacking any Weapon Skills. Thus, she has no Load score to speak of, so has an Encumbrance of 0.

**Step Seven:** Salistra as a character is essentially complete. All she needs are some minor details that make her mortal. Everyone has a background and little quirks, and Salistra is no exception.

She appears as a plain woman of rounded build, but is not overweight by any means. Rather, her shoulders roll into her torso. She is of pallid complexion and constantly bears an expression of disinterest, no matter how exciting or dramatic events are. She has a marvellous poker face. Her dull, grey eyes only reinforce her bland look, and her mousy, unkempt hair suggests she does little to alter her appearance. Salistra's arms and legs are somewhat short for her build (but she's still Size 0), and her fingers are stunted, though steady and nimble.

As for quirks, Salistra always goes barefoot, even in winter. Strangely enough, she never suffers abrasions or frostbite. This peculiarity has given Salistra the nickname of "Cold Feet"

amongst the Grogs at her Covenant.

Salistra was born in a mining village and was put to work in the mines at an early age. Called upon to enter a narrow new passage, she had to be hauled out, screaming of something terrible beyond. The miners feared they had dug too deep and that the demons of Hell were upon them, and thus immediately sealed the tunnel.

After the incident young Salistra did not speak and was feared as demon-tainted, so it came as no surprise that her parents were willing to trade her to a peculiar stranger who came to the village. That man was Mostrensa, who recognized the girl's newborn magical Gift, and goaded her back into the world to teach her the art of magic.

To this day Salistra cannot remember what she saw in the tunnel, but flashes of memory still come to her, suggesting that she and the earth are one, and that they must ultimately join.

And, that's it. Salistra is complete. Going back to the original concept you'll note that she's changed somewhat over the creation process, but that's part of what character creation is about — characters becoming independent and alive.

# raits

## chapter three

his Chapter describes and lists all the qualifiers and quantifiers that define and give your character identity. Generally anything that has a number attached to it, and describes a character in some way, is called a trait. This Chapter describes all the traits used in **Ars Magica**, and explains how they might be used in play.

There are many different categories of traits. These categories are described in the following order in this Chapter: Characteristics, Virtues and Flaws, Abilities, Reputation, Confidence, Personality Traits, and Health. Magical Arts and Spells receive coverage in their own respective Chapters.

# Characteristics

There are eight Characteristics in **Ars Magica**: Intelligence, Perception, Strength, Stamina, Presence, Communication, Dexterity and Quickness. Characteristics establish the physical and mental capabilities of your character. They establish how strong you are, suggest how fast your reflexes are, and indicate how good you are at persuasion. Each Characteristic has a number associated with it, describing the degree of your aptitude in that

area. These scores are used as modifiers to rolls in the game, depending on the situation. For example, if you are trying to move a large bolder, Strength is used. A 0 is average for any Characteristic. Positive numbers indicate higher than average ability, and negative numbers indicate below average ability, with -3 to +3 being the normal range.

Remember that your Characteristics represent your inborn capabilities at their optimum, so they cannot rise by normal means. You can, however, improve skills and capabilities that complement your Characteristics.

The following is a breakdown of all Characteristics, with Specialties included:

**INTELLIGENCE** represents both your memory as well as your ability to learn and think. It is important for Abilities that require thought power and is paramount for the magical Arts. A character is not necessarily stupid if he has low Intelligence; common sense, street savvy, and wisdom are not part of the Intelligence score — these are facets of the characters that are portrayed by the player.

**Negative:** *dull-witted, ponderous, forgetful, lazy, doddering, addled, asinine, stupid, slow learner, bored, decadent, immature.*

Positive: *broad shoulders, strong grip, bulging biceps, powerful stride, massive chest, husky build, able body, hearty, big.*

**STAMINA** indicates how long you can continue to exert yourself as well as how much physical punishment you can sustain. It is your staying power, both mental and physical, and one of its most important components is simply the will to live. Some people are too mean to die. Stamina also helps determine how well you carry a load, ignore fatigue, and withstand wounds.

Negative: *nagging cough, frequent illness, short winded, delicate constitution, no self-discipline, weak-willed, enfeebled, tremulous, slothful.*

Positive: *tireless legs, strong constitution, iron willed, forceful personality, enduring, tough minded, tenacious, stalwart, durable, large hearted.*

**PRESENCE** describes your appearance, demeanor and charisma. Personal tastes vary, but within a culture good looks are standard enough that what is attractive, interesting or impressive to one person is likely the same to others. Presence is also indicative of how imposing or intimidating you are; you might not be physically attractive but your demeanor might command respect. Presence is important for making a good impression, as well as for leading people.

Negative: *carbuncles (acne), greasy hair, scarred face, timid demeanor, shifty eyes, slouching posture, despairing expression, unassuming, flighty.*

Positive: *sexy, luminous eyes, alluring, straight posture, confident stride, mean, imposing, intimidating, honest face, comforting, imposing beard, dignified, captivating, regal manner, commanding stare, look of the eagles, genial.*

**COMMUNICATION** represents your aptitude for self-expression. It is important when you are attempting to verbally influence or communicate with another, or when trying to do so through body language. Communication is the basis of most human interactions, and a positive Communication score suggests a character who is comfortable with or confident in his relationships with other people.

Negative: *poor diction, slurred speech, faltering voice, guttural voice, lisp, boring speaker, rambling, inconsiderate, vile manners, bland expression, heavy accent, laconic personality, no sense of humor, garrulous, foul mouthed.*

Positive: *smooth talker, glib tongue, honeyed voice, expressive hands, sophisticated sense of humor, captivating speaker, orator, eloquent.*

**DEXTERITY** indicates the physical ability to move with agility and to manipulate what you are holding with accuracy and grace. It includes hand-eye coordination, fine motor manipulation, and bodily grace. Dexterity helps determine how well you swing a sword or throw a knife.

Positive: *quick-witted, shrewd thinker, sharp minded, discerning, creative level-headed, wily, bookworm, knowledgeable, clever, pragmatic.*

**PERCEPTION** indicates how well you notice things going on around you, as well as your powers of intuition. While sometimes a conscious thing, Perception often works intuitively — you simply notice something. Besides letting you notice things, a Storyguide may have you roll Perception with various knowledge abilities to see if you have the insight to understand or know about a certain fact or concept. Perception is important for Abilities such as Alertness, Track, and Folk Ken.

Negative: *distracted, unobservant, absent-minded, preoccupied, inattentive, unheeding, careless.*

Positive: *insightful, attentive, patient, probing, keen-eyed, perceptive, intuitive, visionary, astute, apprehensive.*

**STRENGTH** is a measure of your physical power. It is your lifting, pushing, shoving, heaving and moving ability. Strength is important when hefting a melee weapon, and when using brute, physical force against something or someone. People with higher Strength are often bigger than those with lower Strength, assuming they are within the same Size category.

Negative: *scrawny arms, weak grip, rounded shoulders, weak chest, puny, decrepit, indolent, small frame.*

**Negative:** *trembling hands, clumsy, awkward stance, all-thumbs, graceless movements, plodding step, gawky limbs, can't dance, gangly.*

**Positive:** *nimble fingers, smooth motioned, lithesome walk, steady hand, deft hand, graceful dancer, agile, adept athlete, cat-like grace.*

QUICKNESS indicates your reaction speed and reflexes. It is simply how fast you are. Quickness helps determine who acts first when two people are trying to do something with great haste. It also determines how well you do something when you do it rapidly. Whenever Quickness modifies a roll, Encumbrance, the measure of how loaded down you are, is applied as a penalty. In other words, you react more slowly when carrying a heavy load.

**Negative:** *slow reflexes, torpid, flat-footed, languid stride, ungainly, lethargic, overweight, slothful, lumbering.*

**Positive:** *quick reflexes, surefooted, energetic, jumpy, nimble feet, fleet-footed, fast, breakneck sprinter, swift, nervous.*

# Virtues and Flaws

Virtues and Flaws are purchased during the character creation process. Virtues are the exceptional attributes of a person. Since Magi, Companions and many Grogs are exceptional people, they have many Virtues. Normal people, on the other hand, have only one Virtue, or none at all. Flaws are the exceptional attributes that hinder or limit characters, and are used to balance out the Virtues a character has. Virtues are each assigned a positive value, and Flaws are each assigned a negative value. The value indicates how much the Virtue or Flaw affects your character.

Some Virtues and Flaws have notes for Magi who choose them. Some of these have different values for Magi than they do for Companions and Grogs, and some Virtues and Flaws are not available to Magi at all. For instance, Fast Learner is more valuable for a Magus than it is for a Companion, so a Companion must pay 3 points for it while a Magus must pay 5. However, some Virtues and Flaws are exclusively available to Magi.

Your Virtues and Flaws are often central to your character, so choose them thoughtfully. Decide what your character is like, and choose Virtues and Flaws that advance that concept. Virtues and Flaws that somehow work against each other can create an interesting inner struggle, such as Compulsion to Drink, which can conflict with being Dutybound. Virtues and Flaws that are directly contradictory, as well as those that deal directly with the same aspect of your character, are mutually exclusive. You cannot have Poor Eyesight and Keen Vision, or be Lithe as well as Obese. Neither can you be Large and Stocky, since both describe your body type. Likewise, you cannot have both a Knack for picking pockets and a Light Touch, since they essentially cover the same kind of endeavor. Some Flaws are perverse versions of Virtues, in which case the two are mutually exclusive. For example, Dutybound describes those who think they have a true Code of Honor, but do not. Sometimes you may take more than one Virtue or Flaw that refer to the same aspect of your character. You might have a Driving Goal to overthrow a local baron, and a Hatred of that baron. In such a case the Virtue and Flaw combine and make you much more obsessed with killing the baron than you would be with only one of them.

Below is a list of the Virtues and Flaws you may purchase. They are organized according to the following categories: Hermetic, Passions, Physical, Mental, Supernatural, Social, Traits, Background, and Equipment.

## HERMETIC

It is a rare Magus whose natural Gift for magic perfectly fits the structured theory of Hermetic magic. This means you can have special magical proficiencies and deficiencies. Almost all Magi therefore have Hermetic Virtues and Flaws. To simulate this, it's suggested that at least half your total points devoted to Virtues and Flaws must be spent on Hermetic Virtues and Flaws. The remaining Virtues and Flaws may be chosen from the other lists.

*Restrictions: Hermetic Virtues and Flaws can only be taken by Magus characters.*

## Virtues: variable

**CAUTIOUS SORCERER:** You have learned to be very careful with a specific kind of magic, giving you one less Botch roll with *all* magic of that type (even in laboratory work), but you must at least roll one Botch die. The cost of this Virtue is the same as the cost for an Affinity (see below) with the type of magic you are careful with. This Virtue combines well with the Flaw of Slow Caster (see below).

**CYCLIC MAGIC:** Your magic is attuned to some cycle of nature (the sun, the moon, the tides, the seasons), and itself cycles from low to high strength with given phenomena, like the phases of the moon. The cycle of your magic must be regular, and your overall magical power must balance out over the course of the cycle (so, if you gain +4 to magic during the peak, you must suffer -4 during the low). The cost of this Virtue is half the bonus you gain to your magic during the peak of the cycle (so if you peak at +4, the Virtue costs +2).

**HEART-BEAST:** Each Bjornaer Magus has at least one Heart-Beast, which is the animal form you can take at any time, without casting a spell. Your master actually probed your heart to see what shape lay within, so your Heart-Beast is not a matter of choice, but one of your nature. Rare apprentices can take more than one form, or the form of an inanimate object (in which case the form is called the Heart-Shape). Over time, you maintain more and more aspects of your Heart-Beast in human form, including personality and physical shape. You have a Personality Trait named after the form you take (e.g., "Bear"). A high score means you are closely attuned to the shape and strongly identify with it. Cost: +2 if form is battleworthy (e.g., wolf, stag, bear), and +1 if the form is not battleworthy.

**MAGICAL AFFINITY:** You have an affinity (which is treated like an ordinary Ability) with a specific kind of magic, and you may add your score in the Affinity to all spell rolls and Lab Totals involving that kind of magic. You buy this Ability along with your other Abilities and can gain Experience in it as you can any other Ability. Affinities are important because you cannot assign Experience Points to your Arts, but you can assign Experience Points to affinity Abilities, increasing your magical power in an indirect way.

**Example +1 Affinities:** fighting demons, water creatures, ghosts and corpses, death and aging, wind, self-transformation. **Example +2 Affinities:** healing, forests and forest animals, faeries, passions, rock. **Example +3 Affinities:** any Form, such as Terram or Mentem. **Example +4 Affinities:** any Technique, such as Creo or Perdo.

**WILL OVER FORM:** This arcane talent functions as a *Magical Affinity* (i.e., you have to purchase an Ability score in it as a trait). That score counts as a bonus toward spells that turn you into a different shape — those willingly cast on you. It also acts as a bonus to Natural Resistance rolls against spells that change your shape — those you don't want cast on you. This score also modifies rolls to determine if you can resume human form, or one of your other natural forms (if you have any), when you have been turned into another shape. When forced into another form, as with a transformation spell cast upon you, you make a stress + Will Over Form roll every Round. If you roll 9+ you can resume one of your natural forms. Cost: +2 if your other natural forms are battleworthy animals, and +1 if they are not.

**THE HIDDEN SHAPE:** Allowed for Bjornaer Magi only. Hermetic magic cannot determine your Heart-Beast. Spells such as *Sight of the True Form* only reveal your current shape as if it is your natural shape. Magic of other kinds, such as faerie magic, might be able to detect your Heart-Beast, at the Storyguide's discretion. Cost: +2 if your Heart-Beast is battleworthy, and +1 if it is not.

**METHOD CASTER:** You are very good at Formulaic magic, having perfected a consistent method for all your castings. You get half the cost of this Virtue as a bonus on every Formulaic spell you cast. However, if you alter from your standard tone of voice and use of gestures, you do not get this bonus. The score of the Virtue, and therefore your bonus, is decided by you based on how many Virtue and Flaw points you want to spend.

## Virtues: +1

**ADEPT STUDENT:** You get +5 on Lab Totals when learning spells.

**BOOK-LEARNER:** You have a knack for figuring out what people mean when they write about magic — the capacity to read between the lines. Treat all magic books that you study as if they are 2 levels higher than they actually are.

**DEFT ART:** You are facile with one Art. You get half the ordinary penalties for casting spells in that Art in physically awkward circumstances. For example, if you need to Fast-Cast a spell without words or gestures, you get at a -10 rather than -20 penalty.

**BONUS WITH FAMILIARS:** You get +10 purchase points when determining the strength of the three cords for your Familiar.

**EXTRA SPELLS:** You start with 10 extra Levels of spells. This Virtue may be taken more than once.

**EXTRA ARTS:** You start with 10 extra purchase points in the magical Arts. This Virtue may be taken more than once.

**FAERIE MAGIC:** As with a *Magical Affinity* Virtue, you have a score in an arcane Ability, Faerie Magic, that you must purchase with starting Experience Points, and can raise with further Experience. The Ability represents your training in faerie ways. It is used as a bonus to Resistance rolls against faerie magic, and as a bonus to your spell rolls that deal with faeries. The higher your score in the Faerie Magic Ability, the stranger and more faerie you are.

**THE GENTLE GIFT:** The ability to work magic at all is called the "Gift," and it usually disturbs normal people and animals. That is why Magi suffer -3 on rolls involving social interaction with normal people, and dealings with animals. However, yours is a "gentle Gift;" it does not bother people or animals and you do not suffer the -3 penalty.

**HERMETIC PRESTIGE:** Because of your famous and well-respected master, other Magi look up to you, even if you haven't earned their respect. Some envy you, and most expect more from you than they do from other Magi. Take a Reputation of +3 with a Specialty of Hermetic Prestige.

**QUAESITOR:** This Virtue includes the equivalent of the Hermetic Prestige Virtue (but that bonus costs you no extra Virtue points), and gives you some legal powers in the Order of Hermes. But, you have certain restrictions too. For instance, you may not

vote at Tribunal, nor develop bonds to others that may bias your judgement.

**INVENTIVE GENIUS:** You receive +3 on rolls for inventing new spells, crafting magic items, and inventing longevity potions. If you experiment, you get +6.

**MASTERED SPELLS:** You have 20 Experience Points that you can use to Master spells.

**PERSONAL VIS SOURCE:** You have a regular source of *vis* which you can claim as your own. You gain one pawn of *vis* per Season (four pawns per year) of a specific type chosen when you create your character. Some Magi gain this *vis* from their own hair or blood, and others know of independent sources in secret places. No matter what the source, your *vis* may at some time cause you problems, as the source may be put in danger or used against you (especially if your source is part of your body and it falls into the hands of an enemy wizard). You start the Saga with no personal *vis* — your master got it all while you were an apprentice.

**SPECIAL CIRCUMSTANCES:** You are able to perform magic better in certain circumstances, gaining a +3 bonus to your rolls to cast spells or resist them. Example circumstances: during a storm, while in the air, while touching the target.

**STRONG WRITER:** You write about magic with great speed and enthusiasm. You may write about 4 points of Arts each Season instead of 3, and may write up to 2/3 of your Art scores per Season. You may also write out 80 Levels of spells that you know in one Season, or copy 240 Levels of spells that are already written. As for lab texts, you can make 100 Levels of your own readable, or copy 250 Levels that are already readable, in a Season. (This Virtue can be combined with the *Incomprehensible* Flaw, below, leaving you with a lot of valuable books that nobody can understand but everyone wants to.)

# Virtues: +2

**INDEPENDENT MAGIC:** Your magic is closely tied to your own internal power, lessening your vulnerability to (and dependence on) external powers. Halve any bonuses or penalties imposed by supernatural Auras, which include those of Magic, Faerie, Divinity, Reason and the Infernal.

**FREE STUDY:** You are a free thinker, ill suited to learning from others. You are better at figuring things out for yourself than you are at studying from books. You gain +2 on your rolls when studying from *vis*, but if you

study from books, their rating is halved to determine how much you can learn.

**QUIET MAGIC:** Your spells require only soft verbal components, so you may cast them using only a Soft voice at no penalty, and you are only at a -5 penalty if you use no voice at all. You gain no benefits for using your voice fully, though you may take that as a *Special Circumstance* Virtue. You do, however, gain full benefits for using a Booming voice.

**SIDE EFFECT:** Your magic has some side effect that is primarily useful, though it might occasionally be a nuisance to you. The intensity of the side effect increases with the power of the magic being used (maybe with spells of Level 20 or higher). For example, you might gain a commanding presence when you use magic (+1 to Presence for 10 minutes after a spell is cast), acquire a pleasant scent following spell casting (dispelling foul odors), or achieve a calm state of mind (bonus to Concentration rolls) after you cast spells. Side effects almost always prove a minor nuisance with very powerful magic or in certain circumstances.

**SUBTLE MAGIC:** Your spells do not require gestures, so you may cast them without using gestures at no penalty. You gain no benefits for using gestures, though you may take that as a *Special Circumstance* Virtue. However, you still gain full benefits for using Exaggerated gestures.

**FAST CASTER:** Your magic takes less time to perform than that of other Magi. You gain no advantages for casting spells at the normal rate, but your Casting Time of Fast-Cast Spontaneous spells (p.184) gains a +3 bonus. If you cast a Formulaic spell simultaneously with another Magus, yours is assumed to go off first (though your spell still goes off at the end of the Round, after other actions). If both casters have this Virtue, make a simple roll, modified by +3, to determine who casts first. The casting time of Ritual spells cannot be reduced by means of this Virtue.

# Virtues: +3

**STUDENT OF FAERIE:** You have been trained in the various rites and observances of faerie magic. You receive a +4 modifier in rolls involving Faerie Lore, whether you have that Ability or not. You also know how to behave around different kinds of faeries. For instance, you know the rituals to communicate with clackers, the looks and uses of faerie plants, and faerie etiquette. You also have *Common Sense* (as the +1 Mental Virtue) when dealing with faeries. If you

teach your knowledge of Faerie to someone other than an apprentice, the faeries may be angered.

**ENDURING MAGIC:** Your spells tend to last longer than usual (though Instant spells still take an instant and Permanent spells remain just that). The Storyguide secretly rolls a stress die; your spell lasts that many times longer than usual. If a 0 is rolled by the Storyguide, the spell lasts the standard Duration. If a Botch results, the spell immediately fails and the caster loses a Short-Term Fatigue Level. A Spontaneous Intéllego Vim spell of Level 10 tells you roughly how long the magic lasts. This Virtue may work against you at times, especially when you want a spell to have a short Duration. This Virtue lengthens the Duration of spells that involve *vis* in their casting.

**LIFE-LINKED SPONTANEOUS MAGIC:** Your Spontaneous magic is linked with your life force, allowing you to do more with Spontaneous magic than most Magi, but only at a very high cost. This extra power is tapped when you decide to exert yourself in a spell casting roll, but the usual Fatigue Level is not spent yet. Rather, when exerting yourself while casting a Spontaneous spell, you declare the Level of effect you wish to produce with the spell. After all factors are added to the roll and the total is divided by two, the Level rolled is subtracted from the Level declared. You cast at the Level declared, but at a cost of one Long-Term Fatigue Levels for every five Levels, or fraction thereof, by which you failed to reach your declared Level. The Short-Term Fatigue Level normally spent for exertion is not spent if your spell casting result is lower than the declared Level of the spell; Long-Term Levels are spent as described above. If your spell casting roll is high enough to meet the declared Level of the spell, no Long-Term Fatigue Levels are spent, but the usual Short-Term Level is.

Any Long-Term Fatigue Levels left over after dropping you to Unconsciousness are taken as Body Levels. (Yes, it is quite possible to kill yourself by casting an overly powerful spell!) On a single Botch in the spell casting roll, the spell still goes off, but based on a spell casting roll of 0 (so all the power behind the spell is paid for by you, with a Long-Term Fatigue Level for every five Levels of the declared spell). On double or higher Botches, you suffer the above effect, plus other Botch effects.

# Virtues: +4

**APTITUDE WITH ELEMENTS:** You have an innate knack for casting spells which

deal with any of the four elements (Aquam, Auram, Ignem and Terram). Whenever you engage in magical activity involving these Forms, you gain +4 to your die rolls.

**CONTINUOUS SPONTANEOUS MAGIC:** You have greater control over Spontaneous magic than most Magi, allowing you to cast more powerful spells by building up power for several Rounds. With this Virtue you therefore use rules different from the standard Spontaneous ones. When you exert yourself (i.e., spend a Short-Term Fatigue Level), you may delay completion of a Spontaneous spell for several Rounds. For each Round you wait, and expend another Short-Term Fatigue Level, a multiplier is applied to your spell casting roll, rather than a divisor (of 2, by the standard rules). After the first Round, your spell casting roll is multiplied by 50%. After the second, it's multiplied by 75%. And, After the third Round, your Spontaneous spell casting roll is multiplied by 100% (it's taken at face value). It's not Hermetically possible to build up power for more than three Rounds before casting.

As you Fatigue yourself for every Round that you build up power, you accumulate Fatigue penalties based on your current Fatigue Level. The Level you reach when you cast your spell dictates the penalty to your spell casting roll.

**LIVING MAGIC:** You may use human life force to power your magic. Each Body Level worth of energy you draw from a willing target may be used in place of one Fatigue Level you would normally lose in performing magic (Long-Term or Short-Term Fatigue Levels). You may also use your own Body Levels to cast spells. The person whom you draw Body Levels from makes a Stamina roll of 6+ to resist your drain. Thus, even if your

subject is willing, his body may resist your efforts. Magic Resistance also defends against Body Level drain, based on the Form of the spell being cast.

**SILENT MAGIC:** Your spells do not require verbal components, so you may cast them without speaking at no penalty. You gain no benefits for using your voice, though you may take that as a *Special Circumstance* Virtue. You still gain the bonuses of using a Booming voice, though.

## Virtues: +5

**FLAWLESS MAGIC:** You learn Formulaic spells perfectly every time. Whenever you learn or invent a Formulaic spell, it is automatically Mastered; you do not need to expend any Experience to Master it. Obviously, all your beginning spells are Mastered.

**NIGHT READER:** You have the habit of reading magic at odd times of day and night. You get one extra Season's worth of studying magical Arts at the end of every year. In that "extra" Season you must study a different Art from any you are studying during normal, waking hours in that year.

**ELEMENTALIST:** You are an elementalist, and have a natural Magical Affinity (like the +1 Hermetic Virtue) when working with any of the natural elements (Aquam, Terram, Ignem, and Auram), so have an Ability in the elements, in this case with a starting score of 6. However, due to your extensive work with the elements, your ties to Hermetic magic are weak. As a result, all rolls that involve Vim are divided in half, and you are unable to cast Ritual spells (including those that involve elements).

## Flaws: variable

**POOR FORMULAIC MAGIC:** You are simply not very good at Formulaic magic. Subtract the cost of this Flaw from every Formulaic magic roll that you make (e.g., a -2 Flaw means -2 on all rolls).

## Flaws: -1

**FLAWED PARMA:** Your *Parma Magica* is defective and provides poor protection (1/2 of the normal Resistance) against one Technique. That is, it is weak against any spell with that primary Technique; it has usual power against spells for which that Technique is only a Requisite. This Flaw may be taken repeatedly with different Techniques.

**LIFE-LINKED MAGIC:** Your magic is powerfully linked to your life force, and expires completely when you die. All spells (including Ritual spells) of Permanent or shorter Duration expire immediately upon your death (making a Duration of Permanent essentially a Duration of "Life"), and any items you have enchanted lose their magical properties. (This Flaw is only applicable if your Troupe assumes spells persist after their caster's death, at least for a while.)

**TWILIGHT POINTS:** During apprenticeship you suffered an encounter with wild, strong magic that has given you Twilight Points (see the Saga Chapter, p.356). Divide a simple die by 2 (rounded up) to see how many points you have. You can gain more points even before you start taking your longevity potion. Decide the nature of the experience that gave you these beginning points, as any temporary Twilights you undergo are undoubtedly related to the first.

**HEDGE WIZARD:** You have a bad Reputation, level 2, with a Specialty as a hedge wizard, though you are a member of the Order. Other Magi distrust you, and, more importantly, grant you no respect.

**THE BLATANT GIFT:** Your Gift (the ability to do magic) is easily noticed by others. You suffer -6 on all social rolls involving normal people, and on rolls involving animals — animals are extremely disturbed, frightened, and possibly enraged by your presence. People immediately realize there is something strange about you, even if they do not realize you are a Magus. (You must have led a lonely life even before becoming an apprentice.)

**VIS OBLIGATION:** You have a personal *vis* obligation, independent of any your Covenant may have. You must pay someone four pawns of *vis* a year, and failing to meet your obligation may lead to very serious consequences, such as Hermetic punishment.

**WEAK WRITER:** You write about magic very slowly and awkwardly. You can only write one point of Arts each Season (up to a score of 1/3 your level), transcribe 15 Levels of spells, or copy 40 Levels of spells that are already in readable form. Furthermore, you can only copy your own lab texts into readable form at a rate of 40 Levels per Season, and can only copy already readable lab texts at a rate of 100 Levels per Season. You are also unable to use Verditius runes (see House Verditius in the Mythic Europe Chapter, and see the **Ars Magica** supplement **The Order of Hermes**) or other magical writings.

**DELETERIOUS CIRCUMSTANCES (UNCOMMON & MINOR):** Your magic rolls are at -5 in certain uncommon circumstances, such as when in a large city or when underground.

**INFAMOUS MASTER:** Your master is widely despised or held in contempt, and most Magi expect little better from you. Even if you've done nothing out of the ordinary, other Magi treat you as if you don't deserve to be among their number. Your master could have been a diabolist, a bumbler, or a fool. You have a bad Reputation of the appropriate type, level 2, with a Specialty among Magi.

**LOOSE MAGIC:** You lack the concentration, will, or ability to Master spells.

**NO SIGIL:** Your sigil (the symbol of your membership in the Order of Hermes) is held by your *Parens* (your former master). You cannot vote at Tribunal and the Magus who holds your Sigil can call on you to perform whatever tasks or missions she wants. If you have *filii* (former apprentices of your own), they do not hold their sigils until you hold your own. You must defeat the holder of your sigil in *Certámen* to claim your right.

**MINOR MAGIC DEFICIENCY (RARE):** You have trouble with a particular Art, and its score is treated as one-half its true value, rounded down. (Treat the Art normally when studying.) For example, if you have a score of 9, it acts as a 4, but you still cannot learn from a book with a score of 6. Do not choose Córporem, Vim, or a Technique.

**NECESSARY CONDITION:** In order for your magic to work, you must do something that is (thankfully) relatively easy to do. For instance, maybe your magic only works if you sing or if you spin around once.

**STINGY MASTER:** Your master trained you less thoroughly than most masters train their apprentices, so you have only 130 points with which to buy spells and 130 points with which to purchase Arts.

**WARPED MAGIC:** Your magic is accompanied by some annoying side effect, always of the same type, but with increasing intensity according to the Level of the spell you cast. Possibilities are noises, smells, flashes of light, the disturbance of animals, winds, smelly slime, or a tendency for you to become edgy or easily angered after using magic. The Flaw should cause trouble from time to time, but is mainly just annoying.

**TORMENTING MASTER:** Your master does not yet believe you have successfully passed the Apprentice's Gauntlet (the test of becoming a Magus). Thus, he periodically troubles you with political moves and indirect attacks.

**VERDITIUS MAGIC:** You need a small device called a Spell Focus (see p.187 in the Magic Chapter) to cast each Formulaic spell you know. Whereas other Magi gain bonuses to spell casting rolls when using Spell Foci, you gain none. On the other hand, you have special skills at crafting magic items. Take a new Arcane Skill, Verditius Magic (buy a score in it as you do other Abilities). Add this Ability score to your Lab Total when it applies to magical devices, including longevity potions. You may also choose a Specialty in the Ability (e.g., potions, any Technique or Form). Verditius Magi have no problems dealing with with Arcane Skills, *Parma Magica* or *Certámen*.

# Flaws: -2

**DISCREDITED LINEAGE:** The Quaesitoris suspect your Hermetic line of some terrible crime, such as diabolism or descent from House Diedne. It's unlikely that your name will ever be cleared, and if bold accusations are ever made against you, many may shoot first and ask questions later. The Quaesitoris keep a close eye on you and are suspicious of anything you do or say. If wrongdoing takes place, you are the first they suspect. The Quaesitoris try very hard to prevent any member of your line from achieving a position of authority. Take a bad Reputation of an appropriate type with Specialization among the Quaesitoris at level 1. The only way to lose this Reputation is to repudiate your tradition, or to clear it of the crime.

The suspicion may or may not be true. If it is true, and you know it, you may take the *Dark Secret* Flaw as well (though that Flaw must be purchased normally).

**DELETERIOUS CIRCUMSTANCES (COMMON & MINOR):** Your magic rolls are at -5 in certain reasonably common circumstances, such as when in a town of 200 or more people, or during the night. These circumstances are difficult or impossible to avoid.

**DELETERIOUS CIRCUMSTANCES (UNCOMMON & SEVERE):** Divide your magic rolls by 2 in certain uncommon circumstances, such as when casting on wild animals or when you are not standing.

**LACK OF CONCENTRATION:** You cannot possess the Concentration Ability and cannot cast Ritual spells due to your profound inability to focus your mind.

**LACK OF CONTROL:** After casting a spell, you must spend a Round recovering your mental faculties before casting another. If you cast a spell after casting one the previous

Round, divide the second spell casting roll by 2. Magic items are probably most useful to you.

**RESTRICTION (RARE):** Your magic does not work under rare circumstances, such as when touching an animal, or does not work on certain targets, such as avians.

**WILD MAGIC:** You cannot control your magic with as much finesse and surety as other Magi. You get an extra Botch roll when dealing with magic. You must also spend twice the normal Experience Points to Master a Formulaic spell.

**SHORT-LIVED MAGIC:** Your spells of long Duration do not last as long as they should. Permanent spells last a Year, Year last Moon, Moon last Sun, and Sun last only an hour or two. Short-term spells, like those with a Duration of Ring, and Instant spells are unaffected. Furthermore, spells with their Duration enhanced by *vis* are not affected by your Flaw.

**DISJOINTED MAGIC:** You cannot use previous knowledge to help you with the creation or learning of new magic. You gain no benefit from knowing a spell which is Similar to a spell you are learning or inventing, and you gain no bonuses to enchantment based on the Techniques and Forms of powers already enchanted into an item.

**WEAK MAGIC:** You are particularly weak with a certain type of magic, making it difficult for you to overcome the Natural and Magic Resistance of targets. Halve your spell rolls for purposes of magic Penetration, and increase Natural Resistance rolls made by your victims by 3.

**INCOMPATIBLE ARTS:** For some reason you are unable to use certain combinations of Techniques and Forms. Choose one combination in which you are totally incapable. This Flaw may be taken repeatedly with different combinations, though it should not be taken with either Vim or Córporem.

**INCOMPREHENSIBLE:** You have an eccentric understanding of magic, which you are almost completely unable to communicate. Subtract 4 from your Communication when talking about magic. This assumes that you are trying to communicate clearly. If you are trying to be obscure, well, it's not hard. This Flaw also affects other magic-related matters:

• People reading your notes must make an Intelligence + Scribe Latin roll of 12+. Even if they make the roll they still suffer the penalties below.

• Writing about Arts: If you write a book about a magical Art, it is hard to understand.

Anyone trying to read it must make an Intelligence + Art roll of 18+ each Season of study, or they get no benefit from it. Book Learners get a +5 bonus on the roll. (So, novices have almost no chance of understanding your writings; experts don't have too much trouble.)

• Transcribing Spells: Spells that you have written down are half again as hard to learn as their Level indicates. (So, a rank 20 spell requires a Lab Total of 30 to learn.)

• Training Apprentices: Your apprentice usually has the Flaw of Stingy Master (even if you are generous), as she cannot understand you. You must roll 3+ on your Communication about magic + your apprentice's Intelligence to teach her a point of Magic Theory in a Season. She is likely to get impatient and leave you before she is fully trained.

**NO FAMILIAR:** Because of a flaw in your magic or nature, it is impossible for you to create the cords that bind you and Familiar. You cannot have a Familiar. This Flaw does not apply to Bjornaer Magi as they compensate for their lack of Familiars in other ways.

**CLUMSY MAGIC:** You have trouble getting your magic to go where you want it to. A Targeting roll result of 0 is automatically a Botch.

**NO NATURAL RESISTANCE:** You have limited Resistance to magic of Arts which you are proficient in (i.e., those you have scores in), gaining no bonus to your Magic Resistance rolls for your Form scores. If you are caught without your *Parma Magica*, you still have a Magic Resistance of +0. If a spell cast at you involves a Natural Resistance roll, you are still entitled to that roll.

# Flaws: -3

**MAGIC ADDICTION:** You are addicted to the rush of casting and holding power over magic, and whenever you use it, you must focus your will to avoid using it again (and again, and again), draining yourself into Unconsciousness. Whenever you cast a spell, you must make an Intelligence + Concentration stress roll of 3 + half the Level of the spell or you immediately cast another spell (which can be no lower, or as close as you can manage to the Level of the previous spell). This roll is continued after each spell until you regain control of yourself. If the roll Botches, you continue casting spells until you pass out.

**DELETERIOUS CIRCUMSTANCES (COMMON & SEVERE):** Divide all your magic rolls by two in reasonably common

circumstances, such as when under clouds or in a building.

**MAJOR MAGIC DEFICIENCY (RARE):** You have great difficulty with any one Art (do not choose Córporem, Vim, or any of the Techniques). Any sum that includes the Art (including any spell casting rolls, Lab Totals, and the Art when considered alone) is divided by 2. For example, if you have a Major Deficiency with Terram and are trying a Rego Terram spell, you must divide the total of Rego + Terram + Stamina by 2 before rolling for the spell. With a *Minor Magic Deficiency*, you only divide the Terram score.

**UNIMAGINATIVE LEARNER:** You have trouble figuring things out for yourself, so subtract 4 from your rolls or scores when studying magic. When studying from a book, lower the score of the book by 4.

**ISOLATED FROM THE ORDER:** You have been trained in isolation from the Order, but are still a member. You have no score in Speak or Scribe Latin, nor in Hermetic Lore or History, and may not start with a score in *Certámen* . You do have an initial score in *Parma Magica*. You are likely to be afraid of normal Hermetic Magi. You do, however, have a starting score of 3 in scribing your own obscure magical language (ogham, runes or similar). Requires the *Hedge Wizard* Flaw.

**WEAK PARMA:** Your *Parma Magica* is weak (protection 0, but other modifiers, like Form, still apply) under some relatively common circumstances which are fairly easy for your opponent to utilize (e.g., when the caster of the spell is pointing a wand at you, or singing).

**PAINFUL MAGIC:** Each spell you cast causes you the equivalent of one Body Level in pain, which reduces all your actions by the appropriate wound penalty (though you do not actually suffer any wounds). You recover "pain levels" as if they are Short-Term Fatigue Levels (though pain levels for Ritual spells are considered long-term, like Long-Term Fatigue). Wound penalties for actual wounds are cumulative with wound penalties for pain levels.

It is suggested that you mark pain levels via some new type of mark in the Body Levels boxes on the character sheet. For example, use a vertical line or an asterisk, so that pain levels aren't confused with genuine Body Levels (which are marked with Xs).

**OLD:** You started your apprenticeship late in life, or were held far too long by your begrudging master, and are now old as you become a Magus. Your age is 40 + Stamina, which means you may have to make rolls on the Aging chart (without the aid of a longevity

potion) before play even begins. You may begin even older if you wish, adding three years to age for each additional -1 point of Flaw. Your first year as a Magus is undoubtedly spent in creation of your longevity potion.

**DISGUSTED BY MAGIC:** You find casting magic unpleasant and physically unsettling. Whenever you cast any sort of spell, you must perform a small personal (non-magical) ritual as soon as possible afterwards. Examples include touching your head to the ground three times, taking a swig of sour wine, washing your hands — something simple but not always easily performed. This is a psychological ritual that allows you to be comfortable with yourself again, and should be roleplayed. Until you perform your ritual, your next magic roll is at -3. Each time you use magic before you perform your ritual, this penalty gets one point worse, but the ritual eliminates it completely. A Round of *Certámen* counts as a spell.

**POOR READER:** You don't like to read, and don't read very well. The effects include:

• Treat all books of magic as if they are three levels less than their actual score.

• You get -8 on Lab Totals when learning spells from books, or when working from lab texts.

• When you cast spells from books, you roll five extra Botch dice.

• You get -3 on rolls to understand other Magi's writings.

**SLOW CASTER:** Your magic is slower than that of other Magi, requiring extra time to prepare and execute. Your Formulaic spells take two Rounds to execute, and your Spontaneous spells take two Rounds unless you Fast-Cast, in which case they take place at the end of the first Round (with other, normal spells). Ritual spells are performed at normal speed as all Magi must cast them slowly and carefully.

**STUDY REQUIREMENT:** You are unable to study magic (including spells, Arts, and maybe even enchanted items) from books or *vis* alone. You must study in the presence of the Form of the magic, and experiment with it. For example, you need to sit next to a brook or pond to study Aquam, or a large fire to study Ignem. Growing things are good for Creo, decaying ones good for Perdo. (This imperils your books, and probably restricts the Arts you can study.) As your knowledge grows, the presence of the Form you need gets larger. While a brook suffices for beginning Aquam, or a modest library for Intéllego, you may discover you need to study on the ocean or in the world's greatest library to learn higher level magic. This may put a limit on your ability to learn some Arts. For example, there simply may not be anywhere in the world with enough creation to learn Creo to level 15, or the volcano that you need for Ignem 20 might be too dangerous to work near.

**RIGID MAGIC:** You cannot use *vis* when you cast spells. Thus, you cannot extend the Duration or Range of spells, increase your spell rolls, cast Ritual magic, or create permanent effects with your magic. You can, however, use *vis* in the lab.

# Flaws: -4

**DEPENDENCE ON PROPS:** You need props of some kind (trinkets, certain attire, herbs, gems, magical artifacts) to properly work your Formulaic spells. You require different props for each Formulaic spell you learn, and you cannot use the spell if you do not use your props. Spontaneous and Ritual spells are not affected. Required props do not include Spell Foci.

**MINOR MAGIC DEFICIENCY (COMMON):** You have trouble with an important Art; it is always treated as half its true value (round down), though is considered full strength for the purposes of studying. Affects only Córporem, Vim, or one of the Techniques.

**SUSCEPTIBILITY TO DIVINE POWER:** You are especially sensitive to the Dominion and suffer twice the normal penalties (i.e., magic roll modifiers and Botch rolls) to your magic when in an area of Divine power.

**SUSCEPTIBILITY TO FAERIE POWER:** You are especially susceptible to the Fay powers and their magic. Whenever you enter a Faerie area, you must make a Stamina roll equal to or greater than the Aura of the area or become disoriented, strongly expressing (score of 3+) one Personality Trait chosen at random, or manifest another side effect appropriate to the situation. If you already have the Personality Trait acquired, increase your score in it by two. Your Magic Resistance, including that of your *Parma Magica*, against faerie magic is also divided by 2. If someone else protects you with their *Parma Magica*, it is not affected, and protects you normally.

**SUSCEPTIBILITY TO INFERNAL POWER:** You are especially susceptible to the dark powers. Whenever you enter an area of Infernal influence, you must make a Stamina roll equal to or greater than the power's Aura or become ill (-1 on all rolls).

Positive Personality Trait rolls (such as Brave) in the face of demons are at -3. You get only half your normal Magic Resistance against Infernal magic, though if someone else's *Parma Magica* is protecting you, it counts normally.

**SUSCEPTIBILITY TO RATIONAL POWER:** You are especially susceptible to the logical power of the realm of Reason. Whenever your enter an area of Rational influence, your magic tends to fail you. All spell casting rolls suffer a -5 modifier (regardless of Aura strength), and require twice the normal number of Botch dice. You are also incapable of reading any magical text in an area of Rational power; it all looks like gibberish.

**CHAOTIC MAGIC:** Your magic is very wild. When you cast a Spontaneous spell, you must specify a desired Level of effect. If you fail to achieve that Level, or exceed it by more than 5 Levels, the spell still works, but its effects are beyond your control — the Storyguide decides the results. Furthermore, you are automatically considered to have both *Wild Magic* (roll an extra Botch die when dealing with magic) and *Loose Magic* (cannot Master spells). Extra Virtue points are not gained from these Flaws. And, when using *vis*, you roll twice the normal number of Botch dice. The only good part of all this is that your Botches tend to be more strange than bad. In other words, you Botch more often, but the results are more likely to embarrass you than cause you harm (though your friends are under no special protection).

**PURE MAGIC:** You cannot cast or learn spells with any sort of Requisites. Only one Technique and Form may be used per spell.

**UNPREDICTABLE MAGIC:** You must always roll a stress die when casting spells, even if you are completely relaxed. Your lab work always requires a roll on the experimentation *Extraordinary Results Chart* (without the Risk Modifier), though you do not get the experimentation bonus of an extra simple die. If you do experiment, roll twice on the *Extraordinary Results Chart* for each Season you experiment. You may not Master Formulaic spells.

# Flaws: -5

**NON-SPONTANEITY:** Your magic is so strongly tied to the formulas and rituals of the Order of Hermes that you cannot improvise magic — you cannot cast Spontaneous spells. This is not totally bad, as your training compensates by giving you 200, not 150, Levels of Formulaic spells after

your apprenticeship. You may also purchase an *Affinity* with Formulaic spells as a +3 Virtue, but at the cost of only 2 Virtue points.

**RESTRICTION (COMMON):** Your magic does not work under certain common circumstances, such as when underground or inside a building. The circumstances must not be more rare than these.

**MAJOR MAGIC DEFICIENCY (COMMON):** You have great trouble with one common Art, such as Córporem, Vim, or a Technique. Any sum that includes the Art (including any rolls or Lab Totals, and the score when considered alone) is divided by two.

# Flaws: -6

**UNSTRUCTURED CASTER:** You have never quite mastered the intricacies of spell casting, and are unable to perform Formulaic magic without extreme effort. You may learn non-Ritual Formulaic spells only, and you cast all Formulaic spells as Ritual spells, including the need for *vis*. You can cast Spontaneous spells normally, though.

**PERSONAL MAGIC:** Your magic is very personal, and you have a -5 penalty to affect anything other than yourself with spells. This penalty also applies to laboratory projects that deal with anything but yourself. This includes working on a Familiar.

# PASSIONS

Passions are driving goals and manners of behavior that rule your character's actions. They are intrinsic to your identity and cannot be eliminated or changed, except by powers beyond man's comprehension. By choosing one of these Virtues, you determine how your character behaves most of the time; Passions control you constantly. When you are not casually discussing your Passions in idle conversation and acting on them in mundane events (i.e., through roleplaying), you can make them more dynamic by adding the fire of your Passions to your actions.

When selecting a Passion, decide on the type you want to have. It's recommended that you take no more than three Passions as Virtues. More than three causes you to be too severely torn by your varying compulsions. Only excellent roleplaying can see you through such an eventuality.

Remember that Passions rule your personality, and must be roleplayed constantly, but your personality is not limited to them. There are other facets of your identity that they do not demonstrate. These facets may be represented by Personality Traits (see p.106). However, where a Passion and Personality Trait may both apply to a situation, your Passion takes precedent and influences your behavior. Personality Traits do not function while a Passion is "activated." Personality Traits are also different from Passions in that Personality Traits only modify rolls to determine how you behave in a situation. They do not work in conjunction with Confidence, and cannot modify all your rolls in a scene as Passions do.

Passions manifest themselves in the game by allowing you to use Confidence Points to get scene bonuses. In extreme, stressful circumstances, you can use the value of a Passion score to modify all your rolls in a scene. Keep in mind that a scene lasts about as long as the current setting or time frame remain the same. The Passion called upon must somehow be appropriate to the situation, and can only be applied if the Storyguide agrees.

The application of a Passion to an entire scene requires the commitment of a character's whole being and will. A Confidence Point is therefore spent.

For example, if you have the Passion Honor, and have been entrusted with a secret that you promised not to tell, you can use the strength of your Passion to resist revealing the secret. If you are being tortured for the secret, you may spend a Confidence Point and add the score of your Passion to all rolls in the torture scene, hopefully holding your tongue and maintaining your code.

In modifying all your rolls in a scene, Passion scores even modify rolls related to magic, such as Magic and Natural Resistance rolls. Your conviction makes you more resilient to magic that affects you directly, even to spells intended to help you. (In the case of helpful spells, like healing spells, if a high roll is required for the spell to work on you, your Passion score applies as a negative modifier to the roll). For example, you have a superior chance to resist a faerie princess's enchanting allure if you are in Love with another person, and summon up the joy of that love for strength of will.

While a Passion's score can help you accomplish much when applied as a modifier to all rolls, it can also hinder you. That is, your driving emotions can lead you to rash decisions and oversights. For example, a Hatred score adds to a roll to disbelieve a lie from your greatest enemy. However, if your enemy is telling the truth, your Hatred score also adds to a roll to disbelieve him. Thus, your Hatred makes you refuse to accept the truth.

There's another danger to activating Passions. If you ever Botch a roll during a scene in which your Passion is activated, you permanently lose the Confidence Point invested for the activation. At that moment, you also lose all Passion bonuses for the remainder of the scene; your Passion modifier is dropped. No Passion may be called upon for the remainder of that scene. And, on top of all that, you suffer the normal results of the Botch.

Passions must also be roleplayed constantly. If you activate a Passion, and receive a scene bonus from it, but digress from your Passion, you automatically lose the Confidence Point invested in the scene. For example, if you have the Honor Passion, and activate it in combat with your most hated enemy, you must behave with honor throughout the battle. If your enemy loses his sword and you strike him unarmed, you defy your honor, so your Passion fails you. Not only do you lose the scene bonus, but you lose the Confidence Point invested. The Storyguide is the final arbiter in determining what constitutes a break in Passion.

Keep in mind that Passions also have Specialties. These Specialties are like those of Characteristics, Abilities and Reputations. They indicate one object which is the prime focus of your Passion, effectively raising your Passion score by 1 when that object is involved in a scene. If that object is not involved, your Passion still applies to other realms of your life, so is not dependent on that object alone.

COST: Passions all cost the same flat amount, 1 Virtue point per point of Passion. Thus, if you spend 3 Virtue points on a Passion, it has a score of 3. Unlike most other Virtues, you may increase the score of your Passion by spending Experience Points on it. The number of Experience Points needed to increase your Passion score is determined as for Characteristics and Abilities. Note that you can only spend Experience Points on a Passion if you use that Passion in a story — your Passions are flared by your latest encounter with them. The Saga Chapter provides more information about the allocation of Experience Points after a story.

LOVE: You repeatedly fall desperately in love with people whom you grow close to. Indeed, you are in love with being in love, and seek after it. There may be one person whom you particularly cherish, or you may fall in love with new people wherever you go. Regardless of who you love, you are constantly drawn to him or her. The object of your ardor occupies your mind constantly. You breathe his or her name under your breath and go to bed each night with visions of the two of you

together. Your passion is purely aesthetic and no lust is involved — it is pure and it is true. Your beloved need not be someone you know, either. He or she could be a person you once spotted in a crowd and have since longed for. (Though it is usually reserved for other people, Love need not be felt for people alone.)

Whenever you are suffering, are in danger, or feel dejected, the thought of love gives you the strength and determination to persevere, adding your Love score as a scene bonus.

Specialties: *one man, one woman, a symbol, an ideal, a province, a faerie, a faerie king or queen, an idealized animal, a nun or priest.*

JEALOUSY: The emotions of green envy have easy rise in your spleen, and you find it difficult to control them. You envy anyone who seems superior to you, or who possesses some object or power that you lack. You may envy a particular person or quality, chosen by you, over all other things. You seek to humiliate or show up the person you envy, in order to equalize the two of you (to your mind). You might even go to the extreme of murder.

Whenever you fear you cannot avenge yourself on, or bring someone or something that you envy down to your level, you find the determination to fight on and placate your emotions. As a result, your Jealousy score is added as a scene bonus.

Specialties: *another person, titles, social standing, wealth, power, favor, loved ones, magical resources.*

HATRED: You come to hate people and things with terrible swiftness and profound intensity. You may hate a particular object, like a person or the Muslim faith, more than other things, but you also discover something new to loathe with every passing day (it's suggested that you find one object for hatred in every story). Given an opportunity, you strike out against the object of your hatred, and seek to destroy the person or ideal no matter the cost to you or others.

Whenever you have the opportunity to strike out against something you hate, your vigor is intensified by the application of your Hatred score as a scene bonus. You may also apply that bonus if you fear defeat or are downtrodden, calling upon your anger to fire you.

Specialties: *a town council, a bounty hunter, diabolists, Moors, faeries, Magi, the English, Celts, Jews, Norsemen, feudalism.*

VENGEANCE: You seek revenge against any person, group or organization whom you feel has betrayed you, or even slighted you, and are constantly concocting plans to strike out against them. In fact, you often fantasize about killing the latest object of your revenge. To your mind, the means justify the ends, no matter who is hurt in the process. Once in battle with your foe, it's highly unlikely that you break it off.

When down and beaten, your desire for revenge renews your strength, your Vengeance score acting as a scene modifier. In the face of your latest object of revenge, you almost always apply your scene bonus, even if your intent at that point is not to kill.

Specialties: *nobles, your parents, siblings, a torturer, a king, murderers, Moors, Pagans, a House of Hermes.*

**LUST:** You desperately crave carnal knowledge of other people. The reasons are many and varied and depend on your identity. You may desire a person for that person's innocence, unblemished beauty, social standing, or maybe you just lust after all objects of the opposite sex. Of course, you need not limit your craven urgings to the opposite sex, adults, or even humans. In fact, you could lust after an ideal or goal, like power or the throne, for your own perverse ends. There may also be one object that you desire more than all others, and you pursue it with vehemence.

When in the presence of an object you lust after, your passions take command of you, insuring that you achieve physical knowledge of that object—your scene bonus helps you get what you want. Your Lust also invigorates you when you fear defeat before fulfilling your desires.

Specialties: *a single man or woman, men, women, a princess, a particular virgin, a faerie, animals, children, wealth, magical tomes, spells.*

**LOYALTY:** You commit yourself wholeheartedly to those whom you meet and agree to aid or work with (but that doesn't mean you're stupid or easily duped). Indeed, you pride yourself on being true to causes. There may be one particular cause or a group that you refuse to forsake or act against, regardless of the consequences. Often times Loyalty is expressed through a spoken vow, though it could also arise from a personal pact made by yourself to act on behalf of another. Whenever your loyalty is called into service, whether by summons from a patron or personal decision, you must respond.

Whenever your devotion to an object is threatened, you may summon the fury of your Loyalty to persevere and preserve your obligation; apply a scene bonus. If near defeat, or spiritually broken, you may also call upon your Loyalty, and its scene bonus, to see you through hard times.

Specialties: *Church, a Covenant, a Magus, a noblewoman, a family, the residents of certain lands, the king, your family, friends.*

**GREED:** You covet material wealth and power for yourself. You may also desire a particular object with a fury, and do anything necessary to get your hands on it. Oftentimes the objects of your cravings are worldly, physical items, like gold or jewelry. However, you can also be greedy for intangible objects, like souls or magical power. If your values are not overly upright, you may resort to theft and murder to get what you want. Note that Greed differs from *Jealousy* in that the latter involves craving for something purely because someone else possesses it; the desire is not for the object itself, as is the case with Greed.

When an object that you desire presents itself, your Greed drives you to pursue it relentlessly, and you receive a scene bonus in that pursuit. You may also call upon inner desires in the face of death and adversity, finding the strength to survive in order to acquire the objects you crave.

Specialties: *gold, magic items, spell books, jewelry, faerie treasures, souls, followers, land.*

**HONOR:** You have a commitment to chivalry and possess a personal code of ethics. No matter where you go or what you do, you must show respect and fairness to others, including commoners and enemies. In battle with a foe you might return his sword if he's disarmed and at a disadvantage. Knights are often impassioned by Honor, but not all are, and others besides knights can follow a strict code of ethics — anyone can. Honor may derive from outside teachings, like those of the Church, or can also arise from personal convictions.

Whenever your personal honor or that of another is at stake, you may add the conviction of your values to your actions, adding a scene bonus to your rolls. Sometimes, however, doing the honorable thing means self-sacrifice, and your scene bonus helps you fulfill that sacrifice.

Specialties: *chivalry, toward women, toward the innocent, toward the defenseless, honoring promises, paying debts, toward the Church.*

**RAGE:** You are prone to losing your temper with little provocation, and can sometimes become frenzied. You may choose a specific object that automatically raises your ire, but you are enraged by any frustrating experience. The source and nature of your Rage is dependent on your identity, history, and life experience. Rage differs from *Hatred*

because the latter demands that you seek the source of your Passion, while the former does not; Rage results from your immediate environment. Rage and *Hatred* may be taken in conjunction with one another.

Roleplaying determines when you're enraged. As a rule of thumb, when frustrated, insulted, hurt or threatened you go into a fury. At these times your Passion offers you a scene bonus. You may also inspire Rage in yourself by calling up heated emotions, particularly when the odds are against you and you need an edge. Note: when you become enraged you suffer a penalty to all Communication rolls equal to your Passion score.

If, during a scene in which your scene bonus is activated, you Botch a roll or get a result of 20+, you behave as described under the *Fury* Flaw. Your Passion scene bonus is added to the modifiers that *Fury* applies, and calming from *Fury* still leaves you enraged (your Passion scene bonuses continue to apply until the end of the scene).

The Rage Passion is incompatible with the *Berserk* Virtue.

Specialties: *pain, personal insults, remarks against Order of Hermes, poor manners, evil, public brutality, diabolists, Jesuits, Moors, fire.*

**VALOR:** This Passion not only describes your outward expression of courage, but your desire to attain legendary status for being dauntless. Valor can only be used when there is a direct danger to your person, danger that can be directly faced, and prevented by your actions. Such danger can also be posed to comrades or to other people of a particular identity, like nobility or Magi, whom you resolve to defend.

This Passion is different from the Brave Personality Trait in that Brave only determines

how willing you are to risk harm. You can act Bravely, but still feel fear. Valor makes you completely fearless; its rating determines the degree to which you are aware of your fearlessness (i.e., at +1 you suspect you fear nothing, while at +3 you know there is nothing in the world that scares you).

Characters with Valor are never frightened into retreating; if you retreat it's by choice (but the Storyguide must determine if you lose any invested Confidence Point by retreating). When you decide to apply your convictions of courage (i.e., apply your Passion), you receive a scene bonus to all your acts. If events conspire against you and defeat seems possible, you may also summon your convictions to become victorious.

Specialties: *standing ground, multiple foes, fantastic beasts, Magi, diabolists, criminals, Pagans, undead, large animals.*

COMPASSION: You feel tremendous pathos for those who suffer. You do everything in your power to help those beings, whether they be human, animal, faerie, or even demonic. Indeed, you can feel particularly intense compassion for certain beings, but still feel for all others. This Passion is extremely demanding on your time for Mythic Europe is rife with those in anguish. Maybe your Compassion is the motivation for your life of travels — to help others abroad.

When someone is suffering and needs your help, you do everything in your power to be there for them. Activating your Passion, you gain a bonus in all acts when striving to help that being. This might include rolls to fight an enemy, and rolls to apply Chirurgy to the being. Note that the suffering of others need not always be physical, but can be spiritual or mental.

Specialties: *children, the elderly, the mad, the wounded, faeries, magical creatures, animals.*

REBEL: You refuse to conform to the dictates of authority, maybe because you hate authority, or maybe because you recognize your individuality and don't want it stifled. Naturally, you do not get along with those who claim superiority over you, which may mean fiery social dynamics at the Covenant. You refuse to so much as compromise with authority, so face a hard fate if those with power cannot be manipulated.

Whenever you sense your independence is jeopardized, you immediately assume a defensive position, and may add your scene bonus to rolls to preserve your freedom. That may mean rolls to convince a leader to give you autonomy, or may mean combat rolls if your superior physically frowns upon your attitude. You may also activate your Passion when things look bleak and death and harm are imminent; you refuse to let yourself be controlled by the will of another, fighting back with new vigor.

Specialties: *freedom of others, Magi, noble authority, Church officials, Grog captains, Praeco (leaders of the Order of Hermes).*

# PHYSICAL

Physical Virtues and Flaws make a statement about the physical capacities and often appearance of your character. If you are a fine physical specimen, you are more likely to survive in the brutal world of Mythic Europe. If you are physically weak or misshapen, you had best have a quick mind or wit if you intend to live.

## Virtues: variable

IMMUNITY: You have an innate resistance to some sort of affliction. For diseases and poisons, this could be a complete immunity; for other things, it is a bonus to Soak rolls. Really weird stuff like fire resistance should be limited to characters with magical backgrounds or divine blessings. You and the Storyguide must determine your immunity and its rating, based on how often your immunity comes into play (e.g., immunity to disease is a +3 Virtue).

## Virtues: +1

STOCKY: You are short, but broad and thick. Add +1 to Strength

VERSATILE SLEEPER: You can fall asleep at will, any place, any time, lapsing into deep sleep within a few minutes. Thus, each day you get the equivalent of a full night's sleep without sleeping the night. You can be awakened normally when napping. A good Virtue to combine with *Light Sleeper.*

ENDURING CONSTITUTION: You can withstand pain and fatigue. Deduct a point from each of the negative adjustments in both your Body and Fatigue Levels, so Medium Wounds, for example, means only a -2 penalty, not -3. You also get +3 on rolls to resist pain.

BERSERK: Any time you lose a Body Level or wound an enemy, you must make a stress roll and add your Angry Personality Trait score (so you must assign yourself that Trait). If you roll a 9+, you experience battle lust and go berserk. The Storyguide can also call for a roll when you are strongly frustrated. While berserk, you get a +2 on Damage, Soak, and Fatigue scores, but suffer a -2 penalty on Defense; you cannot retreat, hesitate to attack, or give quarter. Calming down requires a Perception - Angry stress roll of 3+, one roll allowed per Round. If you are still berserk while no more enemies are present, you attack your friends. If you Botch a roll to become berserk or recover from berserk rage, you completely lose control and have to be physically restrained before you can try to recover.

KEEN VISION: Get a +3 bonus on all rolls involving sight.

LIGHT SLEEPER: You can wake up almost immediately when disturbed, and take no penalties for the first few Rounds of activity. The Storyguide may also allow you to make generous Perception rolls while you are asleep to see if noises wake you up.

LITHE: You are slightly built and agile. Your Size is -1, but you add +1 to both Dexterity and Quickness. You also have one less Body and Fatigue Level; cross off the Hurt Body Level and the Winded Fatigue Level from your character sheet.

LONG-WINDED: You have a high endurance and gain +3 on all your Fatigue rolls. Magus: The bonus does not apply to casting spells.

HARDY CONVALESCENCE: You get a +3 bonus on all rolls to recover from wounds.

SHARP EARS: Get a +3 bonus to all rolls involving hearing.

## Virtues: +2

LARGE: Your Size is +1 instead of 0, which makes you a very large person. This extra size gives you an extra Hurt Body Level and an extra Winded Fatigue Level. (Divide the line for these Levels in half with slash marks; both sides must be marked before you drop to the next lowest Level.) You also get a +1 bonus to your Strength. If your Presence is positive, it increases one point; but if it is negative, it decreases one point. Magus: +4 Virtue.

**LIGHT TOUCH:** You have especially good hand-eye coordination and an aptitude for using your hands in precise, fast ways. Gain +3 to all rolls involving subtle use of the hands and fingers (like picking pockets) and roll one less Botch die than you normally would. Does not apply to archery.

**LIGHTNING REFLEXES:** You have extremely fast reflexes which respond to surprises almost instantly. In fact, your reactions are sometimes so fast you don't have a chance to think about how you are going to respond — your reflexes make that decision for you. Whenever you are surprised or startled, make a Quickness roll. A result of 3+ indicates that you respond reflexively. You may choose one type of action (attacking, dodging, blocking, running) which you are most likely to do, but your reaction is finally up to the Storyguide (though it is always in the best interests of your immediate self-preservation). You only react to threats that you are not fully aware of (e.g., if you watch an assassin for two minutes as she sneaks up on you, your reflexes do not kick in). Note that you do not get a choice about whether to react. If your best friend is sneaking up on you to play a joke on you, you are just as likely to skewer her reflexively as you are to skewer an assassin. Also note that you must perceive an action to react to it; this Virtue gives you no special powers of perception (so you can still be easily killed in your sleep).

**RESERVES OF STRENGTH:** Once per day, when in need, you can put forth an incredible show of strength. For the duration of your current need, add +4 to your effective Strength. Afterwards you must make two Short-Term Fatigue rolls. You may use this reserve while battling one enemy, lifting one boulder, or wrestling one opponent.

## Virtues: +3

**NEED NOT DRINK:** You do not need to drink to survive. You never feel thirst, and you are doubly resistant to dehydration of all types (cf. *Curse of the Desert* [PeAq 25]). You may drink things if you wish. This Virtue requires that you have some sort of supernatural background.

**NEED NOT EAT:** You are magically energetic, and do not need to eat to survive (though you still need to drink). You never feel hunger, though you may still eat normally if you wish, and may enjoy eating simply for the taste. This Virtue requires that you have some sort of supernatural background.

**AMBIDEXTROUS:** You can use either hand equally well. When using two weapons in combat, you only suffer a -1 penalty with each, rather than the standard -1 for the dominant hand and -3 for the off hand.

## Virtues: +5

**NEED NO SLEEP:** You need no sleep to function, and you resist spells which induce sleep as though you have a Magic Resistance of +50. You get an extra 8 hours a day to do with as you like, giving you an extra Season for study and training. This Virtue requires that you have some kind of supernatural background. Magus: +7 Virtue.

## Flaws: -1

**MISSING EAR:** You cannot locate the direction of sounds, -1 to hearing rolls.

**MISSING EYE:** You cannot judge close distances easily and get -2 on missile weapon and thrown weapon Attack scores. You have a blind side on which people can approach you without you seeing them. In melee combat you suffer -1 on Attack rolls because your field of vision is limited.

**MISSING FOOT:** You have a wooden peg for a foot; you cannot run quickly and suffer a -3 penalty on rolls that involve walking or balancing on your feet. You also suffer a -1 on Defense scores because you cannot maneuver well.

**OBESE:** You are large because of fat, not muscle. Your Size is +1, but you must subtract 2 from Quickness. You also suffer -3 on Fatigue rolls (not including casting spells). You get an extra Hurt Body Level, but you get no extra Fatigue Level.

**FRAGILE CONSTITUTION:** You suffer a -2 penalty on all rolls to recover from wounds and diseases.

**EVIL EYE:** One of your eyes is bloated and deformed, casting an evil look across your face. Reduce your Presence by 3. People generally regard you as evil, and hide their children's faces from your gaze. The Virtue of *Entrancement* works well with this Flaw.

**POOR EYESIGHT:** Subtract 3 from rolls involving sight, including Attack and Dodge scores. New environments are disorienting and perhaps frightening for you.

**POOR HEARING:** Subtract 3 from rolls involving hearing. Speech that is hard for others to understand because of language, dialect, or accent is very difficult for you to understand. You often pretend to be listening to people when indeed you are not.

**DEEP SLEEPER:** When you sleep, you don't do it halfway. You can sleep through loud noises and generally only wake up when shaken or when you're good and ready. Even then you suffer -3 on your rolls for half an hour or so, and you're likely to head back to bed if at all possible.

**DISFIGURED:** A visible disfigurement makes you ugly and easy to recognize. Subtract 3 from your Presence rolls that involve good looks and gaining respect. You probably have a cruel nickname that refers to your unfortunate appearance. Magus: Your disfigurement probably comes from an accident during your apprenticeship. Let your imagination run wild.

## Flaws: -2

**CLUMSY:** You are not very graceful and tend to drop things. Play this up as much as you can, reduce your Dexterity by 1, and make an extra Botch roll with Dexterity-related rolls.

**MUTE:** You cannot speak; perhaps your tongue was cut out. You probably use rudimentary hand gestures and grunts to get your needs across. Magus: n/a, your master would have restored your voice magically.

**HUNCHBACK:** You have a deformed body that gives you a grotesque appearance and hinders your movements. Presence is -3 and Dexterity is -1. Magus: -1 Flaw.

**DECREPIT:** You have 1 Decrepitude Point (see *Aging*, p.354) from old wounds or a past serious illness.

**GANGLING:** You are scrawny and awkward. Subtract 1 from Strength, Presence, and Dexterity.

**LAME:** As a cripple either from birth or through some accident, you move slowly and clumsily. Anyone can outrun you. Take -5 on rolls involving moving quickly or with agility, -4 on Dodge score, and -1 on other combat scores. Your base speed is a mere one mile per hour. Decide precisely how and why you are lame.

**MISSING HAND:** You can only use one hand for climbing, combat, and other activities; take a -2 to -4 penalty to any such actions. Magus: You suffer -3 on spell casting rolls, except for spells you invent specifically for one-handed casting (-2 on Lab Totals to invent such spells).

**SMALL FRAME:** Your frame is smaller than average. Your Size is -1; subtract 1 from

Strength. Body and Fatigue Levels as for *Lithe*, above. Magus: -3 Flaw.

## Flaws: -3

**ARTHRITIS:** Your joints are stiff and often painful, making prolonged movement of almost any kind a task. Reduce you Dexterity and Quickness by 1 each. Occasionally, your joints become so painful that you are seriously disabled. On any movement or combat Botch one of your joints may lock up, making the limb effectively useless (-5 to all rolls involving it), until you have a chance to rest it for a day or two.

## Flaws: -4

**MIDGET/DWARF:** You are the size of a child, and though your muscles are mature, you lack the leverage that benefits larger folk. You Size is -2; subtract 2 from Strength. Your comfortable walking speed is two-thirds normal. Even if you are strong, leverage prevents you from using any weapons that require a positive Strength. Cross off the Hurt and Medium Wounds Body Levels and the Winded and Tired Fatigue Levels from your character sheet.

## Flaws: -5

**BLIND:** You have no or almost no sight. Use of missile weapons is futile, reading is impossible, and navigation in unknown territory is difficult. Magus: n/a, your master would have restored your vision magically. It's that important.

**ENFEEBLED:** You cannot exert yourself for longer than a few seconds. Any need for rapid movement, such as combat or a chase, leaves you helpless. Long hikes are likewise beyond your capability. You are unable to learn combat skills, since you cannot train in them. Magus: You lose double Fatigue Levels from casting spells; -6 Flaw.

## Flaws: -8

**LEPROSY:** You have the dreaded disease leprosy. Everyone shuns you (most Magi included), mothers grab their children and run when you come into view, and people would prefer to see you dead and your cursed form burned. Of course, there are physical problems as well. Your skin is in a constant state of decay, producing a constant stench to identify you as a leper, and requiring constant vigilance on your part to prevent it from rotting away. Every wound you receive has the potential for contracting gangrene, and

you heal slowly (if at all). For each wound you take, roll for wound recovery at -3, and then roll another die — on a 0, the wound does not heal all the way, and you gain a Decrepitude point (and probably some disfigurement as well). You start with one Decrepitude point (see the *Aging* rules in the Saga Chapter), and reduce your Stamina by 2. Since no healers touch you, you are likely to die an early death. Hope for a miracle.

# MENTAL

Mental Virtues and Flaws are a reflection of your state of mind and capacity to pursue your own will.

## Virtues: variable

**BOOKS:** You have your own library containing Knowledges from which you can study. For each point of the Virtue, you get 10 Experience Points to spend in Knowledge Abilities — which Knowledges is left for the Storyguide to decide — at the beginning of the game. You need not invest all these points right away, but those spent during the Saga must be accounted for by time devoted to study (one Season accounts for about 5 Experience Points with this Virtue, so 10 Experience is accounted for in two Seasons).

**SELF-CONFIDENT:** You begin the game with more than the normal number of Confidence Points. You start with 3 points, plus the level of the Virtue in Confidence Points. Of course, you must take this Virtue at +1 at least.

## Virtues: +1

**STRONG PERSONALITY:** For any three Personality Traits, you may have scores from -6 to +6, instead of the usual -3 to +3.

**STRONG-WILLED:** You cannot easily be coerced into activities, beliefs, or feelings. You get a +3 on any roll which may require strength of will, such as resisting temptation, torture, or the effects of a magical ability or spell that attempts to dominate your will.

**STUDENT:** You have access to books and possibly teachers from which you can study, and have adequate time to do so. You get 1 Experience Point per Season to apply to your Knowledge Abilities.

**CAREFREE:** You are unshakably cheerful and happy in all circumstances. You receive +5 on all rolls to resist despair and sorrow (e.g., against spells like *The Pains of a Thousand Hells*), and receive +5 to Communication rolls with those who

appreciate your disposition (i.e., not with those who are grumpy). You cannot take (or later acquire) Flaws like *Lost Love* — you take cheer at the thought of your love watching you from Heaven.

**CLEAR THINKER:** You think clearly and rationally. You get a +3 bonus on all rolls to resist lies, confusion, befuddlement, and subterfuge, whether those attempts on you are magical or mundane.

**COMMON SENSE:** Whenever you are about to do something contrary to common sense, the Storyguide has the task of alerting you to what you are doing. This is an excellent Virtue for a beginning player, as it legitimizes any kind of help the Storyguide may give. It is also valuable for explaining what is sensible in a fantasy world.

**FREE EXPRESSION:** You have the imagination and creativity needed to compose a new ballad or to paint an original painting, and have the potential to be a great artist.

**LEARN FROM MISTAKES:** You learn from your mistakes in one particular Ability (mundane or arcane). The first time in a given story that you Botch a roll or fail by exactly one point, you gain one Experience Point in the Ability. You may take this Virtue several times for different Abilities.

## Virtues: +2

**PIERCING GAZE:** By staring intently at someone, you make them feel uneasy, as if you are staring into their heart and soul. Those with ulterior motives, uneasy consciences, and those who are lying must make Personality rolls, Guile rolls, or whatever the Storyguide deems appropriate to remain calm. Faeries and demons are unfazed by your power.

## Virtues: +3

**TRUE REASON:** Your mind has transcended religious and superstitious thought. You contemplate the truths of life and existence on their own merit, using science, logic and deduction as a basis. You have 1 Reason Point and can gain more, but have no Confidence Points.

**FAST LEARNER:** You get an extra Experience Point per story and an extra Experience Point per year because of your ability to learn quickly and pick up ideas faster than normal. You begin the game with 10 extra points with which to purchase Abilities. Magus: you get 1 extra Experience Point per story and +1 on rolls to study from vis; but don't get the extra yearly Experience Point. This is also a +5 Virtue for you.

**INTUITION:** You have a natural intuition which allows you to make decisions that are correct more often than luck allows. Whenever you are given a choice or decision in which luck plays a major role (such as choosing whether to take one of two unexplored corridors), you have a good chance of choosing the correct one. To determine the accuracy of your intuition, the Storyguide makes a secret, simple die roll. If the result is 6 or more, intuition kicks in. Otherwise, you don't get a sense of what the correct course of action is. Thus, if you come to four tunnels, the die roll gives better than even odds of helping you decide which tunnel to take.

**JACK-OF-ALL-TRADES:** You can attempt things that are more difficult for those who share your lack of training. You suffer no adverse penalties for making Ability rolls when you have no score in an Ability, provided you have some time to consider what you are about to do. Those Abilities that are exclusive of a particular group, as Arcane Knowledges are to Magi, are still beyond you, unless you belong to that group.

**VISUAL MEMORY:** You remember everything you see as pictures, giving you an increased chance to remember things, and a very precise memory for those things you can remember. You gain +2 to all Intelligence rolls to remember a scene, and if that Intelligence roll succeeds, you get another memory roll at an additional +3 (+5 total) to remember details about the scene, making you unlikely to miss any but the slightest of details.

# Virtues: +4

**MASTERED KNOWLEDGE:** You have a Knowledge Ability at which you are exceptionally learned. All rolls involving this Knowledge receive a +4 modifier, and you never roll more than one Botch die with the Knowledge. You are undoubtedly a master in your field, and may have a Reputation to reflect that.

# Flaws: -1

**OBSESSED:** You are obsessed with some prized object, action, or ideal. Examples: you keep your sword with you at all times, polish it hourly, and let no one touch it; you protect the Magi from all dangers, becoming furious when they are insulted or hampered; you keep yourself spotlessly clean and look down on those who do otherwise.

**DRIVING GOAL:** You have some personal goal which you feel compelled to follow, even if it gets you into trouble or jeopardizes the group's goals. Examples: to free the peasants from oppression, to harass and kill Norman warriors, to make everyone regard you as more intelligent than they are, or to amass as much personal wealth as possible. The goal is limitless in extent, something that you can never finally accomplish.

**DUTYBOUND:** You adhere to a restrictive code of conduct, probably including prohibitions against lying, killing prisoners, stealing and other occasionally useful actions. Unlike the *Honor* Passion, you follow this code out of guilt or fear, so it does not provide moral support. You are more likely to spend your energy justifying your conduct than keeping your conduct pure.

**POOR MEMORY:** You have a bad memory, especially for one thing, such as names, faces, or places. You must make a roll of 6+ to see if you remember anything related to your special difficulty, and you get a -2 on any other memory rolls. Magus: it takes twice as long to learn spells. You begin the Saga with half the normal spell Levels; -6 Flaw.

**SENSITIVE:** Something that others find unpleasant you find completely intolerable. If you are the violent type, you may start fights with those who offend you. Examples: impiety, insults to women, poor manners, lack of civilized niceties (such as a warm bed), and arrogance.

**SHORT ATTENTION SPAN:** You must earn double the normal Experience Points to raise your Knowledge Abilities, and must expend double the normal number of Experience Points to buy them in the first place. Keeping watch, listening to complex orders, following the plot of a story, or performing other such tasks that require continued attention are usually not within your ability. Magus: n/a, you'd never have survived apprenticeship.

**SIMPLE-MINDED:** You can only keep your mind on one thing at a time — guarding the bridge, hunting for a missing ring, or hiding in the trees. You become easily confused unless others give you very clear instructions. When unexpected circumstances pop up, you find them difficult to deal with.

**SOFT HEARTED:** You cannot bear to witness suffering and causing it can bring you days of sleepless grief. You avoid danger and try to keep your friends out of it as well. You value life and health so strongly that you would rather give up important goals than have another person risk combat for you.

Even the deaths of enemies are painful for you. On the positive side, you are sensitive and easily moved by song and story.

**UNCOMMON FEAR:** Something that others find innocuous, perhaps disturbing, or even pleasant makes you nervous, edgy, and unable to concentrate. In the presence of the object you fear, the only thing you can comfortably do is get away. The feared object is not something you're likely to meet on a daily basis. If you are prone to violence, you might respond to the thing you fear by attacking or destroying it, but only when you cannot get away. Examples: wild animals, strange sounds, clergy, enclosed spaces, the full moon, the open sea, foreigners, Jews.

**WEAK SELF-CONFIDENCE:** You begin the game with 1 fewer Confidence Points than normal (thus, 2 points). Not available to Grogs.

**WEAKNESS:** You have a weakness for some object or kind of person. In the face of this thing, all else is unimportant. Promises are forgotten, duties are neglected, and common sense is cast to the winds. Examples: poets & storytellers, a pretty face, alcohol, flattery.

**WEAK-WILLED:** Instead of looking to yourself, you look to others for guidance. Those who try to fool, intimidate, or manipulate you gain +3 to their rolls. You have great difficulty gaining Confidence Points, requiring monumental tasks (at least to your eye) to do so. Take a positive Follower Personality Trait. What you need more than anything else is to find someone you can trust to put all your faith in.

**COMPULSION:** You have an unfortunate compulsion which causes you problems. Examples: drinking, sex, perfection, bragging, gambling, eating

(perhaps you could combine this one with obesity), to champion the Grogs, to always get the last word, to "exaggerate" (lie), or to challenge authority.

**DELUSION:** You believe wholeheartedly in something that just isn't so. For example, you might believe that you are a Magus (if you aren't), that round rocks are extremely valuable, that you are the long-lost son of a baron, or that your imaginary friend is actually real.

## Flaws: -2

**COMMON FEAR:** As *Uncommon Fear*, above, but the thing that frightens you is common, such as dogs, night, woods, women, men, people in authority, weapons, or fire.

**OVER-CONFIDENT:** You have an exaggerated and unshakable opinion of your capabilities, and you do not hesitate to try things that promise only defeat. (This is a dangerous Flaw where combat is concerned.) If you are convincing in your speech, you can infect others with your overconfidence.

**TERRORS:** Some specific thing fills you with overwhelming dread. You can do nothing but scramble and fight to escape the presence of the terrible thing, and if escape is impossible, you are likely to become a pile of quivering pudding. Make the object of your fear common enough that it comes into play, but rare enough that you still have a playable character. Examples: criminals, deep forests, heights, wide open spaces, storms, caves.

## Flaws: -3

**FURY:** A violent temper sometimes overwhelms you, sending you into a destructive, uncontrollable rage. Choose some offense that is likely to bring on your temper, such as being insulted, being hurt, or hearing the Order of Hermes disparaged. You must roll 9+ on a stress die or fly into a

rage, and you can attempt a similar roll every Round to try to calm yourself. If you ever Botch, you try to kill everyone around you until all are dead or gone. While enraged, you get +3 to Damage, but -1 on all other scores and rolls, and you must make a Short-Term Fatigue roll every Round. Such a furious temper may well be the result of a curse.

**NONCOMBATANT:** You cannot learn any combat skills and suffer -2 on all Attack and Damage scores. You cannot pick the *Poor Equipment* Flaw. Magus: -2 Flaw.

# SUPERNATURAL

Supernatural Virtues and Flaws assume you have some tie with powers beyond the mundane, either in your past, present, or very being. The supernatural powers include Magic, Divinity, Faerie and the Infernal. If you have more than one supernatural Virtue or Flaw, all should derive from the same supernatural power, unless you can justify a combination of different realms. For example, you can have True Faith (a Divine Virtue) and Demon Plagued (an Infernal Flaw) if you explain that a demon is trying to sway you from your higher faith. The Ars Magica supplement Faeries offers several more Virtues and Flaws for Fay characters.

## Virtues: variable

**MAGIC ITEM:** You begin with a magic item, perhaps an a heirloom or one gained on an earlier adventure. The Storyguide designs the item. The item can range in power from a minor trinket to one created in the lab of a Magus. The cost of the Virtue is +1 per 10 Levels of spell effects (see *Invested Devices*, in the Laboratory Chapter) invested in the item. This Virtue is particularly appropriate for older characters.

**PURIFYING TOUCH:** You have the ability to cure a certain type of affliction by touch. This ability can be a gift from the Divinities (like the English kings' ability to cure the King's Evil, scrofula), a faerie power, or can arise as an inherited ability. The cost of the Virtue depends on how common the affliction you can cure is, and how severe it is. The ability to cure something both common (or potentially epidemic) and deadly (the Black Death) should not be allowed. Examples of things that can be cured (choose one): snake venom, lightning burns, rabies, the common cold, injuries by demons, flu, frostbite, or sunstroke, but not conventional weapon or accidental wounds. For each person purified, you must expend one Long-Term Fatigue Level.

## Virtues: +1

**FAERIE EYES:** You can see normally in deep woods or at night. Your eyes are unusually bright in color and reflect light, like a cat's. It's another +1 Virtue to have Faerie Eyes that look "normal," though they are usually an unusual color, such as bright green. Inhuman eyes give you a -3 Presence and Communication modifier when dealing with mundanes, though Magi and faeries don't usually mind your eyes. This Virtue is usually only available to those with the *Faerie Blood* Virtue.

**FAERIE SIGHT:** This is similar to the Ability *Second Sight*, except that you are automatically specialized in seeing faeries and faerie things. With Faerie Sight you can see through faerie illusions on a roll of 12+. This Virtue requires that you also possess the *Faerie Blood* Virtue.

## Virtues: +2

**LATENT MAGICAL ABILITY:** You have a magical quality that has not yet manifested itself. At some point it might appear, either spontaneously or because of some relevant event, like drinking faerie wine. You have the capacity to become a Magus as long as some magical talent does not manifest itself strongly first. You probably do not realize you have this capacity. The Storyguide determines when and how the talent appears. Magus: While developing your magical ability, your master failed to identify some power hidden in you, and it remains latent.

**LUCK:** You are very lucky, performing well in situations where luck is more a factor than skill or talent. You get +1 to +4 (Storyguide's discretion) on rolls in such situations, depending upon how much luck is involved in the rolls. You do very well at games of chance, but are likely to get yourself in trouble if you play them too often, as you may be labelled a cheater.

**FAERIE FRIEND:** You have a faerie as a companion. The faerie is created by the Storyguide and can be of any sort, though it probably isn't malicious, at least not toward you. The faerie is fully sentient, has its own powers, and can speak when it chooses. Whether your faerie friend is a constant companion is up to you. It may covertly follow you, protecting you like a guardian angel. Maybe the faerie feels it owes you a favor and refuses to leave your side until it fulfills its duty. If poorly treated your companion may leave you, or could even develop a hatred for you and curse you. Keep in mind that a faerie companion can be a great boon, but can also be a terrible burden. If your companion is particularly nasty or mischievous, it could cause trouble for you everywhere. If the Troupe complies, another player may assume the role of your companion.

**MAGICAL ANIMAL COMPANION:** You have, as a companion, a magical animal that's smart enough to follow your orders. The smaller and more innocuous the creature, the more intelligent it is. A ferret or crow is as intelligent as a human, though it cannot talk, while a wolf is merely very cunning, and a horse is simply a bit smarter than normal. Subject to the Troupe's approval, you may give the animal a mystical Virtue or two, balancing any Virtues normally with Flaws of your own. The creature has a Magic Might score of +10, minus its Size.

**WITHSTAND MAGIC:** You are innately non-magical and can resist many magic spells. You have a +6 bonus to Natural Resistance rolls and apply the bonus to your Soak score against damage from spells. You resist good magic as well as bad, so if there is a spell in which a high roll means the magic affects you (like a healing spell), you suffer a -6 penalty on the roll. You can have no magical powers. Magus: n/a.

**BEGINNING VIS:** You start the campaign with some *vis* stores, perhaps a gift from your mentor, perhaps gained on some earlier adventure. You have 5 pawns of any type. (You can take the Virtue more than once.) If you are a Companion, you may have already traded some of this *vis* for services from Magi (e.g., you might only have 4 and an *Edge of the Razor* spell on your sword). Magus: n/a. You already have a similar Hermetic Virtue, *Personal* Vis *Source.*

# Virtues: +3

**TRUE FAITH:** Through piety and holy devotion you have received the faith that, it is said, can move mountains. You have 1 Faith Point and can gain more, but you have no Confidence Points.

# Virtues: +4

**CHARMED LIFE:** Fortune protects you from the most terrible injury and harm. Whenever you Botch, you may reroll the Botch dice. Take whichever of the two Botch results is better. For example, if you roll three Botch dice and get a 0 (a Botch), you can reroll all three dice. If there is no 0 in the reroll, you do not Botch, but if you get a 0 on the reroll, you still Botch. You must describe in (possibly outrageous) detail how you

manage to miss the grave fate that was almost yours. The Storyguide should also keep this trait in mind during the story and be more lenient in scenes of your rescue or protection. Magus: This luck does not count for spell casting rolls; magic is too unpredictable and powerful to be influenced in this manner.

**GHOSTLY WARDER:** A ghost watches over you. It might be your grandmother, a childhood friend, or anyone else who would care for you enough to stay around you after death. The ghost is invisible and silent to all but you (and those with the *Second Sight* Ability). The ghost can see and hear what is going on around you, and can leave your presence once per day for up to half an hour, making an excellent spy. Each time the ghost leaves your presence, however, roll a stress die to see how well it manages. It needs to roll a 3+ to come back with anything coherent. Below that, it loses touch with the living world and finds out nothing. On a Botch, it loses touch with you and never returns. Make an extra Botch roll for each point of the Divine, Infernal, Faerie, or Rational Aura you might be in. Death does not leave people in their normal state of mind, so your ghost no doubt has some quirks that make it less than dependable. The ghost has 20 points of Experience in various Abilities that it can use to advise you. The ghost might even encourage you to join it over on the Other Side.

**MAGIC RESISTANCE:** You have an innate +20 Magic Resistance, incompatible with a *Parma Magica* (they're not cumulative). Some physical sign may accompany this Resistance, such as a birthmark or iron fingernails.

**WEREWOLF:** When the full moon shines in the night sky, you take the form of a wolf. While you are in wolf form, add the Characteristics listed for wolves (p.336) to your own, and give yourself a Personality Trait of Violent +3, or add three to the Trait if you already have it. You also get +8 on your Soak score versus all non-silver and non-magical attacks. You must also take an Ability called Werewolf, with a score purchased like any other Ability. When that Ability score is applied to stress die roll, and the result is 12+, you may voluntarily take the form of a wolf (one try per day). If you Botch the roll you cannot make another attempt throughout the current story. Your clothes do not transform with you, and you are not healed when you change. This ability is very rare and mysterious; it is often seen as evil. Invent a good story to explain the origin of your lycanthropy: a bite, a family trait, or a curse. Muto Córporem Level 35. For more rules

and Virtues and Flaws about shapechanging characters, see the Ars Magica supplement The Medieval Bestiary.

# Virtues: +5

**RELIC:** You own a holy relic with one Faith Point in it. The relic can be built into any other item you possess (a sword, for instance).

**GUARDIAN ANGEL:** You have learned to hear the words of your guardian angel, who gives you practical and spiritual advice. Your angel guides and protects you. Thus, any time you do something of which the angel approves, and you roll a 1 in stress, you automatically succeed in the action (provided the action's Ease Factor is 20 or lower, otherwise you keep rolling normally). The angel whispers in your ear and tells you what is best for you spiritually, which may not be what is best for you materially. When you speak aloud, your angel can hear you, and you can hold conversations. The angel is aware of your thoughts, but other than that has a limited view of the world. If you act against the angel's moral advice, it may leave you, perhaps until you correct your ways, perhaps forever. The angel approves of violence only when there is a holy reason for it, and that is often difficult to provide.

# Virtues: +7

**IMMORTAL:** You cannot die of anything but natural causes. You heal wounds normally, unless you suffer a killing blow. If you suffer a killing blow, you cannot heal it fully. You recover normally from an Incapacitated state, but bear the marks of your injury. Killing wounds leave you debilitated, maimed, mangled, sickly, or just plain disgusting in appearance, and give you at least 1 Decrepitude Point. This Virtue can even be extended to say that you can never die, but you still age, and after a while become quite disgusting and frail. In any case, if anything can destroy you completely (like Infernal destruction), you can still die, and you are in no way immune to miracles. If and when you do die, you will have a very, very persistent ghost.

# Flaws: -1

**MAGICAL AIR:** You look and act like a magical person — Magus, witch or priest. You need not do anything to persuade people that you are magical. Magus: n/a, you undoubtedly suffer from this Flaw already.

**STRONG FAERIE NATURE:** The blood of faeries is so strong in you that you feel the full effects of Divine and Infernal power. Instead of using the Magic column of the *Power Interaction Chart* (p.308), as most characters do, you use the Faerie Column, with its greater susceptibility to Divine and Infernal powers. Magic areas also aid you less, but you get full bonuses in a Faerie area.

**MAGIC SUSCEPTIBILITY:** You are easily affected by magic. You suffer a -3 penalty on all Magic Resistance and Natural Resistance rolls, and to Soak direct damage from magic (opposite of *Withstand Magic,* above). If the magic is good, the penalty may become a bonus, as you are more likely to be affected by good magic as well.

**CURSED:** Somehow, for some reason, you are cursed, either magically, divinely, or perhaps through the influence of dark powers or faeries. Example -1 Curses:

• Everything you say, that you really mean, is taken in the worst possible way.

• Smile, laugh, frown, and cry always in the wrong circumstances.

• Can only eat living things.

• A toad appears in your mouth when you speak a direct lie.

• All food tastes like ashes and all drink like stagnant water.

• Music causes you pain — the more beautiful, the more painful.

**OFFENSIVE TO ANIMALS:** You are somehow tainted with magic, and this disturbs animals. Horses do not let you ride them, and dogs growl or cower in your presence. People may well suspect you of being a Magus or devil-worshipper. Magus: n/a, you automatically have this trait.

# Flaws: -2

**CURSED:** You suffer from a severe curse given you by one of the great supernatural powers. Example -2 Curses:

• Stutter uncontrollably when you try to say something important.

• If you ever tell a secret that was entrusted with you, the secret somehow, in some way, harms you.

**MINOR DISCOMFORT FROM IRON:** Due to your faerie blood, you are uncomfortable touching things of iron. Touching iron does not harm you; it just doesn't feel good. You suffer a -3 penalty to use any weapon or tool if you have to touch iron to use it. If you wear iron armor, you are -2 on all Fatigue Level rolls. This Flaw cannot

be taken with *Vulnerability to Iron.* This Flaw is usually taken with *Faerie Blood.*

**SUSCEPTIBILITY TO DIVINE POWER:** Because of your faerie blood your tie to the mortal world, especially the religious world, is so weak that you are vulnerable to the power of the Dominion. The touch of holy water, sacramental incense, or a crucifix hurts you, and actually burns your skin if it remains there for any longer than a few seconds. Your lack of faith and your impure (from the Church's point of view) nature drives you away from holy items. You cannot use any magical or faerie powers you have on people bearing items blessed by the Church (incense, water, hosts, possibly a crucifix or cross) nor can you use those powers while on consecrated ground (churches and cemeteries). This Flaw must be taken with *Faerie Blood.*

**HAUNTED:** You are haunted by a ghost that only you can see and hear. It insults, berates, and distracts you, especially when you need to keep your cool. In addition, it often uses one of the following powers against you: takes and hides small items; "chills" others around you and makes them ill at ease (-3 on your Presence and Communication rolls); causes a buzzing in your or someone else's ears to prevent proper hearing (-3 on hearing rolls); moves small items, like knives, to cause them to fall on you, trip you, or otherwise hamper or endanger you; or makes eerie noises, such as chains clinking. Yelling at the ghost sometimes drives it away but also confuses those around you. Unless you are exceptionally strong-willed, you may sometimes do as the ghost commands to get relief from its hauntings. If you aid the ghost in completing its final purpose, you may be able to get rid of it. The ghost has no powers when more than seven paces away from you. Magus: the ghost is particularly powerful, so you may have trouble controlling it even with spells. It can interfere with your lab work; -3 on all Lab Totals.

**TAINTED WITH EVIL:** Something you, your parents, or your ancestors did has tainted you with evil. Others naturally feel very ill at ease around you, and people easily grow to hate you. Gaining a positive Reputation is impossible. Magi do not react as strongly to this attribute as normal people. Magus: -1 Flaw; it doesn't matter much what people think of you.

# Flaws: -3

**CURSED:** You have been cursed by one of the great supernatural powers. Examples of -3 Curses:

• Pained by light — the greater the light, the greater the pain.

• See shapes and phantoms in the night that terrify and immobilize you.

**VULNERABILITY TO IRON:** Due to your faerie blood the touch of iron burns you. You take no actual damage from just touching iron, but it hurts. You cannot use iron weapons or tools where you must touch the iron, and you cannot wear iron armor. In addition, iron weapons do +2 damage to you. Furthermore, your faerie blood is so strong that your blood probably does not look like human blood. It might look like black ichor or white wine. If you choose this Flaw you cannot choose that of *Poor Equipment.* You cannot take this Flaw in conjunction with *Minor Discomfort from Iron.* This Flaw must be taken with *Faerie Blood.*

**SENSE OF DOOM:** You have gained knowledge best left unknown, perhaps a vision of your demise or eternal fate, perhaps secrets about your true nature. At times you are listless, as no ambition can shake your sense of doom. Whenever you are defeated somehow, whether in combat or a more mundane effort, you are incapable of taking any energetic action for up to a day. If forced to defend yourself during this time, you suffer -2 on scores, and are incapable of using your Confidence Points.

# Flaws: -4

**CURSED:** You have been terribly cursed by one of the great supernatural powers. Examples of -4 Curses:

• Doomed to be wounded in every battle in which you partake (and in many that you try to avoid).

• Your wounds bleed horribly, so that for each unbandaged wound you have, you lose one Short-Term Fatigue Level per Round, and then lose Body Levels once you are Unconscious.

• Normal tools (including weapons) often break when you try to use them.

• The touch of sunlight burns painfully (lose one Body Level per minute).

**DEMON PLAGUED:** You have come to the special attention of a minor demon, who is set on capturing your soul and making your life a living hell. This demon has a specialty that it uses against you, such as rage, greed, sloth, or dishonesty. The demon can use its powers directly against you and against others with intent to harm you. For instance, a demon of lies can make you lie or make others lie to you. The demon is too busy (or lazy) to harass you constantly, so it usually only affects you during important times of your life (like adventures). The Storyguide should keep in mind the subtle nature and sinister purpose of the demon's plans. Secretly, you wonder what evil (or good) you or your family has done to deserve such a fate. For overcoming Magic Resistance, assume the demon has +12 on its magic Penetration roll, though it may grow in power or be replaced by a superior demon if it fails to carry out its plans. Magus: Hell takes a special interest in Magi; the fiend's Infernal Might is at least 24. Don't forget the attendant problems this might cause you in the Order.

## Flaws: -5

**AGE QUICKLY:** Probably due to a curse or a magical disaster, you age twice as fast as normal men. Increase your age by two years every year, and when you begin to age, make two Aging rolls each year. There is no way to halt this aging or slow the pace except with longevity potions. Magus: The aging is beyond the ability of a single longevity potion to control, so unless you have two longevity potions, the second Aging roll you make is not modified by your longevity potion.

## Flaws: -8

**DEMON TAINTED:** You have been tainted by demons, but have somehow managed to break free of their grip. You automatically have the *Demon Plagued* and *Dark Secret* Flaws (but gain no Virtue points for them), and constantly have to struggle to prevent yourself from sliding completely into corruption and losing your soul. You have one unsavory Personality Trait with a score between +4 and +6, and it is very difficult for you to reduce it (though you may increase an opposing Trait normally). Eventually, some miracle of faith or devotion may save you, but chances are that the Devil will eventually take your soul. Magus: If the Order finds out about your Flaw, you will surely be cast out.

# SOCIAL

Social Virtues and Flaws describe the things which your character is capable of in terms of the rest of society, both mundane and magical.

Restrictions: Except for a few exceptions, Magi can take none of the following traits, unless you can provide the Storyguide with strong justification for possessing a trait.

# Virtues: +1

**SOCIAL CONTACTS:** You have a broad range of acquaintances, accumulated over years of travel and socializing. Almost everywhere you go, you meet someone you know, or you know how to get in touch with someone who can help you. Whenever you are somewhere new, you know someone who is in town or in the area if you can make a Presence simple roll of 10+. You must pick the kind of contacts you have: underworld, noble, merchant, town guard, Church, peasants. This Virtue may be taken more than once, representing contacts in more than one part of society.

**VENUS'S BLESSING:** You get a +3 on Communication and Presence rolls with sexually compatible characters in appropriate situations. People are often attracted to you; the Storyguide should play this out. At times you can put this to good use, at other times it's an annoyance.

**TRUE FRIEND:** You have a very close friend who is your confidant, supporter, and ally in all things. Your friend does not hesitate to help you, and you do not question your friend's needs. You feel much more confident and at ease with your friend by your side — add one to your Confidence score when helping your friend, and when receiving his help. Remember that friendship brings obligations as well as benefits, and if anything bad happens to your friend, you are extremely distraught (and, if appropriate, extremely vengeful). You and your friend have *Loyalty* Passions toward each other with scores of +3 (this is a free Virtue).

**WELL-KNOWN:** You have a good Reputation in a particular area and are well-liked. Choose an appropriate Reputation in a specific location near the Covenant. You begin at level 2.

**INSPIRATIONAL:** You can inspire people, giving them a +3 bonus to Bravery and other related Personality Rolls, and to Natural Resistance rolls versus certain Mentem spells.

**ANIMAL COMPANION:** You have a loyal, intelligent animal for a companion. Your relationship with it is a meaningful one; you are very close. The animal can at least obey simple commands. If it should die, you are profoundly distraught.

**BUSYBODY:** You want to know everything that is going on among your friends and acquaintances, especially in private matters. You are always interested in rumors and gossip. You are frequently able to extract personal secrets from people. To convince

another to tell a secret, each of you makes a simple die roll, yours modified by +4 and the other's modified by an appropriate Personality Trait or Passion. If you roll is higher, the secret is revealed. You usually know what is going on, and who is sleeping with whom. Magi: the language is more dignified, but the idea is the same. The community you keep tabs on is probably Hermetic — the Magi of your Covenant, your House, and nearby Covenants at the least. You probably don't have much knowledge of what's going on among your covenfolk, unless you tailor this Virtue to those people.

**GANG MEMBER:** You are a member of a small (4-7 person), close-knit group of some sort. You may gain support from your group, but must help others in your group in return, and must do whatever the leader of the group tells you to do (within reason). Your group may, at your option, have a Reputation of your choice at level 1 in the local area, and other members' Devotion Personality Trait scores are typically positive.

In general, any Virtue or Flaw that normally involves family can be applied to a small group instead. So, you may be a *Black Sheep* from a group instead of a family, with some different and interesting implications.

# Virtues: +2

**TEMPORAL INFLUENCE:** You wield some political influence in society. You have the ear of some leader and may lead common folk at times, if they respect your position. The more influence you have, the more responsibility you have, and the harder it is to work with Magi unopposed. Examples of people with such temporal influence are the mates and children of leaders, courtiers, and worthy subordinates.

**FAMOUS:** You have a good Reputation with a score of 4. Choose the specific Reputation and pick one or more noteworthy deeds that are part of this fame.

**GOSSIP:** You have regular social contacts in the local area that provide you with all kinds of information about social and political goings on. You know interesting details of local intrigues — on a simple roll of 8+, you hear interesting news before almost everyone else. You treat all local Reputations as though they are twice their level for purposes of your recognizing them, and with some well-placed words, you may be able to create new Reputations for people, whether they are deserved or not. You may very well have a Reputation in the local area as a gossip.

**GANG LEADER:** You are the leader of a small (4-7 person) group of some sort. The members of your group look up to you, and do what you tell them to, within reason. You are, however, responsible for your group, and must occasionally stick up for the group or one of its members. You may also occasionally have to deal with challenges to your leadership in one form or another. Group members' Devotion Personality Trait scores toward the group, and you, are typically positive.

# Virtues: +3

**LEADERSHIP:** You have risen in power and prestige in whatever organization or entity you have chosen to work within. A Magus may be the head of a major Covenant, or a leading scholar in one of the Arts (make sure you have the actual Art level to back this up — at least 20). A Companion may be a baron, or an influential merchant. A Grog is the leader of a turb, or belongs to a group of Grogs assigned to a special Magus, such as the *Primus* of a House, or the *Praeco* of a Tribunal.

# Virtues: +6

**GREATER LEADERSHIP:** Like *Leadership*, above, you have gained a high position and a great deal of power and respect in your profession. Your decisions are listened to and often followed, and you can sway other powerful individuals with your opinion. You have many responsibilities and duties, and time for adventuring and experimentation is very hard to find. A Companion might be a duke or a merchant lord of a great trading city. A Magus is a *Praeco* of a Tribunal, an Arch-Mage, or possibly a *Primus* of a House. Grog characters cannot take this Virtue. Note: you must have the skills to hold the position.

For example, a Magus must have created a 31+ Level spell to qualify for the position of Arch-Mage.

# Flaws: -1

**BAD REPUTATION:** People in the area know of you and hold you in ill regard. Choose a specific Reputation. The beginning score of the Reputation is 2. The Storyguide should be sure to bring the Reputation into play; it can make things very interesting.

**SOCIAL HANDICAP:** You have some trait that keeps you from interacting easily with other people. Possibilities include body odor, a morose temperament, unworldliness (difficulty understanding such trivial and mundane concerns as money), unclean habits, or outspoken atheism. The trait you choose impairs your social dealings with most people in society, causing penalties of -1 to -3 on appropriate rolls. Magus: n/a, being a Magus is a social handicap in and of itself.

**DEPENDANT:** You have a dependant, like a young child or a decrepit grandmother, whom you take responsibility for. This restricts your freedom and requires your time in a variety of ways. The effects of this Flaw may change with time — when your child grows up, she may move away; when your grandmother gets seriously ill, all your time must be devoted to her. If you have several dependants, like a family, this Flaw may be taken with a lower rating, like -3.

**EXPENSES:** You must pay a significant portion of your wealth and income (25% to 50%) to a person or organization, or devote it to expenses. Failure to pay your dues brings unpleasant consequences — perhaps the loss of other privileges, or the acquisition of a significant enemy. If your expense is some kind of taxation, you may be able to hide some of your wealth, like grain, from the expense, but the tax collector has ways of finding out, and if your evasion is discovered, you must suffer the consequences. Expenses can arise from tithes, blackmail, protection money, or just bribes to support social contacts.

**FAVORS:** You owe favors to someone (or to a great many people), and these favors may be called upon at any time. The consequences of ignoring a favor is up to the Storyguide to determine.

**MEDDLER:** You want to fix other peoples' lives — arrange matches, teach peoples' children to sew (because you do it right and they don't), and tend the sick. Assign yourself a Personality Trait of Meddlesome, rated +3. You waste a lot of time and energy on such endeavors, and

people usually resent it. You have a bad Reputation as a Meddler (level 1). Magus: you probably interfere in the affairs of Magi, Companions, and apprentices. While dabbling in private lives you don't violate Hermetic Law often or maliciously, but you probably come close, and you almost certainly irritate the Magi of your Covenant.

**RECLUSIVE:** You prefer to be left by yourself, whether to study or to perform any other action. You do not like being interrupted, and feel that an intrusion by another upon your time is generally unnecessary at best, and an insult at worst. Assign yourself a Personality Trait of Reclusive +3. If someone persists in interrupting you, make a Reclusive stress roll. If 6+, you rudely show them the door. If you Botch, you lose your temper completely and get rid of the pest as fast as possible. A double Botch is the same as above, but you probably use violence. You may also intensify your reclusiveness if a double or triple Botch occurs (adding to your Personality Trait score), at the discretion of the Storyguide.

**JUDGED UNFAIRLY:** Somehow you come across wrong to people, and they universally distrust and underestimate you. You catch no one's eyes, impress no one, and can get no one to take you seriously. You might find one exceptional person who somehow sees you as you want to be seen. Cling to that person.

**OATH OF FEALTY:** You owe service to someone or some organization outside the Covenant. It could be a lord, the Church, political leaders in a city, or your family. You must justify your actions to those to whom you owe fealty, and sometimes there is a conflict between your activities with the Covenant and your oath.

# Flaws: -2

**INFAMOUS:** The locals know you well and curse you in their prayers. Take a Level 4 bad Reputation, and decide what horrible deeds you did to gain such ill will.

**CURSE OF VENUS:** You are very attractive to people whom you do not wish to attract (add 4 to Presence rolls concerning attractiveness). People whom you detest are constantly getting crushes on you, and tend to overlook your rejection of them. On the other hand, people you wish to attract or endear tend to think you are vain and shallow (subtract 1 from Presence and Communication rolls with them).

# TRAITS

A number of Virtues and Flaws deal with gaining higher and lower traits during character creation. These traits include Characteristics, Reputations, and Personality Traits. Virtues are also listed here that allow you to have exclusive Ability traits. Trait scores reflect your capacity to function in the world of Mythic Europe in terms of game statistics.

## Virtues: +1

**TOUGH:** You can take physical punishment better than most people. You get a +3 bonus on your Soak score.

**ARCANE LORE:** You are privy to Hermetic knowledge, so you can choose Arcane Knowledges (which are normally restricted to Magi) as beginning Abilities.

**EDUCATED:** You may choose Formal Knowledges as beginning Abilities.

**EXCEPTIONAL TALENT:** The following Exceptional Talents may be taken as +1 Virtues: Direction Sense, Herbalism, Empathy, Read Lips, Alchemy, Premonitions, Second Sight, Sense Holiness/Unholiness, Dousing, Magic Sensitivity, Weather Sense, Hexing, Contortions, Mimicry, Perfect Balance, Healer.

**GOOD CHARACTERISTIC:** You may replace any one Characteristic with a number derived by making a simple roll and referring to this chart: 1-5: +1, 6-8: +2, 9-10: +3. This Virtue is only available if you roll your Characteristics.

**KNACK:** You have an innate knack for some specific activity which gives you a +2 on rolls dealing with that activity. Examples include: mechanics, music, bows, swords, woodlands, mountains, cities & towns, languages, noble courts, and swamps. Whenever you are in this environment or pursuing this activity, you get the bonus. A bonus on weapon type applies whenever a skill for that weapon applies; the bonus applies to either Parry or Attack Skill, your choice. Knacks, as +1 Virtues, can be no more broad than those listed here.

**RECKLESS:** You tend not to notice that situations are threatening. You have a Reckless Personality Trait of +3, and can never have a positive Careful Personality Trait. Whenever the Storyguide asks for a Brave Personality Trait roll (or such a roll otherwise seems appropriate) you instead make a Reckless roll and can use Confidence with it. If you roll whatever is necessary to make the Brave roll, you do not realize the situation threatens

you, and no Brave roll is necessary to perform the actions in question. If the Reckless roll fails you make a Brave roll normally — you realize the situation is dangerous, but may have the resolve to deal with it. Note: this Virtue *is* compatible with a negative Brave Personality Trait.

## Virtues: +2

**APTITUDE +1:** You have an aptitude with a broad class of things or actions, such as combat, business and finance, arts and crafts, travel, or animals. You gain +1 to all rolls involving your aptitude. The class you choose may be no broader than these, and the bonus due to your aptitude is incompatible with any bonuses due to the *Knack* Virtue or other Aptitudes — you get the highest applicable bonus, not the total of them.

**TRAINING:** You receive regular training in a limited set of Abilities from some source. You receive twice the normal amount of Experience Points you normally gain in a year (see *Experience*, in the Saga Chapter), and the extra Experience gained may only be applied to the Abilities in which you are already trained. Magus: n/a — You can receive most any training you wish anyway, and must spend normal time to do it.

**EXCEPTIONAL TALENT:** You can take the Abilities of Enchanting Music or Visions as a +2 Virtue.

**KNACK:** As the +1 Virtue, but your bonus is +4.

**SUPERIOR CHARACTERISTIC:** As *Good Characteristic*, above, except bonuses are: 1-6, +2; and 7-10, +3.

## Virtues: +3

**HIGHLY TALENTED:** You have 20 additional Experience Points to spend on Talent Abilities.

**HIGHLY SKILLED:** You have 20 additional Experience Points to spend on Skill Abilities.

**VERY KNOWLEDGEABLE:** You have 20 additional Experience Points to spend on Knowledge Abilities.

## Virtues: +4

**MASTERED TALENT:** You have a normal (non-Exceptional) Talent Ability at which you are naturally proficient. You receive a +4 to rolls involving the Talent and never roll more than one Botch die with it.

**MASTERED SKILL:** You have a Skill Ability at which you are naturally proficient. You receive a +4 modifier to rolls that involve

the Skill and never roll more than one Botch die with it.

**MASTERED KNOWLEDGE:** You have a Knowledge Ability at which you are expressly learned. You receive a +4 modifier to rolls involving the Knowledge and never roll more than one Botch die with it. You have a Reputation reflecting your knowledge.

**APTITUDE +2:** As the +2 Virtue, *Aptitude +1*, but the bonus of your Aptitude is +2.

**EXCEPTIONAL TALENT:** You may take Entrancement or Divination as a +4 Virtue.

## Virtues: +5

**MYTHIC CHARACTERISTIC:** You have one Characteristic of epic proportions, raising a Characteristic score to +6. In addition, once per day, you may perform an incredible feat related to your Characteristic. For example, if you have Mythic Strength, you may, once per day, lift and toss a huge boulder or use a huge log as a club. This Virtue is only available if you roll your Characteristics.

# BACKGROUND

Every character has a background. For many background is very simple: they were born and raised at the Covenant. Others, however, come from a more traditional background: they were once part of mundane society. Still others hail from more exotic backgrounds (after all this is a fantasy game, despite the historical trappings). It's possible that your character was raised by wolves or faeries, or that your character is not completely human.

It's impossible to list all the possible backgrounds. You may create others, but they must be approved by the Troupe. For instance, if you are playing Ars Magica with a high fantasy setting, you probably allow characters to be Elves and Dwarfs. You have to come up with rules for such backgrounds on your own, but that's part of the fun.

If you want to get really bizarre you can play a Familiar or some sort of high-powered faerie. You have to negotiate with the Troupe for such extreme characters, likely trading your "Magus spot" for the exotic character.

## Virtues: +1

**FAERIE UPBRINGING,:** Perhaps you were abandoned by your true kin, and the faeries found you. Perhaps your family actually lived in a faerie forest, or maybe faeries took you as a babe. In any case you are now back in human society, but feel at home with faeries, magic, and other strange things, and receive +3 to all your Personality Trait rolls when dealing with such things. However, you find human society, especially religion, bizarre. You cannot have Social Skills as starting Abilities.

**CIRCUS UPBRINGING:** You were raised among a troupe of entertainers, spending much of your childhood (except the winters) traveling from town to town. Rolls involving Performance Skills and Physical Talents receive a +1 modifier.

**WELL-TRAVELLED:** You have traveled extensively in this part of the world and find it easy to get along with people throughout the land. You are familiar with their dialects, can pick others up quickly (+2 to appropriate speaking rolls), and you know something of local habits and traditions. You get a +1 bonus to Knowledge rolls connected with being well-traveled, such as when making Legend Lore rolls.

**CLOSE FAMILY TIES:** Your family is one of the most important things in your life, and they still support and aid you whenever they can, even if it means personal risk. They do not hesitate to do you any favor that is within their power, and can call on their friends and neighbors to help them. It works both ways, however; your family may call on you for help some day.

**HIGHER PURPOSE:** Let others concern themselves with petty matters; you have a higher goal, such as freeing an oppressed people or bringing peace between the Order of Hermes and society — your feelings must be altruistic. When pursuing this goal you receive a +2 bonus to rerolls and scene modifiers (from Passions) allowed by Confidence Points; you see beyond your momentary purposes to a higher end. You also gain +3 on Personality Trait rolls made to pursue your goal.

**HEIR:** You have little power or wealth now, but your are heir to land, titles, and wealth. You need do nothing special to remain in a position to inherit, but others may occasionally attempt to remove you from the line of succession, one way or another. When gain your inheritance you inherit its responsibilities as well, so your freedom may be restricted.

**PRESTIGIOUS FAMILY:** Your family is well-known and respected. When in dire need, others may help you because of your family ties, or your family itself may provide assistance. You begin the game with a Reputation of your choice at level 2.

**SECRET HIDING PLACE:** You know of a place which is well hidden or just very difficult to get to, making it unknown to all but a few (or just yourself), and an excellent hiding place when you are in trouble. You may occasionally have trouble getting to your hiding place, but once you are there, you are basically safe. At some point, someone may find your hiding place, putting you in some kind of a predicament.

# Virtues: +2

**FAERIE BLOOD:** Somewhere in your ancestry there is a faerie, and this relation gives you an intuitive grasp of the motivations and personalities of faeries.

Faeries are more comfortable around you than they are around other humans and, given time, may even forget the mortal blood in your veins. Precise results of this possibility are up to the Storyguide (and the faeries). Add +1 to all your rolls to avoid losing Characteristics to Aging, and add +3 to all Natural Resistance rolls (for those spells you want to resist). The line of faeries you are descended from also influences your talents and predilections. Choose one of these or create your own line, with its own capabilities.

*Sidhe Blood:* One of your ancestors, perhaps even a parent, was one of the noble elves who rule the faerie lands. This relationship exhibits itself in your appearance, for you are slight of build, fair of face, and likely to have white or blond hair. Take a +1 bonus to your Dexterity, even if that brings your total over +5, but scratch your Hurt Body Level from your character sheet. Faeries who you meet may often treat you with great respect, believing you to be a noble of their kind.

*Satyr Blood:* Satyrs are a promiscuous sort, and sire many children in many different races. Though you are fully human in build, some features of your father exhibit themselves in you. You are extremely hairy, possess aquiline features, and are cursed with cloven hooves/feet (you need special shoes). You automatically have a *Lust* Passion of 1 (though a higher score is suggested, and the Passion can be raised normally).

*Goblin Blood:* You are short, squat and ill-favored by humanity. Your ancestry has marked you with ugliness and a predisposition for dark and hidden places. Your Presence and Communication cannot be higher than -1, but you can see in the dark as if it's twilight.

The **Ars Magica** supplement **Faeries** offers many more ideas on the traits and capabilities of faerie characters.

**BLACKMAIL:** You have information which some powerful person would prefer left unspoken. You receive payments or services in return for your silence, and you may occasionally leverage special favors, but don't push your luck, as your victim may decide it isn't worth the cost, or may decide to silence you permanently. You gain wealth or services with a yearly value of about 50 silver pennies, plus anything else you can leverage.

**INDENTURED SERVANT:** You have an indentured servant to attend to your everyday needs and desires. The servant is not trained to fight, and is not highly skilled (points in Abilities equal to age), but generally follows your commands. The relationship you have with your servant is up to you, but there must be some strong motivation for the servant to remain with you. If your servant ever dies, you have no replacement, and your servant may, in any case, have only a limited term of service with you.

**INDULGENCES:** You have a number of indulgences which have been bequeathed upon you by the Pope (indulgences are remissions of sin which you can sell to others). You may sell these indulgences, keeping a small amount of the money gained for yourself, or you may grant the indulgences to individuals in return for services to the Church (i.e., have them do something for you). Each indulgence allows the remission of one sin, and you have no more than 20 indulgences at any time (roll two dice). When your indulgences are all granted, you may gain more by returning to Rome.

These are minor indulgences. Full indulgences (remission of all sins) are reserved for very wealthy people or for those needed by the Church. For example, during the Albigensian Crusade, the remission of all sins was offered to anyone fighting 40 days in the war against the heretics.

**MENTOR:** A person of some importance, wealth, or wisdom has taken an interest in your life, and at times provides you with material aid and advice. Your mentor does not necessarily like or even know of your relationship with the Covenant. At some point your mentor may have a small favor to ask of you…

**PATRON:** You have a patron who funds you and provides you with materials and a handsome (by medieval standards) salary, in return for services of some kind. The relationship is one of business more than friendship, and you may occasionally have to walk on eggshells with your patron, due to any (real or imagined) unacceptable behavior.

# Virtues: +3

**KNIGHT:** You are a knight, though you do not necessarily hold any land or titles. You are entitled to bear arms, and are a member of the nobility (though you are at the bottom of the pecking order). You have the Virtue *Good Armaments* (it's free), and may purchase the Virtues *Superior Armaments* and *Wealth* at one less point than they're worth (i.e., Wealth, as a +4 Virtue, costs 3 points), during character creation. If you choose any of the Virtues *Close Family Ties*, *Patron*, *Prestigious Family*, *Temporal Power*, *Superior Armaments*, *Wealth*, or anything else the Storyguide considers appropriate, you have your own mount as well. You automatically have the *Oath of Fealty* Flaw, however, and are required to spend one Season a year in service to your lord, often fighting his wars. Possession of this Flaw does not give you more Virtue points to work with.

**BUSINESS:** You own or run a business which generates significant wealth for you, but which provides you with little (if any) political clout, and which you must manage and protect. You have a yearly excess income of about 250 silver pennies, and may own your own mount (though you may not own land unless you have the *Wealth* Virtue). You may purchase *Wealth* (a +4 Virtue) for 2 points, but the land and titles are still tied to your business (i.e., you still have to work to maintain them).

**CLERGY:** You are a member of the clergy, and thus fall under the protection of the Church (even if you regularly fail to fulfill your Church vows). You are accorded some respect (or at least fear) due to your position, by both nobles and common folk alike, but nobles still usually outrank you in a sense, as the nobility have a great deal of political power in the Church. Magus: n/a.

**PROTECTION:** You are under the protection of a powerful person, usually a noble or high-ranking Church official (though other options are certainly possible). Those who know of your favored status are careful about how they treat you, while those who don't know who you are, and who treat you poorly, often pay the price. Take a Reputation (good or bad, your choice) of level 3. Note: if the protector is particularly great or well-known, increase the Reputation score accordingly.

# Virtues: +4

**DESTINY:** Your life is heading toward a definite culmination. Prophecies and dreams may give you clues as to the culmination's nature, but you are not yet sure what it is. This sense of direction gives you the surety to overcome fear, depression, and discouragement caused by anything not relevant to your destiny (and therefore not, in the end, relevant to you); +2 on appropriate rolls. If it ever seems your destiny will fail because of your untimely demise, something, somehow, preserves you. When the time is right, your destiny will be fulfilled, though it may cost you your life.

**FAILED APPRENTICE:** You began apprenticeship to become a Magus, but something keeps you from ever being able to continue your studies. Perhaps your master found that your Gift of magic was incomplete or some grievous mishap robbed you of it altogether. You may have Arcane and Formal Knowledges as beginning Abilities, and you are familiar with a Magus's life. Magi welcome you and have compassion for you (those Magi who are given to such emotions, anyway). You may still work for your former master. If your Gift was not completely destroyed, you most likely have some Exceptional Talents. Magus: N/A.

**REDCAP:** You are a Redcap, a messenger of the Order of Hermes. You may be assigned to one Covenant or you may wander among the Covenants delivering messages, in turn receiving a moderate stipend. Strangely enough, you are considered a full member of the Order of Hermes; you possess a Sigil, and your representatives attend most Tribunals (although, out of deference to true Magi, they do not vote). Most folk do not harass or harm you, and even Magi think twice before hindering your mission. Essentially this gives you a high degree of protection when you travel, even when you travel alone. You may choose Formal and Arcane Knowledges as beginning Abilities. Magus: +3 Virtue.

**WAYS OF THE WOODS:** You have a deep understanding of the woodlands, feeling more natural and at home there than anywhere else. You get a +4 bonus to rolls that directly involve the woods and its inhabitants, mundane or faerie. In addition, you suffer one less Botch than normal (but always at least one) in rolls that pertain to your woodland understanding. Particularly vicious creatures may still attack you, but at least they'll accord you proper respect.

This understanding of nature may be adapted to apply to areas other than woodlands. For example, you could have Ways of the Seas, Ways of the Mountains, or Ways of the Deserts. Each such Virtue must be purchased separately.

**WEALTH:** You own land and other valuable things and have a yearly income of about 700 silver pennies. You can have a mount of your own and automatically receive the *Superior Armaments* Virtue (at no cost to your Virtue and Flaw point pool).

# Virtues: +5

**GIANT BLOOD:** You are part giant, and the blood of that ancient race flows in your veins. Though you do not stand as tall as your ancient ancestors, you are at least seven feet tall (but not more than eight) and weigh up to 500 pounds. Your Size is +2. Add +2 to your Strength, even if that brings it over +5, and take two additional Hurt Body Levels. You may not know that you have giant blood in you, thinking only that you are an abnormally large human. If you even meet giants, they are aware of your ancestry and may even accept you as a "runt" of their own kind.

# Flaws: variable

**VOW:** You have sworn a vow to do or not to do something difficult, such as fight all demons, live in poverty, never raise a weapon, or not to speak. Obedience to this vow is determined by your roleplaying; to break your vow is a high crime. When tempted to break your vow, make an appropriate Personality Trait roll with a +6 modifier. The Ease Factor is 12. If you break your vow (fail your roll), some kind of penance is called for, whether it be religious penance or just coming to terms with your own failure. Either way, you lose all Confidence Points and can only regain any by redeeming or avenging yourself (the means by which you do so is decided by the Troupe).

People respect your dedication, and you begin with a good Reputation, as chosen by you, of level 1.

The cost of the Flaw is determined by the Troupe depending on the severity of your vow.

**FOREIGNER:** You are of a race which is both identifiable by sight and distrusted or disliked by the Church or most people (e.g., an Arab, Jew, Gypsy). You are shunned and often persecuted because of your race, and your life and freedom may occasionally be put in peril. Take a level 1 to level 3 Reputation for your race (depending upon how easy it is to identify you as a member of that race). There is no way for you to ever remove your Reputation; you are branded by it wherever you go. Cost: Zero minus the level of the Reputation. Magus: -1 Flaw if the Reputation is level 2 or higher, no points otherwise.

# Flaws: -1

**OBLIGATION:** You are obligated to perform certain services for someone. These services typically occupy at least one Season out of every year, and may occasionally require more time than that. Your duties may arise from personal choice, like the protection of a family member, or a true duty, like the duty of a knight to his lord. Whatever your duties, failure to perform them may have serious or lasting consequences.

**ENEMIES:** You have an enemy or enemies who cause you trouble, such as a local baron or bishop, a band of outlaws, or perhaps a really nasty innkeeper. The enemy must be powerful enough to endanger you; make sure you get the Troupe's approval.

**DARK SECRET:** You have some secret that haunts you and would lead to shame, rejection, and possibly revenge if discovered. Hints about the secret continually arise, and there might be others who know the secret and could betray you. If people were to find out about your secret, your life would change drastically. The secret makes you avoid certain places, dislike certain people, or fear certain things. A few examples are: your parents are diabolists, you once murdered a knight (or maybe a Magus), or you are fleeing from mundane or Hermetic justice.

**HIRED SWORD (GROGS ONLY):** You are an experienced mercenary, but you are new at the Covenant. You don't know the Magi or their strange ways very well, and you might not fit in with the community of Grogs just yet. You cannot have a Personality Trait that involves devotion toward the Covenant.

**INFAMOUS FAMILY:** You come from a family that is very well known, but not very well liked. You have a bad Reputation at level 3, and have a particularly hard time losing it because it is seen as a family trait, not a personal one. You have trouble trusting others because others in your community have always acted against you.

**LOST LOVE:** You have lost your true love to death, distance, or marriage. You take little joy in life's pleasures and give up easily in the face of difficulty, since you've already lost the most important struggle. On those occasions when you forget yourself and have a good time, you inevitably feel sorrow afterwards as you think about how it could have been if your true love were with you. Incompatible with the *Love* Passion.

**PERSONAL HATRED:** You bear an all-consuming hatred for some person who is so powerful that exacting proper vengeance is impractical or impossible. Nevertheless, you constantly pursue opportunities to gain power over or hurt the object of your hatred, so much so that your reason is clouded. This Flaw is different from the *Hatred* Passion as this focuses on one person, and does not dictate as much of your personality.

**CRIMINAL BRAND:** The brand of a criminal has been burned into your cheek, imposing a -1 penalty on all rolls involving others' reactions to you. You have a Reputation (level 2) as a criminal. Perhaps some old enemies are still on the watch for you. Magus: n/a. Who cares? You're a wizard.

**RECRUIT (GROGS ONLY):** You have been trained at the Covenant, but you have never fought in a real battle. You cannot have the Valor Passion or a positive Bravery Personality Trait score; increasing your Bravery score is important for your character development.

**BLACK SHEEP:** You come from a prestigious family, but you have somehow estranged yourself from your relatives. They have nothing to do with you, unless they feel the need to punish you somehow. Those who might resent your family's power can take safe revenge by assaulting you. You begin the game with a bad Reputation of your choice at level 2.

**ORPHAN:** You have no family. You were either raised by the Church or you simply made your own way on the streets. You are a loner and have trouble working with others. You are also used to a world in which one must be selfish, sneaky, and heartless to survive.

**POOR:** You have almost no wealth or money, and for some reason, you can never seem to long possess the valuables you do gain. You automatically have the *Poor Armaments* Flaw (its possession does not offer you more Virtue points), and whenever you gain something of value, you can bet you don't get a chance to keep or use it.

**FAERIE ENMITY: FAERIES** hate you and take every opportunity to harm or pester you. Faerie forests are extremely dangerous places for you, but even in rural areas faeries often spoil your food, plague your dreams, or otherwise torment you. Luckily, they prefer to let you live so they can continue to hassle you.

# Flaws: -2

**DIABOLIC UPBRINGING:** Your parents were diabolists, and, though you have escaped their evil ways, you are still haunted by your upbringing and the memory of acts best left unspoken. The thought of demons fills you with dread and hatred. Hell might maintain a special interest in the well-being of your soul.

**SHELTERED UPBRINGING:** You grew up completely separated from society, knowing only your parents or mentor. Recently you have been introduced to a wondrous new world of strangers, and you are overwhelmed. You are unable to function normally because you cannot understand most human customs, motivations, and mentalities. Take -3 to most tasks involving social interaction, and you may have no Social Talents or Skills as beginning Abilities. Depending on your personality, you might react to the world with contempt, fear, or wonder. Eventually you may overcome your upbringing.

# Flaws: -3

**FERAL UPBRINGING:** You grew up in the wilderness, either being raised by wild animals or by surviving on your own. For much of your life you could not talk or speak and knew nothing of the ways of man. Now that you have reentered human society (or the Covenant) you have learned to understand some basic spoken phrases, but normal civilized life is still a mystery you want little part of. As for beginning Abilities, you may only choose those that you could have learned in the wilds. You may have picked up a few skills at the Covenant, such as how to use a mace instead of a club, but you have neither the inclination nor the capacity to learn more refined skills. You have no Speak Own Language Ability. Magus: n/a.

## Flaws: -4

**OUTLAW:** You are an infamous criminal, and although no one is devoted full-time to your capture, you can be sure that someone is sent after you whenever you come to the attention of the authorities. You have a level 4 Reputation as an outlaw. If you are caught, there might be a debate about whether to kill you outright or save you for public execution, but your death is assured. Magus: n/a — You're a wizard, and the authorities give you a wide berth. The worst you have is a very bad Reputation.

# EQUIPMENT

The quality of equipment, particularly armor and weapons, you use can be instrumental to the identity of your character. This is particularly true of Grogs and some Companions. In order for you to have above average gear, you must purchase a particular Virtue, though you can have a Flaw for poor quality equipment. Your background often determines the quality and nature of your gear.

*Restrictions: Virtues and Flaws that deal in bronze armor and faerie iron are only available to characters with faerie ties or ancestry, unless your character has come in contact with a faerie treasure trove, or has been awarded the armor by the Fay.*

## Virtues: +1

**GOOD ARMAMENTS:** You can have any standard armament and one expensive armament. For armament expenses, see the weapons and armor charts in the Combat Chapter.

**STANDARD EQUIPMENT OF BRONZE MANUFACTURE:** All of your equipment, which would normally have iron parts, utilizes bronze in its construction, thereby being less inimical to your faerie nature (assuming iron has adverse side effects upon you).

## Virtues: +2

**SUPERIOR ARMAMENTS:** You can have expensive arms and armor. For armament expenses, see the weapons and armor charts in the Combat Chapter.

**SUPERIOR EQUIPMENT (ONE PIECE) OF BRONZE MANUFACTURE:** All of your equipment which normally would have iron parts utilizes bronze in its construction, thereby being less inimical to your faerie nature (assuming iron has adverse side effects upon you). One piece of your armament (a single weapon or your armor) may be of the expensive variety. For armament expenses, see the weapons and armor charts in the Combat Chapter.

## Virtues: +3

**SUPERIOR EQUIPMENT OF BRONZE MANUFACTURE:** All of your equipment which ordinarily would have iron parts utilizes bronze in its construction instead, thereby being less inimical to your faerie nature. Your armaments and armor can be of the expensive type. For armament expenses, see the weapons and armor charts in the Combat Chapter.

**STANDARD EQUIPMENT OF FAERIE IRON:** All of your equipment which normally would be manufactured with iron has been constructed out of faerie iron instead. Your armaments are only of standard expense, but add 1 to all Protection (for armor) and Damage (for weapons) totals.

## Virtues: +4

**QUALITY ARMAMENTS:** Your weapons and armor are of high quality, adding 2 to your armor's Protection rating, and 2 to Damage for weapons. However, it takes a skilled craftsman (Blacksmith skill of at least 4) to properly repair your armaments. Others are able to mend them, but not restore them to their full strength, so they only receive +1 bonuses, if that.

**SUPERIOR EQUIPMENT (ONE PIECE) OF FAERIE IRON:** All of your equipment which normally would be manufactured from iron has been constructed from faerie iron instead. One piece of your equipment (a single weapon or your armor) may be of the expensive variety. For armament expenses see the weapons and armor charts in the Combat Chapter.

## Virtues: +5

**SUPERIOR EQUIPMENT OF FAERIE IRON:** All of your equipment which normally would be manufactured from iron has been constructed from faerie iron instead. Your armaments and armor can be of the expensive type. For armament expenses see the weapons and armor charts in the Combat Chapter.

## Flaws: -1

**POOR EQUIPMENT:** You can only have inexpensive arms and armor, and can only have inexpensive equipment relevant to your occupation.

# Abilities

Abilities represent what you can do beyond the outline provided by your Characteristics. All mundane skills, talents, and knowledges are covered in this area, as well as some exceptional and mystical talents.

Each Ability you have is assigned a score representing how good you are at that Ability. The number is used as a bonus or penalty to die rolls when you attempt to use the Ability. This section of the rules guides you in determining what Abilities you have and how high or low each Ability may be rated.

## USING ABILITIES

An Ability score is used as a bonus (or sometimes penalty) to a die roll when you attempt an action covered by that Ability. For almost all Ability rolls, take one Characteristic and one Ability, and add them to a roll to exceed an Ease Factor. The Characteristic chosen to go with the Ability depends on how the Ability is used. Many Abilities have standard Characteristics that are almost always used with them. For example, it is difficult to imagine a situation in which Intelligence does not modify a Legend Lore roll. Other Abilities are more variable. For example, if you are trying to lie you use Guile + Communication to determine success. But, if you are trying to detect someone else's lie, you use Perception instead of Communication.

The Storyguide must also decide how to determine success. When you use an Ability against a static force, as in the case of picking a lock, the Storyguide assigns an Ease Factor that you must beat with your roll, based on the difficulty of the task. When your attempt is directly opposed to another person's actions, such as when you chase someone, your roll is compared to the other person's roll. If the two of you are trying the same thing, like running at top speed, you use the same Characteristics and Abilities for your rolls. If you are attempting different, opposed acts (one is lying and the other is attempting to see through the lie), you may employ different Characteristics and Abilities in the rolls. The Storyguide takes into account any other modifiers that apply, such as Encumbrance, Virtues and Flaws, Personality Traits, or modifiers based on the circumstances. In case you need help determining an Ease Factor, refer to the *Ability Activities Table*.

You and the Storyguide must also decide whether the roll is stress or simple (see p.20). If your character is feeling pressured and is likely to make mistakes or do exceptionally well because of that pressure, the roll is stress. Once the die is rolled and the result announced, the Storyguide determines the result in terms of the story.

## Ability Activities Table

This table gives you some standards by which to rate the Ease Factors of various activities. Some activities require straight Ease Factors, while others must be compared to the indicated roll to be made by other characters involved.

| Task | Modifiers | Ease Factor |
|---|---|---|
| Break open a wooden door | Strength + Size | 9+ |
| Track a person through woods for one day | Perception + Track | 9+ |
| Identify a major demon | Intelligence + Occult Lore | 12+ |
| Know lore about a major demon | Intelligence + Occult Lore | 18+ |
| Stand guard all night | Stamina | 3+ |
| Make a good first impression | Presence + Charm | 8+ |
| Persuade a neutral person to help you | Communication + Charm | 7+ |
| Tell a convincing lie | Communication + Guile | Perception + Guile |
| Sneak up within two feet of someone | Dexterity + Stealth | Perception + Alertness + 5 |
| Hide in thick cover | Dexterity + Stealth + 3 | Perception + Scan |
| Leap to safety as trap door falls away | Quickness - Encumbrance + Athletics | 9+ |
| Judge a sword-wielder's skill | Perception + Sword Attack | 6+ |
| Identify a distant Covenant by insignia | Intelligence + Hermes Lore | 9+ |
| Running leap of ten feet | Strength + Athletics - Size - Encumbrance | 6+ |

Note that the Storyguide need not tell you ahead of time of the circumstances behind a roll, its modifiers, or the results of success or failure. Indeed, the Storyguide may make up the result with little forethought. The Storyguide usually has an idea of what can happen in the story and bases the results of die rolls on that idea. Furthermore, the Storyguide may make rolls on your behalf from time to time. She does so because your character is not aware of the conditions that warrant a roll. The Storyguide may simply announce the results of a roll "out of the blue."

If you attempt an action covered by an Ability, but do not have that Ability, there are three possible effects. For Talents, roll normally as if you have a score of 0 in the appropriate Ability, and make 3 additional Botch rolls if you roll a zero. For Skill Abilities, you receive a -3 penalty to the roll, as well as 3 extra Botch rolls. You cannot attempt feats that involve Formal or Arcane Knowledges without the appropriate Ability. The only exception to this rule applies to Casual Knowledges; if, during your life, you learn something that is common knowledge, like who Pope Constantine was, you might get a roll to see if you recognize the name, even if you don't have a Church Lore Casual Knowledge score.

The Storyguide can also set a minimum score that must be met to even attempt certain rolls. For instance, following a faint trail through the woods might require a Track score of 3+, no matter how good your Perception is.

Ability descriptions are general because they categorize human endeavor, something that is not easily divided into discrete units. You may try something and not know which of your Abilities applies. As a rule of thumb, if your action is covered under one Ability, it is not covered by another. For example, suppose that you want to know whether you can use your Charm Ability to win over a large gathering of peasants. You can't because Charisma, not Charm, covers presentations to a group.

# ABILITY DESCRIPTIONS

Abilities fall into three basic categories: Talents, Skills, and Knowledges. Each of these is divided into subcategories, such as Arcane Talents and Social Skills. The differences between these categories and subcategories are described in their headings.

Each description shows what actions an Ability covers. It's up to the Storyguide to determine how difficult a successful roll is to make, and just what the results of one are. Descriptions also list sample Specialties and (in parentheses) the Characteristics most often used with the Ability in question.

Feel free to invent your own Abilities. Unique Abilities, added with Troupe approval, make a character distinct and help elucidate her personality.

## Talents

Talents are untrained, intuitive capabilities. They can only be raised through direct experience, usually gained on adventures.

## Arcane Talents

Only Magi can have these Talents.

**FINESSE:** Manipulating your spells and performing special feats with them. You have to make rolls with this Ability to place objects delicately with your *Unseen Arm*, for example. The Ability is also useful for Targeting spells and other such maneuvers described in the Magic Chapter. Specialties: *grace, precision, any one Form (but not a Technique)*. (Perception)

**PENETRATION:** Getting your spell through the target's Magic Resistance. Add your Ability score to the number rolled to cast your spell, and compare the total to the target's Resistance roll. Specialties: *any one Form or Technique.*

## Awareness Talents

**ALERTNESS:** Noticing something that you're not looking or listening for. Use it when you might be surprised by someone sneaking up on you, or when something interesting is happening that you aren't yet aware of. The Ability tells you something's there, but does not give the specific information that the *Scan* Ability does. Specialties: *bodyguarding, traps, ambushes*. (Perception)

**SCAN:** Noticing things that you're looking or listening for. Used to catch or identify faint sounds, to hear someone whispering to you, or to see the riders approaching across the moor. Specialties: *keeping watch, quick scan, sea, woods*. (Perception)

**SEARCH:** Looking for something in a small area, such as trying to find a ring in a castle larder or searching for concealed doors, objects, or even people. Specialties: *in the dark, sounds, plants*. (Perception)

## Exceptional Talents

You can have an Exceptional Talent only if you buy it as a Virtue. For the purposes of interacting with magic, some Exceptional Talents are given Techniques, Forms, and spell Level equivalents. When Penetrating Magic Resistance (as described in the Magic Chapter), the Level equivalent is used as a bonus to your die rolls.

**ALCHEMY:** Creating potions, poisons, and elixirs, as well as refining alchemical substances. Non-Magi can make a potion as per the rules for Magi; your Lab Total is Intelligence + Alchemy. Alchemy is especially suited for some purposes, so you get bonuses when making certain types of potions: poisons +5, antidotes +4, healing and health +3, and transformations +2. You may also wish to indulge yourself in more esoteric pursuits, such as discov-

ering the secret of the philosophers' stone. Magi with Alchemy may add it to Lab Total when creating potions, and they get the bonuses described above (such as +5 for poisons). Specialties: *potions related to any one Technique, such as Perdo or Muto*. (Intelligence)

**ANIMAL KEN:** A profound empathy with animals that allows you to understand their motivations and feelings. Such empathy engenders a solemn love and respect for animals of all kinds. By touching and speaking softly to a wild (but not violent) animal and rolling 12+, you can tame it to your touch within a matter of minutes. Adds to *Animal Handling* rolls. Specialties: *wolves, falcons, horses*. (Intelligence, Perception)

**CONTORTIONS:** Add your score to any roll to break free of a hold or restraint, squeeze into a small space, or to get through a small opening. Specialties: *ropes, breaking people's holds, crawl, squeeze*. (Dexterity, Strength)

**DIRECTION SENSE:** You can determine which way is north on a roll of 9+. Specialties: *underground, in towns, in woods, at sea*. (Perception)

**DIVINATION:** You have some method of divining the future, which you can use to give you greater power over future events. You may influence any one die roll during a story, dictating before the die is rolled that the outcome will be a great success (roll of 20+), or a Botch. However, to affect that roll you must make a Divination roll of 8+. If your roll fails, you have no effect on the story and cannot attempt to influence events again until the next story. If your roll Botches, the opposite of your predicted event occurs. You should choose the method of your divination, which may affect how your power manifests itself. Specialties: *astrology, pyromancy (reading flames), crystal gazing, haruspication (reading entrails of slaughtered animals), prophetic dreams, rune casting, examining cracks in bones*. (Intelligence, Perception)

**DOUSING:** You have the ability to find things beneath the earth through the use of a dousing rod (usually a forked stick) and your own intuitive sense. To douse, you concentrate on the thing to be found, hold your dousing rod out in front of you, and follow the subtle motions of the rod that lead to the intended target. To find something common, like water within 15 paces, requires a Perception + Dousing roll of 9+.

The Ease Factor of your roll is higher when searching out more complex targets (i.e., water is easier to find than oil, oil is easier to find than lead, and lead is easier to find than silver). Your Ease Factor is also higher when searching for something over a large area, and when searching out a specific target (e.g., running water). If you're looking for something specific, your search fails unless you have an appropriate sympathetic connection to the thing sought (e.g., bottled water from a stream when searching for a subterranean source of running water).

When you set out to search for something, you must first designate the area in which you are searching (e.g., a field, hilltop, mountain slope). If the item sought after is not present in that area, your search is in vain (though the Storyguide may make rolls anyway to keep you guessing). When searching, make a roll at the beginning of the effort, and if successful, the Storyguide leads you to your target. If the roll fails, you fail to find anything in the designated area, and if you Botch, you may think you've found the sought-after item when it's not really there. The Storyguide usually makes these rolls for you as you don't know if the item you seek is present until you find it.

Time required to search for something depends on the size of the area searched, as determined by the Storyguide. This time must be invested whether your Dousing roll is a success or failure. Specialties: *silver, water, coal, gold.* (Perception)

**EMPATHY:** You can intuitively understand the emotional needs of others and can therefore respond to them correctly. Add your score to appropriate Communication, Presence, and Folk Ken rolls. Specialties: *warriors, those in need, anger.*

**ENCHANTING MUSIC:** When you set your mind to it, you can influence others in a *specific* way by trying to enchant them with your music. After a successful roll with a musical Ability, such as Sing or Play Lute, make a stress roll + Enchanting Music + Presence and compare the result to the following chart to see how well you affect your audience. The harder the effect sought, the higher you must roll. For a specific (as opposed to general) effect, you must sing words that people can understand. You can calm the grieving with tunes alone, but you need lyrics to convince peasants to rise up against the local lord. If you Botch, you inspire an unwanted emotion. If you, the player, actually compose and sing appropriate lyrics (and the result is somewhat pleasant), a positive roleplaying modifier should be applied. (MuMe 25) Specialties: *love, anger, pride, sadness.*

| Roll | Possible Effect |
|------|-----------------|
| 9 | Calm someone who is upset |
| 10 | Rouse someone in anger |
| 11 | Raise the morale of warriors |
| 12 | Win someone's love |
| 15 | Incite a riot |
| 17 | Calm a wild animal |
| 18 | Touch a Magus's heart |
| 24 | Win back a soul from the Prince of Darkness |

**ENTRANCEMENT:** The power to control another's will. First you must stare deeply into the other's eyes for several seconds — generally impossible in combat. Then you can verbally command the victim to perform a certain task. At that point, roll a die versus the target's Stamina to see if the command is carried out. You roll Presence + Entrancement versus the victim's Stamina roll. In addition, the victim gets a bonus according to the command, as rated by the Storyguide. (ReMe 40) Specialties: *seduction, domineering, with the prideful.*

| Command | Example | Victim's Bonus |
| --- | --- | --- |
| Innocuous | Talk to me | +3 |
| Questionable | Meet me alone at night | +6 |
| Dangerous | Put away your weapons | +9 |
| Heinous | Kill your fellows | +12 |
| Suicidal | Jump out the window | +15 |

**HEALER:** Empathic understanding of how to aid the wounded, the sick, and the suffering. Add your score to any roll to tend wounds or disease, and to the recovery rolls of any whom you tend regularly. You can also use this Ability to calm the grieving, and to soothe pains. Specialties: *disease, childbirth, broken bones.* (Presence, Communication, Dexterity)

**HERBALISM:** The combination, distillation and refinement of plants to release their inherent magical properties, for use in potions, elixirs, pastes and powders. Non-Magi can make these substances using Magi lab rules; your Lab Total is considered Intelligence + Herbalism. Magi add Herbalism score to their normal Lab Total. However, in order for Herbalism to apply as a modifier for Magi, the Form you use in the substance must be Herbam. Herbalism is particularly suited for some purposes, so you get bonuses when making certain kinds of substances: poisons +5, antidotes +5, healing and health +5, hallucinogens +3. These modifiers also apply to Lab Totals of non-Magi. This Ability also lets you identify plants, lets you know when to harvest them, and tells you plants' special properties. Specialties: *substances related to any one Technique, such as Perdo or Muto.* (Intelligence)

**HEX:** Hexes can bring injury or ruin to your enemies. You must wish a specific calamity upon a person by cursing him aloud, and the Storyguide (based on your die roll modified by Hex score) determines how much of it comes true. The full extent of your Hex strikes your victim within a day to a month. Protection by the Church or magic might prevent a hex, but a hex can often bypass Magic Resistance by affecting the victim indirectly. Sometimes the Church punishes those whose curses are widely known to have come to pass. Specialties: *revenge, fear, crops, children.* (PeMe, PeCo, PeAn, etc. 20)

| Hex | Roll |
| --- | --- |
| Cause a calf to be born with only three legs | 9 |
| Bring a debilitating illness to a family member | 15 |
| Cause the victim to be killed in a strange accident | 21 |

**MAGIC SENSITIVITY:** Sensing the aura of magic in order to identify a place or object as magical. A roll of 9+ lets you sense magic in the general area, and a roll of 15+ lets you pinpoint it in a certain object. Because you are sensitive to magic, you must subtract your Ability score from all Natural and Magic Resistance rolls you make. Specialties: *any one Technique or Form.* (Perception)

**MIMICRY:** Mimicking others' voices as well as animal sounds. Mimicry is far from perfect, and you have to make good rolls (usually 9+) to convincingly mimic a specific person's voice. Specialties: *wolf howl, specific person, sounds of pain.* (Communication)

**PERFECT BALANCE:** Keeping your balance, especially on narrow ledges or tightropes. Add your Ability score to any roll to avoid falling or tripping. Specialties: *ropes, ledges, high winds.*

**PREMONITIONS:** Sensing danger intuitively; you have the feeling that something is wrong, or likely to go wrong soon. For example, a roll of 12+ lets you anticipate an ambush the Round before it is sprung. Specialties: *cities, forests, caverns, natural disasters, ambush.* (Perception)

**READ LIPS:** You have the limited, self-taught ability to read lips. It is far from perfect, and you get many words confused. However, the Ability is vital to a deaf, illiterate person who needs to communicate, and is extremely handy for a thief. A roll of 9+ lets you catch the gist of a person's speech. Specialties: *conversations, whispers, speeches.* (Perception)

**SECOND SIGHT:** Seeing ghosts, demons, and other invisible spirits, usually on rolls of 9+. Specialties: *ghosts, demons, at night, while concentrating.* (Perception)

**SENSE HOLINESS & UNHOLINESS:** Feeling the auras of good and evil. A roll of 12+ lets you sense holiness or unholiness in a general area, and 18+ lets you sense it in a person or object. If you roll 20+ in a Divine area, you feel safe and at peace, probably losing interest in previous concerns. If you roll 20+ in an Infernal area, you are paralyzed with fright.

**VISIONS:** Receiving visions related to emotionally- or magically-laden events. Whenever it is appropriate to

the story and the setting, the Storyguide can have you make a roll to see if you have a vision. Roll a die and add the level of any realm Aura you're in; you have a vision if you roll 12+. The Storyguide must make up the vision, which could be of the past, of a possible future, or of a related but distant event. Usually visions are symbolic or confusing. Interpreting a vision correctly requires an Intelligence + Visions roll of 9+ (which the Storyguide may make secretly). Visions usually come to you at quiet times when you are in a place connected with a powerful emotional or magical event, such as the site of a patricide or diabolic sacrifice. Specialties: *past, future, over a distance, grief, death.*

**WEATHER SENSE:** On a roll of 9+, you can sense what the weather will be like the next day, or sooner if the weather is rapidly changing. Specialties: *storms, sea, temperature.* (Perception)

## Physical Talents

**ATHLETICS:** General athletic prowess, not as specialized as modern athletics. It includes moving smoothly, confidently, and with grace, and improves most gross body movements. Specialties: *grace, jump, long distance run, sprint.* (Stamina, Dexterity, Quickness)

**CLIMB:** Climbing all manner of difficult surfaces, including trees, cliffs, mountainsides, and walls. Specialized equipment is necessary for more difficult climbs. A Botch usually means a fall. (See *Falling* rules in the Combat Chapter.) Specialties: *cliffs, trees, walls.* (Dexterity, Strength)

**DODGE:** Getting out of the way of attacks and other dangers. See the Combat Chapter for the Ability's use. Specialties: *reaction to surprise attack, versus one type of attack (thrown, thrusting, unarmed).*

## Social Talents

Social Talents are closely tied to your personality and to aptitudes developed when you were very young. Therefore, during play, it is nearly impossible to gain a score in a Social Talent that you did not choose as a beginning Ability. You may, through experience, raise the Social Talents you already have as you can any other Talents.

**CHARISMA:** Possession of a certain indelible force of presence, which causes people to trust you and want to follow you. It works on audiences and groups of people the way the *Charm* Ability works on individuals. Specialties: *demagoguery, war, politics, inspirational, religion.* (Presence)

**CHARM:** Enticing, fascinating, and endearing others to you, but only on a personal basis. It can be used to win someone over to you emotionally, especially those of the opposite sex. The Ability is more a facet of your charming personality than an overt manipulation of others. Specialties: *love, first impressions; being brash, sly, or witty.* (Presence)

**GUILE:** Telling convincing lies. If you understand the person you are lying to (such as by a Perception + Folk Ken roll of 10+), you may gain a bonus to your Guile roll. Specialties: *lying to authority, elaborate lies, quick lies.* (Communication, Perception)

**FOLK KEN:** Understanding the motives, background, and personality of another person. Predictions of a person's actions, when possible, are never, ever certain. The Storyguide should secretly roll a die when this Ability is used. A "0" means that your use of the Ability fails, despite your own roll. This kind of uncertainty keeps players on their toes. Specialties: *peasants, townsfolk, nobles, clergy, wizards, the opposite sex.* (Intelligence, Perception)

**PRETEND:** Feigning an emotion, a belief, or a certain frame of mind. This Ability is similar to the *Acting* Ability because you pretend to be that which you are not, but unlike *Acting*, you do not pretend to be someone other than yourself. Specialties: *tears, anger, friendliness, passion.* (Communication)

**SUBTERFUGE:** Subtly getting the upper hand in your relations with others. Subterfuge involves figuring out the motivations and temperament of others, and then manipulating those motivations and that temperament to your own ends. Subterfuge never simply involves lying, but is a clever rendering of certain selected truths chosen for their bias in your favor. Subterfuge can be used to justify conduct, to escape the full force of an argument, or to evade condemnation or censure. Because it is such a tricky and fickle art, always make an extra Botch roll. Specialties: *bluff, cajole, whine, con, arguments.* (Presence, Communication, Perception)

## Skills

Skills are trained or possibly self-taught Abilities. You can increase them through training or direct experience.

### Arcane Skills

Only Magi may have these Skills.

**CERTÁMEN:** Fighting magical duels. Your score applies to your rolls in *Certámen.* (See the Magic Chapter for details.) Specialties: *any one Form or Technique.* (Intelligence)

**PARMA MAGICA:** Performing a magic ceremony to protect you from magic. The ceremony takes about a minute to perform. Once performed, the ceremony lets you add 5 times your Ability score to Magic Resistance rolls until sunrise or sunset, whichever comes first. You may also protect one other person for each point in your Ability score, but your score is effectively 3 points lower when protecting others (so you need a score of 4+ to do any good at all). You may cancel the effect of the ceremony at will. Specialties: *protection from any Form or Technique.*

## Forester Skills

**ANIMAL HANDLING:** Handling and use of animals, including raising them, tending them, grooming them, and dealing with their medical problems. Specialties: *falcons, dogs, horses, veterinary.* (Intelligence, Perception)

**SURVIVAL:** Finding food, water, shelter, a direct route, and relative safety in the wilderness, a very dangerous and "wild" place in Mythic Europe. The Ability covers such mundane tasks as lighting a fire (without matches) and cooking food without implements. Specialties: *woodlands, grasslands, mountains, leading groups.* (Perception, Intelligence)

**TRACK:** Following and identifying the tracks of creatures and beasts of all varieties. The Ability also involves covering your own tracks, or never leaving any in the first place. Specialties: *woodlands, mountains, swamps, tracking humans, hiding tracks.* (Perception)

## Mental Skills

**CONCENTRATION:** Focusing your mental faculties on one task, particularly for extended periods of time. If you are attempting a feat that demands your extra attention, or if you have just failed a feat and are trying again, the Storyguide can call for a Concentration roll before you can make the attempt. This Skill is especially important for Magi because it helps them maintain concentration on spells despite distractions. Specialties: *ignoring pain, ignoring sounds, concentrating for long periods.* (Stamina, Intelligence)

**DEBATE:** Proving your view superior to your opponent's through use of facts, logic and presentation. It has little effect when countering emotions because emotional people are little swayed by logic. Depending on the needs of the story, die rolls can be modified by Debate score for precise maneuvers, such as spotting an opponent's *non sequiturs* and convincing key members of the audience, or it can be used to indicate a general victory.

Specialties: *philosophy, Hermetic Law, conversation.* (Communication, Presence, Intelligence)

**MEDITATION:** Focusing on your mind and ignoring outside influences. The Ability is helpful for recovering Fatigue, for certain magical activities, and for praying. Specialties: *prayer, composing your thoughts, resting the body, controlling emotions.* (Intelligence)

## Performance Skills

**ACTING:** Playing a role before an audience. Acting incorporates the ability to mimic gestures and accents, and allows you to change your apparent personality to create a believable character. The Ability is often as useful off stage as on. Specialties: *improvisation, tragedy, soaring passions, a specific role.* (Communication, Presence)

**STORYTELLING:** Choosing an appropriate story from your repertoire (which grows with your score) and telling it well. Masters of the art can tell different stories for weeks without repeating themselves. Specialties: *poems, romances, tributes, improvisations.* (Communication)

**JONGLEUR:** Covers the skills it takes to be the professional, all-purpose entertainer and minstrel of the Middle Ages, the jongleur. Includes juggling, showy acrobatics, and slapstick humor. Jongleurs can be found in both the marketplace and noble courts — some even frequent the homes of wizards. This sort of amusement is often very coarse. Troubadours supply the more serious poetic and musical entertainments. Specialties: *antics, jesting, pranks, juggling.* (Communication, Dexterity)

**SING:** Singing well, and knowing a repertoire of songs. Everyone can sing, but this Skill indicates a level of competence that allows others to enjoy listening to your voice. Specialties: *solo, choral, ballads, lullabies, war songs.* (Communication)

**PLAY** (Specific Instrument): Performing with a certain instrument and familiarity with a repertoire of music appropriate to the instrument. Specialties: *solos, group, improvisation, vast repertoire.* (Dexterity, Communication)

## Physical Skills

**BRAWL:** Fighting unarmed and with casual weapons, such as jugs and chair legs. The Ability includes punching, kicking, grappling, throttling, gouging, and biting. See *Brawling* in the Combat Chapter. Specialties: *tackling, pinning & holding, punching, ambushing.*

**RIDE:** Riding and controlling a horse, especially under stress. Specialties: *performance, speed, in battle.* (Dexterity, Strength)

**SWIM:** A refinement of the skill most folk already have. Specialties: *rough water, diving, swimming deep, long distance, underwater.* (Dexterity)

## Rogue Skills

**DISGUISE:** You have the know how to mimic other people, or no one at all in order to fit into the crowd, by adopting special clothes, appearance, voice and behavior. Perception + Disguise rolls are required from you to convey an image. Those who might see through your disguise make a Perception + Disguise roll against your Disguise roll. The party with the higher roll wins, maintaining the disguise or seeing through it. Each party gets a modifier to their roll based on familiarity with the person mimicked (-3 for an unfamiliar person, +3 for a highly familiar person, and +3 to your Disguise roll if you have the subject for modeling). Generally speaking, rolls are made whenever someone could see through your disguise (i.e., on initial meeting, and every time you do something to give yourself away — Storyguide's discretion). A Botch on behalf of either party means your disguise is faulty but you don't realize it, or your opponent is completely duped and never sees through your disguise (no further comparison rolls are made). Specialties: *men, women, nobles, Magi, peasants, one person in particular.* (Perception)

**FORGERY:** Forging documents and wax seals. The ability to scribe helps but is not always a requirement. A roll of 12+ lets you forge a missive from a baron to one of his loyal vassals if you have a sample of one of his letters. Specialties: *ecclesiastical documents, signatures, wax seals.*

**LEGERDEMAIN:** Sleight of hand and a mind oriented towards discovering ready sources of income. It requires a delicate grace and great hand-eye coordination. Legerdemain is usually the province of petty thieves, who often get a hand cut off for their troubles. Legerdemain includes filching things from market stalls and cutting purses, as well as simple "magical" trickery — often used in confidence games, such as the shell game, to raise money from the credulous folk who play them. Stealing is usually a tricky task, so victims often get a +2 modifier to their Perception + Legerdemain rolls to catch you. Specialties: *filch, pick pockets, prestidigitation.* (Dexterity, Quickness)

**PICK LOCKS:** Opening locks without the convenience of a key, and usually without the permission of the owner. Certain locks are so intricate that a minimum skill level is required to even to attempt to open them, but these locks are very rare. Medieval locks are much larger, bulkier, and simpler than their modern counterparts. Specialties: *traps, speed, in darkness.* (Dexterity)

**STEALTH:** Sneaking about without being seen or heard. The Ability includes following people without their noticing you. This Skill may be judged according to an Ease Factor, or may be rolled against another person's Perception roll. Specialties: *hide, sneak, tail, forest, towns.* (Dexterity)

## Social Skills

**BARGAIN:** The know-how of getting the greatest return for a service or product, and of paying the least for something. It involves reading the person with whom you haggle, and presenting yourself in certain ways. A good bargainer can easily overcome resistance in an inexperienced customer. Specialties: *textiles, dealing with Flambeau Magi, dealing with superiors.* (Presence, Communication)

**DIPLOMACY:** Negotiating successfully and getting along with other people without putting on an act, overt manipulation, or letting your own desires fall by the wayside. Diplomacy Skill involves knowledge of the informal rules of conduct and politeness. Because of the value of a player's actions and speech in Diplomacy, always try to apply a roleplaying modifier. Specialties: *negotiation, politics, etiquette, tact.* (Communication)

**DRINKING:** Drinking prodigious amounts of alcohol without passing out, a familiarity with expected and acceptable drinking behavior, as well as enjoying drinking without debilitating yourself. With this skill, a person is able to have fun in a tavern, even in one of a different culture. A roll can be made to see how small a penalty is given to a character who has been drinking. Specialties: *guzzle, drinking songs, vulgarity, keeping your head about you.* (Stamina, Communication)

**ETIQUETTE:** You know the social graces and know accepted behavior in different social situations. Successful Etiquette rolls might grant you bonuses in Social Talent or other Social Skill rolls that follow. Specialties: *nobility, the court, peasants, faeries, the Church.* (Presence, Communication)

**INTIMIDATION:** Inspiring fear in others and scaring them into submission, manipulating their own fears and weaknesses to use as weapons against them. (*Folk Ken* Ability may be of help in many complimentary rolls). Specialties: *overt, subtle, threats, violence, intellectual.* (Presence, Strength, and even Intelligence)

**INTRIGUE:** Dealing and plotting, including subtle use of power in non-confrontational ways to achieve your own ends. Intrigue also involves the ability to pick up important facts about those in power, separating those facts from endless amounts of false and useless gossip. Intrigue is a vital talent for those who frequent a king or earl's court, or a Hermetic Tribunal. Specialties: *gossip, plotting, rumormongering, alliances.* (Presence, Communication, Perception)

**LEADERSHIP:** Getting people to obey your orders and to follow your lead. With a successful Leadership roll, you may add your Ability score as a modifier to another's appropriate Personality Trait rolls. For instance, you can encourage Grogs to be Brave or Cautious. Specialties: *giving orders, engendering loyalty, combat, inspiring bravery.* (Presence)

## Weapon Skills

When you choose a Weapon Skill, you pick a specific weapon. You must choose Attack and Parry Skills separately. You cannot have parry scores with throwing weapons or missile weapons. The Storyguide may allow you to use this skill at a small penalty when you wield a weapon similar to one with which you are trained. In a single Round, you cannot both attack and parry with a single one-handed weapon, but you can with a two-handed weapon. The use of Weapon Skills is explained in the Combat Chapter. Melee Specialties: *charging, tournaments, bodyguarding, fighting beasts, formation fighting, wild melees, night fighting.* Missile Specialties: *tournaments, moving target, still target, rapid fire.*

## Work Skills

**BOATING:** Handling small watercraft of all types, vital for most fishing. Specialties: *directing others, handling storms, repairs.* (Dexterity)

**CHIRURGY** [kyRURjee]: This Skill is surgery, Middle Ages style. It encompasses tending and binding wounds of all varieties, and the rather brutal, though necessary, skill of cauterization. You can use this Ability to help others recover from wounds. (See *Wounds* in the Combat Chapter.) Cauterization is necessary any time you fail, by normal means, to stop the flow of blood and requires that you have a fire and the proper implements at hand. You must make Chirurgy stress rolls for cauterization, with two extra Botch dice if you roll a "0." If you Botch, your patient loses another Body Level. A person skilled in Chirurgy is called a chirurgeon. Because the Church prohibits touching corpses and blood, chirurgeons are looked down upon, and many of them are non-Christians. Still, even good Christians find them useful. Specialties:

*bind wounds, cauterization, diagnose, set bones, poison.* (Intelligence, Dexterity)

**CRAFT (SPECIFY):** A general term for countless unrelated Skills, all dealing with handiwork of some type. Choose a craft from this list, or make up your own: baking, blacksmithing, bowmaking, carpentry, chandlery, clothiery, cooperage, engineering, embalming, fishing, glassworking, goldsmithing, hide-working, jewel-working, leather-crafting, locksmithing, masonry, millery, portrait painting, perfumery, pottery, sculpting, silversmithing, shipbuilding, smelting, woodcrafting, weaponry, wine making. Specialties: *appropriate for craft.* (Intelligence, Dexterity)

**EVALUATE (SPECIFIC ITEMS):** Knowledge of the general worth of a certain class of items and an ability to figure the worth of an item in that category. You may evaluate items of other categories with a -3 penalty. Some common categories are arms and armor, distances, artwork, foodstuffs, machines, animals, and clothing. Specialties: *appropriate for the category chosen.* (Intelligence, Perception)

**WAGONEERING:** Handling carts and wagons of all kinds, vital for trade and most farming. Specialties: *avoiding accidents, rough terrain, repairs.* (Dexterity)

# Knowledges

Knowledges are Abilities that require applications of the mind, not the body, so they almost always use Intelligence as a modifier. Many knowledges that 20th Century people take for granted, such as counting and reading, are not common among medieval folk.

You usually use stress rolls for Knowledges, even when you are not under stress. The variability of the stress roll simulates the variability of the facts you know. It is possible for someone with limited knowledge to have picked up little-known facts and for someone with lots of knowledge to miss a few bits of information.

## Arcane Knowledges

Only Magi and Companions with the Arcane Lore Virtue can have these Knowledges. The Knowledges can all be increased through study.

**ENIGMATIC WISDOM:** An understanding of the world in all its manifestations, as a Criamon Magus possesses. You have a far-reaching perception into strange and baffling phenomena, helping you understand their nature. Your score is applied to rolls to interpret dreams and riddles, and to understand phantasms and arcane or mysterious situations (such as a faerie festival). The Ability score can also be used to impress Criamon Magi, applied to social rolls in which you demonstrate a mastery over the mysterious. However, your enigmatic understanding may seem strange or even ludicrous to the uninitiated.

Whenever you roll for *Wizard's Twilight* (see The Saga Chapter), add your Enigmatic Wisdom to the roll. If you go into Twilight, you may add your Ability score to the roll for control over the experience, and may subtract it from the roll to determine how many Twilight Points you gain (though you always gain at least 1). Thanks to this Ability, Criamon Magi go into Twilight more often, but survive it better than other Magi. Specialties: *faeries, interpreting dreams, explaining the Enigma, writing verse.* (Perception, Intelligence)

**HERMES HISTORY:** Knowledge of the Order's known history, including its founders, major tomes, and pre-Hermetic roots. Experience is obtained only through study. Specialties: *tomes, Houses, legal processes.*

**HERMETIC LAW:** Judging events according to the Code of Hermes and the Peripheral Code. In addition to the memorization of important precedents, this knowledge includes the practical ability to enforce Hermetic Law — when to push for a vote, and how to present an argument. Specialties: *apprentices, dealings with mundanes, Tribunal etiquette.* (Intelligence, Presence, Communication)

**HERMES LORE:** Knowledge concerning the mystical Order of Hermes. It includes the general history of the Order of Hermes; the local, unofficial history of Magi in your specific region; the intrigues and goings on among members of the Order in your area; and a general idea of how the Order of Hermes functions as an organization, including its rules, hierarchy, and formal traditions. You can get 1 Experience Point for participating in a relevant activity, such as a Tribunal, if you decide to allocate Experience to the Knowledge. Specialties: *history, politics.*

**MAGIC THEORY:** Knowledge of what magic is and how it works, used primarily for work in the laboratory. You can sometimes gain experience through experimentation (see the Magic Chapter). Specialties: *potions, enchanting items, inventing spells.*

## Casual Knowledges

These can be studied, but one can also pick them up through direct experience — about 1 Experience Point for a month of exposure to, or participation in, a significant event, such as a faerie party.

**(AREA) LORE:** Knowledge specific to one particular region, or Covenant, or village. Includes knowledge of where things are located in the immediate area (deer trails, good fishing holes, the "hanging oak"), of the area's history and legends (the saga of a local hero, Dedra the Red), and of the centers of power and their organization in the region ("Sir Tarbil holds the real power here!"). Specialties: *geography, history, politics, personalities.*

**CHURCH LORE:** Knowledge of Christianity, especially as expressed locally, including Church politics. Specialties: *saints, clergy, history, corruption.*

**FAERIE LORE:** Familiarity with enigmatic faeries, partial knowledge of some of their powers and weaknesses, and a sense for their needs and motivations. Even with this knowledge, categorizing faeries neatly and making sense of their behavior is difficult. Specialties: *faerie forests, the Unseelie Court, faerie mounds, faerie festivals.*

**FANTASTIC BEAST LORE:** Familiarity with the magical creatures of the world, such as dragons, unicorns, and ogres. Specialties: *giants, werewolves, dragonkind, weaknesses, motivations, habitats.*

**LEGEND LORE:** Familiarity with legends and folklore, some of which may even be true. Use this lore when you are trying to remember information about some mythical place, beast, or hero. Legend Lore can often give vital insights into the weaknesses of a monster or the location of a mystic oak. Specialties: *beasts, heroes, faeries, a particular place.*

**OCCULT LORE:** An understanding of the sinister side of the world of its darker aspects. Occult Lore includes knowledge of demons, their habits, and their weaknesses; of the undead and their habits; and of the sinister power of curses. Specialties: *demons, undead, curses.*

**SPEAK (SPECIFIC LANGUAGE):** Actually speaking a particular language. Your language score is not usually used as a die roll modifier. Instead, it serves as a general measure of your ability to communicate. When two people attempt to use a language, their lower Ability level counts to see how well they get their ideas across.

Note that there is no "common tongue" in Mythic Europe; each kingdom, and often each province, speaks a different language or dialect. A skilled interpreter is often vital to the success of a journey!

Specialties: *class, expansive vocabulary, colorful phrases.*

| Score | Fluency |
|-------|---------|
| 1 | Basic ideas only |
| 2 | Basic ideas w/grammar |
| 3 | Functional, but difficult |
| 4 | Functional, but with lapses |
| 5 | Fluent |
| 6 | Impressive, worth listening to |
| 7+ | Perfect clarity and understanding |

## Formal Knowledges

Formal Knowledges are available only to Magi and to Companions with the *Educated* Virtue. Formal Knowledges can be trained or studied, but cannot be learned through direct experience alone.

**CHURCH KNOWLEDGE:** Knowledge of orthodox religious teachings and interpretations, of the history of the Church and its inner workings and hierarchy (essential for working within the Church and manipulating it to one's own needs), of the important texts of the Church and how to interpret them, of heresy against the Church (and of the Church's methods to contain, restrain, and punish it), of the Church's underlying theology, and of the ability to debate on the subject. Specialties: *doctrine, history, politics, exegesis, heresy, theology*.

**HUMANITIES:** Familiarity with all the branches of higher learning, including the Classics. Most books are rare Latin copies, and, thanks to the Arabs, some Greek texts. Specialties: *arts, science, philosophy*.

**MEDICINE:** The art of healing at a level not commonly found in medieval society. Includes knowledge of the structure and functions of the human body (the study of which the Church punishes by burning), the use of elixirs and herbs in healing (which can aid a Magus in obtaining materials for potions and other laboratory procedures), and the diagnosis and treatment of disease. Some wounds and diseases can only be cured by a person knowledgeable in the art of medicine. The Knowledge of Medicine may give you a bonus on Chirurgy rolls because you know of better salves and ointments to apply to wounds. Specialties: *anatomy, apothecary, physicianry*.

**SCRIBE (SPECIFIC ALPHABET):** Reading and writing a specific alphabet. In Western Europe, Latin serves as the common alphabet for all civilized languages. Note: in the Middle Ages reading silently is unheard of and is thought to be impossible for normal mortals, if considered at all. If you have a score of 6+ in Scribe, you have the option of being able to read silently. Also, people usually read standing up, with the book on a reading stand.

# REPUTATION

Reputation is the social aspect of your personality. Your Virtues, Flaws and Personality Traits describe how you act, and your Reputation describes how others expect you to act, and how they act toward you. It's unlikely that you have a Reputation at the beginning of the Saga (unless you have a particular Virtue or Flaw that gives you a Reputation), but you can certainly acquire one as the Saga progresses. If you have a Reputation before play begins, choose it from or roll it on the *Good* or *Bad Reputation Lists*, below, and assign it a score that you feel best describes it. You may create a new Reputation that suits your character, but the Storyguide should approve it before the Saga begins.

People normally have only one Reputation. Once you're known for a particular quality, it's difficult for people to perceive you in different ways. However, the Storyguide may allow you more than one Reputation based on your actions and Saga events. Magi, for example, sometimes have Reputations among mortals that differ from their Hermetic Reputations. Remember that Reputations are not always reflections of your true nature. They can be forced upon you by a group needing a symbol, they can come to you accidentally (e.g., you unwittingly kill as assassin who's stalking the king), or they can be made up by others (e.g., an enemy spreads word that you are adulterous).

Reputations have Specialties. These are particular qualities you are known for, even more so than your "general" Reputation. A character known for being Cunning might have a Specialty in *spying*, and so gains added notoriety for intrigue and maybe even patriotism. Reputation Specialties offer a +1 modifier to rolls where that aspect of a Reputation applies (see *Applying Reputation*, below). Specialties don't increase the area throughout which you are known, they just specify the nature of your Reputation in the area designated by your original Reputation score.

## Applying Reputation

Each Reputation has a score from 1 to 10 (5 being a practical maximum) which reflects how well you are known and how widespread your fame or infamy is. Refer to the *Realms of Reputation Table* to determine how far your name reaches. If your Reputation is high enough, it may precede you in distant lands and in foreign circles. To determine whether you are known by Reputation in a particular place, make a simple roll and add your Reputation score. The Ease Factor of the roll is usually 6, though the Storyguide may raise or lower it based on the nature of your Reputation and the likelihood of it being known in a place. If the roll succeeds, people in that place have heard of you and respond to you based on your Reputation (i.e., your Reputation score modifies social rolls you make with others).

Note that your Reputation does not extend beyond those lands or circles specified on the *Realms of Reputation Table*. People outside those lands or circles don't know you. So, those distant lands and circles are where you may develop new Reputations, if the Storyguide agrees, which stand separate from any others.

If your Reputation is known in a place, its score acts as a modifier to people's behavior toward you and to your social interaction rolls (i.e., Communication and Presence). For example, the Storyguide may award you a bonus on Subterfuge rolls if you have a Reputation for Honesty. Or, if you have a Reputation for being Vengeful, the folk of a village may be hesitant to betray you. Your Reputation can also be used as a modifier to the villagers' Personality Trait rolls to see if they tell the authorities you're in town. Keep in mind, though, that not everyone you deal with cares about your Reputation. If you are known as an Adulterer, a merchant isn't deliberately going to cheat you, unless he suspects you of sleeping with his wife. . .

Your Reputation can also be dangerous because it may incite people to interfere with your actions or act against you. For example, if you are known for being Fair-Minded, people may hassle you constantly to resolve their disputes. Or, if you are known for your Fearlessness, young upstarts may frequently challenge you, hoping to win glory as the person who bests you. And, of course, the higher your Reputation score, the more often you are called upon to fulfill or defend your Reputation. These distractions and confrontations are largely products of the Storyguide's tale. They are introduced by her when you enter a region in which you are known.

## Gaining a Reputation

To gain a Reputation you generally must be in the presence of people, and in an area, with whom and in which you have no Reputation. If you do anything worthy of public gossip or admiration, such as return taxes taken by a greedy nobleman, you gain a Reputation for your actions, usually with a score of 1 (centered on the region where the noteworthy action is performed). Fellow Troupe members and you may suggest the nature of this Reputation, like Fair or Just, but the Storyguide has final

say. As a rule of thumb, you can decide if a character gains a Reputation if she is a topic of conversation in a locale, even if just for a day or two. If this conversation affects people's understanding of your character, she probably gains a Reputation, maybe even a bad one.

The Troupe may also decide that you gain a new Reputation in a place, or with a group, wherein you already have a Reputation. Such a change requires that you perform a deed of greater notoriety than that which spawned your first Reputation (i.e., the score of your new Reputation must be higher than that of your old). Your old Reputation is generally forgotten.

It's also possible to have more than one Reputation in a region if those Reputations are restricted to isolated groups — groups that have no dealings with each other. A Magus, for example, can have a Reputation in his Tribunal and a completely different Reputation in the barony in which he lives. Magi and mortal folk within those common areas simply perceive the Magus differently, maybe with no inkling that the Magus has another "face."

## Increasing a Reputation

To increase a Reputation you must do something that exceeds the Reputation you already have. This action must also occur within the realm of the Reputation you already hold. If the Troupe deems the action noteworthy

### Realms of Reputation

| Reputation Score | Areas You Are Known |
|---|---|
| 1 | Your Covenant |
| 2 | Lands within a mile of your Covenant |
| 3 | Your Tribunal/Lands within 5 miles of your Covenant |
| 4 | Your House/Lands within 10 miles of your Covenant |
| 5 | The Order of Hermes/Your province, dukedom or barony |
| 6-7 | A magical Order other than Hermes/Your kingdom |
| 8-9 | A second Order other than Hermes/neighboring kingdoms |
| 10 | Mythic Europe |

If a Reputation is gained away from your "home," the "radius" of its influence is centered on the region or group in which or for which you perform the notable action.

## Bad Reputations

These are some unsavory Reputations that you may use. It's suggested that you select your Reputation based on your background and history. However, if you're stumped for a Reputation, or need one in a hurry, roll percentile dice on this chart.

01-07 Bad at a skill (e.g. Bad Cook, Bad Warrior)
08-09 Cruel
10-11 Violent
12 Cold
13 Impulsive
14-15 Rude
16-17 Cowardly
18 Quitter
19-20 Greedy
21 Easily Angered
22 Abusive to Animals
23 Vivisectionist
24 Arsonist
25 Warlock
26 Pushy
27 Arrogant
28-29 Brown-noser
30 Troublemaker
31 Paranoid
32-33 Cheap
34-35 Crazy
36-37 Treacherous
38 Bloodthirsty
39 Overly Curious
40 Gullible
41 Faerie Friend
42 Stupid
43-44 Pervert
45 Vengeful
46-48 Lustful
49-50 Selfish
51 Lazy
52-53 Liar
54-55 Thief
56-57 Drunkard
58 Suspicious
59 Masochist
60 Dead ("Wait. . . Didn't I hear you were dead?")

61 Dirty, Mean and Nasty
62-63 Killer
64 Cruel to Inferiors
65 Criminal
66 Disrespectful
67 Gossip
68 Sadist
69 Bumbler
70-71 Religious Zealot
72 Overconfident
73 Trickster
74 Morbid
75-76 Backstabber
77 Leave Friends to Die
78 Weak-Willed
79 Bad at *Certámen**
80 Flee in Battles
81 Child Molester
82-83 Snob
84 Easy Mark
85 Manipulative
86 Mediocre (at everything)
87 Uncaring
88 Con Man
89 Diabolist
90 Demon Spawn
91 Atheist
92 Gypsy
93 Barbarian Lover
94 Lecherous
95 Rapist
96 Adulterer
97 Sinner
98 Disloyal
99 Careless
100 Not Possessing the True Gift (for Magi) — or — Unlucky

* Reroll if not appropriate

## Exempli Gratia:

### Reputation

Robin is a Point Grog in an entourage of covenfolk who have traveled near the village of Pasaquine, a village plagued by wolf attacks. When the group is near a farmer's fields, a wolf cry is heard in the distance, and it startles a bull out grazing. In a panic, the bull charges the vulnerable party. Robin realizes what's about to happen and instinctively uses his natural strength to stop the brute. He bears down on the beast, becoming something of a bull himself. In the collision of man and beast, the bull is stopped in its tracks, and runs off defeated.

The local farmer witnesses the event and goes back to the village, intent on earning free ale with his tale of a man more powerful than a bull! Before long the farmer is exceedingly drunk, and Robin has gained a reputation for being "as strong as an ox" (1 point Reputation in the village).

When Robin gets back to the village, people are careful not to anger him, and offer their barstools lest he try to take one by force.

## Good Reputations

As with the *Bad Reputation Chart*, this chart allows you to roll up a Reputation, but it's advised that you choose your rep instead, remaining true to your character's identity, not luck.

| | | | |
|---|---|---|---|
| 01-03 | Good at a Skill (e.g. Good Teacher, Good Swordsman) | 53 | Perceptive |
| | | 54 | Hard Bargainer |
| | | 55-56 | Good Friend |
| 04 | Brave | 57 | Nobleman * |
| 05 | Loyal | 58 | Joyful |
| 06-07 | Reliable | 59 | Caring |
| 08 | Dragon Slayer | 60 | Patient |
| 09 | Wizard Slayer | 61 | Helpful |
| 10 | Good-Natured | 62 | Inventive * |
| 11-12 | Pious | 63 | Powerful |
| 13 | Compassionate | 64 | Clean |
| 14 | Just | 65 | Peaceful |
| 15 | Honorable | 66 | Optimistic |
| 16 | Chaste | 67 | Sweet-tempered |
| 17 | Forgiving | 68 | Kind to Animals |
| 18 | Generous | 69 | Civic-Minded |
| 19 | Honest | 70 | Intelligent |
| 20 | Merciful | 71 | Respectful |
| 21 | Modest | 72 | Strong-Willed |
| 22-23 | Prudent | 73 | Confident |
| 24 | Trusting | 74 | Demon Slayer |
| 25 | Valorous | 75-77 | Good Christian |
| 26 | Self-Sacrificing | 78 | Charitable |
| 27 | Loving | 79 | Noble Blood |
| 28 | Polite | 80 | Careful |
| 29 | Protective | 81 | Knowledgeable |
| 30-33 | Heroic (did something wonderful) | 82 | Strong |
| | | 83 | Lively |
| | | 84 | Well-read * |
| 34 | Faerie Slayer | 85 | Thrifty |
| 35 | True Believer | 86 | Good Warrior * |
| 36 | Excellent Orator | 87 | Determined |
| 37 | Practical | 88 | Tries Hard |
| 38 | Lawful | 89 | Friendly |
| 39-40 | Good Leader * | 90 | Easy Going |
| 41 | Good Follower * | 91 | Fun to be Around |
| 42 | Handsome | 92 | Intuitive |
| 43-44 | Well-Travelled | 93 | Temperate |
| 45 | Tough | 94 | Good Lover * |
| 46 | Witty | 95 | Nimble |
| 47 | Saintly | 96 | Crusader * |
| 48 | Chivalrous * | 97 | Hospitable |
| 49 | Good at *Certámen* * | 98 | Authoritative |
| 50 | Excellent Magic Item Maker * | 99 | Orderly |
| 51 | Virile | 100 | Arch -Mage (For Magi) — or — Lucky |
| 52 | Charming | | |

\* Reroll if not appropriate

enough, you gain another point in that Reputation, and word of your deeds spreads. To gain above a score of 3 requires a truly impressive performance, something people remember and talk about for years to come. If your spreading Reputation infringes on areas where you have another Reputation, that with the higher score prevails. The Reputation with the lower score is largely forgotten with the latest news of your exploits.

## Losing a Reputation

If you ever commit a notable deed that runs contrary to your Reputation, you lose 1 point from its score. By losing a point when you have a Reputation of 1 you lose the Reputation altogether. The Storyguide and fellow Troupe members decide when you've acted contrary to your Reputation. However, if that action occurs in a private place, and is kept from public knowledge, your Reputation does not change. Even if you do lose your Reputation, you can still acquire a new one in the region of the old one.

If you are uncertain whether your Reputation should suffer, make a Reputation stress roll. The Ease Factor is 8 (it's easier to lose a Reputation than it is to gain one; such is the way of society). If the roll succeeds, your Reputation remains true. If you fail the roll, your Reputation loses a point. If you Botch, you lose 3 points, if not the Reputation itself. Though rolling for such an image change helps you determine the change, rolling should not be relied upon. Die rolls are a last resort to roleplaying.

# CONFIDENCE

Confidence is a measure of your ability to surpass your own limits, whether they be physical or mental. It is your faith in yourself, a coolness under fire, a determination to do your best, and a command over your full potential. In terms of game mechanics, Confidence Points are used to modify stress rolls.

Most people in the world have 1 Confidence Point, profoundly defeated people have 0 points, and exceptional people have 2 or more points, with a universal maximum of 10. At the start of the game all characters begin with 3 Confidence Points. A person with high self-confidence (a score of 5 or more) is self-possessed and has a noticeable air of self-assurance, though some might see it as arrogance. Such individuals are strong enough to rely on themselves, and that faith in their own capacity translates into better chances of success in game terms — or a second chance for success.

## Using Confidence

When your character fails a stress roll you can actually make a second attempt by using a Confidence Point.

Essentially this gives you two chances at success — if at first you don't succeed, try again. You must spend a Confidence Point in order to do so, however. If the reroll succeeds, you retain your Confidence Point and may use it again during the current story. If you fail your reroll, you lose the invested Confidence Point for the duration of the current story (see *Gaining and Losing Confidence* for more details). If you Botch the reroll you lose the invested Confidence Point permanently, besides the normal effects of the Botch. You cannot use more than one Confidence Point to attempt success at a single action.

Note: Use of Confidence to get a reroll must be declared as soon as an attempted action fails. If the roll of a failed action is a zero, you must declare use of Confidence before Botch dice are rolled for the initial roll. That is, you can't discover that your initial attempt triple

Botches, and then try to escape the disaster by declaring Confidence use.

In terms of the story, a successful reroll based on Confidence is explained by your realization of imminent failure. You realize the action you are attempting is about to fail, and throw all your being into it, hoping the added effort helps you succeed. If the reroll still fails, your added effort is of no avail.

You can also use Confidence Points in connection with your Passions. Passions are Virtues and Flaws that fire your spirit and form the foundation of your identity. When you invest a Confidence Point in a situation where a Passion applies, the score of your Passion is added to all rolls you make in that scene. For example, if you have the Passion Vengeful against a corrupt priest, and want to invest all your being into acts made against him, you may invest a Confidence Point. You therefore get bonuses to all rolls that oppose the intentions and desires of the priest. These rolls include offensive rolls made against the priest and his allies, and include all defensive rolls made against his attacks on you. For complete details on the use of Passions with Confidence, see *Passions*, p.73, in the Virtues and Flaws section of this Chapter.

## Exempli Gratia:
### Confidence

Robin, the Point Grog, is on another expedition, this time with a group of Companions and Grogs from Mistridge. Their journey leads them to a small fortress occupied by the bandit Mazain and his men. The group has to rush the fortress gate to get to Mazain, and Robin leads the way. The Storyguide decides a Strength + Size stress roll of 12+ is needed to break down the door. Robin rolls an 8. Crashing into the wooden door, he is stunned by the blow and fails to burst through. Looking up, he sees archers preparing to fire from above, which will mean the death of his trailing comrades. To preserve his allies and protect his reputation as a human battering ram, Robin spends a Confidence Point to get a reroll. This time he gets a 14, and manages to burst through the gate, forcing a path for his friends to make it safely inside the fortress.

Having succeeded in the reroll, Robin retains the Confidence Point he invested, and may use it again elsewhere. He doesn't gain any new Confidence Points, though. The Storyguide decides he only performed the action expected of him and didn't get a resounding, dramatic success.

Had Robin failed his reroll, he would have lost the Confidence Point for the remainder of the story (although his allies might not have lived long enough to know their friend failed them...).

The actions into which you invest your Confidence are an expression of your personality. Putting Confidence into a roll is, in a way, putting your heart into an effort. Before you use Confidence ask yourself if your character would put his or her heart into the action in question. Some people are more likely to push themselves in desperation, others only when threatened, and others only when trying to impress the opposite sex. Use your Confidence to express the true nature of your character, for in doing so you gain new insights into the identity of your character.

## Gaining and Losing Confidence

Confidence can only be gained as an element of the story (there is no die roll to make and Experience Points cannot be used to purchase Confidence). A new Confidence Point is simply awarded by the Storyguide as reward for extraordinary success and/or prolonged unwavering effort. The point reward is also based on your character's identity. If you are afraid of ghosts, but find the courage to face one in order to protect your friends, you may be eligible for a Confidence Point. However, if you have no such fear and face the ghost, you gain no Confidence. Members of your Troupe may also help decide when your are eligible for a Confidence bonus.

At the start of a story the Storyguide may even announce that if you succeed in your mission, your character gains a Confidence Point. It's advised that no more than one point be awarded per story. So, if a character performs an action during a story that vastly increases her self-esteem, 1 Confidence can be awarded then. The one promised for successful completion of the story is made redundant by the self-esteem the character has already gained, so the second point is not awarded.

Confidence Points temporarily lost during a story (i.e., from a failed reroll) return at the beginning of the next story. They may also return if you have complete rest for a week or two, or if you decisively succeed at a vitally important task. Aside from permanently losing points to Botched rolls, the only way to lose all your Confidence is to suffer extended, dehumanizing treatment, such as slavery or torture, or through extreme trauma, such as the loss of one's true love. Grogs who are neglected and abused by Magi may lose all their Confidence, if they don't desert or rebel first.

# PERSONALITY TRAITS

In **Ars Magica** your character's identity and nature are translated into game mechanics through Personality Traits (and many Virtues and Flaws). Personality Traits are indicative of the inclinations and predilections you have. (They are more general in nature than Passions — a type

of Virtue and Flaw—which are very specific and demanding in nature.) If a Passion and Personality Trait apply to a situation at the same time, the Passion always takes precedent. Personality Traits develop your character's identity by indicating what she is like outside her Passions. They are also different in that they operate under different rules: Personality Trait scores are added to rolls to determine your behavior in a situation. Passions modify the rolls of an entire scene and can only be "activated" through the expenditure of Confidence (see Passions, p.73, to learn how they function).

## Personality Traits

The types of Personality Traits you may choose or create are unlimited. For this reason, Traits are simply listed below, and it is left to you to determine how they influence your character's identity and behavior at any given moment. Personality Traits cannot have the same names or parameters given to Passion Virtues (see p.73).

Brave
Dependable
Devoted
Honest
Kind
Violent
Respectful
Scrupulous
Upright
Wise
Cunning
Practical
Empathetic
Unreliable
Undependable
Gullible
Pensive
Distrustful
Hotheaded
Seditious
Sly
Faithless
Scornful
Naive
Witless
Frivolous
Insensitive

You can take as many or as few Personality Traits as you like. (For a listing of some of the Traits possible, see the *Personality Traits Table*.) You can even choose Traits that are somehow opposed. For example, you can choose "Leader -2" and "Follower -3." With a negative Leader score alone, people might guess you're a follower, but with both of these scores, it's obvious that you have distanced yourself from the entire leader/follower dichotomy. Another character, with a fascist-like personality, might have positive scores for both Leader and Follower, indicating both a desire to be in charge and a deference to superiors. Even when Personality scores are "opposites," a high score in one doesn't necessarily imply a low score in the other.

It's suggested that you limit yourself to five Personality Traits, with only one or two having extreme values (scores of 4 or more are only attainable by having a Virtue or Flaw that states otherwise). Otherwise you run the risk of turning your character into a caricature. Rather than playing him as a mortal human, you may find yourself chained to powerful natures running in opposite directions.

Personality Traits are integral to character identity, and you should know how they arise from your character's background, upbringing and life experience. In terms of roleplaying, Personality Traits serve several purposes. They provoke you to think concretely about the identity of your character, to better understand the true identity of the person your are pretending to be. Characters with no strong Personality Traits tend to be apathetic, indifferent creatures—freed from the chains of emotion, but without a real connection to anything outside themselves.

In terms of the rules, Personality Traits sometimes allow the Storyguide influence over your character's actions, outside your own interpretations of how your character behaves. However, they also legitimize "acting out of character." When a Reaction roll (see below) comes up that states a normally timid character suddenly behaves with bravery, the aberration is acceptable because the die calls for it. Without a concrete Personality system, any player who has a timid character act bravely is often accused of acting "out of character," even though real people surprise us all the time.

You should roleplay your Personality Traits constantly, working them into every story, using them as guides to your character's behavior. For example, if you have the Personality Trait Steadfast, you should strive to accomplish all tasks you set yourself to. If you frequently digress from this code of behavior — you become lazy or careless — and cannot adequately justify your actions, the Storyguide may penalize you with a roleplaying penalty (lowering your Experience Point award for the story). On the other hand, players who skillfully follow their Personality Traits, or admirably justify aberrant behavior, are often awarded a roleplaying bonus at the end of a story.

Sometimes Personality Traits result in confrontations between your motives and those of the Troupe. That's something you have to come to terms with, hopefully not at the expense of your character's identity, or the unity of your gaming group.

## Reaction Rolls

Sometimes, during roleplaying, situations arise where there is some ambiguity as to character action. You simply cannot decide what your character does. In those situations you may act based on the results of a Personality Trait roll. For example, if a frightening beast confronts your Grog, you must decide what action is taken. Your better judgement (and that of your friends) tells you to run. However, you have the Personality Trait Brave +3, so your spirit tells you to stand and fight. The Storyguide assigns

## Exempli Gratia:
### Choosing Personality Traits

Because she is not physically impressive, Isabel can use some interesting Personality Traits. So far it has been determined that she is practical above all else; Isabel should have Personality Traits that not only support this trait but that go beyond it.

Devoted +2: she is unlikely to be tempted to betray her commitments to others by such distractions as fear, greed, or laziness.

Practical +5: Her Virtue of Strong Personality lets her have three Personality Traits with scores as extreme as +6 or -6.

Appreciates Art +2: Her appreciation of art creates the possibility of interesting internal conflict with her practical bent. A Trait like this keeps her personality from being completely one-sided.

Frivolous -6: She takes the lowest possible score for this Trait. It coincides with her Practical Trait, indicating her aversion to silliness.

Isabel runs the risk of being a caricature because her practical side is so strong. Isabel's player will have to be careful to develop other sides of her identity. As Isabel is still entitled to one more Personality Trait of extreme score, as offered by her Strong Personality Virtue, she may acquire that Trait during the game, but such an extreme score in it may not alleviate her caricature problems.

Giving your character a strong, almost exaggerated personality allows you to get into the persona at first, but a more rounded personality must be developed to keep the character interesting.

# Exempli Gratia:
## Personality Rolls

Isabel sits quietly as the others in her group enjoy themselves at an inn. She expects the Grogs to handle themselves with reserve and dignity. However, they are drinking, joking, bragging and generally carrying on. Since she is sensitive to frivolity and tends to speak her mind, Isabel feels like berating them for undisciplined behavior. She tries to hold back out of loyalty to Grimgroth, though, who gave them leave to have fun.

She decides that a Personality Trait roll is in order — Practical +5 versus Devoted +2. Since this is her first journey with the covenfolk, she wants to make a good impression. The die turns up 9 + 5 = 14 for Practical, and 6 + 2 = 8 for Devoted. Since the Devoted roll is lower, Isabel invests a Confidence Point to make a reroll, which results in 8 + 2 = 10. Since both Devoted rolls are lower than the Practical roll, Practicality rules the moment. Isabel stalks over to the Grogs and other Companions, assumes a superior demeanor, and scolds them cuttingly. (The player roleplays the scene out.) Appeased, she returns to sit by Grimgroth, who looks at her puzzledly.

Since Isabel failed the roll she invested Confidence in, she loses a Confidence Point for the duration of the story. This loss of confidence is explained by a disappointment in herself for being unable to follow Grimgroth's lead.

an Ease Factor and you must roll a stress die, modified by your Brave score, to determine what happens. If your roll exceeds the Ease Factor, you stand and fight. If it fails, you turn and run. Characteristics and Abilities, as well as circumstantial modifiers, may also apply to these Personality Trait rolls. A Personality Trait usually manifests itself with a roll of 6+.

If you have two opposed Personality Traits, like Leader and Follower, as discussed above, you may have to make comparison rolls between the two to determine what action you take. The Trait that receives the higher roll is the one that determines your behavior. See the example provided for a demonstration of this rule.

A Personality Trait roll that results in a Botch causes the character to act in a manner opposite to the type of Personality Trait she has. For example, if you are Deceitful +2, and get a Botch using that Trait, you behave as if Honest +2. If a character gets a result of 20+ in a Personality Trait roll, she cannot be made to relent from the Trait for the entirety of the scene, unless physically restrained (in which case she may even turn on her friends). In such extreme cases "Brave" becomes "Foolhardy," and "Devoted" becomes "Fanatic." Roleplay it out.

If the results of a successful Personality Trait roll shortly prove suicidal (maybe the monster cannot be beaten), the Storyguide may allow another roll, assuming a Botch was not made. The roll may be the same as that made earlier, or may be different, reflecting common sense (e.g., Brave - Intelligence; courage is tempered by common sense, making you realize the folly of further brave actions). Such a "strategic withdrawal" is not necessarily a sign of weakness. However, if the foe you face is your greatest enemy, it's probably considered cowardice to withdraw, regardless of imminent death.

The results of a Personality Trait roll may also have drastic effects on your character's life. In the above example, if you stand and fight as a result of a Brave roll, you might die. But, if you turn tail and run, you may feel shame for what you consider cowardice. After a failed Brave roll the Storyguide might impose a penalty to successive Brave rolls, until you make another successful one, at which point you regain your self-esteem. The effects of other successful or failed Personality Trait rolls are different, but all have a significant impact on your character's self-perception and spirit.

Though this rolling system is effective for determining character action, it should not be resorted to frequently. Rather, the Storyguide may demand a choice from you, forcing you to decide and contend with the results of your choice. If your choice defies character identity as the Storyguide perceives it, and cannot be adequately justified, you may suffer an Experience penalty.

# Gaining and Losing Personality Traits

When you create a character you establish the basic zeal — Personality Traits — that puts fire in his belly. Those Personality Traits can only be changed by major events in the character's life. It's up to the Troupe to determine if one of your Personality Traits changes score after a story event. If you are Violent, for example, and are grossly humiliated by a baron who lives to tell the tale, the Storyguide may decree that your Violence score increases by 1 point. Alternatively, if you are Respectful to other people, but a particular maiden is cuttingly scornful in return, you might lose 1 point of your Respect for others. The two can certainly be combined. If the maiden scorns you in favor of the baron, you might lose 1 point of Respect and gain 1 point of Violence. Also keep in mind that a Personality Trait cannot exceed a value of +3 or -3, unless you have a Virtue or Flaw that states otherwise.

If you think a Personality Trait change is valid you can petition the Storyguide for the change. If you already have a score of +1 in a Trait and want that score lowered, your Trait score can drop to zero. Further changes in the Trait may increase it again, or decrease it even further. For example, if an abused Grog drops from a Devotion score of +1 to zero, he may drop again to -1 or lower, becoming increasingly disloyal to his masters. Alternatively, a Grog with a Devotion score of -1 can accumulate positive Trait points, acquiring a positive Devotion score. The Storyguide has final say on all such changes.

Personality Traits as a whole can also be lost or gained during the course of the Saga, though it's rare. Again, the Storyguide must agree that the loss or acquisition is justified, and you must insure that the change suits your character's identity. If you exact revenge on the baron and others who mock you, you may purge all the Violence from your soul. Their destruction constitutes the loss of your Personality Trait.

Personality Traits can be gained through epic, heart-wrenching story events, after which your character's soul is forever touched. For example, if you witness wide-spread human injustice, as in an unfounded witch hunt, the Storyguide may decree that your Respect for others is lost. But, you may acquire the Personality Trait Jaded instead. In most cases where a Personality Trait is lost it should be replaced by another appropriate to the situation. If no new Personality Trait readily comes to mind, it's suggested that you adopt a new one sometime soon in the Saga. The new Personality Trait may be justified as an emotional replacement for the last, filling your spiritual void.

# SIZE

Every creature and person in Ars Magica has a Size rating, which is an indication of how tall and/or broad they are. Average Size is 0, which is about that of an adult human. Size determines the number of Body and Fatigue Levels (see below) a creature has. Its score is also added to your Soak total (which is used to absorb weapon damage) and is subtracted from your Defense total (used to avoid being struck in combat). Size can also, at the Storyguide's discretion, influence such rolls as Stealth and Intimidation. By and large, Size score is more important for comparisons between creatures of different species than it is for creatures of the same species. The *Size Table* gives some standard scores.

# HEALTH

The health of your character is instrumental to his survival. There are many ways to jeopardize your survival in **Ars Magica**; Mythic Europe is a harsh, violent place. Disease, famine, exposure, and premature decrepitude are all threats to your character, but as you are a traveler and explorer, death in battle and by magic are by far your greatest worries. Though rules for suffering harm are largely covered in the Combat and Magic Chapters, some of the mechanics behind those rules are presented here so you have an understanding of how your character is vulnerable.

## Body Levels

When combatants fight, the damage they deal out and receive is kept track of in terms of Body Levels. After receiving a certain amount of damage (i.e., losing a certain number of Body Levels), your character is impaired and may be killed. You have a certain number of Body Levels, but if you have a higher than average Size you have more Body Levels. The average person has one of each of the following Body Levels: "Unhurt," "Hurt," "Light Wounds," "Medium Wounds," "Heavy Wounds," and "Incapacitated." As you suffer more wounds and lose more Body Levels, you suffer penalties to many of the rolls you make, as pain clouds your mind and inhibits your body. If you lose Body Levels beyond "Incapacitated" your character is dead or wounded so badly that death is imminent and inevitable.

## Fatigue

When your character exerts herself she runs the risk of tiring, and extended exertion heightens the chance of exhaustion. Your capacity for exertion is reflected in Fatigue Levels. As with Body Levels, there are six: "Fresh," "Winded," "Weary," "Tired," "Dazed," and "Unconscious." When you exert yourself, whether through combat, spell casting, some prolonged effort, or daily labor, you must make Fatigue rolls, based on your Stamina and Encumbrance scores. If these rolls fail, you lose Fatigue Levels. Sometimes the loss of Fatigue Levels is automatic, as it can be with spell casting. Any loss of Fatigue Levels results in mounting penalties to the efforts you make. These penalties are cumulative with those incurred from lost Body Levels. If you lose enough Fatigue Levels, you are "Unconscious."

| Size Table | |
|---|---|
| **Size** | **Example** |
| -5 | Mouse |
| -4 | Crow |
| -3 | Infant, Cat |
| -2 | Child, Dog |
| -1 | Adolescent |
| 0 | Adult Human |
| +1 | Huge Human |
| +2 | Horse, Bear, Stag |
| +3 | Ox, Heavy Horse |
| +4 | Elk |
| +5 | Elephant |
| +6 or more | Dragon |

## chapter four

ne of the most distinguishing and intriguing features of **Ars Magica** is the concept of the Covenant. While other roleplaying games may touch on the idea of a home base for the characters, few embellish upon the concept or make it an integral part of the ongoing campaign. The Covenant is the most important character of your Saga, for the Covenant is the constant character in your Saga. Players' characters may come and go, but the Covenant remains and is the refuge of those transient people who reside in it. It's therefore important to understand and develop every aspect of your Covenant, for it is the foundation of your game. Otherwise, your game may suffer from shallow stories and uninspired narratives. This Chapter tells you what a Covenant is, talks briefly about the role it plays in Mythic Europe, leads you through the steps necessary to create your own Covenant, and furnishes a concrete example of such a Covenant and how it might change with time.

Readers interested in expanded Covenant creation rules, along with detailed examples of Covenants, are referred to the **Ars Magica** supplement **Covenants**.

# What is a Covenant?

Simply put, a Covenant is a group of Magi who live together. That's all there is to it. They can live in a hole in the ground, in a castle, in the tops of trees, or on the deck of a ship — it doesn't really matter. What does matter is that these Magi, whether they like each other or not, have gathered together, pooling their resources to provide themselves with a relatively safe haven from the intrusions of the outside world. It's a natural enough thing, for the world isn't always kind to Magi. Nobles find them a threat to their authority, peasants fear them and have been known to form mobs to hunt them down, and the Church, of course, believes them emissaries of the Dark One.

In this harsh environment a solitary, inexperienced Magus is hard pressed to do more than stay alive, much less find time to develop his skills or research new spells. So, upon completing their apprenticeship, most Magi seek the safety of their own kind. Some are drawn towards the stability of an established, older Covenant, knowing that they have to fight for respect and acknowledgment from the older, more knowledgeable Magi. Others, intrigued by their freedom after a long, trying apprenticeship, find other young Magi willing to embark with them upon the adventure of creating a new Covenant. Whatever their individual choices, all but the most eccentric and egotistical of Magi realize the benefits of the "system" and eventually join the Covenant of their choosing.

The ideal Covenant provides each Magus with a comfortable and safe place to live, an extensive library (both magical and mundane) to assist in research, and a spacious, well-appointed laboratory in which to conduct arcane experiments without disturbance. Unfortunately, few Covenants ever reach this idealized state, and the few who come close do so only after decades, if not centuries, of struggle and hardship. Many problems waylay such utopia: a proper site must be found, plans made, money obtained to build or buy the structure (which must also be able to withstand attack), laborers and skilled craftsmen hired to perform necessary work, books collected into a meager library, agents sent to purchase the proper laboratory equipment, servants hired, and last but not least, a force of men-at-arms convinced to live at the Covenant to provide for its defense. The formative years provide a Covenant with most of its problems, which loom constantly: a source of income must be found; alliances (or at least uneasy truces) need be made with neighboring villages, nobles, and clergy; and those living at the Covenant must be provided with food, safety and shelter. All of these factors counteract efforts to provide the ideal work and living place for Magi.

While a Covenant revolves around its Magi, it could not exist without the help of the numerous mundane folk who also make the Covenant their home. Of greatest importance, at least superficially, are its men-at-arms, or Grogs. They are the strength of the Covenant, and serve a myriad of roles. They man its defenses in times of need, and patrol the area, keeping it clear of bandits, wild animals and other potentially dangerous foes. Some have more pedestrian roles at the Covenant, like the cook, manservants, and stable hands. Select Grogs, known as *custos*, serve as bodyguards to Magi when travel is necessary, and perform a variety of other tasks as needed, like running to town for supplies or hunting for fresh meat in the winter.

In addition to Grogs, a handful of Companions make the Covenant their home. These are people who, for various reasons, live or spend a great deal of time at the Covenant. They typically have the freedom to come and go as they please, but often have fairly strong reasons for aligning themselves with the Covenant. In return for food, shelter and services the Companion is allowed to call the Covenant home. Examples of Companions include a forester recently declared an outlaw by the local nobility, a recently orphaned street urchin (with a quick wit and nimble fingers), a heretical priest who hopes to convert the Magi, or, the bored, youngest son of a minor noble who is cursed with a strong intellect, ready wit, and visions of the future.

# THE COVENANT'S PURPOSE

While the definition of the Covenant as a group of Magi who live together is certainly true, it doesn't convey the depth or importance of the entire concept. "So all of the characters live together," you might say, "what's the point?" The point is that the Covenant is more than a bunch of Magi, Grogs and Companions living in a small castle — the Covenant is a character itself, a meta-character if you will, that serves many essential functions in the game.

First of all, the Covenant provides a rationale for your characters to live together and be considered a cohesive group. This may seem obvious, but it is an important fact. Without the structure of the Covenant there is little reason for a group of temperamental Magi, general misfits, and mercenary henchmen to live together. Within the Covenant, these people have

a reason to coexist, regardless of personal conflicts and problems — which can get quite heated at times. The Covenant serves as the glue that binds together these outcasts from medieval society.

Second, the Covenant gives all characters a set of common goals and interests. The most basic of these is survival, for if the Covenant is destroyed, the characters, both magical and mundane, most likely come to great harm as well. Thus, each person living there has a vested interest in the continued well-being of the Covenant. If there is friction between the Grogs and the Magi it is likely to be forgotten in the face of an angry mob of peasants or a plague of Hellish demons.

A longer-term goal of the Covenant is progress. Improving the defenses, finding new sources of *vis* or income, building up the mundane or magical library, and raising or training new Grogs benefits all. Regardless of individual priorities, improving the Covenant's overall power can serve to focus individual ambition into unified purpose. All the Magi might not agree, for example, on the particulars of how to obtain a powerful magic item from a band of local faeries, but all agree that getting it will be useful. Thus, they are willing to put aside their differences (well, mostly anyway) for their common goal.

Besides unifying the characters and giving them common goals, the Covenant provides an identity for your Saga that persists throughout all but the most catastrophic disasters. If your Magus or Companion dies, simply make up a new one that has reason to join the Covenant, show up at the gate and request admittance. Introducing new characters can be as easy as that. Though some memories, knowledge and skills are certainly lost when a character dies, the Covenant as a whole continues much as before. In this fashion, the story of your Covenant can far outlast the lifetimes of the founding characters. While the lives and adventures of individual characters are important in the short term, it is the life of the Covenant that unifies them all and is of overriding importance in the long-term.

In essence, the Covenant is a character, the *primary* character of **Ars Magica**. From the moment of its creation, the Covenant begins to grow, evolve and change in response to the goals, successes and failures of the individuals who create it. And when (or rather, if) it is destroyed, the Saga of all the characters who form the Covenant also comes to an end, for without the Covenant to hold them together, they certainly drift apart to follow their own particular goals. The exciting thing is that while it lasts, you and your friends are working together, overcoming threats and dangers to your mutual home, trying to make your Covenant work in spite of the forces arrayed against you. This feeling of community and common purpose is rare in the harsh reality of Mythic Europe, and can make your life worth living in an otherwise desperate world.

# THE FOUR SEASONS

The following is an excerpt from the folio *Magic, Mysteries and Musings: Vol. I* by Davnavolus, Follower of Bonisagus. This particular section contains his musings upon the commonly held "four seasons" view of Covenant development first postulated by the Magus Dionasius of House Bonisagus in *The Changing of the Seasons of a Covenant."* This excerpt has long been the favorite of apprentices for both its clarity and style.

*I often wonder upon the meshings of the universe, its hidden cogs and gears whirring beyond sight, for what other causes can there be for such synchronicities as so often appear between man and nature? It is as though we humans, and to a lesser extent animals, cannot help but mimic those great invisible gears and wheels that we nevertheless perceive in some unfathomable way. For aware of them we are, and aware of them we have always been, as evidenced in the pagan rites of the eldest religions. Even our most distant ancestors understood that life, like the seasons, turns on a great wheel. Again and again my thoughts return to this subject. But perhaps the reader does not follow my logic? Allow me to clarify, by example, with elucidations upon the theories of Dionasius, who first placed this theory to parchment.*

*Cycles surround us, engulf us, and permeate our very beings from the day we are born to the day we die. Life and death, in fact, is the cycle of which we are most keenly aware, but there are countless others, both here on the solid earth and high above within the heavenly aether. Some argue that the cycle of day and night is most influential in shaping our natures, but I (and others) would argue that the yearly progression of the seasons is that which has enchanted our souls, guiding our actions and thoughts far beyond the simple realm of planting and reaping. For what is a day but a year in microcosm?*

*Many have applied the analogy of the seasons to human and animal life as follows. When we are born, we are as the Spring, growing and full of vigor, though weak in both body and mind. We are quite vulnerable at this stage, both to dangers from without, like disease and wild animals, and to our own foolishness and inexperience with the world. As we age and our bodies mature, we pass into Summer's realm, full of highest strength and confidence, though this may not yet be recognized by our elders. In Summer we have reached the peak of body and intellect, strong yet flexible, having learned from our mistakes of Spring and not yet succumbed to the rigidity of Autumn. In Autumn, our peak of Summer is past, though is not yet forgotten by those around us. We begin to close our eyes and ears to new things and our strength declines, but we may still hold great power, arising from our previous experience and knowledge. Autumn lasts as long as we can harvest the fruits of our youthful labors.*

*Eventually, our bodies and minds decline such that this reputation fades and we slide slowly into the relative quiet of Winter. No longer strong in body or supple of mind, we are left with our memories and a lifetime of knowledge. We may live in quiet obscurity, watching the distant world through agéd eyes, or kingdoms may seek our sage advice, swirling and toppling through our machinations. However Winter treats us, we are all one before the irresistible, final pull of time's tide. Or is it final? Certain faiths believe in the rebirth of the spirit into other forms and other lives —*

a continuation of the cycle anew, paralleling the rebirth of Spring we ourselves know so well.

So too may this cycle of the seasons be applied to kingdoms, dynasties, empires, and other human endeavors. The Romans, for example, had a turbulent Spring and a short but strong Summer followed by a long, drawn-out Autumn based on the strength of that Summer. Even our very own Order of Hermes is not exempt from the pull of the pattern. Our Spring was filled with persecution and uncertainty, a transition to the true strength of Summer with the invention of formulaic magic and Parma Magica by the esteemed Bonisagus. And then what? Where are we now? Some would say we are stagnating into an Autumn with the roots of transition in the schism war, while others insist we still grow and prosper in the strength of Summer. I leave my own musings upon this question for a later date, for still, in my own circular way, I have not come to the point I so wish to make.

And that is: Covenants too, follow this pattern. A new Covenant is as fresh, weak, inexperienced and naive as Spring. Its members are quick from apprenticeship and have little knowledge of the world beyond their masters' stern glare and a few dusty tomes (of which, I dare say, this is one). Now they must learn and grow, and do so quickly, if they wish to reach the safer waters of Summer. Many Covenants, like human and animal infants, do not live past childhood. And beware, young ones, not only of the dangers of

mundane society with its petty nobles, feuding clergy and ignorant peasants, but also of the Order itself. Some Covenants (especially those in Autumn) are filled with beings just as petty and cruel as the mundanes they abhor, and think nothing of pinching a young Covenant in the bud if given reason or inclination. Make quickly for Summer if you wish to survive!

Those Covenants surviving to Summer may rest a while, though they usually choose not to. Now they are strong and presumably wise enough to avoid most overt confrontations, while still being filled with the vigor of youth. Most have resolved any difficulties with nearby mundanes, and spend their time in the quest for magical knowledge. During Summer they reach their peak of magical prowess, and now other, more established Covenants begin to see them as a true threat. In this they are correct, for your needs, desires and plans often coincide or conflict with those of other Covenants, putting you at odds. But don't expect a direct magical assault. The Code forbids it, and older Covenants are often filled with agéd Magi tottering on the brink of Twilight, afraid of using their full magical power for fear of toppling over the edge. Thus, they may attack you not with magic, but instead seek to stunt your growth with incessant political pressure from the within the Order and, to a lesser degree, from mundane sources. Members of a Summer Covenant must weather this political storm, all the while gathering their own allies and weeding out their enemies, in addition to continuing to strengthen their magical might.

A sure sign of transition into Autumn is the Covenant's increased reliance upon magical power from without (in the form of magical items and artifacts) rather than from within (its own aging Magi). Internally, the Covenant often becomes hierarchical as the older members tighten the reins on incoming younger Magi to insure they remain comparatively weak. Elders in an Autumn Covenant also pursue this course on the level of the Order itself. They seek to intimidate and dominate younger Covenants while maintaining their own position within the Order. Thus, political motives often consume the lives of powerful Magi, denying them the opportunity to pursue and further improve upon their own magical arts. It is during this time, when magical power wanes, that the Covenant is strongest politically. The chief danger to an Autumn Covenant is internal—watch ever vigilantly for the stagnation and corruption that can lead to Winter.

Eventually, Autumn Covenants are shouldered aside by younger Covenants into the cold of Winter. This transition can be slow and gradual, as a mighty Covenant's power base slowly ages and erodes, or it can be triggered by a catastrophic event that shatters the Covenant's might in a matter of moments. When the Magi no longer have the strength or inclination to further their Covenant's aims, the transition is complete. This is the mark of a true Winter Covenant — the apparent loss of its magical and political might. The Covenant's Magi may still hold great power, but simply forget they have it or lose all desire to use it for anything but their own unfathomable goals.

But, you must still be wary of Winter Covenants, for though they may seem doddering and powerless, they can strike as swift and true as the serpent when sufficiently aroused from their dazéd slumber. Of course, they may also be content to bask in the slowly setting sun, warily guarding their hard-earned knowledge from those who would see it destroyed. Nevertheless, I repeat my warning — beware! Instead, if you dare brave their ancient halls and eccentric customs, seek the treasure of their immense knowledge and vast experience. Ofttimes hard to find and harder still to comprehend, this treasure is usually wasted as the Covenant drifts further and further from the world, its memory fading until it is lost forever, its halls in ruin and its inhabitants long dispersed or buried. And so in Winter the cycle ends.

Or does it? For many, the wheel stops and the Covenant becomes a mere memory, a collection of names and events passed from Parens to apprentice. For other Covenants, however, the wheel keeps turning and phoenix-like, it may leap anew from the ashes of its ruins. Such cases are rare, but young, dedicated Magi in sufficient numbers may provide enough strength, vigor and courage to break the icy grip of Winter's frost and allow Spring to begin again.

And so I, Davnavolus, come to the end of my musings, having said much, but leaving much unsaid. For who can predict the turnings of the great wheel? Its gears and intricacies affect us all, but how shallowly we know this, how adroitly we avoid thinking upon it. Even I choose only to see the rising crests before me, looking always to the peak and never to the downward slopes that follow. The night is upon me and my head and hand are weary, so now I must leave until the morrow, my friend. Until the wheel turns unto dawn once more.

## The Oath

Joining a Covenant is a serious business, perhaps the most important point in a young Magus's life. The Covenant becomes his home, the covenfolk his family, and the Covenant's reputation his own. The Covenant shapes his views and, in turn, he has a hand in shaping the Covenant's. The Covenant's strengths make him stronger and its weaknesses provide numerous challenges. In short, the bond between a Magus and his Covenant is immeasurably intimate and strong, one that cannot be broken without invoking the wrath, not only of one's fellow covenfolk, but of the entire Order of Hermes. In rejecting your Covenant, you also reject the Order and all that it stands for.

Thus, it is not surprising that most Covenants enforce a lengthy ceremony of initiation upon new member to impress upon them the seriousness of this bond. Each Covenant's initiation is a highly personal, highly secret affair usually only observed by senior Magi. In general, however, it usually culminates in an oath spoken before the entirety of the assembled covenfolk, both magical and mundane alike. Though the oath's particulars may vary from Covenant to Covenant, most are similar enough in style, wording and content to make it worthwhile to present a representative oath here.

"The Oath," as composed by Consuelia, founder of Mistridge, in the year 1067. To be memorized and solemnly repeated to the gathered Covenant at the conclusion of initiation rites. Upon its completion, the entrant signs in full view a manuscript containing the words spoken, which is then placed in the Covenant's archives.

I, Grimgroth of House Jerbiton, do humbly ask for acceptance into the Covenant of Mistridge. I do so of my own will, under no influences other than my own; no magicks or powers mundane force me here today. I understand that my life is forfeit should this or any other part of my oath be found false. Here I stand, with full knowledge of what I do.

I swear by the Order, my life, and all I hold dear, that I am Grimgroth follower of Jerbiton, filius of Vlaria, fully trained solely in the ways of Hermetic Magic and none other. I here truthfully state I have never consorted with or aided demons, diabolists, or practitioners of magic other than those sanctioned by the Order, and will continue this practice as long as I live.

I further swear the title of Magus is properly mine, being conferred upon me by Nostrorum in the year 1067, at the Covenant Duresca, within the Iberian tribunal. I, Grimgroth, do now renounce all ties, oaths and loyalties, binding or otherwise, to my filius and the Covenant of my apprenticeship.

Now I begin anew, and give myself wholly to Mistridge. I understand all that this entails, and agree to all terms within the Covenant charter for now and for all time. In addition, I swear to follow both the Code of Hermes and the Peripheral Code, lest I lose my title of Magus, position within my House, and place within this Covenant.

From this day forward, Mistridge shall be my home. I agree to make Mistridge's goals mine own, its allies mine own, its enemies mine own, its riches mine own, and its hardships mine own. I swear never, by action or inaction, to allow the Covenant to come to harm, in the physical, magical, spiritual, or personal sense. I agree never to represent Mistridge to others, sign binding pacts, or make oaths regarding its members or its welfare without first being so empowered by the Covenant. In all respects I will uphold the reputation and honor of this, my new home, and consider its welfare above my own.

This is my solemn covenant. Mistridge's very life is now mine own,

Grimgroth.

## THEME

During the character creation process it is often helpful to have a central theme around which your character is built. This can be something as simple as "I want a wizard who specializes in Auram spells," or as complex as "I'm picturing a person who is driven by the need to gather knowledge, but is incapable of using it effectively for her own ends." Regardless of complexity, a theme tells something about your character and provides a skeleton upon which to base all other aspects of character creation. A theme also helps answer questions about your character. At each step during creation you can ask, "How does this relate to the theme of my character?" and may make the appropriate decision.

A Covenant should have a theme, like a character, and since the Covenant is the Troupe's character, all members of the Troupe should agree upon the theme. Provided here is a selection of Covenant themes you may choose from. Of course, you may create more, and you may select more than one if your Covenant has disparate or complex motivations. Keep in mind that these themes are supposed to aid you in Covenant creation, not restrict you. They are available to use or not use as you see fit. As an alternative, you can just start creating your Covenant and see what happens, allowing the theme to form during the creation process. Note that these themes can be as pervasive or unassuming as you like. Some may deal with the entire Covenant, while others may only apply to a few members.

## Covenant Themes

**Improvement:** Your Covenant, or some group of people within your Covenant, is devoted to improving itself. This is a common theme for Spring Covenants (all Magi) and Winter Covenants (the young Magi).

**A Need to Belong:** For some reason, your Covenant feels like it doesn't belong in its surroundings, be they Hermetic, social, or physical, and wants to change that. Or, someone or something wants desperately to join your Covenant.

*Examples:* A Covenant or group of Ex Miscellanea Magi who want their tradition accepted as a full House within the Order. A Covenant of Merinita Magi who wish to be accepted by the High Faeries. A group of Magi who want to be accepted by the Church, the nobles, or the peasants. An extreme case of this might be the secret remnants of House Diedne seeking acceptance in the Order. Or, a hedge wizard or other magical being wishes to join your Covenant.

**Mystery:** Some mystery is central to your Covenant. You are either trying to solve the mystery, or keep the mystery hidden from others.

*Examples:* Your Covenant is built on the ruins of an older Covenant. Who destroyed it and how? Or, your Covenant is experimenting with magic that is not Hermetic in origin. If the Order were to find out, there would be trouble. Or, perhaps your Covenant itself is a mystery to either mundanes or the Order. Your Covenant might exist within the sewers beneath a town or within the court of a local noble. Or, your Covenant possesses a powerful artifact which it does not know how to use.

**Power:** Your Covenant seeks after pure power, usually of a particular type. Some seek power for selfless reasons, while others seek it to dominate or destroy.

*Examples:* Your Covenant craves political power, and hopes to force the Order/nobles/Church to follow your own agenda. You seek immense magical power in the form of new spells, *vis* or artifacts. You are diabolists seeking to control hordes of demons.

**Dominance:** You wish to dominate some person, place or organization. This dominance can be benevolent or your goal may be to destroy them utterly. This is closely related to *Power* (above). Note that your Covenant can be on the receiving end of this theme.

*Examples:* Your Covenant wishes to have its own serfs and fiefdoms like any other noble (this is tied to *A Need to Belong*). A group of diabolists trying to infiltrate the Order and bring it down. A Covenant with a desire to control all animals/people/ plants for miles around. Or, perhaps someone (a powerful enemy like a demon, a secret society or other organization) is trying to dominate *your* Covenant.

**Unorthodox:** Your Covenant differs in some significant fashion from others within the Order. This difference shapes much of day-to-day life within the Covenant.

*Examples:* Your Covenant is nomadic, wandering according to whim or need. It could be based on a ship, on horseback, or in wagons that roam the plains. Perhaps your Covenant lives in a tent city in the desert, relying on stealth rather than stone walls to resist foes. Or, your Covenant has an odd source of income. Perhaps it supports or even runs a thieves' guild in a nearby city. Or, like Bellaquin, you could have an unusual location, like at the center of a city, or at the bottom of a lake or river, or in a *regio*.

**Evangelists:** Some Magi within your Covenant have strong beliefs and spend much of their time attempting to spread those beliefs to others.

*Examples:* A Covenant of Flambeau Magi who wish all-out war with the mundanes. A Covenant of Criamon Magi who like disrupting people's everyday lives in odd ways so those people experience life more fully. Or, your Covenant could simply be trying to establish or reestablish its prestige within the Order.

**Seekers:** Your Covenant is devoted to gathering something it treasures. This may be for selfish or selfless reasons.

*Examples:* A Covenant of Magi devoted to investigating legends of the Old Ones. A group of Magi determined to find a way to create life. A group of Magi set upon creating and casting a vastly powerful spell. Or, a Covenant full of worldly Magi who are merchants and wish to become as wealthy as possible. Note that the thing your Covenant seeks could be a secret to the rest of the world.

**Erosion:** Something is eroding at your Covenant's power base, and you must stop it to survive.

*Examples:* Bickering nobles, offended clergy, unhappy faeries or a strange magical phenomena (like *regio*) can all erode or affect your Covenant's power in different ways. Or, your Covenant could be full of warring factions that threaten to tear it apart.

**Balancing Act:** Your Covenant walks a thin line between survival and destruction. This can easily be linked to several other themes, like Mystery, Survival, or Unorthodox.

*Examples:* Your Covenant receives much of its power and Aura from a magical being it managed to trap many decades ago. Large amounts of yearly vis are required to keep it subdued. If it ever escapes the Covenant will be destroyed. Or, for years the Covenant has played the local nobles and clergy against each other to insure survival. If this balance ever shifts, they may come after the Covenant.

# Creating a Covenant

Creating your Covenant is the most important step in beginning your **Ars Magica** Saga. It is the character that most influences the events of your Saga, as well as the one likely to outlive any of your individual characters. Because of its importance, be prepared to take your time in creating your Covenant — an evening should suffice. Gather your Troupe and review with them the basic concepts presented earlier in this Chapter (if they aren't familiar with them already).

## SEASON

Before you can begin to design your Covenant, you must decide what Season it's currently in. Are you interested in accounting for and roleplaying all the aspects of the Covenant's growth and maintenance? Choose a Spring Covenant. Do you like roleplaying politics? Try an Autumn Covenant. Choosing your Covenant's Season is the most important step in creating your Covenant, as it sets the tone of your Covenant and determines what problems you will face, so take your time. Be sure that everyone in the Troupe has their say. Remember that this is a group effort. Also keep in mind that there is no right or wrong choice of Season for your Covenant, though some Seasons may be easier to handle for new groups. If you've never played before, we suggest you try a Spring or Summer Covenant, simply because they are usually smaller, with fewer Magi and inhabitants to worry about. Don't let us stop you from trying a Autumn or Winter Covenant, though, if that strikes your fancy.

Once your Season is chosen, you're finished with the hard part. Now you just have to fill in the details. To help you along, four Covenant "templates" are provided, one for each Season. These templates offer the basics of what your Covenant might have in its current stage of development. The templates are like the Vocations of the Character Chapter in that they help you make decisions and make the creation process quicker.

Basically, each template lists the attributes of a "typical" Covenant for that Season, along with alternatives to that basic choice, both good and bad. You simply work your way through the template, category by category, making your choices. If you aren't happy with the default choice, take a look at the Options listed beneath each entry. If one or more *Options* appeal to you, choose them, but keep tabs on whether they are "good" or "bad"

## The Basics of Covenant Creation

Creating a Covenant for the first time can be an exciting but daunting process. To help you on your way, here's a short list of points you should consider.

• Look over the Covenants Chapter. Make sure you understand the important concept of a Covenant's Season.

• Talk with your fellow Troupe members and decide what generally appeals to each member. Looking over the Themes and Seasons sections helps here. Make sure that *everyone* has a chance for input.

• If you so desire, choose a Theme to help guide your Covenant's creation.

• Choose your Covenant's Season. Spring or Summer is recommended for your first Covenant.

• Talk about possible locations for your Covenant. Be as specific or as general as you like. It's more important to think about and describe the *surroundings* than actually pin down the location. Things to think about: local terrain (hilly, forest, plains, mountains), water sources (rivers, streams, wells), nearby settlements (villages, towns, farms), local politics (nobles, Church, other Covenants), weather (harsh/mild winters, hot summers). Come up with a general feel for the place you want, then pick a place in Mythic Europe that seems to fit your description.

• Choose a general time period for your Covenant. Don't worry if you don't know real dates and times of actual medieval events. You can always come back and change the period of your Covenant if you so desire. For those of you with no particular date in mind, the late 12th Century (circa A.D. 1197) is suggested for its political intrigue and impending mayhem. This is also considered the "official" Ars Magica Saga starting date.

• Start working through the template for your Covenant's Season. Choose good and bad options (or make up your own) to customize your new home. The numbers of good and bad options should balance out in the end. Use your common sense and sense of fairness here.

• Detail the Covenant further, as desired. Sometimes it helps to divide the work up amongst the Troupe. For example, one person can make up a map, another detail the covenfolk, and one choose appropriate spells for the library.

• Keep in mind that these Covenant creation rules are just guidelines to help you along your way. We suggest that you follow them until you are familiar with **Ars Magica**, but they should only serve to augment your imagination, never to restrict it.

• Above all, remember that the Covenant is a character. Spend the same time and care on it as you do with an individual character. In the end you are rewarded with a solid, believable haven that can provide many, many years of enjoyment.

options. When all is said and done, you should try to balance the number of good options with bad options. Additionally, feel free to make up options of your own; the ones listed are merely suggestions to help spark your imagination. Just be careful to keep your Covenant trait strengths or weaknesses commensurate with the options that are listed. You and your Troupe have to keep yourselves honest about this.

As you come to each category in the template, consider the category carefully. Talk it over with the other members of your Troupe and see if anything clicks. After a few decisions your Covenant begins to take form before your eyes. Feel free to go back and change previous choices if you need to, and feel free to make up new options if none of the existing ones fit your Covenant. Just try to make them roughly equal in "goodness" or "badness" to the existing ones. When you get to the end of the template, you're almost done. Just take a brief look over what you've created, make sure that your options roughly balance out, and make any needed adjustments. Then, if you haven't already, choose a name for your Covenant, its time period, and rough location in Mythic Europe, and you're through.

If you need a concrete example of Covenant creation, see the example near the end of the Chapter.

# The Four Seasonal Templates

## SPRING

Spring Covenants are newly formed, usually by a handful of Magi just out of apprenticeship. These early years of Covenant life are usually filled with struggles for survival and a maturing of the Magi's powers. Choose a Spring Covenant if you want your Magi to be in complete control of the Covenant and don't mind the accompanying responsibilities. Your Covenant doesn't have much power or respect, but the Covenant is completely yours to do with as you wish. Does your Covenant grow in power and pass into Summer, or does it perish in the attempt?

## The Setting

**Location:** Unfortunately, most locations combining desirable, defensible terrain with a strong Magical Aura have already been settled by Covenants now in their Summer, Autumn, or Winter Seasons. Thus, unless you are willing to attempt survival in the wilderness far from any hint of civilization, Spring Covenants usually have to settle for a less than optimum site. Typical locations include the middle of a swamp, the bottom of a ravine, the middle of a searing desert, or the center of a primal forest. Feel free to chose another location, but make sure it has several disadvantages.

*Options:* Your Covenant is lucky. Choose a Summer location. Or, your Covenant is built on the ruins of a previous Covenant. This could be one that went through Winter and made it to Spring, or its demise could be a source of mystery (and of stories). Another option is to do something fairly different, like basing your Covenant on a medium-sized ship or in a band of roving wagons and carts. Be prepared to ad-lib and adjust the rest of the Covenant creation process if you do.

**Magic Aura:** Spring Covenants tend to be located in areas of fairly weak Magic Aura (roll on the *Aura Table*, p.129).

*Options:* Adjust your Aura strength upward by one. Or, roll as a Winter Covenant and ignore all results giving an Aura of less than six (remember that an Aura of 6+ warps those living within it for extended periods of time).

**Fortress:** Most Spring Covenants must start from scratch, spending money from meager resources to build what they can. This usually entails a two or three-story stone tower surrounded by a wooden palisade. The tower provides cramped housing for the Magi and a handful of Grogs. Everyone else must sleep outside, usually within wattle-and-daub or wooden buildings. The tower and wooden palisade are well-built and in good repair.

*Options:* The Covenant is built upon the remains of an older fortress. This means there's a lot more space, but it lies in partial ruins.

## The Inhabitants

**Internal Politics:** The atmosphere within a newly formed Covenant is usually one of excitement and cooperation. The Magi are on their own for the first time, and are likely to revel in their newfound freedom, at least for a time. The Magi probably get along fairly well and hesitate to impose strict rules upon each other. It is a time of growth and exploration, a time when council meetings are informal affairs, filled with heartfelt discussions and arguments that decide the course of the newly founded Covenant.

*Options:* The founding member of the Covenant is an older Magus, perhaps one who felt stifled at an overly hierarchical Autumn Covenant. This means the younger Magi have someone experienced to guide them, but it also means losing some freedom since one Magus is clearly the leader.

**Grogs:** To find the number of Grogs living at the Covenant, roll on the *Grog Table*, p.129. These Grogs are usually inexperienced and may only have inexpensive arms and armor. To represent their lack of training, they may only have their age in Experience Points to spend on Abilities (though Grogs played regularly by players have the normal number of Experience Points to work with). Additionally, while fairly enthusiastic about their new jobs, these Grogs are fairly undisciplined — give each a negative score in a Discipline Personality Trait.

*Options:* The Covenant has hired two to three experienced mercenaries to train and discipline the Grogs. Create these mercenaries as standard Grogs, with the Flaw of Hired Sword. Or, take the best (or worst) of three rolls on the *Grog Table*. Or, give a few of the Grogs standard armaments.

**Covenfolk:** A newly created Covenant has a minimum of covenfolk, most with minimal skills. These might include: a cook, a gardener, a shepherd (if the Covenant has flocks), and possibly a tinkerer/handyman. Some such folk can also belong to the Grog complement of the Covenant, so are slightly more skilled than their peers. Any tasks requiring special skills (glassblowing, scribing, blacksmithing) must be performed by locals at nearby towns.

*Options:* Several Grogs have useful Abilities at adequate skill levels (3-4). Of course, this means they might not be available for normal duty. Or, the Covenant has managed to attract a single specialist (Ability level of 4-5). This person may have ulterior motives for joining the Covenant.

## Mystical Attributes

**Arcane Library:** A Spring Covenant's library usually consists of books transcribed by an apprentice or, more rarely, donated by one's *Parens* (former teacher). Your library has the

equivalent of one die in all the Arts, and a total of fifty Levels of copied spells. Reroll three rolls of your choice.

*Options:* Your fellow Magi were quite diligent scribes. Take 1 die +5 in three Arts and 1 die in the rest, and 100 Levels of spells. Reroll three rolls of your choice. Or, a particularly kind *Parens* donated some books (or perhaps you stole them). Take two Arts at 1 die +6. Or, your previous Covenants frowned upon such scribing. Take only five Arts with 1 die each, and thirty Levels of spells.

**Magical Laboratories:** Space is another thing Spring Covenants don't have much of. Laboratory space is cramped and equipment is often the bare minimum needed to conduct research. Take -1 to all Lab Totals until more equipment is purchased and more space made available.

*Option:* Your Covenant is especially cramped. Some or all of the labs are shared, meaning that not all the Magi may conduct research at the same time. Or, your Covenant has plenty of space and equipment. Lab totals are normal.

**Magical Artifacts:** Unless built on an extremely Magical area or upon the ruins of an older Covenant, Spring Covenants usually have no magical artifacts or enchantments.

*Options:* Take one minor natural enchantment that the Magi have no control over, like a perpetual mist that surrounds the Covenant, or a friendly forest. Or, place a stronger enchantment nearby that the Magi know of but do not know how to use (e.g., a scrying pool, a cave wall covered with strange runes that can prophesy).

**Sources of Vis:** The Covenant has managed to find a steady source of *vis* nearby which provides 10 pawns yearly. Up to 20 additional pawns may be gathered at a different site, but this supply is not guaranteed — it is difficult to obtain. It might require negotiation, combat, *Certámen*, or trickery to gather each year.

*Options:* 10 more pawns may be gathered each year. Or, no steady source of *vis* is available — it is all contested in some fashion.

**Aegis of the Hearth:** The Covenant's *Aegis* is fairly weak. It is +15. Every Covenant has this spell (see the spell of the same name, p.233).

**Option:** Take an *Aegis* of +10 or +20.

## Mundane Attributes

**Mundane Library -** A Spring Covenant's mundane library is likely to be small. Choose three Knowledge Abilities represented by the library and roll a simple die on the *Mundane Library Table*, p.129, to determine the scores of those Knowledges.

*Options:* Your library is pathetic. Choose one Knowledge and take one roll on the *Table*. Or, your library is fairly nice. Take five rolls on the *Table*.

**Equipment:** Most beginning Covenants have had little time to gather a stock of standard expedition equipment, but it

isn't too hard to remedy the situation with a few purchasing trips to a good-sized city. The equipment the Covenant does have is simple, consisting of a few packs, ropes, torches, flint and steel, and other bare essentials.

*Options:* The inexperienced Grogs sent to purchase the Covenant's equipment were swindled by wily merchants. The Covenant has a larger than normal variety of equipment, but most is of inferior quality and is likely to wear out or break quickly. Or, the Covenant is fairly well-equipped. Take the equipment of a Summer Covenant.

**Income:** Money is another item in short supply at Spring Covenants. Most is spent early on building, food, armaments, and setting up the Magi's labs. Essential supplies like food and basic repairs are paid for, but no more than 20 silver pennies may be used for other items each Season. Without a source of income, the Covenant can continue spending at this rate for five years before running out of money. Finding a steady source of income probably takes several game sessions.

*Options:* The Covenant has a small source of steady income that requires some supervision. The Covenant has about fifty silver pennies to spend each Season as desired, but in return one Magus or a handful of Grogs must spend the equivalent of a Season overseeing it. Or, the Covenant is dirt poor and struggles

to keep all the covenfolk fed. No money is available for extraneous items.

## The Outside World

**Contacts:** Spring Covenants normally have some contacts in the outside world, consisting chiefly of people met while apprenticing. Other covenfolk may round these sources out, but in general, most news the Covenant receives is stale. Redcaps rarely visit the Covenant, and then only for important reasons.

*Options:* You have an extremely well-connected person living at the Covenant (create this person as a Companion). This person insures that news and information is fairly current. Or, your Covenant has little contact with anyone. You rarely, if ever, hear news of any kind.

**Status/Reputation:** A new Covenant might pose a threat to the balance and established order of the area. Most nearby Covenants subtly test the new Covenant within the first few years to determine how to treat the newcomer. Beware lest taking sides in an ongoing conflict completely determine your friends and enemies. Covenants farther away have no reason to take an interest in you.

*Options:* Some or all of the Magi forming the Covenant were troublesome apprentices. This reputation is now transferred to the Covenant and might make it difficult to find allies within the Order. Or, the Magi forming the Covenant were gifted apprentices. It could be hard to live up to their reputation, and other Covenants are leery of helping such a potentially powerful Covenant.

**Relationships:** A Spring Covenant has had little time to make friends or enemies. Nevertheless, you may roll or choose up to one friend/ally and one enemy from the *Relations Table* (see p.129).

*Options:* Choose up to two friends/enemies from the *Table*.

**Obligations:** This varies considerably from Covenant to Covenant, but Spring Covenants are the most likely to have outside obligations. This can take many forms, ranging from making yearly payments to local lords, to payments of vis to a Covenant, or serving a time each Season as judges for the locals. The possibilities are endless. Choose one if you so desire, and it fits with your Covenant's history.

# Summer

Summer Covenants have survived through the trials of Spring and soon reach the peak of their magical power. The founding Magi often bring in new blood (the players' characters) to take care of matters not demanding their close attention. By choosing a Summer Covenant you surrender some freedom of action (the older Magi make all the important decisions) but you gain a measure of stability as well as greater access to magical resources.

## The Setting

**Location:** Summer Covenants typically have slightly better locations than their younger Spring cousins. These might be on a hilltop, on a small bluff overlooking a river, or on a promontory partway up a mountainside. Overall, the location should be fairly defensible.

*Options:* Choose as a Spring or an Autumn Covenant.

**Magic Aura:** A Summer Covenant's Magic Aura is usually moderate in strength. Roll once on the *Aura Table* (p.129).

*Options:* Roll as a Spring or Autumn Covenant.

**Fortress:** Summer Covenants have usually had some time to strengthen and expand their once humble fortress. The central tower has been expanded to include such niceties as a great hall, a kitchen, a council chamber, and a small library. The timber palisade has been replaced with a sturdy stone wall and a small watchtower or two. Overall, the defenses are well-maintained and are equal to those of a small castle. Note that in times of trouble at least thirty Grogs are needed to properly defend the walls.

*Options:* A cave complex has been discovered beneath the Covenant and might be used for further expansions. Or, your Covenant is extremely lucky and managed to build on the remains of a previous castle. Add several watchtowers and a gatehouse.

## The Inhabitants

**Internal Politics:** Most Summer Covenants have fairly subdued internal politics. After all, the Covenant wouldn't have made it past Spring without its members working together in some fashion. Thus, while individual Magi may have personal disputes among themselves, they usually set aside those troubles for the good of the Covenant. Politics are likely to become much more of an issue, however, as the Covenant grows and moves toward Autumn.

**Grogs:** Roll once on the *Grog Table* (p. 129) to determine the number of Grogs at the Covenant. These Grogs are likely to be loyal and fairly committed to their work. Give the turb an overall Trustworthy Personality Trait of +1. Most are not particularly experienced — give them their age in Experience Points with which to purchase Abilities. A few, however, have become fairly proficient at what they do. To reflect this, start two dice worth of the Grogs at their age +5 in Experience Points. Note that Grogs often played as characters are created by the normal character creation rules. The turb is equipped with a mixture of inexpensive and standard armaments, with a few select Grogs possessing an item or two of expensive equipment.

*Options: The turb is exceptionally* large or small. Roll on the Spring or Autumn *Table*. Or, the majority of the Grogs are equipped with standard equipment. Or, the Covenant has managed to attract or train a handful of excellent Grog sergeants. Create 3-5 Grogs, adding 10 to their age for Experience Points.

**Covenfolk:** A Summer Covenant has had time to recruit a few essential specialists, but the overall number of covenfolk is still limited. In addition to a dozen or so people who work in the kitchen, clean the rooms and do other odd jobs, the Covenant is likely to have a blacksmith or weaponmaker, a scribe/librarian, a carpenter, and someone who oversees all matters of money and the staff — the autocrat. These specialists have Ability levels of 4 or so in the appropriate skills. Skilled covenfolk may also be counted among the Grogs based on their importance in the Covenant.

*Options:* You have lots and lots of covenfolk, but none are particularly skilled.

## Mystical Attributes

**Arcane Library:** The library at a Summer Covenant has grown since its Spring days. Take 1 die + 5 to determine the score in three Arts represented by the library, and one die in all the rest. Reroll three rolls of your choice. 100 Levels of spells can also be found in your books.

*Options:* Your fellow Magi have worked hard on the library. Take 1 die +7 in three Arts, and 1 die +2 in the rest. 200 Levels of spells. Or, a local Covenant is willing to let you copy spells or books in return for some favor. A Magus must take the time to copy the books, then the favor must be performed.

**Magical Laboratories:** The labs at a Summer Covenant are still somewhat cramped, but at least everyone has their own lab space. They are adequately equipped — no modifiers to Lab Totals.

*Options:* For one reason or another, you still must share lab space. There is one less laboratory than Magi. Or, you have spent quite a bit of time and money to equip your laboratories. They are fine enough that each Magus may add +1 to his Lab Total.

**Magical Artifacts:** By now the Covenant has acquired, discovered or made several minor magic items. These might include a magical alarm system, a door that talks, or magical lanterns or torches. In addition, some minor magical enchantment might lie near the Covenant, like a scrying pool, a well that never goes dry, or a spot of ground that grows crops at twice the normal rate.

*Options:* Instead of several minor magics, take one major item or magical enchantment. This single item might be a magical map that shows the position of friends or enemies, a powerful magical guardian, or a door that is impervious to magic and requires a password to open.

**Sources of Vis:** Now the Covenant has a fairly regular supply of *vis*. You may collect 20 pawns of *vis* per year without a problem, and 30 more is contested in some fashion. These pawns can be guarded by faeries, beasts, or claimed by a rival Covenant.

*Options:* None of your *vis* is contested. Collect 30 pawns per year.

*Aegis of the Hearth* : Your *Aegis* is +25 (Each Covenant has this spell. See the spell of the same name, p.233).

Options: It is weaker (-10) or stronger (+10).

## Mundane Attributes

**Mundane Library:** In the years since it was founded, the Covenant's mundane library has grown substantially. Choose six Knowledge Abilities that the library's books represent, and roll a simple die on the *Mundane Library Table,* p. 129, to determine the ratings in those Knowledges.

*Options:* Your library is lacking. Choose only three Knowledges. Or, your Covenant has acquired a special collection of some kind. This is fairly large and has not been cataloged, so specific information may be hard to find. Appropriate rolls and time must be spent to glean any useful information. The collection should have a particular theme, such as maps, histories, or religious documents.

**Equipment:** Your Covenant is well-equipped for routine expeditions. It has plenty of ropes, packs, lamps and torches, oil and other necessary items. In addition, the Covenant has half

a dozen pack animals (ponies or mules). If the Covenant is near water, you probably have a few small boats as well.

*Options:* The Covenant has a horse or two (for patrols and quick trips to town). These horses are *not* accustomed to the Magi. Or, the Covenant has acquired a magical beast of some kind that willingly bears a Magus. This beast should still be difficult to control/ride. Or, if the Covenant is near a large body of water, it has purchased or built a medium-sized boat. This boat is not suitable for long ocean voyages, but can handle placid rivers, lakes and short ocean voyages.

**Income:** Most Summer Covenants have found a steady source of income. This means that food, replacement Grogs (within reason), and normal maintenance is taken care of. Seasonally, about 100 silver pennies are available for extraneous use.

*Options:* The Covenant's supply of money is contested. The source of the problem could be local peasants, robbers, nobility, a rival Covenant, faeries, or even a natural phenomenon of some kind.

## The Outside World

**Contacts:** A Summer Covenant's contacts are adequate, but nothing extraordinary. You are kept abreast of important Hermetic news by Redcap visits, and learn of more mundane news at the same time as minor nobles in the area. You probably have a few friendly sources in most of the nearby villages, and perhaps a spy in a nearby nobleman's household, but that's the extent of it.

*Options:* For one reason or another, the Covenant's sources are still lacking. Take your contacts as a Spring Covenant. The local peasants or nobility, for example, might have an open hatred of the Magi and their friends. Or, the Covenant has proven exceptionally adept at politics. Take your contact score as an Autumn Covenant.

**Status/Reputation:** Whether they deserve it or not, Summer Covenants are often viewed with suspicion and distrust by older, more established members of the Order. This is simply because Summer Covenants are the rising stars in the Order, and pose a threat to the status quo. Summer Covenants are growing in magical power, while Autumn and Winter Covenants struggle to keep what they have. If a Summer Covenant appears to gather too much power too quickly, its folk may find themselves harassed and persecuted in Tribunals by blocs of politically powerful Covenants. You have to tread carefully to avoid the attention of the powerful.

**Relationships:** Summer is a time of gathering friends and making enemies. Choose or roll two enemies and one friend from the *Relations Table* (p.129).

*Options:* Your Covenant is particularly well-liked or hated. Choose an additional friend or enemy.

**Obligations:** Summer Covenants usually have either no obligations or are working toward eliminating same. If it fits your Covenant history, or you need an additional "bad" option, create one obligation for your Covenant. This could be a yearly gift of some sort —vis, potions, or money are all likely candidates. Or, it could be something else entirely, like a requirement that all the Magi grovel before a noble (mundane or faerie) every five years.

# Autumn

Autumn Covenants have grown into their political prime within the Order. As Autumn Covenants are usually large and fairly hierarchical, new Magi (the players) have little say in the running of the Covenant and have to work hard to gain respect and privileges from their elders. Choose an Autumn Covenant if you like politics, intrigue, and don't mind allowing others to run the Covenant.

## The Setting

**Location:** Autumn Covenants had a wide selection of locations to choose from when they were first built. Thus, they usually have a fine, defensible site. Examples include: a large bluff overlooking a river, the top of or on the side of a cliff, a small pinnacle on a mountainside, or a rocky island in the middle of a raging river.

*Options:* Choose as a Summer or Winter site.

**Magic Aura:** The Magic Aura of an Autumn Covenant is usually quite strong, without being too strong (i.e., not greater than 6), for it is known that powerful Auras tend to warp those living within them for long periods of time. Roll once on the *Aura Table* (p.129) to determine your Covenant's Aura rating.

*Options:* Your Covenant is situated in an area of fairly weak Aura — roll as a Summer Covenant and take a Winter location in return. Or, the founding Magi chose to ignore warnings about powerful Auras — roll as a Winter Covenant and create some strange results that have arisen from your locale, such as mutations of and aberrant behavior in covenfolk.

**Fortress:** Added to and improved upon throughout the decades of Summer, Autumn Covenants are usually quite large and well-defended. The smallest house over 100 Grogs and a dozen or more Magi with ease. The largest are more like small cities, encompassing more than five acres within their walls and requiring 200 to 300 Grogs to man those walls properly. Most have a formidable central keep (the home of the Magi), surrounded by a tower-studded outer wall. Some even have an additional inner wall — almost unheard of in medieval times. The senior Magi have spacious apartments and roomy laboratories, and the library, great hall and council chambers follow suit. The defenses are constantly maintained and improved.

*Options:* Your Covenant has found little need for defense. It consists of a large central tower with no outer wall. Almost all the covenfolk and Grogs live outside in wooden buildings. Or, your Covenant has taken defense to an extreme — it is equal to (if not better than) the best castles of the period, but your paranoia allows almost no visitors. Alternatively, your Covenant can be an entire town, with a population of up to 5000.

## The Inhabitants

**Internal Politics:** Politics are usually quite extreme in an Autumn Covenant. The founders (those still alive, anyway) are beginning to wane in power and often try to enforce their desires on younger Magi with strict rules and regulations. Thus, Autumn Covenants are often hierarchical in nature — older Magi have many privileges with few responsibilities, while young Magi may have to scribe and perform other undesirable work for the chance to glance at the occasional spell book. Apprentices in Autumn Covenants are likely to regard each other as rivals rather than friends. Additionally, entrance requirements for new Magi are usually fairly prohibitive — many years of scribing and large gifts of vis for the elders are not uncommon.

*Options:* Over the years, unresolvable differences have arisen between the elder Magi. As a result, the Covenant is sharply divided into several camps, each supporting a particular Magus's view. These politics can be extremely dangerous to the uninitiated.

**Grogs:** To determine the number of Grogs present at the Covenant, roll once on the *Grog Table* (p.129). These Grogs are likely to be well-trained and fiercely loyal to the Covenant (or to one of its factions). Half of the Grogs have one piece of expensive equipment, while the rest are equipped with standard arms and armor. When creating the Grogs, divide them into three groups to reflect their age and experience. One group has Experience Points to spend on Abilities equal to age. The next group has points equal to age + 5, and the last has points equal to age + 10. Grogs who are frequently played by the players are designed with the normal creation systems.

*Options:* Due to exceptionally charismatic leaders, the Grogs are more loyal to their captains than the Magi. The Magi are completely unaware of this. Or, Covenant politics have interfered significantly with the morale of the Grogs. They do their jobs, but their hearts aren't in it. Give most a positive Apathetic Personality Trait. Or, the Grogs are motivated not by respect, but fear of the Magi (they probably have a history of ill-treatment at the hands of the Magi). The Grogs are fairly disloyal and may rebel if given the chance. The turb has an overall Trustworthiness Personality Trait score of -3.

**Covenfolk:** Autumn Covenants usually have a large and varied contingent of covenfolk. These include many unskilled workers who clean or perform other necessary jobs, and special-ists, like scribes, glassblowers, and blacksmiths, who are often Grogs as well. Choose five specialists and give them Ability levels of 5 in the appropriate areas. An autocrat (and his staff) almost certainly controls the day to day operation of the Covenant.

*Options:* The Covenant has hundreds of covenfolk, but none are particularly skilled. Give each an Ability of level 2 to 3 in an area of choice. Or, your Covenant has a particularly ambitious autocrat. This person has a stranglehold on the Covenant and carefully controls all information given to the Magi.

## Mystical Attributes

**Arcane Library:** The Covenant's arcane library usually reaches its pinnacle during the Season of Autumn. Added to first by the founding members, then by more and more young Magi, it can be truly impressive — a library that other Magi travel far to visit, hoping to spend a Season in study. The books' scores in the Arts are determined as follows: take 1 die +10 in three Arts and 1 die +5 in the others. 300 Levels of spells are recorded in the books. Keep in mind, however, that the Covenant's politics may place restrictions on access to these wonderful tomes.

*Options:* Your library is truly exceptional. Take 1 die +12 in three Arts and 1 die +8 in the others, with 500 Levels of spells. Or, due to the divisive nature of the Magi at your Covenant, the library is fragmented, a few books being jealously guarded by each Magus. Access to books belonging to a faction other than your own is truly difficult to achieve.

**Magical Laboratories:** All of the older Magi have excellent facilities, allowing them to add +3 to their Lab Totals. Younger Magi have lesser facilities, mostly +1, while the youngest may not have access at all.

*Options:* In an overly hierarchical Covenant the young Magi have several hidden labs worth +1 each. If discovered, the consequences could be dire. Or, allow the young Magi +3 labs, but they must be shared, making a Season's project take twice that time to complete. Or, the young Magi all have their own labs, but must use the cast-off equipment of their elders; -1 to all Lab Totals and add an extra Botch die.

**Magical Artifacts:** The Covenant has probably gathered or manufactured several magical artifacts during its years of growth. Take one major item (a magical portal, a powerful demon or faerie ward, an unseen but powerful guardian) and several minor items (talking doors, a scrying pool, magical alarms). Permanent spells are common throughout the Covenant and provide illumination, running water and other conveniences.

*Options:* The Covenant has numerous small magical arti-facts, many of which don't work or are on the verge of breaking. Or, the secret of using the Covenant's most precious magic item was lost when the last founder recently died. The item is immensely powerful, but no one knows how to activate it. Political jockeying to be the first to study the item is fierce.

**Sources of Vis:** An Autumn Covenant usually has quite a large amount of *vis*. Of course, most of it is used by the senior magi for study or for making magic items. The Covenant can expect to gather 40 pawns annually. Twenty more pawns may be gathered, but are contested in some fashion.

*Options:* The Covenant gets its *vis* from an individual or group, and this group charges use of the Covenant's facilities in return. The group provides 50 pawns a year, but is susceptible to political tactics like boycotting, interference from wars (restricting travel), and the like. Or, the Covenant has an income of 80 pawns, but 60 of it is contested. The contest should be commensurate with the Magi's powers.

*Aegis of the Hearth:* The Covenant's *Aegis* is quite strong (+35). All Covenants are protected by this spell. See the spell of the same name, p.233, for details.

*Options:* Your *Aegis* is phenomenal (+45), but unknown to the Order, it requires a ritual that uses some aspects of non-Hermetic magic (perhaps requiring a human sacrifice or the active participation of powerful demons or faeries). This secret is known only by the Covenant's most powerful Magi and would cause tremendous repercussions if it became widely known. Or, your Covenant's *Aegis* is quite weak (only +15), also a closely held secret. Most rival Covenants assume your *Aegis* is higher and don't bother trying to test it.

## Mundane Attributes

**Mundane Library:** Your library is quite excellent. Choose ten different Knowledge Abilities that are represented by your library and roll a simple die on the *Mundane Library Table* (p.129) to determine the scores in those Knowledges.

*Options:* Your library is fairly modest. Choose six Knowledges only. Or, take a special collection of some sort: maps, demons, faeries. In this area your Covenant is unequaled.

**Equipment:** Autumn Covenants are usually well-equipped. You have more than you'll ever use for traveling and exploring, and anything you don't have can be manufactured quickly by one of your skilled craftsmen. Additionally, the Covenant has a stable of pack animals and riding horses, though these are still skittish around magical folk. If your Covenant is located near water, it has a half dozen boats (up to ten feet in length).

*Options:* If near water, the Covenant owns a medium-sized (thirty foot) boat. Or, the Covenant has a handful of horses trained to carry Magi without problems.

**Income:** Autumn Covenants usually have plenty of money. The senior Magi may spend as they wish (though not too extravagantly) and the younger Magi are given adequate allowances from Covenant coffers when traveling on Covenant business. The Covenant may even have such luxuries as a commissioned tapestry in the great hall, and paintings of more illustrious members on the walls.

*Options:* Through political machinations, your Covenant's enemies are cutting off your source of money. Each year your Covenant must overcome some difficulty to obtain any money at all. Or, unknown to outsiders (and most within the Covenant), some dark scandal is draining the coffers faster than they can be filled. This loss could result from payoffs to cover up some indiscretion or blunder by a senior Magus, or from overzealous embezzling by an ambitious autocrat. Or, your Covenant could be extremely wealthy, allowing the Magi to live like minor nobles at court. Such a Covenant might own comfortable estates in all the nearby cities.

## The Outside World

**Contacts:** A typical Autumn Covenant has an extensive system of friends, contacts and spies. They keep you abreast of all the important news, both Hermetic and mundane. Specific information can be gathered from this network within a few days or weeks, depending on the obscurity of the question.

*Options:* The Covenant has an amazing network of informants, so amazing that the information must be sifted by underlings before reaching the ears of Magi. The autocrat and Magi so inclined learn of important events throughout the known world as fast or faster than important clergy and nobility. Or, your network of informants has recently undergone a concerted attack by enemies of the Covenant (clergy, nobility, rival Covenants). Information is scarce or just plain wrong. Or, you have a spy within your Covenant who reports all important actions and decisions to your enemies.

**Status/Reputation:** This can be highly variable depending on the personality of the Covenant, ranging from revered and respected to outright hostility. Autumn Covenants hold great political clout within the Order, and most of their reputation hinges on how they use their power. Are they forceful and domineering, often resorting to dirty tactics to get their way? Or do they place themselves above conflict, often acting as arbiters in inter-Order disputes? Think carefully upon the personality of your Covenant before deciding.

**Relationships:** Autumn Covenants usually have a number of allies and enemies. Choose or roll three enemies from the *Relations Table* (p.129), and two allies. One of the enemies must be a rival Covenant (not a Spring one).

*Options:* Your Covenant is particularly well-liked. Take three friends/allies and one enemy. Or, your Covenant made many enemies while gathering its power. Take four enemies and one friend/ally.

**Obligations:** Autumn Covenants rarely have obligations, unless they are to an extremely powerful magical or mundane force, like the Pope, a king, or a prince of Faerie or Hell. Choose this option only if it works well with your Covenant's history.

# Winter

Winter Covenants are past their prime in political and magical power, but have a vast amount of experience and knowledge to draw on. Older Magi are often eccentric and reclusive, not wanting anything to do with the outside world. Any new Magi (the players' characters) have to strive mightily to breath new life into the Covenant. As long as they respect any customs or eccentricities of older Magi and covenfolk, the characters should nearly have free reign. Choose a Winter Covenant if dealing with eccentric, elderly Magi intrigues you and you don't mind taking more and more control of the Covenant's activities. Can you bring the Covenant full circle from the depths of Winter to a newborn Spring?

## The Setting

**Location:** Founded long ago when Covenants were few, the founders of your Covenant had their choice of location. As a result, Winter Covenants are usually situated in the most desirable of spots. In most cases, this means the location is easily defensible, somewhat removed from mundane population centers, and extremely private. Standard locations include mountain tops, islands, or on the edge of a rocky outcropping or cliff, though any spot fulfilling these criteria can be used.

*Option:* Choose an Autumn location.

**Magic Aura:** In the case of Magic Auras, first is not always best. Most Winter Covenants are built on areas of strong Magical Aura, sometimes stronger than the human body can safely endure (Aura rating of 6+). To determine your Aura strength roll a simple die and consult the *Aura Table* (p.129).

*Options:* Adjust your Aura upward by one, or downward by one or two.

**Fortress:** Winter Covenants have had plenty of time to add to their once humble size and defenses. The Covenant is usually a sprawling affair, with mighty walls and towers added haphazardly in centuries past. Everyone is easily housed within the Covenant with room to spare. However, large portions of the Covenant are often abandoned and general upkeep on walls and towers is poor — the Covenant now relies more on its location for defense.

*Options:* Overall maintenance is good. Defenses still aren't in optimum shape, but there are no major breaches or holes. Or, maintenance is so bad that it affects lab work (due to leaking roofs and other disturbances). Each Magus subtracts a simple die, divided by two, from Lab Total.

## The Inhabitants

**Internal Politics:** The majority of Magi in a Winter Covenant are elderly and often become fixated on something to the detriment of everything else in their lives. This something could be inventing a particularly powerful spell, studying an esoteric problem in magic theory, or something bordering on the insane like collecting the legs of insects. Many of these Magi may be on the verge of final Twilight (see p.356 for details). Other Magi may live at the Covenant as well, with the older ones being apathetic and unproductive — often the last apprentices of the Magi described above (if they were industrious the Covenant

would still be in Autumn). Politics in these Covenants vary considerably, and range from being nonexistent (little contact between the Magi at all) to being dangerously bizarre. In any case, younger Magi have to tread carefully and are well-advised to quickly learn each Magus's eccentricities and customs.

*Option:* A competent, middle-aged Magus lives at the Covenant. Or, the elderly Magi are quite coherent and are still quite aware of mundane affairs. Perhaps they were thrown into Winter for reasons other than decay, like the loss of the entire library, orvis sources, or by being forced to abandon their Covenant and most of their belongings. Now they are trying desperately to regain their lost power and status.

**Grogs:** To determine the number of Grogs living at the Covenant, roll once on the *Grog Table* (p.129). The morale of these Grogs can vary considerably, from fiercely loyal to slovenly complacent. Much of this depends on the particulars of the Covenant's other inhabitants. The Grogs were probably born and raised at the Covenant. Because of this, if the Aura of the Covenant is 6+, they might have common physical or mental mutations/deformities. The quality of their equipment can vary considerably, but is likely to be standard with a scattering of poor (due to bad maintenance) and expensive. Older Grogs are likely to have slightly enchanted weapons (permanent *Edge of the Razor*, MuTe 5, for example). Their training is distributed in the same fashion as in an Autumn Covenant. Keep in mind that resident Grogs used by players should have Virtues and Flaws that reflect the influence of any strong Magic Aura.

*Options:* The Covenant has a loyal and healthy contingent of Grogs; roll for the number of Grogs as an Autumn Covenant and make their equipment uniformly standard except for one expensive arm or armament each. Or, the turb is slovenly and ill-trained; roll for the number of Grogs as normal but give each only their age in Experience Points, give them all poor arms and armor, and give them each a negative Trustworthy and Brave Personality Trait score. Another interesting option is to say that the leader of the Grogs is slowly wresting control of the Covenant from the Magi. If allowed to continue, the Covenant becomes the equivalent of a small castle with a feudal lord.

**Covenfolk:** The quality and number of a Winter Covenant's covenfolk can vary considerably. There is likely to be a handful of competent folk still about (useful Abilities rated 3 to 4), though they may be as eccentric as their masters. These are the folk who are likely to meet Grog status. There is also a variety of less skilled folk (2 to 3), both young and old. If the Covenant's Aura is 6+, small physical or mental abnormalities are common.

*Options:* An extremely efficient autocrat lives at the Covenant, ruling it absolutely (except for the Magi's quarters). Any visitors have to deal with this autocrat to get anywhere at all. Of course, the autocrat can be slightly insane or have a few disquieting quirks. Or, the covenfolk are basically unskilled peasants who just happen to make the Covenant their home. Little order exists and they do the bare minimum necessary to keep their eccentric masters happy.

# Mystical Attributes

**Arcane Library:** The magical library in a Winter Covenant is likely to be fairly amazing, but difficult to gain access to. Over the years, most of the books have been removed (all but one die's worth in number) by eccentric Magi and never returned. Some have been forgotten, others are used constantly, and a few are probably unreadable due to neglect. If all the books are gathered together, they embody scores of 1 die +12 in three Arts, and 1 die +8 in the others. They also contain 500 Levels of spells.

*Options:* A possessive librarian has kept the books together and in good condition; take 1 die +14 in three Arts, 1 die +11 in the rest, and 600 Levels of spells. Or, take 1 die +10 in three Arts, 1 die +5 in the others, and 300 Levels of spells. Or, all the books have been removed from the library. It is difficult and time-consuming to find them. Or, the Magi revere and guard their library jealously, never allowing access to any but a chosen few.

**Magical Laboratories:** The laboratory situation in a Winter Covenant is similar to that of an Autumn Covenant. The older Magi's labs are often sprawling affairs, with centuries of accumulated equipment spread liberally throughout. Younger Magi have to scrounge for what they can get as resources for new equipment is limited. Depending upon the efficiency and senility of Magi and covenfolk, take a penalty of -1 to -3 to Lab Totals. At least space is not a problem.

*Options:* Enough lab equipment can be refurbished to provide for a number of fairly decent laboratories. No overall modifier to Lab Totals. Or, a young Magus may choose to use the lab of a master who has passed on. Start your Lab Total at -5 and decrease this penalty (make it more positive) by one for every year you use the lab for at least two Seasons (you are gaining familiarity with it). Your Lab Total continues to increase to a maximum of +3. As long as you have a penalty for using this lab roll two extra Botch dice.

**Magical Artifacts:** Winter Covenants are likely to have a number of magical artifacts, though many may be lost, broken, or work in odd ways. Take four minor enchantments (scrying pool, magical illumination, surrounded by mist) and one average enchantment (magical alarms, magical doors, or the like).

*Options:* The enchantments are easy to fix, or a few work without problems. Or, the magical enchantments are dangerous, and often harm those attempting to use them. Or, the Magi have an extremely powerful item upon which they depend for much of their remaining power or strength.

**Sources of Vis:** While a Winter Covenant might have had great sources of *vis* in the past, many sources have dried up or have been lost to younger, more energetic Covenants. Even so, 25 pawns of *vis* may be collected each year.

*Options:* Fifteen additional pawns of *vis* may be collected each year. Or, all the sources of *vis* are contested by a magical creature or enemy Covenant; only 15 pawns may be collected each year. Or, the Covenant no longer collects any *vis* at all, depending entirely upon its immense, secret stockpile for all its

needs. This stockpile consists of 500 pawns of assorted types. Or, the Covenant has no primary sources of *vis* but gathers 30 pawns or more a year by charging visiting Magi to use the library.

*Aegis of the Hearth:* The Covenant's *Aegis* has probably weakened over time. Most Winter Covenants have an *Aegis* of +15. All Covenants have this spell. See the spell of the same name, p.233.

*Options:* The *Aegis* is +25. Or, the *Aegis* is +5.

**Mundane Attributes**

**Mundane Library:** The mundane library in most Winter Covenants is likely to be fairly extensive, though it may be in poor condition due to age or neglect. Choose 10 different Knowledge Abilities that the library represents with its books and make a *stress roll* on the *Mundane Library Table* (p.129). A zero or Botch result indicates that the books have decayed beyond use. In addition, whenever a book is used, roll a stress die. On a Botch the book decays beyond use.

*Options:* A competent librarian has taken care of the books through the years. None of the books are decayed or fragile. Or, the books are extremely fragile. When they are used, make a stress roll. A result of 3 or lower results in the book's destruction.

**Equipment:** A Winter Covenant's equipment is likely to be extensive but fairly worn out. Nothing new may be made or built, though much may be found or salvaged with an investment of time.

*Options:* A cache of unused, well-kept equipment lies in a forgotten storeroom. It is found on a simple roll of 9+ each Season equipment is used.

**Income:** With its lack of political might, a Winter Covenant is likely to have few sources of income. Many sources carefully built up and maintained during earlier Seasons are now untended, or have been stolen by local lords or rival Covenants. On the other hand, Winter Magi have little need for money. Overall, the Magi are poor and have little to spend on exotic supplies and new lab equipment.

*Options:* A hidden reserve of 10,000 silver pennies lies forgotten in a Covenant vault. It is discovered on a simple die roll of 10+, made each year. Or, the Covenant is completely broke. No money is available for purchases beyond simple food and supplies.

## The Outside World

**Contacts:** Winter Covenants are often quite removed from the outside world. All but the most earth-shattering of news may take years to make it to the Covenant, and Redcaps rarely visit or bother to inform the Magi of anything other than important Tribunals.

*Options:* The Covenant is considered "lost." No one visits the Covenant and most believe its inhabitants dead. Or, a local Redcap has made it his (or her) business to keep tabs on the

Covenant and visits fairly often — up to twice a year. Or, the covenfolk have made it their business to keep up the network of spies and informants created during Autumn. Thus, while the Magi are in the dark, some of the covenfolk know quite a lot.

**Status/Reputation:** Early in the Winter Season, Winter Covenants are respected by the Order for their past accomplishments, but this respect soon erodes as impertinent young Covenants begin testing the powerful, both politically and magically. In time the Covenant's previous might becomes a memory. The Covenant's overall reputation is usually a faded version of its previous glory.

*Options:* The Magi still take an active part in the politics of the Order. They wield little power, but hold a considerable block of votes (though even these are diminishing). Or, strange rumors of the Magi's doings have spread throughout the Order. No one from the Covenant is taken seriously, and might be shunned or even actively attacked.

**Relationships:** A Winter Covenant has had many years to build up both friends and enemies, but even more friendships and feuds have been forgotten. Choose or roll a balanced

number of friends and enemies from the *Relations Table* (p.129). Up to five of each may be taken.

**Obligations:** Winter Covenants rarely have any obligations to anyone, either mundane or magical. However, a failure to fulfill former obligations may have contributed to the Covenant's passage into Winter, but those obligations are now forgotten or of little consequence anymore.

## Grog Table

### Season

| Roll (simple die) | Spring | Summer | Autumn | Winter |
|---|---|---|---|---|
| 1 | 15 | 20 | 50 | 10 |
| 2-3 | 20 | 30 | 75 | 30 |
| 4-5 | 25 | 40 | 100 | 45 |
| 6-7 | 30 | 50 | 150 | 60 |
| 8-9 | 40 | 60 | 200 | 75 |
| 10 | 50 | 75 | 300 | 100 |

## Aura Table

### Season

| Roll (simple die) | Spring | Summer | Autumn | Winter |
|---|---|---|---|---|
| 1 | 1 | 2 | 3 | 4 |
| 2-5 | 2 | 3 | 4 | 5 |
| 6-9 | 3 | 4 | 5 | 6 |
| 10 | 4 | 5 | 6 | 7 |

## Relations Table

### Possible Friends and Enemies:

| Roll (simple die) | Friend/Enemy |
|---|---|
| 1 | A Minor Nobleman |
| 2 | The Nearby Peasants |
| 3 | A Magical Creature |
| 4 | A Wealthy Merchant |
| 5 | The Local Clergy |
| 6 | A Spring Covenant |
| 7 | A Band of Faeries/Demons |
| 8 | A Faerie King or Queen/Prince of Hell |
| 9 | A Summer Covenant |
| 10 | An Autumn Covenant |

## Mundane Library Table

| Roll (stress die) | Knowledge Rating |
|---|---|
| 0 | Books Ruined |
| 1-3 | 1 |
| 4-6 | 2 |
| 7-9 | 3 |
| 10-12 | 4 |
| 13-15 | 5 |
| 16+ | 6 |

Modifiers to roll: Spring +0, Summer +2, Autumn +5, Winter +7

# THE COVENANT OF MISTRIDGE

This section, written from a player's perspective, presents a sample Covenant, that of Mistridge, taking you step by step through its creation as a Spring Covenant. This example should help clarify any questions you have about the Covenant creation process, and shows how options may be used creatively to enhance your Covenant. (Note: Mistridge is only used as an example in this instance. The Covenant is described fully in its Summer Season in the **Ars Magica** supplement **Mistridge**.)

## Creating Mistridge

First, our Troupe gathers together and skims over the rules. We decide to make up the Covenant first, then create our characters. Armed with one player's knowledge of southern France, we decide to place our Covenant there, in the foothills of the Pyrenees (the mountains dividing France and Spain). After talking a while, we look at some history books and pick a date of 1067 for the starting date (for no real reason), and set out to create our Covenant.

The first series of choices deal with the setting: location, Magic Aura, and fortress. We aren't too thrilled with the locations listed for Spring Covenants, so we take a good option, a Summer location, on a hilltop. We figure that fits with our concept of being in the foothills. One of us starts a running tally of good and bad options for future reference. Someone else comes up with the idea of our hilltop always being shrouded in mist, giving it the name Mistridge. Next, we take the standard Aura, and roll a 7, which translates to an Aura of strength 3 — not bad for Summer. We also opt for a fortress, picturing a stone tower on the edge of a low cliff, surrounded for now by a low wooden palisade.

Now we move on to the next part: Inhabitants. Looking over the idea of internal politics, we are intrigued by the listed option, and decide to take it – another good option. One of the players says he'd be happy to create and play an older Magus and even has a name picked out: Consuelia. The idea sits well with the Troupe because this person also plans on running many of the stories. Next, we take everything standard for the Grogs and

end up with 25 of them armed with inexpensive armaments. Likewise, we take standard covenfolk and decide we have a few drudges to do the cleaning and cooking, with no one else being especially skilled.

Next comes mystical attributes. We've taken two good options so far, so we feel the need to take some negative ones. We decide to take a poor option for our arcane library (though we'll probably regret it later). For the rest of the entries, we take the standard: adequate laboratories, no artifacts, and a +15 *Aegis of the Hearth*. On second thought, we decide to use our last negative option on our *vis*, making some of our *vis* contested. We aren't sure with whom – probably another Covenant. We do decide to make the *vis* of the Herbam variety, in the form of magical mushrooms in a nearby forest.

The next section is easy: standard library (containing scores in Provencal Lore, Hermes History and Hermes Lore Abilities) and equipment. We aren't too excited about being poor, so we come up with the idea of a silver mine nearby, but also aren't keen on taking another positive option. As a compromise we decided to make the silver mine currently abandoned for unknown reasons. It will be quite a challenge (and will take several stories) to open it again, though once opened it will provide a comfortable income. Our record keeper

marks this down as a good option, though one to be made use of at a later time.

Coming upon the last part, we need to take an extra bad option to balance our excess good one. We take standard contacts, standard status/reputation, and choose one enemy from the *Relations Table*. We decide this enemy goes well with our contested vis, and settle on our enemy being a rival Autumn Covenant, named Windgraven. This enemy should provide lots of story opportunities in the future.

All that remains is to go back and flesh out our Covenant, map its layout and that of the surrounding lands, create our characters, and begin play.

## Progression Through the Seasons

The following section provides an example of how a Covenant can evolve as it ages through the Seasons. To be precise, it shows developments from Spring to Summer, with hints at what is to come in Autumn and Winter. Note that this is merely an example, and should not be taken as *the* way to advance through the Seasons. Some Covenants move faster, some slower, while others may not survive more than a few decades, and some may never die.

The progression through the Seasons presented here takes the form of an annotated history. It is written in journal form by one of Mistridge's Magi, Grimgroth, as he experiences the growth of the Covenant. He takes us from the Covenant's birth to the year 1197, the "official" starting date of **Ars Magica** Sagas. Thus, his writings can be used as a basis for Covenant history in your own Saga. Indeed, you may use Mistridge as your Covenant, picking up its tale where Grimgroth's words end, in the Summer Season.

Provided with Grimgroth's writings are *Player's Notes*, which describe in game terms the changes to the Covenant. These notes make Grimgroth's tale concrete and palpable.

Note: The development of Mistridge provided here is only one possible progression. The Mistridge supplement presents the Covenant in a more complete and genuine light.

*Being an annotated history of the Covenant of Mistridge as recorded by Grimgroth, follower of Jerbiton.*

*Welcome, gentle reader, to this my private testament. I am afraid you have the advantage of me, for though you hold within your hands not only the story of my life and innermost thoughts, you remain a stranger to me, veiled by this barrier of paper and ink. I must presume upon your good nature to look kindly upon my scribblings, and ask you to treat this tome with all the respect due an elder, regardless of your own age or stature. Upon one point I must insist: if you must notate as you read, keep your musings well to the sides of the text! Many a notable book has been ruined in such fashion. Do not make this one of them. And reader, if you should find this work dull or pretentious beyond mortal endurance, may your dreams be sweet.*

*I am,*

*Grimgroth.*

*1066: What may I write of the year of the Lord, 1066? If a scholar you know it as the year of the great battle at Hastings and, if a noble, the crowning year of King William, and, if a mystic, the year in which the immense, traveling globe of fire transfixed the lunar sphere. Unfortunately, few note the most important event of the year, at least to me: my passing the gauntlet and thus shedding the bonds of apprenticeship. It is a time of great joy and confusion, for many paths lie before me and all are clouded in mist. My Parens urges me to devote my magics to the Crusades here in Iberia, but I do not know. While my mind sees the reason in such a path, my heart urges me otherwise. I would like to seek out my family in Val du Bosque again, whom I was so rudely snatched away from to begin my initiation (though I see the reasoning behind it now).*

*1067: Now I follow the middle path, wherever it may take me. I did not join an older Covenant, nor yet rush off headlong to form a Covenant of squabbling apprentices. It happened thusly: at the last Tribunal I was approached by one Consuelia, an older Magus in her prime. For reasons beyond my perception, she wished to break with her current Covenant and found a fresh one in the foothills of the Pyrenees. It seemed she understood my longing to return home and knew I could not resist her offer. Seeing a way to placate both heart and mind, I accepted. Now I sit within the*

*sparsely appointed walls of Mistridge, a cold draft upon my feet and a feeble candle throwing into shadow my once clear decision. My parents, I have learned, are long dead, and so, have I learned, are my feelings toward my brother and sister. I feel the burden of my coldness toward them.*

*I had no idea of the multitude of tasks necessary to begin a Covenant. We have worked ceaselessly since the thaws of spring to make our new home. A site was chosen (one I approve of, a mist-shrouded hillock), the local nobles and clergy briefly contacted (Consuelia's chief task), the tower verily summoned from the rock, Grogs found, laboratory equipment ordered, and so on to the exclusion of sleep, food and good humor. Consuelia is sometimes forceful, sometimes strangely uncaring, but still alluring. She remains a mystery to us all. Ah, yes. Allow me to introduce the rest of our little group: Felix Necromius, an odd, gangly fellow with a fascination with death; Clavius, a studious Magus of the mind that hides a keen intellect behind a mask of calm; and Oculo, an enigmatic person with a keen eye for the intentions of others and future events. All in all, not too bad a group. I think I will like Mistridge, provided they repair the roof of my study!*

**Player's Note:** We begin our first evening of **Ars Magica** by creating our Covenant. After completing that, we glance over the rules for magic and talk about the type of Magus we each want to play. We want to be sure to have a balanced group of Magi whose strengths complement each other. Luckily, each person has a different concept for their Magus and we end up with: Consuelia the elder, Mistress of Illusion (Imágonem), Grimgroth, Master of the Four Winds (Auram), Felix Necromius, Master of Life and Death (Córporem and Intéllego), Clavius, Master of the Mind (Mentem), and Oculo, Gatherer of Knowledge (Intéllego). This certainly doesn't cover all of the Arts, but it suffices for now.

Similarly, we talk about and create our Companions. Once again, we try to place our Companions' strengths in different areas we think important. The Companions we create are: Dexter the one-armed bard (good social skills and contacts with nobles), Robért the Friar (healer and champion of the common folk), Kip the street urchin (a nimble-fingered street orphan with underworld contacts in cities), Toadwart the doorman (a hideously deformed dwarf with several magical abilities and high scores in many Knowledges), and Homer the woodsman (lots of combat and outdoor skills).

Before we break up for the evening, we each agree to put the finishing touches on our characters in time for the next session, and to do our part in creating our turb of Grogs — we agree to each design five Grogs.

*1078: Eleven long years have passed since last I wrote to you, my friend. You must excuse my lapse, for never have I worked so hard. Where is the time spent? Pondering great questions, and in uncountable hours spent for love of research and experimentation. Where is the quiet, unbroken stillness of a season spent improving one's art or developing one's supposedly growing number of spells? Gone! Shattered by the harsh intrusions of the mundane world and the demands of Covenant life. Certainly, I have wrested some time for myself and others, but my Pater never hinted it would be so little. Do I seem overly bitter? Perhaps it is because I can only blame myself for much of my troubles.*

*It all began quietly enough. I was curious of Consuelia's doings away from the Covenant (in fact, we all were) and I asked to accompany her on her next trip. Thus was my life changed forever. That first excursion was to the local Baron, in an attempt to purchase the rights to a decrepit silver mine in the nearby hills. The Baron took a liking to me (I suppose because of my so-called "gentle gift") and strangely, I too enjoyed the exchange. On the way home I made the mistake of mentioning this fact to Consuelia and from that moment onward she found an excuse to include me in on every visit, however trivial, to every petty noble, quivering reeve, or bland-faced clergyman she felt it necessary to placate "in the interests of the Covenant." I gather her late Covenant (of which she never speaks) had rather bad relations with the mundanes. I shall have to pry into that later. So successful was I in those dealings that soon the mundanes would hear nothing of talking to anyone from the Covenant but me. Flattering, it is true, but not conducive to quiet study.*

*Still, I must say I'm proud of the results. We purchased the rights to the mine and have begun to restore it to working condition with but a promise to keep the area free from ravenous beasts and roving bandits — and a fifth of the income for the next twenty years. In addition, we bought the indentures of a group of hardy peasants to work the mine (each and every one a troublemaker, we soon discovered). The clergy have not been so understanding, but mutual fear and respect should keep matters in hand.*

*In other matters, our Grogs are recruited and trained, the hills cleansed of bandits (evidently in the pay of a rival nobleman), and our presence is now known throughout the valley. Ah yes! I had nearly forgotten one important piece of news. Five years past, Felix journeyed to gather our yearly vis from near Pasaquine, and found it already harvested! Through diligent magicks we found the culprit to be Windgraven, a Covenant much older than ourselves, located some miles to the southwest. Since then, a small, undeclared war has sprung up between us. With the exception of a few dead Grogs, some disrupted shipments of foodstuffs, and a number of Certámens, little has occurred. Of course we shall present our grievances at the next Tribunal, but have little hope of finding justice given our relative infancy. At least Windgraven, with its unorthodox and questionable practices, is as powerless as we in the politics of the Order.*

**Player's Note:** Our first few sessions of actual play develop themes that become central to the Saga of Mistridge. Initially, most of these stories serve to introduce us to the area and its inhabitants. Our first story, for example, deals with a magical creature discovered near a local village. We have to deal with the creature and persuade the peasants we aren't devils ourselves. Further stories involve the local nobility, a band of roving brigands in the area, and exploring the abandoned silver mine. One Troupe member runs some stories involving conflicts with our new-found enemy, Windgraven. The person

who made up Consuelia runs many of the stories, but at times other Troupe members step in with stories of their own. On average, we tell two stories per game year. The number of stories we experience is bound to decline shortly, as we get ourselves established in Val du Bosque and no longer need to account for every threat that faces the Covenant.

One thing that helps us plan future sessions, and chart the growth of the Covenant, is to make a "wish list" for the Covenant, as well as a separate list of story ideas or conflicts that need to be resolved. Troupe members wishing to run a story can easily look over the list to see if anything sparks their imagination. After a few sessions, for example, our list reads: "explore and make silver mine safe for workers, deal with bandits in hills, visit local lords and barons (Grimgroth). Long-term: deal with Windgraven. Perhaps trick them into violating the Code? Look for allies at the next Tribunal. For Covenant: housing for Grogs, training for Grogs, better library, improve defenses, create steady source of income (mine), hire specialists, and where are we getting our food?"

*1100: A new danger faces us all. Five years ago Pope Urban II declared a Crusade to free the Holy Lands from the 'infidel' Saracens. I vainly hoped little would come of this proclamation, but the petty nobles did not disappoint. They swarmed to the cause like flies to a sweetmeat. Within a year, a great host had set out and in three had captured Antioch. I can only hope that the Crusaders are soon defeated, for each new victory only strengthens their cause. If the Pope, by preaching on Crusade, can defeat the Saracens in Arabia, what is to keep him from defeating the Order throughout civilized lands? So alarming are these events that a special Tribunal was called last year.*

*Of course, nothing was resolved, with hotter heads urging an immediate confrontation with the Church, and cooler ones urging a migration of Covenants out of all civilized lands. In the end we all pledged to respect the Church and its servants. Many wished to make it a high crime to break this pledge, arguing that it endangered the Order itself, but others quickly voted that down. I suspect that most Covenants will watch themselves carefully for the next few years, then conveniently forget the whole matter.*

*Many other matters were discussed at the Tribunal, including our dispute with Windgraven. The older Covenants clearly had little interest in our squabble and, seeing no way to profit themselves, deftly shelved the unresolved issue in a matter of minutes. Consuelia grew angrier than ever I've seen (I believe she responded to the implied snub from her old Covenant). She sweetly exchanged frost-laden words with Cellemon of Windgraven, and soon goaded him into challenging Certámen over the matter, which she won handily. Little else of interest occurred, though I did spend a great deal of time discussing philosophy with Augustus of Bellaquin. In exchange for my copy of* The AlMagust, *he loaned me his copy of* La Chanson de Roland, *evidently a recently penned poem popular with the local nobles. I am hoping it will give me insights into their particular ways of thought. We've also agreed to share the tomes of our libraries. I look forward to expanding our Covenant's knowledge and sharing what we have with others.*

Onto more mundane matters. Overall, Mistridge is healthy and hale. We have purchased and are training a new contingent of Grogs, as well as starting to build them permanent living quarters at the base of our tower. Additionally, our silver mine is now open and providing us with an ample income. A large part of it is being used to refurbish lab equipment, provide us with food, and keep us supplied with vellum, ink, and other necessities.

One area needing drastic improvement, as I have already suggested, is our library. Already each of us has learned all that can be gleaned from our well-thumbed pages, leaving us hungry for more. Since the chances of acquiring new magical texts are slim, we have agreed to vigorously search for new sources of vis to help in our studies. Hopefully there is some to be found nearby — closer than Bellaquin — else Windgraven will hold more power over us.

**Player's Note:** We have lots of fun roleplaying the Tribunal. As a Troupe we decide who represents Mistridge (Consuelia and Grimgroth), then allow everyone else to play Magi from other Covenants, each with their own goals and motivations. Things get a bit chaotic at times, and it takes some extra effort on the Storyguide's part to coordinate everything, but it is worth it in the end. Now, whenever we need a change of pace we have a Tribunal session.

Our Covenant improves a lot in twenty-five game years, though not enough to warrant calling ourselves a Summer Covenant. How do we decide that? Basically, we look over the template for a Summer Covenant and compare it to our own Covenant. In many ways the Mistridge of 1100 is found lacking. So, we keep updating our Covenant wish list and applying time and money to the needed/desired improvements.

Over this period we average one story per year, with a good variety of politics, mysteries, puzzles, exploration, and good old-fashioned combat. Stories are increasingly motivated by individual characters' desires and past histories, not all of those characters being Magi. In fact, several of the stories involve Companions and/or Grogs alone.

*1125: Another quarter of a century finds Mistridge still prospering. My earlier fears of a crusade upon the Order have proven unfounded. For now, at least, the mundanes seem content to fight in the Holy Lands. Nevertheless, we are careful not to offend the priesthood and try not to give them cause to notice us.*

*Recently, an order of monks calling themselves Cistercians were gifted lands northwest of us. They have now built a monastery there, most simple and unadorned. I must confess I was most curious about these monks, for their monasteries seem to parallel our Order's Covenants in many ways. I resolved to visit them as a matter of courtesy and was quite pleased with the result. Their Abbot, Vincent, is a friendly, educated person with a sharp wit and keen intuition in matters of politics. I had some inclination to present myself as a traveling scholar, but soon found myself warming to his genial charm and eventually told him of our true nature. He did not seem alarmed and was rather pleased to have a small community of well-educated people nearby. He even entertained the notion of exchanging representatives to observe firsthand how the other lives. The meeting was pleasant, and I am looking forward to further meetings between our kind. It gives me hope that one day the Order will someday be accepted by the Church and indeed, all mundanes.*

*Clavius, being deeply interested in matters of philosophy, is most interested in the Abbot's offer and well may accept. It will be a matter of some debate (to put it mildly!) if we are to allow a monk within our Covenant for a season. I am inclined to welcome him, for so popular is Friar Robert among the locals that he has little time to perform proper services for the covenfolk (several Magi included) here.*

*Here at home the construction of the Grogs' quarters is complete. No longer need our servants worry about ravenous wolves while carrying out their duties. The Covenant proper and the Grogs' quarters are connected by a stairway spiraling upward through the tower, though the Grogs rarely climb very high, where the Magi quarters are, unless ordered to some service. The morale of our turb has improved considerably, a yearly contest of Grogs, with winners rewarded, being an immense help. Our silver mine is now firmly established, and we continue to pay the Baron a small amount each year, to seal our friendship.*

of Grogs, our new alliance with Bellaquin, and the maturing magical abilities of our Magi. Once again stories set in this time are a mix of politics (Tribunals, and dealings with the nobles, peasants and clergy), action (further explorations of the mines and local area, fighting bandits, and hunting and/or trapping an occasional magical creature), and pure fun (a band of local faeries have provided much amusement, to the Magi's chagrin). We usually run one story each year, though things are occasionally quiet, when nothing happens requiring the Magi's direct attention. Several stories set in these times develop the personalities and histories of our Companions. And, players of Magi feel a shortage of vis in these quiet periods, so pursuit of it assumes priority on the wish list.

*1165: Events in the world continue to make things interesting. Another crusade was called and is now at its height. We shall see how it ends. A special Tribunal was held to discuss the matter and, as usual, little was resolved. However, Mistridge was given considerable voice, evidence of our growing reputation and respect within the Order. Still, I sometimes I wonder if we shouldn't adopt the style of the mundanes' monarchies, with a single person making all important decisions. Surely it must be more efficient.*

*Civilization and enlightenment continue to make inroads despite formidable forces arrayed against change. A university was recently founded in Paris. We shall see what men of learning flock to its doors. If it does well, who knows? I might be tempted to pay it a visit. Nearer to home, my friends at Bellaquin tell me that Toulouse has become a hotbed of religious activity. Evidently a new religious movement there is quite popular and on the verge of being accepted by the nobility. They call themselves Albigenses, and evidently preach against the evils of worldly possessions. We have heard this before.*

*Our search for vis in the local area has turned up a magical pool in the mountains to the east. As of yet it is unclear what its powers are, but we are all hard at work attempting to discover them. As soon as we discover its powers we shall be all the more formidable. And, toward that end, we have turned our efforts from improving the Covenant to improving our magical arts. We continue to add to our debt to Bellaquin by studying their texts and have, on occasion, traded silver for the right to study at other Covenants.*

*And yes, I dare mention it. We have admitted a new Magus to our Covenant, one Vulcris, may the Lord help us.*

**Player's Note:** Since the players are currently most interested in researching new spells and increasing their Arts, we average one story every two years. This seems to work well now that much of the Covenant's relations have stabilized. We are experiencing the prosperity of Summer and are a force to be reckoned with.

*1185: Consuelia has left us. Words cannot convey the chaos that is now Grimgroth, and Mistridge. We squabble about everything: vis, rights to books, and who shall travel to pick up needed supplies ad nauseum. Never before has there been Certámen between the Magi of Mistridge. In the last three months there have*

*Windgraven continues to cause problems whenever possible. Their latest ploy was to cause trouble in a nearby village, claiming they were from Mistridge. They've even gone so far as to kill peasants on the Baron's lands! Thankfully, Oculo found concrete proof of their involvement and between us we have managed to placate the understandably furious noble. At the next Tribunal, Windgraven Magi were severely chastised for their actions, though no just penalty was declared. Though old and twisted, Windgraven still has power that other Magi are wary of. As for us, we have formed a strong friendship with Bellaquin, and continue to support the other's motions in Tribunal.*

*Indeed, as I had hoped, Bellaquin has been generous in allowing our Magi to study their magical texts. (Our own library is pathetically deficient and has long since become useless.) Hopefully this will help us keep pace with Windgraven's Magi; in recent years we have lost more Certámen than we have won. In return, Bellaquin has asked for nothing, though it is understood we owe them a great favor some time in the future. I cannot help but wonder what this favor will be, and what part it will play in the fate of Mistridge.*

**Player's Note:** During the last game decade we have decided that Mistridge has earned the right to be called a Summer Covenant. We base this decision largely upon our improved defenses, our larger, better trained and equipped turb been three! Never did I realize how strongly and surely she guided us; with a gentle, disarming phrase in the council chambers, or a quiet look of intense displeasure that caused tempers to cool. I try to do my best, but fear that Mistridge may tear itself apart before a new order is established. I long to follow Consuelia in her escape.

Much of our problems are caused by Consuelia herself. It is truth! She did not warn us or prepare us in any way. We do not know precisely what occurred. All that Oculo can glean is that Consuelia gathered a few personal things and departed for the top of nearby Tierné. There the trail ends with nary a clue; she simply vanished. Was this a plot of Windgraven's or does she now wander in some mysterious Twilight realm? I fear we shall never know.

One thing is clear: our inner turmoil must never become apparent to Windgraven. If they strike decisively, we will lose much of our strength and might never recover. I see no point in asking my friends at Bellaquin for aid. What could they do in any case? I can write no more.

**Player's Notes:** This is a time of great change in our Saga, especially in contrast to the previous period of relative quiet and stability. The disappearance of Consuelia gives rise to several roleplaying sessions involving each of our Magi at the Covenant, as we try to establish a new pecking order. It also serves to jolt us out of thinking only of our own Magi, and to start thinking about the Covenant again. Consuelia's disappearance is also a reminder of Covenant vulnerability. Even though the Summer Season is the height of vitality, it ultimately leads to the sedation of Autumn and eventually the stagnation of Winter.

*1197:* Mistridge has survived once again. We have managed to settle most of our internal problems, and have recently decided that an influx of young blood is needed to take care of the tedious tasks we no longer have the inclination to perform. Thus, we are sending word to many nearby Covenants to locate new Magi to supplement our aging ranks (none of us is willing to accept new apprentices at this time, wanting to pursue our own ends). In preparation for this influx, we have begun major expansions of the tower, both above and below ground. While this construction is noisy and distracting, it does make one proud to be part of Mistridge. We have also decided to expand our turb of Grogs, build new council chambers, and expand our library. I have some trepidations about doing all of this at once, for though we have much silver stored away in the coffers, our mine has been plagued by goblins in recent years and its output has dropped steadily. I'm sure our new Magi will take care of the problem.

Our bonds with Bellaquin continue to strengthen, with much travel and trade between us. Augustus and I have taken an active interest in the Albigensian movement, and its followers often give us shelter when passing through. Word of our camaraderie has somehow reached the nearby monastery, much to my consternation. The Abbot has responded in a most alarming way. He warns me of my defiances of God, aligning myself with what he calls heretics. I believe that he speaks not of his own heart, but on behalf of the Pope. This possibility truly frightens me. The Crusade I feared against the Order years ago may now be a threat to the lands of Mistridge itself.

**Player's Note:** With the coming of Autumn, the Magi of Mistridge find themselves preoccupied with their own studies, becoming somewhat isolationist and argumentative. The Troupe agrees that new construction makes old problems seem dead, though they are only buried to arise again in a later Season. New blood is also a necessity to take care of minor problems now too insignificant to be dealt with by higher minds. The power and obsession of magic are surely alive and well in Mistridge. Thus, Mistridge is still great in power, but already shows the signs of decline. In deference to medieval history, we decide that the coming Albigensian Crusade, a crusade to southern France itself, will have immense destructive impact on the Covenant, and may even bring about its destruction.

# Combat

## chapter five

he focus of most roleplaying systems is combat. It is a time of teamwork and excitement, and provides a chance to achieve a definitive victory. Each battle is a story in its own right, with its own heroes, villains, and plot. Thus the basis of **Ars Magica's** combat system is "narrative combat," which emphasizes roleplaying over wargaming-style mechanics. When playing out a battle, use the rules to strike a balance between combat as a contest to be won and as a scene in the ongoing plot. It is easy to stage a no-nonsense, gung-ho battle, but to truly experience battle's drama and excitement is much more stimulating.

**Ars Magica** offers two combat systems for your use. The first is the Action System, which allows you to resolve struggles quickly and easily. Its use is recommended at times when tensions run high and you want the pacing of a fight to reflect that desperation, such as when Grogs make a made dash through enemy lines to reach their goal. The Action System is also handy for organizing large struggles, when many combatants are involved, and can be used when you simply don't want to get bogged down by a long melee.

The Dueling System is more complicated than the Action System. It allows you to account for every little factor in a conflict, like maneuvers and environmental conditions, that influence the scene. The Dueling Combat System therefore makes for a more accurate and precise battle. The Dueling System is recommended when you want combatants to savor their struggle, so they may relish every blow and parry. It's particularly useful during

dramatic fights where the heroes come face to face with a story's primary villains, and the groups' parting will leave both sides lacking in number.

Depending on the scene of each battle, you may alternate between combat systems throughout a story. Of course, if you prefer one system over the other, you may use it at all times. Though the two systems are different, they are based on the same premises. Indeed, the Dueling System is simply an elaboration on the Action System. Thus, if you plan to use the Dueling System you should be familiar with the Action System, for many foundations for Dueling are described under Action.

Regardless of the combat system you use, the Storyguide controls the battle, ruling on who gets to attack when and where, as well as taking the role of non-player combatants. When you run a battle, play it by ear; ditch the rules when they get in the way. Use miniatures only as long as players continue to imagine the setting of the melee; their imagination should go beyond the battle map. Work especially hard at helping the players properly visualize the scene. If you do so from the start, and everyone listens, you avoid much confusion — "Wait a minute, I never knew there was a cliff there!" Read a few novels and see how authors describe a fight; borrow a few adjectives. Try to imagine exciting and varied settings for battles, and figure out how they affect the melee. Battle is a time of peak emotions, so try to elicit every last scrap of excitement and agony.

The unit of time in combat systems is called a Round. A combat Round is usually about six seconds, but it can be up to 12 seconds if the action is very slow (as in a methodical duel) or as short as three seconds if the action is extremely fast (desperate Grogs trying to break through enemy ranks.) When in doubt, figure that a Round is enough time for each character to perform one quick action, such as an attempt to connect with a sword or dash to another part of the battle — enough time to do something interesting.

# The Action System

## INTRODUCTION TO THE COMBAT SCORES

There are six scores that apply to combat. It's important at this point to understand the basics of what each is and does, to insure better understanding of the rules that follow. These six scores receive complete coverage later on in the Combat Chapter.

**FIRST STRIKE:** First Strike is a score that helps determine when you act in a combat Round, usually during melee. One roll often determines when you act throughout a battle. All weapons have a First Strike score, which influences when in a Round you act (i.e., long, heavy weapons are slower than short, light ones).

**ATTACK:** Your Attack total represents your ability to connect with a weapon. There are several factors that apply to this score, including your weapon skill and the type of weapon you use.

**DEFENSE:** Your Defense total represents your ability to avoid being struck. It's determined by your speed if dodging, and your weapon skill is parrying.

**DAMAGE:** This score indicates how much harm you inflict when your weapon connects. Damage is influenced by the weapon you use, your ability with it, and your strength.

**SOAK:** This score reflects the amount of physical punishment you can endure before being genuinely hurt. Your armor and resilience determine your Soak score.

**FATIGUE:** When you exert yourself in combat and other strenuous activities you run the risk of exhausting yourself. Your Fatigue score determines when this exhaustion sets in, and determines its severity.

## COMBAT SEQUENCE

Now that you have a basic understanding of the combat scores, we can discuss the combat sequence. There are five stages to each combat Round, and they must be coordinated for a battle to run smoothly and quickly. These stages are Between Time, Movement, Missiles, Melee, and Magic. These phases are described below for your convenience, and you can use them very casually if they are not needed.

### I. Between Time

At the beginning of the combat Round, you and the other players take care of certain aspects of the battle, including bookkeeping and any rolls that come at the ends of or beginnings of Rounds.

In this phase the Storyguide asks for declarations of actions for the coming Round, in order to better coordinate the actions of the combatants. These declarations force players to decide quickly what their characters do, and make it easier to structure the confusion and chaos that a battle can become.

Indeed, conflict, in which men, metal and magic clash, is chaos incarnate. Combatants are caught up in the events that surround them, and are constantly driven to perform deeds that exhaust the body. Indeed, all combatants who, from one Round to another, switch from one physically demanding action to another, such as running and then attacking, must make a Short-Term Fatigue stress roll of 6+ or lose a Fatigue Level. See Fatigue, p.157, for a complete discussion of Fatigue and how it works.

As your character's actions are determined for the coming Round in the Between Time phase, it is during this phase that you determine the Fatigue rolls your character makes. If you choose to attack when you spent the previous Round running, you must make a Fatigue roll between the events because you are changing strenuous actions. If you do not want to make a Fatigue roll, you can

### Combat Sequence Chart

1. Between Time
2. Movement
3. Missiles
4. Melee
     First Strike vs. First Strike
     Attack vs. Defense
     Damage vs. Soak
5. Magic and 2nd Missiles

decide to stroll across the battlefield instead of running. However, in that case you must spend at least one Round without attacking or running before your attack.

## II. Movement

At this time, each of the characters may move. The most common form of movement in combat is hustling, moving quickly but slowly enough to keep an eye on what is happening around you (and beneath you, so you don't fall). You can move up to 12 paces (yards) per Round while running, or less if on broken ground or in the dark. Walking cautiously moves you 6 paces per Round. An all-out sprint, in a straight line on a flat surface, takes you paces equal to 30 + Quickness + Athletics - Encumbrance - Wound and Fatigue penalties (the last two are explained under *Effects of Combat*, p.155).

## III. Missiles

In any given combat Round, all missiles that are ready to fire do so before melee takes place. If your crossbow is loaded and aimed, all you need to do is release the bolt. If you have to aim or load your weapon, your shot goes after the melee, in the Magic phase (see below).

In the Action System, you may fire one missile per Round. When you fire a missile, the Storyguide rates the difficulty of the shot and decides the Ease Factor. Sample Ease Factors are given on the *Missile Fire Table*. You then make an Attack roll to see if your missile hits the target. Roll a stress die and add the Attack Bonus of your weapon, your Weapon Skill score, and your Perception. (**Missile Attack = stress die + Weapon Attack Bonus + Weapon Skill + Perception.**) The Attack Bonus of your weapon is listed on the *Missile Weapons Chart*, later in the Combat Chapter.

If your missile Attack total at least equals the Ease Factor of the shot, you have scored a hit, otherwise you miss your target. If you hit, you must roll to determine the damage you do. Damage equals the result of a stress die, plus the Weapon Damage score (your Weapon Skill and Strength do not apply). (**Missile Damage = stress die + Weapon Damage.**) The Damage score of your missile weapon is listed on the *Missile Weapons Chart*, located at the end of the Combat Chapter. The target tries to resist the damage you inflict. His Soak score is modified by +6 to determine his Soak total; the defender does *not* make a Soak roll in the Action System. The topic of Soak scores is fully discussed under the Melee phase, below.

As missile Attack and Damage rolls are made on stress dice, it's possible to Botch those rolls. When you Botch, roll on the *Combat Botch Result Table* (p.156), and tailor the result to suit your weapon.

### Defending Against Missiles

If you try to dodge an archer's arrows, the archer's Ease Factor is modified by the score of your Dodge Ability.

# MISSILE FIRE TABLE

| Difficulty — Ease Factor of Shot | Example Conditions |
| --- | --- |
| Free Shot — Automatic Hit | You are standing over a prone, unmoving target |
| Simple Shot — 6+ | Point-blank range, slow or unmoving target |
| Easy Shot — 9+ | Point-blank range, target moving<br>Person standing at 20 to 50 paces |
| Medium Shot — 12+ | Small or quick target at point-blank range<br>Moving, human-sized target at 20 to 50 paces |
| Hard Shot — 15+ | Quickly moving target at 20 to 50 paces<br>Tiny, quick target nearby, like a bat<br>Long-range shot with long-range weapon, such as a bow |
| Very Hard Shot — 21+ | Long-range shot with short-range weapon, such as a sling<br>Target obscured by darkness, underbrush, dust |

(**Dodge Missiles = Dodge score added to attacker's Ease Factor**.) If you have no Dodge Ability, you can still go through the dodging motions, though aren't as hard to hit as a target with Dodge skill; you are treated as a moving target on the Missile Fire Table. For example, if an archer has an Ease Factor of 7 to hit you, you dodge, and your Dodge score is 2, the archer needs an Attack roll of (7 + 2) 9 to hit you. To dodge missiles, you must do nothing but watch for the missiles, you must have room to dodge, and you must make a Dodge roll of 3+ (to insure you don't slip). If you fail this roll, you lose all benefits of dodging and are considered a stationary target on the Missile Fire Table to determine the attacker's Ease Factor to hit you.

If you defend against missiles by hiding behind a shield, the archer's Ease Factor increases by the shield's Parry Bonus score (the number that is usually added to your Defense score, as will be discussed). The Parry Bonus score of your shield is listed on the *Melee Weapon Chart*, located later in the Combat Chapter. Additionally, your Size is normally subtracted from the archer's Ease Factor. The larger you are, the easier it is to hit you, but if you're small (e.g., Size -1) you are more difficult to hit. (**Shield Defense against Missiles = Shield Protection - Size, added to attacker's Ease Factor**.)

### Preparing Missiles

In order to have your missile weapon ready to fire at the beginning of a Round, you must spend time loading and aiming at the end of the previous Round. This usually means you do nothing more in the previous Round than shoot another missile, or forego any other action to prepare your missile. After having prepared the shot at the end of the previous Round, you announce the shot in the Between Time phase, choosing a target. Having done all this in advance of the next Round, you get to shoot your missile before the Melee phase of the next Round.

If, in the Between Time phase, you do not state your next target, or if that target is no longer available after the start of the next Round, you have to wait until the end of the Round (the Magic phase) to fire. If you only draw your missile weapon once melee begins, you fire during the Magic phase of the Round. You may then fire before melee in the next Round if you prepare your next shot in advance.

## IV. Melee

After the ready missiles have been released, the main part of the Round comes: melee.

Because combat can be complicated, the Storyguide should divide large battles up into small units, and resolve each sub-melee separately in each Round. A sub-melee is one whose outcome for the Round is not affected by the actions of any other character. If you are fighting a zombie while the rest of your group is otherwise occupied, you and the zombie are one sub-melee. The faster of you (hopefully you and not the zombie!) strikes first, and then the other returns the favor. This sequence should be played out by itself, rather than having players involved in other battles rolling their dice between your strike and the zombie's response — that only confuses matters. If a Magus in your party is casting a spell to decompose the zombie, then that Magus becomes part of your sub-melee, because the effects of that spell are important to the outcome of your battle this Round.

There several stages to the melee procedure. Each is described in sequence below:

**FIRST STRIKE:** As previously discussed, First Strike determines who makes the first blow in your sub-melee. First Strike is rolled for each combatant. Roll a stress die and add the Weapon Speed of your weapon, your Quickness, your Weapon Skill score, and subtract your Encumbrance score. (**First Strike = stress die + Quickness + Weapon Speed + Weapon Skill - Encumbrance.**) For speed of play these modifiers should be calculated and recorded on your character sheet, to be added to a stress die at any time. The Weapon Speed of your weapon is listed on the *Melee Weapons Chart*, located later in the Combat Chapter.

The highest First Strike roller attacks first, followed by the second highest, and so on. Uninterrupted combat continues from Round to Round in the same order as that decided in the first Round; you usually roll First Strike only when you first close with your opponent.

The order of melee only changes if you take command of the First Strike. To take command you must make a higher Attack roll than all your opponents, and must strike at least one of them in a Round. In the next Round you attack first and force your opponents backward with the force of your onslaught. They step back one pace per Round. As long as your opponents don't make a higher Attack roll than you, and don't strike you with it, you continue to attack first on each successive Round. The only way to lose control of the First Strike is to be exceeded by an opponent in an Attack roll, and to be hit by his attack. If neither you nor your opponents hit each other, the combatant who controlled First Strike in the previous Round continues to control it in the next.

If a tie ever results between First Strike rolls, reroll until one combatant emerges as the quicker.

It's suggested that you use miniatures to keep tabs on combatant positions, particularly as combatants may be forced back by others. A combatant who has control of the First Strike may force his enemies into dangerous areas, like cliff edges.

As First Strike rolls are made on stress dice, it's possible to Botch them. If you Botch your First Strike roll,

## Exempli Gratia:
## FIRST STRIKE

Torlen, the Grog Sergeant, closes for battle with a bandit. Torlen's First Strike score (before the stress roll) is 4. He rolls a 7, for a First Strike total of 11. The bandit's First Strike score is 3, and he rolls a 13, for a total of 16. The bandit strikes first in each Round of the battle unless Torlen can take control of the battle. In one Attack roll, Torlen gets a total of 15 and hits the bandit, while the bandit only gets an Attack roll of 5. Torlen therefore takes control of the melee, becoming the first attacker of each successive Round. In each Round he forces his opponent back one pace. But, in a later Round, the bandit makes a higher Attack roll and hits Torlen, so resumes control of the First Strike, forcing Torlen back each Round.

you attack last throughout the entire combat scene, regardless of how many combatants are involved in the scene, of how slow the others are, and of how high your Attack rolls are. Attacking last in each Round, you are always driven backward by your attackers.

**ROLLING TO HIT:** When you strike at an opponent, you make an Attack roll. An Attack roll consists of a stress die, plus your Dexterity, Weapon Skill, and the Attack Bonus of the weapon you're using. (**Attack roll = stress die + Dexterity + Weapon Skill + Weapon Attack Bonus.**) Your weapon's Attack Bonus is listed on the *Weapons Chart*, located later in the Combat Chapter. All of the above modifiers to the stress die should be recorded on your character sheet for each weapon you carry, allowing you to quickly add their total to a stress die at any time.

If your Attack roll exceeds your target's Defense total, you have made a solid hit. The defender's Defense total varies depending on whether she attempts to parry or dodge your blow. If parrying, her Defense total equals 6, plus her Parry Skill, plus the Parry Bonus of her weapon, minus her Size (larger targets are easier to hit and smaller ones more difficult). (**Action Parry Defense Total = 6 + Weapon Parry Bonus + Parry Skill - Size.**) Weapon Parry Bonus is listed on the *Melee Weapons Chart*, located later in the Combat Chapter. If the defender lacks the Parry Skill, it is treated as zero for this calculation. If dodging,

## DAMAGE EFFECTS CHART

| Damage in Excess of Soak | Body Levels Lost |
|---|---|
| 1-5 | Drop one Body Level |
| 6-10 | Drop two Body Levels |
| 11-15 | Drop three Body Levels |
| 16-20 | Drop four Body Levels |
| 21-25 | Drop five Body Levels |
| And so on… | |

her Defense total equals 6, plus Dodge Skill, plus Quickness, plus Quickness, minus Encumbrance and Size. (**Action Dodge Defense Total = 6 + Dodge Skill + Quickness - Encumbrance - Size.**) If the defender lacks the Dodge skill, it is treated as zero for this calculation. Both parry and dodge totals should be recorded on your character sheet for quick reference during play. In the case of parrying, a Defense total should be calculated for each weapon you carry. You'll note that Defense does not involve a roll in the Action Combat System.

Since Attack rolls are made on stress dice, it's possible for you to Botch a roll. If you do, refer to the *Combat Botch Result Table* (p.156). As Defense involves no rolls in the Action system, it cannot be Botched.

If you exceed your opponent's Defense total with your Attack roll, you may determine the damage you cause her.

Note: You cannot both attack and parry with a single one-handed weapon in one Round. You are allowed to attack with a one-handed weapon and parry with another (such as a shield), or attack and dodge. However, you can both attack and parry with a two-handed weapon in a single Round.

**DAMAGE:** To determine Damage from a successful hit, roll a stress die, plus your Weapon Skill, Strength, and the Weapon Damage score of your weapon. (**Damage = stress die + Weapon Skill + Strength + Weapon Damage.**) Your Weapon Damage score is listed on the *Weapons Chart*, located later in the Combat Chapter. The modifiers of this roll should be recorded on your character sheet for each weapon you carry, ready to be added to a stress roll at any time. Note that Damage modifiers for missile

weapons are different from those of melee weapons, as discussed above (p.139).

Your Damage roll is compared to the target's Soak total. His Soak total equals 6, plus his Armor Protection, Stamina, and Size. (**Action Soak = 6 + Armor Protection + Stamina + Size.**) Armor Protection is listed on the *Armor Chart*, located later in the Combat Chapter. Soak total should be calculated and recorded on your character sheet for easy reference.

If your Damage roll exceeds your opponent's Soak total, you harm your opponent. For every 5 points, or fraction thereof, that your Damage roll exceeds the target's Soak total, your opponent loses one Body Level (see the *Damage Effects Chart* for a plan of how this works). If the defender's Soak total matches or exceeds your Damage roll, the defender suffers small cuts and bruises, but no more serious harm. The section on Wounds (p.159) discusses the results of lost Body Levels.

As Damage rolls are made on stress dice, it's possible to Botch them. If you Botch, refer to the *Combat Botch Result Table* (p.156) to determine the results. You'll note that Soak does not involve die rolls in the Action Combat System. Botches, therefore, cannot result from Soak.

### Brawling in Action Combat

Brawling is fighting unarmed. In Action Combat you can simulate unarmed combat by using the "Unarmed" weapon listing on the Weapons Chart (p.164). The variables of "Unarmed" are applied to your First Strike, Attack and Damage rolls, and Defense total. References to Attack and Parry Skill for combat calculations are considered Brawl Skill instead.

WOC
92

**THROWN WEAPONS:** Thrown weapons are different from missile weapons in that they are far more unwieldy, have a much shorter range, and can be parried whereas missile weapons cannot. The low Attack Bonuses of thrown weapons represent the difficulty of hitting someone at a distance as opposed to hitting someone directly in front of you. Thrown weapons are therefore considered part of the Melee phase of combat, not the Missile phase. Thus, characters can use their attacks to throw a dagger or hand axe rather than attack in "genuine" hand-to-hand combat.

As part of melee combat, thrown weapons use all the modifiers and rolls of hand-held weapons. They can also be parried and dodged as normal for melee. However, the Storyguide may wish to rule that certain weapons cannot parry incoming thrown weapons, thus reducing the target's Defense total. For instance, imagine parrying a thrown knife with a morningstar. It's virtually impossible, so no Parry Bonus is allowed for the morningstar's use as a parrying weapon.

## V. Magic

After melee, missiles that were not fired in the first part of the Round are resolved, followed by Formulaic spells and normally-cast Spontaneous spells. (Fast-Cast Spontaneous spells have no established place in the combat schedule; they're cast whenever they're needed). Rules for casting Formulaic and Spontaneous spells are found in the Magic Chapter.

If you need to know who casts a spell first in the Magic phase, compare the totals of Quickness + Finesse - Encumbrance of the two Magi. The caster with the higher score gets his spell off first. If you need to know whether a spell caster or missile attacker acts first in the phase, compare the above score of the caster to the following

## THE SIX BASIC ACTION COMBAT SCORES

**FIRST STRIKE:** The First Strike roll of each combatant is compared when they enter combat, and the combatant with the higher roll strikes first for the duration of the the fight with that opponent. Any ties are rerolled. Another combatant may seize control of First Strike honor by making a higher Attack roll than, and striking, the fighter who currently controls First Strike. For each round that you retain control of the First Strike honor, you force your opponent backward one pace.

Your First Strike total is **stress die + Weapon Speed + Quickness + Weapon Skill - Encumbrance**.

**ATTACK:** The Attack roll represents your ability to connect with a weapon. The result is compared to the target's Defense total (see below). If your attack roll exceeds the Defense total, you connect and may make a Damage roll.

For melee and thrown weapons, the Attack roll is **stress die + Weapon Attack Bonus + Dexterity + Weapon Skill**.

For missile weapons the Attack roll is **stress die + Weapon Attack Bonus + Perception + Weapon Skill**.

**DEFENSE:** The Defense total represents your ability to avoid being struck in combat. When you are attacked, compare your Defense total to the result of your opponent's Attack roll. If your Defense total at least matches the Attack roll, you avoid the attack.

If you defend by parrying with a weapon or shield, your Defense total is **6 + Weapon Parry Bonus + Parry Skill - Size**.

If you dodge, your Defense total is **6 + Dodge Skill + Quickness - Size - Encumbrance**. Neither Defense total applies directly to missile weapons; other scores apply to missile weapons when you defend against them (see *Missiles*, above).

**DAMAGE:** This roll indicates how much damage you do when your weapon connects. A Damage roll is compared to the target's Soak total, and if the Damage result exceeds the Soak total, the target loses Body Levels, representing wounds and possibly death. For each five points, or fraction thereof, by which your Damage roll exceeds the target's Soak, the target loses one Body Level.

The Damage roll for melee and thrown weapons is **stress die + Weapon Damage + Weapon Skill + Strength**.

Missile weapons use only a **stress die + Weapon Damage**.

**SOAK:** This total represents your ability to withstand damage without being wounded beyond negligible cuts and bruises. If your Soak total at least matches the Damage roll of the attacker, you do not drop a Body Level.

Your Soak total equals **6 + Armor Protection + Size + Stamina**.

**FATIGUE:** Your Fatigue score represents your ability to exert yourself continuously without tiring. Whenever you switch actions from one strenuous activity to another without taking it easy for at least one Round in between, you must make a Fatigue roll of 6+ or lose a Fatigue Level.

Your Fatigue total is **stress die + Stamina - Encumbrance**.

## Summary of Movement Distances

**Walking Cautiously in Combat:** 6 + Quickness in paces (yards)

**Running in Combat:** 12 + Quickness

**All-Out Sprint:** 30 + Quickness + Athletics - Encumbrance - Wound and Fatigue penalties

score of the missile attacker: Quickness + Attack Skill - Encumbrance. The character with the higher total acts first. Who acts first is important in determining the results of conflict. See the *Fast-Cast* rules, p.184, in the Magic Chapter for the results of "who acts first" situations, as applied to the Magic phase.

**Miscellaneous Activity:** You might find yourself doing non-combatant things during combat, such as looking for the axe you accidently threw into the bushes or rummaging through your backpack for an important magic component. The Storyguide must determine how long such activities take. Each character should be allowed one activity and roll per Round, simply because it keeps players involved in the activity at hand. Normally you have to give up your attack for a Round to do anything else. Miscellaneous activities are usually taken care of in the Round's Magic phase.

Note that though the above material comprises the bulk of Action Combat, there are factors involved in

## Exempli Gratia: Action Combat Stats

The following are Torlen's Action combat statistics:
**Mace (one-handed)**
**First Strike:** Speed + Skill + Quickness - Encumbrance = +2 +3 +0 -2 = +3

**Attack:** Weapon Attack Bonus + Skill + Dexterity = +3 +3 +0 = +6

**Damage:** Weapon Damage + Skill + Strength = +6 +3 +1 = +10

**Defense Total (parrying with knight shield)**
**Defense:** 6 + Weapon Parry Bonus + Skill - Size = 6 +4 +3 -0 = 13

**Defense Total (dodging)**
**Defense:** 6 + Skill + Quickness - Size - Encumbrance = 6 +3 +0 +0 -2 = 7

**Soak Total (with hauberk of ring mail)**
**Soak:** 6 + Armor Protection + Size + Stamina = 6 +7 +1 +0 = 14

**Fatigue**
**Fatigue:** Stamina - Encumbrance = +1 -2 = -1

Action that also apply to Dueling Combat. These factors, such as wounds and their results, Fatigue, and Botches, are described on p.155, after an explanation of Dueling Combat.

## An Example of the Action Combat System

Torlen and some of his Grogs are charging a nest of bandits, who are entrenched in a ruin. Torlen and his men have to break through the bandits' defenses quickly, in order to get inside before any other bandits kill their hostages, the mundane allies of the covenfolk. Given the desperation of the Grogs' charge, the Storyguide decides the Action Combat System is appropriate.

Some bandit archers outside the ruin fire on the approaching Grogs. The Storyguide decides that two archers attack each Grog, and each gets one shot off before closing into melee — before forming sub-melees, each of three combatants.

**Round 1:** Two archers fire on Torlen with self bows, while Torlen's Round is spent charging (for ease of play, all the bandits are assumed to have the same statistics). Since Torlen is moving directly at the bandits without dodging or hiding behind his shield, the Ease Factor of the bandits' shots is 12. The archers' missile Attack scores, before stress rolls, are +3 (+0 Weapon Attack Bonus + 2 Weapon Skill + 1 Perception). Their stress rolls are 3 and 14, for a total of 6 (misses) and 17 (hits). No Defense totals are applied in missile combat.

Damage is determined for the second shot. The Weapon Damage score of a self bow is +8, modified by a stress die which results in a 5, for a total of 13. Torlen's Soak total, 14 (see the earlier insert), is compared to this result. Since 14 is higher than 13, Torlen shrugs off the grazing wound without losing Body Levels.

One archer spends the remainder of the Round reloading to fire again before Torlen closes.

**Between Time:** As one of the bandits is shooting again, he acts before Torlen arrives. The other draws his sword and waits for Torlen to close with him.

**Round 2:** The single archer fires again, getting a result of 9, another miss.

As Torlen is switching from charging in the last Round to attacking in this, he must make a Fatigue roll. His Fatigue score is -1 (+1 Stamina and -2 Encumbrance). He rolls a 6 on the stress die, for a total of 5, which is lower than 6, so he loses a Short-Term Fatigue Level, falling to Winded, but that loss involves no penalties.

Torlen closes on the two with his mace. His First Strike total is 8 (stress roll of 5 + 3). The bandit with sword drawn gets a First Strike of 6 (stress roll of 4 + 0 Quickness + 2 Speed + 1 Weapon Skill - 1 Encumbrance). The bandit with the bow has already acted in the Round so cannot attack again; he can only defend.

As Torlen's First Strike is highest, he attacks first, swinging at the bandit with the sword. His Attack total is 9 (stress roll of 3 + 6). The bandit parries and his Defense total is 9 (6 + 2 Weapon Parry Bonus + 1 Skill - 0 Size), which equals Torlen's attack, so the attack is deflected.

The bandit strikes back, getting an Attack roll of 11 (stress roll of 6 + 4 Weapon Attack Bonus + 1 Skill + 0 Dexterity). Torlen parries with his knight shield, and has a Defense total of 13, which exceeds the Attack roll, so Torlen is safe.

**Between Time:** All combatants are now in melee; the remaining bandit drops his bow and draws his sword

**Round 3:** As Torlen won the First Strike roll, and was not hit by an Attack roll higher than any of his own in the last Round, he retains control of First Strike.

Torlen swings at the bandit who just joined the melee. Torlen gets an Attack roll of 18 (stress roll of 12 + 6). The bandit tries to dodge the blow, and has a Defense total of 7 (6 + 2 Skill + 0 Quickness - 0 Size - 1 Encumbrance). Torlen hits and rolls Damage of 15 (stress roll of 5 + 10). The bandit's Soak total is 8 (6 + 1 Armor + 0 Size + 1 Stamina). As Torlen's Damage roll exceeds the bandit's

Soak total by 7, the bandit loses 2 Body Levels (one for every five points, for fraction thereof, of damage suffered), suffering Light Wounds (-1 to successive rolls, as discussed on p.159).

The bandit struck is knocked back a pace by Torlen's blow. However, as Torlen is locked in combat with two bandits, he doesn't want to leave himself open to the first bandit's attacks by advancing on the injured one. Thus, the bandit that was forced back may again close with Torlen to attack (the battle continues normally). Had Torlen pursued the wounded bandit, the bandit would be forced to step a pace back from his original position. If a cliff edge was within a pace, he would be dead now!

Now the bandits strike back. The first gets an Attack roll of 9 (stress roll of 4 + 5 for Attack modifiers), and the second gets a roll of 6 (stress roll of 2 + 5 for Attack modifiers -1 for Light Wounds). Neither exceeds Torlen's parry Defense total of 13.

**Between Time:** All combatants continue the melee.

**Round 4:** Torlen still controls the First Strike and thus attacks first. He swings at the wounded bandit and gets an Attack roll of 10 (stress roll of 4 + 6). The bandit dodges again, but his Defense total is now 6 (one less than usual) because of his Light Wounds. Torlen hits and rolls Damage. He gets a result of 20 (10 stress roll + 10)! The bandit's Soak total of 8 (his Wound penalty does not apply to his Soak) still leaves him with 12 damage, so he loses 3 more Body Levels. The bandit falls to the Incapacitated Body Level, collapsing at Torlen's feet.

The remaining bandit swings at Torlen for an Attack roll of 12 (stress roll of 7 + 5 for Attack modifiers), which fails to exceed Torlen's parry Defense total of 13.

In the Rounds that follow, Torlen kills the remaining bandit at about the same time the remainder of his turb dispatch their opponents. The Grogs who are still on their

WOC 92

## Making Attack and Damage Rolls

When making Attack and Damage rolls, it is a good idea to use two differently colored dice simultaneously. One is designated as the Attack and the other the Damage die. This combined roll reduces the number of total rolls required in a combat Round. Even if your Attack roll fails to hit your target, eliminating the significance of the Damage roll, the Damage roll can still be applied to the narrative of the battle. Your Damage roll tells you how forceful your attack is. So, even though the attack misses the target, the damage rolled may be applied to something else hit by the blow, like the floor or a bannister against which you are leaning. The Storyguide decides any incidental effects from a particularly weak or powerful blow that misses your target.

feet then charge into the ruin to rescue the folk being held hostage, but the would-be saviors are too late. Their friends were slaughtered days ago, their remains lingering about to decay in the open air, and their souls trapped in this world without absolution.

# Dueling Combat

The Dueling System is based on the structure of the Action System. Indeed, the Dueling System mainly functions to make the Action System more accurate and realistic. This means factors like battle maneuvers and the environment come into play. Every axe stroke and bolt shot is made important and dramatically exquisite. However, this also means combat as a whole is slowed as a game event; determining who strikes and who hurts who takes longer and involves more modifiers. The Dueling System is therefore reserved for scenes of dramatic battle between bitter enemies, scenes that involve, well. . . a duel to the death.

## COMBAT SEQUENCE

The Sequence of events in Dueling Combat is the same as that in Action Combat. Many of the rules that apply in Action Combat apply here. However, some new rules are introduced to Dueling Combat that supersede those of Action. These new rules are presented below.

## I. Between Time

The announcement of action for the coming Round is made here, as usual.

## II. Movement

Movement in combat is a dangerous affair, as you have to keep a constant eye out for enemies and obstacles that could put you at a disadvantage, such as tree roots, corpses, and other debris. These dangers do not preclude a person's natural speed, though; some people are faster than others, regardless of distractions or dangers. To reflect this, movement can be modified by your Quickness score. You can move up to 12 + your Quickness score in paces (yards) per Round while running through a combat scene. The Storyguide may reduce this distance if there are particularly daunting distractions that interfere with your movement. Walking cautiously moves you 6 + your Quickness score in paces per combat Round. And, if you sprint in a straight line, on flat terrain, you can travel a number of paces equal to 30 + Quickness + Athletics - Encumbrance - Wound and Fatigue penalties (the last two are explained under *Effects of Combat*, p.155).

## III . Missiles

For the most part, combatants who fire missile weapons are only of sufficient skill and ability to fire one missile per Round. However, those who are naturally quick or adept are capable of firing more often, and should be entitled to do so. A special missile weapon, designed for a high rate of fire, may also increase the number of shots you get per Round. To determine your rate of fire, total the Rate listed for your weapon, your Weapon Skill, your Quickness, and subtract your Encumbrance. (Missile Rate of Fire = Weapon Rate + Weapon Skill + Quickness - Encumbrance.) The Rate of your weapon may be found on the *Missile Weapon Chart*, located later in the Combat Chapter. Compare the total number calculated to the *Missile Rate Table*. If the table states you are able to fire

| MISSILE RATE TABLE | |
|---|---|
| *Rate Total* | *Shots/Round* |
| -20 and lower | 1/4 |
| -19 to -10 | 1/3 |
| -9 to 0 | 1/2 |
| +1 to +10 | 1 |
| +11 or better | 2/1 |

## EXCEPTIONAL BLOW TABLE

| Body Levels Lost | Severity | Example |
|---|---|---|
| One | Minor | Leg wound: movement hampered (reduce to 50% normal) |
| Two | Major | Head: knocked unconscious for 15 minutes, unless reduced to the Incapacitated Body Level, which takes precedent over this effect |
| Three or more | Grave | Arm: maimed (-3 to rolls involving arm) or severed (-5 to rolls involving arms) |

twice per Round, you can fire one in the Missile phase. After you fire in the Missile phase you can choose another target, and fire at that target in the Magic Phase. You cannot fire both arrows in either the Missile or Magic phase alone. Thus, if you don't fire in the Missile phase, you can only fire once in the Round, during the Magic phase.

If two or more combatants fire missile weapons in the Missile or Magic phases, you may want to determine who shoots first. The attacker with the highest Quickness score shoots first. If there's still a tie, the weapon with the

highest Rate score (as shown on the *Weapon Chart*) is the first to fire.

Taking extra time and care with a missile attack improves its chances of hitting the target. If you spend an entire Round aiming your missile weapon (giving up any opportunity to fire, move, or act during that Round), add +3 to your Attack roll when you make the shot in the following Round.

As missile Attack and Damage rolls are made on stress dice, they have the potential for extraordinary failures (Botches). To determine the results of Botches, refer to the *Combat Botch Result Table* (p.156). The results found on the chart have to be tailored to missile weapons. Stress Attack rolls can also result in extraordinary successes. If your Attack roll exceeds the required Ease Factor by at least 10 points, you may hit a certain spot on the target, with the Storyguide determining any special results. You may choose the spot you hit. Exceptionally high Damage rolls from missile attacks have their own inherent benefits.

Also note that the Dueling System involves a new use for Soak, which applies to both missile and melee attacks. See the description of the Dueling Melee phase, below, for a discussion of that new Soak rule.

## IV. Melee

**FIRST STRIKE:** If combatants tie their initial First Strike rolls, made at the beginning of melee, neither combatant takes control of the initiative. Rather, the two attack each other simultaneously, which means that the weapons used to attack cannot be used to parry that Round. Shields and weapons in the other hand can still parry, though. Simultaneous attacks persist in each Round that follows until one combatant strikes the other, and gets a higher Attack roll than the other in the same blow. When that happens, the attacker takes control of the First Strike for the battle that follows. However, he may lose it again if his opponent gets a higher Attack roll, and strikes with it, in a later Round.

In Dueling Combat, the combatant who controls the First Strike gains an additional benefit from it. Not only does he force his opponent back one pace each Round, but

## Making Defense and Soak Rolls

The use of a stress die in Defense and Soak makes Dueling Combat more complex as it adds another two rolls to each combatant's actions in a Round. If several combatants are involved, that can mean a lot of extra rolls. To rectify things somewhat, it's suggested that two dice be rolled simultaneously by the defender whenever attacked. The dice should be of different colors, one designated for Defense and one for Soak. Thus, you only really make one overall roll, and the game is not so terribly impeded. If your Defense roll is successful in repelling an attack, simply disregard the result of your Soak die.

he receives a noncumulative +1 bonus to his Attack rolls for each successive Round that he controls the First Strike. Thus, if you get the First Strike in Round 1, you gain +1 to Attack rolls in Round 2, and in each Round thereafter (these +1 bonuses do not accumulate to become +3 after three Rounds, though). If your opponent steals control of the First Strike, he gains a +1 modifier to hit you each Round thereafter.

If you Botch your initial First Strike roll, you attack last each Round, are driven back a pace each Round, and are +1 to be hit each Round.

**ROLLING TO HIT:** The act of rolling to hit remains the same in Dueling Combat as it is in Action Combat. However, if you get a particularly good, and successful, Attack result (15 or more than your opponent's Defense roll), you strike a vulnerable spot on the target. Choose a general location: head, limb, chest, or abdomen. The target's Soak roll (discussed below) only counts the armor covering that part of the body. Furthermore, since you have struck a vulnerable spot, your attack can have a greater than normal effect. See the *Exceptional Blow Table*.

Though Attack rolls change little between the Action and Dueling systems, Defense changes significantly with the Dueling System. The target makes a Defense roll rather than applying a Defense total. Thus, the Attack roll of your opponent must exceed your Defense *roll*, not total, to have a chance to hurt you. If the target parries, her Defense roll equals the sum of a stress roll, Weapon Parry Bonus, and Parry Skill, minus Size (**Dueling Parry Defense = stress die + Weapon Parry Bonus + Parry Skill - Size.**) If the defender lacks the Parry Skill, it is treated as zero for this calculation, and three extra Botch dice are rolled for the action. If the target dodges, her Defense roll equals the sum of a stress roll, Dodge Skill, and Quickness, minus Size and Encumbrance. (**Dueling Dodge Defense = stress die + Dodge Skill + Quickness - Size - Encumbrance.**) If the defender lacks the Dodge Skill, it is treated as zero for this calculation, and three extra Botch dice are

rolled for the action. The scores that contribute to your defenses should be calculated and recorded on your character sheet, ready to be applied to a stress roll whenever needed. For parrying, you should determine your Defense modifiers for each weapon or shield.

As Defense rolls are made with stress dice in the Dueling System, it's possible to get extraordinarily bad or good results. If you Botch your Defense roll, refer to the *Combat Botch Result Table* (p.156) to determine the results. Exceptionally good results have their own, obvious merits.

**DAMAGE:** Dealing out damage changes little from the Action System. It's in the Soaking of Damage that the Dueling System differs from the Action. The target of an attack makes a Soak roll, rather than utilizing a Soak total. Thus, your opponent's Damage roll must exceed your Soak *roll*, not your Soak total, to hurt you. Your Soak roll equals the sum of a stress die, Armor Protection, Stamina and Size. (**Dueling Soak = stress die + Armor Protection + Stamina + Size.**) The scores that contribute to your Soak roll should be calculated and recorded on your character sheet, in order to quickly be added to stress rolls as needed.

**THROWN WEAPONS:** Thrown weapons function like melee weapons, as they do in the Action Combat System. However, in the Dueling Combat System, Defense and Soak *rolls* are used to resist their attacks.

**MAGIC:** As per Action Combat.

# Brawling

Brawling is fighting unarmed, but can include close combat with small or available weapons (including knives and rocks). In Action Combat you can simulate unarmed combat by using the "Unarmed" weapon listing on the Weapons Chart. However, to portray the brutality of and possibility of maneuvers in unarmed combat, unarmed combat is fully developed under Dueling Combat. The "Unarmed" listing is not used in the Dueling Combat System.

Brawling is as deadly as fighting with weapons, but it has several interesting options. These options slightly change the nature of Dueling Combat. When brawling, select a maneuver (listed below). You then have to make a successful Attack roll (one that exceeds your opponent's Defense roll) to see whether you make contact with the target. Once you have made contact, you may execute the maneuver chosen above.

As brawling is a different form of combat from genuine melee, First Strike, Attack, Damage and Soak rolls are different than usual (only Defense rolls remain the same). Your First Strike roll in brawling equals the sum of a stress die, Quickness, and Brawl Skill, minus Encumbrance. (Brawling First Strike = stress die + Quickness + Brawl - Encumbrance). Your Attack roll in brawling equals the

## Brawling Maneuvers Table

| Maneuver | Replacement Damage Roll | Replacement Soak Roll | Close Combat |
|---|---|---|---|
| Strike | Strength + Brawl | Soak | 0 |
| Throw | Strength + Size + Brawl | Quickness + Size + Brawl - Encumbrance + 5 | -4 |
| Tackle | Strength + Size + Brawl | Quickness + Size + Brawl - Encumbrance | +4 |
| Wrest Weapon | Strength + Brawl | Strength + Brawl | 0 |
| Immobilize | Strength + Brawl | Strength + Brawl +5 | +4 |
| Closing | Quickness + Brawl - Encumbrance | Defense | n/a |

sum of a stress die, Dexterity and Brawl Skill (Brawling Attack = stress roll + Dexterity + Brawl.) Damage and Soak rolls are replaced by ones appropriate to the type of maneuver you attempt on your opponent. The Brawling Maneuvers Table lists the Damage and Soak replacement rolls.

When your brawling Damage roll exceeds the target's brawling Soak roll, you perform the intended maneuver on the target, and do him damage in the process. Otherwise, the target resists your move and is not hurt. Brawling damage is different from standard damage. For every 10 points, or fraction thereof, that you exceed your opponent's Soak roll, he suffers the loss of a Short-Term Fatigue Level instead of a Body Level. For every second Fatigue Level lost, whether in one Round or over several, a Body Level

is also lost. If your brawling Damage in one blow exceeds your opponent's Soak roll by 21 points or more, your opponent is automatically reduced to a state of Unconsciousness (see Fatigue, p.157), assuming such a blow doesn't reduce him to that anyway. He also loses a Body Level.

The following are explanations of the maneuvers on the Brawling Maneuvers Table:

**STRIKING:** Hitting your opponent in an attempt to cause damage, possibly with the fist, knee, or foot. You can increase damage by using a cestus or other weapon, at the Storyguide's option.

**THROWING:** Unbalancing and toppling your opponent while remaining standing yourself. Your opponent lands 1d10 feet away.

**TACKLING:** Knocking an opponent down while falling down yourself. Upon landing, the two of you land apart from each other; you are not in Close Combat (see below). If you take a running start before you tackle, you get a -1 modifier to your Attack roll, but receive a +4 bonus to your tackle Damage roll.

**WRESTLING FOR AN ITEM:** Grabbing an opponent's possession, like a weapon, and pulling it away. If your Attack roll succeeds, you have made contact with the item. To wrench it from your opponent's grip your Damage roll must exceed his Soak roll by at least 5 points. If your Damage roll is the lower of the rolls, the two of you continue wrestling over the item. Further attempts to wrench the item free in subsequent Rounds do not require Attack rolls, simply Damage and Soak rolls to determine who becomes the possessor. Of course, your opponent may make an attempt on the item himself in his part of the brawling Round. Note that damage is not inflicted between combatants who wrestle for an item.

The person who has control of First Strike at the beginning of a wrestling match is assumed to control it throughout. He only loses First Strike if his opponent takes possession of the item being fought for. The person who wins the item acts first in subsequent Rounds. While wrestling, the combatant who attacks first each Round cannot force his opponent back, nor does he gain the +1 modifier to hit on Attack rolls.

If the weapon you wish to grab does not have a long wooden haft, you suffer a -5 penalty on your initial Attack roll to grab it. It is suggested that you not try this maneuver with a bladed weapon.

**IMMOBILIZING:** Holding or pinning, making your opponent unable to move. To get free your opponent must deliver Damage in excess of your Soak score. To deliver that damage he attempts another brawling maneuver, like Strike or Throw. The immobilized combatant's Attack and Damage rolls suffer a -3 modifier until free. Until he gets free, you continue to hold your opponent and retain control of the First Strike, even if you didn't control it before immobilizing your opponent. Furthermore, for every Round that you maintain the hold, you need not make Attack rolls to hit your opponent; you simply apply pressure and compare your brawling Damage roll to the other's brawling Soak roll.

**CLOSING:** Coming close enough to an opponent that you can use the rules for Close Combat (below). A brawling Attack roll is made to get close to your opponent. The Damage roll indicated on the *Brawling Maneuvers Table* is for getting a Close hold on your opponent. You inflict Damage in the process, based on your roll to get the hold. The Round after a Close hold is achieved, Close Combat is used. If your Damage roll to Close does not exceed your opponent's Soak roll, you fail to achieve Close Combat. The same is true if your brawling Attack roll is lower than your opponent's brawling Defense roll. If you want to Close again in the next Round, you have to make another Attack roll. As soon as you successfully Close with and get a Close hold on someone, you gain control of the First Strike in the following Round, whether you controlled First Strike in the previous Round or not.

Breaking away from Close Combat involves the same rolls for closing into it. You make an Attack roll to find an opening and hurt your opponent when you break free (through your Damage roll). If your Attack roll is less than your opponent's Defense roll, your opponent blocks your path and you remain in Close Combat. If your Damage roll does not exceed your opponent's Soak roll, you do not push free and are still locked in Close Combat.

**CLOSE COMBAT** — Sometimes you may fight in full contact with an opponent, such as when you roll around on the ground and wrestle. When in Close Combat you can use all the brawling maneuvers listed on the *Brawling Maneuvers Table*, but each defender's Defense and Soak rolls suffer a modifier because you are in Close Combat. These modifiers are listed on the table. Attack and Damage brawling rolls are not modified in Close Combat.

While Close fighting, your Defense roll is the sum of a stress die, Quickness, and Brawl, minus Encumbrance. (**Close Combat Defense = stress die + Quickness + Brawl - Encumbrance.**) Your usual Defense roll is not used. You cannot use weapons other than knives, or those of similar size (their combat modifiers from the Weapons Chart, p.164, are applied under the *Strike* maneuver), with which you get an additional +3 to Attack and Damage rolls. Animals also get this +3 bonus with their natural weapons when Close fighting.

First Strike in Close Combat is controlled by the combatant who wins it; the combatant who had the higher Attack roll, and struck the other, in the previous Round. The combatant who controls First Strike in Close Combat does not receive the usual +1 modifier to subsequent Attack rolls, and does not force his opponent back a pace; the two are intertwined.

You can initiate Close Combat or break away from it by using the *Closing* rules, above.

# OTHER DUELING COMBAT CONSIDERATIONS

## Combat Maneuvers

Though you usually fight simply by swinging your weapon at opponents as explained in the Action Combat rules, sometimes you may want to make use of special combat maneuvers. These maneuvers are possible in Dueling Combat. Some possible maneuvers are explained below:

**TWO-WEAPON USE:** You may strike with two weapons each Round. You can only use one-handed weapons in each hand, and your Strength must be two points higher than that listed on the Melee Weapon Chart (p.164) to wield a weapon in your off-hand. Unless you have the *Ambidextrous* Virtue, you suffer a -3 Attack penalty with the weapon in your off-hand, and a -1 Attack penalty with the weapon in your good hand.

Your Parry and Attack Skill scores with a weapon in your off-hand are 0, as long as you have a positive Parry and Attack Skill score (whichever is appropriate) with the weapon in your good hand. If your Parry and Attack Skills with your good hand are zero or negative, those of your off-hand are one point worse. You can raise your Parry and Attack Skill scores in off-hand use just as you can raise any other skill.

If you attack with two weapons in the same Round, you cannot dodge or parry in that Round. Your Defense score thus equals the higher Parry Bonus of your two

weapons, minus your Size. (**Defense when attacking two-handed = highest weapon's Parry Bonus - Size.**)

When you enter combat using two weapons, roll First Strike for the weapon in your good hand. The result of the roll determines when you attack in each Round. If you have the *Ambidextrous* Virtue, you may roll First Strike for both your weapons and use the highest. The Attack rolls of both your weapons may also be used to take First Strike from a combatant who controls it. That is, if either weapon gets a higher Attack roll than your opponent's, and you hit your opponent, you resume control of the First Strike.

**DESPERATE DEFENSE:** If you have not yet attacked this Round you may decide to forego your attack and devote your effort to defense, calling out "Parry" or "Dodge" to the Troupe (say it aloud); this gives you a +5 bonus on your Defense rolls for the rest of the Round. This action may even be taken if you announced a different action during the Between Time phase.

**GREAT BLOW:** You can put extra force into a blow, making it more effective than usual. You must forgo your Attack roll for a Round in preparation for the blow. In the Round that follows, your Attack roll receives a +3 bonus, and Damage from the blow, if it hits, is twice the amount remaining after the target's Soak. However, you must make a Short-Term Fatigue roll immediately after

the blow, even if your Attack roll fails. While preparing for your Great Blow you are only allowed to parry incoming attacks, but cannot parry or dodge in the Round that the attack is made. Your Defense score in this Round consists of your weapon's Parry Bonus - your Size.

**HOLDING YOUR GROUND:** By suffering a -2 penalty to Defense rolls, you can hold your ground in a battle. When doing so you are not forced backward by an opponent when she has control of First Strike (however, you are still +1 to be hit, and still attack after your opponent). The Defense penalty is suffered for every Round you hold your ground, and you must announce the action in the Between Time phase to perform the action in the Round that follows.

**MOUNTED COMBAT:** If you are engaged in combat while on a horse, any Ability used while riding cannot be used at a level higher than your Riding score. For instance, if you have Broadsword Attack at level 5, but a Riding of only 3, you use your Broadsword at level 3 instead of 5 while riding. When mounted you gain +1 to hit opponents on foot; however, when mounted, you always take an extra Botch roll. People who lack the Ride Ability suffer a -3 modifier to *all* rolls when mounted, and must make three additional Botch rolls.

**KEEPING AT BAY:** When you are armed with a longer weapon than your opponent (i.e., your weapon is at least three feet longer), you can choose to keep your opponent at a distance rather than harm her. Your opponent, on the other hand, tries to get past your weapon and in so doing cannot harm you unless she succeeds. Each Round is therefore devoted to determining whose intentions prevail. The combatant who gets the higher Attack roll, and would normally hit the other, wins the contest.

If you have the longer weapon you receive a +5 modifier to Attack rolls as long as the other is at a distance. If you get a higher Attack roll than your opponent, and would normally hit her, you get control of the First Strike (if you already have it, you maintain it). As a result you attack first in the next Round, drive your opponent back *three* paces, not just one, and receive another +1 Attack roll modifier in the next Round. No damage is delivered by your "attack," and no Soak rolls are made by your opponent.

If your opponent with the shorter weapon makes a higher Attack roll than you and would hit with it, she takes control of the First Strike (assuming she doesn't already control it). She does not damage you in this Round, but evades your weapon and closes with you. In the next Round she attacks first and may harm you, drives you back a pace, and receives a +1 Attack roll modifier.

If neither combatant would normally hit the other, regardless of how high Attack rolls are, the status quo is maintained; the combatants maintain the distance held between them in the previous Round.

If you have the longer weapon and your opponent gets inside its reach, you have to move away from her if you want to keep her at bay again. This assumes she gives you the opportunity to get some distance. . .

**CHARGING:** You can charge with any thrusting weapon by running before you strike. You get a Damage bonus of +5, plus your Size. If you miss your blow, the defender gains +1 on her Attack roll that Round (or in the next if she has already attacked in this Round and if you are still nearby). If the defender has a thrusting weapon, and has time to set it against your charge (i.e., knows you're coming), the defender's Damage roll receives a bonus of +5, plus the attacker's Size; your bonuses are equal. If you charge on a horse, add the Size of your horse to the Damage delivered by charger and defender. The attacker in a charge must make a Fatigue roll of 6+ or lose a Short-Term Fatigue Level. If you're mounted, the roll is made for your horse.

**MONSTROUS COMBAT:** Beasts often have special attacks best developed individually by the Storyguide. Unorthodox attacks often affect the way the combat rolls work. For example, imagine a fire drake that pounces on its opponents. A Defense roll based on Dodge skill lets you evade the creature, but a Defense roll based on Shield Parry skill merely means that the shield is between you and the beast. You are still knocked to the ground, pinned, and likely crushed, but the shield might at least protect you from some of the creature's claws. Because of their special attacks, monsters are often exceedingly dangerous to battle.

**ATTACKING OBJECTS:** Sometimes you may want to direct your weapon against an inanimate object, such as an enemy's magic item, or even a door. If the object is held or carried by someone, you need to make an Attack roll versus an Ease Factor set by the Storyguide, but otherwise you do not need to exceed the carrier's Defense roll. The Storyguide also assigns the object a Soak score (or simply an Ease Factor), to be rolled against by your Damage score, as well as a number of resistance levels (equivalent to Body Levels) to determine whether the object is damaged by your attack. For every 5 points that your Damage roll exceeds the object's Soak roll, the object loses one resistance level. The Soak scores and resistance levels of objects are symbolized as follows, using a wooden door as an example: door (+10/5). The number before the slash is added to a Soak stress roll. The number after the slash is the number of resistance levels an object has. Once all an object's resistance levels are depleted, it is irreparably damaged. The more frail an object, the lower a Soak and the fewer resistance levels it has. The sturdier an object, the higher the Soak and the more levels it has.

# COMBAT MODIFIERS

The Action Combat System is designed under the assumption that combatants are armed and able to defend themselves, that they are fighting on even ground in full daylight, that they are all human or nearly so, and that they are content merely to exchange blows without trying any tricky maneuvers. Some battles fit these criteria, but for entertainment value, exceptions are the rule in the Dueling System. The following are elaborations that allow you to make Dueling Combat true to its circumstances, making it more interesting.

## Striking from Advantage

When you can strike a foe from a superior position, such as from behind, above, or the side, you get an advantage. It's easier to hit your opponent and easier to place the blow in a damaging spot on the body.

Striking from Above: +1 to Attack rolls

Striking from the Side: +1 to Attack rolls

Striking from Behind: +3 to Attack rolls; Damage after Soak is doubled

Surrounding Opponent: +1 to Attack and Damage rolls for every extra person on your side attacking a single opponent. These bonuses are cumulative based on the number of allies helping you. If you and two others attack, you all gain +2 to Attack and Damage rolls.

Striking Defenseless Opponent, Hurriedly: Automatic hit (unless you Botch), Damage after Soak is doubled.

Striking Defenseless Opponent, Surely: Automatic kill (barring unusual circumstances.)

## Combat Environment

The physical environment can hamper combatants' abilities.

Heat: -1 to -4 on Fatigue rolls.

Darkness: -1 to -4 to Attack rolls, one or two extra Botch rolls.

Complete Darkness: First Strike is rolled normally at the beginning of the fight. With each Round a comparison roll is made between combatants, consisting of a stress die + Stealth + Perception. The combatant with the lower of the two rolls suffers a -5 modifier to Attack, Defense, Damage and Soak rolls for the Round. Even if your roll is the highest of the two compared, you still receive a -2 modifier to all the above combat rolls. If you Botch the comparison roll, you're hit automatically that Round (skip Attack and Defense rolls, moving on to Damage and Soak rolls, but still with the above modifiers). Combatants in complete darkness cannot attack in a Round that they move in.

Obstacles in Battlefield: These include anything like corpses and undergrowth. They result in whatever seems appropriate, like extra Botch rolls or movement penalties.

Strong Winds: Penalties on missile fire and thrown weapon Attack rolls.

## An Example of Dueling Combat

Torlen has been sent into the abandoned town of Mercille to see what he can find. While Torlen is exploring the smithy, a man who was hiding in the back room attacks him with a club. Because Torlen is expecting danger from diabolists, and to trick Torlen's player into thinking that danger has arrived, the Storyguide announces this battle will be fought with the Dueling System, suggesting a significant fight. Thus, before Torlen even knows who's attacked him, Torlen's player expects an impressive combatant. When Torlen attacks with corresponding violence, the pathos of the scene is only heightened. The Storyguide is nasty indeed.

For a listing of Torlen's Dueling Combat scores, see the insert on p.154.

Between Time: The attacker's Stealth + Dexterity roll, made to sneak up on Torlen, is 7. Torlen's Alertness +

153

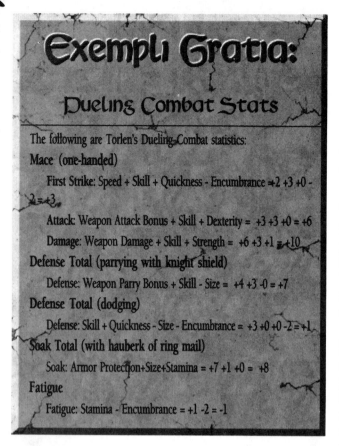

# Exempli Gratia:

## Dueling Combat Stats

The following are Torlen's Dueling Combat statistics:

**Mace (one-handed)**

First Strike: Speed + Skill + Quickness - Encumbrance = +2 +3 +0 - 2 = +3

Attack: Weapon Attack Bonus + Skill + Dexterity = +3 +3 +0 = +6

Damage: Weapon Damage + Skill + Strength = +6 +3 +1 = +10

**Defense Total (parrying with knight shield)**

Defense: Weapon Parry Bonus + Skill - Size = +4 +3 -0 = +7

**Defense Total (dodging)**

Defense: Skill + Quickness - Size - Encumbrance = +3 +0 +0 -2 = +1

**Soak Total (with hauberk of ring mail)**

Soak: Armor Protection+Size+Stamina = +7 +1 +0 = +8

**Fatigue**

Fatigue: Stamina - Encumbrance = +1 -2 = -1

Perception roll, made against the smith's roll to detect his approach, is only 5, so the ambusher attacks with the advantage (+3 to his Attack roll and double damage). The Storyguide decrees that in the first Round, Torlen can only spin, counter the attack, and call out for help.

**Round 1:** The smith's Attack roll is a 3, modified by +3 for the club's Attack Bonus, +1 for his Skill, +0 for his Dexterity, and +3 for attacking from behind. Total: 10. Torlen's Defense roll is 4 (roll) + 7 (Shield Parry score), for a total of 11. Torlen's total is higher, so he parries the attack.

**Between Time:** The attacker decides to swing his club and dodge Torlen. Torlen attempts a Perception roll to realize he's being attacked by a poorly-armed civilian, not a diabolist at all. The Storyguide sets the Ease Factor at 6, and Torlen rolls a 5. So, in his confusion he responds instinctively as he would to a better-armed attacker, striking back with his mace.

**Round 2:** Since Torlen didn't even attack in the last Round, the smith still controls the First Strike, so he attacks first. He therefore pushes Torlen back a pace and receives a +1 modifier to his Attack roll.

The smith rolls a 1 on his Attack die, rolls again and gets a 6, which doubles to 12, and makes a total of 17 with his Attack and First Strike modifiers. Torlen's Parry is only 6 (roll) + 7 = 13, so he is hit. The smith rolls Damage. He gets a 9 (roll) + 2 (Weapon Damage) + 1 (Strength) +1

(Skill) = 13. Torlen's Soak is 4 (roll) + 8 (Soak modifiers) = 12. Torlen loses one Body Level, dropping to Hurt, with a strong blow to his right arm (as ruled by the Storyguide).

Torlen replies with an Attack roll of 5 (roll) + 6 = 11 and a Damage roll of 8 (roll) + 10 = 18. The smith's Defense roll is a mere 7, with no modifiers, so he is hit, and his Soak depends merely on his +1 Stamina. His Soak roll is 4 (roll) + 1 = 5. Since damage exceeds Soak by 12 points, the target loses 3 Body Levels. The smith is now at Medium Wounds, with a -3 penalty to his actions.

**Between Time:** The Storyguide makes a Bravery Personality Trait roll for the smith to see if he flees. The roll is 8 + 2 (he's a very brave peasant) - 3 (wound penalties), for a total of 7, above the Ease Factor of 6, so the smith keeps fighting. The Storyguide also decides that Torlen now realizes he is fighting a resident of Mercille, not a diabolist. Torlen decides to drop his mace and shield and wrest the club from the smith's hand.

**Round 3:** In the previous Round the smith had the highest Attack roll, so he maintains the First Strike advantage. That means Torlen is driven back another pace, and the smith receives a +1 modifier to his Attack roll this Round. Even if Torlen had won control of First Strike, the Storyguide might have given First Strike advantage to the smith because Torlen is changing his attack strategy this Round.

The smith's Attack roll beats Torlen's Defense roll, which is easy to do when Torlen doesn't have his shield, but Torlen's Soak protects him.

Torlen is grabbing the smith's weapon, which is a brawling maneuver, so brawling rules are used. Torlen gets a 9 on his brawling Attack roll (Brawl + Dexterity) to grab the club, but the Storyguide rules that the club is short enough to give him a -2 penalty on the roll. The modified roll of 7 is still good enough to overcome the Defender's roll of 4 (Defense roll doesn't change with most brawling rules). Now that Torlen grips the club, he tries to pull it away. His brawling Damage roll (Strength + Brawl) is 7 (stress die) + 1 Strength + 3 (Brawl) = 11. The smith's brawling Soak roll is only 8 + 1 (Strength) + 1 (Brawl) - 3 (wounds) = 7, but Torlen needs to win by at least five points to get the club, so both combatants retain a grip on it, with no one person possessing it.

**Between Time:** Both combatants struggle for control of the club.

**Round 4:** The smith controlled the First Strike in the last Round. Since the two are wrestling for an item, the smith continues to control the First Strike, acting first in each Round for the duration of the struggle, until one combatant takes possession of the club. While wrestling, the smith does not gain the usual +1 bonus to Attack rolls (there are no Attack rolls), and does not force Torlen back a pace.

Now that both combatants have a hold on the club, Attack rolls are not used to determine who gets control of the club; only brawling "Damage" and "Soak" rolls are used. The Smith's brawling Damage roll (Strength + Brawl) is 3, which is lower than Torlen's brawling Soak roll (Strength + Brawl), so the smith fails to wrest the club away. On his turn, Torlen's brawling Damage roll is 9 and the smith's brawling Soak roll is 4, a difference of 5 points. Torlen pulls the club free and hurls it across the room, trying to get across the point that he is not an enemy.

**Between Time:** Torlen thinks his job is done, so he decides to address the fellow he has just bested. However, the Storyguide makes a successful Daring Personality Trait roll for the smith, who jumps for Torlen's dropped mace. Torlen changes his action and brings down his doubled fists on the man's exposed back. Given this sudden change, the Storyguide decides Torlen's action suffers a -3 penalty to the Attack roll.

As Torlen assumed possession of the club in the previous Round, he now has control of First Strike. He brings down his doubled fists as the smith begins to reach for the fallen mace. Torlen's brawling Attack roll for a Strike Attack is 8 (stress roll + Dexterity + Brawl +1 for controlling First Strike), but the result is reduced to 5 because of his -3 penalty for changing tactics. The smith's brawling Defense roll (normal Defense since the attack is a brawling Strike) is higher, so Torlen's fists bounce off their target.

The Storyguide decides the smith needs a Dexterity roll of 8 to get the mace, and rolls a 0. As the smith's shop is littered with tools, the Storyguide decides that two Botch rolls are required. A 5 and 0 result, the second roll indicating a Botch. The Storyguide decides that the smith falls on the mace, losing a Body Level and dropping to Heavy Wounds.

The Storyguide rules that the smith now surrenders. When the aid that Torlen called for at the beginning of the fight arrives, they find their friend tending to the smith's wounds.

# Effects of Combat (Both Systems)

The results and possibilities of combat described below apply to both the Action and Dueling Systems. They are therefore provided together for easy reference.

## Botches

The Action and Dueling Combat Systems tell players who wins a fight, and indicate how much damage each side suffers. However, they do not take into consideration all the debilitating, life-threatening, anxiety-provoking, and even humorous things that can happen on a battlefield. Botches take these unpredictable possibilities into account.

Combat Botches follow the same rules as normal Botches, though they tend to be more dangerous. There are three "Botchable" rolls in Action Combat: First Strike, Attack, and Damage. First Strike Botches allow your opponents to attack before you throughout a battle. Therefore, they don't require coverage here. The other two rolls, Attack and Damage, do require explanation. The same is true for the remaining two Botchable rolls of the Dueling System: Defense and Soak.

When a die in any of these four rolls results in a 0, roll another die (if not more, as dictated by the Storyguide). If a number other than 0 turns up, you don't Botch. However, your result for the Attack, Defense, Damage or Soak roll is still 0.

If another 0 does turn up on a Botch die, you've Botched and must make a roll on the *Combat Botch Result Table* to determine the results. The *Table* dictates the intensity of your Botch.

# COMBAT BOTCH RESULT TABLE

## Damage/Soak Botches

2 You are thrown 1d10 paces from your opponent. In the next Round you can only dodge and parry.

3 The blow knocks the wind out of you. Make a Fatigue check against an Ease Factor of 6 or lose a Short-Term Level.

4 You overextend yourself and collapse to the ground. You can only dodge or parry next Round.

5 Your arm shudders with the blow. Your Dexterity suffers a -2 modifier for the next 1d10 hours.

6 Your weapon flies out of your hand if you're striking. It lands 1d10 paces away. Part of your armor flies off if you're Soaking. Reduce your Protection score by 2.

7 Your weapon caroms off your opponent if you're striking, throwing you off balance for your next attack; next Round's Attack roll suffers a -3 modifier. If you're Soaking, your armor is dented, limiting your mobility; your Attack and Defense scores suffer -2 modifiers for the remainder of the combat.

8 Your arm is smashed by the blow. You cannot use it at all for 1d10 hours. You suffer an overall -2 modifier to Dexterity and Strength.

9 Your weapon is damaged if you're striking. All Attack, Damage and Parry rolls suffer a -3 modifier until the weapon is repaired. If you strike unarmed, your hand is smashed; your Dexterity suffers a -2 modifier for 1d10 hours. Your armor is damaged if you're Soaking. Reduce its Protection score by 3 until repaired.

10 You reel out of control, making yourself vulnerable to your opponent's attack. In the next Round his Attack roll receives a +5 modifier.

12 Your weapon is broken and useless if you're attacking. If striking unarmed, your hand is crushed; your Dexterity suffers a -3 modifier for 1d10 hours. Your armor is destroyed and rendered useless if you're Soaking.

14 The blow absolutely devastates you. You stagger backward, seeing stars and gasping for breath. Lose a Short-Term Fatigue Level.

16 The blow stuns you. You stand prone for the following Round. You cannot act at all; you're a sitting target. Any attack made against you hits you automatically (just roll Damage and Soak), unless Botched.

18 You put everything you've got into the move and exhaust yourself. You automatically lose two Short-Term Fatigue Levels.

20 If striking, your weapon rebounds back at you. Roll Damage against your own Soak score. If Soaking, double the attacker's Damage, after subtracting your Soak.

24 You risk every ounce of vitality you have and waste it. You lose all remaining Fatigue Levels and are Unconscious.

28 Your arm is broken by the blow. It's useless, resulting in an overall -4 modifier to Dexterity and Strength. To determine how long it takes for the arm to heal, roll on the *Wound Recovery Chart*, assuming Heavy Wounds.

32 As a result of bad footing or a powerful blow, your leg is broken. Your Quickness suffers a -4 modifier. To determine how long it takes for the leg to heal, roll on the *Wound Recovery Chart*, assuming Heavy Wounds.

36 A loose piece of steel blinds you in one eye. You gain the Poor Eyesight Flaw and automatically lose a Body Level.

40 A deflection or powerful blow destroys an ear, hand or foot. You acquire one of the Missing Ear, Missing Hand or Missing Foot Flaws. You automatically lose 2 Body Levels.

48 A deflection or powerful blow destroys a leg or arm. You acquire one of the Lame or Missing Hand (with a -5 penalty to all actions and spell casting) Flaws. You automatically lose all remaining Body Levels and are Incapacitated.

56 A wildly swung weapon plunges into your chest, shattering your sternum. Fragments of bone scatter to the winds as your spurting blood muddies the ground at your faltering feet. The earth grows richer with your corpse.

64 The clash of bodies and wills is too much for your frame to endure. Your pounding heart bursts, sending a cascade of blood gushing from your mouth. May the Divinities accept your soul.

72 Rising after yet another resounding exchange of blows, you look to your weapon and realize it's broken short, the lethal end impaling you from abdomen to spine. For a moment you feel the sinews of your back slide from their moorings before you fall lifeless to the ground.

80+ You are sent recoiling from the fray, your arms flailing in the air. As you try to recover your footing, you lunge for the nearest ballast. Before you can stop yourself, you realize you have plunged onto the weapon of your nearest ally, and that your weapon has struck him as well. You're beyond the mortal coil. To determine whether you damage your ally, make normal Attack and Damage rolls. Your ally's Defense and Soak attempts each suffer a -5 modifier due to surprise.

If the Storyguide requests several Botch checks on a roll of 0, you must make all of them. For example, Pierre is fighting in a heavy wood, where he has plenty of chances to make mistakes. The Storyguide states that Pierre's player must make three Botch tests when he rolls a 0. The number of zeroes you roll with your Botch dice determines how many times you roll on the *Combat Botch Result Table*. The highest of your rolls on the *Table* is the one you suffer from. So, if Pierre gets two zeroes on his Botch rolls, he must roll twice on the *Combat Botch Result Table*, suffering the worst of the effects rolled (i.e., taking the highest roll).

When rolling on the Combat Botch Result Table, make a stress roll. If a 1 is rolled, the die is rolled again until a number other than 1 is rolled, with the total calculated as usual. With this stress roll, 0 is treated as 10, though, unlike normal stress rolls.

The *Combat Botch Result Table* is divided into two sections: Attack/Defense Botches and Damage/Soak Botches. Look up the result of your stress roll in the section that applies to your action. The results described are generic in nature, so they may need to be tailored to the weapon you use (e.g., a missile weapon) or the action you attempt.

## Fatigue

By exerting yourself in both Action and Dueling Combat, and in other strenuous activities, you can tire and even exhaust yourself. Your level of exhaustion is measured in Fatigue Levels. Each character has a certain

# COMBAT BOTCH RESULT TABLE

## Attack/Defense Botches

Note that references to "weapon" apply to attacking weapons and shields, and defending weapons and shields, whichever is appropriate to the scene.

2 Your swing buries your weapon into the ground. A Strength roll of 6+ is needed to withdraw it, performed in the next Round in lieu of other actions. If unarmed, your fist is snared in surrounding clutter and must be pulled free.

3 Your weapon flies from your hand, landing 1d10 paces in a random direction. If unarmed, you fall down and lose a Round of action.

4 You overextend yourself and are thrown off balance. Your Attack and Defense scores are modified by -3 in the next Round.

5 With a wide sweep of your arm you wind yourself. Make a Short-Term Fatigue roll against an Ease Factor of 6.

6 Your weapon is damaged. Attack, Damage and Parry rolls suffer a -3 modifier until the weapon is repaired. If unarmed, you bruise your hand. Your Attack and Defense scores suffer a -3 modifier in the next Round.

7 You pull a muscle and suffer a -3 modifier to your Attack, Damage, and Parry rolls throughout the combat.

8 Your weapon is broken and useless. If unarmed, your arm is crushed and you suffer a -2 modifier to Dexterity for 1d10 hours.

9 You flail wildly and crash to the ground. Your Attack and Defense scores suffer a -5 modifier in the next Round.

10 You move left, your opponent moves right. Disoriented, you automatically lose control of the First Strike, if you have it, in the next Round. If you don't already control the First Strike, you cannot win it for the next three Rounds.

12 You step off balance and leave yourself completely open to your opponent's next attack. His next Attack roll receives a +5 modifier.

14 You crash into your opponent, falling to the ground before him. You cannot act for a Round, except to parry his next attack. His next Attack roll receives a +5 modifier.

16 You put everything into your action, and in missing strain yourself. You automatically lose one Short-Term Fatigue Level.

18 You strain yourself to your very soul. Lose two Short-Term Fatigue Levels.

20 You strike your own arm if attacking, and make your arm vulnerable if defending. Your own Damage, or that of your attacker, is rolled normally against your Soak. Regardless of

damage suffered, your Dexterity suffers a -3 modifier for 1d10 hours.

24 You strike your own leg if attacking, and make your leg vulnerable if defending. Your own Damage, or that of your attacker, is rolled normally against your Soak. Regardless of damage suffered, your Quickness suffers a -3 modifier for 1d10 hours.

28 You strike yourself in your own eye if attacking, and make your eye vulnerable if defending. Your own Damage, or that of your attacker, is rolled normally against your Soak. Regardless of damage suffered, your Perception and Presence each suffer -3 modifiers for 1d10 hours.

32 You fall on your own weapon. Roll Damage as if attacking yourself, against your own Soak. You cannot act on the next Round, except to parry or dodge. If you're unarmed, you fall on your own arm, suffering a -4 Dexterity modifier for 1d10 hours.

36 You overreach all your physical limits and expend almost every ounce of energy you have. You are now Unconscious. Lose all remaining Fatigue Levels.

40 As you move your weapon it's deflected off a nearby obstruction; you strike yourself. If unarmed, you move wildly, causing limbs to be disjointed. In either case you automatically lose a Body Level.

48 You stumble and fall upon your own weapon with all of your weight. You lose all remaining Body Levels and are now Incapacitated. If unarmed, you twist your body out of shape in falling and lose all Body Levels.

56 In a tragic turn of events, you crash into your opponent, bury your own weapon into your chest and blunder to the ground. You die a terrible death, your last sight that of blood pumping from your body.

64 Your weapon glances harmlessly off your opponent, rebounding back into your face. Fragments of bone shatter backward into your brain! You die horribly. Your friends mourn.

72 You lunge at your opponent and fall upon his weapon. Steel rends through your vital organs, spewing them out onto the ground around you as a fountain of blood showers your allies.

80+ You flail wildly with your weapon and miss your opponent completely. Out of control, you tumble toward your nearest ally. Collapsing upon his weapon, your skull is smashed, and your weapon simultaneously crashes down upon your friend. Roll Attack and Damage normally to determine whether your ally is hurt. Your ally's Defense and Soak are modified by -5, given his surprise at your mishap.

while a character who has hiked all day is weary until the next morning.

**SHORT-TERM FATIGUE:** Before any Round in which you switch from performing one strenuous activity to performing another, you must roll for Fatigue. Thus, if you spend one Round running and switch to fighting in the next, you must make a Fatigue roll of 6+ in between or drop a Fatigue Level. The most common way to avoid this is to rest a Round between changing strenuous activities. The Storyguide can call for extra Fatigue rolls when you exert yourself mightily, even if you do not change from one form of exertion to another.

You recover from Fatigue one Level at a time, starting with your lowest (most exhausted) Level. Each Level's recovery takes a certain amount of time depending on the Level you are currently at. Short-Term Fatigue recovers at the following rates: Winded, 2 minutes; Weary, 10 minutes; Tired, 30 minutes; Dazed, 60 minutes; Unconscious, wake up at Winded in 2 hours. You can recover a Level in half the time by making a Stamina roll of 9+. If you meditate to recover your wind, add your Meditation score to your Stamina roll to recover from Fatigue. If you are active while recovering from Fatigue (i.e., you fight, run or cast spells), the duration of each Level's effect is doubled.

**LONG-TERM FATIGUE:** Long-Term Fatigue results from extended activities, such as hiking and performing Ritual spells. These special cases are

number of Fatigue Levels; most people have six. They are: Fresh, Winded 0, Weary -1, Tired -3, Dazed -5, and Unconscious. For each Fatigue test you fail (usually made an a stress roll + Stamina - Encumbrance, against an *Ease Factor of 6*) you lose one Fatigue Level. If you Botch a Fatigue roll, you lose two Fatigue Levels, both of the same variety, Short- or Long-Term.

When you fall to a Fatigue Level of Weary or lower, the penalty listed with that Level is applied to all the rolls you make, including magic rolls, but not Soak attempts. This penalty represents the effects of your growing exhaustion. These penalties are cumulative with those resulting from lost Body Levels (discussed below). That's right, cumulative; be careful.

There are also two kinds of Fatigue, with effects that accumulate against you. The two types are Short-Term and Long-Term. Short-Term Fatigue represents temporary windedness, as one might suffer during an athletic contest or melee. It is also the Fatigue that Magi suffer when casting spells. Long-Term Fatigue represents weariness caused by prolonged exertion, such as hiking. The major difference is that Long-Term Fatigue affects a character longer than does Short-Term Fatigue. A character who has just sprinted recovers in a few minutes,

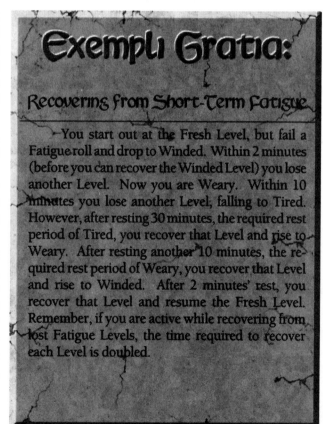

## Exempli Gratia:

### Recovering from Short-Term Fatigue

You start out at the Fresh Level, but fail a Fatigue roll and drop to Winded. Within 2 minutes (before you can recover the Winded Level) you lose another Level. Now you are Weary. Within 10 minutes you lose another Level, falling to Tired. However, after resting 30 minutes, the required rest period of Tired, you recover that Level and rise to Weary. After resting another 10 minutes, the required rest period of Weary, you recover that Level and rise to Winded. After 2 minutes' rest, you recover that Level and resume the Fresh Level. Remember, if you are active while recovering from lost Fatigue Levels, the time required to recover each Level is doubled.

covered in their respective sections. Long-Term Fatigue is only recovered by sleep and sufficient food. A full night's sleep usually recovers all lost Fatigue Levels, Long or Short.

RECORDING FATIGUE: Short- and Long-Term Fatigue combine to lower your Fatigue Levels; they don't have separate pools of Levels that they decrease. If you are at Winded after a Short-Term loss, and lose another Level due to Long-Term Fatigue, you are now at Weary, the next lowest Level. It's recommended that you use one type of symbol to record Short-Term Fatigue loss on the character sheet (perhaps a slash) and another for Long-Term (an X).

### Using Short- and Long-Term Fatigue

It's possible to lose several Fatigue Levels to Short-Term Fatigue, and then lose one to Long-Term Fatigue, say through a Ritual spell. Let's say you lose three Levels to Short-Term Fatigue, becoming Tired. Before recovering all those Levels you also lose a Long-Term Level. You have now lost four Levels in total, so are Dazed. Since Short-Term Levels recover more quickly than Long-Term, you recover the lost Levels from lowest to highest, Short-Term Levels being recovered first. Thus, you recover from Dazed after 60 minutes, recover from Tired after another 30 minutes, and recover from Weary after another 10 minutes. However, as your fourth lost Level is Long-Term, it cannot be recovered without a night's sleep, so you remain at Winded throughout the day. Of course, you can suffer more Short-Term loses, but they recover to leave you at Winded again. If you ever suffer another Long-Term Level, you are lowered to the Weary Level until you sleep.

If you go to sleep when you still suffer from a combined loss of Short- and Long-Term Fatigue Levels, all are recovered by morning.

## Wounds

When combatants fight, the damage they deal out and receive is kept track of in terms of Body Levels. After receiving a certain amount of damage (i.e., losing a certain number of Body Levels), a character is impaired and eventually killed. If characters are not killed, they can recover with proper medical attention and rest.

Each being has a certain number of Body Levels, with more Body Levels for a larger Size. The average person has one of each of the following Body Levels: Unhurt, Hurt, Light Wounds, Medium Wounds, Heavy Wounds, Incapacitated. Anyone who loses Body Levels beyond Incapacitation is dead, or wounded so badly that death is imminent and inevitable.

For every Size level a creature is below 0, it has one less Body Level. A human of Size -1 has no Hurt Body Level, and a human of Size -2 has neither Hurt nor Medium Wounds. It's up to the Storyguide to decide what Body Levels a small, non-human creature does and does not have. This connection between Size and Body Levels means that any creature with a Size of -5 or below has only one Body Level: Unhurt. Any missed Soak attempt by that creature results in death. Any creature with more than 0 Size has extra Body Levels. A human with Size +1 has an extra Hurt Body Level, but for other creatures, it is up to the Storyguide to assign extra Body Levels. If a creature has two or more of a given Level, it must lose all of those Levels before dropping to the next, lower Level of wounds. For instance, imagine that a creature has three Hurt Levels. From Unhurt it can drop one, two, or three Body Levels and still only be Hurt. When it drops the fourth Body Level it suffers Light Wounds.

The typical way to lose Body Levels is to receive damage in excess of your Soak (as previously discussed). Whenever you take a certain amount of damage, whether by spell, arrow, or axe, you can try to resist the damage by equalling the Damage roll with your Soak (total or roll, depending on the combat system you're using). If your Soak at least matches the damage done, no significant wounds result. You may still be bruised, scraped, or singed, depending on the type of attack, but the damage is not enough to count in game terms.

When you are Unhurt, and even Hurt, all abilities function normally. When you are Incapacitated, no actions are possible. Each Body Level in between has some penalty associated with it that is applied to rolls requiring physical or mental exertion. Soak totals and rolls are a notable exception; Body Level penalties do not affect your Soak attempts. Wound penalties are: Light Wounds -1; Medium Wounds -3; Heavy Wounds -5. These penalties have a strong effect on combat, because they apply to Attack, Defense, First Strike, and Damage totals and rolls (again depending on the combat system you use). Magi beware: they also apply to all aspects of spell casting. Furthermore, they apply to all Ability rolls you attempt. Remember also that penalties from lost Body Levels are cumulative with those from lost Fatigue Levels.

## Recovering From Wounds

There are several means by which you may recover from your injuries. Rest and natural healing are effective if your wounds are slight. More grievous injuries require more specialized attention.

CHIRURGY: Chirurgy is the most common sort of aid for wounded people. With this skill, you can tend the wounds of another character. (You can use Chirurgy on yourself as well, but at a -2 penalty.)

# WOUND RECOVERY CHART

## Die Roll

| Wounds | 0 | 1-2 | 3-5 | 6-8 | 9-11 | 12-14 | 15-17 | 18+ |
|---|---|---|---|---|---|---|---|---|
| Light | X | 14 | 10 | 7 | 6 | 5 | 4 | 3 |
| Medium | X | 60 | 40 | 21 | 18 | 16 | 14 | 12 |
| Heavy | X | X | 80 | 45 | 35 | 28 | 25 | 21 |
| Incap. | See *Recovery in the Field* | | | | | | | |

When referring to the Wound Recovery Chart, roll a stress die + Stamina + chirurgeon's Skill score; compare the roll to the type of wound you suffer. If the result is a number, that is the number of days it takes you to recover to the next Wound Level (e.g., from Heavy Wounds to Medium Wounds). The same roll is also used to continue healing until healthy again. For example, if you have Heavy Wounds and roll a 10, it takes you 35 days to heal to Medium Wounds, another 18 days to heal to Light Wounds, and another 6 days to heal fully. If the rolled result is X, roll on the *Catastrophe Subchart*, below. If you Botch your roll on the Wound Recovery Chart, you recover Body Levels at the slowest rate listed for your wound type, and must roll twice on the *Catastrophe Subchart*.

## Catastrophe Subchart

After you roll on this chart, roll on the *Wound Recovery Chart* again to see how long it takes to recover from the affliction gained here (unless the affliction is permanent). If you roll another X on the *Wound Recovery Chart*, you have to roll on the Catastrophe Subchart again, accumulating afflictions. When rolling on the Catastrophe Subchart, roll a stress die + Stamina + chirurgeon's Skill score.

### Roll    Result

0    Death

1    You fall into a coma. Your roll to determine recovery time is at -2, and the time rolled is doubled. You then have to make two Aging rolls. 2  Permanently Enfeebled, as per the Flaw.

3-4    You are permanently crippled in some manner. Perhaps amputation is necessary. Choose an appropriate Flaw, such as Missing Foot.

5-6    Festering wounds, infection, gangrene. Drop a Body Level.

7-10    Make an Aging roll.

11-12    Wounds fail to heal completely; gain 1 Decrepitude point.

13    Nightmares or flashbacks torment you for a long time to come. Three extra Botch dice on any kind of Brave Personality Trait rolls.

14+    Slow recovery. The recovery time rolled on the Wound Recovery Chart is doubled.

If a roll on the Catastrophe Subchart Botches, you die. If the Storyguide is particularly nasty, she might have your soul linger on the earth rather than go to its reward.

When tending the wounded, you roll a die and add Chirurgy + Intelligence + the victim's Wound Penalty. For Incapacitated characters, the penalty is -5. If your total is 9+, the wounded character immediately rises one Body Level. If the total is 3+, the wounded character is bandaged and the wounds are stabilized. Now the character receives a bonus on wound recovery rolls (discussed below) equal to your Chirurgy skill. If wounds are not stabilized, strenuous activity can cause the loss of more Body Levels.

The die roll for Chirurgy is usually a simple die, assuming that medical attention is applied *after* a battle or accident, when drama is low. However, when you perform Chirurgy in the heat of battle, or when on the run from pursuers, the Chirurgy roll is made on a stress die. If you Botch the roll, your subject loses a Body Level for every Botch you get.

**HEALING SPELLS :** Certain Creo Córporem spells also aid recovery and are described in the Spells Chapter. They do not have a permanent effect unless raw *vis* is used. Note: A character does not heal at all while any of her Body Levels are temporarily healed, as through magic, though she can recover normally after permanent healing.

## Fire Damage

| Fire Size | Damage |
| --- | --- |
| Candle | none |
| Torch | +6 |
| Campfire | +9 |
| Bonfire | +12 |
| House Fire | +15 |

## Falling Damage

+1 per 2 feet
X2 for hard surface
one-half for soft surface
one-fourth for water

# COMBAT HINTS

Combat can be very demanding on the Storyguide, and risky for the characters, so here are some tips for better and more interesting battles.

### For the Storyguide:

1) As a general rule, the more you prepare for a combat the more interesting it is and the more smoothly it runs. Having tactical maps of the battlefield and a chart listing important stats for the combatants certainly helps.

2) For simplicity, you can assign most or all the monsters in a group identical stats. The players probably won't notice the difference. You can distinguish monsters in a group by specific physical features such as "dark skin," "warty face," or "misshapen arm" instead of using numbers. As long as you can still keep the different opponents straight, you add detail with no loss of playability. Plus, the players can help you keep track of who's who ("I'm on Wart Face!").

3) Rolling simultaneous Attack and Damage and then Defense and Soak dice (the latter two with the Dueling System) vastly speeds up combat (use two differently colored dice).

4) In a battle, include actions in the situation other than combat. Ability and Characteristic rolls, to perform actions during the battle, can be as tense and important as combat rolls, and in the end perhaps more satisfying.

### For the Players:

1) Magi must always be protected from physical threats, and shield Grogs should never leave the side of their charge.

2) Those involved in a battle should know their priorities: who should protect whom, what the object of the battle is (such as to capture, kill, or drive off), and what to do should the battle turn against you, forcing a retreat. Perhaps a tactical leader, other than the Magi, can lead the Grogs.

3) Carefully planned tactics can often swing the most disastrous dilemma in your favor. Use your brains and you just might succeed — don't underestimate the value of cunning.

4) Keep in mind that combat is very risky because you can always Botch. No one is invulnerable; luck can turn against the mightiest of warriors and heroes (and enemies, too).

5) In large battles, make your relevant rolls after the Storyguide sanctions your statement of intent, but before you are called on for the results. Speed of play is increased in this fashion; other players don't have to wait while you roll.

6) Be sure to add up your combat totals when designing your character, not during a battle.

## Hanging in There

If your character is killed, you might (at the Storyguide's approval) hang on long enough to do one more thing, such as whisper a few last words or curse your killers. The device is simply for the purpose of drama. Don't abuse it.

**RECOVERY IN THE FIELD:** If you are Hurt, you automatically recover to Unhurt in one day. More serious wounds do not recover in the field on their own. In fact, the Storyguide can rule that certain strenuous activities might aggravate your condition, especially if your wounds have not been stabilized by a chirurgeon.

If you are Incapacitated, the story is grim. You are on the edge of death, and could die at any time. Each day at sunrise and sunset, you must make a stress Stamina roll to see if you have died or recovered a Body Level. If your wounds have been stabilized by Chirurgy, you get a bonus on your roll equal to the chirurgeon's skill. A 0 or less indicates that you have died. A roll of 9+ means you are at Heavy Wounds. A roll of 1 to 8 indicates that your condition has worsened slightly, and all subsequent recovery rolls are made at a cumulative -1 penalty until you rise a Body Level or die. After recovering to Heavy Wounds you recover normally.

**RECOVERY AT HOME:** Recovery from serious wounds requires rest and care. When you have a suitably long time to recuperate you can make a roll on the *Wound Recovery Chart*.

## Other Ways to Get Hurt

There are plenty of ways to get hurt in **Ars Magica**; combat isn't the only way. It's a hard, cruel world.

**ILLNESS AND DISEASE:** Simulate the weakening effects of illness by dropping Fatigue Levels. A head cold might drop you one Long-Term Fatigue Level unless you make a Stamina roll of 8+. A more severe illness might force you to make four Stamina rolls of 9+, with each failure meaning the loss of one Long-Term Fatigue Level. Your energy (and Fatigue Levels) return when you shake the illness (which might require more Stamina rolls or another character's Medicine rolls).

Illnesses can also hamper your Characteristics, temporarily or permanently reducing them. These effects can be mimicked with Aging rolls (see p.354).

The precise effects of a disease are up to the Storyguide who puts the disease in a story. Just hope that the Storyguide isn't familiar with diseases; that way, maybe you won't suffer through any of the more malign ones.

**FIRE:** Each fire has its heat rated with a Damage modifier, a number added to Damage rolls when you are burned by a fire (these rolls are made on a simple die; fire can't Botch in hurting you). The first Round you are exposed to fire, your Soak includes armor, but in subsequent Rounds your armor is assumed to have heated up and no longer protects you. Furthermore, after the last Round you are in a fire, you take damage from your armor, which is still hot. To determine damage resulting after a fire (because of hot armor), roll a simple die and add the Protection value of your armor. If you are in a fire for an extended period of time, the Storyguide can rule that your armor burns away. Other bad things can happen in a fire, such as disfiguring burns and the loss of valuable, flammable items. Such tragic ends are best left to the devious imagination of the Storyguide.

**FALLING:** If you fall, you take damage, which you can resist using a normal Soak total (but your armor's Protection value is halved for the roll). For each two feet you fall, damage is +1 on the Damage die. The Damage die is a simple one; gravity can't Botch in hurting you. If you fall onto a hard surface, such as rock, the Damage suffered, after Soak is applied, is doubled. Soft surfaces cushion the blow, as shown on the *Falling Damage Table*. You can try to break your fall, possibly slowing your descent and protecting yourself. If you make an Athletics roll of 6+, the first five feet of the fall do not count toward the Damage roll.

**POISON:** As there are a great many different poisons, there are a great many different effects. Each poison has two relevant factors: the amount of time it takes to work, and the possible effects. Typically, the possible effects depend on a Stamina roll by the victim, attempting to match an Ease Factor representing the strength of the poison. A simple poison has two effects: a powerful effect that happens if the Stamina roll fails, and a weak effect that sets in if the Stamina roll succeeds. The Storyguide may wish to craft a more complex poison, with a greater variety of results depending on how many points by which you fail your Stamina roll, and whether you Botch.

**DEPRIVATION:** An inability to get the necessities of life, such as air, water, warmth, and food, can cause weakness and death. Deprivation is simulated by reducing Fatigue Levels until you are Unconscious. This is usually determined through Stamina rolls, failure of which costs you a Fatigue Level (Short- or Long-Term, depending on the nature of your deprivation). The Ease Factor of Stamina rolls is determined by the Storyguide, based on the nature of your deprivation. That nature also determines how often you make Stamina rolls; if you're deprived of water and shelter you make rolls more often than if simply deprived of water. When you run out of Fatigue Levels (i.e., you drop to Unconscious), your body keeps suffering. Thus, you continue to make Stamina rolls, but lose Body Levels when those rolls fail. Thus, slowly or quickly, depending on the type of deprivation, you die. Good Stamina rolls can delay the end, but not even the

# ARMOR CHART

| Armor | Expense | Protection | Load |
|---|---|---|---|
| *Cuirass Armor:* | | | |
| Leather/Fur/Quilted | inex | 1 | 0.5 |
| Heavy/Hard Leather | inex | 2 | 1 |
| Ring Mail | stan | 4 | 1.5 |
| Scale Mail | stan | 5 | 2 |
| Chain Mail | expn | 8 | 3.5 |
| *Hauberk Armor:* | | | |
| Leather/Fur/Quilted | inex | 3 | 1.5 |
| Heavy/Hard Leather | inex | 5 | 2.5 |
| Ring Mail | stan | 7 | 3 |
| Scale Mail | stan | 9 | 4.5 |
| Chain Mail | expn | 12 | 5 |
| *Full Armor:* | | | |
| Leather/Fur/Quilted | inex | 4 | 2 |
| Heavy/Hard Leather | inex | 6 | 2.5 |
| Ring Mail | stan | 8 | 4 |
| Scale Mail | stan | 11 | 5.5 |
| Chain Mail | expn | 14 | 6 |

## Type of Armor

Cuirass armor covers only the chest, abdomen, and back. The arms and legs are left completely unprotected. This very basic armor does not include a helm (which makes aimed blows particularly effective against people wearing cuirass armor).

Hauberk armor covers the torso, as well as the shoulders and upper arms. It also includes a short skirt that protects the thighs and groin. It includes a half helm that protects only the crown and the back of the head. The helm subtracts 1 from all your Perception rolls.

Full armor covers the entire body, even the forearms, shins, feet, and hands, and it includes a full helm which covers the neck and part of the face. Subtract 3 from all Perception rolls when wearing the helm.

### Armament Availability

Statistics for a wide variety of weapons and armor are provided here to cover as many possibilities as, well. . . possible. Not all the listed armaments are readily available in all regions, and some types of armament (notably plate mail) are only available late in the medieval period (which encompasses the Thirteenth Century). If you want to create armaments not listed here, use the stats provided as models for your own.

# BRONZE ARMOR PROTECTION

Some characters, particularly those of faerie blood, have armor made of bronze or faerie iron. Bronze armor functions as follows (there is no bronze chain mail).

| Type | Cuirass | Hauberk | Full |
|---|---|---|---|
| Ring | 3 | 6 | 7 |
| Scale | 4 | 8 | not used |

The Load for bronze armor is the same for steel armor of the same type. Bronze armor is always "expensive," no matter the type. Armor made of faerie iron is very rare. Armor made of faerie iron offers one more point of Protection than steel armor, and can be forged into any armor type. Its Load is the same for steel armor of the same variety. Faerie iron armor cannot be purchased, so expense is a moot point; you have to win or earn faerie iron.

**EXPENSE:** inex = inexpensive, stan = standard, expn = expensive.

**PROTECTION:** The value that modifies your Soak total (for Action Combat) or your Soak roll (for Dueling Combat).

**LOAD:** Represents the weight and awkwardness of the armor, used to calculate Encumbrance.

toughest can go without basic necessities for long. Ale does not count as a basic necessity.

Here's an example of how deprivation rules work: If you are drowning in churning water, the Storyguide might say you must make Strength + Swim + Stamina rolls of 9+ or drop a Fatigue Level. If you can succeed twice before losing all Fatigue Levels, you swim to safety, but if you fall Unconscious from loss of Fatigue, you lose Body Levels until you drown.

# MELEE WEAPON CHART

| Weapon | Expense | Speed | AtkB | WpnDam | ParB | Str | Load | Space |
|---|---|---|---|---|---|---|---|---|
| Unarmed | N/A | 0 | 0 | 0 | 0 | N/A | 0 | 0 |
| Dagger(1h) | inex | +1 | +4 | +2 | +1 | n | 0 | 0 |
| Shortsword(1h) | stan | +2 | +4 | +4 | +2 | -2 | 0.5 | 0 |
| Broadsword(1h) | expn | +3 | +4 | +6 | +3 | 0 | 0.5 | 1 |
| Bastard Sword(1h) | expn | +4 | +3 | +8 | +3 | +2 | 0.5 | 2 |
| Bastard Sword(2h) | expn | +4 | +3 | +10 | +4 | 0 | 0.5 | 2 |
| Greatsword(2h) | expn | +5 | +3 | +11 | +5 | +1 | 1 | 3 |
| Short Spear(1h) | inex | +5 | +2 | +3 | +1 | -1 | 0 | 1 |
| Short Spear(2h) | inex | +6 | +3 | +5 | +2 | n | 0 | 0 |
| Long Spear(2h) | inex | +8 | +2 | +6 | +3 | -2 | 0.5 | 0 |
| Lance (mtd)(1h) | stan | +7 | +2 | +8* | +1 | 0 | 1 | 1 |
| Hand Axe(1h) | inex | +2 | +2 | +7 | +1 | 0 | 0.5 | 1 |
| Battle Axe(2h) | stan | +4 | +2 | +12 | +2 | 0 | 1 | 3 |
| Pole Axe(2h) | stan | +5 | +1 | +13 | +3 | 1 | 1.5 | 4 |
| Halberd(2h) | expn | +5 | +1 | +15 | +3 | +1 | 2 | 4 |
| Club(1h) | inex | +2 | +3 | +2 | +1 | -2 | 0 | 2 |
| Club(2h) | inex | +2 | +3 | +3 | +2 | n | 0 | 2 |
| Quarterstaff(2h) | inex | +5 | +2 | +4 | +6 | -2 | 0 | 2 |
| Mace(1h) | stan | +2 | +3 | +5 | +1 | 0 | 0 | 2 |
| Mace(2h) | stan | +2 | +3 | +7 | +2 | -2 | 0 | 2 |
| War Maul(2h) | stan | +3 | +3 | +10 | +2 | 1 | 1.5 | 2 |
| Morning Star(1h) | stan | +3 | +2 | +8 | +1 | +2 | 0.5 | 3 |
| Morning Star(2h) | stan | +3 | +2 | +10 | +1 | 0 | 0.5 | 3 |
| Military Flail(2h) | expn | +4 | +3 | +10 | +2 | -1 | 1 | 4 |
| Throwing Knife | inex | -2 | -1 | +0 | N/A | n | 0 | N/A |
| Javelin | stan | -5 | -1 | +5 | N/A | -2 | 0 | N/A |
| Throwing Axe | stan | -4 | -2 | +6 | N/A | -1 | 0.5 | N/A |
| Target Shield | inex | +1 | +3 | -2 | +2 | n | 0 | 1 |
| Round Shield | inex | +2 | +2 | -1 | +3 | -2 | 0.5 | 1 |
| Knight Shield | stan | +2 | +1 | +0 | +4 | 0 | 1 | 0 |
| Kite Shield | expn | +1 | +1 | +0 | +5 | +1 | 1.5 | 1 |
| Tower Shield | expn | +0 | +0 | -1 | +6 | +2 | 2 | 1 |

**EXPENSE:** There are three types of weapons, classified by the cost of making and maintaining them: Inexpensive (marked "inex"), standard (stan), and expensive (expn). Weapons available to you depend on your background, Virtues, Flaws, and Covenant.

**SPEED:** The bonus to your First Strike roll when using the weapon, based on the weapon's length, weight, and style of use. A long, light weapon held in front of the user has the edge over a short, heavy weapon that's swung from over the shoulder.

**ATKB, ATTACK BONUS:** The weapon's modifier to your Attack roll.

**WPNDAM, WEAPON DAMAGE:** The weapon's modifier to your Damage roll.

**PARB, PARRY BONUS:** The weapon's modifier to your Parry Defense score (if using the Action Combat System), or roll (if using the Dueling System).

**STR, STRENGTH:** The minimum Strength required to use the weapon effectively. An "n" means no minimum Strength score is required.

**LOAD:** Represents the weight and awkwardness of the weapon. It's used to calculate Encumbrance.

**SPACE:** Feet needed around the wielder for effective use; think of it as a zone. If the zones of two people overlap there could be trouble.

**NOTE:** Some characters, particularly those of faerie blood, have weapons made of bronze or faerie iron. Bronze weapons do one less point of damage than normal steel or iron ones, and are always "expensive," regardless of the weapon type. Weapons made of faerie iron do one extra point of damage, and cannot nor-

mally be purchased — they are usually won or given — so expense is a moot point. The Load for bronze or faerie iron weapons is the same for steel ones of the same variety.

\* See the Dueling Combat section on Charging.

## MISSILE WEAPON CHART

| Weapon | Expense | Rate | AtkB | WpnDam | Str | Load | Range |
|---|---|---|---|---|---|---|---|
| Sling | inex | +2 | 0 | +4 | n | 0 | 100 |
| Self Bow | inex | +3 | 0 | +8 | 0 | 0 | 120 |
| Long Bow | stan | +6 | 0 | +14 | +2 | 0.5 | 250 |
| Composite Bow | expn | +4 | +1 | +9 | -1 | 0.5 | 225 |
| Light Crossbow | expn | -8 | +1 | +10 | 0 | 0.5 | 200 |
| Heavy Crossbow | expn | -15 | +1 | +15 | -3 | 1 | 300 |
| Arbalest | expn | -23 | +1 | +19 | 0 | 1.5 | 400 |

**EXPENSE:** inex = inexpensive, stan = standard, expn = expensive.

**RATE:** The bonus to Rate total (for Dueling Combat), which determines how often you can fire the weapon.

**ATKB, ATTACK BONUS:** The weapon's modifier to your Attack roll.

**WPNDAM, WEAPON DAMAGE:** The weapon's modifier to your Damage roll.

**STR, STRENGTH:** The minimum Strength needed to use the weapon.

**LOAD:** Represents the weight and awkwardness of the weapon, used to calculate Encumbrance.

**RANGE:** maximum firing range in paces.

# chapter six

n the Eighth Century the wizard Bonisagus developed a "universal" theory of magic, and with his invention wizards could share their knowledge freely. The Order of Hermes was born. Until then magic had been highly individualistic and limited in scope. With the ability to share and accumulate knowledge, Hermetic Magi have gained an immense advantage over other wizards. Some believe, however, that the strict regimentation of Hermetic magic helps mediocre Magi who need an exact system to guide them, and robs truly brilliant Magi of the chance to discover the modes of power that best suit them.

One of the innovations of the Order is the *Parma Magica*, a magical shield that has not been duplicated by other supernatural powers. This protection was instrumental in bringing the Order to power over other wizards in the Eighth Century.

The Order of Hermes, however, is only a small part of the magical world. Magical beasts, many of them intelligent, also belong to this category, and many wizards who have not joined the Order continue to practice their obscure arts. Non-Hermetic Magi are less flexible, but more specialized and powerful in specific talents. The rules for magic in **Ars Magica** are for Hermetic magic only. Storyguides should be sure to use non-Hermetic magic to create monsters, wizards and magic items beyond the bounds of these rules, and thus keep magic a mystery even to those who think they know it all.

Magic is an earthly force, and as such can only affect things below the lunar sphere – things on earth and in Hell. Magic can never affect the moon or anything beyond it. Nor can magic change anything's true nature. It cannot, for example, raise the dead or force a demon to tell the truth.

Hermetic magic is a useful but imperfect theory. These rules represent what Magi expect to happen when they work with magic, and while the expected usually occurs, the exact effects of magic can be influenced by countless factors. Some factors include the phase of the moon, the intangible nature of the target, and the mental state of the caster. Storyguides who occasionally bend the rules and interpret magical effects imaginatively, therefore, are simulating the magical world better than those who follow the magic rules to the letter.

# The Magic Arts

Fifteen Magic Arts describe your mastery of the various fields of magic: five Techniques and ten Forms. The Techniques describe what you do, and the Forms describe what you affect. Each spell combines one Technique and one Form. Thus, a "create fire" (Technique of "create" and Form of "fire") spell produces light, heat, or fire, and a "transform fire" spell transforms light, heat, or fire into a new shape or structure. Each of the fifteen Arts has a Latin name.

## Exempli Gratia:
### Bonus for Forms

In Mercille, Grimgroth touches a plague-ridden corpse and must make a Stamina roll of 3+ (judged by the Storyguide) to keep from catching the plague himself. His Córporem score of 7 gives him a +1 (his Córporem score is above 5, but not above 10) bonus to the roll. His roll is 3 + 0 (Stamina) + 1 (bonus) = 4, so he retains his health.

Later on, another Magus casts a healing spell on Grimgroth. The spell requires that Grimgroth make a Stamina roll of 3+. However, his Córporem Form bonus resists the spell because his Form bonus naturally protects him. Thus, Grimgroth's Form bonus is added to the Ease Factor of the Stamina roll, raising it to 4 (3 + 1), and making the success roll more difficult.

You have a score in each Art, just as if they are Abilities. These scores represent your aptitude for working with the various types of magic. Arts are not, however, mere knowledges; your Arts are actually a part of you. True magical prowess requires native talent, long-term theoretical study, years of practice, a comfortable familiarity with and intuitive understanding of magic, high confidence in one's own skills, and much courage.

Your score in a Form helps you resist spells of that type (see *Magic Resistance*, p.174) and withstand mundane danger related to that Form. For instance, an Ignem (fire) score gives you a bonus to resist damage from fire and cold — your Soak rolls are modified by your Ignem score. For every full 5 points you have in a Form score, you get a +1 bonus to relevant rolls. As a Storyguide, you may wish to extend the Form bonus to other activities related to a Form. For example, the Ignem bonus could be added to a roll to perceive a change in temperature — the Form bonus is added to Perception and rolled against an Ease Factor — rather than limiting it just to protection. Form bonuses are even added to Natural Resistance rolls against spells, including those that penetrate your Magic Resistance. For instance, if a *Ball of Abysmal Flame* penetrates your Magic Resistance, your Natural Resistance roll receives a bonus based on your Ignem score. However, this bonus also "protects" you against spells that are beneficial to you. For example, your Form bonus for Córporem adds to the Ease Factor of a Natural Resistance roll against

a healing spell; your Natural Resistance is reinforced by your Form bonus, even if you don't want its added protection. The whole concept of Natural Resistance is discussed later in the rules.

Each of the Arts is listed with its abbreviations, translation from Latin, scope of effect, and perhaps a mnemonic device to help you remember it. The Hermetic pronunciation (close to that of Classical Latin) is also given. Along with Forms are listed some mundane things they protect you from, as discussed above.

# TECHNIQUES

## Creo (Cr) "I create"

This Art allows you to create something from thin air. It turns dreams into reality. Creation is concerned with the instantaneous production of objects from nothing. When using a Creo spell, you enter a momentary state of transcendent meditation and contact the realm of Forms, in which all the objects that ever were and ever could be — chairs, dogs, anger, quills — exist as perfect Ideas. Your magic finds the proper form and makes it real. Objects

created this way are closer to the world of Forms than are normal objects, so they are always perfect and flawless. You can also use the Art of Creo to perfect things that have deteriorated from their ideal nature, such as healing a broken arm or mending a broken vase. Magi who study Creo intently see the world filled with growth, birth and creation. Pronounced "CRAY-oh," think: creation.

# Intéllego (In) "I perceive"

All things in the world are connected to each other, and Magi who pursue the Art of Intéllego learn how to see these connections, read them, and learn from them. What others hear as wind in the branches is to an Intéllego Magus the language of the trees. Pronounced "in-TEL-le-go," think: intelligence.

# Muto (Mu) "I transform"

The Art of transformation and transmutation. Muto Magi tend to view the world as being in the constant flux of change. They see each apparent state, such as "sleeping," "young," or even "dead," as one step in a perpetual process of change. Through this Art, they learn to direct and control this natural process. Transformations are easiest when there is a strong connection between the original form and the result of the transformation, such as turning a leaf into an apple. On the other hand, turning a leaf (living flexible, and vegetable) into a sword (inert, unyielding, and mineral) is quite difficult. Pronounced "MOO-toe," think: mutate.

# Perdo (Pe) "I destroy"

The one trait held in common by all objects and creatures in the temporal world is that some day they will come to an end; their demise is inevitable. The Magus who understands the Art of Perdo knows this, and uses magic to control this universal process. Aging, disease, decay, rust, and death are all subjects of manipulation through this Art. Deep study of Perdo often leads Magi to perceive everything about them as being in some stage of decay. Pronounced "PAIR-doe," think: perdition.

# Rego (Re) "I control"

You can move things with this Technique, but not change them. The Magus of Rego attempts not to change things, but to control their motions and positions. Since this Art affects an external factor, such as action, rather than an internal factor, such as shape, it is versatile. A Rego spell that moves a person can be used to lift someone out of danger, or to slam someone into a wall. Those who devote their lives to this Art often become obsessed with ordering the world around them, though the order they

seek may be unfathomable to others. Pronounced "RAY-go," think: regulate.

# FORMS

## Animál (An) "animal"

This Art affects animals of all kinds, from the fish of the sea to the birds of the air. Animál magi develop a keen appreciation of the power of the animal spirit and form, and some prefer the company of beasts to that of humans. Nevertheless, an uncrossable chasm separates humans from animals: humans have souls. Bonus: animal poisons or other special abilities, like a cobra's hypnosis (but not claws). Pronounced "ah-nee-MAUL."

## Aquam (Aq) "water"

Affects all manner of liquids. Through this Art, one gains access to the might of a roaring flood and the gentleness of a clear pool. Studying Aquam can teach one flexibility and strength. Bonus: drowning and dehydration. Pronounced "AH-kwahm," think: aquatic.

## Auram (Au) "air"

Air, wind, and weather. The heart of an Auram Magus is in the sky, among the roiling storms, rushing winds, cool fog, and gentle rains. To them, the earthbound world is slow, dull, ponderous, and static. True flight is only possible through this Art. Bonus: effects of weather and suffocation. Pronounced "OW-rahm," think: aurora.

## Córporem (Co) "body"

Human and human-like bodies. Magi of this Art see the human body as the most refined and perfect creation in the physical world, a combination of the elements that is above all of its components. Some use their arts to heal, others to harm, but both kinds of Córporem Magi develop an appreciation for the body's intricacy. Bonus: disease. Pronounced "CORE-pore-em," think: corpse.

## Herbam (He) "plant"

Plants and trees of all types, including dead wood. The trees of the forest are old and mighty, and their roots reach deep into the secrets of the earth. Herbam Magi appreciate the many virtues of plant life: bountiful fruit, strong wood, powerful herbs, and ancient trees that can tell much to those patient enough to listen to them. Many Herbam Magi develop an antipathy toward fire. Bonus: herbal poisons. Pronounced "HAIR-bahm," think: herbal.

## Ignem (Ig) "fire"

Fire, heat, and light. Fire is the most lifelike of the four elements: it moves, it devours, and grows, much like a living thing. Also like living things, it can be killed by the other three elements: smothered by earth, quenched by water, or blown apart by wind. Though fire can be destroyed by the other elements, its position midway between inert matter and living being gives it the advantages of both. Ignem Magi are often passionate and fickle. Bonus: heat, cold, and blinding light. Pronounced "IG-nem," think: ignite.

## Imágonem (Im) "image"

The art of illusions and phantasms. This Art affects only sensations and can never affect matter. Masters of this Art have learned to separate an object from its apparent features, and many of them likewise become separated from what those around them see as reality. Many Imágonem Magi become more interested in colors and sounds themselves than in the actual things that produce them. Bonus: being fooled by appearances. Pronounced "i-MAH-go-nem."

## Mentem (Me) "mind"

Minds, thoughts, and spirits. This Art comes as close as magic can to affecting souls. Through this Art, Magi manipulate what they call the "body of the soul": memories, thoughts, and emotions. They can also affect the "spiritual bodies" of noncorporeal beings, such as ghosts. Mentem Magi who think too deeply on the implications of their Art do not make good company. Bonus: confusion or mental weakness. Pronounced "MEN-tem," think: mental.

## Terram (Te) "earth"

Solids, especially earth and stone. Terram Magi see their Art as affecting the very foundation of the world, and they can wield powerful spells. Though Terram magic is mighty, the earth proves resistant to manipulation. Just as stone is heavy and hard to lift, it is inert and hard to change, even through magic. Many Terram Magi learn patience and stillness from the earth they study. Bonus: damage from earth, such as avalanches and falling. Pronounced "TAIR-rahm," think: terrain.

## Vim (Vi) "power"

Magic and demons. All the Arts rely on the power of magic to function. This Art, however, is on a higher level; it manipulates the power of magic itself, allowing Magi to assume more control of their spells. The Art also affects demons, which are innately magical creatures. Dealing with demons, however, is dangerous because of the risk of corruption, and because it is against the code of the Order of Hermes. Bonus: none. Pronounced "WEEM"

# LIMITS OF MAGIC

Magic, though a very powerful force, is not omnipotent. Even though a power of immense proportions, there are certain laws that magic must conform to, and certain limits that spells can never cross.

Every spell in **Ars Magica** fits within the framework of the medieval paradigm, as understood in terms of post-Aristotelian, pre-Copernican physics of the medieval world. Magic must therefore stay within certain boundaries, no matter what the potency of the spell or the talents of the caster. Hermetic magic cannot do any of the following:

Affect the Lunar sphere or anything above it.

Overcome the power of the Highest Divinity or the deceptions of Infernal powers, including:

Affecting the outcome of a miracle.

Affecting the mind or body of someone buried in piety by the Church.

Detecting the presence of the deceptions or illusions of a demon, and detecting the purposes behind those deceptions or illusions.

Affect anyone's immortal soul, including:

Creating true human life.

Restoring the dead to life.

Alter or determine something's essential nature, including:

Halting or reversing natural aging.

Preventing or removing Twilight Points or Decrepitude.

Affecting the Heart-Shape of a Bjornaer Magus.

Creating, destroying or altering any supernatural Aura.

Create anything permanently without raw *vis*, including curing permanently without raw *vis*.

Alter the passage of time, including:

Affecting anything in the future.

Restore physical energy (i.e., Fatigue Levels, raw *vis*) so that one can cast more spells.

Affect an unseen target without an Arcane Connection.

Affect True Faith or True Reason.

Restore Confidence.

Inspire a Passion.

Always keep in mind that the "laws" of post-Aristotelian, pre-Copernican physics are not just laws, they are facts, and their essence cannot be altered by magic in any way. For example, you can lift an object in the air, defying

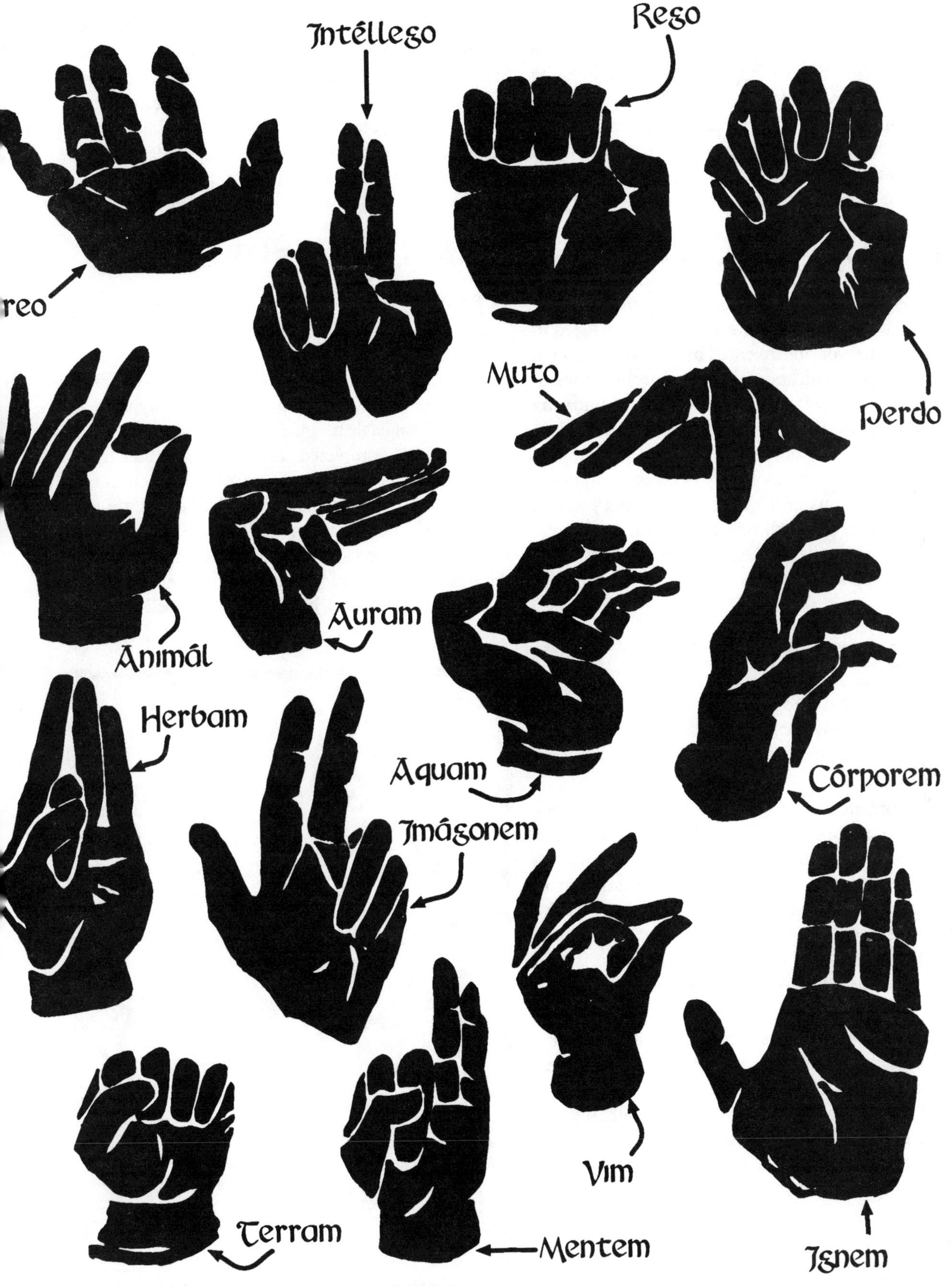

Intéllego

Rego

reo

Muto

Perdo

Animál

Auram

Herbam

Aquam

Córporem

Imágonem

Vim

Terram

Mentem

Ignem

171

gravity, but you cannot eliminate gravity itself. Thus, such things as gravity and time cannot be overcome in any way, though the past can be viewed.

The boundaries of Hermetic magic are well known to the Order, but that doesn't stop Magi from challenging them. Indeed, many Magi spend countless years searching in vain for a way to transcend these limits. Certainly, any Magus who actually succeeds in surpassing any of these boundaries will become famous, perhaps even as famous as the Order's very founders.

# Casting Spells

As a Magus, you find yourself casting many spells. You can cast a Formulaic spell, such as the ones listed in the Spells Chapter, or one invented by another person, if you know the spell. You know all spells you choose when creating your character, and come to know more by learning or inventing them during the course of the Saga (see *Spells* in the Laboratory Chapter, p.239). You may cast a Spontaneous spell any time you please; you never "know" a Spontaneous spell, though, and even if you cast the same Spontaneous spell repeatedly, you may never learn how to cast it reliably (i.e., as you can a Formulaic spell) without spending laboratory time to learn or invent it.

## TYPES OF MAGIC

Magic is divided into two types: Spontaneous and Formulaic. Both draw upon your mastery of the magical Arts and use magical words and gestures to obtain a supernatural effect.

With Spontaneous magic, you combine on the spot the words and gestures you think will produce a desired magical effect, taking into account the specific circumstances you are in such as time of day, astrological correspondences, and the specific shape and size of the target. Spontaneous magic is therefore flexible, but unpredictable. The nature of Spontaneous magic is also transient, ultimately limited in duration and scope.

With Formulaic magic, you repeat magical formulae (including words and gestures) that almost always have a given effect, and which affect more general circumstances. Formulaic magic is more powerful than Spontaneous magic, but much less flexible, as you may not change the formula in any way (though the formula itself may allow for the Range and Duration to be extended). Unlike Spontaneous magic, Formulaic magic may, with the proper expenditures, produce long-lasting and even permanent effects.

In addition, Formulaic magic encompasses Ritual magic, which involves very complex ceremonies and raw vis (raw magical power in physical form) to produce effects of greater extent than are possible with normal magic (Spontaneous or Formulaic). Ritual magic is more powerful than normal Formulaic magic, but just as inflexible, and more expensive in terms of time, effort, and magical resources.

# CASTING A FORMULAIC SPELL

To cast a Formulaic spell, you recite the magic words in a firm voice and boldly execute arcane hand gestures memorized as part of the spell. This activity shapes and directs the magical energy that pervades the world. Once these acts are completed, roll to see whether the spell works and whether you are fatigued by your efforts. With each spell cast, roll a **die**, modified by **Technique + Form + Stamina - Encumbrance**. If the total equals or exceeds the spell Level, the spell works without fatiguing you. If the total falls short of the spell Level, you automatically lose one Fatigue Level, but still cast the spell. If you miss

## Fatigue in Spell Casting

Fatigue is described in the *Effects of Combat* section of the Combat Chapter. Fatigue from spells is normally Short-Term, although it is always Long-Term where Ritual spells are concerned (see *Ritual Spells*, below).

Short-Term Fatigue recovers at the following rates: Winded — two minutes, Weary — 10 minutes, Tired — 30 minutes, Dazed — 60 minutes, Unconscious — wake up at Winded in two hours (three hours if a result of Ritual spell casting). You can recover a Fatigue Level in half the time by making a Stamina roll of 9+. Only one such roll may be attempted per Level of Fatigue that you suffer from. Long-Term Fatigue is only recovered with sleep.

the spell's Level by more than 10, the spell does not take effect, and you still automatically lose a Fatigue Level. The die rolled for the casting is a stress die if you are in stressful circumstances; otherwise it is a simple die.

When you successfully cast a spell, remember what number you roll because it might be used immediately to see if you overcome the target's Magic Resistance (see p.174).

The more powerful or difficult a spell is, the higher its Level. Look at the Muto Córporem spells on p.208 for examples.

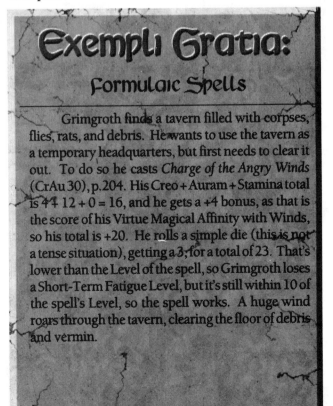

## Exempli Gratia:
### Formulaic Spells

Grimgroth finds a tavern filled with corpses, flies, rats, and debris. He wants to use the tavern as a temporary headquarters, but first needs to clear it out. To do so he casts *Charge of the Angry Winds* (CrAu 30), p.204. His Creo + Auram + Stamina total is 4 + 12 + 0 = 16, and he gets a +4 bonus, as that is the score of his Virtue Magical Affinity with Winds, so his total is +20. He rolls a simple die (this is not a tense situation), getting a 3, for a total of 23. That's lower than the Level of the spell, so Grimgroth loses a Short-Term Fatigue Level, but it's still within 10 of the spell's Level, so the spell works. A huge wind roars through the tavern, clearing the floor of debris and vermin.

# CASTING A SPONTANEOUS SPELL

Casting a Spontaneous spell is more flexible, but more complex and less predictable than casting a Formulaic spell. You decide what effect to attempt and invent a spell on the spur of the moment to achieve that effect. To determine the results of a Spontaneous spell, you and the Storyguide first determine the Technique and Form that are appropriate for the feat being attempted. Then, decide whether you are exerting yourself (i.e., expending a Fatigue Level). Finally, roll a **die + Technique + Form + Intelligence - Encumbrance**. If you expend a Fatigue Level, divide the result by **two**; if not, divide it by **five**. Any bonuses or penalties are applied to the roll before it is divided. The result is the Level equivalent of the Spontaneous spell. Compare this number to spells of that Technique and Form and near that Level to see what effect the Spontaneous spell has. The spell should be as powerful as other spells of its Level (the Storyguide's judgement is paramount in deciding the effects of a Spontaneous spell). If the result is 0 or lower, there is no effect.

Remember the Level of effect of your spell, because if the target has Magic Resistance, the Level is used to see whether you overcome the target's Magic Resistance (see p.174).

If you do not Fatigue yourself, you roll either a stress or simple die depending upon the circumstances. However, whenever you choose to Fatigue yourself, you are pushing your limits; you must roll a stress die, whether you are in a stressful situation or not.

If you know a Formulaic spell — a spell that's in your repertoire — which produces effects similar to those you are trying to produce with a Spontaneous spell, you may get a bonus on your Spontaneous spell roll by spending one full minute considering the similarities between effects of the Formulaic and Spontaneous spells. See the *Similar Spells* insert for complete details. Of course, combat rarely offers the opportunity for a minute's contemplation. If you are at all disturbed during this period, an Intelligence + Concentration stress roll of 6+ is required

## Spell Levels

In game terms, spells are ranked according to Levels, but characters never use that term. Magi use the term **magnitude** to rank their spells. The magnitude of a spell equals the number of pawns of *vis* needed to give it its longer Duration or Range (i.e., 1 pawn per 5 Levels). A first magnitude spell is therefore Level 1 to 5, and a second magnitude spell is Level 6 to 10.

to maintain contemplation. Otherwise, you fail to pin down the similarities between your spell and a Formulaic one, and receive no spell roll bonus.

# CASTING RITUAL SPELLS

Some powerful spells require much more energy and concentration than standard spells, and thus the process of casting them is different. These spells, called Ritual spells, perform major feats, exceeding some of the limits of normal — Formulaic and Spontaneous — spells.

Normal spells are limited in the following ways:

• They cannot affect an area larger than you can see (though the effects may move out of your sight and control once a spell is cast).

• Duration cannot be longer than one month without expenditure of *vis*.

• They cannot be used to perceive anything in the past or future.

Ritual spells can surpass these limits, and thus create farther-reaching and longer-lasting effects. Formulaic spells may surpass the limit on Duration and Range only, and only through expenditure of *vis*. Spontaneous spells cannot exceed any of these limits, and thus the effects of Ritual spells cannot be produced with Spontaneous magic.

## Similar Spells

When attempting to create magical effects Spontaneously, it is helpful to know a Formulaic spell which produces similar effects to those you are trying to create, or which is so similar to the effects you are trying to create that it may be considered a version of the same spell.

Similar spells may only differ in the following ways:

| Difference | Examples |
|---|---|
| Details of spell | Range; Duration; aiming modifier |
| Details of effect | shape of a wall; direction of motion |
| Requisites | learning or Casting Requisites |
| Restriction | need for Arcane Connection; need for eye contact |
| Strength of effect | amount and heat of flame; damage done |
| Type of target | stone vs. metal; fish vs. bird; fog vs. smoke |

A spell may be considered similar to another spell so long as it differs in no more than one of the above ways. However, Ritual spells may never be considered similar to Spontaneous spells or regular Formulaic spells. And, spells of different Forms may never be considered similar; no matter how close the effects are, the underlying material is fundamentally different.

When casting a Spontaneous spell that is similar to a Formulaic spell, you get a bonus to your Spontaneous spell roll equal to one-fifth the Level of the similar Formulaic spell. If you are casting a Spontaneous spell that's similar to the 15th Level spell *The Captive Voice*, you receive a +3 modifier to your Spontaneous spell roll. You may only get the bonus from one spell at a time.

If you describe exactly what your Magus does to cast a Spontaneous spell, and if it's interesting, colorful, eminently sensible, or uses the laws of magic appropriately (see p.195), you get a bonus of up to +5 on your casting roll (Storyguide's discretion).

To attempt to cast a Ritual spell, you must spend 15 minutes in uninterrupted concentration for every 5 Levels of the Ritual spell. You must also spend one raw *vis* point (see Raw *Vis*, p.181) for every 5 Levels of the spell. That *vis* must match the Technique or Form used in the spell. Then you make a casting roll as you do for Formulaic spells, but you may add your Meditation Ability score to that roll. Ritual spells are both physically and mentally demanding. If your spell casting roll is a success, you must still spend a Fatigue Level. If your spell casting roll is up to 10 points short of the spell's Level, you lose two Fatigue Levels, and the spell proceeds. If you miss the spell's Level by more than 10, the spell fails, you lose two Fatigue Levels, and all the *vis* used is wasted. Fatigue Levels lost in Ritual spell casting are Long-Term. If you drop below Unconscious due to this Fatigue loss, you are unconscious for an extra hour. However, if your Ritual spell succeeds, remember your roll, as it may be required to determine whether the spell penetrates an opponent's Magic Resistance (see p.174).

Many Ritual spells have two Ranges or Durations listed. For each level of either Range or Duration that you wish to extend, you must spend an additional 15 minutes and one additional pawn of *vis* per 5 Levels of the spell. Thus, if you wish to extend both the Range and Duration to the second (longer) shown, you have to spend a total of 45 minutes and three pawns of *vis* (15 minutes and one pawn of *vis* for each Level of the basic Ritual, for extended Range, and for extended Duration) per 5 Levels of the Ritual spell.

# REQUISITES

Most spells involve a simple combination of two Arts, one Form and one Technique. Some spells, however, involve more than two. For instance, a spell that turns a human into a bird uses Muto (because you are transforming something), Córporem (because you are affecting a human body) and Animál (because you are turning the human body into an animal body). In addition to the two primary Arts, Córporem and Muto in this case, casting the spell involves your Animál score as well. The third Art is a Requisite.

Requisites, if any, are listed for each Formulaic spell in the Spells Chapter. (See *Curse of Circe* on page 208 for an example.) The Requisite limits one of the primary Arts, either Form or Technique (i.e., the spell's Technique is limited when the Requisite is a Technique, and the spell's Form is limited when the Requisite is a Form). So, if you cast *Curse of Circe*, and your Animál is 6 while your Córporem is 13, you treat you Córporem score as if it is only 6. Note, however, that if your score in the Requisite exceeds that of the primary Art, the lower primary Art is used. So, if in the above example your Córporem is 6 and your Animál is 13, your Córporem score remains at 6 and is applied to the spell.

Sometimes a spell has a Requisite for both its Technique and Form, so that both are limited. And, if several Requisites apply to the same primary Art (e.g., there are two Requisites that are Forms, so both limit the primary Form), the lowest one serves as the limit.

Requisites listed at the beginning of a spell apply when you are learning, inventing, or casting that spell, but do not apply for determining the defender's Magic Resistance. The defender's Magic Resistance is determined by the spell's primary Form, not that listed as a Requisite, even if the caster's Requisite Form score is higher than that of his primary Form score.

## Casting Requisites

Some Requisites are not listed at the top of a spell because they only count when the spell is being used in a certain way. They sometimes count when casting the spell, but never when learning of inventing it, so they are called **Casting Requisites**. Look at *Shape of the Woodland Prowler* (p. 208) for an example. When learning the spell or using it to transform only your body, you need an Animál Requisite, but if you want to transform your wooden staff along with you, you need a Herbam Requisite as well. You might, therefore, be able to transform your staff as well if you have a good Herbam score, but be unable to transform your metal dagger if your Terram score is low. You choose which Arts you use as Casting Requisites when casting the spell, so what you can affect

is limited by your choice. The lowest score among all the chosen casting Requisites is the one used when you cast the spell.

Any Magical Affinities or Deficiencies you have with an Art which is a Requisite apply. Thus, if you have the Major Magical Deficiency Flaw with an Art which is a Requisite, then you have to divide your entire spell roll by 2, because your weakness with the underlying concepts and magic of the spell interferes with your control of the primary Arts.

Look at the various spells in the Spells Chapter to see how Requisites are determined.

## Spontaneous Requisites

Requisites are similar for Spontaneous spells. When the Arts used are determined, determine also whether Requisites are involved. If so, they limit your Arts just as they do for Formulaic spells; you may choose which Casting Requisites to use.

# TARGETING

Some spells, especially Animál, Córporem, and Mentem spells, affect a target directly. While casting *Curse of Circe* (p.208), for example, you must concentrate on the body that you are transforming into a pig, and if you

## Spell Targeting Table

**Free Shot:** Target is standing still, in plain view, at short range. No roll required; automatic.

**Easy Shot:** Target is moving slowly or is standing at a distance. Targeting roll of 6+ necessary.

**Hard Shot:** Target is engaged in combat, is obscured by darkness or cover, or is at a great distance (200 paces). Targeting roll of 9+ necessary.

**Very Hard Shot:** Target is visually obscured and moving quickly. Targeting roll of 12+ necessary.

**Incredible Shot:** Distant target is barely visible. Targeting roll of 15+ necessary.

Other factors have effects as the Storyguide sees fit.

successfully cast the spell, it affects the target directly (though the target may resist magically.)

Other spells, however, conjure some type of medium, such as fire, which in turn affects the target. To have their desired effect, both types of spells need to be targeted. For instance, if you are trying to blind an enemy temporarily with *Flash of the Scarlet Flames* (p.216), you have to get the flash right in the target's face. No problem if the victim is standing still and in plain sight, but someone sneaking through the bushes or dodging around in a melee is a more difficult target. Sometimes spells have bonuses or penalties (Targeting modifiers) depending upon how hard they are to aim, such as the -3 penalty of *Flash of the Scarlet Flames* (indicated at the top of the spell). Spells that need to be Targeted are indicated as such in their descriptions, by the word "Aimed," followed by the Targeting modifier for that spell.

To see whether your spell comes up where you need it, roll a **die** and add **Perception + Finesse + Targeting modifier**. If the roll equals or exceeds the Ease Factor set by the Storyguide (see the *Spell Targeting Table*), the spell hits the right target.

The die rolled for Targeting depends on the situation. If you're aiming the spell in the heat of combat, or under tense conditions, a stress die is rolled. If there's no pressure on you, a simple die is rolled. The results of a Botched Targeting roll can be horrible. Rather than affect the intended target, you might affect a friend, yourself, or something you're trying to protect. The Storyguide has final say in such a situation. Even if you don't Botch your Targeting roll you can still fail it, missing your intended target. In that case, the spell takes effect behind or to the side of the target, failing to affect him. Of course, the spell still goes off, so it may affect others and have various side effects.

# MAGIC RESISTANCE

There are two kinds of protection from magic: Natural Resistance and Magic Resistance. Natural Resistance is a defense inherent to the target of a spell. It derives from his essence and is completely non-magical. It functions constantly; it is not summoned into activity. If a spell can be defended against with Natural Resistance, that spell's description describes how the Natural Resistance works. For instance, *Trust of Childlike Faith* (p.224) can be resisted by an Intelligence roll. Even if the spell strikes you, Natural Resistance can keep it from affecting you (just as a Soak roll can keep a sword that hits you from hurting you). Most people and creatures have only Natural Resistance, and since most spells are impervious

## Exempli Gratia: Magic Resistance

Grimgroth grasps a staff that he finds in Mercille. Unfortunately, it has been warded with *Blessing of the Childlike Bliss*, held in a *Waiting Spell*. The Magus who placed the ward rolled 29 (spell casting roll) + 3 for Penetration Talent = 32, the Penetration total. Grimgroth's *Parma Magica* score is 4, giving him 20 points of protection, plus his Mentem score of 3 (his score in the Form of the attacking spell), for a total of 23. Grimgroth rolls a 9, for a total of 32, exactly matching the Penetration total. *Blessing of Childlike Bliss* is repulsed, and Grimgroth realizes a spell attack has been made against him. Being a clever man, he realizes the staff is the source of the spell.

## Penetration Total

This table illustrates the various kinds of Penetration totals that different spells or magical attacks use.

| *Type of Spell* | *Penetration Total* |
| --- | --- |
| Formulaic spells | Formulaic spell casting roll + Penetration Talent |
| Spontaneous spells | spell Level + Penetration Talent |
| Spell-like powers | As specified by the power's description; Level of power if not specified in description, or Might score of creature using power |

## Spells: Resisted & Not Resisted

This chart provides some examples of which spells can be Magically Resisted, and indicates some that can't be. Use these examples to determine whether other spells of similar design can be Resisted or not.

### Resisted

> *Incantation of the Milky Eyes* (PeCo 20)
> *Pilum of Fire* (CrIg 20)
> *The Chirurgeon's Healing Touch* (CrCo 20)
> *Frosty Breath of the Spoken Lie* (InMe 20)
> *Broom of the Winds* (ReAu 15)
> *Weight of a Thousand Hells* (CrMe 25)
> *Visions of the Infernal Terrors** (MuIm 30)
> *Eye of the Sage*** (InCo 30)

### Not Resisted

> *Pit of the Gaping Earth* (PeTe 15)
> *Strike of the Angered Branch* (ReHe 15)
> *Cascade of Rocks* (PeTe 25)
> *The Shadow of Human Life* (CrIm 40)
> *Neptune's Wrath* (ReAq 50)
> *Transmogrify Spell* (MuVi Gen)
> * because of the Mentem Requisite of the spell
> ** detected but not countered

to Natural Resistance, normal people fall easily to the power of spells.

Natural Resistance rolls are made on stress dice. If the defender Botches, his Natural Resistance can be overwhelmed by the magical attack. Refer to the *Magic Botch Suggestions Table*, below, to determine the results of a Natural Resistance Botch.

Magic Resistance is a defense against spells that is created through sorcery, or arises from the innate magical nature of a being. Magi and magical beings often have Magic Resistance on top of Natural Resistance, which can counter a spell before it even hits its target (like a shield that blocks a sword). Magic Resistance comes from innate magical abilities (for faeries, demons, and the like), from blessings of the Church, from black blessings of the Infernal powers, from *Parmae Magicae* (see below, p.180) and from a Magus's Forms.

## Spells That Can Be Magically Resisted

All spells that attack you directly, or attack you by magically forming a medium (like a lightning bolt), can be resisted. However, not all spells can be magically resisted.

Spells that affect you by changing your environment (maybe by causing an earthquake) cannot be resisted. Most illusions cannot be resisted because they exist in your environment; they don't affect you directly, though you may still see through them by other means.

Intéllego spells can be resisted. If an Intéllego spell gives the caster a vision of another person without first probing the target person, successful Resistance merely detects the spell. When you resist this type of Intéllego spell, you know you are the subject of some type of detection magic, but you do not know what specific spell was cast, or who cast it. Spells like *Eye of the Sage* work like this. Intéllego spells that probe the target's person or anything else protected by the target's Magic Resistance, such as spells that read minds or attempt to determine if the target's possessions are magical, are blocked when resisted.

Another way to protect yourself from a spell is to cast a quick counterspell against the attacking spell (see *Fast-Cast Spells*, p.184).

# Resisting Hostile Magics

When a spell that can be resisted strikes a character with Magic Resistance, the target must roll a **stress die + Magic Resistance** (for a description of what makes up Magic Resistance, see below) to see if the spell is resisted. The result is compared to the Penetration total of the attacking spell (see the *Penetration Total Table* for the factors involved in Penetration totals). If the Penetration total exceeds the Magic Resistance roll, the spell penetrates (but may still be Naturally Resisted, if the spell allows.) If the Magic Resistance roll equals or exceeds the Penetration total, the spell is countered and does not affect the target. If the target Botches the Magic Resistance roll, refer to the *Magic Botch Suggestions Table*, below, to determine the results.

For a Magus, Magic Resistance is 5 times your *Parma Magica* score + your score in the Form of the attacking spell. That means your total Magic Resistance defense equals a **stress die + 5 times your *Parma Magica* + your score in the Form of the attacking spell**. Without a *Parma*, only the score you have in the Form of the spell applies. The reason the Form of the attacking spell is included in the Resistance rating is because command over a Form means protection from it. If you are a master of the Art of Ignem, you are not easily affected by flame spells; they flare around you but do not usually burn you, unless extremely potent.

For non-Magi, Magic Resistance is just a straight number. For instance, a faerie with a Faerie Might of 22 has +22 Resistance, modified by a stress die.

Your Magic Resistance covers only you and anything that you wear or hold in your hands. Just touching something does not convey your protection on it, and things extended far from your body (such as a fully extended staff) may not be covered by your Magic Resistance. The Storyguide has the final judgement on what is protected by your Magic Resistance.

Magic Resistance is automatic, assuming a Magus's *Parma Magica* is active. No one need ever decide to resist, nor does doing so require concentration. Magi may, however, decide not to resist a given spell. You may suppress the bonus provided by your score in an appropriate Form by concentrating, and you may drop your *Parma Magica* by concentrating. If *Parma Magica* is temporarily dropped in this way, it resumes protection over you when you will it to, and remains until it wears out at the next sunrise or sunset, as usual (see below).

You do not need to lower your *Parma Magica*, however, to affect yourself with most spells. Any spell of range Self or Body (see p.193) which you cast automatically circumvents your Magic Resistance. However, for you to be affected by any other spell, it must penetrate your Magic Resistance, or you must drop your *Parma Magica*.

## Parma Magica

*Parma Magica* is an Ability, and as such is described in the Abilities section, but as it is integral to the ways of Magi, it is described here as well for easy reference. *Parma Magica* is unique to Magi of the Order of Hermes, but is not a genuine spell. Rather, it is a form of ritual that focuses magical energies into a shield around you and others you designate it to protect. It takes about a minute to perform this ritual, and all to be protected by it must be present for the performance.

Once performed, the ritual lets you add five times your score in the Ability to your Magic Resistance rolls. The ritual protects you until the next sunrise or sunset, whichever comes first. At that time you may perform the ritual again, renewing your protection.

You may also protect one other person for each point you have in the Ability, but your score is effectively 3 points lower when protecting others, no matter how many people you protect (so you need a score of 4+ to do any good at all). Therefore, if your *Parma Magica* score is 5, and you are protecting three other people, you all have a partial Magic Resistance score of 10 (5 - 3 = 2, multiplied by 5 = 10). Furthermore, if your *Parma Magica* protects others, your score in the Form of any attacking spell applies to the Magic Resistance of all you protect — your Form score is not reduced. Finally, if a spell is directed at a group under the protection of a Magus's *Parma Magica*, or at an individual in the group who is not the Magus, each individual in the group or the individual rolls for Magic Resistance. The Magus does not make one Magic Resistance roll for the whole group, nor does she make individual rolls for the people under her protection.

People protected by a Magus's *Parma Magica* must remain within 15 paces (yards) of the Magus to maintain their Magic Resistance. If a person leaves that 15 pace radius, the Magic Resistance score of those still protected remains the same — when the ritual is performed it's designed for specific people and their number, so it remains that way until the next sunrise/sunset. Also, if a person leaves the 15 pace radius, she may return and regain the Magus's magical protection. Newcomers cannot be included in the Magus's protection after the *Parma Magica* ritual has been performed. They may be added after the next sunrise/sunset, when the ritual is performed again, or if the Magus elects to perform a new ritual right away.

## Awareness of Attack

Whenever your Magic Resistance succeeds in protecting you from intruding magics, you immediately become aware that hostile magics have been repelled. However, you do not know what type of magic is repulsed, nor the source of the intrusion. If your Magic Resistance fails to repel the attack, your awareness is overcome along with your protection, and you do not automatically become aware of the attack; you are only aware of the attack if its effects are noticeable (e.g., you burst into flames).

# CONCENTRATION

It takes concentration to cast a spell, so if anything distracts you while you are casting, you must make a successful Concentration roll or the spell automatically fails (though you must still roll for a disrupted spell to determine if you Botch it). Whether your Concentration roll succeeds or fails, you have to make the spell casting roll with a stress die and with one extra Botch die. The Concentration roll is **stress die + Intelligence + Concentration skill**, and the Ease Factor depends on the distraction suffered; see the *Distraction Table*. If you are moving, subtract your Encumbrance from the roll. You must also make a Concentration roll when you are distracted while trying to maintain a spell. If your Concentration roll Botches, you automatically lose a Short-Term Fatigue Level, or can refer to the *Magic Botch Suggestions Table.*.

# SPELL EFFECTS

The Range, Duration, and effects of spells are all explained in general and specific terms in the Spells Chapter.

## Distraction Table

| | |
|---|---|
| Walking | 6 |
| Jostled | 9 |
| Sudden noise or flash of light | 9 |
| Running | 12 |
| Imminent personal threat | 12 |
| Fall | 12 |
| Knocked Down | 15 |
| Dodging | 15 |
| Blown Over | 21 |
| Damaged | 12 + 1 per point by which you miss your Soak roll |

The numbers are the Ease Factors for a Concentration roll. If more than one distraction applies, use an Ease Factor equal to the most difficult one that applies.

# DANGERS

Despite the Order's attempts to regulate it, magic remains an Art, not a science; no matter how skilled a practitioner you are, and no matter what precautions you take (short of not using magic at all), your magic will sometimes get out of your control. From the occasional danger of casting a spell improperly to the more enigmatic danger of Wizard's Twilight, magic is filled with hazards.

## Botches

The most common danger you face when performing magic is a Botch while casting a spell. The results of a given spell cast under stress are not entirely predictable, and a Botch on a spell roll means that you've made a mistake which, rather than just causing your spell to fail, causes your spell to produce different effects than you intend. A Botch means you lose control of your magic, and losing control is almost never a good thing. Thus, though the effects of Botches can vary widely, they are almost universally detrimental. See *Magic Botch Suggestions* for common Botches for different types of spells and spell-related rolls like Magic Resistance and Natural Resistance.

## Wizard's Twilight

When your magic gets beyond your control, or you are overwhelmed by the powerful magic of another, you can succumb to what is known, and largely feared, as Wizard's Twilight. Twilight tends to be a phenomenon that occurs during the course of a Saga, as events unfold in your life. Twilight also tends to drastically alter the course of your life, or marks it in some unmistakable way. Wizard's Twilight is therefore discussed fully in the Saga Chapter, p.356.

# RAW VIS

Magic power (vis) is sometimes stored in physical objects, either because a Magus has trapped it there or because of natural magical processes. When in physical form, this power is called "raw vis," and Magi have many uses for it.

Raw vis is always associated with a particular Technique or Form. Thus, there is Ignem vis, Creo vis, Imágonem vis, and so on. There is even Vim vis, pure magical power stored in physical form. Raw vis comes in many forms, including blood, skins, horns, plants, sap, crystals, and minerals. When vis is used, it is permanently lost, and its physical form usually changes. It dissolves, withers, crumbles, shrivels, or whatever is appropriate to the material in which the vis is trapped.

As vis is always associated with an Art, that vis can only be used with spells that involve the same Art. For instance, if you are using raw vis to strengthen a Creo Ignem spell, you must use Creo or Ignem vis. Vis of any other Art is used up, and its power is wasted and uncontrolled (see below). If a spell involves a Requisite, vis of that Requisite can be used in the spell. For example, if you cast a Creo Córporem spell that involves an Animál Requisite, Animál vis can be used in the spell.

Raw vis can be used to strengthen a spell, perform a Ritual, create a magical enchantment, make a spell permanent, increase one's power in *Certámen* (a magical duel), provide a source for study of a magical Art, or aid several other magical activities. Because it is so versatile, vis is used as currency among Magi.

Raw vis is measured in "vis points." More powerful actions require more vis points. Magi measure raw vis in "pawns," each equal to one point. Ten "pawns" make a "rook," and ten "rooks" make a "queen."

When you expend raw vis, you must be touching it. This is why Magi often wear magical sources of vis in necklaces or rings; it is a visible sign for all who might challenge them that they have vis to use if threatened. When you choose to use raw vis, you must determine the number of pawns that are to be invested in the magical activity. Once you have established the number you cannot change it, and if the spell is disrupted, fails, or Botches, all vis dedicated to it is lost. Of course, you can cast spells without expending any vis.

There are limits to the amount of vis you can utilize at one time. You cannot spend more pawns of vis than you have a score in the Art that the vis is attuned to (i.e., If your Herbam score if 4 you can't spend more than four Herbam vis). This limit is imposed for a single Round of action, and for the casting of a single spell. For laboratory activities, which take an extended amount of time, Vim + Magic Theory is the limit to the number of pawns of vis you may use in one Season. Vim is used because it's representative of magic as a whole, so imposes a limit on the amount of magic you can work with over an extended period.

If you try to use more vis than your appropriate Art or Vim score allows, whether casting a spell or working in the lab, the extra points are used up, but you do not gain any benefit from them. They do not count towards the action attempted, but they do count to determine the number of extra Botch rolls you make (see *Using Raw* Vis, p.187). At the Storyguide's option, the uncontrolled magical power that you release may affect your surroundings, causing magical side effects in proportion to the amount of uncontrolled vis expended.

# Magic Botch Suggestions

Look at the suggestions for the Technique and Form of the Botched spell, and the explanations that follow those suggestions. Those effects marked with an asterisk are also appropriate results for Botched Magic Resistance or Natural Resistance rolls.

## Techniques

**Creo:** Out of Control, Too Powerful *, Reverse Effect (healing spells), Improper Creation, Flawed Creation, Target Turns on Caster.

**Intéllego:** Caster Addled, Misleading Information, Overwhelming Vision, Attract Unwanted Attention, Connection with Target, Senses Overwhelmed, Roll for Twilight.

**Muto:** Related but Unwanted Effect, Reverse Effect, Permanent Side Effect*, Too Powerful*, Constitution Broken*, Undying Spell*, Incomplete or Improper Effect.

**Perdo:** Spell Affects Caster, Wrong Target, Reverse Effect, Too Powerful*.

**Rego:** Affects Wrong Target, Out of Control, Reverse Effect, Undying Spell*, Target Turns on Caster.

## Forms

**Animál:** Target Deranged*, Target Turns on Caster.

**Auram:** Storm Created.

**Ignem:** Target Turns on Caster.

**Imágonem:** Undying Spell.

**Mentem:** Attract Unwanted Attention, Target Deranged*, Target Turns on Caster, Uncontrolled Faculties*.

**Terram:** Earth Rebels, Target Destroyed.

**Vim:** Demon Summoned, Roll for Twilight, Caster Overwhelmed.

**All Elements (Aquam, Auram, Ignem, Terram):** Out of Control (especially Ignem), Elemental Summoned.

**All Living Things (Animál, Córporem, Herbam, Mentem):** Death and Destruction*, Constitution Broken*, Debilitating*.

**Spells Which Affect the Caster:** Caster Overwhelmed.

## Suggestion Explanations

**Attract Unwanted Attention:** The attention of someone or something, perhaps the target of your spell, is drawn to you.

**Caster Addled:** The caster is insane, confused, or demented. You acquire the Flaw Simple-Minded for an indefinite duration.

**Caster Overwhelmed:** You are overwhelmed by your own magic. Make a Stamina stress roll of 6+ or be knocked unconscious, possibly losing magical ability for a while. It can, albeit rarely, obliterate the caster's mind.

**Connection with Target:** Your target becomes aware of your investigations, and may learn something about you through the arcane link that is temporarily established.

**Constitution Broken:** The target loses the faculties related to the spell, such as a Muto spell that leaves the target with no natural shape so the target's form droops and decays without a spell to support it.

**Death and Destruction:** The target "falls apart" under the supernatural pressure of the spell, such as a Rego Córporem spell that leaves the body lifeless or a Mentem spell that causes complete insanity.

**Debilitating:** The spell pushes the target too hard and does permanent damage, such as a Rego Animál spell that forever leaves the beast without its natural instincts and urges.

**Demon Summoned:** You inadvertently summon a demon of a power proportionate to the Level of the spell. Good luck.

**Earth Rebels:** The earth rebels against being manipulated, causing a localized earthquake. All creatures and structures in the immediate area are affected.

**Flawed Creation:** The creation is heavily flawed, though the flaw may not be obvious until the creation is used.

**Improper Creation:** The wrong thing is created, or the right thing is created in the wrong way (such as a stone wall that is created lying down).

**Incomplete or Improper Effect:** A spell, for example, intended to transform you into a wolf, but which only transforms your head and hands.

**Misleading Information:** False or misleading information, perhaps the answer to the wrong question.

**Out of Control:** The spell creates or calls forth something beyond the caster's ability to control.

**Overwhelming Vision:** The caster is overcome with a mystical vision, and is completely incapacitated until the vision is over.

**Permanent Side Effect:** For example, a spell that transforms you into a wolf, but leaves you with fangs afterward.

**Related but Unwanted Affect:** For example, a spell intended to transform you into a wolf, but which turns you into a pig.

**Reverse Effect:** The spell does exactly the opposite of what is intended.

**Roll for Twilight:** Roll to avoid Wizard's Twilight. If you avoid it, you still suffer another Botch result.

**Senses Overwhelmed:** One or more of your senses are completely overwhelmed, leaving them useless for an indefinite period of time.

**Spell Affects Caster:** instead of the intended target.

**Storm Created:** A storm or some other weather phenomenon is created from thin air. It may last minutes or days, depending on the Level of the spell attempted.

**Target Deranged:** The target becomes deranged, going completely out of control.

**Target Destroyed:** Whatever you are attempting to affect is completely destroyed, in whatever manner the Storyguide deems appropriate.

**Too Powerful:** The spell does more than it should and thereby causes problems.

**Target Turns on Caster:** The subject being manipulated turns on the caster, attacking or otherwise harming him in whatever way possible.

**Uncontrolled Faculties:** The target loses control of his emotions or thoughts, his faculties changing frequently and randomly for an indefinite period of time.

**Undying Spell:** You cannot stop the spell by concentrating, it does not end at the normal time, and it proves resistant to being dispelled.

**Wrong Target:** Pick a new one at random.

Note: the more spells a person has been influenced by, especially for long periods of time, the more likely she is to suffer ill effects from Botches. So, a Covenant that uses spells to make its Grogs loyal may soon have a turb of insane or feebleminded Grogs. Sometimes even beneficial spells can have detrimental effects on those affected by them.

# Spell Casting Options

## Mastering a Spell

When you gain Experience Points at the end of a story or year, you can use them to Master spells. You may put Experience Points on spells you have used under stress or dedicated yourself to study, instead of on Abilities (no more than one point per spell per story, though more than one point may be assigned with a year's Experience). When you accumulate one-fifth the spell's Level in Experience Points, it is Mastered.

When casting a Mastered spell, you always roll a simple die, unless you are using vis to boost the spell (see p.187). If you are using vis to boost the spell, roll one less Botch die. In addition, you gain a bonus of +1 to all Concentration and Meditation rolls involving the Mastered spell, and may attempt to Multiple Cast it (see below).

## Multiple Casting

You can cast a single Mastered spell so that it affects more people, objects, or areas (as applicable) than normal. Only Mastered spells may be Multiple Cast.

First, you must make a **Finesse + Intelligence** stress roll of 9+, with a penalty on the roll equal to the number of spells cast. If you fail the roll, your time is wasted (no spells are cast), and if you Botch, you automatically lose a Short-Term Fatigue Level and must roll on the *Magic Botch Suggestions Table*. If your roll succeeds, you must make a casting roll for each spell, subtracting from each roll a number equal to the number of spells cast. If a spell roll is 10 lower than the spell's Level, that single spell is not cast, but the rest may be. As you make spell casting rolls as usual, you may lose Fatigue Levels for low rolls. If you drop below "Unconscious" because of this exertion, you are Unconscious for an extra hour for each Fatigue Level you lose past Unconsciousness.

Subtract the number of targets from any Targeting rolls made when Multiple Casting. Even if all the spells are aimed at one target, you receive a -1 penalty.

For example, if you cast three *Balls of Abysmal Flame* (p.216), two at one target and the other at a second target, you have a -3 penalty (the number of spells) on the Finesse roll to succeed with Multiple Casting, and a -3 penalty to the rolls to cast the spells. You also have a -2 penalty (the number of targets) on each Targeting roll.

The Storyguide can penalize or prohibit Multiple Casting that is especially difficult, such as casting two spells in opposite directions.

## Fast-Cast Spells

To cast a spell safely you need time to draw together and control the energy that powers the spell. Formulaic spells always require an expenditure of time. Even Spontaneous spells need some measure of control. However, if you're daring or desperate, you can cast a Spontaneous spell more quickly. Fast-Casting a spell entails gathering the energy and expending it before the normal precautions are taken to control it. You may have to take this risk to defend yourself against an incoming attack or spell, or to prevent an event which is underway at the moment (e.g., one of your friends is falling and you want to magically catch him). Fast-Cast spells are also used to defend against attacks that Magic Resistance and Natural Resistance cannot defend against. For example, if an enemy Magus causes a tree branch to swing down and strike you, you can Fast-Cast a Spontaneous spell in response, to make the branch swing wide.

There are three steps to determine the success of a Fast-Cast spell: Casting Time, Casting Roll, and Spell Potency.

### Casting Time

To get a Fast-Cast spell off when you need it, combine your **Quickness + Finesse - Encumbrance**. That score is compared to the total of the Magus you're fighting, if you're defending against a spell just cast. If your score is higher, you may attempt your Fast-Cast and hope it counteracts the magical attack (see *Spell Potency*, below). If you fail the contest, the incoming spell takes effect before you can stop it. Your spell may be made useless at that point, and you may choose not to cast it. However, you must still make a spell casting roll to insure you don't Botch (make three extra Botch rolls), and you must still expend any vis invested in the Fast-Cast spell.

If you choose to proceed with your Fast-Cast spell, even if you've lost the speed contest with your opponent, you may cast the spell. You must make an Intelligence + Concentration stress roll to do so, though, based on any interruptions you've suffered (see the *Distraction Table*, above).

If you're Fast-Casting to avoid incoming mundane attacks (i.e., to divert approaching arrows, or to throw aside axe strokes), compare your **Quickness + Finesse - Encumbrance** total against the **Quickness + Attack Skill - Encumbrance** total of each of your attackers. If you are faster than all of them, you may cast your spell and hope to avoid all their attacks (see *Spell Potency*, below). If your speed total is lower than some or all of your attackers' totals, the faster attackers proceed unhindered. You may still get your Fast-Cast spell off against attackers who are slower than you, but you must make a Concentration roll, based on the amount of damage you've taken.

## Fast-Cast Defense Summary

| To Defend Against | Level Required |
|---|---|
| Hostile Magic | Half Penetration total |
| Mundane Attacks: | |
|    Single Known Attack | 10 |
|    Up to 3 Known Attacks | 15 |
|    Any Number of threats | 20 |
|    Any Number of Known or Unknown Attacks | 25 |

When defending against multiple mundane attacks with a single spell, the spell must be of appropriate Form and effect to defend against all types of weapons and attacks.

If your enemy in Fast-Casting is time (e.g., you're trying to save a falling friend), your speed rating is compared to an Ease Factor set by the Storyguide. The average Ease Factor is about 3, given that die rolls are not involved in this comparison.

There are no dice involved in this speed comparison system to avoid another roll in the game, and to save time in the whole Fast-Cast procedure. Fast-Casting is supposed to be *fast* after all.

### Casting Roll

A Fast-Cast spell is rolled for as a normal Spontaneous spell, but with a -5 penalty because it is so hasty. This penalty is applied *before* the Spontaneous spell casting roll is divided. If you roll a 0, you make three extra Botch rolls to determine the results. No one said Fast-Cast spells are safe.

Fast-Cast defenses have very limited Range, Duration, and potential for targets, as their Levels tend to be low. The Duration of most Fast-Cast counter spells is Instant.

### Spell Potency

The exact effects of any defensive spell you cast are always up to the Storyguide, but the following guidelines can be used by the Storyguide to determine the effectiveness of your defense. In all cases, you must use a Technique and Form appropriate to defend you from the attack, and you must describe your spell fully, just as if you are casting a normal Spontaneous spell. For example, if you are defending yourself from flame, you might use Creo Aquam or Perdo Ignem to put the fire out, or Rego Ignem to deflect the flame. Failure to use an appropriate Technique and Form makes your defense useless.

If you are defending against a magical attack, you may completely ward off the attack if the Level of your Spontaneous spell equals or exceeds half the Penetration total of the attacking spell.

If you are defending against mundane attack, a Level 10, 15, or 20 spell normally completely protects you from a single attack, a few known attacks, or any number of known attacks, respectively. A Level 25 spell normally protects you from any attacks of a given type, whether you are aware of the attacks or not. Thus, if you are quick enough to Fast-Cast a defense spell against several mundane attacks, but don't get a high spell casting roll (a high enough spell Level), some of those attacks may still hit you (but your spell still functions against those it can, as determined by its Level; the spell is not disrupted unless you fail a Concentration roll). If you are defending against multiple mundane attacks with a single spell, your spell must be general enough (both in the Form used and in the specific effect) to encompass all the different types of weapons and types of attacks you are defending against.

Fast-Cast counterspells which fail to completely defend against the attack (i.e., the Fast-Cast is quick enough to beat the attack, but isn't powerful enough to stop the attack cold) usually still provide some protection, in the form of reduced damage from the attack, a more difficult Attack Roll for the attacker, a greater Natural Resistance roll, or something similar. The Storyguide should be careful to consider the side effects of the defense used. For example, a Fast-Cast Perdo Ignem defense might destroy the incoming attack completely, but a Rego Ignem defense might protect the Magus, only to have the fire deflected into another combatant.

## Recognizing Spells

The Form required for Fast-Cast defenses against mundane attacks is almost always obvious (e.g., ReTe if redirecting sword swings), but for Fast-Cast defenses against magic, you must at least be able to determine the Form of the magic you are defending against, or you are unable to construct an appropriate defense.

If the attacker is a Hermetic Magus, and is using either voice or gestures which you can perceive, then you can determine both the Technique and the Form of the attacking spell automatically. However, Perception rolls may be required for you to perceive the words or gestures used if the Magus is using soft speech or subtle gestures (see below), or if there are distractions, such as loud noises on the battlefield.

In all cases where the Form and Technique are not obvious, you must make a Perception roll of 9+ to recognize the Form and Technique of the attacking magic. If the attacking spell is Hermetic, then you may add your Magic Theory to this roll.

If you fail to determine the Form of the attacking magic, and still want to chance a Fast-Cast defense, you

## Magic Activities Table

| Action | Roll Modifiers | Notes |
|---|---|---|
| Cast Formulaic Spell | Technique + Form + Stamina | Level of spell or lose Fatigue Level, within 10 or fail spell |
| Cast Spontaneous Spell | Technique + Form + Intelligence | divide by 2 for exertion, divide by 5 for non-exertion |
| Casting Speed of Simultaneous Spells | Quickness + Finesse - Encumbrance | vs. that of opponent |
| Cast Ritual Spell | Technique + Form + Stamina + Meditation | lose one or two Long-Term Fatigue Levels |
| Magic Penetration | roll to cast spell + Penetration | beat target's Magic Resistance roll |
| Magic Resistance | Form + 5 x *Parma Magica* | stress roll |
| Targeting | Perception + Finesse + modifier | see *Spell Targeting Table* |
| Concentration | Intelligence + Concentration | see *Distraction Table* |
| Fast-Cast | Speed: | |
| | Quickness + Finesse - Encumbrance | against opponent's Fast-Cast score |
| | Weapons: | |
| | Quickness + Attack -Encumbrance | to deflect attacks |
| | Spontaneous Spell | -5 and 3 extra Botch rolls |
| | 0 means side effect and roll for Botch | |
| Recognizing Spells | Perception + Magic Theory | roll 9+ |
| Multiple Casting | Intelligence + Finesse - # of | roll 9+, penalty on casting and targeting spells rolls |
| Casting a Spell while Maintaining Another | Intelligence + Concentration | roll 15+, +3 if the same spell or target |
| Casting from Text | As for Formulaic | stress & twice normal Botch rolls |
| *Certámen*: Basic Roll | Technique + Form + Intelligence + *Certámen* | compare w/ opponent's roll |
| Weaken Opponent | Intelligence + *Certámen* + bonus points | vs. Stamina + *Certámen* |

**Using Raw Vis**

Ritual Spell: requires 1 pawn per 5 Levels of spell

Increase Spell's Duration or Range: requires 1 pawn per 5 Levels of spell

Strengthen Formulaic or Spontaneous Spell: +5 per pawn on roll

In *Certámen*: +5 per point in basic roll

**Requisites**

A Requisite limits the Form (if the Requisite is a Form) or the Technique (if the Requisite is a Technique). A Casting Requisite limits the Art only when the spell is used in a certain way.

must guess at the Form, or find some other means of defending yourself.

# Words and Gestures

It is possible to cast either a Formulaic or Spontaneous spell without the firm voice and strong gestures that are typical, but doing so is difficult. You can also exaggerate your motions and yell at the top of your lungs in casting a spell, making spell casting easier; the elements of magic respond more obediently to your commands. Use *The Words and Gestures Table* to determine your penalty when casting subtly, or with excessive vigor. The modifiers listed are cumulative. For example, if your are using soft words and subtle gestures, your penalty is -7. Also note: if you cast a spell without any gestures, you do not suffer penalties to your spell rolls for being Encumbered.

## Words and Gestures Table

| Voice Modifier | Modifier | Gesture | |
|---|---|---|---|
| Booming | +1 | Vigorous | +1 |
| Firm | 0 | Bold | 0 |
| Soft | -5 | Subtle | -2 |
| None | -10 | None | -5 |

## Extra Care

You may wish to spend extra time preparing to cast a Spontaneous spell or a non-Ritual Formulaic spell, in order to be more careful, and to increase your chances of casting the spell correctly. Ritual spells may not be aided in this manner, since the extra time for preparation is already accounted for in the time to cast the spell.

You spend one minute per 5 Levels of the spell in preparation, considering the symbols you are about to use, considering the laws of magic, and carefully gathering the energy that powers the spell. When the preparation time is over, you cast the spell, adding your Meditation score to your spell roll. In addition, if you are making a stress roll, you may reduce the number of Botch dice (if any) by 1 (but never below one Botch die).

## Spell Foci

Most Formulaic spells have certain special ingredients, called Spell Foci, which aid in their casting, and which, when used, supply some of the magical energy needed to cast a spell. When you use the Focus specified in the description of a spell (see the Spells Chapter), you gain a specified bonus to your roll when casting the spell. Failing to use these Foci causes no ill effects or penalties.

Certain powerful spells may require the mandatory use of certain Spell Foci, in which case the spell description notes the requirement. In this case, failing to use the specified Focus results in failure of the spell.

Note that the creation of a Focus through magic (probably a Creo spell) does you no good. The magically created Focus offers no spell casting bonus, unless its existence is made permanent through the use of vis . A functioning Focus must otherwise exist naturally, and does not have to possess magical properties.

Spell Foci continue to exist after the casting of a spell — a single Focus can be used over and over — unless a spell's description states otherwise.

## Using Raw Vis

Raw vis is magical power in physical form. It is required to cast Ritual spells, and you can use it to strengthen spells. With Spontaneous spells, you may only use raw vis to increase your spell roll (and thus increase the Level of the resulting spell). With Formulaic and Ritual spells, you may use raw vis to extend Range, extend Duration (making permanent spells possible), or increase your spell roll. (Of course, in the case of Ritual spells, vis expended due to these things is in addition to that needed to perform the Ritual itself). You must always use Art-specific vis with spells, and the total number of pawns of vis you may use when casting a spell is limited by your score in the Form or Technique that matches that of the vis (see Raw Vis, p.181).

When using vis to increase your spell roll, add +5 to it for every pawn of vis expended. When casting Spontaneous spells, this bonus is added before the roll is divided.

Some Formulaic and Ritual spells have two Ranges or Durations listed, and you can only achieve the second (longer) Range or Duration by expending one pawn of raw vis per 5 Levels of the spell or fraction thereof. For some spells, the second Duration listed is "Perm.," meaning that the spells can be made permanent. If you wish to extend both Range and Duration, you must expend vis for both.

Using raw vis to strengthen a spell in any of the above ways is tricky, and you must always roll a stress die when strengthening a spell with vis, even if you have Mastered the spell. In addition, if you roll a zero, you must roll one extra Botch die per pawn of vis expended.

## Casting a Spell While Maintaining Another

To cast one spell while concentrating on another, make an Intelligence + Concentration stress roll of 15+. You get a bonus of +3 if the second spell is the same as the first, or if the target of the second spell is the same as the target of the first. If you fail the Concentration roll, you fail to cast the second spell. If you Botch the Concentration roll, the first spell fails you as well.

## Casting from a Text

It is possible to cast a Formulaic spell that you do not know yourself if you have a readable copy of it. Indeed, many powerful spells have never been learned by anyone but their inventors; they are cast almost exclusively from texts. To cast a spell from a text, you spend one Round for every 5 Levels of the spell, and make a spell casting roll on a stress die with double the normal number of Botch dice. If your spell casting roll does not equal or exceed the spell Level, you lose one Short-Term Fatigue Level for every 5 points, or fraction thereof, by which you miss the spell Level. The spell succeeds, whether you make the spell casting roll or not, unless you go Unconscious from

Fatigue loss. If you go Unconscious and the spell fails, you must roll to see if you Botch, even if the spell casting roll was not a zero.

Ritual spells may be cast from a text, but they take much longer. You must spend 30 minutes for every 5 Levels of the spell, and must expend raw *vis*, just as you do for casting the Ritual from memory.

## Counteracting Spells

Sometimes you may want to nullify the effects of another Magus's spell. There is no hard and fast means of doing so. Fast-Cast spells (see p.184) are one means, but as those spells are unrefined, their ability to dispel other magics is limited.

Another, more common, means of nullifying another Magus's spells is with a prepared spell of your own. There are numerous spells described in the Spells Chapter which are designed to dispel other magics. Most of these spells are tailored to affect spells of their own Form and Technique. Most also involve Rituals, so *vis* is a necessity. Some Vim spells, like *Wind of Mundane Silence*, are capable of counteracting any kind of spell or magic. In addition, spells like *Aegis of the Hearth* provide protection from magic in the first place.

# CERTÁMEN

*Certámen* (CareTAHmen, Latin for "duel") is the ceremony by which two Magi voluntarily create a magical "dueling ground," where they pit their magical talents against one another. *Certámen* is solely an institution of the Order of Hermes; non-Hermetic wizards do not have the ability to participate in the ceremony. Within the Order, *Certámen* serves as a non-lethal way for one Magus to establish dominance and precedence over another. The ceremony has formal restrictions to keep it from disrupting the unity of the Order. You may challenge anyone to *Certámen* once, but the Code prohibits you from challenging the same person again unless she challenges you in the meantime. Thus, you cannot hound an unwilling opponent into *Certámen*.

To engage in *Certámen*, you must first find a magical middle ground with another Magus, and must use your magical arts to overcome your enemy's. The middle ground consists of a Form and Technique combination, which is the medium through which the struggle occurs. You and your opponent must agree on the Form and Technique, or the duel cannot take place. Thus, either combatant can decline to enter *Certámen*. (It is possible

# Exempli Gratia:
## Certámen

Grimgroth meets the Magus who is behind the mystery at Mercille. She is a sullen wizard who refuses to explain her actions. Grimgroth is concerned for the inhabitants of Mercille, given that signs of diabolism have been found. Grimgroth insists that the intruder explain herself, and she responds by challenging Grimgroth to *Certámen* (which in itself at least proves she is of Hermetic background). Implicit in the contest is the agreement that the intruder will divulge her secrets if she loses, and that Grimgroth will leave if he loses.

The intruder chooses the Rego Technique. Luckily, this is Grimgroth's best Technique. Grimgroth then chooses his best Form, Auram, and decides that the contest will involve controlling a whirlwind phantasm. This allows Grimgroth to use his Affinity with winds on his rolls. The two Magi face off while the others watch in anticipation. The Storyguide allows the duelists to ignore the -2 penalty for being in the Dominion since the penalty applies equally to both of them.

Round 1: Grimgroth's Rego + Auram + Intelligence + *Certámen* + Affinity total is 6 + 12 + 3 + 2 + 4 = 27. He rolls a 1, and rolls again for a 7, which doubles to 14. His first Round total is 41. His opponent only rolls a 32, so Grimgroth has a healthy advantage of +9. He decides to keep his advantage and add it to his next roll.

Between the duelists arises a swirling cone of air, which each of them struggles to control.

Round 2: Grimgroth rolls a 7 + 27 + 9 (bonus from last Round) for a total of 43. His opponent rolls a 35, so Grimgroth's bonus drops to 8. Grimgroth realizes he should use the points he scored from his first, lucky, roll before he loses them entirely, so he

tries to tire his opponent now. His roll to reduce her Fatigue Levels is 8 (roll) + 2 (*Certámen*) + 3 (Intelligence) + 8 (bonus) = 21. The other Magus's *Certámen* + Stamina roll is 10, which means she drops three Fatigue Levels (based on their 11 point roll difference). Grimgroth's opponent now suffers a -3 modifier to her *Certámen* rolls due to Fatigue, which puts her at a serious disadvantage.

The maelstrom of air suddenly lunges at Grimgroth's enemy, striking her soundly before she can force it back to the middle of the magical battlefield.

Round 3: Grimgroth rolls a 30. The intruder rolls a 37, but expends four pawns of raw Rego vis, which gives her an extra 20 points! Her total thus equals 57, giving her a 27 point advantage. The unknown Magus immediately uses these 27 points to tire Grimgroth. Her roll to do so is 36, and as Grimgroth's defense roll is only 8, he drops six Fatigue Levels, to Unconscious. The woman declines the opportunity to cast a spell at Grimgroth, seeing no point in Fatiguing herself further.

A bolt of wind flies from the intruder's ring, the source of her raw vis, and joins with the whirlwind. Under the control of the intruder, the vortex of wind pummels Grimgroth into unconsciousness. The ring turns to blackened metal and breaks, falling to the ground.

*Certámen* ends.

Grimgroth's allies carry him from the scene of the battle, back to the tavern where they've made their camp. When the Magus awakens, the group trudges back to Mistridge, with little to show for their efforts.

to decline *Certámen*, but not always socially acceptable.) By tradition, the aggressor in the duel chooses the Technique and the defender chooses the Form, but this system is purely artificial, and any system for determining the Arts used is possible as long as both Magi agree to it.

Once the middle ground is chosen, you and your opponent concentrate for a moment, and both enter trances (during which you have no defense against physi-

cal attacks). You become attuned to the magical forces around and between you, and these forces take shape as phantasms, controlled by you. If the middle ground is Muto Animál, the phantasms might be two animals, one yours and the other controlled by your opponent. The animals change form at your mental command, turning into various animals in an effort to defeat the other. A Creo Ignem *Certámen* could consist of two fiery beings fighting.

An Intéllego Aquam contest is not spectacular; it might appear that the combatants are in hazy water, each trying to find his way around.

The illusionary battle is the tangible result of the magical battle taking place. What happens between the phantasms affects the minds of the combatants, and the minds of the combatants affect the phantasms. This being the case, *Certámen* is a good situation in which to apply roleplaying modifiers. If you describe your phantasm's appearance and actions in dramatic or colorful detail, the Storyguide may give you a bonus to your rolls. You may also gain a bonus if you convincingly enact your character's reactions to the duel, reacting to events as your character does.

Bonuses also apply to *Certámen* rolls if you have a *Magical Affinity*, or other related Virtue, that applies to the duel. The Magus who chooses the Form of the battle chooses the shapes of the phantasms used. So, if you have an *Affinity* for wolves, and choose wolves as the phantasms, you get your *Affinity* bonus with your *Certámen* rolls.

In game terms, the duel is simulated by opposed die rolls of a **stress die + Technique + Form + Intelligence +*Certámen* Skill**. The duel is measured in terms of Rounds, as in combat, with each duelist making a single die roll. In any Round you win the contest, count the points by which you exceed your opponent's roll. You can do one of two things with these points: attempt to weaken your opponent, or save them to add to your next roll.

If you use your excess points to weaken your opponent, roll a **stress die + Intelligence + *Certámen* + the points**, and compare the total to your opponent's **stress roll of Stamina + *Certámen***. For every five points, or fraction thereof, by which you exceed your opponent's roll, your opponent drops one Short-Term Fatigue Level (like losing Body Levels in physical combat). Penalties incurred from lost Fatigue Levels apply to all further rolls made in *Certámen* .

If you save your excess points for your next roll, you hope their addition to that roll gives you an even greater excess score in the next Round. However, if your next comparison roll against your opponent is low, you may lose the advantage you had in the previous Round. It's a gamble to hold onto points from one Round to the next, but if you roll high or your opponent rolls low in the following Round, the gamble can pay off with an even higher excess. Note, however, that points saved for the next Round are not cumulative *per se*; they do not automatically accumulate to form one big bonus over several Rounds.

There are three ways to win *Certámen*. The first involves wearing your opponent out until she falls unconscious — she loses all Fatigue Levels. When this happens,

the victor is entitled to cast a single spell at the loser. This spell circumvents the loser's *Parma Magica* (but the loser still gets a Magic Resistance roll based on the Form of the spell), and the spell must be of the same Form and Technique combination used in *Certámen*. In most *Certámen* contests, this "free" spell is unnecessary because your opponent's collapse already designates your victory. However, some duelists still use it to intimidate and embarrass those who fight them. (This spell could also be used to harm your fallen opponent, but, remember, *Certámen* is intended to be a *harmless* way to resolve disputes.)

The second way to win *Certámen* involves your opponent surrendering. He realizes he is outmatched, or wants to walk away from the duel, and concedes the contest. Such a submission means the loser is still capable of defending himself, though, so he still has his full Magic Resistance (i.e., any final spell cast at him is defended against normally).

The third way to win *Certámen* results from a lapse in your opponent's concentration (see the *Concentration* rules, p.180). If your opponent fails a Concentration roll (sometimes necessitated by events or conditions surrounding the duel) during *Certámen*, the fight ends. (Note: Concentration rolls are not necessitated by the loss of Fatigue Levels during *Certámen*). Your opponent's loss of concentration causes her phantasm to disappear, indi-

cating your victory. If this happens you are entitled to cast a "free" spell at your opponent, disregarding her *Parma Magica*.

Loss of concentration, however, does not necessarily mean *Certámen* is over and a victor decided. If the usual "victor" refuses the honor, and the combatant who lost concentration agrees, the battle may resume until a clear victor emerges. A Magus might refuse his "victory" for reasons of honor, or if he has the intent to do more harm, refusing to let his opponent off easy.

You can also use raw vis at any time during *Certámen*, even if your opponent doesn't use it, or doesn't expect its use. For every pawn you expend, add five to a single contest roll. This bonus only applies to your rolls that involve Form and Technique, not to rolls that determine Fatigue Levels lost by your opponent. Raw vis used must

be attuned to one of the Arts used in the duel, either Form or Technique, and you cannot use more pawns in a single Round than you have a score in the appropriate Art. For example, if the duel is based on Perdo Córporem, you can use vis attuned to either Art, but cannot use more pawns in a Round than you have a rating in Perdo or Córporem, whichever is appropriate. You can, however, choose the number of pawns you use, just as you can in any other magical situation.

Rolls for *Certámen* are made in the Magic phase of a Round, if the duel is integrated into a melee situation. Magi involved in *Certámen* can do nothing else until the magical duel is resolved.

# Spells
## chapter seven

The Order of Hermes has collected hundreds of spells that have been invented, improved upon, and passed down by Magi through the centuries. Those listed here are the most generally useful, interesting and exemplary of the spells. However, in no way should these spells be taken as a definitive list of spells available to the Order. Rather, they should be used to help you form guidelines, so that you may invent spells of your own. Many of these spells serve as good examples for several others. For example, a spell to turn you into a wolf can be used as a model for a spell to turn you into another land animal.

# Spell Format

Each spell has several factors that describe it for game use.

**TECHNIQUE AND FORM:** The Technique and Form are shown in the heading under which you can find the spell. Spells are arranged first by their Forms, in alphabetical order, and then within each Form by Technique. There are also general notes provided for each Form and for some Form-Technique combinations. Read the notes, particularly those covering Forms and Techniques your Magus often deals with. The notes help you interpret the possible uses of your spells, and offer ideas on how to invent your own spells. Techniques and Forms are often abbreviated by the first two letters of each word; thus a MuTe spell is of Muto Technique and Terram Form.

**TITLE:** The titles given are the actual names of the spells, as known by Hermetic Magi. Titles are often metaphoric or figurative as they describe effects not easily portrayed in mundane terms. When inventing new spells, try and give your spells interesting names. *Ball of Abysmal Flame* is a colorful name, which gives the game flavor, while *Fireball* is kind of boring.

**LEVEL:** Most spells are assigned a Level, which is usually a multiple of 5. A 5th Level spell is very weak, a 15th Level spell is of moderate power, and a 30th Level spell is quite powerful. Level depends on both the power of the spell and its casting difficulty. For Example, *Gift of Reason* (CrMe 30), a spell which temporarily gives one the ability to think without bias or distraction, is not very powerful, but is difficult to accomplish, so the Level is high. The section explaining Guidelines gives more information on how to choose spell Levels.

Some spells are General spells (abbreviated: Gen), which means they may be learned at any Level of difficulty, with increasingly powerful effects. A ward against faeries of the woods (ReHe Gen), therefore, might, at Level 40, be able to keep out the lords of that realm, while the same General spell, learned at 10th Level, is lucky to discourage Sprites. While the spells listed have Levels at multiples of 5, there is no law of magic that requires new spells to follow this pattern. Thus, you can have a General spell of 13th Level.

The Level you know or learn a General Formulaic or Ritual spell at depends on the source from which you obtain it. If your master has a General Level spell in his grimoire, and it's designed for effectiveness at Level 15, then that's the Level at which you learn the spell. You cannot exceed Level 15 effects with that spell. The only way to get higher results with a General Level spell is to find or invent a version of it that functions at a higher Level, say 25. All this means you cannot utilize a General spell at any Level you want simply because it's General. General Level spells are open ended, so can have affects on a small or large scale, but still have Levels to indicate where your version of the spell is on that effectiveness scale. You cannot simply cast your General Level spell at Level 5 and later cast it at Level 15. Your spell has a set Level, but there are other versions of the same spell out there with lower or higher Levels.

**RANGE** (labelled **R** in spell descriptions): There are seven basic Ranges of spells. Regardless of Range, a target must be seen or distinctly sensed to be affected directly. Thus, a *Pilum of Flame* can be thrown into the bushes in hopes of burning a bandit hiding within, but that bandit is safe from *Curse of Circe*, which requires direct eye contact. Most spells have two Ranges. The one before the slash is the standard Range. The one after the slash is the Range if *vis* is used to boost it (one pawn is required per 5 Levels of the spell). When a Ritual spell may have its Range boosted, the criteria are specifically listed in the Ritual.

**BODY:** affects the caster's body or mind only, not clothing or possessions.

**SELF:** affects only the caster and his clothing and possessions.

**TOUCH:** affects only the caster or whatever the caster touches.

**REACH:** within two paces (a pace is considered a yard).

**EYE:** eye contact; once you establish eye contact, even momentarily, you can hold it by casting the spell, and the target cannot look away until the spell is cast. Normally, eye contact is almost automatic if your target is within ten paces. However, someone who is avoiding eye contact at all costs manages to avoid your spell. Those who avert their eyes but still look in your general direction (as in a social setting) must make Intelligence rolls to avoid eye contact. Spells maintained through concentration only require actual eye contact for the first few seconds of spellcasting.

**NEAR:** within fifteen paces (yards).

**SIGHT:** You must be able to see the target. If the effect has a radius or diameter, you need only see the center of the circle. Sight is the maximum Range which Hermetic magic can normally affect. Only Rituals, spells taking advantage of the Law of Contagion, and spells boosted by vis may ever exceed this Range. In Rituals and when using vis, you must still be able to see the center of the area that you are affecting.

**SPECIAL** (Spec.): A unique Range, described in the spell's text. Many of these spells have long Range, and thus necessitate Arcane Connections or vis.

# DURATION

(labelled D in spell descriptions): Standard Durations are described below. This is how long the effects of a spell last. If a spell has two listed Durations separated by a slash, the first (shorter) is the normal Duration and the second (longer) is the Duration if the spell is supported by raw *vis* — one pawn per 5 Levels of the spell. In the case of Ritual spells, an extra pawn must be spent for the longer Duration, which makes for a total of two pawns per 5 spell Levels, as one pawn must be spent to make the Ritual possible.

Only spells that produce normal results can be made permanent (see *Using Raw Vis* in the Magic Chapter, p.187). Spells that produce unnatural things can be made to last longer with raw *vis*, but they cannot be made permanent. For example, you can turn someone into a dog indefinitely, but if you turn someone's head into a dog's head, the effect does not last forever. A spell's effects usually wear off gradually, not at the instant a spell's Duration ends. Created things weaken and slowly crumble to dust, while transformed things slowly shift back to normal.

By concentrating for a Round, you can automatically cancel any spell (except spells with a Duration of "Instant," see below) that you have cast on yourself.

**INSTANT** (Inst.): The spell works for only an instant, after which nature takes its normal course; the final effects of the spell are permanent and cannot be dispelled. If you burn someone with an instant spell, the magic is gone in a moment, but the burns remain. If you calm a raging bull with an "Instant" spell, the bull can become angry again normally, because the magic of the spell does not continue to affect the beast.

**CONCENTRATION** (Conc.): The spell lasts as long as you concentrate on it. When distracted or when you attempt to do something else in addition to concentrating, you need to make Concentration rolls to maintain the spell (see p.180 for the guidelines on Concentration). If a Concentration spell explicitly involves speaking (such as *Tongue of the Beasts*, InAn 20), such speech requires no Concentration rolls.

**RING**: The spell creates an invisible magic ring which remains in effect as long as the caster does not leave it.

**SUNRISE-SUNSET** (Sun.): The spells lasts until dawn or dusk, whichever comes first. Dawn and dusk, for the purposes of these spells, last about ten minutes, while the sun is on the horizon.

**MOON**: Lasts until both a new moon and a full moon have come. Thus, if cast on the night before the new moon, it lasts until the rise of the next full moon, and if cast before the rise of the full moon, it lasts until the night of the new moon. Moon is the maximum time that a Formulaic or Spontaneous spell may last. Only Rituals, or spells with duration boosted by *vis*, may exceed the Moon limit.

**YEAR**: Lasts until the fourth seasonal change. Thus, a spell cast in the spring lasts until the vernal equinox. Only by casting one of these spells on a solstice or equinox can the spell be made to last a full year. If the spell is temporarily cancelled, the effects return at the next sunrise or sunset, whichever comes first.

**PERMANENT** (Perm.): The spell can be made to affect its target on a permanent basis, with the expenditure of raw *vis*. Permanent spells are different from "Instant" ones in that nature does not resume its course after the casting of a Permanent spell. If, for example, a Permanent spell is used to calm a bull, the bull remains calm forever, whereas it can become enraged again after the casting of an Instant spell. Permanent spells can be dispelled. Permanency is usually possible with the longer of a spell's two listed Durations.

**SPECIAL** (Spec.): Some spells have unique Durations detailed in their descriptions.

**RITUAL**: Ritual spells (designated by the word "Ritual") require fifteen minutes and one raw *vis* point for each 5 Levels of the spell. See *Ritual Spells* in the Magic Chapter (p.174).

# REQUISITES

(labelled Req in spell descriptions): Requisites make it more difficult to cast spells as they demand greater knowledge of the caster. Some apply whenever a spell is learned or cast, and these are listed at the top of the spell description. Other Requisites, called Casting Requisites, only affect the casting of the spell and are listed within the body of the spell description.

# AIMED

: Spells that affect targets indirectly (i.e., spells that use a medium, like fire, to strike the target) require Targeting rolls. You have to place the spell in the right spot to affect the target. Such spells are labelled "Aimed," and may list a modifier to Targeting rolls when appropriate.

# SPELL FOCUS

: Most Formulaic spells (not Ritualistic) have some Spell Focus which aids in the casting of the spell. When such a Focus is used, a variable bonus is gained on the spell casting roll, which is listed under each spell. These Spell Foci are based upon both the Law of Sympathy and the lore of Mythic Europe. See *Spell Foci* in the Magic Chapter for more details.

# DESCRIPTION

: The effects of the spell. Since magic is variable and unpredictable, and can be used in a number of ways, the responsibility for determining the effects in unusual situations lies with the Storyguide. Descriptions cover about 95% of the circumstances in which spells are used. Under exceptional conditions (Storyguide's option), spells may have different effects.

Spells can range from flashy displays, like those you're used to in the movies, to subtle workings with results that can often be seen, but with a medium that's not always apparent. You and the Storyguide are free to choose the glamor of every spell cast. However, once a spell is described as having a flashy or subtle display, it always has that display — at least in the case of Formulaic and Ritual spells — unless the caster strives to alter the casting (see *Words and Gestures*, p.186).

The term "target" means the subject of the spell. The target can be a person, animal, monster, object, area, or yourself.

# NATURAL RESISTANCE

(often Stamina, Size, or Intelligence rolls) is described under spells that allow it.

Many of the spell descriptions include visual descriptions, hand gestures, Spell Foci and Wizard's Sigils. It should be noted that these are all examples. Don't feel bound by the examples in this book. Simply use them as guidelines, and then customize all your spells in ways appropriate to your own Magus. When you give special details to your own customized versions of these spells, you are rewarded with more interesting game play.

There are also hand gestures that are common to each Technique and Form, and usually used in all spells of the appropriate types. Typically, they are worked into a spell, along with any other gestures which may be mentioned in a specific description. These gestures are depicted in a full-page illustration (see p.171).

**SPELL GUIDES:** Among the spell listings are numerous simple spell descriptions, which are not fleshed out. They are usually guides for spells that you might need at any time during the game, and thus are named Guides. These spells are considered to have a Range of Near, and Duration of Sunrise-Sunset, or Instant. Occasionally, a spell name is listed right after the presentation of a Guide. This spell gives an example of one of the Guide's aspects. Guides are meant to help you invent your own Formulaic spells, and are also to be used as guidelines for Spontaneous spells.

# NOTES ON TECHNIQUES

**CREO:** Things created are either independent or a natural part of a larger being or object. For instance, a Creo spell can grow back a severed hand or can create a bird, but it can not grow wings on a person (that would be a Muto spell). Independent objects usually appear in your hand or directly in front of you. You cannot create things inside of people to kill them, nor can you perform other tricky maneuvers (unless a spell specifies you can, and in the aforementioned case has a Perdo Requisite). Nothing created by magic is ever permanent, unless vis is used to extend the duration of the spell.

**INTÉLLEGO:** Lets you perceive things or see through them. An Intéllego Terram spell, for instance, can let you see through walls. Intéllego cannot affect the subject of its spells (the person you're watching), but those who are sensitive to such things (i.e., those with Magic Resistance) might realize they are being spied on magically. Intéllego spells are always of limited Duration, even when extended with vis.

**MUTO:** There are two types of Muto spells, those that change the shape of an object, and those that change the substance of an object. Although all Muto spells are of limited Duration when vis is not used, the shape of an object may be changed, if the substance is altered. Though the original substance eventually returns, the shape does not. For example, a Muto Terram spell can be cast to change a stone wall into dirt, which falls to the ground. The dirt eventually becomes stone again, but is now a pile of stone, instead of the wall it once was.

Muto spells that change the size or weight of a target cannot be used multiple times, to cause the target to continue to change. A spell that doubles a creature's size, for instance, doubles its normal size, not its current size. To triple a creature's size, a more powerful spell is needed.

**PERDO:** Most Perdo spells affect their targets directly, using no intervening medium. Therefore, you usually need no Targeting roll to strike something with a Perdo spell. Since Perdo spells are almost all instantaneous, there is no removing them once they are cast. Thus, a Magus should consider carefully before he blinds or deafens someone, for that person may only be restored with the application of vis and a Creo spell.

**REGO:** A Rego spell does not change the target; it merely moves or controls it. For instance, you can slam someone into a wall with a Rego spell. The easiest way to move things is to move the whole object evenly. To spin the object or to move just part of it is more difficult.

# THE WIZARD'S SIGIL

When you invent a spell, a little of your personal affinity for magic is likely to make itself known. If nothing else, some little quirk in the spell makes it different from the spells listed in this Chapter. Magic is unpredictable and idiosyncratic; to precisely duplicate another Magus's spell is nearly impossible. For instance, in Arridere of Jerbiton's version of *Blessing of Childlike Bliss*, the spell works as normal, but has the added detail that the victim babbles "Bama bama bama. . ." This detail doesn't usually change the effectiveness of the spell. Many Magi have recurrent quirks in their spells. Once known, these quirks can identify certain Magi as having cast certain spells. This recurrent mark or quirk in a Magus's spell is termed by the Order of Hermes "the Wizard's Sigil." Throughout this Chapter, various sample Sigils are listed for spells. Keep in mind that these are just guidelines; they're meant to give you ideas to better personalize your spells, and perhaps to aid you in choosing your own Sigil.

# SPELL LAWS

When casting a spell, a Magus uses his Gift to manipulate magic in the world around him. For most spells, there are certain vocalizations and gestures that help a Magus control and define this manipulation. There are also certain laws which aid a Magus in his spell casting. These laws are based on observations of how magic works; Magi understand them intuitively without actually vocalizing them. By incorporating the laws into spells, Magi may strengthen Formulaic magic, or even surpass its normal limits.

The Law of Contagion states, quite simply, once together, always together.

Items which were once part of a whole maintain a mystical connection, even when separated. Thus, while Formulaic Hermetic magic is usually restricted by the Range of sight, this limitation may be overcome by having some part of the subject you are trying to affect. For instance, to find a person, you can use a strand of his hair, or a drop of his blood, clippings from his fingernails or even something that is intimate to him, such as clothing or a prized possession. *The Inexorable Search* is a spell that makes use of these magical laws, and allows Magi to exceed the usual bounds of magic. At the same time, a spell used to instantly return you to your laboratory requires a tile from its floor, or a piece of its wall. *The Leap of Homecoming* is a spell that lets you exceed the normal Range of Hermetic magic in this way, thanks to a Magus's knowledge of the workings of spell law. Items used to improve magic through the Law of Contagion are known as Arcane Connections.

Another magical law that Magi often use to strengthen their spells is the Law of Sympathy. It declares: that which looks alike is alike. Thus, a representation of someone can aid you if you wish to control her, while starting a small bonfire might help in casting a spell to make a huge one. Quite often, this law of magic is seen in the Spell Focus of a spell, or in the gestures used with a spell.

Spontaneous magic is also affected by these two laws. To gain great Range with a Spontaneous spell, you must have some Arcane Connection to what you are trying to affect. Additionally, you may utilize the Law of Sympathy to strengthen Spontaneous spells, similar to the way Spell Foci strengthen Formulaic spells.

These two laws are present throughout the spells in this book, and should be considered when creating new spells.

# ANIMÁL SPELLS

Animál spells affect all manner of natural living things besides plants and humans, doing to animals what Mentem and Córporem spells do to people. Any animal-like body or animal-like mind may be affected by an Animál spell.

When a person is shape-changed, or a beast is intelligent (as opposed to Cunning), Animál spells that affect the mind are not effective. Instead, Mentem spells are needed. However, the body of such a being may be affected by Animál spells, including spells like *The Falcon's Hood* (PeAn 20) and *The Immaculate Beast* (MuAn 15).

If a human body has animal parts (such as bat wings), those parts can be affected by Animál spells, even though the rest of the body is only affected by Córporem spells.

## Creo Animál Spells

Animals created by Creo Animál spells are inherently magical and have a Magic Might of 5 + Size. These animals are not afraid of Magi as normal animals are, and are somewhat loyal, but do not automatically follow your orders. They die and rot away at sunrise/sunset, whichever comes first, unless *vis* makes the spell permanent.

Unless *vis* is also used to make food produced permanent, the food provides no nourishment, and feelings of being sated vanish when the spell wears off.

In general, it is easy to create dead animals (and related products, like leather), a bit harder to create living animals, and hardest of all to repair living animals. Thus, while a 50th Level spell can create a griffin, a spell to heal it completely is several magnitudes higher. The Guidelines for CrAn are very similar to those for CrCo, and that section may be referred to for further spell Level ideas.

### Full Health of Beast and Bird: Gen.

R: Touch, D: Sun./Inst., Ritual

Cancels the effects (short of death) of a malign Animál spell, such as *The Falcon's Hood* (PeAn 20) if the spell is less than or equal to the Level of this Ritual.

**Lv 5:** Create a bear's pelt.

**Lv 10:** Produce enough meat for five people (*Conjuration of Savory Beef*) or create the full corpse of an animal.

### Soothe Pains of the Beast: Lv 20

Spell Focus: Piece of Amber (+3)

R: Touch/Near, D: Sun./Inst.

This spell looks much like a ritualistic "laying on hands," seen in many churches. The Magus kneels and presses his hands to the wound while reciting a quiet incantation. A piece of amber, which is routinely used by common folk both to cure and protect, often rests around the Magus's neck, giving aid in the casting. The animal touched recovers a lost Body Level by making a Stamina stress roll of 3+ (apply penalty resulting from lost Body and Fatigue Levels).

Asaron of Flambeau believes his mission in life is to repopulate the world so there will be more to kill, and thus spends seasons healing animals and people throughout Europe. In his version of this spell, a black patch in the shape of a tongue of fire is left where the wound was. A symbolic flame is seen in almost all of Asaron's spells, making it his Wizard's Sigil.

### Weaver's Trap of Webs: Lv 20

Spell Focus: A Spider Web (+1)

R: Near/Sight, D: Sun./Inst.

In casting this spell, the Magus points at an area; if using a Spell Focus, the Magus commonly flings the web at the desired spot. From this initial location, a huge net of spider webs grows, filling an area 5 paces by 5 paces by 6 feet high. With supports, the webs can hang vertically, forming a wall; otherwise they act like a net. When the webs are through growing after a few seconds, they are as thick as string and as strong as iron. Everyone caught in the area of the webs is immobilized. Breaking free requires a Strength roll of 12+, or someone who is not trapped using an edged weapon to free a victim, which takes three Rounds. Contrary to widespread opinion, fire is ineffective against these webs. Webs created "instantly" may continue to trap victims in the future, as long as they don't decay and aren't completely hacked apart.

**Lv 25:** Create a cat (*Twin Eyes of the Stalking Shadows*), a dog, or another creature of similar size; the animal must be non-magicial, and no larger than Size -2.

**Lv 35:** Create a horse (*Conjuration of the Quick Retreat*) or other similar non-magical creature, no larger than Size +2.

**Lv 40:** Create an elephant (*Conjuring the Behemoth*) or other very large non-magical creature.

### Curse of the Ravenous Swarm: CrAn 40

R: Spec.; D: Moon; Req: Perdo, Herbam; Ritual

Calls a swarm of locusts or other destructive insects upon an area, ravaging plant life and fields. The pestilence does not extend past one square mile, and at the end of the Ritual's duration the insects all die, leaving many thousands to rot.

**Lv 45:** Utterly heal a beast no larger than a horse.

**Lv 50:** Create a griffin (*Conjuring the Lord of the Air*) or other magical fantastic beast.

# Intéllego Animál Spells

When you try to get information from an animal, remember that its memories are filtered through its particular senses. For example, dogs remember much about odors of various things, but often forget details of how they looked. Animals do not remember human words, but might remember tone of voice and such. You are not likely to get the exact information you are looking for.

To communicate with an animal you must bring yourself to the animal's mental level, which might have strange, though temporary, effects on you. For example, you might have a craving for raw meat or

speak very slowly for a moment after communicating with a bear.

Since Animál includes aspects of both Córporem and Mentem with regard to beasts, guidelines that apply to the latter two may apply to Animál. InCo and InMe may be referred to for additional ideas.

A common Wizard's Sigil for an Intéllego Animál spell is to have the information reported in some quirky way. For example, all spells cast by Chavin of Tytalus can be recognized because they promote or advocate war or violence. In his version of *Image of the Beast* (InAn 5), claws and teeth of the beast appear more dangerous, while his version of *Tongue of the Beasts* (InAn 20) has problems translating words such as peace and love.

**Lv 5:** Sense the state of consciousness of a beast (asleep, awake, insane) or learn the most general information about a beast's body.

## Image of the Beast: Lv 5

Spell Focus: A Sapphire (+5)

R: Body, D: Conc.

Gives you a hazy mental image of an animal if you hold some significant piece of its body, such as a bone or a severed paw (an Arcane Connection). If a Sapphire (commonly associated with wisdom or knowledge) is used with this spell, the image of the beast is seen within the stone.

**Lv 10:** Sense the dominant emotions felt by a beast (hunger, anger) or one specific fact about a beast's body.

## Shiver of the Lycanthrope: Lv 10

Spell Focus: A Silver Necklace (+3)

R: Reach/Near, D: Conc./Moon

You feel a sudden shiver if you are next to a person or beast that is actually a lycanthrope. If you use a silver necklace when casting the spell, it becomes extremely cold against your flesh.

**Lv 20:** Speak with any animal (*Tongue of the Beasts*). Flying creatures require an Auram Requisite (*Tongue of the Birds*), and aquatic creatures require an Aquam Requisite (*Tongue of the Fish*). Read the surface thoughts of a beast. Find a beast by use of an appropriate Arcane Connection.

## Vision of the Marauding Beast: Lv 20

Spell Focus: A Catseye (+3)

R: Body, D: Conc., Inst.

By touching wounds created by a beast, you get a mental image of the beast from the perspective of the creature attacked — handy for finding out what killed your Grog. If the victim didn't see the creature, you can't see it either. If the attacker wasn't a beast, the spell refuses to function (though you must make a spell roll anyway to check for a Botch, and lose any vis spent). If the body of the victim is human, there's a Córporem Requisite. A catseye helps you focus on the attacker, being attuned to the nature of all predators.

## Opening the Tome of the Animal's Mind: Lv 25

Spell Focus: The Tail of a Sphynx (+3)

R: Touch/Near, D: Conc.

You touch the head of the animal in question and read its memories of the past day. The further the animal is from human, the harder it is to read its memories accurately. If you simply scan the beast's memories, not looking for anything special, you get the memories the beast thinks are most important. If you are trying to get a specific fact, you need a Perception roll of 6+, or 12+ if the fact is obscure. Since normal animals are sensitive to magic, they strongly resist your touch, and try to shy away from you both when the spell is cast, and while the spell continues to function. This can be quite a problem with larger animals. The Sphynx is alleged to be a fantastic beast of great intelligence, and thus its tail is thought to bring wisdom to the bearer, aiding in the spell.

**Lv 30:** Thoroughly probe and understand the mind of a beast (*Peering Into the Beastly Mind*). See a beast and its surroundings by use of an appropriate Arcane Connection.

## Hunter's Sense: Lv 30

Spell Focus: The Eye of a Griffin (+3)

R: Near/Sight, D: Sun./Year

You sense the shapes and motivations of all animals above a certain size that come within 15 paces of you. You decide the size threshold when you cast the spell, such as all animals of Size -1 or greater. If you're asleep, you see the animal in a dream, but that might not awaken you. If cast with the eye of a griffin, the eye must be kept with you for the duration of the spell.

## Calling the Council of the Beasts: Lv 45

R: 20 miles, D: Moon, Ritual

This spell calls all of the animals of a particular type, specified at casting, to "awaken" from their bestial state, come together, and have a council to discuss the problems affecting their kind. In council the animals can call upon ancient powers, which take forms similar to theirs, to help them resolve their difficulties. Thus, a council of wolves may call up spirit wolves or very powerful magical wolves. The results of this conference may not be entirely in your favor. The animals remain awakened for only a month, and may seek to return home before the end of this period.

# Muto Animál Spells

Animals are not infinitely mutable, and using too many of these spells for too long on an animal can warp its natural constitution and even destroy it. Muto Córporem spells may be examined to get additional ideas and guidelines for Muto Animál Spells. Common Sigils seen in Muto Animál spells involve animals being changed in some strange way. Beasts transformed by Julian of Flambeau, with *The Beast Remade* (MuAn 25), might have bright red hair in their new form, while toads created by Silva of Merinita, with *Transformation of the Ravenous Beast to the Torpid Toad* (MeAn 20), might have a comical coloration.

**Lv 5:** Gradually turn meat into maggots, flies, beetles, and other vermin. Since this is what happens to meat anyway, the duration is Instant.

**Lv 10:** Change an animal's limb.

## Growth of the Creeping Things: Lv 10

Spell Focus: A Basil Sprig (+3)

R: Touch/Near, D: Sun./Perm.

Causes an insect, mouse, toad, or other small (Size -5) creature to grow to four times its normal size. If it was poisonous before, it is even more poisonous now. Semi-poisonous creatures, like most spiders, do +8 points of poison damage in larger form.

**Lv 15:** Make a major change in a beast.

### The Immaculate Beast: Lv 15

Spell Focus: A Topaz (+3)

R: Touch/Near, D: Sun./Perm.

Transforms an animal into a flawless specimen of its type, enhancing its outstanding features and giving it +3 on rolls related to its strongest feature. It improves a hawk's vision, a racehorse's speed, or a draft horse's strength, for example. The topaz which may be used with this spell is associated with the lion, and thus the beast in question is given the best of the animal kingdom's qualities.

**Lv 20:** Utterly change a beast.

### Beast of Outlandish Size: Lv 20

Spell Focus: A Giant's Heart (+5)

R: Touch/Near, D: Sun./Perm.

Changes the Size of a land animal by +1 or down to -2. If the beast grows this change modifies Damage by +2, Soak by +1, Defense by -1, and adds one Body Level. If the beast shrinks, reverse the signs of these modifiers and apply them for each point of Size decrease. If enlarged, the new beast is of huge size, and looks much more impressive than its former self. Townspeople may run in fear of it, and there is little doubt among them that it is a creature of magic. If shrunk, the beast appears to be little more than a runt, unfit to live.

### Steed of Vengeance: Lv 20

Spell Focus: The Hoof of a Pooka (+5)

R: Touch, D: Sun./Perm.

Turns a horse into a ferocious magical mount. Its coat becomes a deep black, and its eyes a fiery red. The horse's teeth transform into fangs, and its hooves become razor-sharp. Occasionally breathing steam from its mouth, the horse seems a creature from Hell itself. All Attack and Damage rolls get a +5 bonus. The horse tolerates a Magus rider. When the spell wears off, the horse must make a Stamina stress roll of 10+ or die from shock. Pookas are shape-shifting hobgoblins that enjoy playing tricks on mortals. They may be found in Faerie forests.

### Transformation of the Ravenous Beast to the Torpid Toad: Lv 20

Spell Focus: A Toadstone (+3)

R: Near/Sight, D: Sun./Perm.

Turns any animal into a toad, unless it makes a Size stress roll of 9+. Birds are so dissimilar to toads that they get a +2 bonus to their roll. The toadstone that may be used

with this spell is a rock that is either shaped like or colored like a toad. You can tell if you have a real toadstone by placing it in front of a toad. If the toad tries to leap forward and grab the rock, you have a genuine toadstone. A newly created toad may be used to terrorize peasants and serfs, for many believe toads exude a poisonous substance from their skin.

### The Beast Remade: Lv 25

Spell Focus: A Shapeshifter's Heart (+3)

R: Touch/Near, D: Sun./Perm., Req: Córporem

Gives one land beast a human form, though its mentality remains the same. Some feature of the animal is retained in the human form. A former dog might have an exceptionally hairy human body, and a former cat might let loose an occasional "meow." Once transformed, the beast is disorientated for a while, before it becomes used to its new body.

**Lv 35:** Change a bird or fish into a human.

# Perdo Animál Spells

Perdo Animál spells are very dangerous because their Durations are often Instant. This should be considered before harming a beast for the rest of its natural life. A common Sigil among Flambeau Magi, and others who cast Perdo spells, is to leave some type of mark with the damage they do. For example, a beast's eyes might bear a faint silhouette of a flame if *The Falcon's Hood* is cast upon them by Asaron of Flambeau.

When inventing a new spell, Perdo Córporem may be consulted for guidelines and ideas.

**Lv 5:** Do superficial damage to a beast, such as removing its fur, causing it to sneeze, or making it tired.

**Lv 10:** Cause an animal pain, but do no real damage. Destroy objects that were parts of animals.

### Agony of the Beast: Lv 10

Spell Focus: Branch of Holly (+3)

R: Sight, D: Conc.

After pointing at a beast and casting this spell, the beast begins lashing wildly about, upsetting any nearby objects, and howling in great pain. In order to do anything else, the beast must make a Stamina + Size stress roll of 9+ each Round. Holly,

believed by many to be a harmful plant, may be used in this spell to inflict pain. If a Magus is noticed with a twig of it, and other obvious wizardly apparatus, villagers may mistrust him, and may blame him for any local problems.

### Decay Fur and Hide: Lv 10

Spell Focus: A Bit of Animal Fur (+3)

R: Sight, D: Inst.

Destroys an object made of animal fur or hide, including wool and leather. Each casting decreases leather armor's Protection value by 3 points, and any armor dropped to 0 Protection is destroyed completely. When cast with a Spell Focus, a bit of animal fur is destroyed, which strengthens the spell through the Law of Sympathy.

Marius of Tremere invented this spell with an Auram Requisite, which causes the target to disappear in an impressive puff of smoke. When using a Spell Focus, he burns it at casting time.

### Alleviate the Serpent's Bite: Lv 10

Spell Focus: Branch of Ash (+3)

R: Touch/Near, D: Inst.

Makes one dose of animal toxin harmless. If cast on toxin already in someone's body, the spell requires a Córporem Requisite, and keeps the person from suffering further damage. The spell can render poison in a poisonous animal inert if you touch the animal in question. In order to affect herbal or mineral poisons, an appropriate Requisite is needed. The branch of ash, which may be used with this spell, is commonly known by folk to provide protection from both snakes and poison.

**Lv 15:** Do minor damage to a beast. Destroy entire corpses of beasts no larger than humans.

### Cripple the Howling Wolf: Lv 15

Spell Focus: Legbone of a Wolf or Dog (+3)

R: Sight, D: Inst.

When casting this spell, the Magus commonly makes an abrupt snapping motion with his hands, sundering the legbone if he has the Spell Focus present. If the beast fails to make a Stamina + Size stress roll of 12+, its leg is cleanly broken. At this point, the beast falls to the ground and dies from shock if it fails a Stamina + Size stress roll of 3+. Even if the roll succeeds, the animal loses a Body Level.

**Lv 20:** Destroy a major sense in an animal (sight, smell, touch, taste, or hearing).

### The Falcon's Hood: Lv 20

Spell Focus: A Falcon's Hood (+1)

R: Sight/Near, D: Sun./Inst.

Destroys an animal's vision. The title refers to the hood used to cover a falcon's eyes when it is not hunting. If such a hood is used with the spell, the casting is made more effective.

### Cleanse the Verminous Infestation: Lv 25

Spell Focus: A Sprig of Basil (+1)

R: Sight/Spec., D: Inst.

All spiders, snakes, rats, mice, lice, and other little creatures emerge from their hiding places, if they exist within Sight range of the Magus, and begin to emit a high-pitched shriek. As the creatures emerge, they begin to either kill themselves or attack each other until slain. Many cruel Magi cast this spell at festivals, so Grogs may place bets on which creatures survive longest. Any animal of Size -3 or greater is not affected by the spell. If raw vis is used to expand the Range, the spell broadens to include the entire residence that the Magus casts the spell in.

### The Hunter's Lethal Arrow: Lv 30

Spell Focus: Destroying Angel (+3)

R: Touch/Near, D: Inst.

Enchants an arrow to slay an animal. When cast with the Spell Focus destroying angel, which is a poisonous mushroom found only in faerie forests, the arrow is rubbed with the pulp from the mushroom. The arrow must be fired in the Round after the spell is cast; otherwise, the spell dissipates. If the arrow hits an animal, the beast must make a Stamina + Size stress roll of 12+. If the animal fails, it falls to the ground and convulses for several minutes before finally expiring. If the animal makes the roll, it still suffers normal arrow damage + 10. The target gets a normal Magic Resistance roll.

**Lv 40:** Kill an animal at near range.

# Rego Animál Spells

Córporem spells may be referred to for ideas and guidelines on controlling an animal's body, while Rego Mentem spells may be referred to for ideas and guidelines on controlling an animal's mind.

Typical Sigils for Rego Animál spells may cause beasts to act in certain ways. For example, if Chavin of Tytalus casts *Mastering the Unruly Beast,* the target might act surly and unfriendly while going about its tasks, even if Chavin doesn't specifically tell it to do that.

### Ward Against the Beasts of Legend: Gen.

Spell Focus: A Star Ruby (+3)

R: Spec., D: Ring

Creates an invisible ring seven paces across with you at the center; it lasts as long as you remain within it. When the ring is created, the Storyguide rolls a secret simple die and adds it to the Level of the spell. No magical beast whose Magic Points are equal to or less than the roll result can enter the ring. When making this, and most other wards, a common gesture is the Fig Sign. This sign involves balling the right hand into a fist, and then putting the thumb in between the pointer and middle fingers of the fist. The Italian Magus should be warned that this sign is a deadly insult in his country. The star ruby is a very powerful and rare gem that aids in controlling some types of entities.

### Disguise of the Putrid Aroma: Lv 5

Spell Focus: A Corked Bottle (+1)

R: Self/Near, D: Conc./Sun., Req: Auram

The target takes no interest in you as long as you do not threaten it. A carnivore treats you as if you are simply something it does not eat. It retains normal interest, however, in anyone else nearby. A corked bottle is representative of you and your contained odor. An animal isn't interested in what it can't smell.

### Soothe the Ferocious Bear: Lv 10

Spell Focus: A Piece of Red Mullet (+3)

R: Near, D: Conc./Inst.

Calms an animal until it is threatened or aroused again. You must speak soothingly or musically to it. Red mullet is a fish known for its capacity to calm those who consume it, though the animal need not eat of it.

### Panic of the Elephant's Mouse: Lv 15

Spell Focus: A Mouse (+2)

R: Eye/Near, D: Sun./Perm.

Makes an animal afraid of you by preying upon its instinctive fears, causing it to attempt escape by the quickest, most feasible means possible. Size roll of 9+ to resist. The title refers to the elephant's legendary fear of mice, and that fear applies, as a Focus, to all animals through the Law of Sympathy.

### Viper's Gaze: Lv 15

Spell Focus: Two Seized Bones (+3)

R: Eye/Near, D: Spec./Sun.

Holds an animal rigid as long as you can maintain eye contact and concentration (assuming no vis is used). The seized bones are Sympathetic to those in the animal's body.

### Circle of Beast Warding: Lv 20

Spell Focus: A *Ligurius* Stone (+5)

R: Spec., D: Ring

Creates a magical circle fifteen paces across that no natural animal will enter. Lasts until you leave the ring. A *Ligurius* Stone, urinated by a Lynx, helps form a territorial boundary to animals.

### The Gentle Beast: Lv 20

Spell Focus: A Divine Mushroom (+4)

R: Eye/Near, D: Sun./Perm.

Calms an animal, making it nearly fearless. It does not resist being ridden, shaved, or whatever else you can think of. Combat, extremely frightening circumstances, or any kind of wound ends the spell. The animal must be Size +3 or less. A mushroom picked from Dominion lands puts the serenity of the Divinities into the animal.

### Mastering the Unruly Beast: Lv 25

Spell Focus: A Lion's Tooth (+5)

R: Eye/Sight, D: Conc./Inst.

You can mentally control an animal as long as it is in sight, making it perform any act it is capable of. It is difficult to maintain control of particularly stubborn or fierce animals, such as mules or boars. The target creature must make a Ferocity roll of 9+ to resist. As the lion is the king of the beasts, his tooth adds to your ability to command.

### Commanding the Harnessed Beast: Lv 30

Spell Focus: A Lion's Tongue (+5)

R: Touch/Near, D: Sun./Moon

You implant a complicated command into an animal, which it carries out to the best of its abilities. The command must involve completing a certain task, such as finding a certain person. Vague orders, like "protect me," do not work. If the animal does not complete the task as the end of the spell approaches, it becomes desperately ferocious, especially at night. A lion's tongue gives you royal command over animals.

**Lv 50:** Enslave a beast's mind for Sun./Moon.

# AQUAM SPELLS

Aquam spells affect water and all other liquids. They cannot affect liquids in a body, such as blood; that requires a Córporem spell.

## Creo Aquam Spells

Water created without raw *vis* quenches the thirst but provides no lasting benefits to the drinker. Common Sigils for Creo Aquam spells include water with a specific scent, color or flavor. Creating flammable liquids, such as oil, involves an Ignem Requisite.

**Lv 5:** Create enough water to fill a bucket.

**Lv 10:** Create enough water to utterly saturate a person.

### Creeping Oil: Lv 10

Spell Focus: A Pinch of Lantern Oil (+3)

R: Sight, D: Sun./Perm., Req: Ignem

Saturates a porous material with oil. When casting this spell, the Magus often makes a flicking motion with his index finger and thumb, as if he is propelling something at the victim. A dot of oil appears on the target after the spell is finished, and slowly spreads over the target, saturating enough cloth to cover a person. If used on a person's clothes and ignited, the oil does 1d10+12 damage the first Round, +6 the second, and +0 the third.

**Lv 15:** Create enough water to cover about ten square paces.

### Footsteps of Slippery Oil: Lv 15

Spell Focus: Snake Fat (+1)

R: Self/Touch, D: Spec., Req: Ignem

Nonflammable grease spreads out from each of the next twenty footsteps you make, leaving a slick area ten paces wide. The effects of the grease on movement depend on the surface covered. Quickness- Encumbrance stress rolls are required to remain upright whenever a character on the oil does something more challenging than walking. A roll of 6+ is needed for the average maneuver, with rolls of up to 15+ needed to (for example) make a right turn at full speed on a smooth, greased surface. Using fat from a snake makes casting slightly easier.

The spell was invented by a rather good-natured Magus, and the gestures associated with the most common variations of the spell are as comical as the effects themselves. You can stand first on one leg, and then the other, vigorously rubbing the bottom of each upturned foot, as if spreading on a salve.

**Lv 20:** Create enough water to soak all in Near Range.

### Mighty Torrent of Water: Lv 20

Spell Focus: An Aquamarine Stone (+3)

R: Spec., D: Spec., Aimed (-3 to +1)

A three foot diameter cone of water sprays from your outstretched arms towards a target for up to five Rounds. During theses Rounds you must maintain concentration. Anyone hit by this gusher of water takes 1d10+14 damage and must make a Strength + Size roll of 10+ or be sent flying back. Targeting is at -3 for the first Round, increasing by +1 for every Round it is aimed at the same target thereafter. The aquamarine stone aids the spell due to its strong ties to the element of water.

Marbaid of Flambeau's Wizard's Sigil arises given his obsession with blood. In his version of the spell, which has a Córporem Requisite, the target is hit by a gush of blood, and the stains do not go away until Sunrise/Sunset.

### Deluge of Rushing and Dashing: Lv 25

Spell Focus: A Drop of Water From a Water Elemental (+4)

R: Spec., D: Conc.

Causes a stream to flood, starting at the stream's nearest point to you and continuing one mile downstream. If the Spell Focus is present, it is flicked into the stream, and the flood begins at that precise point. As long as you concentrate, the stream remains at flood levels. Anyone caught near the stream when it floods is struck by the rush of water (+18 damage), caught up in the flood, and dragged along. Every Round, a victim makes a stress roll of Strength + Dexterity + Swim - Encumbrance. A roll of 9+ means the character escapes the flood. Otherwise the character drops one Short-Term Fatigue Level and takes +10 damage. Any who fall Unconscious drown. This roll is repeated until the character either escapes the flood or dies. The results of this spell are generally quite impressive. As the river overflows its original bed, it becomes a raging torrent, sucking in everything near it. Damage from the spell can last for many years.

### Breaking the Perpetual Drought: Lv 30

R: 1 mile, D: Inst., Ritual

Breaks a drought, restoring normal rainfall to the region. The region may be expanded by half a mile for each extra pawn of *vis* used in the spell.

### Lungs of Water and Death: Lv 35

Spell Focus: Black Onyx (+1)

R: Near/Sight, D: Inst., Req: Perdo

Fills a target's lungs with water. The target falls to the ground and can do nothing but cough up water; Stamina roll of 8+ to avert drowning within three minutes. Casting Requisite is Animál for beasts and Córporem for people. Black onyx, which may be used with this spell, is known to bring both malediction and death.

## Intéllego Aquam Spells

Most Sigils that are seen in Intéllego Aquam spells report the information in some slightly quirky way, such as a version of *Voice of the Lake*, invented by Chavin of Tytalus, which always makes the lake sound strong, masculine and arrogant.

**Lv 5:** Learn one property about a liquid.

### Touch of the Pearls: Lv 5

Spell Focus: A Pearl (+5)

R: Touch/Reach, D: Conc./Moon.

Tells you whether a liquid you hold or touch is poisonous, just as a pearl sometimes does. Not surprisingly, having a pearl present makes it very hard to fail when casting this spell.

In Verdan of Ex Miscellanea's version of the spell, poisonous liquids turn a faint green. According to his Sigil, all his spells involve the color green. Many of his spell variants have Imágonem or Muto Requisites.

**Lv 10:** Have a natural intuition in the water.

## Subtle Taste of Poison and Purity: Lv 10

Spell Focus: A Sapphire (+5)
R: Touch, D: Inst.

Determines all the mundane properties of a liquid that you touch with your tongue. The sapphire, which may be used with this spell, provides wisdom.

**Lv 15:** Make your senses unaffected by water (e.g., see through murky water).

## Call of the Rushing Waters: Lv 15

Spell Focus: A Divining Rod Made of Hazel (+1)

R: Spec., D: Moon/Year.

Guides you to any natural body of water for which you have an Arcane Connection (e.g., a vial of water from it), if the water is within 100 miles of you. Once you cast the spell, you can hear the water whenever you concentrate. Following the sound eventually brings you to the water, but you must make Perception simple rolls of 6+ to follow the sound accurately (roll once per day for long journeys). Bodies of water which do not move or make little noise require rolls of 9+ to be traced. If you construct a Y-shaped rod out of hazel wood, you get a bonus not only to the casting roll, but to Perception rolls as well.

## Voice of the Lake: Lv 25

Magic Focus: A Rock From The Lake Bottom (+3)

R: Near, D: Conc

You can hold a conversation with a body of water. A body of water usually knows about things directly in contact with it, such as boats and fish. By the Law of Contagion, any item from the body connects you to the body.

## Enchantment of the Scrying Pool: Lv 30

R: Reach (500 miles), D: Year., Req: Imágonem, Ritual

Turns a body of water into a scrying pool. Innately magical people (including most Companions with mystical powers) who look into the pool can see any spot that they know of that is within sight of some body of water. The view is from the perspective of that water. Maximum range is 500 miles. This Ritual is not entirely of Hermetic magic. It is an old Mercurian Ritual that has become known throughout the Order.

# Muto Aquam Spells

Some Muto Aquam spells involve heat and cold, but are not Ignem spells.

The distinction is that an Ignem spell uses heat as an intermediary to effect a change while a Muto Aquam spell effects the change directly. For example, you can turn ice into steam by applying heat with an Ignem spell, but you can probably make the change faster by using a Muto Aquam spell, making the change directly.

You cannot transform liquids within someone's body unless the spell is designed that way (and has a Córporem Requisite).

The Guidelines given are for turning water into another liquid, or into ice, or, in general, into some other structure that is still based on the Aquam Form. To change something beyond Aquam usually takes about 5 more Levels.

Common Muto Aquam Sigils guide transformations in specific ways. For example, in Silva of Merinita's version of the Level 5 Guideline, the wine is always quite potent, though has an innocuous flavor.

**Lv 5:** Change a bottle of water into wine.

**Lv 10:** Change a man-sized amount of water into another liquid.

## Lungs of the Fish: Lv 10

Spell Focus: Powdered Scales of a Fish (+3)
R: Body/Touch, D: Sun./Year, Req: Auram

Turns water into air as it enters your lungs, allowing you to breathe water as you do air. If using the Spell Focus, place a small bit of it on your tongue, and swallow it at the completion of the spell.

## Breath of Winter: Lv 15

Spell Focus: Beryl (+5)
R: Near/Sight, D: Inst.

Turns a circle of water up to five paces across into snow. Beryl is a gem associated with water.

**Lv 20:** Change any amount of water in a Range of Near into another liquid.

**Lv 20:** Allow another you touch to breathe water like air (*Grant Lungs of the Fish*).

## Bridge of Frost: Lv 20

Spell Focus: Beryl (+3)
R: Sight, D: Spec.

Causes a thick layer of frost (firm enough to walk on) to form on a surface of water. The frost can take any shape up to 15 paces in any direction. The bridge collapses after 6 to 15 creatures have crossed over it (roll a simple die + 5). Only the Storyguide knows the number of creatures that can cross. The bridge begins to melt normally after an hour.

In Cralian of Tremere's version of this spell, the frost is so crystal clear that it can hardly be seen. All of his spells are very subtle.

## Ice of Drowning: Lv 25

Spell Focus: A Piece of Ice from a Frozen Ocean (+3)

R: Sight, D: Conc./Sun., Req.: Rego

Turns water in a circle 10 paces across into jagged chunks of ice that pound against anything on the water's surface. The ice can punch holes in small boats but does not damage ships. Any swimmers in the area take 1d10+15 damage, and suffer -5 and two extra Botch checks on Swim rolls. If a piece of ice from waters north of England is available, it is thrown into the water where the spell is cast.

**Lv 30:** Change an amount of water in Range of Sight into another liquid.

## Cloak of Winter: Lv 30

Spell Focus: Drop of Water from an Elemental Made of Ice (+3)

R: Sight/Spec., D: Spec.

Over the course of an hour it snows and sleets on a body of water up to the size of a small lake (no more than two miles in diameter), causing it to freeze. Every pawn of vis used to expand the Range of the spell adds one half mile to the diameter of the body of water that may be covered. If the water is running, it either freezes up (if of small volume) or fills with ice floes (if of large volume). The Spell Focus is flicked into the body of water that is to be frozen, to help bring down snow and sleet.

## Perdo Aquam Spells

As magnitudes in these spells rise, the destruction caused becomes more subtle, or more pervasive. Sigils commonly seen in Perdo Aquam spells usually involve destruction in some specific way. For example, Silva of Merinita's version of *Incantation of Putrid Wine* might not change the smell at all, making the wine seem fine until tasted.

**Lv 5:** Utterly dry an object no larger than man-sized (*Breeze of the Sandy Wastes*).

**Lv 10:** Remove some water from a man-sized inanimate object.

### Parching Wind: Lv 10

Spell Focus: A Pinch of Dust (+1)

R: Reach/Near, D: Inst.

Removes all water from any inanimate object of Size -1 or less, including plants (with a Herbam Requisite), possibly making the object brittle and fragile. A pinch of dust can be tossed at the target, driving water from it.

**Lv 15:** Destroy an amount of water within Range of Near.

### Incantation of Putrid Wine: Lv 15

Spell Focus: Venom From a Spider (+1)

R: Near/Sight, D: Inst.

Makes all liquids in your presence vile, malodorous, and mildly poisonous. The room where this spell is cast may not lose the stench for weeks or months.

### Break the Oncoming Wave: Lv 20

Spell Focus: An Aquamarine Gem (+3)

R: Near, D: Conc./Moon

Breaks all waves and torrents of water (including magical ones) as they come within 10 paces of you. The water either crashes to the ground or flows around you in a truly impressive display. The gem, which may be used, has strong associations with water.

In Ferramentum of Verditius's version of this spell, the water breaks at precisely ten paces, leaving a very clean line showing where the waves stopped. All of his spells may be recognized by their orderliness.

### Curse of the Desert: Lv 25

Spell Focus: A Breeze from a Desert (+3)

R: Near/Sight, D: Inst.

Removes most of the fluid from the target's body, doing 1d10+16 damage, which can only be Soaked with Stamina + Size. The target must drink within an hour of being struck with this spell or die. Casting Requisites are Animál for beasts, and Córporem for humans. If you have managed to trap a breeze from a desert, you can open the container in which it is carried, and have it blow towards the victim, draining him of fluid.

**Lv 30:** Destroy an amount of water within Range of Sight.

### Vile Water of Sterility: Lv 30

Spell Focus: Venom From a Greater Worm (+5)

R: Sight, D: Inst.

Ruins a body of water up to the size of a small lake, making it unfit for natural life or consumption. The water becomes dark and murky, and noxious fumes emanate from it. Vegetation on the banks either dies or becomes corrupt. Nearby trees become gnarled and blackened, and any land animals flee the area. If the venom from a greater worm (i.e., dragon) is available, a drop is let into the lake. The corruption begins there, and is always strongest at that spot.

### Calling the Odious Drought: Lv 40

R: 1 mile, D: Year/Perm., Ritual

Causes a drought over the land within Range. Only one-tenth the normal rain falls, streams dry up, rivers dwindle, and famine stalks the land. The area of effect may be increased by half a mile for each extra pawn of *vis* used.

## Rego Aquam Spells

### Ward Against Faeries of the Waters: Gen.

Spell Focus: A Star Ruby (+3)

R: Spec., D: Ring

Creates an invisible ring seven paces across with you at the center; it lasts as long as you remain within the ring. When the ring is created, the Storyguide rolls a secret simple die and adds it to the Level of the spell. No water faerie whose Faerie Points are equal to or less than the rolled result can enter the ring. A gesture often used with the spell is the Fig Sign. The Magus balls his right hand into a fist, and places his thumb in between his pointer and middle fingers. The Star Ruby is a rare gem that aids in controlling many types of entities. Seen from certain angles at night, the ring appears as a light blue dome.

**Lv 5:** Control an amount of water that could fit in a small box.

### Cloak of the Duck's Feathers: Lv 5

Spell Focus: A Duck's Feather (+3)

R: Touch/Near, D: Sun.(Spec.)

Makes water run off one object or creature, protecting the target and the target's apparel from dampness. It lasts until the target is submerged in water or until the next sunrise/sunset.

**Lv 10:** Control an amount of water no larger than a man.

### Gift of the Floating Wood: Lv 10

Spell Focus: A Piece of Wood (+3)

R: Near/Sight, D: Sun.(Spec.)

Lets any object or creature of Size +3 or smaller float in water. Lasts until the object leaves the water or the next sunrise/sunset.

### Push of the Gentle Wave: Lv 10

Spell Focus: A Sliver From an Oar (+3)

R: Near/Sight, D: Conc.

A low wave is formed to propel a small boat slowly through the water. When casting this spell, a pushing gesture is commonly made by the Magus. If a sliver from an oar is available, it is thrown into the water behind the boat, and the wave originates from that spot.

In Silva of Merinita's version of this spell, the wave occasionally drifts or bobs about, as if it is happy and playful.

**Lv 20:** Control an amount of water within Range of Near.

### Chaos of the Angry Waves: Lv 20

Spell Focus: An Emerald (+3)

R: Sight, D: Conc.

Causes water to churn wildly, overturning small water craft in a circular area 20 paces across. The emerald has associations with water.

### Waves of Drowning and Smashing: Lv 20

Spell Focus: A Vial of Water (+3)

R: Sight, D: Inst.

Raises a five foot high, 30 pace wide wave that can submerge swimmers, overturn rowboats, and damage sailing ships. It starts as a small, curved wave and grows for the first ten paces, at which point it reaches maximum size. If it travels 100 paces without striking an object large enough to break it up, it dissipates. The vial of water must have been taken from a large body of water during a storm.

### Pull of the Watery Grave: Lv 25

Spell Focus: A Piece of a Boat Long Buried Below the Waves (+3)

R: Sight, D: Conc.

Creates a strong undertow which pulls any object smaller than a rowboat 25 fathoms (150 feet) into the depths. Those caught in the undercurrent must make stress rolls of 9+ on a Strength + Dexterity + Swim - Encumbrance to avoid being dragged down. Rolls are made per Round that the spell is maintained.

Lv 30: Control an amount of water within Range of Sight.

### Parting the Waves: Lv 30

Spell Focus: A Vial of Water from the Sea (+1)

R: Spec./Spec., D: Conc.

Parts a body of water up to 50 paces across, revealing a dry path five paces wide along the bottom. For every pawn of *vis* used to increase the range of the spell, the water body parted may be another 25 paces across.

### Tower of Whirling Water: Lv 30

Spell Focus: Beryl (+1)

R: Near/Sight, D: Conc.

From a large body of water you form a waterspout which moves under your mental direction. It causes 1d10+14 damage to anyone it hits (no Attack roll necessary). In addition, those struck must make a Quickness - Encumbrance roll of 8+ to avoid being sucked up by the waterspout. Those that fail are helplessly pulled into the spout and begin to drown immediately. When the waterspout fails, they fall up to 20 feet to the water's surface. If you direct the waterspout to move across land, you must make an Intelligence + Concentration roll of 10+ each Round to maintain it.

### Neptune's Wrath: Lv 50

R: Sight, D: Inst., Ritual

A gigantic wave is created in a very large body of water. The wave, which is only 20 feet high and up to a mile wide, is capable of capsizing ships at sea, smashing and drowning people near shore, and utterly destroying coastline communities. The tidal wave needs five miles of water surface to build itself up to proper proportions.

# AURAM SPELLS

Auram spells are powerful because the element of air is ubiquitous. Their weakness is that air is not usually violent, like fire, nor strong, like earth. Auram, however, incorporates most weather phenomena such as storms, lightning, rain, mist, and falling snow.

Auram spells usually affect air as phenomena (winds, odors) rather than as gases (a modern concept).

By their nature, Auram spells cover large areas with poorly defined borders. The areas given in the spell descriptions are not exact, but describe the general boundaries of effects. For example, consider the task of making a storm. Storms are naturally large things, and making a small one that affects a room-size area is no easier than making a more natural, large storm.

## Creo Auram Spells

When creating only one aspect of air (such as forming its mistiness, its smell, or its winds) spell Level is usually 5 lower than the Guidelines given below. These Guidelines are appropriate for creating air as a whole, or for creating multiple aspects, as in *Wreaths of Foul Smoke* (CrAu 15), in which both smoke and smell are created. Common Sigils seen in Creo Auram spells give the air specific properties, such as special scents or colors.

Lv 5: Create enough air to fill a small box.

### Air's Ghostly Form: Lv 5

Spell Focus: An Opal (+5)

R: Spec./Near, D: Inst.

A thick fog forms around you. A breeze can push the fog around. The fog dissipates at its natural rate, which can be as rapid as a minute. The opal has associations with Mercury and the air.

Lv 10: Create air in a small, no larger than man-sized area.

### Stench of the Twenty Corpses: Lv 10

Spell Focus: A Piece of a Rotting Corpse (+3)

R: Near/Sight, D: Inst.

Makes the surrounding air stink horribly of rotting corpses until the odor dissipates naturally. All those within 10 paces of

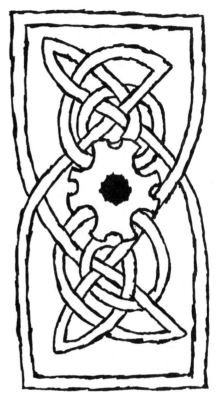

the target point must make Stamina stress rolls of 6+ or act with a -3 penalty on all rolls. Anyone who Botches the roll vomits and is temporarily incapacitated.

Lv 15: Create air in an area no larger than a medium-sized room.

### Chamber of Spring Breezes: Lv 15

Spell Focus: An Agate (+3)

R: Near/Sight, D: Sun./100 years

Creates a breeze of fresh air that continually moves throughout a room, keeping the air breathable even if the room is airtight.

Rose of Jerbiton has a version of this spell that always causes the air to smell of roses.

### Wreaths of Foul Smoke: Lv 15

Spell Focus: A Dollop of Mud from a Marsh (+1)

R: Near/Sight, D: Inst.

Thick, yellow, sulphuric smoke rises up from the spot you designate, filling a circular area nine paces across. It blocks sight, and for each Round anyone breathes the smoke, a Stamina roll of 9+ must be made or a Short-Term Fatigue Level is lost. Once a character is Unconscious, further Levels lost are Body Levels.

The smoke dissipates naturally. The area where the spell is cast is also damaged. Small plants wilt and die, and tree growth is stunted. There is a faint stench in the air for days after the spell is cast.

**Lv 20:** Create enough air to fill the entire area Near the Magus.

## Clouds of Summer Snow: Lv 25

Spell Focus: Ice Shavings (+3)

R: Sight, D: Inst.

Creates clouds that drop snow over four square miles. Once created, the clouds behave as normal snow clouds and dissipate within an hour. The spell does not affect temperature.

## Clouds of Rain and Thunder: Lv 25

Spell Focus: The Essence of an Air Elemental (+3)

R: Sight, D: Inst.

Creates a severe rainstorm, including lightning and winds, covering four square miles. It takes half an hour for the clouds to form and start raining. The storm rages for ten minutes and calms down to nothing over the next twenty minutes.

## Charge of the Angry Winds: Lv 30

Spell Focus: An Agate (+1)

R: Spec., D: Conc. (5 Rounds)

A wall of wind roars away from you, starting up to 10 paces away and continuing up to 30 paces. The wind is five paces wide. All within the area must make a Dexterity + Size stress roll of 10+ or fall down. The rolls must be made at the start of the gale and each subsequent Round that the wind is maintained. You must concentrate on the gale and can maintain it for up to five Rounds. Missile fire into or out of the gale is futile, and marching against the gale requires a Strength + Size stress roll of 16+. Failure in this attempt demands another Dexterity + Size stress roll of 12+ to keep from falling.

### The Incantation of Lightning: Lv 35

Spell Focus: An Oak Wand (+3)

R: Near/Sight, D: Inst., Aimed -3

A lightning bolt shoots forth from your outstretched hand in the direction you are pointing, doing 1d10+45 damage to the target it hits. Those next to the bolt must make Size rolls of 6+ to remain standing. The oak wand need not be magical, but must be from a tree struck three times by lightning.

### Breath of the Open Sky: Lv 40

R: Sight, D: Conc., Ritual

You can call up a wind capable of devastating the countryside. You must stand under the open sky to cast this spell. Once you have completed the Ritual, a breeze picks up from behind you. As long as you face in the same direction, the wind grows in speed and breadth. After an hour has passed, the wind is a gale roaring over the visible countryside. If you turn away from your original facing for more than a few seconds, you have to make a Concentration roll of 12+ to maintain the spell. If you turn away for a minute or more, the spell ends.

### Wrath of Whirling Winds and Water: Lv 60

R: Sight, D: Inst., Ritual

Creates a hurricane 45 miles wide. The winds and rain cause immense damage along shorelines. The spell can only be cast at sea or at the coast. You must be able to see the position where you want to center the spell.

# Intéllego Auram Spells

**Lv 5:** Sense one property of air, such as if the air is poisonous.

**Lv 10:** Learn all mundane properties of the air. Have a natural intuition of air.

**Lv 15:** Your senses are unhindered by the air (e.g., can see into strong wind).

### True Sight of the Air: Lv 15

Spell Focus: A Four-Leaf Clover (+1)

R: Sight, D: Conc./Moon

Lets you see clearly through all manner of obscuration in the air, including smoke, fog, and dust, even if the obscuration is magical. The clover is said to help you see through deceptions and obstructions.

### Whispering Winds: Lv 15

Spell Focus: Three Leaves From an Oak Tree (+1)

R: Sight, D: Conc./Moon, Req: Imágonem

You can hear words spoken by anyone within your line of sight, provided no solid barrier (including glass) intervenes.

### Sailor's Foretaste of the Morrow: Lv 20

Spell Focus: The Liver of a Pig (+1)

R: Sight, D: Inst.

You know precisely what tomorrow's weather will be and can get a general impression about the weather for the week ahead. The liver is known to be very useful for divinations.

**Lv 25:** Speak with the air, although it is usually flighty and has a short attention span (*Speak with the Spirits of the Air*).

### Eyes of the Bat: Lv 25

Spell Focus: The Eyes of a Bat(+1)

R: Body/Touch, D: Spec., Req: Imágonem

You can move about confidently in complete darkness by sensing air and its boundaries (e.g., where solid objects are). The spell ends when you can see normally, or when, for any reason, you stop using blind navigation.

# Muto Auram Spells

Changing air into some other element is usually 5 Levels higher than the changes presented by the Guidelines. Minor transformations, such as doubling a phenomenon or changing rain clouds into storm clouds, are usually about 5 Levels lower than Guidelines that present major transformations.

**Lv 5:** Change enough air to fill a small box.

**Lv 10:** Change a man-sized amount of air.

### Blasting Wind, Blinding Mist: Lv 10

Spell Focus: Air Bottled During a Storm (+1)

R: Near/Sight, D: Inst.

Doubles the strength of one minor air phenomenon, including fog, smoke, and odor.

## Rain of Stones: Lv 15

Spell Focus: A Hailstone (+1)

R: Sight, D: Conc., Req: Terram, Aimed

Turns raindrops into stones just before they strike the target, causing 1d10+15 damage per Round of exposure to the "rain." The Spell Focus must be thrown into the air somewhere above the target if used.

**Lv 20:** Transform any air that is Near you.

## Clouds of Thunderous Might: Lv 20

Spell Focus: The Essence of an Air Elemental (+5)

R: Sight, D: Inst.

Turns rain clouds into a full-fledged storm.

## Talons of the Winds: Lv 20

Spell Focus: Claw of a Hawk (+1)

R: Near/Sight, D: Inst.

Transforms a wind into an abrasive medium that tears and claws at everything in its path. It is up to 20 paces wide and blows through 40 paces before ending. Soft materials like leaves and cloth are shredded, and people take 1d10+5 damage from innumerable bloody cuts and abrasions. Not surprisingly, this spell has a certain demoralizing effect on its victims.

In Ossium of Bjornaer's version of this spell, which has an Imágonem Requisite, a strange keening can be heard in the air as it cuts through targets. According to Ossium's Wizard's Sigil, many of his spells are eerie or frightening, even if the spell is not usually so.

**Lv 30:** Change the air within Sight.

## Fog of Confusion: Lv 30

R: Sight, D: Year/Perm., Req: Imágonem, Ritual

Turns all the fog within five miles of the center of the spell into a silvery mist too thick to see through. Random screams, thumps, hisses and other noises harass and confuse anyone within the fog, perhaps even leading them into danger. People have extreme difficulty navigating through the fog, especially through unknown territory. No more than seven people, who must be present at the Ritual, can see normally through the fog.

## Heat of Hell's Impending Doom: Lv 35

R: Spec., D: Conc./Moon, Req: Ignem, Ritual

A huge wave of heat comes rolling over the area in a mile's radius around you, with the exception of the area within 10 feet of you. Those caught in this heat must make a Fatigue roll of 8+ every Round or lose a Short-Term Fatigue Level. Body Levels are lost once Fatigue Levels are gone.

## Infernal Smoke of Death: Lv 40

Spell Focus: The Breath from a Poisonous Sheep (+3)

R: Spec., D: Conc., Req: Perdo

Turns smoke into a vile poison that eats through soft material (like cloth) and contaminates all who breathe it. Anyone in the cloud of smoke takes 1d10+35 poison damage (once only), and various material objects are damaged or destroyed. While you concentrate any new smoke formed becomes poisonous, but even after you stop concentrating the poisonous smoke remains deadly. It dissipates only after several hours. If not controlled, it rolls along the ground poisoning everything in its path.

## Rain of Oil: Lv 50

R: Sight, D: Spec., Req: Ignem, Aquam, Ritual

Turns the rain of a storm into droplets of oil. The rain of oil continues as long as the storm does, drenching the landscape with flammable liquid. A Spontaneous Creo Ignem spell of Level 25+ can ignite the storm so that the oil burns as it falls.

# Perdo Auram Spells

Destroying just one small phenomenon of air is a bit easier than destroying air outright. Treat the destruction of such small phenomena as 5 Levels lower than the Guidelines presented (which discuss removing large air phenomenon, and air in its entirety).

**Lv 5:** Destroy a man-sized amount of air. Stop breezes.

## Thief of the Stolen Breath: Lv 10

Spell Focus: A Branch of Holly (+3)

R: Near/Sight, D: Inst.

Takes a creature's breath out of its lungs, causing panic and the instant loss of a Short-Term Fatigue Level, plus a second Level unless a Stamina roll of 7+ is made.

Casting Requisite is Animál for beasts and Córporem for people.

**Lv 15:** Destroys the air in a room-sized area. Destroys smoke, haze and odor (*Air Clean and Pure*) within that Range.

## Room of Stale Air: Lv 15

Spell Focus: Agate (+3)

R: Near/Sight, D: Inst.

Makes the air in a room stuffy and uncomfortable. Any creatures that breathe air suffer a -3 penalty on all rolls. In addition, for each Round of exertion, a character must make a Fatigue roll of 6+ or lose a Short-Term Fatigue Level. This may cause panic in some creatures or people. When using agate, a stone associated with both Mercury and the air, you must crush the rock. Through the Law of Sympathy, this helps destroy air within the area.

## Quiet the Raging Winds: Lv 25

Spell Focus: A Branch of Ash (+1)

R: Near/Sight, D: Inst.

Stops the wind near you, leaving only calm air. Calms any force of wind, magical or otherwise. The branch of ash is said to provide protection from storms.

**Lv 30:** Destroys air within Sight.

## The Cloudless Sky Returned: Lv 30

Spell Focus: A Branch of Ash (+1)

R: Sight, D: Inst.

Clears the sky within your vision of any clouds or other meteorological activity.

In Ferramentum's version of this spell, the clouds clear from the sky in an orderly manner, as if they are soldiers marching on parade.

# Rego Auram Spells

Trying to do really fancy things with air (e.g., *Circling Winds of Protection*) usually causes spell Level to increase. Common Sigils seen in Auram spells usually involve the element acting in some quirky way.

## Ward Against Faeries of the Air: Gen.

Spell Focus: A Star Ruby (+3)

R: Spec., D: Ring

As *Ward Against Faeries of the Water* (ReAq Gen), but for faeries of the air. From some angles at night, the ring may be seen as a violet-hued dome.

**Lv 5:** Control a small amount of air (enough to fill a small box).

### Wind at the Back: Lv 5

Spell Focus: A Hand Fan (+1)

R: Reach/Near, D: Spec.

A breeze follows you until you stop traveling. It causes phenomena you pass through (fog, haze) to follow you.

**Lv 10:** Control a man-sized amount of air.

### Jupiter's Resounding Blow: Lv 10

Spell Focus: A Violet Amethyst (+5)

R: Near/Sight, D: Inst., Aimed

Creates a thunderclap; anyone directly underneath must make a Stamina stress roll of 9+ or be deafened. If deafened, the target gets another Stamina simple roll each minute and recovers with a roll of 8+. If the first roll Botches, the victim is permanently deafened. Violet amethyst is the stone of Jupiter.

### Broom of the Winds: Lv 15

Spell Focus: Splinter from a Broom (+1)

R: Near/Sight, D: Inst.

Whips up violent, swirling winds around the target, who must make a Size stress roll of 10+ to remain standing. The target can also resist by making a Strength stress roll of 9+ if holding onto a strong support. If both rolls fail, the target is knocked in a random direction; roll a simple die: 1— down; 2 or 3 — left; 4 or 5 — forward; 6 or 7— right; 8 or 9 — backward; 0 — up twelve feet and dropped. Damage depends on what obstructions are struck.

**Lv 20:** Control a Near amount of air.

### Circling Winds of Protection: Lv 20

Spell Focus: Bottled Breath of a Zephyr (+5)

R: Reach, D: Spec.

Surrounds you with winds that circle you at great speed. Since the wind picks up dust, you may be obscured. Anyone standing near enough to attack you with a hand weapon must make a Size stress roll of 9+ at the beginning of each Round or be blown away. Melee Attack rolls against you are at -2, and missile or thrown weapon Attacks are at -10. The winds continue for 5 Rounds after you end concentration. The zephyr's breath is released to encourage winds to blow faster.

### Wings of the Soaring Wind: Lv 25

Spell Focus: A Feather from a Bird of Legendary Size (+3)

R: Self/Near, D: Conc.

Generates a massive gust of air around you which supports and pushes you along through the air at speeds up to 40 miles per hour. It is dangerous for extended travel, because you might easily lose your concentration.

**Lv 30:** Control air in Range of Sight.

### Gathering of the Stormy Might: Lv 30

Spell Focus: The Essence of an Air Elemental (+3)

R: Sight, D: Inst.

Calls the surrounding clouds into a storm within one hour. The size of the storm depends on the amount of cloud cover available. This spell cannot be used on an utterly clear sky.

### Pull of the Skybound Winds: Lv 40

Spell Focus: A Captured Gust of Wind from a Tornado (+3)

R: Sight, D: Conc.

Makes winds rise upward, pulling one object, creature or person 50 feet into the sky before letting it drop. Even a small building can be torn from its foundation. Such a building can be no larger than 20 feet to a side and cannot be built out of a material heavier than stout wood. Uprooted objects fall randomly, but perhaps a Finesse stress roll of 12+ will let you choose.

# CÓRPOREM SPELLS

Córporem spells deal with human or human-like bodies and anything that involves those bodies. Most faeries are humanoid enough to be affected by Córporem spells.

## Creo Córporem Spells

Many Creo Córporem spells are most useful as permanent (or Instant) spells, requiring raw vis. A spell that binds your wounds without using raw vis lets your wounds open again by the next sunrise/sunset. As long as a wound is temporarily healed by magic, it cannot begin to heal normally. No Hermetic spell can restore Fatigue Levels.

Creo Animál spells may be used as guidelines and examples for Creo Córporem spells.

### Free the Accursed Body: Gen.

R: Touch/Near, D: Inst., Ritual

Cancels the effects (short of death) of a malign Córporem spell, such as Twist of the Tongue (PeCo 20), if you can match the Level of the spell with the Level of this Ritual.

**Lv 5:** Prevent decay of a body.

### Charm Against Putrefaction: Lv 5

Spell Focus: A Piece of Preserved Flesh (+3)

R: Touch/Near, D: Moon/Perm.

Prevents decay of a human corpse. Necromancers use it to preserve their revived corpses.

**Lv 10:** Creates an entire human corpse.

### Bind Wound: Lv 10

Spell Focus: A Spider's Web (+3)

R: Touch/Near, D: Sun./Inst.

Typically, the Magus places his hands on the target and passes them over the wound, which magically seals itself and stops bleeding. If a spider's web is available, it is laid over the wound and disappears as the wound seals itself. Any subsequent recovery rolls required by the wound are made at +1.

**Lv 15:** Stops the progress of a disease.

### Gentle Touch of the Purified Body: Lv 15

Spell Focus: A Pouch of Healing Herbs (+3)

R: Touch, D: Sun./Inst.

Stops the progress of any disease of typical strength. It does not remove damage that has already occurred, nor does it cure such dread illnesses as leprosy.

### The Chirurgeon's Healing Touch: Lv 20

Spell Focus: Bloodstone (+3)

R: Touch/Near, D: Sun./Inst.

The person touched can recover a lost Body Level by making a Stamina stress roll of 3+, to which is added the highest Chirurgy skill of anyone who has successfully tended the wounds. Also, subtract the wound penalty from the roll. Does not heal damage from poison or disease.

### Restoration of the Defiled Body: Lv 25

Spell Focus: Garnet (+1)

R: Touch/Near, D: Sun./Inst.

Removes the crippling or malignant effects of any poison, disease, or premature aging. The effects of natural aging cannot be undone by this or any spell. Garnet is reputed to help against diseases and other afflictions.

### The Severed Limb Made Whole: Lv 30

Spell Focus: Carnelian (+1)

R: Touch/Near, D: Sun./Inst.

A limb which has been detached from the body can be reattached, but any decay that has occurred on the severed limb remains after the limb is reattached. After a day of decomposition, a limb is weak. After seven days, it is nearly useless and infects the character on whom it is replaced (Stamina stress roll of 6+ or lose a Body Level). If it's been severed for more than two weeks, the limb is completely useless.

### Incantation of the Body Made Whole: Lv 45

Spell Focus: Chips from a Unicorn's Hooves (+3)

R: Touch/Near, D: Sun./Inst.

Heals all damage to a human body at the rate of one Body Level per Round. You must maintain concentration for the Rounds during which the spell is cast. A cloak, blanket, or similar covering must be laid over the target to cast the spell.

### Healer's Ring: Lv 70

R: Spec., D: Ring/Inst., Ritual

Creates a ring seven paces across. Every Round, every person in the ring makes a Stamina stress roll of 3+ to regain a Body Level. If a Botch is rolled, a Body Level is lost. Useful for pitched battles, during Covenant defenses, and during especially disastrous adventures, although the *vis* cost is quite high.

### The Shadow of Life Renewed: Lv 70

R: Reach, D: Inst., Req: Mentem, Ritual

Brings the semblance of life to a corpse. During the Ritual, healing spells work on the corpse, and the body must be returned to physical wholeness, or it simply dies again once it is brought back to life. For each day that the person has been dead, roll for Characteristic loss as for Aging. When the Ritual is complete, roll a die to determine the success of the attempt: 1 — body dissolves;

2 — body possessed by a demon, faerie or other supernatural entity; 3 — mindless, useless living corpse; 4 or 5 — automaton with no Abilities over 3; 6 or 7 — automaton, but Abilities unlimited; 8 — person with self-direction but no personality, and somehow dangerously demented; 9 or 10 — person with will, but no personality. In any case, the revived person is not truly alive and is unable to gain Experience Points. Also, the person must make an Aging roll at the beginning of each year of its existence, regardless of age. This is the closest that the Order has gotten to raising a person from the dead.

# Intéllego Córporem Spells

Common Sigils seen in Intéllego Córporem spells usually report information in some strange or quirky way.

**Lv 5:** See the most general information about a person, such as a hazy vision of appearance, from an Arcane Connection.

### Physician's Eye: Lv 5

Spell Focus: Garnet (+1)

R: Sight, D: Inst.

Determines the general health of a single person. Specific afflictions appear to you as areas of yellow coloration on the person's body. A Perception + Medicine roll is required to identify unusual diseases (Ease Factor determined by the rarity of the disease).

**Lv 10:** Sense one bit of specific information about a person.

### Revealed Flaws of Mortal Flesh: Lv 10

Spell Focus: A Sapphire (+5)

R: Sight, D: Inst.

You are able to find any medical defects in a person or being that you see. You must possess something of emotional value to the person (an Arcane Connection). The sapphire used with this spell is said to provide wisdom.

### Sight of the True Form: Lv 10

Spell Focus: A Four-Leaf Clover (+3)

R: Sight, D: Inst.

You see the true, original form of any person whose form has been changed or masked. A four-leaf clover is said to aid its bearer in seeing through deceptions.

**Lv 15:** Hear what a specific person is saying if you have an Arcane Connection to them.

### Whispers Through the Black Gate: Lv 15

Spell Focus: A Green Turquoise (+3)

R: Reach/Near, D: Conc., Req: Mentem

You can, figuratively, speak through the gate that stands between the dead and the living, letting you speak with a corpse that has not yet decayed into a skeleton. The corpse cannot have been buried in Church burial, nor have belonged to a spirit that went straight to Heaven (e.g., a Saint or a Crusader). The spirit that you speak with may not speak the truth unless you come up with a way to coerce it to. All those around you can hear the voice of the corpse. Green turquoise is heavily associated with necromancy. Peasants tend to shy away from one with such an "evil" stone.

### The Inexorable Search: Lv 20

Spell Focus: A Feather from the Target's Pillow (+4)

R: 100 miles/400 miles, D: Conc.

Determines the location of a specific person. To cast the spell you need a map and something intimate to the person sought, such as a lock of hair or a fingernail (an Arcane Connection). After casting the spell, you can move your finger over the map at the rate of one hour per square foot. When your finger passes over the person's location as represented on the map, you sense the person's presence. (If the person is not in the area covered by the map, no sensations result.) You can locate the person to within a thumb's width on the map. Thus, a map with a larger scale provides more precise information. A map of a kingdom reveals what region the target is in. A map of a city reveals what neighborhood he is in. Each casting of the spell allows for the searching of one map. A similar spell allows you to search for a dead body (*Tracing the Trail of Death's Stench*).

### The Eye of the Sage: Lv 30

Spell Focus: A Griffon's Eye (+3)

R: 100 miles/400 miles, D: Conc. (1 hour), Req: Imágonem

Lets you see a specific person and what is within one pace of that person. The image is clear enough to allow reading. The vision lasts for an hour or until concentration is broken. To cast this spell, you need an Arcane Connection to the target.

## Muto Córporem Spells

These spells transform people. There are beneficial spells to cast on yourself and your compatriots, and harmful spells to cast on your foes.

Transformations do not usually completely eradicate the original form; something of the original remains. If you turn a fat, one-armed man into a wolf, the wolf is fat, three-legged and male. Likewise, transformations can have subtle (and sometimes dramatic) permanent effects. Someone who spends a long time, say a month, as an animal begins to act and think like that animal. Eventually, such individuals might lose their human identity altogether. What's more, someone transformed back into a human might temporarily or permanently retain some feature gained in the transformation. Someone turned into a rabbit and

back might keep a fondness for carrots or might retain unnaturally big ears. Transformations are tricky things.

Muto Córporem spells cannot alter a person's mind, so they leave the transformed person's intelligence and knowledge intact. Magi can cast spells while in animal form, but they suffer the normal -15 penalty for casting without hands or voice. Any abilities that the animal form has, the transformed person has as well, though it takes a day or so of experience to get used to the new form.

To change accoutrements along with the body involves Requisites. For example, one needs a Casting Requisite of Animál for leather worn, Aquam for any liquids carried, and Terram for metal objects worn (including studs in armor). Accoutrements are transformed only if they are actually being worn, not just carried in the hand. Anything that does not transform with the body, because the casting Magus chooses not to use the Casting Requisites, or because the Storyguide rules that it is not sufficiently part of the target's worn equipment, falls to the ground.

When the caster is under the influence of one of his shapechanging spells, he may change himself back by concentrating, but this ends the spell.

It is easier to change something and remain within the target's original form (e.g., change a man into another man) than it is to change the target into another form (e.g., change a man into an animal, or into a liquid). The latter usually adds 5 Levels to the difficulty of the spell.

**Lv 5:** Change a small part of a person you touch (e.g., an eye, a nose)

**Lv 10:** Change a limb of a person you touch.

### Evil Eye: Lv 5

Spell Focus: An Oversized Eyeball (+3)

R: Near/Sight, D: Sun./Perm.

Enlarges an eye of the target, deforming the face and producing a grisly image.

### Eyes of the Cat: Lv 10

Spell Focus: Hair From a Cat (+3)

R: Touch, D: Sun./Year, Req: Animál

The target gains the eyes of a cat, which allow him to see in darkness (but not in absolute lightlessness, such as the interior of a subterranean cavern).

**Lv 15:** Change the face of a person you touch.

### Disguise of the New Visage: Lv 15

Spell Focus: A Chip from a Pooka's Hoof (+5)

R: Touch/Near, D: Sun./Year

The target's facial features are transformed to any approximately human configuration.

In Cralian of Tremere's version of this spell, the new visage is always as unassuming as possible.

**Lv 20:** Utterly change the appearance of a person.

### Arm of the Infant: Lv 20

Spell Focus: Lock of Hair From a Baby (+1)

R: Near/Sight, D: Sun./Year

Shrinks a person's arm to half its original length and makes it pudgy, like an infant's.

### Preternatural Growth and Shrinking: Lv 20

Spell Focus: A Giant's Heart (+5)

R: Touch/Near, D: Sun./Year

Adds +1 to your normal Size or decreases it by up to 2 points. An extra Size point gives +1 Soak, +1 Strength, an extra Body Level, and -1 Defense. Each point lost has the reverse effects.

**Lv 25:** Turn a human into a land animal.

### Shape of the Woodland Prowler: Lv 25

Spell Focus: A Wolf's Tooth (+3)

R: Touch/Near, D: Sun./Inst., Req: Animál

You place a wolfskin over the target or yourself and change into a wolf. You or the target may change back at will, ending the spell.

### Curse of Circe: Lv 30

Spell Focus: Mandrake (+3)

R: Eye./Sight, D: Sun./Perm., Req: Animál

Turns a person into a pig. Mandrake, which is also known as Circe's Plant, can be found in faerie forests and at places where a human life has been taken.

### Gift of the Bear's Fortitude: Lv 30

Spell Focus: The Heart of a Black Faerie Bear (+3)

R: Body/Touch, D: Sun./Year

Your flesh becomes resistant to physical damage. You get +10 on all Soak rolls until you Botch one. If the Duration is "Year" and you suffer a Soak Botch, your resistance comes back after the next sunrise/sunset, whichever comes first. Your flesh is tough and insensitive; any rolls that involve a sensitive touch (such as for picking a lock) are at -2.

## Mists of Change: Lv 30

R: Spec., D: Moon/Perm, Req: Animál, Auram; Ritual

As this spell is cast, a whipping wind arises and patches of mist begin to roll across the landscape. Sometimes, a patch of mist suddenly envelops a person for a few seconds, during which time the victim cannot move. When the mist blows away, continuing its course, the person is transformed into a random creature. Roll a simple die to determine the result: 1— Wolf, 2 — Horse, 3 — Brown Bear, 4 — Large Toad, 5 — Ferret, 6 — Viper, 7 — Boar/Sow, 8 — Dog, 9 — Cat, 0 — Other (Storyguide picks, be cruel). People transformed retain their human minds, but inherit all the passions and instincts of their new forms.

The mist covers an area within a one mile radius, the center of which must be in sight when you cast the spell. The mists affect the area for an hour. Generally, the mists affect one in ten of the people caught in the radius. To see whether a given person falls victim, make a simple roll. A 0 indicates the spell affects the person. Once any transformations begin, people realize the nature of the mist and may flee the accursed area.

## The Silent Vigil: Lv 30

Spell Focus: Essence of an Earth Elemental (+3)

R: Self/Touch, D: Spec., Req: Terram

You can move into and become part of a rock formation that is at least twice your size. While in the stone, you can hear what is going on around you, but you cannot use other senses. The spell lasts until you come out, and you must come out where you went in. You have no need for food or drink, though you do age. Rolls to recover from Fatigue or wounds take twice as long to make while you are in the stone. If you plan to take anything you have into the stone, you must apply appropriate Casting Requisites.

**Lv 35:** Turn a human into a bird or a fish.

## Cloak of Black Feathers: Lv 35

Spell Focus: A Cape of Black Feathers (+0)

R: Self/Touch, D: Sun./Inst., Req: Animál, Auram

You hang a small cape of raven feathers on your back or that of the target, and you or the target transform into a raven. Human form can be resumed at will, but ends the spell.

**Lv 40:** Turn a human into a solid inanimate object.

## Stance of the Patient Tree: Lv 40

Spell Focus: A Tree Branch (+3)

R: Self/Touch, D: Sun./Inst., Req: Herbam

You turn yourself or another into a tree about 12 feet high, with a trunk about a foot thick. You can sense only the most basic things, such as night and day, strong winds, and things that affect you physically. You can resume human form at will, but that ends the spell. While in tree form, any wounds or Fatigue Levels remain unrestored. The tree branch you use determines the kind of tree you become.

**Lv 45:** Turn a human into an insubstantial object.

## Transform to Water: Lv 45

Spell Focus: Water That Was Once Ice (+3)

R: Self/Touch, D: Sun./Inst., Req: Aquam

You turn yourself or another into water, one pint for every pound you weigh. As water, you can hold yourself together unless someone makes an effort to separate part of you from the rest. You can roll slowly across the ground, but you cannot move uphill. You can hear sounds, feel things that touch you, and sense temperature. You can resume human form at will, which ends the spell. You can not resume human form if a significant part of your body/water is separated from the rest.

## Cloak of Mist: Lv 45

Spell Focus: Powdered Agate (+1)

R: Self, Touch, D: Sun./Inst., Req: Auram, Aquam

Your body or that of your target becomes a thick cohesive mist of approximately human size. You (or the target) can float through the air at walking speed and can see and hear what is going on around you. You can seep through cracks, but cannot move through solid objects. You can return to human form at any time, but that ends the spell. As mist, you are subject to the forces of the wind. If used, the agate is thrown over you or the target, and as it falls, you fade to mist.

# Perdo Córporem Spells

These spells harm people directly, often permanently, unless outside magics are used to repair the damage.

**Lv 5:** Do superficial damage to a body, such as remove its hair (*Marbaid's Clean Shave*).

## Touch of the Goose Feather: Lv 5

Spell Focus: A Goose Feather (+3)

R: Near/Sight, D: Conc.

The target must make a Stamina stress roll of 7+ or let out a loud sneeze. Spell casters must make Intelligence + Concentration rolls of 15+ to maintain concentration, and others get -1 on most activities at the moment of the sneeze.

## Invocation of Weariness: Lv 5

Spell Focus: A Pinch of Sand (+3)

R: Near/Sight, D: Inst.

The target must make a Fatigue roll of 9+ or lose a Short-Term Fatigue Level. The phrases used with this spell are usually singsong melodies, which lull the victim into drowsiness.

**Lv 10:** Cause a person pain, but do no real damage.

## Grip of the Choking Hand: Lv 10

Spell Focus: Branch of Holly (+3)

R: Near/Sight, D: Conc.

The target feels an invisible, strangling hand on the throat. Each Round the target loses a Short-Term Fatigue Level, or a Body Level, if already Unconscious. Stamina roll of 6+ to break the spell, rolled each Round. If cast with the Spell Focus, the branch of holly is pointed towards the victim while the Magus casts the spell. Holly is dangerous for Magi to carry, as peasant superstition holds it as a harmful plant.

**Lv 15:** Do slight damage to a person, such as make him lame or cause a minor wound.

### Dust to Dust: Lv 15

Spell Focus: Bones Ground to Dust (+3)

R: Near/Sight, D: Inst.

Turns a dead or undead body to dust in two Rounds. The spell is a lifesaver against undead that are mindless corpses, like skeletons and zombies, but it doesn't affect those undead possessed by spirits. Rubbing two or more bones together to make dust during the casting of this spell enhances the effects. Casting Requisite: Animál for animal corpses.

### Confound the Connection: Lv 15

Spell Focus: A Facsimile of the Arcane Connection used Against You (+5)

R: 100 miles/400 miles, D: Inst.

Allows you to destroy an item, used by another Magus, that allows an Arcane Connection. This item may be of your body or possession, or may belong to another person you touch. Use of this spell assumes you know an Arcane Connection has been made to you, though you don't have to know what item is being used to form the Connection. Once this spell is cast, any Arcane Connection to you or the person you touch is permanently severed. Another Connection can only be formed by a Magus if he has another of your personal objects.

### The Wound that Weeps: Lv 15

Spell Focus: A Branch of Holly (+1)

R: Near/Sight, D: Inst., Aimed

When casting this spell, you point at the victim, possibly with a branch of holly, and a large wound opens on his body. The wound may not be a deep one, but it bleeds profusely, forming a gradually spreading dark stain upon the victim's clothing. Every Round the target must make a Stamina stress roll. If the result is a Botch, 2 Short-Term Fatigue Levels are lost. If the result is 2 or less, one Fatigue Level is lost. If Unconsciousness is reached, Body Levels are lost instead. If the result is 3 to 8, no Level is lost. If the roll is 9+, the bleeding stops. A target fighting in melee suffers a -3 penalty to his Stamina rolls. If the victim is completely still, he receives a +1 bonus to them. Of course, accumulated Fatigue and wound penalties apply to all rolls. If outside help is received, a Chirurgy roll of 7+ stops the bleeding.

Lv 20: Destroy a major sense of a person.

### Incantation of the Milky Eyes: Lv 20

Spell Focus: A Blank Glass Eye (+3)

R: Near/Sight, D: Moon/Inst.

Blinds a target, leaving the eyes milky with cataracts.

### Twist of the Tongue: Lv 20

Spell Focus: A Human Tongue (+3)

R: Near/Sight, D: Moon/Inst.

Twists the target's tongue into a spiral, completely destroying the ability to speak. A grave offense to a Magus.

### Bane of the Decrepit Body: Lv 25

Spell Focus: The Heart of an Old Man (+3)

R: Near/Sight, D: Inst.

The target ages a number of years equal to a simple roll + 5. Determine Characteristic loss normally. Only works on adults (age 16+). If casting with the Focus, you slowly crush the heart, draining the years from the target.

### Curse of the Leprous Flesh: Lv 30

Spell Focus: Flakes From the Skin of a Leper (+1)

R: Near/Sight, D: Spec.

The curse of leprosy causes a person's flesh to rot off in a matter of weeks. Every week, over a period of three months, the person must make a stress Stamina roll of 6+ or lose a Body Level permanently. If a roll is ever Botched, an additional Body Level is lost. The target also loses a point of Stamina by the time the spell ends. The magic can be dispelled while it is still in effect, but any damage done cannot be dispelled. The victim of this spell is usually a truly hideous sight. Much of his flesh literally hangs from his frame, and there is a pungent rotting smell about him at all times. If the victim somehow survives this curse, he is shunned by mortal communities. If casting with a Focus, the flakes are blown toward the victim.

### Curse of the Unportended Plague: Lv 35

R: Spec., D: Inst., Ritual

Starts a plague in a city. The plague reaches its height in 6 to 12 months and can spread like any other plague. It is non-magical once begun, and health measures can lessen the effect of the plague. A full-blown plague kills one in ten inhabitants of a city over the course of a few months. Using, or even transcribing, this spell is rigorously discouraged by most of the Order of Hermes.

Lv 40: Kill a person at Near Range

### The Kiss of Death: Lv 40

Spell Focus: None

R: Touch/Near, D: Inst.

The person you kiss dies a sudden death. The only mark on the corpse is the black imprint of your lips. No words or gestures are necessary, though if you apply vis to Range, you can "blow" a kiss of death. Stamina roll of 12+ to resist. This spell is a quiet and effective means of assassination.

### Clenching Grasp of the Crushed Heart: Lv 40

Spell Focus: A Human Heart (+3)

R: Near/Sight, D: Inst.

When casting this spell, the magus makes a clenching motion with the hand, crushing the Spell Focus if using one. The victim doubles over at once, and if fails to make a Stamina roll of 15+, dies with a crushed heart. If the target's roll succeeds, 5 points of Stamina are still lost. The target is still probably crippled for life, and may die an early death.

## Rego Córporem Spells

Lv 5: Make the target lose control of a body part.

### Curse of the Unruly Tongue: Lv 5

Spell Focus: A Branch of Holly (+3)

R: Near/Sight, D: Conc./Sun.

Causes the target to stutter and slur words. Communication rolls are at -4; spoken spells are at -6 to the spell casting roll, with an extra Botch roll.

### Spasms of the Uncontrolled Hand: Lv 5

Spell Focus: A Branch of Holly (+3)

R: Near/Sight, D: Inst.

Target must make a Stamina roll of 5+ or drop whatever is held in hand.

Lv 10: Make the target lose control of his body.

### Despair of the Quivering Manacles: Lv 10

Spell Focus: A Manikin of the Target (+5)

R: Near/Sight, D: Conc./Sun.

Your target shakes vigorously from side to side without falling. Those affected get -3 to combat rolls or other action rolls, and -1 to most other rolls.

### Rise of the Feathery Body: Lv 10

Spell Focus: The Feather of an Eagle (+3)

R: Body/Touch, D: Conc./Moon

Allows you to float up and down to any height, but you cannot move horizontally by means of this spell. You can lift up to 50 pounds with you. You can move as fast as smoke rises, slower if you are carrying a heavy load.

**Lv 15:** Hold another's body absolutely stiff, while you maintain eye contact (R) and concentration (D).

### Endurance of the Berserkers: Lv 15

Spell Focus: Lock of Hair from a Berserker (+3)

R: Touch/Near, D: Conc./Sun.

The target's body acts as though it is unwounded and unfatigued for as long as you concentrate (assuming no vis is used to increase Duration). Keep track of the actual Body and Fatigue Levels that the body loses while "berserk" because as soon as the spell wears off, the target loses those Levels.

Consecutive castings on a character delay the end of the spell — when accumulated wounds take effect — but a body can only take a number of consecutive castings equal to its Size + 2. Further castings have no effect.

### Gift of the Frog's Legs: Lv 15

Spell Focus: Legs of a Frog (+1)

R: Touch/Near, D: 10 seconds

Allows the person on whom it is cast to leap up to 15 feet vertically or 25 feet horizontally (2 feet less for every Encumbrance point). The person must make a Dexterity - Encumbrance stress roll of 6+ to land without injury. A miss indicates the loss of one Body Level, and a Botch indicates a broken ankle or other crippling injury. The person can only make such a leap once for each casting of the spell, and that leap must be made within ten seconds. As with a frog, a running start does not improve the leap.

### Awaken the Slumbering Corpse: Lv 20

Spell Focus: A Green Turquoise (+3)

R: Near/Sight, D: Conc./Moon

Raises a corpse and causes it to function at your verbal command, though commands have to be very simple, like "attack anyone who comes through here." Use the statistics for zombies (if some flesh is still intact) or skeletons (if most flesh is gone) provided in the Realms Chapter. The corpse

used cannot have been buried by Church ceremony.

### The Gift of Vigor: Lv 20

Spell Focus: A Ruby (+3)

R: Touch/Near, D: Inst.

Transfers bodily energy from you to any target who is at a lower Fatigue Level than you. You are thus at the target's current Fatigue Level, and he assumes your previous Level. If you lose a Fatigue Level from casting this spell, the loss comes after the transfer. Magi have long looked for a way to restore their energy in order to cast more spells. This is the closest they've come. The ruby is associated with Mars, and thus represents vigor and strength.

### Lifting the Dangling Puppet: Lv 20

Spell Focus: A Manikin of the Target (+3)

R: Near/Sight, D: Conc.

Lifts a person of Size +1 or lower vertically into the air. Generally, you can make the target rise or descend as fast as smoke rises, but a heavier person rises more slowly and falls more quickly.

### The Walking Corpse: Lv 25

R: Reach, D: Inst., Req: Mentem, Ritual

Turns a corpse into a nearly mindless servant. If the corpse still has most of its flesh, it becomes a zombie; if not, it becomes an animated skeleton (see the Realms Chapter for stats). The creature follows your orders faithfully but unimaginatively. Unless the corpse is preserved with *Charm Against Putrefaction* or the equivalent, the body decays normally.

### Strings of the Unwilling Marionette: Lv 30

Spell Focus: A Manikin of the Target (+3)

R: Near/Sight, D: Conc.

You can control the gross physical movements of a person, such as walking, standing, and turning. If the target resists, the movements are jerky. The target can yell, but you can prevent intelligible speech by controlling the target's mouth. The target must be conscious to be moved about. Strength roll of 12+ to resist, rolled each Round.

### The Leap of Homecoming: Lv 35

Spell Focus: An Opal (+1)

R: Self (150 miles)/Touch, D: Inst.

Teleports you, or one you touch, back to the one place you know best (probably your laboratory), provided it is within 150 miles. You must have an Arcane Connec-

tion with the place you are leaping to, such as a tile from the floor, or a chunk of the wall. The opal is the stone of Mercury, and thought to bring good journeys.

### The Seven League Stride: Lv 35

Spell Focus: An Opal (+1)

R: Self (21 miles)/Touch, D: Inst.

Teleports you or one you touch to any place (within Range) which you can either see or have an Arcane Connection with. If you fail an Intelligence + Finesse roll of 11+, your arrival goes slightly awry. For instance, you might fall when you appear, or just be facing the wrong way. A Botch means you appear in the wrong place, perhaps even in a wall (ouch).

Praefactus of Bonisagus has a version of this spell that always allows him appear in a safe, unembarrassing place (assuming he doesn't fail his Finesse roll). All Praefactus's spells may be recognized in that they make him seem as dignified as possible. This is his Wizard's Sigil.

# HERBAM SPELLS

Herbam spells work on plants and plant matter, both living and dead. Since wood is a common material in weapons, vehicles, and buildings, Herbam spells can be useful in improving or destroying physical things. They can also be used to bring the plant world to your aid.

## Creo Herbam Spells

These spells create and heal plants. Any food created is nutritious only if raw vis is used. The Guideline Levels given below are generally for conjuring the leafy parts of plants. Wood is a bit harder to create, and usually requires a spell about 5 Levels higher.

Wizard's Sigils in many Creo Herbam spells may be seen as quirks in the plant created. Silva of Merinita might make an apple with a strange taste, while Chavin of Tytalus might create a bridge of wood with scenes of wars carved on it.

### Restoration of the Corrupted Plant: Gen

R: Touch, D: Inst., Ritual

Cancels the effects (short of death) of a malign Herbam spell that has its Level matched by the Level of this Ritual.

Lv 5: Create a fruit or a small handful of brush.

Lv 10: Create a man-sized bush, or an equivalent volume of plant.

### Conjure the Sturdy Vine: Lv 10

Spell Focus: A Leaf from a Vine (+3)
R: Reach/Near, D: Sun./Inst.

Grows ten paces of vine from a moderate quantity of wood, or from fertile soil. The vine is extremely strong and pliable, suitable for use as rope. If the Focus is available, it is planted in the ground, and the vine instantly grows from it.

Lv 15: Grow enough brush to fill a room, or a small (man-sized) tree. Cause a tree to bear fruit within the hour, although it is not able to bear fruit again for a year.

### Trap of the Entwining Vines: Lv 15

Spell Focus: A Leaf From a Vine (+1)
R: Near/Sight, D: 1 hour

Causes strong, woody vines to grow rapidly from fertile earth. The vines cover a circle two paces across and reach six feet high. Anything caught within them is im-

mobilized. To avoid the vines, the target must make a Quickness - Encumbrance roll of 9+. To break out requires a Strength roll of 12+ (allowed once a Round). Someone not trapped can cut a trapped person free in two Rounds. The vines weaken and wither to dust after an hour.

Lv 20: Grow a wall of brush.

### Wall of Thorns: Lv 20

Spell Focus: A Single Thorn (+1)
R: Near/Sight, D: Sun./Inst.

Creates a straight wall of woody, thorny bushes up to 20 paces across, one pace thick, and four paces high. The thorns, which are unnaturally resilient, have a +15 Soak and four "Body Levels" (and are cut by edged weapons only). Bodily forcing one's way through the wall requires a Strength stress roll of 9+ and does +15 damage regardless of the attempt's success. If the roll Botches, an additional 5 points of damage are suffered. The wall grows out of existing bushes or fertile soil. A Climb roll of 9+ allows a character to scale the wall, but the character takes +10 damage in the process.

Lv 25: Grow a wall of wood.

### Wall of Living Wood Lv 25

Spell Focus: An Oak Branch (+1)
R: Near/Sight, D: Sun./Inst.

A straight wall of living oak is created, growing quickly from nearby trees, other plant growth, or fertile earth. The wall is 20 paces long, one pace thick, and 5 paces high. It can be scaled by a Climb roll of 9+.

### The Bountiful Feast: Lv 30

R: Spec., D: Year, Ritual

This Ritual, which must be cast at noon on the day after the Winter Solstice, attempts to insure that all crops that grow within its range will be healthy and fruitful. The spell protects against non-magical blight and other diseases. It can't control the weather or prevent others from harming crops, but it does cause crops to be healthier, larger, and tastier than they otherwise would be. The spell affects all plants within one mile, plus one mile for each extra point of *vis* spent in the Ritual. Although food plants are affected most by this Ritual, all plants are made healthier to some degree.

### Bridge of Wood: Lv 30

Spell Focus: A Splinter from a Wood Bridge (+1)
R: Near/Sight, D: Sun./Inst.

Creates an ornate and exquisitely carved bridge made from living leaves, vines, and wood. The bridge can reach up to 50 feet and is sturdy enough to support creatures of up to Size +4.

# Intéllego Herbam Spells

Lv 5: Sense one property of a plant.

### Probe Nature's Hidden Lore: Lv 5

Spell Focus: A Sapphire (+5)
R: Touch/Near, D: Inst.

Lets you know what kind of plant you touch. You get an image of it in its natural habitat. Works with plant products as well as with plants themselves.

Lv 10: Sense all of the mundane properties of a plant.

### Intuition of the Forest: Lv 10

Spell Focus: Chips from a Faun's Hoof (+5)
R: Body/Touch, D: Sun./Year

Gives you an intuitive sense of how to get along in the forest and how to get the most out of the forest without causing it harm. It is a type of communion with the woods. This spell provides a +2 to all nature-oriented rolls (not spells) when in a forest or similar area. Causing significant harm to the forest cancels this spell.

### Hunt for the Wild Herb: Lv 15

Spell Focus: Leaf from a Cypress Tree (+3)
R: Spec., D: Conc./Moon

When you cast this spell, the vegetation of the forest guides you to the nearest specimen of the type of plant you seek. You must have a sample of the type of plant you are looking for. A Perception roll of 6+ is needed to follow the subtle signs, which include pointing branches and inclined trunks. A plant of the type you seek must be within the forest you are currently in, or the spell fails automatically.

### Converse with Plants and Trees: Lv 25

Spell Focus: A Chewed Leaf (+1)
R: Reach/Near, D: Conc.

You can speak with plants for one conversation. The level of conversation depends on the type of plants; longer-lived and more "noble" plants have more to say. A single question and response takes ten to thirty minutes, with slower growing plants speaking more slowly. Typically, plants can talk about the soil, and other plants around them, but have limited awareness of more momentary events, such as the passing of animals or people, unless that passing has a direct bearing on the plant (e.g., a person cut its trunk). News can spread quickly through a forest when it has to, called from tree to tree on the wind. Bystanders cannot understand your conversation.

### Shriek of the Impending Shafts: Lv 25

Spell Focus: A Hazel Wood Rod (+1)

R: Body/Touch, D: Conc./Moon

Lets you know where anything wooden will be in the immediate future (in the next few seconds) by a shriek that sounds in the air in advance of the wood's coming. You get a +8 bonus on Defense scores against wooden weapons, and you can automatically dodge wooden missiles fired from 10 or more paces away (unless so many are coming at you that you can't get out of the way, in which case the Ease Factor of shots is still modified by +3). Missiles from archers closer than ten paces still have an Ease Factor 5 points higher than normal to strike you.

### Calling the Council of the Trees: Lv 45

R: 20 miles, D: Moon, Ritual

All magical and potentially mobile trees within 20 miles of where you cast the Ritual uproot themselves and travel to that spot. Trees in a faerie forest are especially prone to responding. Once gathered, the trees hold meetings, summon ancient powers, and discuss the problems facing their kind. The results of the conference may not be entirely in your favor. The trees remain animated for a month and may seek to return home before the end of that period. The trees can be called only once per decade.

# Muto Herbam Spells

Most Guidelines assume that when you change a plant, it's still a plant in some way. Changing a plant into another form usually involves a spell about five Levels higher than the Guideline most appropriate to the action. Changing a whole tree is also more difficult than just changing a like volume of plants, or other plant material.

Lv 5: Change a small branch, staff, or small bush.

### Transformation of the Thorny Staff: Lv 5

Spell Focus: A Rose Thorn (+3)

R: Touch/Near, D: Sun./Inst.

Causes a length of wood (up to six feet in length) to grow thick, sharp thorns at whatever spots you touch. If the spell is cast on a staff, the thorns provide a +4 damage bonus the first time a hit is scored, after which the thorns break off.

Lv 10: Change something approximately man-sized.

Lv 15: Change a small tree.

### Dance of the Staves: Lv 15

Spell Focus: A Small Twig (+1)

R: Near/Sight, D: Inst.

Causes a pole, staff, haft, or any other long, thin, non-living wooden object to bend and lash about wildly for a few seconds and then stop suddenly, keeping its new, twisted shape. In its new shape, the wooden item is useless. A whirling staff strikes its holder and does +4 damage, with a possible bonus if the weapon at the head of the pole hits the person. If a small twig of wood is available it may be used as a Spell Focus.

### Twist the Living Tree: Lv 15

Spell Focus: A Pearl (+3)

R: Near/Sight, D: Sun./Year

You make a living tree bend into unusual positions. Depending on your needs, you can make a cage, a shelter, or a wall. Even the leaves can be commanded, maybe to form a solid roof that sheds rain. Takes one to ten minutes to complete (depending on the complexity of the new shape), during which time you must maintain concentration.

### Rope of Bronze: Lv 15

Spell Focus: A Bit of Bronze (+1)

R: Reach/Near, D: Sun./Perm., Req: Terram

Turns up to ten paces of rope (made from plant material) into refined, superior bronze, which does not break under normal circumstances. If a bit or bronze is available, it is touched to the rope during the spell, causing the change.

Lv 20: Change as much brush as would fit in a small room.

### Piercing Shaft of Wood: Lv 20

Spell Focus: An Arrow Shaft (+1)

R: Touch/Near, D: Inst., Req: Rego; Aimed +2

Turns a piece of wood into a sleek, barbed, strong shaft that flies through the air at a target. Damage depends on the size of the item from which the shaft is formed: Staff (upper size limit) +20, two-foot branch +15, wand +10. If it pierces a body, removing the shaft causes the target to automatically lose a Body Level, unless a Stamina roll of 7+ is made (add the Chirurgy score of the one who removes the shaft).

### Thaumaturgical Transformation of Plants to Iron: Lv 20

Spell Focus: A Bit of Iron (+1)

R: Reach/Near, D: Sun./Year, Req: Terram

Makes any plant, dead or alive, as hard as iron. Affects any amount of continuous plant material up to the size of a small tree or a small glade of grass. Sharp-edged plants can become deadly when this hard. If a bit of iron is available, it is touched to the plant, bringing about the transformation.

Lv 25: Change a large tree.

### Stir the Slumbering Tree: Lv 25

Spell Focus: A Star Ruby (+1)

R: Reach/Near, D: Sun./Perm., Req: Mentem

Raises any tree into a state of consciousness resembling that of a human. Such a tree can see and hear what is going on around it at a normal human level of perception. Such a tree may share some mental attributes or personality traits with the caster. The tree can move its branches about slowly, too slowly to be detectable by people. Most trees in Magical areas are already awake. It is theorized by some Hermetic scholars that before the Dominion arose, in the days when the faeries danced across the lands with humanity, all the trees were awake and that some even spoke aloud. The star ruby is a gem that may be used for conjuring and controlling occult entities.

Lv 30: Change entire sections of a forest.

### Curse of the Haunted Forest: Lv 30

R: Near, D: Perm., Req: Perdo, Ritual

Turns a previously normal forest into a haunted and dangerous place. The trees become conscious and cruel, capable of sight, hearing, and limited movement. While they cannot uproot themselves, they can move their branches about, reaching the ground in an hour or two. (Only the foolish sleep in such forests.) The trees become gnarled and hideous, and the imaginative can see menacing faces in them. Only ill-tempered animals, such as boars and crows, live in these woods, and nothing in them is left edible. The only knowledge of what might happen, should this Ritual be attempted on a faerie forest, comes from ancient and disputed legends of the Order of Hermes.

## Perdo Herbam Spells

These spells destroy plants and plant material. Since many items are made of wood, these spells can be quite destructive. The Guidelines given are for destroying dead wood. Destroying live wood is usually a bit harder (add 5 Levels).

Lv 5: Destroy a man-sized amount of dead wood. Cover up to a bushel of vegetables, fruit or grain with mold, making it inedible (*Despoiler of Life's Sustenance*).

### Curse of the Rotted Wood: Lv 5

Spell Focus: A Pinch of Sawdust (+3)
R: Near/Sight, D: Inst.

Causes a non-living wooden object to rot and fall apart. Objects up to the size of a single door can be affected, but things that size take up to two Rounds to decay. Usually, large chunks of wood start falling off the target, and slowly crumble to smaller and smaller pieces, until only dust is left.

Ferramentam of Verditius's version of this spell is very orderly — his Wizard's Sigil. The decay of the object starts from the top, and continues to the bottom, causing the object to decay into dust as it goes.

Lv 15: Destroy a Near amount of dead wood.

### Wizard's Autumn: Lv 15

Spell Focus: A Handful of Snow (+3)
R: Sight/1 mile, D: Inst.

Causes all the deciduous leaves (i.e., those that normally fall in Autumn) to turn

brown and then fall to the ground. The full process takes a minute. The trees do not bud again until the next spring.

### Plant's Withering Bane: Lv 20

Spell Focus: A Leaf of Angelica (+1)
R: Near/Sight, D: Inst.

Withers and destroys one living tree which may not be more than twice as tall as a man. The spell may also effect all small, living plants in a radius of ten feet, centered on the caster. If angelica is used as a Focus, it is crushed and cast to the winds.

### The Great Rot: Lv 25

Spell Focus: A Rotten Piece of Wood (+1)
R: Spec., D: Inst.

Rots a large amount of dead wood, up to the amount found in a wooden house or small inn. Wooden structures creak and groan mightily for about a minute before collapsing.

Lv 30: Destroy dead wood that's within Sight.

### Treading the Ashen Path: Lv 30

Spell Focus: A Black Onyx (+1)
R: Spec., D: Inst.

As you walk through a forest after casting this spell, all the plant material ten paces in front of you and five paces to either side withers and dies. Trees are reduced to bare trunks, while their leaves and all smaller plants turn to ash. You can walk for seven miles with each casting of this spell. Use of this spell in faerie woods is not recommended. The black onyx brings malediction and death.

This spell was originally invented by a Magus of House Flambeau, and he was awarded a prize for it by his Primus.

## Rego Herbam Spells

### Ward Against Faeries of the Wood: Gen.

Spell Focus: A Star Ruby (+3)
R: Spec., D: Ring

Like *Ward Against Faeries of the Waters* (ReAq Gen.), but for faeries of the wood. At some angles, at night, the ring appears to be a green-hued dome.

Lv 5: Control a small branch, staff, or small bush.

Lv 10: Control something approximately man-sized. Deflect a single attack by a wooden weapon.

### Repel the Wooden Shafts: Lv 10

Spell Focus: A Staff (+3)
R: Near/Sight, D: Conc./Sun.

Deflects a single blow of any weapon made of wood, up to the size of a two-handed club. You can deflect a different attack each Round. The attack automatically misses, but the attacker still rolls to see if he Botches (with two extra Botch rolls for melee weapons). If you ordinarily carry a staff, it must be tossed aside for the casting.

Lv 15: Control a small tree. Deflect several attacks from wooden weapons.

### Strike of the Angered Branch: Lv 15

Spell Focus: A Whiplike Tree Branch (+3)
R: Near/Sight, D: Inst., Aimed

Causes a large tree branch to swing at a target. You must target the spell for the branch to hit; damage is +10.

### Tangle of Wood and Thorns: Lv 15

Spell Focus: A Small Net (+1)
R: Near/Sight, D: Spec., Aimed +1

Takes a length of wood that you designate and hurls it at a target (Targeting roll is required). The wood wraps around and immobilizes the target (assuming the wood is long enough), who must make a Strength stress roll of 10+ to break free (one attempt per Round). If a roll ever Botches, the victim cannot escape without outside help. If the length of wood has thorns, it does +6 damage when it hits and each time the target tries to break free, whether successful or not. A

small net made out of plants and grass is used to aid this spell Sympathetically.

**Lv 20**: Control as much brush as would fit in a small room. Deflect all known attacks from wooden weapons.

### Coils of the Entangling Plants: Lv 20

Spell Focus: A Small Net (+1)

R: Near/Sight, D: Spec.

Animates all the grass and small plants within a field delineated by your outstretched arms and no more than 15 paces away, causing them to grab and wrap themselves around the people nearest to them (Strength stress roll of 9+ to break free, rolled once per minute). If a roll to break free ever Botches, the victim cannot escape on his own. After an hour's time, the plants release their grip and resume their normal ways. With a Concentration roll of 6+ you can release one individual a Round.

### The Treacherous Spear: Lv 20

Spell Focus: A Drop of Blood (+3)

R: Near/Sight, D: Spec., Req: Auram

Animates a wooden or wooden-hafted melee weapon in someone's hand, and makes that weapon attack its holder until the wielder is dead or the weapon is destroyed. When the spell is cast, the weapon tries to break its wielder's hold (Quickness - Encumbrance stress roll of 9+ to hang on). On subsequent Rounds, the wielder hangs on by making Strength stress rolls of 6+, allowed once per Round. If a roll to hold on ever Botches, the wielder loses control of his weapon and is hit by it automatically (see below). While still in its wielder's grip, the weapon does not strike him, but does not strike on his behalf, either.

Once the weapon breaks free or is released, it floats in the air and attacks its wielder using his Attack and Damage scores (it always strikes after its former wielder attacks, so it suffers the accumulated affects of lost First Strike). The former wielder may fight his rebellious weapon. The weapon has a Defense total equal to 7 minus its Load score. One-handed weapons have +10 Soak and 3 "Body Levels" (with no wounds penalties). Two-handed weapons have +14 Soak and 4 Body Levels. All thrusting and missile weapons used against the floating weapon suffer -5 on Attack and Damage rolls.

The drop of blood that may be used with this spell must be from a person who has betrayed his family.

**Lv 25**: Control a large tree. Keep wood totally away from your person (i.e., deflect all attacks from wooden weapons, whether you can see them or not).

### Lord of the Trees: Lv 25

Spell Focus: Bark From a Century Old Tree (+3)

R: Near/Sight, D: Conc.

Causes a tree to move its branches and bend its trunk in any way you mentally direct. A large tree striking with branches has the following scores: First Strike +5, Attack +7, and Damage +16. Normal weapons are practically useless against large trees.

**Lv 30**: Control large sections of a forest.

### Freeing the Striding Tree: Lv 30

Spell Focus: A Violet Amethyst (+1)

R: Near/Sight, D: Conc.

Like *Lord of the Trees* (ReHe 25), but the tree can walk half as fast as a human can. If you botch a Concentration roll to maintain control, the tree attacks you, having been awakened and disturbed by this spell. The violet amethyst aids this spell because it's the stone of Jupiter and thus aids in the command of others.

# IGNEM SPELLS

As fire is volatile and dangerous, so are these spells. Magi who pursue the Art of fire do so with fine regard for the dangers and also the powers involved, for fire is both dangerous and mighty, to friend and foe alike. Storyguides should make Ignem Botches particularly deadly.

Light and heat are included in this Form. It's important to remember that heat also means absence of heat, so spells that result in cold temperatures are possible through the Ignem Form.

Various Ignem spells have limits regarding the size of the fires they can affect. The following size categories are used to describe fires: candle and torch (CrIg 5), campfire and bonfire (CrIg 10), and house fire (CrIg 15). Unless specified otherwise, a spell that can affect one type of fire can affect all smaller fires as well. Fire damage is explained on p.162, in the Combat Chapter.

## Creo Ignem Spells

Spells that create fires are versatile weapons, destructive to living things, undead, buildings, and morale. Those who depend on fire spells, however, risk the Botch. Fire is an unforgiving element for those who lose control of it, and self-incineration is always a possibility.

Typical Sigils seen in Creo Ignem spells involve the flame being a strange color, or shape, or it may give off a strange smell.

**Lv 5**: Create a small flame, intense enough to do 1d10+5 damage.

### Moonbeam: Lv 5

Spell Focus: Quartz (+5)

R: Spec., D: Spec.

Causes a gentle light, enough to read by, to shine down from above and illuminate the area described by your encircled arms. Lasts as long as you hold your arms in a circle. Quartz is a rock associated with the moon.

### Palm of Flame: Lv 5

Spell Focus: A Piece of Flint (+1)

R: Touch, D: Conc.

A flame leaps up in your palm, which must be upturned for the spell's Duration. Wind can blow out the flame.

**Lv 10**: Create a large campfire, or small bonfire, intense enough to do +10 damage.

### Heat of the Searing Forge: Lv 10

Spell Focus: Chrysolite (+3)

R: Near/Sight, D: Inst.

Makes a piece of metal too hot to touch. Something the size of a breastplate or helmet does +10 damage if in direct contact with the skin for one Round. For each additional Round, more damage is done, the amount dropping by two points each Round (+8 damage on Round two, then +6, and so on). Smaller objects do less damage. Most metal armor has leather or cloth underneath that gives the victim a +2 Soak bonus vs. the heat. Chrysolite is a rock with strong associations to the Sun.

### Lamp Without Flame: Lv 10

Spell Focus: Lantern Oil (+1)

R: Touch, D: Spec.

Creates light (like that of a lamp) that shines forth from some object as long as you hold it. If lantern oil is available, spreading

it over the object strengthens the spell. The oil is absorbed into the object as the spell is cast.

**Lv 15:** Create a house fire, intense enough to do +15 damage.

### Flash of the Scarlet Flames: Lv 15

Spell Focus: Flint (+1)

R: Near/Sight, D: Inst., Aimed -3

A brilliant red flash explodes in the air where you designate. If you target someone's face, the target needs a Stamina stress roll of 9+ to avoid temporary blindness. If the roll is Botched, the target is permanently blinded. If temporarily blinded, one can try to make a Stamina simple roll of 9+ to recover each minute. The Targeting modifier is for creating the flash in someone's eyes.

In Rose of Jerbiton's version of this spell, there is a faint odor of roses in the area where the flash explodes.

**Lv 20:** Create a fire intense enough to do +20 damage.

### Pilum of Fire: Lv 20

Spell Focus: A Javelin (+1)

R: Spec., D: Inst., Aimed +1

A two foot thick spear-shaped jet of fire flies from your palms (consuming your Spell Focus, if you are using one) doing +25 damage (-1 for every pace of distance from you to the target). Beyond 25 paces, the flames dissipate.

**Lv 25:** Create an inferno, or a fire intense enough to do +25 damage.

### Arc of Fiery Ribbons: Lv 25

Spell Focus: A Yellow Diamond (+1)

R: Spec., D: Inst.

A dozen multi-hued ribbons of flame leap from your hands and fly out 15 paces, covering a 60 degree arc. All those in the arc take +20 damage, modified by -1 for every pace the target is from you. The area affected by this spell is so broad that Targeting rolls are only necessary in exceptional circumstances. Anyone who sees the ribbons coming can fall flat and therefore suffer half damage with a Quickness - Encumbrance stress roll of 18+, with a +1 bonus for every pace between the target and caster. If this escape roll Botches, the target suffers an extra +5 damage. The yellow diamond has associations with the Sun.

**Lv 30:** Create a fire intense enough to do +30 damage.

### Ball of Abysmal Flame: Lv 30

Spell Focus: The Heart of a Fire Drake (+3)

R: Near/Sight, D: Inst., Aimed

This spell creates an apple-sized ball of fire in your hand. When you throw it, it bursts into flames as soon as it touches some creature or substance, doing +30 damage to the target and blinding any within 5 paces who are looking at it. Blindness lasts one Round; Stamina stress roll of 12+ to resist (permanent blindness on a Botched roll). You can hold the ball in your hand for up to three Rounds before throwing it, but after three Rounds it flickers out.

Marius of Tremere's version of the spell causes the ball to make a loud bang when it hits the target. His Sigil is a gaudiness in his spells.

### Blade of the Virulent Flame: Lv 30

Spell Focus: The Blood of a Fire Drake (+3)

R: Reach/Near, D: Spec.

Forms a fire along the length of a metal blade. This flame doubles the Weapon Damage score for the blade (or adds +6, whichever is greater), and can start fires as well. Note, however, that after half an hour, the blade becomes so hot that it partially melts. Once this occurs, the spell ends. The user of the flaming blade must wear gloves as the hilt gets hot, or the sword cannot be handled. If using the Spell Focus, the blood is spread along the blade. The +3 Focus Modifier is also added to damage caused by the blade, because the fire is hotter and more intense.

### Circle of Encompassing Flames: Lv 30

Spell Focus: A Cat's Eye Gem (+1)

R: Near/Sight, D: Conc., Aimed

Creates a circle of flames six feet high. The circle begins at a one pace radius, but you can make it shrink to a pillar or grow to a three pace radius. Anyone moving through the flames takes +20 damage. You cannot move the center of the circle. A Targeting roll is needed to encircle someone. The cat's eye gem is associated with the sun.

# Intéllego Ignem Spells

**Lv 5:** Sense one property of a fire.

### Shadows of the Fires Past: Lv 5

Spell Focus: A Lump of Coal (+1)

R: Near/Sight, D: Inst.

Allows you to see where fires have been in the past lunar month. A light red flickering haze appears wherever there was a fire, and you gain an intuitive sense of when the fire was there. This spell is not so much a look into the past as it is a detector of fire traces.

**Lv 10:** Sense all mundane properties of a fire.

### Tales of the Ashes: Lv 10

Spell Focus: A Sapphire (+3)

R: Touch/Near, D: Inst.

Lets you see what the ashes you touch originally were, and how and when the object was burned. The latter two are divined from markings and signs in the ashes.

**Lv 15:** Make your senses immune to fire (e.g. be able to see clearly through a raging house fire). An Auram Requisite may be necessary if smoke is present as well.

### Vision of Heat's Light: Lv 20

Spell Focus: A Cat's Eye Gem (+3)

R: Near/Sight, D: Sun./Moon

Allows you to "see" the heat of objects that are nearly human body temperature or higher. Excellent for use in the dark, but it doesn't give true vision.

### Words of the Flickering Flame: Lv 25

Spell Focus: Ashes in Mouth (+3)

R: Reach/Near, D: Conc.

Allows you to converse with fires, which are commonly very chaotic and distractible. Promising them more fuel to burn might keep their interest. Fires are mostly aware of what they've burned, but they have a limited awareness of what goes on around them as well.

### Sense of the Fires Nearby: Lv 30

R: 1 mile, D: Conc., Ritual

Lets you know the location and size of every fire larger than a candle within one mile. Candle and smaller fires can be detected within one hundred paces. With an Intelligence + Concentration stress roll of 13+, you can concentrate on one of these fires, and get some ideas of what's around it (e.g., people, food, tents). A Botch on the roll may mean that the people spied upon detect you in the fire. A piece of burned wood or wick is needed to see into a specific fire. It acts as an Arcane Connection, through the Law of Sympathy.

# Muto Ignem Spells

Changing fire to another element (e.g., water) usually makes the spell at least 5 Levels higher than a comparable Guideline spell offered below. Making a minor change, such as brightening a fire for an instant, usually involves a spell a few Levels lower than its comparable Guideline.

Lv 5: Change a fire the size of a torch.

### The Many-Hued Conflagration: Lv 5

Spell Focus: A Ruby (+5)

R: Near/Sight, D: Inst.

Makes a fire burn brightly for an instant. Those looking at the fire must make Stamina rolls of 7+ or be blinded for one Round by the multicolored lights.

Lv 10: Change a fire no larger than a bonfire.

### Show of the Flames and Smoke: Lv 10

Spell Focus: Multi-Colored Streamers (+3)

R: Near/Sight, D: Conc.

Causes smoke of different colors, streams of flame, and strange popping and sizzling noises to come from a fire. The effect is so spectacular that onlookers are either entranced or horrified, depending on the circumstances. The pyrotechnics might ignite nearby flammables and cause minor burns to those within two paces of the fire.

### Hornet Fire: Lv 15

Spell Focus: A Stinging Insect (+1)

R: Near/Sight, D: Conc.

Turns a fire into a swarm of fireballs, each the size of a large insect, that fly and harass at your command. Their burning touch gives all those you indicate within seven paces of the fire a -2 penalty on all rolls and two extra Botch dice. If using the Focus, the stinging insect is thrown into the fire.

### Prison of Flames: Lv 15

Spell Focus: A Small Iron Cage (+1)

R: Near/Sight, D: Sun.

Turns a bonfire into a prison shaped like a miniature castle. A person thrown into the middle is not burned, but takes 1d10+25 damage if he tries to escape.

### Trapping the Fire: Lv 20

R: Reach/Near, D: Perm., Ritual

This enchantment places the heat and flames of a campfire into a small, very hard object, such as a gem or a piece of metal. If the object is broken, the flame returns, but dies if there is nothing to burn. The object is as hot and bright as coal.

Lv 20: Transform a house fire.

### Flames of Sculpted Ice: Lv 25

Spell Focus: Essence of a Water Elemental (+3)

R: Near/Sight, D: Spec., Aquam

Turns a house fire into ice. The ice forms beautiful sculptures of leaping flame, until the ice begins to melt. When the ice has melted halfway, the flames start again, but probably don't spread because of wet surroundings.

Lv 30: Change a large number of fires (within Sight).

# Perdo Ignem Spells

Spells to destroy some aspect of fire, such as heat or light, are usually a little more tricky to cast than implied by the Guidelines below. Such spells are therefore higher in Level than the Guidelines for a specified size of fire. Range for the spells remains the same, though.

Lv 5: Destroy a fire no larger than human-sized, such as a bonfire (*Quench the Rippling Flames*)

Lv 10: Remove all of the heat from something no larger than a small box.

### Soothe the Raging Flames: Lv 10

Spell Focus: A Chrysolite (+5)

R: Near/Sight, D: Inst.

Eradicates the heat of a bonfire, which continues to burn until it burns itself out. The remaining flames do not spread or harm things. During the casting of the spell, the chrysolite is crushed, if the Spell Focus is used.

### Winter's Icy Touch: Lv 10

Spell Focus: A Garnet (+5)

R: Near/Sight, D: Sun./Inst.

Causes the target to feel a slight chill, and lose body heat (Stamina roll of 10+ or lose a Short-Term Fatigue Level). Also, makes one susceptible to colds and other minor, but irritating illnesses. If used, the garnet is crushed during the casting of the spell. Garnets provide protection against illness, so destroying one Sympathetically helps the spell. Casting Requisite is Animál for beasts, and Córporem for people.

Lv 15: Destroy a fire up to the size of a housefire.

### Conjuration of the Indubitable Cold: Lv 20

Spell Focus: A Garnet (+3)

R: Spec./Sight, D: Inst.

Cools the air within 10 paces of the caster, leaving it a little below freezing. All non-living things are chilled thoroughly, not just on the surface. All living things (except the caster) lose one Short-Term Fatigue Level and must make a Stamina roll of 6+ to avoid losing a second. House fires become as small as campfires, bonfires become as small as torchfires, and campfires and smaller fires go out.

Lv 25: Remove all the heat from a human-sized creature.

### Well Without Light: Lv 25

Spell Focus: Black Onyx (+1)

R: Near/Sight, D: Ring/Perm.

Creates a 20 pace radius ring in which no light can enter or exist. Only spells greater than Level 25 can create light within this ring. When casting this spell, Magi typically clench a hand into a fist, possibly grasping a black onyx, and the darkness

flows out of the fist, like a living entity, until it grows to encompass the entire area. The black onyx is a stone commonly associated with darkness and death.

**Lv 30:** Destroy all flames in Range of Sight.

### Wizard's Eclipse: Lv 30

R: Spec., D: 5 minutes, Ritual

The sun is eclipsed over a circle of one mile radius by a magical interference that covers the ground with a darkness equal to night. For every extra pawn of *vis* that is added, the Range extends by half a mile. The eclipse is very sudden, and lasts in its totality for five minutes. Superstitious villagers are panicked by this, and are quite sure of the impending end of the world.

## Rego Ignem Spells

**Lv 5:** Control a fire no larger than a torch.

### Tremulous Vault of the Torch's Flame: Lv 5

Spell Focus: A Cat's Eye Gem (+5)
R: Reach (10 feet)/Near, D: Inst., Aimed

Causes a torch fire to quiver a few seconds and then leap up to ten feet. You need a Targeting roll to hit a specific target. The flame stays at the spot it hits if it can burn there. Otherwise, it simply singes the spot and goes out (+6 damage).

**Lv 10:** Control a fire no larger than a bonfire.

### Light Shaft of the Night: Lv 10

Spell Focus: Quartz (+5)
R: Near/Sight, D: Conc.

Collects moonbeams and starlight into a single vertical shaft of soft, silvery light that moves under your control. It illuminates an area fifteen paces across with light nearly equal to starlight (if the moon is out) or moonlight (if the moon is not out). If the sky is overcast, the spell does not work. Can be cast under the night sky only.

### Leap of the Fire: Lv 15

Spell Focus: A Cat's Eye Gem (+3)
R: Near/Sight, D: Inst., Aimed +2

Makes a bonfire jump up to ten paces, where it catches if there is fuel, or burns out if there is none. Make Targeting roll to hit a target; the flames do 1d10+12 damage.

**Lv 20:** Control a fire no larger than a housefire.

### Ward Against Heat and Flames: Lv 25

Spell Focus: Scale of a Flame Drake (+3)
R: Touch./Near, D: Sun./Year

Keeps heat and fire at bay, unable to approach within one pace of the target, making the target immune to damage from flames or heat of intensity less than a house fire. The target gets a +15 Soak on all fire-related damage. Any fire that is smaller than a house fire in intensity (i.e., has equal to or less than a +15 damage bonus) doesn't penetrate the ward. Such fires simply dim at the protected person's passing and flare back up after he's gone.

**Lv 30:** Control a fire with a damage bonus of up to +20.

### Burst of the Sweeping Flames: Lv 30

Spell Focus: A Ruby (+3)
R: Sight, D: Inst., Req: Creo

This spell causes a fire to explode outwards from its source along the ground, as if a giant wind blows on it from above. The fire travels for no more than ten paces and ferociously ignites anything in its path. The original fire is left dead, but in all probability, a number of new fires are started. The flames cause +5 to +20 damage, depending on the size of the original fire.

# IMÁGONEM SPELLS

Imágonem is the Form of sensations and illusion. By using Imágonem, a Magus can alter what others perceive. Imágonem, however, means "image," not "illusion." Thus, one creates, transforms, perceives, destroys and controls images, not necessarily illusions. A clairvoyance spell, therefore, is Intéllego Imágonem because it detects real images. By manipulating sensations, however, a Magus can create effective illusions.

An image works on the senses, not on the mind, so an unthinking beast is as likely to believe an image as an imaginative human. Nevertheless, Imágonem spells are still most effective at fouling the communication on which human society depends.

Fantastic beasts are likely to be fooled by illusions, as are the simpler undead. Demons are very hard to deceive, while faeries often see through illusions and manipulate them to fool the caster in turn. Certain members of the Church have proven remarkably adept at discerning truth from illusion, though the talent is not dependable.

A Ritual for special attention is *Eyes of the Past* (InIm 20). It sees into the past, and is used, when necessary, to find out who deserves Hermetic vengeance. Magi who break the Code of Hermes can be found out through this and other spells.

Imágonem spells require a great variety of Requisites for the specific things they change or mimic. Perception + Finesse rolls are required to mimic a specific image, such as the visage of a duke. The higher the roll, the better you can fool people. You get a bonus to your roll for familiarity with what you are mimicking (-3 for an unfamiliar object, +3 for highly familiar objects, or when you have the subject available for modeling). For mimicking people, a roll of 6+ lets you fool acquaintances of the person, 9+ fools friends, and 12+ fools close friends and relatives. Use a similar scale for mimicking objects. If you Botch the Finesse roll, you may think the image is satisfactory, but it's immediately seen through once in use.

# Creo Imágonem Spells

The Guidelines given generally allow for the creation of a still, noiseless illusion. Sounds usually add 5 Levels to the illusion, and talking, 10 (this includes any specific types of sounds). Other sensations (such as warmth, cold, or pain) add about 5 Levels as well. Having the illusion move adds 10 Levels to its casting. Thus, to create a fire (less than man-sized, 5th Level) that moves and crackles (+5) and warms (+5) takes about 15 Levels. Alternatively, a man (Lv 5) that speaks (+10) and moves about (+10) is 25th Level. Keep in mind, however, that these are just guidelines.

As noted in the general section on Imágonem, all spells have Requisites appropriate to what is created.

Wizard's Sigils can be very obvious in Creo Imágonem spells. The illusions commonly have some small quirk that marks them to a Magus. For example, illusions cast by Fortunatus of Jerbiton often have some small religious icon worked into their structure, due to the manner in which he invents his spells.

## Restoration of the Lost Image: Gen.

Spell Focus: An Icon (+3)

R: Near/Sight, D: Inst.

Cancels the effects of a PeIm spell that masks some sensation, such as an invisibility spell, if you can roll the target spell's Level on a stress die + the Level of your spell. The icon which may be used with this spell must be representative of what is being restored (e.g., a human to destroy invisibility, a rose to restore smell).

Lv 5: Create a still, silent image, no larger than human size (*Fragile Image of the Painted Statue*).

Lv 10: Create an illusionary object up to the size of a room.

## Image of the Inanimate Thing: Lv 10

Spell Focus: A Model of the Item Created (+3)

R: Reach/Sight, D: Sun./Year

Creates an inanimate object up to one pace in each dimension.

## Phantasm of the Talking Head: Lv 10

Spell Focus: A Mask (+3)

R: Near, D: Spec.

Creates an illusionary face on a wall or other flat object. The visage can speak up to 20 words before the spell expires, but cannot sing.

## Phantasmal Fire: Lv 15

Spell Focus: A Ruby (+3)

R: Near/Sight, D: Sun./Year, Req: Ignem

Makes an image of a fire that dances, illuminates, crackles and (apparently) warms. It does not spread, burn, or protect against cold. Makes a great joke at gatherings of House Flambeau, although creating a real fire is even more popular.

## Phantasmal Animal: Lv 20

Spell Focus: A Topaz (+3)

R: Reach/Near, D: Sun./Year., Req: Animál

Creates an image of any animal or beast up to the size of a horse (Size +2). Under your direct mental command, it moves about and makes appropriate noises. You need to be able to concentrate whenever you wish to direct the illusion to move in some manner.

## Phantasm of the Human Form: Lv 25

Spell Focus: A Violet Amethyst (+1)

R: Reach/Near, D: Sun./Year, Req: Córporem

Makes an image of a clothed and equipped person. Under your direct, unspoken command, the person can move about, speak, and behave as a human does.

## The Shadow of Human Life: Lv 40

Spell Focus: A Violet Amethyst (+1)

R: Reach/Near, D: Sun./Year, Req: Córporem, Mentem

The human image created (as in *Phantasm of the Human Form*) has limited freedom and simulated intellect. It functions as an independent human, albeit a stupid one, capable of interpreting general orders in new situations.

# Intéllego Imágonem Spells

Generally, these spells have the least to do with illusions of all the Imágonem spells, because one detects an image without altering or controlling it. These spells improve upon your senses by bringing in images (usually sounds and sights) not normally available.

## Discern the Images of Truth and Falsehood: Gen.

Spell Focus: A Sapphire (+3)

R: Near/Sight, D: Conc./Moon

You can tell whether an image has been created or altered through a spell, seeing both the original and false images in the case of alterations. Roll a stress die + Level + 5 when you cast the spell; any illusion spells higher than your roll are not discerned. If you Botch the roll, you mistake illusions for the real thing and reality for illusion.

## Discern Own Illusions: Lv 5

Spell Focus: A Glass Eye (+2)

R: Body/Touch, D: Sun./Moon

Casting this spell lets you or another touched see through all your own illusions.

## The Ear for Distant Voice: Lv 20

Spell Focus: A Rock Crystal (+3)

R: 100 miles/400 miles, D: Conc.

You can hear what is happening in the place you designate. You must have an Arcane Connection with the place or with a person there.

## Eyes of the Past: Lv 20

R: Near, D: Conc., Ritual

Shows what happened in your present location at a specific time in the past, up to five years ago. You can see what happened in the past as if you had been standing where you are when the events took place. When looking at the past, you must view a continuous slice of time. You cannot scan around or quickly run through events.

## Summoning the Distant Images: Lv 35

Spell Focus: A Rock Crystal (+1)

R: 100 miles/400 miles, D: Conc.

You can see and hear what is happening in a distant place with which you have some sort of Arcane Connection, either to the location or a person there.

### Visions of the Wandering Eye: Lv 45

R: 10 miles, D: Conc., Ritual

Lets you view any area within range that you have an Arcane Connection with, from any perspective. The Connection can be an item from an area, or can be an item from a person. You can change perspectives, but each change requires an Intelligence + Concentration roll of 12+. If beings foreign to the area enter it while you watch, you sense their location. People watched with this spell may detect your action with a Magic Resistance roll.

# Muto Imágonem Spells

These are useful and powerful illusion spells, altering the visual image, noises, smell, or taste of some object or being. The image remains altered without the caster's concentration and adapts itself appropriately to the medium. The accuracy of duplication depends on the caster's knowledge of the subject. For instance, a Magus who wants to make a voice like that of a specific person must be familiar with the voice to be mimicked. Those more familiar with the face, voice, body, or other aspect being mimicked might see through an illusion by mundane means (e.g., "Duke Tybol, didn't your scar used to be on your left cheek?").

All of these transformations involve objects up to the size of a man. To deal with something up to the size of a room takes a spell 10 Levels higher.

### Restore the Image Transformed: Gen.

Spell Focus: An Icon (+3)

R: Near/Sight, D: Inst.

Restores to normal an image that has been transformed with a Muto Imágonem spell, if you can match the target spell's Level on a die + the Level of your spell. If using a Spell Focus, the icon must represent the image that you are trying to restore.

### Taste of the Spices and Herbs: Lv 5

Spell Focus: Spices (+3)

R: Reach/Near, D: Sun./Perm

Food or drink affected by this spell tastes exactly as you designate. Casting Requisite: Aquam for drinks, Animál for meat, Herbam for vegetable. This spell is lower Level than the above Guideline because of the spell's short Range.

**Lv 10:** Change the image of an object to make it appear in a different state. Change something small about an object, such as color or taste. Change a person's voice or hair color.

### Aura of Ennobled Presence: Lv 10

Spell Focus: A Violet Amethyst (+5)

R: Near/Sight, D: Sun./Year, Req: Córporem, Mentem

The target appears more forceful, authoritative, and believable. Numerous subtle changes in appearance effect this change, including slight illumination of the face, a more erect posture, and a louder and smoother voice. The target's Presence increases by +1, or rises to 0, whichever produces the higher result, and others are more willing to follow the character's orders or advice (+3 to Social Talent rolls).

### Illusion of the Altered Image: Lv 10

Spell Focus: An Icon (+3)

R: Near/Sight, D: Sun./Year

Causes an object or illusion up to the size of a door to appear different, but still normal. For instance, a door can appear open instead of closed, or a person can appear dirty instead of clean. You change the apparent state of the object, but not the object itself. The icon used with this spell must represent the image you are trying to create. Casting Requisites: appropriate Form for the target.

### Notes of a Delightful Sound: Lv 10

Spell Focus: A Musical Triangle (+3)

R: Near/Sight, D: Sun./Year

Causes any sounds, particularly music, to sound especially clear and sonorous. The notes are clearer, sharper and more distinct. Add +2 to Communication rolls and +5 to music-related Ability rolls.

**Lv 15:** Change the image of an object as long as it remains the same type of object.

### Disguise of the Transformed Image: Lv 15

Spell Focus: An Icon (+3)

R: Near/Sight, D: Sun./Year, Req: Córporem

Makes someone look different, though at least passably human. The icon must resemble the changed appearance of the person.

**Lv 20:** Utterly change the image of an object. Make an object look transparent (*Transparency of New-Blown Glass*).

### Image Phantom: Lv 20

Spell Focus: A Cocoon (+1)

R: Near/Sight, D: Sun./Year

Any one thing, including a living thing, can be made to look like something else of approximately the same shape and size. The illusion is broken by actions that show it to be false. For instance, a person has to curl up to be made to look like a rock. Standing up or being touched shows the illusion to be false and ends the spell. Casting Requisite: appropriate Form for the target.

**Lv 30:** Cause everything within Range of Sight to be transformed.

### Visions of the Infernal Terrors: Lv 30

Spell Focus: A Hand of Glory (+3)

R: Near/Sight, D: Sun./Year, Req: Mentem

Causes everything that the target sees to look and sound terrifying. The world looks basically the same, but everything is hideously transformed. The target must make a Stamina + appropriate Personality Trait roll to see what the effects are: 0 — scared to death; 1 to 5 — incapacitated with fear, -1 Stamina (permanent); 6 to 9 — incapacitated with fear; 10 to 15 — flee but fight at -5 if cornered or obstructed; 16+ carry on, but at -4 on all rolls. The nature of the Personality Trait used determines how it affects the Stamina roll. A positive Trait, like Brave, makes you resistant to fear, while a Cowardly Trait reduces the result of your roll. A hand of glory refers to the hand of a convicted murderer. It is a very evil Focus, only used in the worst of spells.

# Perdo Imágonem Spells

In addition to destroying created images, these spells mask sensations of things, making wine tasteless, sneaks silent, and Magi invisible.

### Dispel the Phantom Image: Gen.

Spell Focus: Black Onyx (+3)

R: Near/Sight, D: Inst.

Destroys the image from any CrIm spell whose Level you match on a die + the Level of your spell.

**Lv 5:** Destroy something minor about a small image, such as color or taste.

### Taste of the Dulled Tongue: Lv 5

Spell Focus: A Tongue (+2)

R: Reach/Near, D: Sun./Year

Hides the taste of any substance, liquid or solid. Casting Requisite: appropriate Form for the target.

**Lv 10:** Make a small object invisible. Destroy something minor about a man-sized image.

### Removal of the Conspicuous Sigil: Lv 10

Spell Focus: A Fern Seed (+5)

R: Reach/Near, D: Sun./Year

Marks, grooves, runes, writings, and other such things can be obscured so that they are not visible, but the overall shape of the medium remains constant. For example, runes carved into a sword blade can be made invisible, making the sword appear normal. Fern seeds may only be found on Midsummer's Eve; during the rest of the year they are nonexistent. Casting Requisites: appropriate Form for the target.

**Lv 15:** Make a man-sized image invisible.

### Illusion of Cool Flames: Lv 15

Spell Focus: A Coal (+1)

R: Reach/Near, D: Sun./Year, Req: Ignem

A hot object such as a fire seems to lose its heat and drop to the surrounding temperature. It still, however, has its normal beneficial and harmful effects (i.e., a glowing coal still burns someone's hand, though it does not feel hot).

### Invisibility of the Standing Wizard: Lv 15

Spell Focus: A Fern Seed (+3)

R: Self/Touch, D: Sun./Year, Req: Córporem

You become invisible, but the spell is broken if you move (aside from breathing and shifting slightly in place), speak, or are touched by any being larger than a mouse.

**Lv 25:** Make the contents of a room invisible.

### Chamber of Invisibility: Lv 25

Spell Focus: A Fern Seed (+1)

R: Near/Sight, D: Sun./Year, Req: Córporem

Causes a motionless group of creatures to become invisible (affected creatures can see each other). You designate a circular area which can hold up to ten beings. Any affected character who takes a step, makes a noise, or is touched makes everyone become visible. (The required discipline may be difficult for ill-trained Grogs and free-spirited Companions.)

### Silence of the Smothered Sound: Lv 25

Spell Focus: A Feather (+3)

R: Near, D: Sun./Year

Makes one being or object incapable of producing sound by any means. Magi who cannot utter their magic words suffer -10 to their spell casting rolls. Casting Requisites: appropriate Form for the target.

### Veil of Invisibility: Lv 30

Spell Focus: A Fern Seed (+1)

R: Self/Touch, D: Sun./Year, Req: Córporem

You become completely invisible, regardless of what you do, but still cast a reflection in a mirror.

# Rego Imágonem Spells

These spells make things appear to be elsewhere from where they actually are.

### Restore the Moved Image: Gen.

Spell Focus: An Icon (+3)

R: Near/Sight, D: Inst.

Cancels a ReIm spell that moves an image, putting the image back where it belongs, if you can match the spell's Level on a die + the Level of your spell. The icon which may be used with this spell must represent the image that is being restored.

**Lv 5:** Make a small object appear in a slightly different place (up to one pace away) as long as both the original and the image don't move and aren't touched. Shift the position of your voice or of a spell, or something else minor.

**Lv 10:** Make a man-sized object appear in a slightly different place as long as the original and image do not move and are not touched.

### Illusion of the Shifted Image: Lv 10

Spell Focus: An Idol of the Object "Moved" (+3)

R: Near/Sight, D: Sun./Year

Makes any person or object appear to be a pace away from its actual position. The image cannot be placed in a solid object. As soon as the original or image is touched or moves, the spell ends. Casting Requisites: appropriate Form for target.

### The Captive Voice: Lv 15

Spell Focus: A Copper Drawstring (+3)

R: Near/Sight, D: Sun./Year

Captures a person's voice and places it in a bag. The person may not speak unless the bag is open, in which case the voice comes from the bag, not the victim's mouth. If the victim screams while the bag is shut, the bag vibrates visibly. Casting Requisites: Córporem for humans and Animál for animals.

**Lv 20:** Make a man-sized moving object appear in a different place. Move the image of everything that's unmoving within a Range of Near.

### Image from the Wizard Torn: Lv 20

Spell Focus: An Opal (+3)

R: 50 miles, D: Conc., Req: Córporem, Intéllego

Your image separates from your body and moves at your command. It can speak in your voice, and you can see through its eyes. You can use this spell to create a double; to separate from the image, instead of having the image separate from you. Thus, someone watching is unable to tell which is the double and which is you. You must make an Intelligence + Concentration roll for each solid object the image passes through and for each mile it travels. If you wish the image to be able to leave your sight, you must have an Arcane Connection to yourself (e.g., a fingernail or a lock of hair) present when you cast the spell. That Connection becomes an integral part of the image, and falls to the ground when the spell ends, at whatever point the image is last at.

### Wizard's Sidestep: Lv 20

Spell Focus: An Opal (+3)

R: Self/Touch, D: Sun., Req: Córporem

Your image appears up to one pace from where you actually are, so attacks aimed there are likely to miss you. Whenever the image is successfully struck, it disappears and reappears in another spot. Each time it reappears, there is a 1 in 10 chance it returns to your body, ending the spell.

**Lv 25:** Change a small aspect of a large object or area.

**Lv 30:** Change the image of an unmoving object that you can see.

### Confusion of the Insane Vibrations: Lv 30

Spell Focus: Quartz (+1)

R: Spec., D: Sun./Year

Everything within Range of your sight seems to vibrate back and forth at varying high speeds. In addition, sounds and scents are displaced and seem to come from the wrong areas. Anyone trying to fight in these circumstances suffers -3 on Attack and Defense scores, and suffers two extra Botch dice. Navigation is exceedingly difficult. People in the area are likely to become desperate and terribly confused. The visual effects of this spell are negated in complete darkness or by closing one's eyes. Quartz has associations with the moon, and thus lunacy.

### Illusion of the Misplaced Castle: Lv 30

Spell Focus: An Icon (+1)

R: Sight, D: Sun./Year, Req: Terram

Moves the image of any building of castle-size or smaller up to one mile distant from its actual location. The icon must represent the image that is being moved.

### Haunt of the Living Ghost: Lv 40

Spell Focus: An Opal (+1)

R: 300 miles/1200 miles, D: Conc., Req: Córporem

With this spell, you can project your own image to any designated spot. You can speak, hear, and see through the image. The image must appear in some medium, such as a fire or a pool, and the spell has a Casting Requisite appropriate to this medium. You must also have some Arcane Connection with the spot to which you wish to project your image. Each minute requires a Concentration roll of 9+. Very powerful Magi use this spell to attend intercovenant meetings without traveling the intervening distance.

# MENTEM SPELLS

Mentem spells govern thoughts, emotions, minds, and memories. All intelligent minds are affected by Mentem spells, while the minds of beasts are affected only by Animál spells.

Normal people can get better than normal resistance against spells of the mind if they are especially dedicated, impassioned, or desperate. For instance, a parent defending home and family might get a +3 on rolls to withstand a malign spell, or get a Resistance roll where one is not normally applicable.

Since ghosts are essentially minds without bodies, many Mentem spells work on them. Emotions, however, arise from the body's humors and organs (remember the medieval paradigm?), so non-corporeal creatures, such as ghosts, do not have normal passions and are therefore not affected by Mentem spells that influence emotions. However, spells that oppose a ghost's Spirit Might directly (e.g., *Lay to Rest the Haunting Spirit* and *Coerce the Spirits of the Night*) need not make a magic Penetration roll.

Since the effects of Mentem spells are not usually visible, they give you a great deal of power when dealing with the common folk. Even spells requiring eye contact are relatively inconspicuous when cast without voice or gestures, but only more powerful Magi can cast spells this way in the Dominion.

The majority of Mentem spells have a Range of Eye (eye contact).

## Creo Mentem Spells

In addition to healing minds, these spells can also create thoughts, emotions and memories in another person's mind.

Typical Sigils for Creo Mentem spells involve some small quirk in what is created. A specific idea may lie in the background of all memories created, for example.

### Return of Mental Lucidity: Gen

R: Reach, D: Inst., Ritual

Cancels the effects (short of death) of a malign Mentem spell if you can match the Level of the spell with this Ritual's Level + a die.

### Words of the Unbroken Silence: Lv 5

Spell Focus: A Clear Crystal (+2)

R: Near/Sight, D: Inst.

Lets you say two words directly to the mind of the target, who can tell that the words are supernatural and who can recognize your voice.

Lv 10: Make someone understand a concept more easily.

Lv 15: Create an emotion in someone's mind.

### Panic of the Trembling Heart: Lv 15

Spell Focus: A Mouse (+1)

R: Eye/Sight, D: Sun./Moon

Creates an overpowering fear of a specific object, person or place.

### Rising Ire: Lv 15

Spell Focus: A Ruby (+3)

R: Eye/Sight, D: Sun./Moon

Makes the target furious at someone or something (your choice). An appropriate Passion or Personality Trait roll (e.g., Calm) of 9+ can hold the anger in, but the anger is felt strongly regardless of the roll. The ruby is associated with Mars and war.

### Memory of the Distant Dream: Lv 20

Spell Focus: A Sprig of Rosemary (+1)

R: Eye/Sight, D: Sun./Moon

Inserts a full and complete memory into a person's mind. When cast with the Spell Focus, the rosemary, commonly associated with good memory, is crumbled and blown toward the victim. If the target gives your memory some thought and concentration, and makes an Intelligence roll of 8+, the memory is revealed as false.

### Pains of the Perpetual Worry: Lv 20

Spell Focus: Onyx (+3)

R: Eye/Sight, D: Moon/Year

Gives someone a recurrent sense of anxiety, a fear of something one does not know; a fear of everything; a fear of nothing; a nagging, taunting, painful emotion. To have this spell cast on you is truly a curse. (The Western world's first taste of nihilism.) Onyx keeps sadness away from the wielder. By crushing it during the casting, the caster is able to Sympathetically bring sadness to the target.

### Weight of a Thousand Hells: Lv 25

Spell Focus: A Hand of Glory (+3)

R: Eye/Sight, D: Moon/Perm.

Causes the victim to feel the despair and sorrow of a thousand sinners in Hell. One feels despair, anguish and pain. This is a truly horrible spell, for the victim loses almost all motivation and earthly cares. All one can feel is one's own pain — endless, inexorable and searing. Appropriate Passion or Personality Trait rolls suffer a harmful adjustment of 5 points, and the target suffers -2 on any rolls that require thought or concentration. The target has a strong tendency to do nothing but brood. A hand of glory is a very powerful ingredient in many necromantic spells and diabolic summonings. It refers to the hand of a recently dead, condemned murderer. Its use in this spell gives a good indication of the spell's foulness.

### Gift of Reason: Lv 30

Spell Focus: A Sapphire (+1)

R: Eye/Sight, D: Conc./Sun

Gives the target the ability to reason clearly and understand ideas without the bias or distractions that normally interfere with thinking. Strong commitment to a cause, a strong personality, or a stubborn personality nullifies the effects of this spell. Even a relatively stupid person is able to understand difficult concepts. The sapphire used brings wisdom, and is often worn by nobles and rulers for exactly that reason.

# Intéllego Mentem Spells

These spells are superb for cutting through the confusion of social interaction and the endless banter of the rabble. The InAn spells which deal with the mind may also be used for ideas and guidelines for this section. Common Sigils for InMe spells usually involve information being transmitted in strange ways. For example, when communicating with Marlo of Tremere's version of *Tongue of the Folk*, the caster always sounds haughty and arrogant.

Lv 5: Sense the state of consciousness of one intelligent being (e.g., asleep, awake, meditating, dead, drugged, insane, comatose).

Lv 10: Sense the most powerful emotion in a being.

### Sight of the Transparent Motive: Lv 10

Spell Focus: A Clear Crystal (+3)

R: Near/Sight, D: Inst.

Detects the general motive most powerfully influencing the target at the moment. General motives are such things as fear, anger, and greed, not specific things, like the desire to look good before one's superiors.

### Perception of the Conflicting Motives: Lv 15

Spell Focus: A Sapphire (+3)

R: Near/Sight, D: Inst.

You can detect the conflicting motives behind one target's actions. Thus, you can learn that a guard feels conflict between fear and duty. This spell is often used before application of a Muto spell, since it is much easier to change a target's emotions after you've sensed them than it is to create emotions.

Lv 20: Speak with any one human (*Tongue of the Folk*). Read the surface thoughts of a person.

### Frosty Breath of the Spoken Lie: Lv 20

Spell Focus: An Almond (+1)

R: Eye/Sight, D: Conc.

For as long as you maintain this spell, the target exhales a misty breath, as one does during winter, with each spoken lie. Small bits of ice form on the person's lips if the lie is particularly severe. In winter, when breath is visible anyway, lies produce a greater than normal amount of mist (it literally billows out). A target who makes a Communication + Guile roll of 18+ can determine whether any given statement will be taken by the spell as a lie. The spell can be avoided through extensive and judicious application of CrAu and PeAu spells, and a demon is able to manipulate it in any way he wishes, as demons are the embodiment of deception, and are never caught in a lie if they do not wish it. It is House Quaesitor who brought the Order this spell, and it is a very poor Quaesitor who is without it. If the Spell Focus is used, it must be crushed during the casting of the spell.

Lv 25: Read the last day's memory from one person.

### Posing the Silent Question: Lv 25

Spell Focus: A Sapphire (+1)

R: Eye/Sight, D: Spec.

You can ask one silent mental question of the target, the answer to which you then detect. Veracity of the answer is limited by the knowledge of the target. Questions about what the target "would do if. . ." are often inaccurate. You might get what the target thinks he would do, not necessarily what he would really do. The target of this spell does not notice the questioning unless he makes his Magic Resistance roll.

### Thoughts Within Babble: Lv 25

Spell Focus: A Quill (+3)

R: Body/Touch, D: Conc.

You get general ideas as to the nature of human speech and writing in any language, unless the speech or writing is coded. Perception or Communication rolls are needed for difficult exchanges.

### Peering into the Mortal Mind: Lv 30

Spell Focus: A Sapphire (+1)

R: Eye/Sight, D: Conc.

You can thoroughly probe and understand the mind of the target, including immediate and long-term motives, personal strengths, weaknesses, and other pertinent information. The entire process takes about an hour, with half the relevant information available within ten minutes, but more subtle knowledge open only to long-lasting probes. The sapphire brings wisdom.

# Muto Mentem Spells

Since these spells literally change people's minds, they are quite powerful.

### Vision of the Haunting Spirit: Lv 5

Spell Focus: Green Turquoise (+5)

R: Near/Sight, D: Inst.

All spirits within sight and range become visible (if they can do so normally). They can then turn invisible again, but are likely to be interested in whoever has cast this spell on them. Green turquoise has associations with necromancy and other evil magics.

In Asaron of Flambeau's version of this spell, a small patch of the ghost's forehead, in the shape of a tongue of flame, is not made visible, showing his Sigil.

### Subtle Shift of Heart: Lv 10

Spell Focus: A Figure (+3)

R: Eye/Sight, D: Sun./Moon

Subtly change an emotion into a related but different one. For instance, loathing can become hate, and greed can become jealousy. The figure used must represent the spell's target.

### Enchantment of Detachment: Lv 15

Spell Focus: A Figure (+3)

R: Eye/Sight, D: Inst.

Calms and greatly lowers the intensity of the target's current emotions.

### Emotion of Reversed Intentions: Lv 20

Spell Focus: A Ruby (+3)

R: Eye/Sight, D: Sun./Moon

The main emotion influencing a character at the time of casting is replaced by its opposite over the next minute. The new emotion is felt as strongly as the original, but lacks justification, and can therefore be talked out of someone. Intelligence roll of 8+ to resist.

### Recollection of Memories Never Quite Lived: Lv 20

Spell Focus: Rosemary (+1)

R: Eye/Sight, D: Inst.

Changes the target's memory of a detail into a similar, though different memory. The target is no more sure of this manufactured memory than of the authentic one, so strange fabrications may well be discovered to be false.

Lv 30: Utterly change a person's mind.

### Mind of the Beast: Lv 30

Spell Focus: A Topaz (+1)

R: Eye/Sight, D: Sun./Moon, Req: Animál

You turn the mind of the target into that of an animal of your choice. The victim acts and thinks like that animal as much as possible. Usually amusing.

# Perdo Mentem Spells

### Lay to Rest the Haunting Spirit: Gen.

Spell Focus: A Green Turquoise (+3)

R: Near/Sight, D: Inst.

Destroys a single, non-corporeal spirit if your roll on a stress die + spell Level at least equals double the ghost's current Spirit Might. Philosophers concur that the spirit

goes to the afterlife, or is perhaps weakened to helplessness, but is not actually destroyed. (Souls, after all, are immortal.)

### Tip of the Tongue: Lv 5

Spell Focus: A Figure (+5)

R: Near/Sight, D: 1 minute

Causes the target to forget one word of your choosing. The harder the character tries to remember the word, the harder it is to remember. It is incredibly frustrating. The target can come up with the word by making an Intelligence + Concentration roll of 9+. The figure used in the spell must represent the person you are trying to affect.

### Trust of Childlike Faith: Lv 10

Spell Focus: A Lock of Child's Hair (+3)

R: Near/Sight, D: 1 minute/Sun.

The target loses judgement and believes almost any passable lie for the duration of the spell. Intelligence + Stamina roll of 7+ to resist. Truly incredible lies allow easier Resistance rolls.

### Calm the Motion of the Heart: Lv 15

Spell Focus: A Figure (+3)

R: Eye/Sight, D: Inst.

Removes one emotion from the target until it appears again naturally. An angry person stops being angry and a curious one stops being inquisitive (good for keeping an apprentice's nose out of your immediate business).

### Loss of But a Moment's Memory: Lv 20

Spell Focus: Rosemary (+1)

R: Eye/Sight, D: Inst., Req: Intéllego

Removes up to five continuous minutes from a target's memory, leaving a blank. You target the loss of memory to a specific event or time. With an Intelligence roll of 8+, the target realizes that memories of a certain period are missing. This Ease Factor can change, depending on how important the missing memory is and what sort of circumstances surrounded the event. Careful introspection restores memory.

### Passion's Lost Feeling: Lv 20

Spell Focus: A Figure (+3)

R: Eye/Sight, D: Inst.

The target is unable to feel any sort of emotion and acts listlessly, without motivation or cares, until taking an hour's rest or meditation. Intelligence + Stamina roll of 11+ to resist, and dire need allows additional Resistance rolls.

### Blessing of Childlike Bliss: Lv 25

Spell Focus: A Lock of a Child's Hair (+1)

R: Eye/Sight, D: Inst.

Reduces an adult mind to a child's level. The target solves problems, reasons, and expresses emotions as would a three year old. Magi affected cannot cast spells. At first, anyway, the target is likely to be happy at having lost a world of cares and troubles that are no longer imaginable.

### Black Whisper: Lv 30

Spell Focus: None

R: Spec., D: Inst.

You must whisper a magic sentence in the target's ear. It takes several seconds to speak the sentence, so an unwilling, able-bodied target can stop you. If you speak the whole sentence, the target must make a Stamina roll of 15+ or go completely insane. You need not use your hands for this spell, but you must be able to speak.

**Lv 40:** Utterly destroy a mind on command.

### Poisoning the Will: Lv 50

R: Sight, D: Year/Perm., Ritual

The caster curses a place, be it a valley, town, city, or Covenant. The curse gradually saps the will and vitality from the people there. They become less energetic and slowly stop caring about the place, what happens there, other people, and finally about themselves. Colors seem more drab and the days longer, and there is an all-pervading sense of boredom and lassitude. Strong-willed individuals, and those with strong Passions or Personality Traits are less affected, but still suffer to an extent. All Passion and Personality Trait rolls while in the area suffer a -3 modifier. This spell affects only those who are within the cursed area, including visitors to it. Those who leave the area are overwhelmed by the return of their vigor and sense of purpose.

# Rego Mentem Spells

The Rego Animál spells which deal with the mind may also be used as good guidelines for Levels of Rego Mentem spells.

### Coerce the Spirits of the Night: Gen.

Spell Focus: A Green Turquoise (+3)

R: Near/Sight, D: Conc.

Makes a ghost obey you as long as you can coerce it with threats, such as defiling its grave or banishing it to Hell. The more lurid and dramatic the threat, the more cooperative the ghost is. To affect a ghost, you must beat its current Spirit Might on die + Level + Communication + Intimidation. The Storyguide should always give a bonus or penalty depending on the potency of the threat.

### Ring of Warding Against Spirits: Gen.

Spell Focus: A Green Turquoise (+3)

R: Spec., D: Ring

Makes a circle seven paces in diameter, with you at the center. When the spell is cast, the Storyguide rolls a simple die + spell Level. Only ghosts with Spirit Points higher than this total can enter the ring. A common gesture used with this, and all wardings, is the Fig Sign. At certain angles, the ring may be seen as an orange-hued dome.

### Snap of Awakening: Lv 5

Spell Focus: A Twig (+1)

R: Near/Sight, D: Inst.

When you snap your fingers, or the Spell Focus, you instantly awaken a chosen person from sleep to alert consciousness. Does not work on someone Unconscious from Fatigue, wounds, or magic.

**Lv 15:** Control a natural emotion (e.g., calm, fear, or confusion). The target must feel the emotion before you can control it.

### The Call to Slumber: Lv 15

Spell Focus: A Pinch of Sand (+1)

R: Near/Sight, D: Inst., Req: Córporem

The target becomes sleepy and falls asleep within five minutes unless some current need makes wakefulness imperative. Stamina roll of 12+ to resist.

### Confusion of the Numbed Will: Lv 15

Spell Focus: A Speck of Alcohol (+1)

R: Near/Sight, D: Sun./Moon

Confuses a person. An Intelligence roll is needed to take any direct action. A roll of 13+ ends the spell. A roll of 8+ lets the character take the intended action, but the spell remains in effect. Any lower roll means the character is confused and takes some other type of action. When it is imperative for the victim to take an action, the Storyguide

should allow an appropriate modifier to the roll. While under this spell, a character always strikes last in combat and gets at least a -1 on all rolls (not including the above Intelligence rolls).

**Lv 20:** Control an unnatural emotion (e.g., cultivate a person's feelings of bravery where he is usually cowardly).

### Aura of Rightful Authority: Lv 20

Spell Focus: Violet Amethyst (+3)

R: Touch/Near, D: Sun./Moon

Those who listen to the target of this spell have their obedience and tendency to follow orders enhanced greatly. Common people generally do as told without question (as long as the orders are within the realm of reason), but those who are accustomed to giving orders are much less likely to follow the target's. Bishops, dukes, generals and Magi are not affected by this spell unless it is cast on someone of status near to theirs. That person may then command people of power, but an Intelligence roll is still allowed to resist, against an Ease Factor of 20. The violet amethyst is commonly made into a brooch or clasp. The Magus usually gives it to the target of the spell to wear, and makes a shallow bow while casting the spell. Violet amethyst is the stone of Jupiter, and gives political power and ascendancy over the masses.

### Scent of Peaceful Slumber: Lv 20

Spell Focus: A Lilac (+1)

R: Near/Sight, D: Inst., Req: Auram

A very light purple haze, that smells of lilacs, slowly rises from the ground. Those who breathe the haze, and fail a Stamina roll of 8+, fall asleep. You must concentrate for two Rounds before the haze rises to the height of a standing person's nose. The haze has a radius of 10 paces.

### Incantation of Summoning the Dead: Lv 25

Spell Focus: Black Onyx (+1)

R: Reach/Near, D: Conc.

Calls up someone's ghost. You must be on the spot where the person died, or must have the corpse. Alternatively, you can summon up any ghost that haunts the area you are in, if you know the ghost's full name. This is the Law of Names. *Demon's Eternal Oblivion* (PeVi Gen) details it more. Those buried by Church ceremony and those have who gone straight to heaven (i.e., Saints and Crusaders, as opposed to the normal folk who must wait for a time before going on) are not available for summoning.

### Summon the Haunting Spirit: Lv 25

R: n/a, D: Inst., Ritual

Summons someone's ghost, provided you have something intimately connected with the person, such as part of the corpse or a treasured possession (i.e., an Arcane Connection). Once you have summoned the ghost by this Ritual, it haunts the place and can be contacted by the *Incantation of Summoning the Dead* (ReMe 25). Most ghosts do not present themselves in places they haunt; they lurk invisibly and impotently. Rare is the spirit that appreciates being summoned to serve the living. As in *Incantation of Summoning the Dead*, those given a Church burial, and those who have gone on to their reward are beyond the reach of magic and cannot be summoned.

**Lv 30:** Control a human as long as he is in sight (R) and you concentrate (D).

### Exchange of the Two Minds: Lv 30

R: Touch, D: Year, Ritual

This spell switches the minds of two creatures. A new body greatly confuses those who are unprepared for the shock, and even those who are ready take a day to adjust completely. Magi who transport their own minds into younger, healthier bodies usually find that a strong body entails powerful passions, which interfere with the clear thinking needed to pursue the magical arts. Both people involved must make a Stamina roll of 3+ to survive the transfer. The roll is a stress die rolled before the switch is made.

**Lv 35:** Give a human one complex command which he tries to carry out to the best of his ability until the deed is accomplished or until the next sunrise/sunset, whichever comes first.

### The Shrouded Glen: Lv 40

R: Spec., D: Moon/Perm., Ritual

Enchants an area so that anyone moving toward it is subtly diverted, effectively keeping the place from being discovered accidentally. Anyone not actively searching for the hidden place never finds it. Those actively searching can find the place by making a Perception roll of 12+ (allowed once per day). Searchers get a +5 bonus for having a map. If the surrounding terrain is more difficult than the average forest, the Ease Factor increases. Likewise, the Ease Factor drops if the terrain is more open than a forest, and completely open terrain is unsuitable for this spell. Once a searcher spots the hidden place, the spell does not prevent approach. The spell hides up to one square mile of area, and diverts people up to ten miles away. All those who are present for the Ritual are unaffected by the spell. This spell mimics the properties of many faerie forests.

### Enslave the Mortal Mind: Lv 50

Spell Focus: A Violet Amethyst (+1)

R: Touch/Near, D: Sun./Moon

Enables you to completely control the loyalty, emotions, desires, interests, and long-term activities of any person. The target gets one chance to resist by rolling Stamina + Intelligence of 12+. Further Resistance rolls are possible when your control makes the victim do things strongly against that person's former personality.

# TERRAM SPELLS

Terram spells, in addition to covering earth, stone, clay, metal and glass, can sometimes affect inanimate objects in general. For instance, *Wielding the Invisible Sling* (ReTe 10) throws all manners of non-living things.

Though Terram spells affect all manner of solid objects, it is harder to affect certain materials. Here, in increasing order of difficulty, are the materials Terram spells affect: earth (sand, dirt, mud), clay, stone, glass, metal, gemstones.

## Creo Terram Spells

The spell Levels given in the Guidelines are for creating dirt or clay. To make stones, glass and metals requires up to five more Levels. Creation of gemstones is ten Levels higher.

Wizards' Sigils commonly visible in Creo Terram spells involve the object created being bizarre in some way, such as dirt being a specific color or texture.

**Lv 5:** Create enough dirt to fill a small box.

**Lv 10:** Create enough dirt to fill an area approximately man-sized.

### Clenching of the Earth's Mighty Hand: Lv 10

Spell Focus: A Handful of Dirt (+3)

R: Near/Sight, D: Sun./Inst.

Creates dirt to fill in a pit of up to three paces across and three yards deep. (A good follow-up to the *Pit of the Gaping Earth* [PeTe 15].)

### Tooth of the Staff: Lv 10

Spell Focus: A Bit of Flint (+3)

R: Touch/Near, D: Sun./Inst.

Creates a polished flint spearhead. It can appear fastened onto the end of a staff you already possess if you use an Herbam Requisite.

**Lv 15:** Fill a small room with dirt.

### Stone of the Hundred Shards: Lv 15

Spell Focus: A Rock with Several Fracture Marks (+1)

R: Touch/Near, D: Sun., Req: Perdo

Creates a stone the size of two fists which, if thrown, shatters into a hundred pieces, causing +5 damage to all within ten feet, and +15 damage to anyone hit by the stone itself. The stone explodes when it touches anything after it leaves your hands.

**Lv 20:** Create enough dirt to form a large wall.

### Rampart of Protecting Earth: Lv 20

Spell Focus: A Packed Clod of Dirt (+1)

R: Near/Sight, D: Sun./Inst.

Creates a wall of packed dirt up to 15 paces wide, four yards high, and two paces thick. It has a Soak of +15, and 3 "Body Levels." One can therefore knock it down by striking it repeatedly.

**Lv 25:** Create enough dirt to cause a landslide, or other natural disaster, in a relatively stable area.

### Wall of Protecting Stone: Lv 25

Spell Focus: A Chunk of Granite (+1)

R: Near/Sight, D: Sun./Inst.

Makes a wall of granite up to 10 paces wide, four paces high, and one pace thick. One needs miner's tools to break through it, though it can be toppled if it is not connected to a support on its side or top.

### Circle of the Faerie Stone: Lv 30

Spell Focus: A Faerie Mushroom (+3)

R: Near/Sight, D: Sun./Inst., Req: Vim, Aimed

Creates a 12 foot high stone wall in a circle up to ten paces across. It has a Magic Resistance of +20.

### Opening the Earth's Pore: Lv 40

R: Sight, D: Inst., Req: Ignem, Ritual

Opens a hole from the surface of the earth down to the hot reaches of Hell. Molten rock spews forth out of this hole, accompanied by noxious gases. Except for those in the immediate vicinity (30 paces) of the pore, people can outrun the lava flow. The lava spill covers the land within one mile of the pore, doing +20 damage to anyone caught in it each Round. Nasty.

### Conjuring the Mystic Tower: Lv 50

R: Near, D: Moon/Inst., Ritual

An elaborately carved tower, formed from a single block of stone, rises out of the ground. The tower stands 80 feet high and 30 feet wide, with a foundation set 20 feet into the ground. You determine the design of the chambers within.

# Intéllego Terram Spells

Intéllego spells of Terram Form tend to be about 5 Levels higher than their equivalents in other elemental Forms. This is because rock is unusually slow and ponderous, the exact opposite of what one hopes to deal with in seeking intelligence.

### Probe for Pure Silver: Lv 5

Spell Focus: A Chip of Silver (+3)
R: Near/Sight, D: Conc./Inst.

You are guided by a hunch, which is sometimes wrong, to silver nearby.

**Lv 10:** Sense one property of an object.

### Eyes of the Eons: Lv 10

Spell Focus: A Sapphire (+3)
R: Sight, D: Conc./Inst.

Determines the age of any non-living object to within 10% of its actual age. Casting Requisites: appropriate Form for the target.

**Lv 15:** Sense all of the mundane properties of an object. Have intuitive knowledge of the earth.

### Eyes of the Treacherous Terrain: Lv 15

Spell Focus: A Troll's Eye (+3)
R: Sight, D: Conc./Inst.

You can tell intuitively when any natural terrain you see is treacherous, such as a rock field prone to sliding.

**Lv 20:** Have your senses go unhindered by earth (e.g., you can see right through a rock).

### The Miner's Keen Eye: Lv 20

Spell Focus: A Dwarf's Eye (+3)
R: Near/Sight, D: Conc./Inst.

The caster can see any one type of mineral (gold, diamond, sand), specified at the time of casting, through up to three paces of intervening material. The caster has a good idea of how much is there and how pure it is, if appropriate.

### Tracks of the Faerie Glow: Lv 25

Spell Focus: A Mushroom from a Faerie Ring (+1)
R: 30 paces/120 paces, D: Conc.

Causes even faintly perceptible tracks of a specific being to glow with a faint magic light, making them stand out when you are within 30 paces of them. The fainter the tracks are, the more dimly they glow. You need something intimate to the target (an Arcane Connection) to trail him. The glow provides a bonus to Tracking rolls, and the bonus depends on the relationship between the target being tracked and the terrain. If the target is:

| | |
|---|---|
| Magically related to the terrain | +2 |
| Native to the terrain | +4 |
| Neutral to the terrain | +6 |
| Inimical to the terrain | +8 |

In addition, tracking at night without a light source doubles the bonus. The Spell Focus is broken apart over the area where the caster expects to find tracks.

### Stone Tell of the Mind that Sits: Lv 30

Spell Focus: Dirt in Your Mouth (+3)
R: Reach/Near, D: Conc.

Allows you to talk with living stone (but not with statues and such, which have been cut off from the earth and are therefore "dead"). A typical question and response takes one hour; stone speaks slowly. Though a stone is usually willing to talk, its direction sense and awareness of quickly-moving things (such as people) are limited.

### Greeting the Maker: Lv 30

R: Touch, D: Inst., Ritual

Gives the caster a vision of the maker of an item and the process (up to 15 minutes worth) used to create the object. When used in conjunction with magical investigation in the lab, this provides a +5 to the Investigation roll, and, in any case, gives a hint as to the nature of the item being studied.

### Sense the Feet That Tread the Earth: Lv 35

R: 1 mile, D: Conc., Ritual

You touch the earth and feel what is moving along the ground within one mile of you. You can tell direction, distance, weight, number, and manner of movement. For instance, you might sense "a single 50-stone creature slithering toward us, a hundred rods in that direction." For every extra pawn of vis invested in Range, another half mile is added to the radius of sensation.

# Muto Terram Spells

The Guidelines provided below assume you're changing earth, but leaving it in its original form (i.e., sand remains sand, but has a different shape). Changing earth into another form adds another 5 Levels to a Guideline. Small changes (such as slightly weakening or strengthening earth) are usually about 5 Levels lower than listed. Stone, glass and metal are all a bit harder to transform than ordinary earth, so 5 Levels are added to a Guideline that involves them.

**Lv 5:** Transform no more dirt than could fit in a small box.

### Edge of the Razor: Lv 5

R: Touch, D: Inst., Ritual

Sharpens any metal edge to a degree unequalled by manual methods. An edged or pointed weapon gains a +1 bonus to damage. Good-natured Magi reward Grogs by enchanting their weapons thus.

**Lv 10:** Transform no more than a man-sized amount of dirt.

### The Forgiving Earth: Lv 10

Spell Focus: A Handful of Silt (+3)
R: Sight, D: Sun./Inst.

Weakens earth in a 15 pace by 15 pace area, making packed dirt as loose as plowed ground, and soft ground into fine silt.

### Supple Iron and Rigid Rope: Lv 10

Spell Focus: A Bit of Iron or a Bit of Rope (+3)

R: Touch, D: Sun./Inst.

Makes a flexible object stiff and a stiff object flexible. Works only on items easily held in two hands. Casting Requisites: appropriate Form for the material affected.

### Unyielding Earth: Lv 10

Spell Focus: A Clod of Packed Earth (+3)

R: Sight, D: Inst.

Makes the surface of the ground in a 15 pace by 15 pace area become more solid. Mud becomes soft earth, and soft earth becomes packed dirt.

### The Crystal Dart: Lv 15

Spell Focus: A Rock Crystal (+3)

R: 50 paces/Sight, D: Inst, Req: Rego, Aimed +4

Creates a ten inch crystal dart that rises from the ground at your feet, floats into the air, and speeds off like an arrow at your target. Does +8 damage.

### Hands of the Grasping Earth: Lv 15

Spell Focus: A Pair of Brown Gloves (+1)

Ř: Near/Sight, D: Sun., Req: Rego

Earthen hands from beneath the target rise out of the ground and grasp the victim's ankles. The target can avoid the hands on a Quickness - Encumbrance roll of 11+. A roll

of 8 through 10 indicates that only one ankle is caught (the other hand disappears into the earth.) To break free requires a Strength roll of 15+ if both ankles are caught, and a roll of 12+ if only one is caught. (One attempt is allowed per Round, and each requires a Fatigue roll.) Each hand can be destroyed by beating its +25 Soak roll (hacking weapons do double normal damage). Each hand has one Body Level.

### Object of Increased Size: Lv 15

Spell Focus: A Chunk of Masonry from a Castle (+1)

R: Reach/Near, D: Sun./Perm.

Enlarges an inanimate object up to the size of a large chest, doubling each dimension and increasing its weight by a factor of eight. The size increase is based on the object's original, natural size, so casting the

spell more than once on a object has no effect. Noble elements, like gold, silver, and gems, are not affected by this spell. If any part of the item resists growth, the item as a whole does not grow. Casting Requisites: appropriate Form for target.

### Rock of Viscid Clay: Lv 15

Spell Focus: A Bit of a Dwarven Pick (+5)

R: Reach/Near, D: Sun./Perm.

Softens rock enough so that it may be dug out, molded, and otherwise manipulated in the same way that good, hard, river clay can be. The rock is slightly sticky. The spell affects the amount of rock that you can enclose in your arms.

**Lv 20:** Change all rock within 15 paces of you.

### Earth that Breaks No More: Lv 20

Spell Focus: A Chunk of Stone (+1)

R: Near/Sight, D: Sun./Inst.

Turns up to 30 feet square of packed dirt into stone. Works well on a *Rampart of Protecting Earth* (CrTe 20).

### Statue to Animal: Lv 25

R: Reach, D: Sun./Perm., Req: Animal, Ritual

Enchants a hand-size earthen or stone statue of an animal. Later, any time someone gives the command word (decided upon during the Ritual), the statue turns into a life-size specimen of the animal represented. The animal follows the orders of the person who gives the command word, and reverts to statue form when killed or commanded to revert. If killed, the statue is no longer magical. One must touch the statue when giving the command word.

**Lv 30:** Change dirt in Range of Sight.

### Teeth of the Earth Mother: Lv 35

Spell Focus: Ivory Tusk of a Great Elephant (+1)

R: Near, Sight, D: Sun./Year, Req: Rego, Aimed (-3, 0)

You cause twenty pointed pillars of white marble to spring up from the ground to a height of 12 feet, forming a circle three paces in diameter. These pillars can be used to cage people, to form a wall, or simply to skewer enemies. At their tops, the pillars are thin and as sharp as spears. At the base,

where they touch, they are 18 inches thick. To skewer a target, you must make a Targeting roll with a penalty of -3, but to capture a target you must make a standard Targeting roll. Climbing to the top of the pillars requires three Climb rolls of 12+, and the tops break away when the target reaches them, causing the victim to fall. Skewering a target does +25 damage, possibly more on following Rounds if the victim struggles or is exceptionally heavy. When the spell ends, the pillars crumble to dust.

# Perdo Terram Spells

Destroying stone and hard materials is usually more difficult than destroying earth alone. The Levels for destroying those items are given, as are Guidelines for destroying normal earth.

**Lv 5:** Destroy a man-sized amount of earth. Destroy a handful of stone.

### Fist of Shattering: Lv 5

Spell Focus: Bit of a Shattered Rock (+3)

R: Near/Sight, D: Inst.

An object of stone or weaker material that weighs up to five pounds breaks apart. Casting Requisites: appropriate Form for the target.

**Lv 15:** Destroy a near amount of dirt. Destroy up to 25 pounds of harder material.

### Pit of the Gaping Earth: Lv 15

Spell Focus: Earth Taken From a Deep Cavern (+1)

R: Near/Sight, D: Inst.

The dirt in a circle six paces across recedes into the ground, leaving a pit nine feet deep.

### Rusted Decay of Ten Score Years: Lv 15

Spell Focus: A Handful of Rust (+1)

R: Near/Sight, D: Inst.

After the spell is cast, the metal of the target becomes so thoroughly rusted that it breaks if used in any demanding way (e.g., in combat, to pry open a door). It also loses any sharpness it might once have had. Works on up to 25 pounds of metal.

**Lv 20:** Destroy up to 100 pounds of heavy material.

### Obliteration of the Metallic Barrier: Lv 20

Spell Focus: A Handful of Rust (+1)

R: Reach/Near, D: Inst.

Shatters a barrier of metal or stone up to one foot thick. Those within one pace of the barrier, on the opposite side from you, take +10 damage. Alchemically refined and magical metals may be able to withstand this spell. Casting Requisites: appropriate Form for the target.

**Lv 25:** Destroy up to 300 pounds of heavy material.

**Lv 30:** Destroy a vast amount of dirt. Destroy up to 500 pounds of heavy material.

### Stone to Falling Dust: Lv 30

Spell Focus: 100 Year Old Dust (+3)

R: Sight, D: Inst.

One solid object weighing up to 500 pounds turns to a pile of dust. Casting Requisites: appropriate Form for the target.

### Cascade of Rocks: Lv 40

R: Sight, D: Inst., Ritual

Makes a cliff collapse, causing an avalanche. The effects depend on the size of the cliff and what lies below it.

# Rego Terram Spells

Controlling heavier objects such as rock and metal is usually about five Levels higher than the comparable Guidelines given. Doing something subtle (like teleporting an object) is higher than a related Guideline, as well.

### Ward Against Faeries of the Mountains: Gen.

Spell Focus: A Star Ruby (+3)

R: Spec., D: Ring

As *Ward Against Faeries of the Waters* (ReAq Gen.), but for faeries of earth and stone. At some angles at night, the ring may be seen as a dark brown dome.

**Lv 5:** Control or move a handful of dirt.

### Unseen Arm: Lv 5

Spell Focus: A Shaving of Silver (+1)

R: Near/Sight, D: Conc.

Moves non-living things slowly; cannot oppose intentional resistance. Magi use this spell to manipulate things at a distance, but it cannot be used to pull something from someone's hand or to move something that is held. It can only move light things like a mug, instruments or small pouches of coins. The silver Spell Focus must have come from a valued serving platter. Casting Requisites: appropriate Form for target.

Lv 10: Control or move a man-sized amount of dirt. Deflect a single attack by a metal weapon.

### Trackless Step: Lv 10

Spell Focus: Hoof Shaving From a Deer (+3)

R: Self/Touch, D: Spec.

You leave no tracks in the earth until you come to a stop, such as to rest or fight.

### Wielding the Invisible Sling: Lv 10

Spell Focus: A Sling (+3)

R: Reach/Near, D: Inst., Aimed +2

Hurls any nearby object that is normally able to be thrown by a person at any target within 100 paces. The object must be unobstructed (not held down). Damage depends on the object thrown, up to +5 for a fist-sized stone.

Lv 15: Deflect several attacks from metal weapons.

### The Earth's Carbuncle: Lv 15

Spell Focus: A Small Stalactite (+3)

R: Near/Sight, D: Inst., Req: Muto, Aimed + 1

Causes a one pace circle of ground to become jagged, just under the surface, and those fragments burst into the air. Anyone standing on the circle is thrown into the air and hit with flying debris. Damage is +10. On landing, a victim is partially buried.

### Invisible Hand of the Thief: Lv 15

Spell Focus: The Glove of a Convicted Thief (+3)

R: Near/Sight, D: Inst.

Takes an item weighing up to three pounds and teleports it instantly to a sack or pouch you are holding. The spell does not work if the item is worn, held, touched, or seen by anyone but you, if it is made of iron or steel, or if it is a living thing. You must know exactly what and where the object is. Casting Requisites: appropriate Form for the object stolen.

### The Unseen Porter: Lv 15

Spell Focus: A Silver Shaving (+1)

R: Near/Sight, D: Conc.

Like *Unseen Arm* (ReTe 5), but it can carry large objects such as crates. Roughly speaking, it has the capabilities of a very strong person (Str +5). The heavier the object is the slower the unseen porter moves. If delicacy is required, high Finesse rolls (12+ or so) are needed. The spell can only carry inanimate objects, and cannot carry you. It also cannot lift things more than six feet above the ground. The Focus must be from a valued serving platter. Casting Requisites: appropriate Form for the target.

Lv 20: Control a Near amount of earth. Deflect all known attacks from metal weapons.

Lv 25: Keep metal objects completely away from your person (i.e., deflect all attacks from metal weapons, whether you can see them or not).

### The Earth Split Asunder: Lv 25

Spell Focus: Earth From a Deep Cavern (+1)

R: Sight, D: Inst., Aimed

Creates a five foot wide, 60 foot long, 10 foot deep crack in the ground. It opens during one Round, stays open for another Round, and closes at the start of a third Round, crushing all within it for +25 damage. You must maintain concentration for all three Rounds, or the pit slowly closes over an hour's time, rather then shutting quickly and violently. To avoid the pit, victims in its vicinity must make a Quickness - Encumbrance roll of 10+. Falling in causes +10 damage. To escape, another such roll is made. Unless outside help is provided, people in the pit only get one chance to escape.

Lv 30: Control earth within Range of Sight.

### Earth Shock: Lv 30

Spell Focus: Lava From a Recent Volcano (+3)

R: Sight, D: Inst.

Shakes the earth around you. All affected by this spell must make a Quickness - Encumbrance roll of 10+ or fall. Apply these modifiers:

Standing Still +2, On Solid Stone +2, Moving Slowly +0, On Earth +0, Running -2, In Tree -6

### Creeping Chasm: Lv 35

Spell Focus: Earth From a Deep Cavern (+1)

R: Sight, D: Inst., Aimed +6

Creates a chasm that runs from the ground in front of your feet to some target determined by your outstretched arms. The chasm travels about four paces per Round, growing slowly wider as it travels, reaching a maximum width of 20 feet at a distance of 30 paces. The chasm is 20 to 30 feet deep and the sides are likely to collapse, so any caught in it are in a bit of a bind. To avoid the growing chasm, make a Quickness - Encumbrance roll of 10+. The chasm closes naturally in a week. You must maintain concentration for eight Rounds for the chasm to reach maximum length.

### Crest of the Earth Wave: Lv 50

Spell Focus: A Vial of Water From a Tidal Wave (+5)

R: Spec., D: Inst.

Creates a wave in the earth that starts at your feet and travels 100 paces in a designated direction. It starts as a narrow ripple and within five paces reaches its full size of five feet high and 30 paces wide. It moves about 50 paces per Round. Those caught in

its path must make Dexterity - Encumbrance rolls of 10+ to leap over the wave or they are caught underneath it and crushed. Damage is +30. The wave overturns trees and damages buildings in its path.

### Hermes' Portal: Lv 75

R: Reach, D: Perm., Ritual

Creates a magical portal through which people, animals, and objects can travel instantaneously. The Ritual must be conducted simultaneously at two different locations, after which there is a magical connection between them. The Magi conducting each Ritual must have an Arcane Connection (such as a clod of dirt) to the other location when they are conducting the Ritual. After the Ritual, each time the resulting portal is used, one pawn of Terram *vis* per human or human-sized traveler must be expended. The traveler holds the *vis* in hand, and it disappears in transit. The portal is activated by some command word or ritual determined when the portal is enchanted. Inanimate things and unwilling creatures may be transmitted if someone else says the command word, pushes the subject through, and tosses a pawn of Terram *vis* in.

# VIM SPELLS

Vim spells are very useful. They help you use your spells to better effect, and since using spells efficiently is what being a master Magus is all about, these spells are very important. With imagination, you can use these spells to make wards, alarms, one-use magic items and other interesting things.

Vim spells also cover demons. Summoning and dealing with demons is prohibited within the Order, but fighting them is allowed.

Since Vim spells deal with magic in its many forms, Storyguides often have to assign spell Levels to the magical phenomena in their tales; Magi often use Vim to counteract those phenomena. For instance, when you try to break the effects of some magical power that the Storyguide has set up, the Storyguide has to give the effect a number rating to determine whether your counterspell is strong enough. Storyguides, be aware of this possibility and prepare for it.

Many of the Vim spells meant to be cast with other spells have no Spell Foci.

# Creo Vim Spells

There are few Creo Vim spells known throughout the Order.

### Shell of False Determinations: Gen

R: Touch, D: Instant, Ritual

Creates a "shell" of magic on an item, helping to shield it from investigation by other Magi. All attempts to investigate the magic item give false information about its powers unless half of the Level of the shell is exceeded by the Magus's Investigation roll.

### Shell of Opaque Mysteries: Gen

R: Touch, D: Instant, Ritual

This spell is similar to *Shell of False Determinations* (CrVi Gen), but it causes all attempts to investigate the magic item to utterly fail, unless the Level of the Ritual is exceeded by the Magus's Investigation roll. Once a Magus determines the presence of a particular shell (i.e., by overcoming it), it has no more power against him.

### The Phantom Gift: Lv 15

Spell Focus: Bat Wings (+1)
R: Near/Sight, D: Sun./Perm.

The target of the spell becomes tainted with magic as most Magi are. Beasts and people react to the target as though he's a Magus, although those who normally associate with the victim do not become hostile, but do give him a wider berth. The spell has no affect on those already with the Gift, including those blessed with the Gentle Gift.

# Intéllego Vim Spells

Since magic is a tricky thing to understand, spells to detect magic are at once difficult and important.

Although demons deal in Vim, they are made of the essence of deception itself.

If a demon does not wish to be detected, it cannot be (at least to the common knowledge of the Order), and for this reason there are no demon-locating magics.

Magic items cannot be investigated with simple magic spells. Investigation requires at least one Season in the laboratory to discover what magic an enchanted item contains (see the Laboratory Chapter).

### The Invisible Eye Revealed: Gen.

Spell Focus: Eye of Newt (+3)
R: Near, D: Conc./Year

You can see a visual representation of any magical means used to spy on you. The representation varies depending on the spell, but it often looks like some kind of eye floating in the air. For example, a Magus being spied upon with *Enchantment of the Scrying Pool* might see an eye of the deepest blue color, while a Magus who is being tracked by *The Inexorable Search* might see a representation of a small figure of himself moving about a map. This spell detects the use of Intéllego spells of up to double the Level of this spell.

**Lv 5:** Detect if one held object is magical.

### Wizard's Subtle Touch: Lv 5

Spell Focus: Toe of Frog (+1)
R: Touch/Near, D: Inst.

You can tell whether an object is magical by concentrating on it. After a short time the object seems to vibrate softly if it is magical.

### Sense the Nature of Vis: Lv 10

Spell Focus: Sapphire (+5)

R: Touch/Near, D: Inst.

You can tell what Art a supply of raw vis is connected to. To the caster, the vis

appears to glow with an aura that is appropriate to the Technique or Form that the vis is associated with. Creo is white, Intéllego gold, Muto constantly fluctuating, Perdo black, Rego purple, Animál brown, Aquam blue, Auram violet, Córporem dark red, Herbam green, Ignem bright red, Mentem orange, Terram dark brown, and Vim silver. Some of the colors are very similar, but easy to distinguish if the item is held steadily and studied for a few seconds.

### Scales of the Magical Weight: Lv 15

Spell Focus: A Set of Scales (+3)

R: Touch, D: Inst.

When casting this spell, the Magus typically holds his hands straight out from his body, places a known amount of Vim vis in his left hand (usually one pawn), and then places an unknown amount of vis in his right hand. After casting the spell, the Magus may sense how heavy the unknown vis is, in relation to the known. When using the Focus to help empower the spell, the vis is placed in the pans of the scale, and the scale shifts to make obvious the relationship between the two. A common technique is to enchant one of the pans of the scale with a pawn of vis, as if it is being prepared as a magic item, so there is no need to carry a pawn of raw vis about. If the spell is cast without anything to measure the unknown vis against, the Magus only has a very general idea of how valuable it is. The spell cannot be used to determine the amount of raw vis invested in an enchanted item.

### Perceive The Magical Scent: Lv 20

Spell Focus: A Dog's Toenail (+1)

R: Near/Sight, D: Conc./Year

You become sensitive to magical things as if they give off a scent. By sniffing the air, you can sense magical objects within 15 paces of you. You can sense magical objects farther away if the magic is quite powerful.

In the version of this spell created by Verdan of Ex Miscellanea, the nose of the caster becomes bright green, true to his Wizard's Sigil.

### Sense of the Lingering Magic: Lv 30

Spell Focus: A Sapphire (+1)

R: Reach/Near, D: Conc.

Whenever magic is cast, it leaves a magical residue in the area of the casting which may be detected by this spell, for up to ten years. A definite idea of what type of magic was cast is revealed, as is an impression of its powers, and an overview of any distinguishing characteristics (e.g., the Wizard's Sigil involved) it had.

### Sight of the Active Magics: Lv 35

Spell Focus: Ergot (+3)

R: Body/Touch, D: Conc./Moon

The caster can see spells as "auras" around things and people. The color of the aura indicates the Form of the spell working on a subject. The colors match those of *Sense the Nature of Vis* (InVi 10). The Technique of a spell working on the subject is recognized by the aura's shape, not color. Creo and Rego are both very orderly auras. Muto is constantly shifting, and Intéllego usually does so as well, but more slowly. A Perdo aura is usually sundered and broken apart. Thus, a Magus with *Endurance of the Berserkers* and *The Invisible Eye Revealed*, both upon himself, has a very controlled, orderly aura of deep red around his entire body. His eyes are surrounded with slowly shifting auras of a silvery hue. The caster of this spell should be warned: Imágonem spells may be used to disguise auras. The ergot, which may be used in this spell, is a very dangerous faerie plant. It is sprinkled over the head of the caster during the spell.

# Muto Vim Spells

These spells let you change other spells.

### Mirror of Opposition: Gen

Spell Focus: None

R: Spec., D: Spec.

Cast on another spell while the other spell is being cast, this causes the targeted spell to have the exact opposite of its normal effects. Works on spells up to half the Level of the *Mirror of Opposition* spell. This may be cast on another Magus's spell, but you must overcome the Penetration total of the other spell to take effect. To cast this spell at the same time as you cast a spell of your own

requires an Intelligence + Concentration roll of 9+. The effects of the inversion are up to the Storyguide to determine, but the target of the inverted spell usually remains the same as that of the original spell. The inverted spell does not overcome any limitations of Hermetic magic. For example, if an Instant PeCo spell is cast, the inversion is probably a CrCo spell of Sun. Duration. This spell is very dangerous. It demands double the normal number of Botch dice, and cannot be Mastered.

### Shroud Magic: Gen.

Spell Focus: None

R: Reach/Near, D: Sun./Perm.

Changes the outward appearance of a spell, either one that has already been cast or one that is currently being cast. One being cast currently can be made to seem like another spell, its effects can be made invisible, and motions and vocalizations of the casting can be made to seem those of a spell other than the one cast. The spell to be shrouded can be up to double the *Shroud's* Level. You can cast this spell while casting the one to be affected, if you can make an Intelligence + Concentration roll of 9+.

### The Sorcerer's Fork: Gen

Spell Focus: None

R: Spec., D: Spec.

This spell splits another spell into two or more identical spells of reduced power, which may be cast against two or more separate targets. Each of the resulting spells is a fraction of the power of the original spell, so if the spell is split in two, each is at half power. One Penetration die is rolled, and the Penetration total is split between the spells. *The Sorcerer's Fork* must be equal to or greater than the Level of the spell that is to be split. If casting this spell, and the one to be divided, the caster suffers Targeting penalties as per Multiple Casting, and suffers a penalty to the spell casting roll equal to the number of forks made (not the number of Targets). This spell may also be cast by a Magus while he is casting another spell, but he must roll an Intelligence + Concentration roll of 9+.

## Wizard's Boost: Gen.

Spell Focus: None

R: Near/Sight, D: Inst.

You cast this as another spell is cast. The other spell increases five Levels in effectiveness, but not past the Level of the Wizard's Boost. The effects of the extra five Levels of power are for the Storyguide to determine. You can also cast this spell simultaneously with one of your own, if you can make an Intelligence + Concentration roll of 9+.

## Wizard's Communion: Gen.

Spell Focus: None

R: Reach/Near, D: Inst.

Lets Magi combine their power to cast spells. The group of Magi work together to cast a specified spell through the unified power of the Communion. Only one extra Magus may join the Communion for each 5 Levels of the specified spell being cast. One of the Magi in the group must also know the specified spell, or must cast it from a text.

All the Magi in the gathering that know the Communion spell add the Level that they know Communion at to get the effective Level of the Wizard's Communion. This combined total must be at least twice the Level of the specified spell being cast.

Each Magus rolls for Fatigue and for success as if casting the specified spell himself. However, the number rolled against in the spellcasting roll equals the spell's Level, divided by the number of Magi participating in the Communion. If any Magus fails to cast the spell, the whole spell fails. If all succeed, the spell is cast. Communion is a remnant of Mercurian Rituals, so Spontaneous spells may not be cast by this means. This spell is usually used to cast protection spells for the Covenant, spells that are too powerful for a single Magus to cast, or even learn.

## Change the Nature of Vis: Gen.

R: Touch, D: Inst., Ritual

For every 5 Levels of this Ritual the Magus may change one pawn of vis to another Art. A pawn of vis associated with a Technique (e.g., Creo vis) may only be transformed into vis of another Technique, while a pawn of vis associated with a Form (e.g., Herbam vis) may only be transformed into vis of another Form. Thus, at the expense of one pawn for every five Levels of this Ritual, you can change the Art of another pawn.

## Gather the Essence of the Beast: Lv 15

Spell Focus: A Silver Globe (+3)

R: Touch/Near, D: Inst.

Concentrates the raw vis in a corpse into one part of that corpse, which can then be removed. This spell lets you gather all the raw vis you find without lugging around entire corpses of monsters. Note that the vis in many magical creatures is already concentrated in this manner.

# Perdo Vim Spells

## Demon's Eternal Oblivion: Gen.

Spell Focus: Pure Red Coral (+3)

R: Near/Sight, D: Inst.

Weakens and possibly destroys a demon. Roll stress die + spell Level. For every point by which you exceed the target's Demon Points, it loses one Demon Point. If its Demon Points drop to 0, the demon is banished back to Hell for an indeterminate amount of time. If you know the demon's true name, you may double your roll. This is due to the Law of Names, which, like the Laws of Contagion and Sympathy, may be used to strengthen your spells. However, the Law of Names typically has much less application.

## Disenchant: Gen.

Spell Focus: A Pinch of Salt (+1)

R: Touch/Near, D: Inst.

You make a magic item lose all its powers permanently if the Level of this spell can exceed the highest Level of the enchantments in the item. The enchantment is utterly destroyed, as is all of the vis that was used in the magic item. The object left is in all ways a mundane item.

## Masking the Odor of Magic: Gen.

Spell Focus: A Dab of Skunk Oil (+3)

R: Touch/Near, D: Sun./Year

Prevents a magic spell, or power in an item or being, from being detected by InVi magic unless the Penetration roll of the InVi spell exceeds the Level of this spell.

## Wind of Mundane Silence: Gen.

Spell Focus: Amber (+3)

R: Reach/Near, D: Inst.

Metaphorically speaking, you raise a "breeze" that blows the magic away from an area, cancelling the effects of a spell. You can cancel the effects of any spell if, with this spell, you can double the original caster's Technique + Form score (at the time he cast the spell) on a die + the Level of your spell. If the spell to be eliminated was not cast by a Magus, the number to match is double the caster's Might score. If the spell was from a magic item, the value to beat is double the Level of the spell. Parmae can be blown down if the Wind exceeds double the Level of the Parma, times five. Wind of Mundane Silence does not affect spells of Instant Duration. Magical things near the area of the Wind wave slightly from the "breeze."

# Rego Vim Spells

The spell type to repel demons is Rego Vim. Theoretically, it is possible to conjure and control demons through Rego Vim spells, but this knowledge and its use are forbidden by the Hermetic Code. Any who find and dare to use this knowledge face dangers from both the beings they deal with and those in the Order of Hermes who object to such practices.

## Aegis of the Hearth: Gen.

R: Spec., D: Year, Ritual

This ritual protects a Covenant in the way Parma Magica protects a Magus. It affects a circle up to 100 feet across (or the equivalent in area), though the diameter can be increased by another 100 feet for each extra pawn of raw vis used in the Ritual.

If any spell is cast toward the Aegis (originating from outside it) by any Magus who was not involved in the Aegis Ritual, the Aegis resists the spell. Furthermore, spells that bring objects into the Aegis, including teleportation spells such as The Seven League Stride, are also resisted unless the caster was involved in the Ritual. If the "foreign" spell cannot overcome the Level of the Aegis + 5 + a stress roll, it fizzles out. The Aegis is also able to block foreign Intéllego spells, even if they can't normally be blocked by a Parma Magica. Of course, all this means that spells are not interfered with at all if a foreign caster can get within the boundaries of the Aegis.

Demons and faeries cannot enter the area protected by the Aegis unless they have higher Mystic Points than the Level of the Aegis. When crossing the border of an Aegis, a magical person feels a slight tingle in the extremities.

The Aegis is typically cast on the Winter Solstice, since Magical Auras can be slightly higher at that time, and thus allows the Aegis to last for an entire year. The entire Covenant usually participates in the Aegis Ritual, which ends with the participants walking around the perimeter of the protected area in order to define it. Quite often, the Covenant holds a major council meeting, or perhaps a large party, after the Ritual of the Aegis.

### Circular Ward Against Demons: Gen.

Spell Focus: Pure Red Coral (+3)

R: Spec., D: Ring

A magical ring seven paces across forms around you and remains active as long as you do not leave it. When you set up the ring, the Storyguide secretly rolls a die + the spell's Level. All demons with Demon Points equal to or less than this total are unable to enter the circle or harm those within it. If you cast the spell again, the second ring dispels the first, regardless of the relative strengths. Some Magi cast this spell before going to sleep at night. The Fig Sign, mentioned in Ward Against the Beasts of Legend (ReAn Gen) is a common gesture in this, and other, wardings. At night, from certain angles, the ring may be seen as a silver-hued dome.

### Maintaining the Demanding Spell: Gen.

Spell Focus: None

R: n/a, D: 1 minute

You cast this spell on a spell that you have already cast and are maintaining through concentration. The spell that requires concentration is then automatically maintained for one minute (or ten Rounds), whether you concentrate or not. You cannot change the effects of the first spell without concentrating on it again. For instance, you can use The Unseen Arm (ReTe 5) to hold an object in the air without concentrat-ing, but to move the object still requires concentration. An Intelligence + Concentration roll of 6+ must be made in order to cast this spell while keeping the first one going (a lower roll than normal because this is what the spell is designed for). This spell only works on spells of equal or lower Level.

### Opening the Intangible Tunnel: Gen.

R: 100 miles, D: Conc., Ritual

You can open a magical channel from yourself to some target, allowing you to cast a spell at someone or some place not in your presence. First, you need an Arcane Connection, either to the person (a piece of clothing, a lock of hair, or a fingernail), or to her current location (a tile from the floor or a piece of the wall). Then, you cast this spell, which opens the channel between you and your target. Thus, in following Rounds, you can cast a spell at the person at the other end, as if she is in your presence. The spell cast cannot be of higher Level than that of the

Opening.. Note that you must make standard Concentration rolls to maintain concentration on the Opening spell. In addition, a Magus who magically recognizes the tunnel (through The Invisible Eye Revealed or a similar spell) may cast spells back at you.

## Suppressing the Wizard's Handiwork: Gen.

Spell Focus: A Black Onyx (+3)

R: Near/Sight, D: Conc.

Cancels one spell, but only for the Duration of concentration, after which the effects return. The spell temporarily cancelled must have originally been cast by the caster of this spell. The Level of the spell to be suppressed must also be less than the Level of this spell. The effects of the spell being suppressed take about one Round to fade out, and then another Round to return after concentration is broken. The spell to be affected must be active to be suppressed. Common uses of this spell include providing access to some place (for example, having a permanent Muto Terram blocking the door to your lab, and then suppressing it to enter), and avoiding traps (such as suppressing a Waiting Spell [ReVi Gen] on your rear door). This spell is designed to be held while you do something else, so Concentration rolls are easier than normal (3+ walking, 6+ imminent personal threat).

## Waiting Spell: Gen.

R: Reach, D: Spec., Ritual

You place a spell in a specific location where it discharges under conditions that you specify. (These conditions must be immediately obvious, requiring no exceptional modes of detection. Thus, a trap can not be set based on some distant event or obscure fact.) The Waiting Spell must be equal to or greater than the Level of the spell placed in waiting. Several spells can be placed in waiting together, if the Waiting Spell's Level at least equals the sum of the other spells' Levels. If any of these spells is a detection spell, then the other spell(s) can be based on an event detected by the detection spell. Thus, if you put Frosty Breath of the Spoken Lie (InMe 20) into the Waiting Spell, you can also put in a spell that is cast when someone lies. (An Intéllego spell in the Waiting Spell has no effect other than to cast the other spell[s] when the proper condition is detected. Thus, one's breath is not frosty when caught in a lie.) The Waiting Spell is often used for traps; for emergency devices that, for instance, teleport their users away if they are captured; or for spells held in staves, to be discharged at will. The Waiting Spell lasts until it is set off. You cannot store a Ritual spell within a Waiting Spell, but can put Formulaic and Spontaneous spells in.

## Watching Ward: Gen.

R: Touch, D: Spec., Ritual

Puts another spell in suspension on a target, effectively putting that spell "on hold" until triggered. The target of the suspended spell and the Watching Ward must be present for the entire casting Ritual. Under the conditions you specify, the suspended spell takes effect. The Level of the Watching Ward must at least equal the Level of the spell held in suspension. You can put multiple spells in the Ward, provided that its Level at least equals the sum of the Levels of the contained spells. Only one Watching Ward can be placed on any one person or object. If someone tries to dispel the Watching Ward and fails, the suspended spell is cast. Flambeau and Tytalus Magi commonly put highly destructive spells upon their persons, to be cast if they die, so they may have vengeance upon their killers.

# Laboratory

## chapter eight

ost of the magic rules presented so far in **Ars Magica** govern the use of magic during stories, such as casting spells and engaging in *Certámen*. A Magus, however, spends much more time at home studying than adventuring in the lands outside the Covenant. In between stories, Magi study their magical arts and perform research in an effort to advance their powers. Time between stories is recorded in Seasons, each enough time to accomplish a single activity. There are a great number of things Magi can spend their time doing.

# Basic Laboratory Activities

## ARCANE STUDIES

Though anyone can study skills and knowledges (Abilities), as a Magus you have other avenues of study open to you, to strengthen your magical skills. Arcane studies may be performed from books, but you may also study Magic Theory and the magical Arts using *vis*. There

are dangers to such studies, but few limits to the knowledge you can gain.

## Magic Theory

In one form of study, you experiment in the ways of magic to increase your understanding of magical principles; you increase your Magic Theory score. This study requires experimentation with raw *vis*, to learn the secrets trapped within.

You must use raw Vim *vis*, from one to three pawns, to perform such experiments.

You spend a full Season in research, roll a stress die, multiply the result by the number of pawns of *vis* used, and add the level of your magic Aura (usually that of your Covenant). The result is the "level" of your source. The score reflects the amount of magical knowledge to be garnered from your experiment. If the score is high, your experiment reveals new complexities of magical law. If the score is low, you reveal basic magical principles.

These experiments broaden your understanding of magic — increase your Magic Theory score. If the result is at least triple your score in Magic Theory, you gain 3 Experience Points in Magic Theory. If the result is at least double your score, you gain 2 Experience Points. If the result at least exceeds your Magic Theory score, you gain 1 Experience Point. If the result of the experiment is less than your Magic Theory score, you learn nothing from your efforts, and waste the Season. After any experimentation attempt, the *vis* used is lost.

For rules on how Experience Points apply to your Magic Theory score, refer to *Abilities* in the Character Chapter, and *Experience* in the Saga Chapter.

## Studying Arts

Studying Arts involves raising your Form and Technique scores. If you are studying an Art from a book, the book's score in that Art (a rating like that of your experiment, above) must exceed your score in the Art. If the book's score is at least three times your score, you gain three levels in the Art in one Season. If the book's score is at least double yours, you gain two levels in the Art. Otherwise you gain one level. In any case, you cannot raise your Art score above that of the book.

You can also study an Art from raw *vis* of the same type (e.g., you can learn the Art of Herbam from Herbam *vis*). When studying with *vis*, you first decide how many pawns of *vis* to use (up to three). Then make a stress roll and multiply the result by the number of pawns of *vis* used, and add the rating of your Aura. Treat the result as if it's the score of a book you're studying from, so that you gain 1,

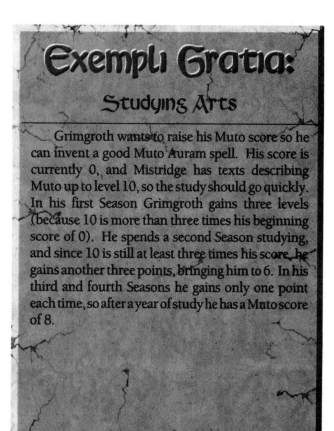

### Exempli Gratia:
### Studying Arts

Grimgroth wants to raise his Muto score so he can invent a good Muto Auram spell. His score is currently 0, and Mistridge has texts describing Muto up to level 10, so the study should go quickly. In his first Season Grimgroth gains three levels (because 10 is more than three times his beginning score of 0). He spends a second Season studying, and since 10 is still at least three times his score, he gains another three points, bringing him to 6. In his third and fourth Seasons he gains only one point each time, so after a year of study he has a Muto score of 8.

### Basic Laboratory Total

You use one total (called the "Lab Total") frequently in calculating your ability to accomplish tasks in the laboratory. The Total varies from task to task because it uses the Technique and Form appropriate to the task at hand. For instance, if you are learning a Rego Auram spell, Lab Total includes your Rego and Auram scores. Depending on the specific task, other modifications, like the Aura of your Covenant, may also apply. Remember, spell Requisites count toward your Lab Total.

Basic Lab Total = Technique + Form + Intelligence + Magic Theory

2, or 3 levels if the total exceeds your score. After study is complete, the *vis* used is gone.

If the score of the *vis* studied is too low for you to learn from it (i.e., you roll low or don't use enough *vis*, and thus can't exceed your Art score), the *vis* is lost, and your Season is wasted in vain attempts to learn.

Raising one's Art score to 30 through study, whether by texts or *vis*, is quite difficult, and beyond 30 even more so. Because of this, books that describe the Arts past level 15 are rare and those with scores of 20 or higher are rarer still (though they do exist), and are incredibly valuable.

## Scribing and Copying Arts

You can write what you know about an Art at the rate of three levels per Season, but you can never write higher than half your score (rounded down). You can copy an existing text on an Art at the rate of nine levels per Season.

## Dangers

If a stress roll ever results in a 0 while you are studying with *vis*, you must check for a Botch. One Botch die is rolled for every pawn of *vis* used. If you Botch, you lose control of the magic you are studying. The Storyguide may apply whatever Botch results are deemed appropriate. The *Magic Botch Suggestion Table*, p.182, indicates possible results, the outcome determined by the type of *vis* you are using. If a Botch demands a roll to avoid Wizard's Twilight (see p.356), add the number of pawns of *vis* used to the strength of your Aura (probably that of your Covenant) to determine the strength of the supernatural power you must control.

# SPELLS IN THE LABORATORY

Formulaic spells are a major measure of your power because they determine those things you can do easily and predictably. As a Magus, you may learn the spells of others and invent your own.

## Learning Spells

If a spell has been written out fully in normal spell fashion, you can try to learn it. (Most Magi's notes are incomplete, so learning spells from their private grimoires is difficult.) In one Season you can learn a single spell if the Level is equal to or lower than your Lab Total. You may get a bonus on your Lab Total for knowing a similar or variant spell (see *Similar Spells*, p.175). Your Lab Total is modified by +1 for every five Levels of the spell you already know.

Requisites listed at the top of a spell's description count for learning and inventing spells just as they do for casting them.

## Inventing Spells

Inventing a spell is more difficult than learning one, but of course you don't need a copy of the spell to do it. First, decide the effects of the spell you wish to invent; you may pick a spell described in the Spells Chapter, or you can make up something completely on your own.

## Guidelines for New Spells

A few general rules should be kept in mind to aid in creating new spells. Increasing the Range of a spell adds about 10 to the Level, while increasing the Duration increases the Level by a variable amount. Non-Ritual spells may not be extended beyond Moon Duration, and many spells cannot be made Instant (see the note on Techniques, p. 195). Overcoming some limitation of a spell increases its Level by 5 to 15. Eliminating major limitations, such as voice, gestures and other significant restrictions, adds 15 or more Levels. Doing something really tricky to a spell increases its Level by a large number, depending upon how subtle the change is. The more drastic the change, the higher the Level increase. Finally, spells that do damage, among other effects, typically end up being at least 10 Levels higher than spells that produce other effects alone. For example, *Lungs of Water and Death* (CrAq 35) only creates about a bucket's worth of water (which puts it on par with a CrAq spell of Level 5), but does it within the body of a person, filling one specific location and causing damage, so 30 is added to the Level (10 for doing damage and 20 for being tricky with the water).

If you want to duplicate an existing spell, use the stats given for it in the Spells Chapter, but include your Wizard's Sigil (p.195). If you create a variant of a spell in the Spells Chapter, extrapolate the stats. Use existing spells and the Guidelines for spells of that Technique and Form in the Spells Chapter to guide you in all respects.

If you invent a completely new spell, you must fully describe the spell, both in terms of mechanics (Range, Duration, Level) and in terms of how the spell fits into the medieval paradigm, limits of magic (p.170), and the Laws of Magic (p.195). The rest of the Troupe or the acting Storyguide must agree on all these elements. Remember to include your Wizard's Sigil (p.195).

You can only invent a spell if your Lab Total exceeds the spell's Level. You may get a bonus to your Lab Total for knowing a Similar or variant spell (+1 per five Levels of Similar spell — see p.175). You also gain your Aura rating as a bonus to your Lab Total. For each point by which your Lab Total exceeds the spell's Level, you accumulate one point per Season. When you accumulate points equal to the Level of the spell, you invent it. (Thus, if your Lab Total is double the spell's Level, you can invent the spell in one Season).

## Copying Spells

All Magi have grimoires containing their spells, which are constantly updated as they learn and invent new spells.

## Inventing Spells and Spell Foci

The concept of Spell Foci is introduced in the Magic Chapter, p. 187. When inventing new spells, the following guidelines should be kept in mind for Foci: +3 is the average bonus for a Focus, and such Foci are relatively common for first or second magnitude spells, rare for third or fourth magnitude spells, and very rare for spells of greater than fourth magnitude. Foci of greater than usual rarity for a spell Level have their bonus raised appropriately. Thus, the bonus of a very rare Spell Focus for a spell of fourth magnitude might be +5. Alternatively, a common Spell Focus for a powerful fourth magnitude spell might be +1. Care should also be taken in choosing a Spell Focus that is characteristic of a spell and its capabilities.

These spells are not immediately useful to others, however, as they include all sorts of personal abbreviations and shortcuts that others cannot understand. (The use of shortcuts is understandable considering how difficult writing can be in the Middle Ages.) In addition, some Magi sprinkle their magic texts with misdirections, which they recognize and ignore themselves, but which endanger others who take these parts of the text as genuine.

If you would like to copy a spell of yours so others can read and learn it, you can spend a Season writing up to 60 Levels of spells to make them useable by others. Also, in one Season, you can copy 180 Levels of spells that are already written understandably.

## Translating Spells

When you acquire a text containing the spells of another Magus, the spells within are often not translated into a form readable by you. Even if they are, the contents of the text may be beyond your ability to fully understand. In addition, some Magi intentionally place traps within their spells, which the original author can recognize and ignore, but which careless or inexperienced Magi may incorporate into the spell, exposing themselves to unknown dangers. Spells copied into readable form by their creators never need to be identified, and almost never contain traps.

If you want to translate the spells of another Magus whose secrets and abbreviations you do not know, you must first roll to "break the code." For most Magi's texts, the "code" is merely the author's personal style, and you only need make an Intelligence + Scribe Latin simple roll of 6+ to figure out the author's style. If the author intentionally obscured the work, add the author's Intelligence to the Ease Factor of your roll, or raise it even higher if the information is actually in code.

Once you have broken the author's code, you must determine the nature of the written spell. Having broken the author's code you automatically determine the Technique and Form of the spell, as long as it is a Hermetic spell. You may then attempt to determine how powerful the spell is (its Level) and what its effects are. You need to read the spell fully and roll a stress die + Lab Total (same Lab Total as for learning the spell), and if your total equals or exceeds the Level of the spell (known by the Storyguide), you determine the Level of the spell and its effects. This means you can write a copy of the spell that may be read and used by others.

You get one roll to decode and one roll to translate a spell per Season. If both succeed, the process takes the length of a Season. If either roll fails, the translation attempt fails and the Season is wasted; the spell remains untranslated (although you may automatically try the second roll again in another Season if you've already succeeded in the decoding roll). If you Botch your translation roll, not only do you lose the Season, but something horrible happens. The copy of the spell may be ruined, or maybe you accidentally trigger a part of the spell, causing it to adversely affect you or others.

You may obscure your own spells by spending a Season, obscuring up to 60 Levels of spells each Season. However, there is rarely any benefit to obscuring a spell unless the spell is created as a trap (a spell like *Curse of the Desert* [PeAq 25], for example, with a Range of Self instead of Near). To create a spell that's a trap, you must invent the spell as you do any other.

You may occasionally acquire a non-Hermetic spell, and wish to identify it. Non-Hermetic spells can be identified in a manner similar to that for Hermetic spells, but they are usually much more difficult to identify. Even determining the Technique and Form may prove impossible without prolonged study. The actions required to identify any non-Hermetic spells are up to the Storyguide to determine.

# Magical Enchantments

Physical creations, as well as mental ones, can increase your power as a Magus. Physical enchantments are very useful devices, but they usually require raw vis to create. In addition to talismans, which you can use to concentrate your magical powers, you can create invested devices, which mimic the powers of spells, potions which affect those who apply them, and longevity potions which extend your mortal life. Since magical enchantments are unique creations of individual Magi, determining how to use one that someone else has created can be a lengthy and even dangerous process.

## Exempli Gratia:

### Inventing a Spell

Grimgroth would like to invent a spell to turn an odor into a pungent, debilitating stench. On consulting the other players, he decides that this is a Muto Auram spell of Level 15 with no Requisites. His Lab Total is 8 (Muto) + 12 (Auram) + 3 (Intelligence) + 5 (Magic Theory) = 28. Each Season he gains 13 points (28 [Lab Total] - 15 [spell Level] = 13) toward completing the spell. So, in two Seasons he invents it, having accumulated even more than the necessary 15 points. If Grimgroth's Lab Total were 30 (only two points more than it actually is), he could have invented the spell in one Season, because one Season would have been enough for him to accumulate all 15 points. He therefore considers studying Muto or Auram a bit more before trying to invent the spell.

Magical enchantments are created through a type of Ritual magic, and as such require a great deal of time, effort, and magical resources. You must take the time to prepare your lab for the task, gather all the necessary materials and equipment, and then craft your work in earnest, taking great care and showing painstaking attention to the details of the enchantment. In the end, you have an enchantment which is independent, generating its own magical energies in order to function, but which is uniquely tied to your magical abilities. Your magical Sigil figures just as prominently in the effects produced by your magical enchantments as it does in the effects produced by your spells.

Magical enchantments often require raw vis to create. The process of enchanting an item transforms the vis, linking the magic power inexorably to the item in which it is instilled. Vis used for enchantments is thus transformed so that it is no longer usable for any other purposes, and it can never be extracted from the enchantment it is used to create. Magi sometimes refer to the magic of enchantments as "cooked," rather than "raw" vis.

Because the act of enchantment is itself a ritual, effects matching those of Ritual spells may not be placed in any magical enchantment. The powerful magics of a Ritual spell cannot be encompassed within the results of another ritual.

# Enchanted Devices

Enchanted devices come in three types: talismans, which enhance and focus your magic powers; invested devices, in which you instill powers which mimic the effects of spells; and lesser devices, which may be instilled with powers as invested devices, but which are more limited in power and require fewer resources.

## Form and Material

The first thing you must do for any magical device is choose the physical form of the item you wish to enchant – both the shape of the item and its component material. A golden ring is more suitable for certain enchantments than a copper ring, and a copper ring is used for different enchantments than a copper wand. Consider well the effects you wish to instill because the form of the item limits you if you choose poorly, and aids you if you choose well (see the *Form & Effects Bonuses Table*).

Pay attention to mundane criteria as well as magical. For instance, enchanting a gold sword might appeal to you, but it is too heavy and soft to use in combat. And while a diamond might be perfect for your ring, do you have a diamond? You might have to go out into the dangerous world to find your materials, especially if your Covenant is poor.

## Preparation for Enchantment

Talismans and invested devices are powerful items which require special preparation before any effective enchantments can be performed.

Once you have the physical item to enchant, you must spend a Season preparing it. You must expend a number of pawns of raw Vim *vis* equal to the number derived from the *Material & Size Table*.

To determine the number of pawns of *vis* needed to prepare the item (which is also the maximum amount of *vis* that can be put into it for powers), find the Base Points on the *Material & Size Table* and multiply by the Multiplier for the item's size. For example, a silver dagger takes 16 pawns of *vis* to enchant, 8 (for silver) x 2 (for the *small* size). Remember that you may use no more *vis* in a single Season than your total of Magic Theory + Vim. If your total is not high enough, you may not prepare the item for enchantment in a single Season.

It is possible to enchant only part of an item. For example, you can enchant a ruby on the end of a staff. Because it is on a staff, the gem gains bonuses appropriate to the shape (but not the material) of the staff (see the *Form & Effects Bonuses Table*), and you don't have to enchant the whole staff. However, any powers which rely on the attachment of gem and staff for a bonus (for example, any

spell in the gem which uses a Form bonus for the staff [maybe Herbam]) are permanently lost if the two are separated.

An item that has been prepared for enchantment is akin to a blank slate; it is utterly useless until it is attuned as a talisman, or instilled with magical powers.

## Talismans

You may create a talisman to help you concentrate and extend your magical powers. A talisman is a very personal item, which contains magics and materials that tie it intimately to you, and that allow you to use it as a channel for your magical power.

To create a talisman, you must first choose the item's physical form and prepare the item for enchantment as described above. Once you have prepared the item for enchantment, you must spend one Season attuning the item's mystical energies to your own; it becomes an extension of your being. At the end of this Season, you have a talisman which may be used to aid your magic.

Your talisman is an extension of your touch as long as you're in contact with it. When you cast a spell of Touch Range, you may reach your target by touching him with your talisman. Thus, if your talisman is a staff, your reach is increased by the length of the staff. You also always have

## Material & Size Table

| Material | Base Points |
|---|---|
| cloth, glass | 1 |
| wood, leather | 2 |
| bone, soft stone | 3 |
| hard stone | 4 |
| base metal | 5 |
| silver | 8 |
| gold | 10 |
| semi-precious gem | 12 |
| precious gem | 15 |
| priceless gem | 20 |

| Size | Example | Multiplier |
|---|---|---|
| tiny | ring, bracelet, pendant, all gems | x1 |
| small | wand, dagger, belt, cap | x2 |
| medium | sword, tunic, boots, skull | x3 |
| large | staff, shield, cloak, skeleton | x4 |
| huge | boat, wagon, human body, small room | x5 |

an Arcane Connection to your talisman (making it easy to find if lost), but it also acts as an Arcane Connection to you, making it very dangerous in enemy hands. Furthermore, your focus is fully protected by your Magic Resistance while you touch it. Thus, while an outstretched staff can be outside your usual Magic Resistance, an outstretched staff which is also a talisman is fully protected. Even when you're not touching your talisman, it receives the Magic Resistance offered by your current Form scores.

In addition to these basic powers, you may, at any time, spend a Season to open your talisman to one kind of magic attunement, based on the shape and material of the talisman. Use the Form & Effects Bonuses Table to determine what attunements are possible. A certain type of item might provide you with many possible attunements, but you only get one that you choose to spend a Season obtaining. For instance, Grimgroth can enhance his staff talisman by spending a Season to attune it to spells that control things at a distance. He then gets a +4 bonus on rolls with spells that control things at a distance (the bonus listed on the *Form & Effects Bonuses Table*). This bonus only applies when casting spells while touching the talisman, not for Magic Resistance or any laboratory activities. There's no limit to the number of attunements a talisman can have at one time, though you can only add one per Season. There's no roll involved in giving your talisman an attunement bonus; you must simply spend the time to get the bonus.

You can only have one talisman at a time; one must be completely destroyed before you can make another. You cannot make a talisman for someone else. You can instill powers into a talisman (see *Invested Devices*, below), receiving a +2 bonus to your Lab Total to instill those powers. You can also turn an item already invested with magical powers into your talisman. You need only prepare an item for enchantment once if you use it both as a talisman and as an invested device.

Note that a talisman is different from a Spell Focus. A talisman is personalized to the Magus and applies to many of his spells. A Spell Focus is personalized to a spell (see those listed in the Spells Chapter). You can, however, make a Spell Focus into your talisman. All you need do is enchant the Spell Focus as you do a talisman. A Spell Focus so enchanted is unique in that it still applies its modifier to the spell(s) it normally effects, and at the same time can be attuned to an ability on the *Form and Effects Bonuses Table*. A Spell Focus can even be invested with spell-like powers and retain the modifier it has as a Spell Focus. Of course, not all Spell Foci can be used in this way; some are simply too vulnerable, like a pinch of dirt or a feather. Obviously, if you want to make a Spell Focus into a talisman or invested device, you have to choose a Focus that will last. And yes, you can enchant a Spell Focus with

the spell it usually modifies. Such a Focus constantly aids in the casting of the spell it contains.

## Invested Devices

Now that you have enchanted a device, you may spend additional time and magical resources to bestow magical powers upon it. When you do so, you create an invested device.

The number of Vim vis points spent during preparation (outlined by the *Material & Size Table*) is a limit on the magical effects that can now be enchanted into your device. Each effect invested requires a number of raw vis points. Their total cannot exceed the overall score established for the device.

## Designing the Effect

First, you choose an effect to be invested in your device, and determine its Level. The effect is like a spell, and must be fully defined, as a spell is. You may base the effect on a spell from the Spells Chapter, or may invent an effect unlike any spell. If inventing a new effect, you must design the effect carefully, as if inventing a new spell (see Inventing *Spells*, p.239). The Level of the effect is the equivalent of its spell Level. If you're inventing an effect,

## Effect Frequency Table

| | |
|---|---|
| 1 Use per Day | 0 |
| 2/Day | +1 |
| 3/Day | +2 |
| 6/Day | +3 |
| 12/Day | +4 |
| 24/Day | +5 |
| 50/Day | +6 |
| Unlimited | +10 |
| Constant Use | +5 |

Add the number listed to the Level of the effect. Only effects, such as invisibility, that function constantly (which excludes all effects with Instant Duration) can have "Constant Use."

its Level can be determined by using comparable spells and Guidelines provided in the Spells Chapter. You should confirm your effect Level with the Storyguide. Also, remember the effect's starting Level. Starting effect Level may change as you define the parameters of the effect, but the starting Level is essential to scores, like Penetration, that are needed when the effect is used.

You must decide how frequently you use the effect. Look at the *Effect Frequency Table* and decide how many times per day you can use the effect. The number you choose corresponds to a bonus, which is added to the Level of the effect.

Next, if the effect is not of Constant Use, you must specify a triggering action or ritual of some kind to activate the power. The trigger must be specific about exactly what actions need to be performed. A trigger can involve a command word or phrase, moving the item in a specific way (e.g., waving or pointing a wand), a stance to be adopted, or anything physical that you can imagine. The enchanted item cannot read thoughts, so the trigger action must be physical, not mental.

Finally, choose any effect modifications you wish to apply to the device (see below), adjusting the Level of the effect for each modification.

## Effect Details

The information provided here is true for effects in all invested devices. This information only changes if modifications are made by the Magus. Effect modifications, discussed below, indicate how these changes can be made.

The technical details (Range, Duration, Casting Requisites, Targeting) of effects you instill in a device usually work the same way for all enchanted devices. If your effect is based on a spell, and two Ranges and Durations are listed for the spell, the shorter of the two is used.

When you use a magic effect against someone or something with Magic Resistance, you have to make a magic Penetration roll, as you do with a spell. It is the power of the effect itself that attempts to penetrate, though, not your own ability. The device's Penetration score equals the starting Level of the effect (the Level of the spell being duplicated, not modified by frequency of use or other factors).

Unless otherwise specified, an effect that needs concentration to maintain when cast as a spell needs concentration when triggered from an invested device as well.

All Targeting rolls demanded by a device's powers are made by the wielder of the device, using the wielder's Finesse score.

If a person gains possession of your magical device, and knows the triggering actions of its effects, that person may utilize your magical device. Even if the possessor does not know the triggering action, he may investigate your item in the lab to learn its powers.

## Effect Modifications

Listed below are several alterations you can integrate into a power when investing the power into a device. These alterations defy the "standards" for invested devices, set above.

### Raw Vis and Invested Devices "in The Field"

When investing an effect, you may open it to the use of *vis* at a later time, to increase the effect's Range and Duration when needed. When the power is activated, you must spend *vis* at the same time. This *vis* is used when needed "in the field," not during device creation. For each factor of Range and Duration that you want to be able to extend, add +3 to the effect's Level. For instance, a healing wand only heals damage temporarily unless *vis* is used with it (the same amount required for the spell being imitated). If you do not design the healing effect so that Duration can be extended "in the field", the use of *vis* with the wand is impossible. The number of pawns of *vis* which may be used in the field to extend Range and Duration is limited by the appropriate current Form or Technique score of the wielder. The Art score used is determined by the type of *vis* used.

## Penetration

You may elect that an effect makes Penetration rolls based on your Form and Technique scores when the effect is originally invested, rather than under the device's own power, by adding +4 to the Level. This means you must record these scores for future use. You may instead elect that the effect Penetrates according to the current Form and Technique scores of its wielder. This option adds +8 to the effect's Level.

## Concentration

When investing an effect, you can arrange to have the device maintain concentration on the effect for you. This option adds +5 to the effect's Level. Note that you still need to concentrate to change how the effect is used. For instance, a levitation belt that does not require concentration can hold you in the air, but to move up or down you have to concentrate. Furthermore, effects left to their own concentration gradually wear off at sunset and sunrise. At these times you must concentrate on the effect for a few moments to perpetuate it until the next sunrise/sunset, whichever comes first.

## Effect Use

You can restrict the use of a device's effect to a specific list of people (for example, you and all your current apprentices), by adding +3 to the Level of the effect. Otherwise, invested devices can be activated by anyone who knows their trigger actions.

### Powers that Affect the Device Alone

Some effects work only on the device in which they are placed, such as a staff that grows thorns like the *Transformation of the Thorny Staff* spell. If the effect only works on the device containing it, the total effect Level, after all other modifications, is divided by 2.

## Instilling the Effect

You have designed the effect that you want to invest in your device. Now you have to perform the ritual of joining. Your Lab Total is compared to the total modified Level of the effect. Lab Total is based on your Form and Technique scores appropriate to the effect, as it is with spells. Several modifiers apply to your Lab Total:

• If the effect you are investing mimics a spell with Casting Requisites, those Requisites apply to your Lab Total.

• Look on the *Form & Effects Bonuses Table* for the device or material being enchanted. If one of the bonuses listed matches the effect being invested, that bonus is added to your Lab Total.

• Add the strength of your magic Aura (probably that of your Covenant) to your Lab Total.

• For each effect already in the device that has a matching Technique and/or Form of the effect being invested, add +1 to your Lab Total.

You can only invest an effect if your Lab Total exceeds the modified Level of the effect. For each point by which your total exceeds the Level, you accumulate 1 point per Season. When you accumulate points equal to the modified Level, you invest the power. (Thus, if your Lab Total is double the modified Level of the effect, you can invest it in one Season.)

For every 10 points, or fraction thereof, of the modified Level of the effect, you must expend one pawn of raw vis, of an Art appropriate to the effect being invested. This vis is expended in the first Season you begin investing

### Effect Modification Table

| | |
|---|---|
| Restricted to specific people | +3 |
| Penetration based on Arts of creator | +4 |
| Penetration based on current Arts of wielder | +8 |
| Item maintains concentration | +5 |
| Range may be extended with *vis* | +3 |
| Duration may be extended with *vis* | +3 |
| Effect works only on item itself | Divide by 2 |

Add the number listed to the Level of the power. If the effect works only on the device itself, divide the Level of the power by 2, after all other modifications to the Level are made.

# FORMS AND EFFECTS BONUSES TABLE

| | | | | |
|---|---|---|---|---|
| Amber | +3 Córporem | | Crown | +3 control people |
| Agate | +3 air | | | +5 gain respect, authority |
| | +5 protection from storms | | | +2 wisdom |
| | +7 protection from venom | | Crystal | +5 water-related power |
| Amethyst | +7 versus drunkenness | | Dagger/Knife | +3 betrayal, assassination, poison |
| | +3 versus poison | | | +2 precise destruction |
| Aquamarine | +3 water | | Diamond | +5 versus demons |
| Animal Bone | +4 harm or destroy animals | | Door | +5 warding |
| Animal Hide | +7 turn into appropriate animal | | Doorway | +7 affect movement through |
| Armor | +7 protect wearer | | | +5 magical transportation |
| Arrow | +2 aiming | | | +7 magical gates and portals |
| | +3 direction | | Down | +3 silence |
| Axe | +4 destroy wood | | Drum | +5 deafening |
| Bag/Sack | +5 trapping things within | | | +2 cause fear |
| | +3 moving things into or out of | | | +3 create storms and thunder |
| Bandage | +4 healing wounds | | Earring | +5 affect hearing |
| Basket | +4 preserve contents | | Emerald | +7 snakes and dragonkind |
| | +5 create food within | | | +4 incite love or passion |
| | +3 create things within | | Fan | +4 create or control winds |
| Bed | +6 affect sleep and dreams | | | +4 banish weather phenomena |
| Bell | +5 warning | | Fired Clay | +4 contain or protect from fire |
| Bellows | +4 create wind | | Floor | +7 affect movement across |
| | +5 strengthen fire | | Glove | +4 affect things by touch |
| Belt or Girdle | +3 affect strength | | | +4 manipulation at a distance |
| Beryl | +3 water | | Gold | +4 induce greed |
| Bloodstone | +4 blood and wounds | | | +4 affect wealth |
| Bookshelf | +3 hide things within | | Green Turquoise | +4 necromancy |
| | +4 protect things within | | Hall | +6 affect movement through |
| Boots | +5 affect walking | | | +3 magical transportation |
| Bow | +5 destroy things at a distance | | Hat | +4 affect image of self |
| Cat's Eye | +3 versus malign Córporem | | Hazel | +3 divination (i.e., many Intéllego) |
| Chalice | +4 detect poison within | | Hearth | +7 create fire and heat |
| | +5 transform or create liquid within | | | +5 destroy things within |
| Clam Shell | +2 protection | | Helmet | +6 affect wearer's sight |
| Clear Glass | +4 invisibility | | | +4 affect wearer's mind and emotions |
| | +5 seeing through something | | Horseshoe | +6 affect horse's movement |
| Cloak | +5 alter or suppress wearers image | | | +2 warding |
| | +4 transform wearer | | Hourglass | +7 timing and alarms |
| | +3 flight | | | +3 increasing speed |
| Coin | +4 induce greed | | Human Bone | +4 destroy the human body |
| | +4 wealth and mercantile | | | +3 destroy the human mind |
| Collar | +6 control wearer | | Human Skull | +4 destroy human body |
| Comb | +7 affect hair | | | +5 destroy human mind |
| | +5 beauty | | | +5 destroy and control ghosts |
| Container | +5 create or transform things within | | Hyacinth | +2 healing |

| | | | |
|---|---|---|---|
| Iron | +7 harm or repel faeries | Rope or Cord | +2 strangulation |
| Iron Shackles | +8 bind faeries | | +4 restraint or magical binding |
| Jade | +4 Aquam | Ruby | +6 fire-related power |
| Jasper | +2 healing | | +3 affect blood |
| | +2 versus demons | | +4 leadership in war |
| Jewelry/Clothing | +4 transform self | Rug | +3 affect those upon it |
| | +4 protect self | Saddle | +7 affect riding |
| | +2 move self | | +4 affect horse |
| Jet | +2 protection | Sapphire | +3 healing |
| | +3 darkness | | +2 versus malign Córporem |
| Lamp | +7 produce light | | +2 knowledge |
| | +4 create fire | Sardonyx | +2 versus malign Córporem |
| Lead | +4 wards | Sea Shell | +2 the sea |
| Lion's Mane | +5 strength, courage, pride | | +3 sea creatures |
| Lyre | +5 affect music | Serpentine | +3 versus infection and animal poison |
| | +3 create sounds | Shackles | +6 restraint or magical binding |
| Magnetite | +3 Animál | Shield | +5 protection |
| Mask | +7 disguise | Ship Sail | +4 affect winds |
| | +3 hiding | | +7 sailing |
| | +2 affect wearer's sight | Silver | +10 harm lycanthropes |
| Necklace | +4 affect breathing and speaking | Snake Tongue | +6 lying |
| Net | +5 immobilization | | +3 deception |
| Oak | +7 protection from storms | Spade | +4 move or destroy earth |
| Oar | +4 affect currents | Star Ruby | +5 conjure and control occult entities |
| Obsidian | +5 darkness | Sword | +4 harm human and animal bodies |
| Onyx | +4 darkness | | +3 block single attack |
| | +4 death | Topaz | +4 strength, courage, pride |
| Opal | +4 travel | | +4 leadership |
| Panpipes | +5 revelry | | +5 controlling wild beasts |
| | +6 affect faerie emotions | Toy | +4 control children |
| | +3 affect emotions | Violet Amethyst | +4 ascendancy over masses |
| | +5 control children | | +7 versus drunkenness |
| Pearl | +5 detect or eliminate poisons | Wand/Staff | +4 destroy things at a distance |
| Pick | +4 destroy stone | | +4 control things at a distance |
| Pin Feather | +5 flight | | +3 project bolt or other missile |
| | +2 Auram | | +2 repel things |
| Quartz | +5 invisibility | Waterskin | +5 create liquid within |
| Quill | +7 Scribing | Whip | +4 control human or animal body |
| Rat Skull | +3 cause disease | | +5 induce fear in animals |
| Ring | +2 constant effect | Wood (dead) | +3 affect living wood |
| Rock Crystal | +3 healing | | +4 affect dead wood |
| | +5 clairvoyance | Yoke | +4 control wearer |
| Room | +6 affect everything within at once | | +5 enhance strength of wearer |
| | +4 create things within | | |

the effect. But remember, a given item can only hold a limited number of effects. If the amount of raw *vis* required to instill an effect brings the total amount of raw *vis* used above the total required to prepare the item for enchantment, the effect cannot be invested. So, if you are enchanting a silver dagger (which takes 16 pawns of *vis* to prepare for enchantment), you can only put 16 pawns worth of effects in it. If the dagger already has 14 pawns worth of powers, a power that requires 3 pawns of *vis* (i.e., a power of Level 21 to 30) does not "fit;" you cannot put it in the dagger.

# LESSER ENCHANTED DEVICES

Invested devices, though very powerful, take a great deal of time and *vis* to create. This extended time, investment, and care is required to insure that the full potential of the item is met, so that one's greatest magical powers can be preserved.

## Exempli Gratia:
### Creating an Invested Device

Grimgroth gets some raw Vim *vis* and decides to enchant his staff with the power to lift people into the air, like the spell Lift the Dangling Puppet (ReCo 20). Unfortunately, preparing a wooden staff for enchantment requires 8 raw *vis* points, and Grimgroth only has a Vim + Magic Theory total of 7. He takes some time to raise his Vim score 1 point, and can then handle the enchantment.

He spends one Season and 8 Vim *vis* points (as directed by the Material & Size Table) to prepare the staff. In the next Season he begins investing the effect into the staff.

The Level of the effect is 20 (the Level of the spell) + 1 (to be used twice a day) + 5 (for not requiring concentration to maintain) = 26.

A staff is a good item to use for a power that controls things at a distance. According to the Form and Effects Bonuses Table, a staff gives +4 on powers like this, so Grimgroth adds +4 when he tries to enchant his staff with the power. Grimgroth's Lab Total is 6 (Rego) + 7 (Córporem) + 3 (Intelligence) + 5 (Magic Theory) + 3 (magic Aura) + 4 (the Form and Effects bonus) = 28. His Lab Total exceeds the final Level of the effect by 2. That means he can invest the

effect in the staff, but it takes some time to do so, about 13 Seasons (2 points accumulated per Season until 26 are attained).

He wants to invest the effect more quickly, and the Storyguide allows him to spend extra *vis* to increase his Lab Total. Grimgroth spends two Córporem *vis*, granting him a +10 bonus to his Lab Total, making his final Lab Total 38 (28 + 10). His Lab Total is now 12 points higher than the modified Level of the power he's investing, so he completes the creation in three Seasons (12 points accumulated over three Seasons makes 26 points, the Level of the effect).

Investing the effect also takes the usual three *vis* (1 point per 10 Levels) to accomplish; Grimgroth uses three Rego *vis*, which applies to the Technique of the effect invested. He spends them in the first Season of his project, along with those devoted to his Lab Total.

Grimgroth decides the effect is triggered by pointing the staff at the target and spinning the staff counterclockwise.

The staff now has 5 (2 + 3) *vis* points worth of powers in it, and since it was enchanted with 8, there is still "room" for 3 more points.

However, you may wish to create enchanted devices that do not require the full potential of you or the item used. In this case, you create a more limited but less expensive type of magical device, called a lesser enchanted device.

To create a lesser enchanted device, choose the shape and material of the item as for an invested device, but you need not take a Season to prepare the item for enchantment. You perform a limited preparation and instill a single power, both within the same Season. That is, no initial Vim vis is spent to "open" the item to enchantment.

You must design the power your are instilling just as carefully as you do when instilling a power in an invested device. Indeed, all the modifiers for invested devices apply here. If your Lab total is twice the Level of the power (after all modifications), you enchant the power into the item. If not, the power is beyond your ability to instill in this limited manner; you must prepare and enchant the item as an invested device, or choose a power that is more within your capabilities (both of which are projects for another Season). If you attempt to instill a power and fail, your vis is wasted.

Though the amount of vis you may use is still limited by the material and size of the item, you do not use vis to "fill" the entire item. You must expend one pawn of Vim vis and one pawn of Art-specific vis for each 10 points, or fraction thereof, of the Level of the power you are instilling. You are still limited to using a maximum number of pawns of vis equal to your Magic Theory + Vim score in a single Season.

After a single Season, your work is complete. You may never instill any other powers into the item, even if the material and size of the item allow for more. A lesser enchanted device may never be used as a talisman.

## Charm Against Magic

Even though there is no spell to do so, Magi can invent magic devices (invested or lesser enchanted) to protect the bearer against magic. Treat this effect as Rego Vim. The Level of effect is the Magic Resistance provided. The charm works continually on the bearer of the device.

The charm works like a Parma Magica, but is incompatible with Parma Magica or any other type of Magic Resistance. Thus, the bearer may not add his score in a Form to the charm's Magic Resistance. If the bearer has a Magic Resistance of his own, the higher of the two protections, that of the bearer or that of the charm, overrules the other.

## Option: Applying Vis to Lab Total

If a Magus has a low Lab Total, she is often slow or ineffectual at investing powerful effects into devices. This means created magical items are somewhat rare, and often the creations of more powerful Magi. If the Storyguide wants more magical items in the game, or feels that an invested item deserves a special chance, he may allow extra vis to be applied to the investment of an effect. For every pawn of Art-specific vis that the Magus spends, she gains +5 to her Lab Total. This vis is above and beyond that Vim vis which must be expended to open an item's enchantment, and is beyond that which must be spent to invest the effect at all.

This extra vis also counts toward the total amount that can be spent on an item's powers (i.e., against the total Vim vis spent to open the item's enchantment). So, if you need to boost your Lab Total with extra vis, your device is able to hold less overall magic. Extra vis used also counts toward the total amount of vis that you can use in a Season.

Extra vis can be applied to Lab Total for the creation of invested devices only, not lesser enchanted items (which are described below).

## The Enchanted Item in Use

You can use one effect from an item each Round, using the appropriate trigger action for each. You must make any Targeting or magic Penetration rolls that are necessary, but you do not have to roll for Fatigue. The Duration is usually the shorter of the two for spells mimicked, but some effects can be boosted by vis for the longer Duration (if that option was made possible during the magic item's creation).

If the enchanted device is broken, all its powers are lost.

You may use an enchanted item before it is "filled up" with powers, and may then add powers later.

# POTIONS

A potion is a specialized, single-use type of enchantment that affects whatever it is applied to. Manufacturing potions is relatively easy, requiring you to alchemically combine, refine, and distill the magical essence of mundane ingredients. Creating potions requires no vis, and you can often brew several doses of a potion in a single Season.

When making a potion, you must fully describe its effect, as you do when inventing a spell. The potion only affects whatever it is applied to, so some spells cannot be

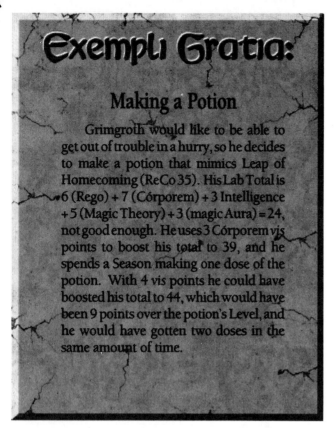

### Making a Potion

Grimgroth would like to be able to get out of trouble in a hurry, so he decides to make a potion that mimics Leap of Homecoming (ReCo 35). His Lab Total is 6 (Rego) + 7 (Córporem) + 3 Intelligence + 5 (Magic Theory) + 3 (magic Aura) = 24, not good enough. He uses 3 Córporem vis points to boost his total to 39, and he spends a Season making one dose of the potion. With 4 vis points he could have boosted his total to 44, which would have been 9 points over the potion's Level, and he would have gotten two doses in the same amount of time.

duplicated by potions. For instance, an *Unseen Arm* potion is not possible. A potion never gives anyone the ability to cast a spell.

Once you have chosen the effect, you spend a Season, add your Aura (probably that of your Covenant) to your Lab Total, and compare the total to the Level of the effect. For every 5 points, or fraction thereof, by which you exceed the Level, you get one dose of potion. If your Lab Total is less than the Level of the effect, and you are not using vis in the potion (see below), the Season is wasted in your attempt.

Though it is not required, you may wish to expend raw vis when creating potions. If you want the potion to have the longer of two Durations listed for a spell (which is especially important for healing spells), you must put Art-specific vis into each potion just as if you are casting the spell. You may also expend Art-specific vis to increase your Lab Total, receiving +5 per pawn used. If you want to use vis to increase the potion's Duration and your Lab Total, you have to pay for each separately. If vis is used, but your Lab Total still doesn't exceed the Level of the effect, the Season is wasted, and you lose all the vis you used.

Note that it's impossible to simulate a Ritual spell with a potion.

Whatever the potion is applied to undergoes the effects of the spell copied. The effect might not be obvious. For example, a potion that lets the drinker fly has no noticeable effect until the person jumps into the air. Targets get normal Magic Resistance rolls against the effects of potions, even if they want the potion to affect them.

Keep in mind that the term potion refers to any salve, incense, paste, powder, ointment or similar substance you wish to make; though potions are often in liquid form, they don't have to be. When you create a substance similar to a potion, you have to indicate how the substance is applied in order for it to work. A salve is applied to the body of the recipient. Dust is sprinkled over the recipient. Incense is inhaled by the recipient. The Storyguide may give you a bonus to your Lab Total if you choose a form for your substance that's especially suited to the effect it produces.

# LONGEVITY POTIONS

As a Magus, you find that your time to study and increase your power has an ultimate deadline: your inevitable demise. In their attempts to gain themselves more time in this world, the Magi of Hermes have developed longevity potions. Though death is still inevitable, these potions can stave off death for a hundred years or more. Magi of two hundred years or older are rare, but not unheard of.

The longevity potion acts as a magical anchor, sustaining the vital life force of the Magus, often by directly affecting the tissues of the Magus's body. This anchor, however, prevents the Magus from expending his life force in normal human fashion, so the Magus becomes sterile. Though called a potion, the longevity effect may be created in any form you desire. Charms, potions, clothes, and tattoos are just some of the forms possible. The means of applying these different forms depends on what effect you want. A longevity charm, for example, has to be worn constantly to provide its preserving power. If it's removed, you could die immediately, or slowly fade away until the charm is returned or a new longevity "potion" is created. A tattoo, on the other hand, is part of you, but might fade when the longevity "potion" in your system fails. Thus, you have a physical countdown of your decline.

The first stage in creating your potion is determining what ingredients you need. You can determine the ingredients, gather them, and brew them in one Season if your Lab Total (based on Intéllego Córporem) and magic Aura total 20 or more. Gathering the ingredients can be part of a story. If your Lab Total is less than 20, you lack the knowledge to form the longevity potion.

Every Magus has a unique formula for a longevity potion, and one Magus's potion is of no benefit to another. The 'standard' Hermetic potion requires one pawn of vis per five years, or fraction thereof, of your current age to

## Summary of Enchanted Items

### Preparing an Item for Enchantment

Spend one Season expending pawns of Vim vis according to Material & Size Table

### Enchanting an Invested Device

1) Select item's physical form
2) Prepare the item for enchantment
3) Choose an effect to instill, including its Level
   - (a) Adjust Level for Effect Frequency
   - (b) Adjust Level for Effect Modifications
   - (c) Detail triggering action
4) Instill Effect
   - (a) Add Aura, Form and Effect Bonuses to Lab Total
   - (b) Accumulated Lab Total - modified effect Level = points per Season. When accumulated point total equals or exceeds Level, power instilled
   - (c) Expend 1 pawn Art-specific vis for each 10 points, or fraction thereof, in Level

5) Repeat steps 3 and 4 as desired, but total pawns of vis used to instill powers may not exceed number of pawns used to prepare item for enchantment.

### Attuning a Talisman

1) Select item's physical form
2) Prepare the item for enchantment
3) Spend one Season attuning as a talisman
4) As often as desired, spend one Season opening one Form and Effects bonus

### Creating a Lesser Enchantment

1) Select item's physical form
2) Choose an effect to instill, as for an invested device
3) Instill Effect
   - (a) If Lab Total is at least twice Level, you succeed
   - (b) Expend 1 pawn Vim vis and 1 pawn Art-specific vis for each 10 points, or fraction thereof, in Level

---

create. The potion functions to improve your chances of weathering Aging rolls (see the Saga Chapter, p.354) unharmed. The potion subtracts 1 from your Aging rolls for every 5 full points in your Intéllego Córporem Lab Total (modified by your magic Aura). For example, a Magus whose InCo Lab Total total is 33 creates a potion that subtracts 6 from his Aging rolls. A Magus can reinvent his potion at a later time to take advantage of increases in his Art scores, but this requires investing another Season of research and the appropriate vis for the new potion.

Normally, only Creo, Córporem, and Vim vis may be used in a longevity potion. However, a longevity potion is a very personal creation, and as such, it is uniquely tied to your magical abilities. You may, with the approval of the Troupe or Storyguide, substitute any type of vis which your magical talents are strongly associated with.

A longevity potion lasts until you actually suffer the effects of Aging, losing a point from a Characteristic or gaining a Decrepitude point. After this, the potion loses its effectiveness, and a new potion must be brewed from the formula of the first, requiring a new investment of vis (an amount based on your current age), but no significant investment in time. This "replacement" potion may be created using your lab text (see below) from the previous brewing. You only need to spend another Season researching and brewing your potion if you wish to improve its effectiveness (i.e., take advantage of your higher Art scores).

When creating a new longevity potion, you can increase its potency by adding extra *vis* to the brew. This *vis* is above and beyond that which you must spend for your current age. For each additional pawn you add to the brew add 1 to your Lab Total. This *vis* must be invested when you originally create the potion. The same amount must be used in potions that duplicate the first — potions made after the original fails. Extra *vis* spent does not increase your Lab Total to determine if you can create a longevity potion in the first place.

If your current longevity potion fails, and you do not or cannot create another, you begin to feel the effects of age. All further Aging rolls you make go without the longevity potion modifier (i.e., your rolls on the *Aging Chart* are not reduced). If you create another longevity potion at a future date, it does not eliminate any Decrepitude points or Characteristic loses suffered when you were "cold turkey."

You can make longevity potions for others, even non-Magi. To determine the ingredients for another person's potion, you and that character must spend one Season of research and brewing. Your Lab Total (based on Intéllego Córporem), plus Aura, must equal 30+. Otherwise, you cannot determine what ingredients need to go into the potion. If your score is 30+, you can make the potion and must invest one pawn of *vis* per five years of the character's current age. A longevity potion made for another Magus functions just as if made for you (-1 to Aging rolls for every 5 points of Lab Total). Non-magical people, however, are not as resilient as Magi. The potion you create for a

## Laboratory Texts

### *You may not change:*

Type of enchantment (invested device, lesser enchanted device, or potion)

Effect produced (the spell mimicked)

Form (shape and material of an item, or form, and method of applying potion)

Scope of the effect (whether the power affects the item itself or something else)

Amount of *vis* used to increase Lab Total

### *You may change:*

Aura in which the enchantment was performed

Enchanted Items:

Frequency (number of uses per day)

Triggering action

Effect Modifications

Potions:

Number of doses produced

## Lab Texts in the Saga

Lab texts are excellent means by which to record the ongoing events of your Saga. As Magi are undoubtedly at constant work in their labs, producing different magical devices, their texts form journals of their experiences and record their magical careers. However, lab texts can also be made to record the events of more mundane events, including the events of your stories. For instance, if characters set out on a journey for Herbam *vis*, a Magus's lab text can refer to that journey when the *vis* is used. A note in the margin might read, "That blasted Herbam *vis* almost destroyed my lab! I swear those damnable faeries are getting the final laugh at my expense." Thus, your notes on your Magus's lab texts can incorporate both game mechanics and fictional pieces, a combination of the conventions and fantasy of the game.

mundane therefore only subtracts one from the character's Aging rolls for every 10 full points in your Lab Total.

Note that longevity potions help forestall loss of Characteristics and acquisition of Decrepitude points due to aging alone. You can still suffer these afflictions by other means. If physical injuries, Wizard's Twilight, or some other harm comes upon you, you may lose Characteristic points and gain Decrepitude points. Your longevity potions do not protect you from this harm, but these afflictions do not cause your current potion to fail. Your current potion only fails you if harm is caused directly through aging.

It is rumored within the Order of Hermes that more powerful versions of longevity potions have been created, but all must either be very dangerous or have significant side effects.

# LABORATORY TEXTS

When you instill a power into an enchanted item or create a batch of potions, your work is not forgotten as soon as the enchantment is complete. You create a laboratory text to record your work, and you can use the lab text to help you recreate your work.

Because of the inflexible, complex nature of enchantments, however, a lab text is not as useful as a spell written out in full. While a written spell aids you in learning a spell and maybe creating other spells with similar effects, a lab text only allows you to duplicate the results of a previous experiment (but does enable you to modify the way the effect is produced).

Essentially, a lab text is a record of a Magus's life in the laboratory. You must therefore record all the factors involved in an invested device or potion you create, so you have them on hand when you refer to your lab texts at a

later date. The factors you must record include the types and amounts of *vis* used in a project, and the effect modifications added to an enchanted device.

## Creating Laboratory Texts

A lab text is automatically created whenever you instill a power in an invested device, create a lesser enchanted device, or create a batch of potions. The lab text you create provides a bonus, equal to your score in Magic Theory, on any further enchantments of the same type, and which produce the same effect, that you attempt. This Magic Theory bonus is equal to your Magic Theory score at the writing of the lab text, not your score when the text is referred to again. If the enchantment recorded in the text is within your Magic Theory specialty (see *Abilities*, p.100), you also add 1 to the score of the lab text.

You can also use the lab texts of other Magi to reproduce their creations. You might copy another Magus's lab text to apply her lab notes to your own projects. Thus, you gain the bonus of her Magic Theory score at the time she wrote the text. However, reproducing another's project (and in so doing creating your own lab text) with the aid of another's lab text is useless unless your Magic

Theory is higher than the Magic Theory of the Magus who created the original lab text.

## Using Laboratory Texts

If you have a lab text describing how to instill a power into an item, you get a flat bonus to your Lab Total when instilling that same effect into the same type of item (i.e., an item that provides the same *Form and Effects* bonuses).

If you have a lab text describing how to create a batch of potions, you get a bonus to your Lab Total when creating a batch of potions with the same powers. Thus, you can create more doses of the potion than you normally would.

In the case of longevity potions, the Magic Theory bonus makes your recent potions more potent and resistant to Aging. However, a lab text for longevity potions is only useful when recreating your previous batch of potions, and that lab text is even valid if you have to add more vis to the new potion based on your increased age. If you're creating a new potion to take advantage of your increased Art scores, your previous lab texts are useless.

written. The Level of the text is *not* equal to the creating Magus's Magic Theory score at the time of your writing.

As previously mentioned, you can use another Magus's lab text to work from. However, you first have to decode that Magus's personal writing style, and then translate her notes into a form you can use. The whole process takes a Season, at the end of which you have the notes for one of the Magus's lab projects — her notes on making a certain potion, or investing a certain device. The rules for decoding and translating lab notes are the same for those of spell notes (see Translating *Spells*, p.240)

## Details of the Enchantment

A lab text helps you to create the same effect in an enchanted item or potion, but you may change many of the details of the enchantment and still receive the benefits of the lab text.

Basic elements of the original project can't change. The type of enchantment (i.e., invested or minor) must remain the same. The form and material of the magic item must remain the same (i.e., *Form & Effects* bonuses must not change), and if the original power affected the device itself, then so must the duplicated power.

If any *vis* was used to increase Lab Total when making the original batch of potions or invested power, you must use the same type and amount of *vis* when using the lab text, but you still gain +5 to your Lab Total per pawn of *vis* used for that purpose. If you do not use the same *vis*, you gain no benefit from the lab text.

# INVESTIGATING AN ENCHANTMENT

If you wish to determine the powers of an enchantment of someone else's creation, you must investigate it in your lab. You inspect the item's physical construction, investigate the Form and Technique with Intéllego magics, and test to see how the enchantment responds to other magics. All of this indicates how the item was created, what its powers are, and how to unleash them.

To investigate an enchantment, you spend a Season, add a stress die to your Intéllego Vim Lab Total, and compare the result to the Level of the weakest power in the enchantment. The Level of a power in an enchanted device includes any effect modifications that apply to the power (see *Invested Devices*, p.243). A device's function as a talisman is treated as a Level 20 power. If you succeed in the roll to identify the weakest power, you discover that function, and may roll again in the same Season for the power immediately above it in strength. Discovering a power in an enchanted device includes discovering the

If you create a longevity potion and make a lab text of it, that text is only of use to you. Longevity potions are too personalized for their lab texts to be used for the potions of others. However, if you're creating a longevity potion for another, and make a lab text of your work, you can refer to that text when making more potions for that individual (assuming the new potion isn't based on your improved Art scores).

## Translating Laboratory Texts

A Magus's lab text notes, like notes for spells, are not originally in a format suitable for others to use. You may copy your own lab texts into a suitable format at the rate of 60 Levels per full Season. You may copy lab texts already in readable format at the rate of 180 Levels per Season. The Level of the text equals the modified Level of the effect invested or potion created when the text is triggering ritual and any restrictions and effect modifications there might be on it.

If you roll well to detect a single power invested in a device (e.g., that with the lowest Level), you do not find the power with the highest Level that your Lab Total beats, and all other powers that have lower ratings. You are simply rolling to discover the lowest-rated power, and must work your way up from there. For example, a device has three powers of Level 10, 20 and 30. If your rolled Lab Total is 25, you do not automatically find the first two powers. As your rolled Lab Total is over 10 (the Level of the first power), you find the first power and may roll again in the Season to find the second power (Level 20), and maybe the third power if you discover the second.

As long as you succeed, you keep rolling. If you roll and find nothing, it either means that there are no more powers in the enchantment, or that you did not roll high enough to find the next one (only the Storyguide knows). In either case, you can keep trying as long as you want, but each failure to discover a power ends the rolls for that Season, and you can do nothing else that Season.

If you Botch any investigation roll, many results can arise, and the Storyguide makes the final decision based on the situation. You can misinterpret a power, thinking it does something different from its actual function. You could misread the triggering action of a power, making it useless to you. Or, you could somehow disturb the enchanted item, setting off its powers. The *Magic Botch Suggestions Table* offers some ideas on what may happen. If you survive an investigation Botch, your Season ends there. However, you may approach the device again next Season to properly identify the power that confounded you.

Magi sometimes use the *Waiting Spell* (p.235) to guard their enchanted devices. The spell held in waiting is often released on anyone who magically examines the item. The *Waiting Spell* is not invested into the device *per se* but cast on it for protection. You therefore cannot detect a *Waiting Spell* in your preliminary "look over" investigations of an item. If you do not cast a spell to detect a *Waiting Spell*, discovering it often means tripping it. Beware.

# ARCANE EXPERIMENTATION

The preceding enchantment rules assume that you are being careful with your laboratory work, staying safely within the bounds of what you know how to do. If you wish, however, you can test your limits and experiment, trying new and possibly dangerous techniques. You can experiment when inventing a spell, creating any magical

## Extraordinary Results Chart

| Roll | Result |
| --- | --- |
| Botch | Disaster |
| 0-3 | Complete Failure |
| 4-5 | No Extraordinary Effects |
| 6-7 | No Benefit from Experimentation |
| 8 | Side Effect |
| 9 | Special or Story Event |
| 10 | Discovery! |
| 11 | Modified Effect |
| 12+ | Roll Twice |

**Disaster**: See the *Disaster Effect Table*

**Complete Failure:** You get nothing from your efforts, not even your basic Lab Total worth of work. If working on an enchanted item or Familiar, roll another die; a 0 indicates that the item or your Familiar is destroyed.

**No Extraordinary Effects:** Your experimentation works without producing any unintended side effects. You get the bonus for experimentation (simple die plus Risk Modifier), but suffer no other effects.

**No Benefit from Experimentation:** Your experimentation may produce no results. You automatically lose the benefits of the experimentation simple die and any Risk Modifier. Recalculate Lab Total without these factors. If the new Lab Total is insufficient to succeed in the project, the project must be abandoned at that point.

**Side Effect:** See the *Side Effect Table*

**Special or Story Event:** Your work is affected in some manner not covered by any of the other choices, or the Storyguide may choose one of the other choices. In any case, a special result usually indicates that your work somehow involves the Covenant in a story. For instance, an emergency might arise and the other Magi find out a secret about you when they come to your aid. The story can involve danger, humor, problem solving, and interaction among those who live in the Covenant, taking up a whole session or just a few minutes of casual roleplaying. Have fun with it.

**Modified Effect:** See the *Modified Effect Table*

**Discovery:** See the *Discovery Effect Table*

**Roll Twice:** Roll two more times, adding the Risk Modifier to both rolls. If either of your second two rolls turns up here again, ignore the result and reroll.

enchantment (device or Familiar), creating a potion, or investigating an enchantment. In any case, you have the chance to perform feats that are normally beyond your capabilities, but you also have the chance to fail utterly, perhaps dangerously.

## The Experimental Premise

At the beginning of each Season, consider the project you're working on and decide whether you want to experiment on it. You may decide to experiment from Season to Season, as long as you're beginning a new project. You can only experiment on a project if you decide to do so from the beginning.

## Disaster Effect Table

You fail miserably, bringing about a disaster. Roll a simple die + Risk Modifier - Perception, on the following chart:

| Roll | Result |
|---|---|
| 0 or less | You manage to spot the disaster before it occurs. You do not suffer the results of a disaster, but your Season is wasted; see Complete Failure. |
| 1 | **Creation Destroyed:** Whatever you are working on and all your notes on it are completely destroyed. You must start over from scratch. If you are working on an enchanted item of any kind, the entire item is destroyed, not just a single power. |
| 2 | **Something Valuable Destroyed:** Your creation is destroyed (see number 1, above), and it takes something else valuable with it (e.g., your Familiar, apprentice, an enchanted item, stores of *vis*, books). |
| 3 | **Creation Turns on You:** Your creation turns on you, attacking you with its most powerful attack capability. If the creation has absolutely no attack capability, you're safe. |
| 4 | **Lab Ruined:** Your creation is destroyed (see number 1, above), taking much of your lab with it. Roll a die for everything valuable in your lab — on a roll of 0, it is destroyed. You must spend the rest of this Season and all of the next repairing your lab and salvaging your notes. If the Covenant is not wealthy enough to provide more lab equipment, you'll have to work or pay to get it from somewhere else. |
| 5 | **Explosion:** Take damage equal to a damage die plus the Level of the spell or power. |
| 6 | **Threat to Covenant:** Your work backfires and threatens the Covenant, causing a fire, leaving the Covenant open to enemy assault, calling up a dangerous creature, or whatever is appropriate. |
| 7 | **Special:** Some disaster not covered in this chart befalls you. A roll on the *Bad Effects Chart* of Wizard's Twilight (p. 357) is appropriate, or anything else the Troupe and Storyguide can come up with. |
| 8 | **Deterioration:** You lose 1 point automatically from one Characteristic or you gain one Decrepitude point; roll on the *Aging Chart* (p. 354). This isn't real aging, but the effects are similar. |
| 9-10 | **Twilight:** Roll for Wizard's Twilight, adding the rank (Level/5) of the spell or power to the Aura to determine the strength of the supernatural power you must control. |
| 11 | **Overwhelmed:** You release too much magic for you to control. Roll a stress die + Stamina - Aura - Risk Modifier. If the result is 6+, you control the magic, but roll for Wizard's Twilight (see number 9-10, above). Otherwise you are destroyed, though a magical shadow of your former self might remain. |
| 12+ | **Roll Twice:** Ignore and reroll if rolled again. |

If you do experiment, add a simple die roll to your Lab Total. This bonus represents the fruits of the risks you take. However, you must also roll on the *Extraordinary Results Chart* for each Season that the project involves. After all, taking chances has its risks. If you experiment over multiple Seasons, inventing the same spell or instilling the same power in a device, the *Chart* results for each Season accumulate and apply to the whole project. For example, if it takes two Seasons to invest a power into your staff, you have to make a roll on the *Chart* each Season. Both results affect the staff or the power you're investing into it.

# Inventing a Spell

Points from the simple die, added to your Lab Total, might let you finish a spell sooner, or even invent a spell that is otherwise beyond your capacity. If your spell comes out flawed or difficult to cast because of your roll on the *Extraordinary Results Chart*, you have two choices: live with it or reinvent the spell. If you re-invent it, use the normal spell invention rules (p.239). However, you gain your Magic Theory score (that at the time of your experiment) as a bonus to your roll to accomplish the invention, having learned something from your nearly successful experiment. Thus, your Magic Theory score is applied twice to your re-inventing Lab Total. The re-invention process must occur in another Season.

If your Lab Total is still lower than the spell's Level, even with the added simple die, you cannot invent the spell, and must still make a roll on the *Extraordinary Results Chart*. Even though your experiment fails, it can still blow up in your face. Having failed to invent the spell, you may try again next Season, and may experiment again.

## Side Effect Table

Your magical creation acquires a side effect, determined by a simple die + Risk Modifier roll on the following table:

| Roll | Result |
|---|---|
| 1 | **Exaggerated Sigil:** Your Sigil is exaggerated to many times its normal strength, becoming a significant portion of the effect. |
| 2 | **Minor Flaw:** Such as a spell to communicate with animals that causes you to retain some speech habits of the animal in question for a while after the spell ends. |
| 3-4 | **Minor Side Effect:** A neutral side effect such as a beast control spell that causes grass to grow under the beasts' feet. |
| 5 | **Minor Side Benefit:** Such as a wind spell that has a sweet scent and makes flying insects uncomfortable. |
| 6 | **Major Flaw:** Such as a healing spell that causes intense pain in the recipient. |
| 7-8 | **Major Side Effect:** Such as a plant control spell that attracts all birds within 100 paces. |
| 9 | **Major Side Benefit:** Such as a spell designed to transform you into a wolf that allows you to speak with all beasts while a wolf. |
| 10-13 | **Fatal Flaw:** Such as an invisibility spell that makes you glow. |

## Invested Devices

Even with the added bonus of a simple die, your lab total may not meet the Level of the effect you're investing. In that case, you lose all the vis involved and must still roll on the *Extraordinary Effects Chart*. You may try again next Season, though, and may experiment again.

If your Lab Total is high enough to invest a power, but the power turns out to be flawed (as determined by a roll on the *Chart*), it still "takes up space" in your device, just like a normal power. Even if you can get the flawed power out of your device, it still denies you the points of vis it "occupied" in the item. Thus, if you risk experimentation and make a mistake, you can permanently limit the effectiveness of your magical item.

## Enchanting a Familiar

When enchanting a Familiar (see *Familiars*, below), the simple die is added to the strength of the bond you create, thus increasing both the number of points from which you purchase ratings in the cords, and the number of Levels of powers exchanged. Any results from the *Extraordinary Results Chart* are applied to all the powers

you both grant and receive. The Troupe may choose to have you roll separately on the *Chart* for each power exchanged, or may apply the results of a single roll to all powers exchanged. Powers that are gained, but altered by the *Chart*, cannot be changed or revoked.

## Inventing Potions

Even with the help of experimentation, your Lab Total may not exceed the Level of the spell being invested into a potion. In that case you fail to produce the potion, lose any vis used, waste a Season, and must still roll on the *Extraordinary Results Chart*.

If the potion's invention succeeds, but comes out flawed according to your roll on the *Chart*, you may attempt the potion again, by normal means, another Season. Your Magic Theory score (that at the time of your experiment) is used as a bonus to your attempt to re-invent the potion, having learned from your nearly successful experiment. Thus, your Magic Theory is applied twice to your re-inventing Lab Total.

You may also experiment on longevity potions, adding the simple die to your Lab Total. This bonus increases the potency of your potion, giving you greater resilience

## Modified Effect Table

The effect is modified in some way. Roll simple die + Risk Modifier on the following chart. If you are investigating a magic item, the item is damaged, one or more of the powers being modified:

| Roll | Result |
|------|--------|
| 1 | **Reduced Effect:** The effect is limited in Range, Duration, or potency, such as a Mentem spell that allows a generous Natural Resistance roll or which cannot be Mastered. |
| 2 | **Restricted Use:** The effect fails to work in certain circumstances, such as a fire spell that sputters and dies in fog or rain. |
| 3 | **Heavily Restricted Use:** The effect only works during special circumstances, such as a healing spell that only works on children. |
| 4 | **Enhanced Effect:** The Range, Duration, or potency of the spell is increased, such as an attack spell with a high Targeting bonus or a power in an enchanted item with enhanced Penetration. |
| 5 | **Enhanced Usage:** The effect works on a greater than expected range of targets, such as a spell to speak with beasts which only needs casting Requisites to speak with birds and fish. |
| 6-7 | **Partial Success:** The spell or power is only one-half the expected Level. Adjust the effect accordingly. If you reinvent a partially successful spell, the Level bonus gained is one-quarter the initial Level of the spell. |
| 8-9 | **Exceptional Success:** Add +5 to the Level of the spell or power. Adjust the effect accordingly. |
| 10-11 | **Modified Effect:** The actual effect is modified, affecting a different type of target than expected, or affecting targets in a different way, such as a *Curse of Circe* spell (p.XX) that turns the target into a goat rather than a pig, or a speak with beasts spell that makes beasts speak Latin to you instead of allowing you to speak with them. |
| 12-13 | **Heavily Modified Effect:** The effect is heavily modified, producing results within the same Technique and Form, but possibly completely different than expected. Your *Curse of Circe* spell could become *Preternatural Growth and Shrinking*, instead. The Level of the effect remains the same or is lowered. |

## Exempli Gratia:
### Arcane Experimentation

Remember when Grimgroth was trying to invent a Level 15 spell and he could almost do it in one Season? Instead of taking up two Seasons or studying his Arts to make the task easier, he chooses to experiment, to push his capabilities, and try to complete the spell in one Season. His Lab Total of 28, plus a simple die roll of 6, equals 34, high enough to invent a Level 15 spell in one Season. But now he has to roll on the Extraordinary Results Chart. He rolls a 8, Side Effect. For the type of Side Effect he rolls 5, Minor Side Benefit. The spell causes a stench, so Grimgroth's player and the Storyguide agree that the smell lingers for hours on the bodies of people who come in contact with it. That means Grimgroth can recognize people by their smell later on, particularly useful for identifying masked attackers. If this side effect was debilitating instead, Grimgroth could attempt to reinvent the spell by normal means. The +3 modifier (his Magic Theory score) he would receive to his Lab Total would let him complete the spell in another single Season, by the normal processes of spell invention.

discover an item's powers. You still have to roll on the *Chart*, though.

When investigating an enchanted item by experimenting on it, you take risks not normally taken, and may damage or destroy the magic item in the process. Any results from the *Chart* indicating damage or changes to the project you are working on are applied to the magic item or one of its powers. It's possible, though, that a magic

against the affects of Aging. If your potion is flawed by a roll on the *Extraordinary Results Chart*, you may recreate your potion next Season and add your Magic Theory score as a bonus to your Lab Total for that potion (thus Magic Theory is applied twice to Lab Total).

## Investigating an Enchanted Item

The simple die is added to every roll made to discover an item's invested powers. Even with the help of experimentation, your Lab Total may not be high enough to

## Discovery Table

Your work has given you a new insight into the art of magic:

| Roll | Result |
|------|--------|
| 1-5 | **Primary Discovery:** Add +1 to your score in one of the Arts used |
| 6-7 | **Related Discovery:** If you are using any Magic Affinity Ability in the lab project, add 3 Experience Points to it. Otherwise, treat as a result of 1-5, above. |
| 8 | **Peripheral Discovery:** Add 3 Experience Points to your score in one Arcane Talent, Arcane Skill, or Mental Skill. |
| 9-11 | **New Understanding:** Add 3 Experience Points to your Magic Theory |
| 12-13 | **Roll Twice:** Ignore and reroll if rolled again. |

item's own protections can preserve it from the dangers of your experiments. If the Level of an item's protecting power (like Magic Resistance or an appropriate spell) exceeds your Lab Total (including any bonus for experimentation), the item resists any damaging effects rolled on the *Chart*.

## Exceptional Risk

You may choose to push your limits even further, adding from +1 to +3 (your choice) to the simple die roll; this bonus is called your Risk Modifier. When you do this, you must add the Risk Modifier to all your rolls on the *Extraordinary Results Chart*, and you get a number of extra Botch dice on your rolls equal to your bonus (rolls made on the *Extraordinary Results Chart* are stress).

## Extraordinary Results

Some of the results listed on the *Chart* are specific, such as +5 to the Level of effect, but others require some interpretation. When interpreting these results, consider the Magus's Sigil, Specialties, and weaknesses. Also take into account the type of spell or power being worked on, and the Laws of Magic. The more aspects of magic that you bring together, the more interesting the result is.

When referring to the *Extraordinary Results Chart*, roll a stress die, adding your Risk Modifier (if any). If you roll a 0, roll one Botch die, plus a number of Botch dice equal to your Risk Modifier. You also get one additional Botch die for each point in your Magic Aura.

# THE LABORATORY IN PLAY

Laboratory activities take up most of your life as a Magus, so you should take some care in deciding both your individual laboratory activities, and your attitude towards your laboratory and your creations. Your laboratory itself is an important reflection of your personality, as it is where you spend much of your time. Take the time to think about what your sanctum looks like, and what's in it. Does your sanctum bear protective spells? Where do you sleep? What do you have in your lab, and where do you keep it? Do you hide your most prized possessions? Is your laboratory clean and well kept, or a disorganized mess in which no one but you can find anything? Answering such questions helps you define who your Magus really is.

## Multiple Laboratory Activities

Sometimes you may wish to perform laboratory activities which, though rewarding, are well within your capabilities, and are not worth an entire Season of effort for a single activity. In this case, you may choose to perform multiple activities within the same Season, splitting your time among them all.

All the activities you perform in a Season must be of the same type (learning spells, instilling powers in an invested device, creating potions) and must use the same Technique and Form for all. For example, you can invent two spells or create three batches of potions in a single Season, but you cannot both invent a spell and create a batch of potions in the same Season.

To perform multiple activities, simply add up the Levels of all activities performed, and apply your Lab Total to the total of the Levels.

If you perform arcane experimentation, you add a single simple die + Risk Modifier to your Lab Total, but any results rolled on the *Extraordinary Results Chart* apply to all activities performed in the Season.

## Help in the Lab

Though the Code of Hermes provides protection for Magi who meet on neutral grounds, the sanctum of a Magus (laboratory and living quarters) is a special place in which Magi hold their greatest treasures and deepest secrets. Thus, the Code of Hermes allows for Magi to exact any toll on Magi who trespass within their sanctums. For this reason, very few Magi ever cooperate in laboratory work, as one Magus has to venture into the sanctum of another and risk attack.

Nevertheless, there are times when Magi receive help in their laboratory work, either from trusting Magi, or from apprentices (see below). Anyone who has the Gift, Hermetic Training (a Magic Theory score), and a positive Intelligence may help you to study Arts or Magic Theory from vis, or to perform any activity which uses your Magic Theory. If you are performing some activity which uses your Magic Theory, you add the helper's Magic Theory + Intelligence to your Lab Total for the Season. If you are studying from vis, you add +1 to your studying roll for the Season. If the assistant has some appropriate Virtue, like Inventive Genius, that Virtue affects the primary researcher's efforts, adding to his scores and rolls in the lab.

Thus, when two Magi cooperate, one must always be the primary researcher and one must be the assistant. Even if Magi are not in danger of attack from one another, very few are willing to spend a Season in the role of lab assistant; the Hermetic social implications are unconscionable.

You may not normally have more than one helper in the lab, as it is difficult to coordinate several helpers with you and with each other. However, if people are exceptionally well-organized and cooperative, more can work together, each helper adding his Magic Theory and Intelligence scores to the primary researcher's scores.

## Distractions From Studies

The rules for what a Magus can do in a Season assume that the Season is uninterrupted. Sometimes, however, Magi take time away from their labs to travel and explore, and this lost time makes itself felt in their lab performance.

You may miss up to 10 days from any laboratory activity, and make up the time by working harder during the remainder of the Season. There is no penalty for this. Your Lab Total is reduced by 1 for each day over 10 that you miss, or, if you are studying, the source you are studying from counts as though it is one level lower for every two days over 10 that you miss.

If the procedure you are performing requires a *full* Season, such as performing multiple tasks of the same kind, any interruption of more than 10 days ruins the procedure, and any *vis* you have expended in the Season is lost.

# Familiars

Protective of their secrets and suspicious of any who might hold power over them, Magi are notoriously distant from other people. They can find some companionship with apprentices, but the master-apprentice bond atrophies after the apprentice becomes a Magus, and sometimes their devotion to each other turns to rivalry. For longer-lasting and deeper companionship, many Magi turn to beings they form and can trust: Familiars.

A Familiar is a magical beast which a Magus befriends, and then magically bonds with, instilling the beast with magical powers and merging the beast's powers and abilities with the Magus's own. Though a Familiar is very close to the Magus that creates it, it always has its own will, and is not under the control of the Magus. The Familiar is the closest friend and ally a Magus ever has, but even friends fight occasionally.

## Finding and Befriending an Animal

The first step in getting a Familiar is finding an animal with inherent magic. With inherent magic, the beast is likely to have a Magic Might score, which may be assigned based on comparable scores of other magical creatures. The means of finding such a creature is ultimately left to the Storyguide. Wandering at random in search of a magical creature is usually profitless; Magi generally follow rumors to the locations of the Familiars they want. Some also receive visions of the animals that are somehow "meant" for them.

Once found, the animal must be befriended. You must genuinely admire or even love the animal in question, and it must trust you freely, under no coercion, magical or mundane. The animal can sense something of your nature when you are in close contact, and if your natures clash, it rejects you. The need for mutual admiration is why air Magi, for example, often take birds as Familiars, and why you can often tell something about Magi by the Familiars they have chosen and that have chosen them.

## Enchanting the Familiar

Once you and the Familiar accept each other, you take the animal to your laboratory and begin a year-long series of enchantments. Any serious distractions to these enchantments ruins them and forces you to start again from the beginning.

Enchanting a Familiar is different from other enchantments, however. The nature of the bond between you and your Familiar causes changes to you both, and you do not have full control over how the enchantment affects you. Your Troupe and Storyguide determine how you are affected  Throughout the enchantment, you do have control over the changes your Familiar undergoes.

## Opening the Enchantment

The first Season of the year-long enchantment is spent attuning the animal's magic to your own. This unification requires a number of pawns of Vim vis equal to 12 + the creature's Size. You also need an Animál score of 10+ to perform this harmonization.

During this Season, the animal often undergoes physical changes, such as a change in hue, shape of limbs, or texture of skin, and it learns rudimentary speech that you, at least, can understand. It may develop a speech trait to match one of yours, and it may acquire Passions or Personality Traits that match yours.

Similarly, you may take on some habits and minor physical and mental characteristics of the animal (such as the propensity of a bird to preen its feathers). You may wish to take a positive score in a Personality Trait that matches the type of animal you are enchanting (for example, "Raven +2").

## Strength of the Bond

In the second Season the bond between you and the animal is secured. The strength of the bond, or Bond Score, that you share is determined by adding your Animál, Mentem, and Intéllego scores, and subtracting the animal's Magic Resistance and Size. If this total is less than 0, your magical abilities are not strong enough to forge the bond, and you cannot make a Familiar of the animal. Your Bond Score is a total used to purchase cord scores (discussed below). It is also used to purchase bond qualities that arise between Magus and Familiar (also discussed below), which occurs in the third Season of the bonding process.

## Forging the Three Cords

Part of the second Season's bonding involves forging three mystic cords that connect you and the Familiar. A golden cord connects your magical abilities, a silver cord connects your minds, and a bronze cord connects your bodies. These cords may be seen by someone with the Second Sight Exceptional Talent, but they are otherwise intangible.

The strength of each of these cords is rated from 0 to +3. To determine their ratings, divide your Bond Score among them. The number of Bond Points required to buy a cord score is listed on the *Cord Strength Table*. The total cost of the cords you buy cannot exceed your Bond Score. The effects of the cords are explained below.

## The Cords

Each cord has a varying effect depending on how well it is forged. The effects apply only when the Familiar is within 100 paces (yards) of you. These benefits also apply to the Familiar. If you and the Familiar are being threatened by the same event, you cannot help each other. Your Familiar, for example, can "breathe for you," giving you a bonus on holding your breath while you are underwater, but if it is underwater too, it can't help you.

### The Golden Cord

The Familiar helps you avoid magical errors, letting you roll fewer Botch rolls when using magic. Your golden cord score is the number subtracted from the number of Botch rolls you would normally make (but you must always roll at least one).

### The Silver Cord

You can apply your silver cord score as a bonus to all rolls that involve Passions, to Personality Trait rolls (or to only one roll when you roll two in opposition), to Natural Resistance rolls against mental magic, and to rolls to protect you from natural mental influences, such as intimidation or verbal trickery. In addition, if your mind is ever overcome by another force, your Familiar may be able to free you. It must roll 9+ (stress) with the silver cord score as its bonus (one attempt per day). If the roll Botches, the animal's mind is overcome with yours.

### The Bronze Cord

You can apply your bronze cord score as a bonus to Soak rolls, healing rolls, and to rolls to withstand deprivation (such as holding your breath or resisting sleepiness). It does not help you withstand Fatigue.

## Tempering the Bond

In the third Season, you strengthen the bond between you and your Familiar by evoking certain magical powers through the bond. These are abilities you and your Familiar manifest together. You choose what qualities you wish to evoke. See the *Bond Qualities Table* for the powers you may choose from. You and the Storyguide then decide how those particular qualities affect you and your Familiar.

# Exempli Gratia:
## Creating a Familiar

Grimgroth seeks out a Familiar and finds himself devoted to a crow. The creature is only slightly magical in nature, having been raised on the Covenant's roof, so has a Magic Might of only 10, and no magical powers. In the first Season of the bird's enchantment, Grimgroth spends 8 (12 - 4 for Size) Vim vis attuning it to his magical energies. Fortunately his Animal score is over 10, otherwise he could not have a Familiar. During this period, both acquire some of the more superficial traits and quirks of the other.

In the second Season the three cords are forged between the two. Grimgroth's Bond Score is 13 (11 Animal + 3 Mentem + 5 Intéllego - 10 Magic Resistance - (-4) Size). Thus, he has 13 points to spend on cords. He wants to be magically and physically rather than mentally bound to his Familiar, so spends his points on the following: golden +1 (5 points), silver 0 (0 points), and bronze +1 (5 points). The remaining three Bond Points are discarded.

In the third Season bond qualities are shared between the two. Once again, Grimgroth has 13 points to spend, his Bond Score. As the crow has no inherent magical powers, points do not have to be spent attuning them to Hermetic magic. Even if the crow had powers, Grimgroth would not have to attune them to Hermetic magic, but that would result in the loss of those powers when the bonding enchantment was closed. The positive bond qualities chosen include: Shared Languages (+5), Sec-ondary Power (+10), and a variant of Shapechange (normally +15) which only allows the bird to assume human form; Grimgroth cannot become a bird (the Storyguide decides to make this +10). This amounts to 25 points of qualities, while Grimgroth only has 13 points. He therefore has to make up for 12 points with negative qualities. Since qualities are rated in units of 5, Grimgroth has to purchase 15 points worth of negative traits to make up for all the positive qualities he's taken.

The negative bond qualities he chooses include: Independence (-5), and At Odds (-10). The former accounts for the latter.

Now that Grimgroth has chosen his bond qualities, he must decide how their connection between he and the crow change each other. These are subjective ideas developed between the player and Storyguide, intended to flesh out the relationship between Magus and bird.

Having done all this, Grimgroth closes the enchantment between he and the bird in the fourth Season. The closing costs 3 Vim vis. The crow is now Grimgroth's Familiar. The bird's game statistics are also devised.

If he raises the traits that combine to form his Bond Score, Grimgroth can open the enchantment between himself and his Familiar again. Any new Bond Points gained are spent to buy new qualities, and negative qualities are taken to account for any excess positive qualities purchased. This action requires a Season's time and three Vim vis.

You have a number of points from which to choose bond qualities, equal to your full Bond Score, as introduced above. Note that your whole Bond Score is used, not just those points left over after cord scores are purchased (those remaining points are discarded in the second Season). Most bond qualities have positive scores, which reduce your Bond Score. Some bond qualities, however, have negative values. These qualities are detrimental side effects of your bond, which may be chosen by you or given to you by the Storyguide. Though these negative bond qualities have detrimental effects, they provide you with additional Bond Points with which you can purchase more positive bond qualities.

Almost all bond qualities affect both you and your Familiar in some related way; they characterize your bond. By characterizing the bond, you are determining how the bond links the two of you, and thus how the physical, mental, and magical qualities of each of you affect the other. In addition, almost all bond qualities are accompanied by the exchange of some minor physical, mental, or (rarely) magical quirk or habit related to a particular bond characteristic. For example, if you choose a bond characteristic that increases your awareness of each other, then you might each gain some minor habit of

each other's perceptions, such as a habit of looking over your shoulder, sniffing people when you first meet them, or perking your ears up when you hear a noise you can't identify.

You and the Storyguide must agree on all changes that you and the Familiar undergo. The powers your Familiar receives may sometimes be based on your magic Arts, in which case the Art you choose indicates the type of power received. In all cases you and the Storyguide must agree on the specific powers your Familiar receives. The qualities you receive from your Familiar are sometimes based on the beast's powers and abilities. In such cases, your new power may be based on either the beast's natural abilities (such as a cat's ability to see in the dark) or on any natural magical powers the beast may possess (i.e., those powers the beast has before it becomes your Familiar).

See the *Bond Qualities Table* for powers you and your Familiar may share. There are many more bond qualities possible. You may create any new bond quality provided it works similarly to those shown, and you get the Storyguide's approval. Some tales tell of Magi who invest Familiars with superior powers and abilities by actually reducing their own powers and abilities. Even if such stories are true, the nature of the bond between Familiar and Magus requires that the Magus gain *something* in return.

## Closing the Enchantment

In the fourth Season of the Familiar's enchantment, you close the enchantment and complete it, which takes another three pawns of Vim *vis*. From then on, you have a Familiar, independent but loyal. At this point determine the remaining statistics for your Familiar.

## The Familiar as a Character

Your Familiar retains any of the natural abilities it had before it became your Familiar, but you must attune all of its magical powers to Hermetic magic with bond qualities. If you don't have enough points to attune all your Familiar's magical powers, those unaccounted for are lost when the animal undergoes the closing ritual.

Your Familiar's Intelligence is now one point lower than yours (assuming it had animal intelligence before).

| Cord Strength Table | |
|---|---|
| **Strength** | **Cost** |
| 0 | 0 |
| +1 | 5 |
| +2 | 15 |
| +3 | 30 |
| Any Bond Points left over from purchases are discarded. | |

263

# Bond Qualities

You may never take the same quality more than once, unless the description says you can.

If a quality is noted as Ranged, it only applies when Magus and Familiar are within 100 paces of each other (though some bond qualities may change this Range).

You may not take bond qualities that are incompatible or which overlap in their scope. The Storyguide's judgement on which bond qualities can be taken together is final.

### +5 Bond Qualities

**Attunement**: You may attune one of your Familiar's natural magical powers to Hermetic magic. You must do this for all your Familiar's natural magical powers (5 points each time) before you can choose any other bond qualities.

**Awareness**: Ranged. The two of you always know where each other are, including direction and approximate distance. You each gain one perception habit or quirk from the other.

**Exchange Virtues**: Your Familiar gains one of your Virtues (and you keep it as well), and you gain a new Virtue related to one of the Familiar's natural abilities or natural magical powers (one it had before becoming your Familiar).

**Extended Bond**: The powers of your bond, including the powers of the three cords and all Ranged bond qualities, work when the two of you are within one mile of each other, not just 100 paces.

**Linked Targets**: Ranged. Whenever either of you is affected by magic (beneficial or hostile), the other is fully affected as well.

**Material Bond**: Your Familiar gains +1 in whatever physical Characteristic is your strongest (i.e., highest), and you gain +1 in whatever physical Characteristic is your Familiar's strongest. Your Characteristic scores may be raised no higher than +7 in this manner. Simultaneously, you each gain some physical appearance trait of the other.

**Mental Bond**: Your Familiar gains +1 in whatever non-physical Characteristic is your strongest (i.e., highest). The Familiar may become as intelligent as you by this means. And, you gain +1 in whatever non-physical Characteristic is your Familiar's strongest. Your Characteristic scores may be raised no higher than +7 in this manner. Simultaneously, you each gain some mental trait or habit of the other, or a Passion or Personality Trait of the other.

**Primary Power**: Your Familiar gains a new magical power related to your strongest magical Art, and you gain 2 Levels in the magical Art most closely related to the Familiar's strongest natural magical power (or its strongest natural ability if it has no natural magical powers). The power gained by the Familiar must be equivalent to a spell of Level 10 or less, and costs 2 Magic Points to use if it affects the Familiar only, or the power must be equivalent to a spell of Level 10 or less, and costs 3 Magic Points to use if it allows the Familiar to affect other things. If the Familiar has no Magic Might score, it can use the above powers three times a day, and twice per day, respectively.

**Shared Ability**: You each gain or increase one Ability that the other possesses, to the Ability score of the other. You may take this bond quality more than once, each time sharing a new Ability. You each also gain one habit of the other, related to the Ability score gained.

**Shared Languages**: Your Familiar's speech becomes intelligible to people other than you (but is still poor). Your Familiar knows only how to speak Latin or your native language (your choice). Likewise, you may speak with beasts of the same species (e.g., wolf, raven, mole, deer) as your Familiar. You each also gain some speech habit of the other.

**Shared Protection**: Ranged. The two of you are protected by each other's Magic Resistance, both getting the better of the two protections. Your Familiar does not control your Parma Magica, but receives its benefits whenever you activate the defense. You each also gain a defensive habit of the other. This habit has no rule implications, it's just a tendency, like an immediate instinct to seek out shelter.

**Sympathetic Emotions**: When either of you feels an emotion, the other feels it too. Whenever one of you makes a Personality Trait roll, or applies a Passion, the other gains the benefits or suffers the same effects of the trait. Your Familiar gains one Confidence Point and one of your Passions with a score of 1, and you gain your Familiar's strongest Personality Trait at the same level it has.

### +10 Bond Qualities

**Mental Communication**: Ranged. The two of you may communicate mentally with each other at will, sharing thoughts, pictures, and simple emotions. You each gain a Personality Trait of the other.

**Secondary Power**: Your Familiar gains a new magical power related to any magical Art you wish, and you gain 4 levels in a magical Art closely related to one of the Familiar's natural abilities or natural magical powers. The Familiar's power must be equivalent to a spell of Level 15 or less, and costs the Familiar 1 Magic Point to use if it affects the Familiar only, or the power must be equivalent to a spell of Level 15 or less, and costs the Familiar 2 Magic Points to use if it allows the Familiar to affect other things. If the Familiar has no Magic Might score, the above powers it gains can be used four times a day, or three times a day, respectively.

**Shared Senses**: Ranged. The two of you may each sense through the other's senses by making a Perception + Concentration simple roll of 9+. While perceiving through the senses of the other, you are completely unaware of your own surroundings. Anything that breaks your Concentration ends the use of this ability. You each also gain some perception habit of the other.

**Shared Speech**: Your Familiar's speech becomes completely clear and intelligible to people other than you (as good as human speech). Your Familiar knows all the human languages that you do. You may speak with all beasts of the same type (land, air, water, or underground) as your Familiar. You each also gain a strong speech habit of the other, or your voices change completely.

**Transfer Fatigue**: Ranged. You may both cause one another to take a Fatigue Level for you, saving yourself from Fatigue, but causing the recipient to lose a Long-Term Fatigue Level (even if you would have only lost a Short-Term Fatigue Level). The one that transfers the Fatigue Level may not use this ability again until the recipient recovers a Long-Term Fatigue Level, though the recipient may use this power at a later time to transfer a Fatigue Level in the other direction. If transfer of the Fatigue Level would knock the recipient Unconscious, the transfer fails. You each also gain some sleeping habit of the other.

**Unlimited Bond**: The powers of your bond, including the powers of the three cords and all Ranged bond qualities, work at any Range.

## +15 Bond Qualities

**Shapechange**: Your Familiar can shapechange into human form, and, with an Intelligence + Concentration roll of 9+, you can shapechange into the form of the Familiar's species. The Familiar must expend 5 Magic Points to change, and you must expend a Long-Term Fatigue Level. (If your Familiar has no Magic Might score, it must also expend a Long-Term Fatigue Level to change shape.) For each hour shapechanged, a Long-Term Fatigue roll is made against an Ease Factor of 8. If it fails, a Level is lost and normal form is resumed. If Unconsciousness is reached, original form is reverted to. You each also gain one physical peculiarity of the other, which is very noticeable.

**Shared Magic**: Ranged. Your Familiar gains a limited ability to use magic in your strongest Art, and you gain a limited ability to use one of the Familiar's natural abilities or natural magical powers. Your Familiar may cast Level 5 Spontaneous spells related to your strongest Art, at the cost of 1 Magic Point each (or at the cost of a Short-Term Fatigue Level if the animal has no Magic Might score). You may, with an Intelligence + Concentration roll of 9+, use a specified power or natural ability of the Familiar, at the cost of one Short-Term Fatigue Level per use.

**Transfer Wounds**: Ranged. You may both cause one another to take a wound for you, saving yourself from injury. Calculate damage normally, assuming you suffer it. The amount exceeding your Soak score is sent to your companion. The one that transfers the wound cannot use this ability again until the recipient permanently heals the damage you send (i.e., the damage cannot simply be healed through a temporary spell), though the recipient may use

this power at a later time to transfer a wound in the other direction. If transfer of a wound would kill the recipient, the transfer fails.

## -5 Bond Qualities

**Exchange Flaws**: Your Familiar gains one of your Flaws (and you still keep it), and you gain a new Flaw related to one of the Familiar's natural or supernatural weaknesses.

**Independence**: Your Familiar is unusually independent, and frequently acts of its own accord, even if you prefer otherwise, though you always band together in times of need.

**Limited Bond**: The two of you gain most benefits of your bond only when you are close to each other. Any positive bond qualities marked as Ranged are only in effect when the two of you are within 5 paces of each other. Negative bond qualities with a Range still function within 100 paces.

**Sympathetic Fatigue**: Ranged. When either of the two of you is Fatigued (Long- or Short-Term), the other must make a stress Fatigue roll of 6+, or lose a Short-Term Fatigue Level. If a Botch results, a Long-Term Level is lost. The two of you almost always sleep together.

**Sympathetic Pain**: Ranged. When either of the two of you is wounded or in pain, the other feels pain as well. For the Round following that in which the original wound is inflicted, both suffer the wound penalty inflicted. If you're already at a lower Body Level than your companion, his lesser wounds have no effect on you. You each also gain a reflex of the other, probably one associated with pain.

## -10 Bond Qualities

**At Odds**: The two of you clash wills on a regular basis, bickering and arguing, occasionally to the point where you refuse to speak. The two of you may purposefully work against each other in many cases, but you always join together fiercely in times of need, with unmatched loyalty (take a free Loyalty Passion with a score of 1, with a Specialization for your Familiar). You each also gain one debate or other mental tactic of the other.

**Tight Bond**: The two of you gain most benefits of your bond only when you are touching. Any positive bond qualities marked as Ranged are only in effect when you are touching. You each gain some physical skin trait of the other.

**Sympathetic Wounds**: Ranged. When either of the two of you is wounded (i.e., takes a Body Level damage), the other must make a Stamina + Size stress roll of 6+, or be wounded for the same amount. If you Botch the roll, an additional Body Level is suffered. You each gain one of the other's instinctive fears (fear of spiders, snakes, fire, certain predators). Take a Flaw or Personality Trait of +3 in the appropriate fear.

If the creature had higher than animal Intelligence before meeting you, it retains that Intelligence after becoming bound to you. However, even with one less Intelligence point than you, your Familiar may be more intelligent than you in a certain way, and thus better than you in certain mental activities.

Your Familiar should have Personality Traits appropriate to its bestial ways, either selected by you, or selected by whomever introduces the beast to the Saga. Most Familiars also have a quirk or two, such as a penchant for recalling irrelevant details, or an obsessive delight in the color blue.

Your Familiar's speech is only intelligible to you, unless you choose bond qualities that state otherwise.

The Familiar uses your Forms or its own Magic Resistance, whichever is better, to resist spells. It can use a *Parma Magica* if you grant it one, but not in conjunction with its own Magic Resistance. You are both able to circumvent the other's Magic Resistance at will.

## The Familiar in Play

You and your Familiar undoubtedly grow closer as the Saga progresses, learning from each other and strengthening the bond between you. Over the years, your Familiar learns what you know, provided you keep it with you when you study, and share your knowledge with it.

In addition, at any time during the Saga, you may spend a Season re-tempering your bond, which allows you to add new positive bond qualities if your total for determining your Bond Score has increased. The new points you're allowed to work with equal those which exceed your previous Bond Score. Thus, if your old Bond Score was 11 and your new one is 16, you have five more points to purchase qualities with. You may never increase the strength of the cords, however, and may never change a bond quality you've already established. Re-tempering the bond also costs 3 Vim *vis*, as the bond is closed once again.

At the end of any story, the Storyguide may choose to award you a new bond quality (good or bad). This usually results if you and your Familiar grew closer together during the story, often a result of your accomplishing some important goal through the use of your bond, or a result of hardship faced together. The Storyguide may choose to give you bond qualities that balance out, one good, one bad.

Your Familiar ages along with you, generally dying a few days before or several weeks after you. The sudden death of your Familiar is warning of immediate danger. Should you ever die while your Familiar remains alive, your Familiar may die from shock, and even if it lives, it is devastated, and never recovers from the shock of your death. Likewise, if you survive your Familiar, you may feel a profound emptiness in your life that may last for months, or echo through your soul for years. A Familiar is a personal, almost private thing, so only those more concerned with status than true companionship use their Familiars as status symbols. You should treat your Familiar much like you would a spouse.

You can only have one Familiar at a time. Your Familiar is with you for a long time, so make it interesting.

## The Participation of Other Players

The Storyguide plays an important role in the creation of your Familiar. If your Troupe has someone who acts as Storyguide for laboratory activities, that person may act as Storyguide while you are creating your Familiar. However, you may wish to use the whole Troupe as the acting Storyguide, since the creativity of a whole Troupe, as opposed to a single person, is especially helpful when creating a unique Familiar.

As you and your Familiar are so close, you may roleplay your Familiar as an extension of your character. After all, you may have similar abilities and personality quirks. However, you may also have the Storyguide or another player act as your Familiar. This alternative assures that your Familiar is at least distinct from you, and is advised if you and your Familiar don't get along very well (see the bond quality, *At Odds*). Ultimately, the choice is left to your tastes and the number of people in your Troupe.

# Apprentices

In your pursuit of the art of magic, you are likely to want an apprentice to help you in your work. An apprentice takes some time away from your studies, as you are obliged to teach as well as research; but the knowledge your apprentice gains in turn helps you with your studies. An apprentice helps you in your laboratory work. In return, you must devote one Season per year to teaching your ward rather than doing research. In addition to service, an apprentice provides close human company and the chance to leave a living legacy after you have died. Apprentices are the closest things Magi ever have to offspring and family.

## Minimum Competence to Teach an Apprentice

You may only have an apprentice if you are competent enough to teach someone every magical Art. This requires a score of at least 5 in each Art. Without a score of at least 5, you are not familiar enough yourself with the Arts to initiate someone else in their use.

# Finding Your Apprentice

If you qualify to teach an apprentice, the next step is to find one. Out among the common people there sometimes appear those rare individuals with the Gift, those who have an innate magical inclination. Only these can become apprentices and eventually Magi. Luckily for those Magi who seek them, these people inevitably stand out from the crowd. They are almost invariably bright, making them fit in poorly with the illiterate society in which most find themselves. Also, most potential apprentices somehow attract supernatural attention to themselves. In many populations there is a youth who is prone to lone wanderings at night, who is the subject of much town gossip, and who displays a precocious wit. Chances are, such a person is your potential apprentice.

Searching for an apprentice can lead to a good story and excellent roleplaying possibilities, especially if the search is complicated by enemy forces or the child's family contriving to thwart your efforts. However, if you do not wish to make a story out of it, you may determine the results of the search with a die roll. For every Season spent searching for a potential apprentice, make a stress Perception roll. If the result is 6+, you find one. If you Botch, you may think you've found an apprentice but are duped by the child, or maybe by a much greater power who replaces your child with its servant. . .

Your student should be between 8 and 17 years old at the beginning of apprenticeship (if you wish, roll a simple die + 7 to determine the age of your apprentice). Children younger than 8 rarely have the discipline required for apprenticeship, and children older than 17 are almost invariably set in their adult ways, no longer fit for Hermetic training.

Being taken away by a Magus to parts unknown is always disturbing and frightening, even if the apprentice is excited or relieved to be free of a miserable life. Some are kidnapped by their masters, some are coaxed away by promises of knowledge and power, while others are actually offered (or sold) to Magi by families who cannot handle the youngsters' strange ways. Though most apprentices come willingly and freely, the Code of Hermes does not require it. Strictly speaking, Magi are allowed to obtain apprentices in whatever manner they wish.

# Training Your Apprentice

Once you have your apprentice, the training begins. Each year, according to the Peripheral Code of Hermes, an apprentice is guaranteed at least one Season's worth of training. If you do not provide this training, the apprentice is free to go to another Magus, and the training you have provided no longer benefits you.

For each Season of training, your apprentice gets one Experience Point (see *Experience Points*, p.350) in Magic Theory (which starts at a score of 0). He also learns the basics in a single Art, granting him a score of 0 in that Art. You choose the order of the Arts that your apprentice learns the basics in. Before learning an Art, it's impossible to cast a spell that involves that Art. Once an Art is learned, even if the score is 0, casting a spell with that Art is possible.

For each year of apprenticeship, your apprentice gets 10 Levels of spells. He uses these to purchase the Formulaic spells he can cast (or to purchase the ones you allow him). The apprentice also gets 10 points to invest in the magic Arts that have been learned.

The apprentice also learns Abilities during the apprenticeship. Essential Abilities, such as Scribe Latin, are learned first, but other than that, it is up to you to determine how your apprentice increases in Abilities. As a guide, assume that after fifteen years of apprenticeship, the student has Abilities like those of a beginning Magus character.

# Fleshing Out Your Apprentice

The basic benefit that an apprentice provides you is the addition of his Intelligence and Magic Theory to your Lab Totals (see *Help in the Lab*, p.259). If all you want is a lab assistant, then you only need to keep track of your apprentice's Intelligence and Magic Theory scores, and after 15 years, your apprentice becomes a full Magus and leaves your service. To quickly determine your apprentice's Intelligence, roll a simple die: 1-5; +2, 6-8; +3, 9-10; +4.

However, if created as a full character and developed as the Saga progresses, an apprentice can become very important to your Magus's character, and a valuable member of the Covenant. If you're going to create your apprentice as a full character, create a normal character, determining Characteristics, Virtues and Flaws, and Passions, as you would for a normal Magus. (Keep in mind the character's young age when determining Virtues and Flaws, though.) You might want to insure that the character has a decent Intelligence (+2 or more), and that the apprentice has a number of Experience Points in Abilities, a number less than or equal to his age. These Experience Points represent the things the apprentice has learned in his short life. Then, as the story progresses, update the apprentice's Abilities, magical Arts, Passions, and other statistics just as you would for any other character.

In most cases it is sufficient to assume that an apprentice is unlimited in what Arts, and what levels in those arts, he may study. The same may be said for the spells he learns. You may, however, limit your apprentice's education to the Arts and their scores found in your books, and

# Laboratory Activities Table

## Arcane Studies

**Magic Theory:** 1, 2, or 3 Experience Points if you roll over your score on a stress die times number of pawns of Vim *vis* used (up to 3), plus Aura.

## Arts

**Study with Book:** 1, 2, or 3 levels, depending on score of source

**Study with vis:** 1, 2, or 3 levels if you roll over your score on a stress die times number of pawns of Art-specific *vis* used (up to 3), plus Aura.

**Write Art:** 3 levels (up to half your score)

**Copy Art:** 9 levels

## Spells

**Learn Spell:** Lab Total must at least equal Level of spell

**Invent Spell:** For each point by which Lab Total + Aura exceeds Level, accumulate 1 point; when accumulated points equal spell Level, spell invented

**Transcribe Spells:** 60 Levels put into useable form

**Copy Spells:** 180 Levels

## Magic Devices

**Prepare Item for Enchantment:** Automatic, requires *vis*

**Instill Power in Item:** For each point by which Lab Total + Aura exceeds Level, accumulate 1 point; when accumulated points equal Level, power instilled; 1 pawn Art-specific *vis* per 10 Levels. Option to increase Lab Total by +5 for every extra pawn spent

**Attune Talisman:** Automatic, full Season

**Open Talisman to One Type of Spell:** Automatic, full Season

**Minor Enchantment:** Lab Total + Aura must equal twice Level; 1 pawn Vim and 1 pawn Art-specific *vis* per 10 Levels

**Make Batch of Potions:** Lab Total + Aura must exceed Level; one dose per 5 points, or fraction thereof, over Level

**Invent Longevity Potion for Self:** Intéllego Córporem + Aura, -1 from Aging rolls per 5 points in Lab Total; requires 1 pawn of *vis* per 5 years of age; +1 to Lab Total per extra pawn of *vis* used

**Invent Longevity Potion for Someone Else:** As potion for self, but -1 from Aging rolls per 10 points in Lab Total

**Investigate Magic Item:** Intéllego Vim, Lab Total + stress die must match Level of weakest power to detect it; continue rolling for next strongest power until all powers found or failure

## Apprentice

**To find one:** stress Perception roll of 6+, or a story

**Per Season:** gains 1 Experience Point in Magic Theory, gets score of 0 in one Art

**Per Year:** gains 10 spell Levels and 10 points in Arts

## Familiar

**Open Enchantment:** 12 + Size in Vim *vis* points

**Bond Score:** Intéllego + Animál + Mentem - Magic Resistance - Size

**Three Cords:** Purchased from points equal to Bond Score

**Exchange Powers:** Levels of powers exchanged in points equal to Bond Score

**Close Enchantment:** 3 Vim *vis*

## Experimenting

Allowed when inventing spells, creating any magical enchantment, enchanting a Familiar, or investigating an item. May choose Risk Modifier of +1 to +3. Add a simple die + Risk Modifier to your Lab Total, but roll on Extraordinary Results Chart, adding Risk Modifier.

## Multiple Laboratory Activities

Add Levels of all activities, which must be of same type and must use same Technique and Form. Arcane experimentation adds once, but applies equally to all activities.

## Help in the Lab

Helpers must have the Gift, Magic Theory, and positive Intelligence. Usually no more than one helper, who adds Magic Theory + Intelligence to your Lab Total, or +1 to rolls when studying from *vis*.

## Distractions From Studies

**Up to 10 days:** no penalty

**Studying:** Reduce Level of source by 1 per 2 days over 10

**Other:** Reduce Lab Total by 1 per day over 10.

to the spells and their Levels found in your grimoires, or those of the Covenant. You should give the apprentice some leeway beyond these limits, though, to take into account his natural talents and interests.

## The Value of an Apprentice

Aside from performing many tedious mundane tasks for you, such as cleaning up your lab, your apprentice helps you in the laboratory. He aids all your Lab Totals that include your Magic Theory, and aids you when you study Magic Theory, or a magic Art from vis. (See *Help in the Lab*, p.259)

## The Apprentice in Play

A fully developed apprentice makes a playable character. If you want to play an apprentice, keep in mind that you have no natural niche in the story. Grogs fight, Companions provide skilled assistance, and Magi have powerful spells. As an apprentice, you are outclassed in all areas. Nevertheless, some stories are made exciting by an apprentice character or characters, as they are interesting individuals, especially if there's no Magus around to overshadow their immature magical abilities.

Attacking another Magus's apprentice is, according to the Code of Hermes, almost as serious as attacking a Magus's Familiar.

When you are a Magus and teacher, some of the best roleplaying opportunities for your apprentice arise when he is interacting with you. You may therefore let another player roleplay your apprentice, or you may consider your apprentice a Troupe character, played by different members of the Troupe at different times, much like a Grog.

## The End of Apprenticeship

Normally, an apprentice leaves after fifteen years of service, though one can leave at any time with the master's permission, or after learning all fifteen magic Arts. In some traditions, an apprentice must undergo tests by a Tribunal of Magi before being officially recognized as a Magus. This famous "apprentice's gauntlet" has come to be dreaded by many a student.

An apprentice who has studied under you, and has become a Magus in his own right, is likely to remain loyal to you, at least to some degree. Even if not played as a full character, former apprentices can aid you in times of need. (But then, we've all heard stories of thankless students who turn against their masters.)

# Mythic Europe

## chapter nine

 t's easy to rely on clichés and stereotypes for our images of the Middle Ages. Some see the medieval era as an age of romance, with brave and honorable knights, beautiful maidens, and a flowering of all the wonders of chivalry. Others see the period as a time of rampant corruption and ruthless oppression, where most people died of hunger or disease before age thirty. While both views have their elements of truth, neither is entirely accurate. It's sometimes difficult to understand what the Middle Ages were really about. Helping you sort that out is one of the purposes of this Chapter.

Yes, the setting of this game is based in history, and we give you background into that history. However, you should know that we are not attempting to provide a realistic perspective of the medieval world so much as we are a mythical perspective. This is not the real historical Europe as described in textbooks. This is Europe through the eyes of the people who were alive then. This is Mythic Europe. Mythic Europe is a setting in which the legendary comes true.

Whether you play in Mythic Europe or not, this Chapter is invaluable in that it explains not only the "facts" about life in the Middle Ages, but it evokes much of the period's flavor and charm. We go to great lengths to explain how medieval society functioned, and how medieval folk thought. We also go to great effort to describe some of the unique and fantastic elements of historical Europe, such as the Order of Hermes. These fantastic elements are things you should know of if you want to play a Magus in all his glory.

# Why Mythic Europe?

The Middle Ages are an essential element of Western culture and there is much we can learn by reliving them. Our thoughts and inner lives are profoundly affected by the myths, legends, and fundamental beliefs of our ancestors from these times. The concepts of love, honor, sworn word, honesty, war and courage all have their roots in medieval culture. And, these concepts are just as alive in us today as they were in the people of centuries ago.

In order to play **Ars Magica** you need to understand the medieval setting. Although you may, of course, use any setting you like, we believe that Mythic Europe is a good starting point, no matter what world you create. It is from our visions of medieval Europe that most of our visions of fantasy come, thus it is to the medieval society we must return, in one way or another, to truly capture the grandeur and flavor of a fantasy world.

All fantasy games, including **Ars Magica**, start with the premise that the game world is in some way related to our own history. In **Ars Magica**, however, we go the full distance. Doing so has several advantages:

• We grow up with the legends of our own history, and they mean a lot to us. It is much easier, for instance, to excite players with a quest to wake King Arthur from his enchanted sleep, and to save England, than it is to make them feel deeply about a quest to find the lost Emperor Khalash, and to save Furdwadia.

• Two thousand years of European history and legend create a more lush game background than the most dedicated Storyguide can hope to invent.

• An unbelievable resource of game detail, from court fashions, to game plots, to exotic legends, is available for free at your local library.

• As storytellers we constantly struggle to make stories seem as real as possible. A Mythic Europe setting is full of real people, real places, and real events whose outcomes have direct impact on the world.

• Reality is stranger than fiction. You will find Mythic Europe to be as exotic a fantasy setting as you have ever read.

## Medieval Paradigm

One of the most difficult feats to perform in **Ars Magica** is the transition from the modern world to a mythic setting. This journey requires that you forget many of the concepts which we have been raised on. Such values as equality, peace, and the separation between Church and state were simply not part of the medieval mindset.

Most fantasy roleplaying games don't require that you make any sort of transition; their worlds, and the people who populate them, share most of the basic mindsets that we do today. Those people really aren't that different from us. The world may be painted a different color, but all the people think the same and speak the same as we do. In **Ars Magica** we expect more.

The mythic mindset is what we call the medieval paradigm. Its premise is this: the world is the way medieval folk perceived it; their fears, dreams, beliefs and legends are manifest in reality. This means the medieval stories and myths that we know of, like the tale of Beowulf, can be true. Indeed, Mythic Europe is a setting in which legends come true — not necessarily all of them, but enough to make it a different reality from our own. You should not feel oppressed by this atmosphere; you don't have to know a lot about medieval history and myth. The world is still yours to create and alter. In truth, all you need to understand about the mythic setting is the medieval paradigm. Beyond that basic approach, you can create any setting you please.

# Historical Europe

Historical Europe is the place you read about in history books. There are no Magi and no dragons, Faerieland is a place in fairy tales, and legends rarely turn out to be true. This is a place of mind-numbing poverty, rampant disease, and immense vigor and passion.

From a historical standpoint, this is the year A.D. 1197 The Thirteenth Century is about to begin. The barbarian and Viking invasions are over, and people are beginning to look beyond their own immediate surroundings once more. The kings of Europe are preparing to go on the Fourth Crusade to the Holy Land (1202-1204), and still remember the Third Crusade (1189-1192), wherein Richard the Lionhearted of England and Saladin the Moor vied with each other in contests of honor and valor.

England is ruled by a single powerful king; the rest of the countries in Europe are not, but support for kings is slowly becoming greater than that for the nobles in most of Western Europe. Feudalism, the rule of individual lands by single nobles, is starting to decline.

This is the beginning of a new age, the age of the city. Towns and cities are being founded at an astounding rate, and the first universities in Europe are coming into existence. Cities and kingdoms are the hallmarks of the new era, and for the first time in modern memory, more peasants are free than indentured, and most nobles can read simple verse and write their own names. In this era the games of power, politics and, most of all, wealth being played between cities and nobles, and even between rival cities, are often as intense as the feuds waged between angry nobles of earlier times.

This is the first great period of art, science, and learning since Roman times. Buried deep in the Middle Ages are the roots of the coming Renaissance, and the stirrings of modern science. Scholars are once again reading Aristotle and Galen. Thomas Aquinas is writing of how there is no innate conflict between faith and knowledge, and that the goal of life is the acquisition of truth, be that truth ethical, artistic, theological, or scientific. While most scholars greet this blossoming of the intellect with joy and relief, there are many hidebound clergy who see newfound interest in secular knowledge as evil and dangerous. The conflict between the two groups runs deep.

In this century, wealth gained by trade and commerce begins to rival the ancient wealth of most noble families. Merchants journey to the far corners of the world, braving savage bandits, raging seas, and scorching deserts to return with the beautiful silks and rare spices to insure their fortunes. Huge trade fairs are held in France, near Paris, where instant cities of tens of thousands are created each summer.

Constantinople is sacked by Christian crusaders (in 1204), and Marco Polo travels to Cathay (China) and back in this century. Also, the Mongols under Genghis Khan conquer all of China, as well as most of Russia and the Middle East. They are only prevented from conquering Western Europe by mere chance. The first part of this century bears no major wars or disasters, but there are, of course, many feuds between nobles, and the usual power and economic struggles that replace war in peaceful times.

The horrors of the Inquisition and the Black Plague are over a century away. People seem more concerned with trade and learning than with mindless slaughter, but religious debate and economic conflict are often as intense as war, and sometimes as bloody. Though the Black Plague has not yet descended, plague still makes its mark on communities, sometimes with horrifying frequency.

This time also marks the modern birth of formal belief in and practice of magic and the occult. Kabbalism had been formalized in Spain and Prague less than 50 years earlier, and Moorish texts on alchemy, astrology, and magic are being translated into Latin at a phenomenal rate.

## Fact into Fantasy

Below is an example of how you can take historical fact and speculation and use it in a mythical setting. You can play **Ars Magica** in either a tight historical setting, or in a really far-out, fantastic setting. The following material illustrates the advantages of each.

**Historical Fact:** The Knights Templar were an order of knights founded in 1119 who took religious vows and went off to conquer the Holy Land, becoming immensely rich in the process. In 1307, the King of France, destitute and worried about the knights' increasing power, had the Inquisition trump up charges against the order, took all its wealth, and had all its leaders imprisoned or put to death. Too bad for the knights. End of story.

In a conventional historical setting, the Templars can be used in stories, either as crusaders or the victims of unfair persecution. Characters might meet the crusaders, or even join them for a while, perhaps gaining some of the order's wealth. Or, Templars might turn to the characters for aid against the Inquisition.

**Historical "Fiction":** The historical information related above stands true, but with some twists added. A Templar named Chretien de Troyes confesses to observing an official Templar act of homage. The ceremony is supposedly performed before a human head — *"flesh from the crown to the nape of the neck, with the hairs of a dog, without any gold or silver covering, indeed a face of flesh. . . bluish in color and stained, with a beard having a mixture of white and black hairs similar to the beards of some Templars."* Quite a few other Templars talk about the same object, called a *maumet* (pronounced, in French, "mummy").

The Inquisitors burn de Troyes, but not for his apparent pagan acts. The paying homage to a *maumet* isn't on the Inquisition's standard list of sins. Obviously the Templars are into some really weird stuff, and the origins behind their penchants can be the means for a strange, but still historically based, medieval story.

In truth, de Troyes's account is historical fact! It just goes to show that history doesn't have to be "conventional" to form the basis of a good story.

With a wider belief in magic, that belief becomes more institutionalized. Magical phenomena and places are identified, and scholars and nobles devote energy to trying to understand them through systems of Christian theology, Kabbalism, natural magic, and astrology. Magic is no longer just the belief of peasants, who look to charms to protect them from raiders, and to whom all lands more

## Noble Titles

### (In Ascending Order of Status)

| English: squire/lady | French: esquire/dame |
|---|---|
| knight | chevalier |
| baron/baroness | baron/baronesse |
| earl/countess | comte/contesse |
| | marquis/marquesse |
| duke/duchess | duc/duchesse |
| prince/princess | prince/princesse |
| king/queen | roi/reine |

than a day's walk from home are magical. Outside of Western Europe, however, many groups are still pagan in their beliefs, and have their own ideas about magic.

# Mythic Europe

Mythic Europe isn't entirely like historical Europe. Sure, the basic dates are all the same, the same nobles rule, and the same Popes pass out decrees, but the texture and scope of the setting are completely different. This is not a world for historians (though the work of scholars is certainly useful). This is a world for those who want to dance to the music of eternal myth.

As you roleplay in Mythic Europe, you need to pick and choose from the legends and stories of the times, deciding which are true and which are not. You can create an incredibly fantastic world by simply decreeing that everything people believed in is true. Or, you can create a world so close to historical "reality" that roleplaying in it is like being in a historical novel. The scope and scale of Mythic Europe is up to you, and your vision of it evolves as the Saga progresses.

The people of the Middle Ages believed in some fantastic stuff. Rumors that circulated were even more exotic than stories of soot-covered dragons and twisted hermits who cast spells. Many people thought Jews had horns and tails, that Saracens built fantastic cities and rode to hunt with giant cats, and that the Ethiopians who lived out somewhere beyond the desert were as black as paint, had one eye, faces in their bellies, and possessed the richest Empire in the world. Medieval folk sometimes thought the Holy Land was like the Garden of Eden, that it was where God walked on earth, and that trees there flowered and bore fruit all at once, throughout the winter. Medieval beliefs about what the world was like and what sorts of things comprised it varied wildly, not only from our view, but from each other's view. It is this paradigm which you base your world on — a paradigm in which legends are truth.

We have all been taught a modern version of medieval reality, which is not the version that medieval people themselves believed in. For instance, most farmers in the Middle Ages left the last shock of grain standing in their fields after harvest, so the faerie of the field had a place to live through the winter. If the shock was cut down, the faerie would die and the field would cease to be fertile. Modern people may look at this practice and either dismiss it as wasteful or praise it as respectful, but we take it for granted that there were never little faeries hiding in the wheatstalks. Much of Mythic Europe is derived from answering the question: what if things really were the way medieval people believed they were?

It is very important to remember that, at first glance, Mythic Europe looks pretty much like medieval Europe would; armies of trolls don't invade France, and demons don't roam the lands. However, subtle differences exist between the two. Perhaps, in Mythic Europe, the farmer who cuts down the last shock of grain never returns home. Perhaps, in Mythic Europe, an oddly shaped birthmark is the sign of demonic possession. The two worlds may seem one, but they're not, and that difference is what you need to evoke to create a mythic setting.

The fantastic elements of Mythic Europe can be as subtle or as obtrusive as you like. On the grand end of the scale, people believe that somewhere in Ethiopia lies the Christian kingdom of Prester John, where the Prester holds court on a golden throne, with leopards at his side. At its most extreme, Mythic Europe's fantasy can claim that the world is divided into three continents, Europe, Asia, and Africa, by the waters of the Tigris, Euphrates, and Nile rivers. At the center, where the three rivers meet, lies the Garden of Eden, protected by a fiery wall and an angel with a flaming sword. However, the maps of England and France still look the same, and you still have to cross the Channel to get from one to the other. The degree to which you accept this fantasy depends on how far you are willing to accept medieval legend.

Whether your game setting is historically accurate or a fantastic excursion from history, there are a few basics to remember. Any worthwhile fantasy world has its terrible opponents, strange people, mysterious objects, and undiscovered lands. In a world of fact or fantasy, it's the Storyguide's job to insure that the unusual is wondrous, and that imagination is eternally vibrant.

# THE THREE CLASSES

In the Middle Ages most folk considered society to be divided into three great classes of people: those who toiled, those who prayed, and those who warred. Each class was supposed to be blessed by God, and worthy of salvation on their own terms. The same people, society, and classes exist in Mythic Europe.

## Those Who Toil

The first of the great classes is the peasantry. A peasant's purpose is to provide the basic needs of life for everyone else, so that clergy are free to deal with God, and nobles free to fight their wars. Even though, in theory, peasants make everyone else's achievements possible, gratitude is hardly bountiful. The upper classes believe that God created their stations, insuring that appropriate people fill them. Since tending to the needs of others is the most ignoble of tasks, the most inferior of humanity are believed to be charged with the duty. Thus, gratitude is not a consideration, as decreed by God.

Just as God decrees a man's social position, so too does He restrict man to that position. Peasants are forbidden to ride horses, nor are they allowed to own swords or armor. To assume the trappings of a superior is blasphemy. Inequality is reality. Disease, malnutrition, crop failure, and taxation are the peasant's bedfellows.

The peasant's social position is bound to that of his superiors by a social contract. The contract says: "If you fight to keep me safe, I'll feed you. If you do your best to save my soul, I'll feed you." Peasants have rights as well as responsibilities. According to God, they have the right to the same chance of salvation as cardinal or king, and therefore have the same access to the blessings of the Church: baptism, consecration, last rites, and Christian burial. They also have the right to decent treatment and full protection from their lord. What they get of that right depends on the mercy of their lord, and the allegiances of the local clergy.

Needless to say, the rights of the peasants are not always observed. However, every time a noble tramples the fields on a hunt, or ravages the countryside in a needless war, the peasants take note. Every time a parish priest is found in bed with somebody's wife, or an order of monks sworn to poverty buys cloth-of-gold, the peasants take note. For the upper classes to break the contract is invitation for the peasantry to do the same. How they demonstrate their defiance is up to them.

The secret nightmare of every abusive noble and hypocritical cleric is that of peasant revolt (though the truth of the matter is that most peasants are very loyal to their Lord). Though poorly armed and organized, angry peasants are made dangerous by their sheer number and anger. The fields can go untilled and unharvested. A dozen armed men can be crushed under the weight of unarmed hundreds. Monasteries can be burned. A city's inhabitants can assassinate their lord. A duke can be struck down by a hexing witch. The natural order of society can be overturned. These are the possibilities, but peasant revolts are rarely so monumental, and usually fail in the end. However, even in their failure, the chaos and famine brought to the land proves the power of a unified peasant class.

## Those Who Pray

The second great class of people in Mythic Europe is the clergy. Their part in the social bargain demands they do the work of mind and spirit. In earlier times, saving souls was the only important job of the clergy. At this time, priests, monks, and nuns assume other important tasks. The first is to control, administrate, and generally meddle with the order of society.

As far as the clergy are concerned, God created society, so God's representatives should run it. When peasants seek to overreach their limits, the parish priest reminds them that their lot is God's will. When nobles fight each other in useless wars, the bishop reminds them of God's will to protect the land against heathen invaders, not one's neighbors. When kings disagree with the Pope, the Pope reminds them that kings only rule by the will of God, and only the Pope knows God's will.

Since the clergy maintain order and conformity in the world, heretics are a threat to both the Church and the

WOC 92

state, and clergy join with nobles to suppress the worst of them.

The second job of the clergy involves the mind. Peasants are supposed to be good farmers. Nobles are supposed to be good warriors. Neither group should have to think any more than necessary — it's not their job. Thinking is dangerous for those not assigned to the task, as it makes them aware of the injustices of life, which can lead to social turmoil. And the thoughts of pagan people — Saracens, Druids, Jews, and Magi — only add to their damnation, for their thoughts are not only blasphemous, but in defiance of God's order.

Some clergy are so certain of their righteousness that they defy conventional laws and morality, establishing their own freedoms. Popes put a price on absolution from sin, taking payment for the assurance of a peaceful afterlife. Cardinals, abbots, and abbesses scheme for temporal power and control of lands. Learned priests and doctors of philosophy traffic with "higher spirits," for demons are simply another kind of angel, and if a man can compel an angel to serve him, it must be God's will. How long such practices are accepted depends upon the moral outrage of society, or that of the few who have power to intimidate the clergy.

WOC
92

Though the clergy tend to draw lines of power outside their number, the clergy are divided by an internal war, one which has been brewing for some time. On one side are those who believe their first task is the most important; they are the defenders of order, the enforcers of orthodoxy. When orthodoxy means restraining mad nobles, or rooting out diabolists, these clergy accept the task and are considered heroes. However, when upholding orthodoxy means excommunicating a noble with a new idea, or fighting benevolent Magi, these clergy are oppressors.

On the other side of the struggle are those who seek knowledge. They are frequently the attackers of orthodoxy. For these clergy, "It's God's will" is not justification for any injustice, for, they say, God made people with the power to think for themselves. Clergy on this side of the Church's dispute fight the bigotry that often arises with the emergence of anything new and different.

## Those Who War

The third great class of people in Mythic Europe is the nobility. Their job is to protect society and maintain order. Being a noble is hereditary, like being a peasant, and both men and women can be nobles.

Every noble has an ancestor who was a barbarian warrior. The common people supported him in return for the power of his sword. These warriors passed their station down to their descendants — the right to bear arms, the right to be supported by the common people, and the obligation to protect commoners in return.

Nobles do not have to be warriors (noblewomen are not expected to be), but only nobles have the power and the right to be warriors. Any noble who supports him or herself through ordinary work forever loses, for all further descendants, the right to be fed, clothed, and housed by the peasantry. Such folk are no longer true to the warrior's blood and purpose.

Every noble wealthy and powerful enough to own a large tract of land keeps a house there. This is a castle in which the arms, armor, animals, and equipment of war are stored. In the early days of war against heathens and monsters, the noble house was but a stone fort. Now, the noble's power demonstrates itself in grand and fantastic manors and castles, with walled gardens and high turrets that dominate the landscape.

The peasants that the lord protects live close enough to his walls that they may take shelter within if danger lurks. Under the system of manor and castle — the feudal system — all of civilization exists within the sheltering shadow of the lord's household, protected by his sword. It is because of this that the nobility rules. They maintain tyranny by protecting rights.

# THE FEUDAL SYSTEM

The social system of the Middle Ages is described as the feudal system. This is a society led by a king who is liege to a group of great nobles, who are in turn liege to a group of lesser nobles, who are in turn liege to villages of peasants. Ultimately, everyone in medieval society is part of this system: everyone in the noble class is the liege of someone, and everyone except the King is a vassal to someone else.

## Pages and Squires

A man of noble birth is called an esquire, or squire, until he proves himself as a warrior, or joins the clergy, or enters one of the trades and ceases to be noble at all. Nobles may be born, but warriors are made. By the age of seven or eight, a young nobleman is no longer a child, but a warrior in training.

Such children are taken from their mothers and fathers and sent into service in a greater noble's house. For the next seven years they are pages, learning to ride and fight, and also serving the lord's household. Pages are servants of the castle, and learn the courtly graces from the ladies of the household.

When they are between eight and twelve, pages are made squires. Each squire now learns from a single knight. Only once a squire has proven his skill in the arts of war is he dubbed a knight. By this time he is a man of at least age twenty-one. What a knight becomes after achieving that honor depends on his place in the hierarchy of nobles.

## Warlord

Noble lords must feed, clothe, and arm the noble warriors who help them protect their lands. The more land and peasants a lord has, the more warriors he or she can support, and the better castles he or she can build. The more warriors and better castles a lord has, the more powerful are the lords he or she can defeat in battle, and thereby gain more lands, castles and warriors. This is how kings and great lords get to be kings and great lords.

All warriors, from the high lord who owns the largest lands to the poor knight who defends a poor lord's single castle, are nobles. However, the poorest knights have no land. They cannot support themselves except by war, and cannot feed and arm other knights to help them get land. All they have to offer is their skill at arms, in exchange for room, board, equipment, and battles to fight. Such a poor knight swears fealty, or loyalty in battle, to a lord who has lands. If such a knight fights with enough intelligence and skill, or with enough frenzy, he can hope to distinguish himself in his lord's eyes.

## Vassal and Liege

Greater nobles have greater ambitions. To win wars, a noble needs knights to make war, and lands to feed and clothe and arm the knights. You can get land and knights by seizing them from your neighboring lord, but it's a dangerous gamble. If your neighbor is more powerful, you might lose your land and knights instead. You might win, but be too weak from the battle to fight the war you thirsted for in the first place.

After a thousand bloody, dangerous gambles, someone found a better way. In exchange for giving another lord a piece of your land, allowing him to be lord of it, he has to fight for you in your wars.

A greater lord requisitions the services of a lesser. In a solemn and holy ritual, the great lord passes a clod of fertile earth into the hands of the lesser, binding forever his gift of land. The lesser lord now places his hands between the hands of his lord and swears an oath of fealty, thereby becoming the lord's man, his vassal. The lesser lord, in turn, can have vassals as well, and so on back down to the poorest knight, who swears fealty for room and board, and hopes someday for a little land and a few peasants of his own as a reward for exceptional service.

Vassals owe their lords a certain number of days of service in war each year (usually sixty). A lord who controls large areas of land, and owes fealty to no greater lord, is a king or queen. In England, the king rules all the lands, for there are no lords equal to him, and none greater in power. In France, the king is lord only over his own domains. Everyone bows when he walks into the room, but he'd better ask the Duc d'Anjou before he takes a walk in Anjou.

## Inheritance

The system of inheritance is complicated in itself. Sometimes only the eldest child gets it all, sometimes other relatives take pieces, and sometimes there's a war and everything goes to another noble. The system is further complicated by the fact that clergy can have vassals and be vassals too, and by the fact that you can owe fealty to two different lords at once, who may happen to be at war with each other (in this case, you can fight for one and send an army to fight for the other, throw in your lot with whoever you think is most likely to win, or conveniently go on a crusade until the whole thing blows over).

A noblewoman may inherit her father's lands if she has the luck, courage, and political acumen to survive the succession. If she gets her father's land, she inherits his titles, rights, and powers as well. If she does not inherit land, her title and position come from her husband. In the latter case she is lord over no lands and cannot have vassals.

WOC
92

Since most noblewomen are not trained in the ways of war, a noblewoman who fails to inherit her father's lands usually can't win her own lands by impressing her lord with swordplay. (There are occasional tales of women who make the attempt, but noble males like to keep those stories quiet for fear of embarrassment, especially those sporting injuries gained "in a hunting accident.") Generally, a noblewoman can be a good wife and mother, or she can be a power behind the throne of her husband, or she can make an outright bid for her husband's lands while he's away, or if he dies while his heir is too young to fight.

Female lords can be formidable, for while their brothers were learning swordplay, they were learning how to be a more subtle kind of threat, becoming skilled in diplomacy, the art of conversation, reading and writing, and foreign languages. By the law, noblewomen have the right to lead armies and go on crusades, though making such an obvious threat of yourself is usually frowned upon.

## Hollow Chivalry

Many nobles have grown bored of their lot in life, now that the age of barbarian invasions is over. Great nobles, left with grand estates but no purpose, have been known to return their lands to a semblance of ancient times, to visions of heaven, or nightmares of hell. The Sire d'Avrine bargained with the Evil One for a twisted imp to sit upon his shoulder as his chatelain. His Infernal black palfrey had the power to ride over earth, fire, water, and air, and also the terrible power of poisonous touch, which blighted all d'Avrine's lands. In his madness, d'Avrine is said to have demanded that the fifty knights who assembled to bring him to justice pay him homage, for it was only the extremity of his evil that allowed them to be heroes beyond all others of the age.

Most nobles are either content to descend into a useless life, or are unwilling to fall into the depths of the Sire d'Avrine. Many doughty knights, in the flower of their youth, choose instead to venture into the far lands of the North or East. For them, the hunger for adventure is unquenchable; without dragons to hunt, crusades to fight, heathen lands to convert, and Infernal taints to cleanse, they have lost the last reason for a knight to live.

# THE CHURCH

The Church is seen as the first line of defense against the ever-present threat of the Infernal Powers. While piety and faith protect many of the clergy from the power of the

Devil, the clergy are often the primary targets for temptation and corruption. While the soul of a cleric may be harder to obtain, it is worth far more since one corrupt cleric can sometimes corrupt a whole parish.

Churchmen and women are the servants of God, but they must choose to serve in one of three ways. The first are the clergy in general, those who minister to the flocks of Christendom and serve their lord, the Pope. The clergy live among lay people of their own station, from the bishop or cardinal who tends the souls of great nobles, to the simple parish priest who baptizes, weds, and rings the bells for the peasants of his village. Regular clergy have a strict hierarchy.

## The Hierarchy

The Pope is the vicar of Christ on Earth, second only to the Heavenly Powers (and certainly not second to any earthly king, if he would have his way). Next come the cardinals, who elect a new Pope when the old one dies, usually one of their own. Archbishops are the chief clerics of large and important lands, bishops are the chief clerics of cities, and below the bishops are the vast numbers of ordinary priests, whose station varies according to the size and prestige of the church and lands they serve, and according to whether they run the church themselves or assist the chief cleric.

As all Christ's disciples were men, so are all those who minister in the general clergy. The most common sinners among this holy flock are those country parish priests too ignorant and unlettered to read the Mass, much less save a soul, and the political bishops and cardinals who would rather fight wars, keep mistresses, and intrigue than pray.

## Monasteries

Monastic clergy are the second group. They live apart from the world in holy retreats: monasteries and nunneries. They must follow only the rules of their order, and need care for no worldly law, not even that of the Pope. They are called monks and nuns (Brother or Sister if you are talking to one), just as clergy in general are called priests (Father if you are talking to him).

The lord of the monastery or nunnery is called an abbot (if a monk) or an abbess (if a nun). Monks and nuns are bound by a great oath to follow the Rule of their holy order, a set of sacred laws set forth by the founder of the order to which they belong. The Rule of the order determines what the monk or nun can and cannot do (e.g., speak, own personal possessions). Rules are different for different orders, and monks and nuns wear robes and hoods of varied patterns, sober blacks, browns and whites, to show which order they belong to.

Some orders take only men, some take both men and women. Every order is based on similar ideals: the holy laws of prayer (applied throughout the day and night), withdrawal from the evils of the world, and celibacy (generally monks and nuns live in separate institutions, though there is a lot of gossip about what goes on behind the walls).

Monasteries and nunneries often hold their own lands. Some have landholdings as great as those of dukes and earls. A noble who fears for his soul may gift the monastery with lands or gold on his deathbed, that the monks may forever pray for his soul. A noblewoman may do the same for a nunnery, though she may have less to give. Generations of such gifts can make abbots and abbesses people to be reckoned with. They bear a higher power, as well, for those who have forsaken the sins of the world are holier than the most pious layperson and the most powerful archbishop alike.

Monks and nuns must bow only to their abbot or abbess, and abbots and abbesses must bow only to God. A true monastic leader walks with Christ and His disciples, and who would dare to doubt or cross their way?

A true monk is the holiest of all men, a false one is the most debased. Their most common sins are the most terrible, for they are violations of their vows. Lecherous and luxury-loving monks and nuns are the subject of a thousand jokes and as many tales of horror. While most of these holy people live lives of pious chastity, an unholy few lie on silk sheets, eat foods as rich as any king, keep lovers, and sometimes even deal with dark and evil powers. The soul of a monk or nun is a true prize for the servants of the Dark One.

## Lay Clergy

The last group of the clergy are the lay clergy. They have stepped into the world of Christ by taking the first holy vows, but they are not yet confirmed in Christ forever as a priest, monk or nun. They must obey all full clergy as their betters and their masters, but have the rights of clergy: they cannot be taxed, cannot be drafted in wartime, and are subject to the laws of the Church rather than those of the local lord or town. Lay clergy do not have to live in a monastery, nunnery, or church, and have taken no vows of celibacy or silence.

To be a lay cleric, for some, is the first step on the road to God. For others, it is a refuge where they can escape from a world they cannot live in, without having to endure the strict discipline of the religious life. Most lay clergy are happy to stay as they are, free to live in the world and subject only to the gentler laws of God.

The other term for these clerics is clerks; they are often civil servants and bureaucrats. The vast majority of students, of whom more is said later, are lay clergy. This status puts them beyond the reach of civil law. The worst of lay clergy are corrupt, worldly, and irreligious, caring only for the freedom from restraint their status gives them.

Lay clerics come in four classes:

• Door keepers, the lowest order, guard and keep the entrances to holy places.

• Readers write and teach, joining the everyday world with the world of the Church.

• Exorcists cast out demons and offer holy cures.

• Acolytes are closest to holy orders, and minister to the altar.

## Heretics

A growing and powerful group of heretics lays claim to the holiness a monastic life creates in man, but renounces the sloth and corruption so often found in the monastic orders. These Albigensians, or Cathars, believe that any peasant can gather holy power, as much as an abbot or cardinal, simply by living in the hermit's fashion, away from the sins of the world. They rail against pope and monk alike, and even denounce the sacred rituals of Mother Church.

The Cathars threaten the very foundations of the world, yet their true faith and their charges of corruption cannot be denied. From their sanctuaries, like the inaccessible mountaintop castle of Montsegur, powerful orators sway the populace against the less heretical monastic orders. In some places they practically rule the countryside, and learned clerics throughout the world debate as to whether they should be brought back into the holy fold by gentle and reasoned persuasion, or burned as tools of the Devil.

# THE COMMONERS' LOT

The commoners live many different types of lives, ranging from that of the spice merchant in his villa to that of the poor villein, starving in his tiny hut. The only thing they have in common is that they're neither noble, nor of the Church.

## Serfs

Serfs are not quite slaves. Serfs are bound to the land, not to a person. Their lord claims ownership, not so much of them, as of their work and the products of their work. It is an indentured servitude in which the term of indenture never ends. The first people to become serfs gave control of their lives and their land to a warrior, undertaking to labor for him in return for safety.

They did this as part of a bargain. In the evil days after the fall of Rome, the world was plunged into darkness. Wyrms, Vikings, howling barbarians, and ravenous hordes

from fallen cities roamed the land, destroying all they met. Those who took on serfdom saved their land and their lives by their bargain.

The bargain does not exist in writing, and its exact details are left up to whomever the lord is at the time, for the bargain is hereditary. Each serf has an ancestor that, at some time in the dark past, agreed to the bargain of serfdom and passed down their burden to all descendants.

As the lord's bound servants, serfs' bodies are their own, but their deeds are not. For every act outside the ordinary bounds of their work, they must have their lord's blessing. Since they have given their land to the lord, serfs must give the lord goods in exchange for being allowed to live and farm on the land. They must also provide for the lord by farming his land before their own, so he can eat, and must provide labor for his cash crops, his building projects, his wars, and his household.

Serfs who break the rules are dead serfs. Lords who destroy those they are bound by tradition to protect, or who raise their serfs' obligations above traditional levels, may or may not be punished by their overlord. Serfs' bodies are their own property, and they must do what they can to care for themselves, as well or as poorly as they may with what their lord allows them. However, since their bodies are their own, serfs cannot be bought, sold, or legally killed without reason.

## Free Peasants

Free peasants are serfs who have been freed, whose ancestors have been freed, or who, through some extraordinary chance, never had ancestors who became serfs. They have the right to do whatever they please whenever they want to, with only two restrictions:

• They must not take on the privileges of their betters (wearing armor; carrying swords; keeping riding horses, hounds, and hawks; hunting on owned land; wearing fancy clothes; making their own laws; and keeping warriors).

• They must, each year, pay rent on the land they farm or be sent packing like any tenant.

Free peasants rent from a landlord, their lord. However, they still have a contract with their lord in which they care for him, his lands, and his household in exchange for protection. They plant and harvest the lord's fields, care for his cash crops, fight in his wars, and wait at his table, just as serfs do. However, they have the freedom to risk starvation and go and do as they please, and freedom is no less cherished for bringing no profits that can be seen.

## Cotters

Cotters are the poorest of the peasants, holding only tiny plots of land from which they seek to scratch just enough to keep them alive and (they hope) to pay the rent. They almost always pay for the use of their land in humble goods — bread, barley and beer — for they have neither the time nor hope to produce anything more that could be sold for silver. Their lives are small and short, poor and cruel, without ease or refinement. Their labor for the lord, defined by tradition if they are serfs and by contract if they are free, is usually the menial scrubbing of pots and cleaning of straw in the darkness of corners and cellars in the lord's house, rather than labor in the clear air of the fields. Most cotters are serfs, for there are few who would keep such a life rather than risk all for a chance at something better.

## Villeins

Villeins are a little better off than cotters. They work larger plots of land. Their work for their lord is usually a certain number of days' labor in the lord's fields each year. If the crops are bad or the rent is high, villeins may be little better off than cotters. However, if they are lucky, they may have a few eggs or wheels of cheese to sell on market day for coins or to barter for an axe or a potter's wheel. If

they can gain wealth, they can buy their freedom if they are serfs, leave the fields to go on pilgrimages halfway around the world, become students, merchants or craftsmen, move to cities, or even marry into the nobility (for some knights are poor enough to be deeply tempted by a lush dowry, even if a peasant wife comes with it).

The Church recruits from the peasant class as well, since passing the priesthood on from father to son is forbidden to truly pious priests. An inspired and dedicated villein boy can even hope to grow up to be Pope, if his parents can afford to lose his labor, and if they can send him to the best monastery, and if he is smart and very, very lucky.

## Peasant Skills

Most of the world's great works come from peasant hands. Free peasants built London and Paris, and bought the cities' right to rule themselves in the same way they bought their own freedom. The knight's proud sword came from the blacksmith's forge in the village at the base of the castle. Doctors, lawyers, artists, craftspeople, and city guards are all peasants. The great cathedrals, monuments to the glory of God, are fashioned by toiling masons. The gold of kings is acquired by the clever minds and skilled hands of merchants and weavers, vintners and

### A Peasant's Obligations

To provide for the survival of my lord before my own survival. To provide certain days (a specified number, generally less than half the peasant's total time) each year of my labor in my lord's service. To provide to my lord, at my death, the heriot (gift of the most valuable thing owned by the peasant). To provide goods to my lord each year in exchange for the use of my lord's land (including mill and laboratory, but rent is never charged for the use of religious facilities).

### A Noble's Obligations

To provide protection at all times from all outside parties (an alternative obligation could substitute, but it must be a permanent, full-time obligation, or the peasant's obligation is temporary as well). To allow all rights as Christians and as peasants. To provide just and fair treatment, and not to inflict suffering or want without just cause. To provide for the administration over the peasant's person and property, as it applies to a person of the peasant's class and station, and to allow no other justice to be applied. To give free days and holidays as provided by the Christian calendar (about eight weeks each year).

tradesmen. Many among the noble class deeply resent peasant wealth and power.

As the power of the peasant's skills and money grows, the power of the noble's land and sword fades. At the same time, however, most peasants are farmers, scraping a living together by the toil of their hands and the sweat of their brow. Short lives, high rents, and heavy taxes (for, as caretakers of all people, they pay all of the taxes levied by nobles and kings) keep most peasants in the role everyone is used to, the role that is said to be ordained by God. Thus, peasants have the power to rise above their current social position, but that transcendence is still centuries away.

# CITIES

In the golden ages of long ago the glorious Roman Empire had scores of great cities which dotted all of Europe and beyond. However, the decadence of the Romans and the hand of God conspired to end that brilliant, yet corrupt, era. The Dark Ages destroyed the Roman cities, and all the civilization they contained. In the Dark Ages the cities were no more.

## Rise of the City

For centuries tiny, ignoble villages clustered close to the castles of the nobles, hiding from the barbarians, Vikings, and others who sought to destroy all order and peace. Even the greatest cities of the past, such as Roma and Londinium, fell into decay, as most of the inhabitants left to seek safer homes. As the barbarians were driven off or civilized, merchants began to travel the newly safe roads, craft and trade fairs sprang up outside many of the larger castles, and some free peasants began to return to the long-deserted cities.

Many nobles saw that the taxes they placed on the trade fairs often brought more silver and gold than the meager taxes they took from the mouths of overburdened peasants. In return for the greater profit gained from a permanent center of trade, many nobles granted the inhabitants of trading towns the right to freedom and self-government. Sometimes armed rebellions, staged by angry townspeople, forced other nobles to give these brave towns their freedom. Whatever the reason, lords often signed a town charter with the inhabitants of a town, promising the townspeople many rights in return for taxes given to the lord.

From these humble beginnings many hundreds of towns and cities were born. Now there are hundreds of towns of more than a thousand inhabitants. London and Genoa boast over 50,000, and Paris, Milan, and Venice, jewel of the southern seas, all have more than 100,000 residents. Of course, none can yet rival far Constantinople, with its population of more than half a million inhabitants.

## Perils of Freedom

In the city, no one is lord or serf. All people have the right to marry, move, and inherit property as they please. A serf who can live within the walls of a city for a year and a day is free, and no one can be called out to fight and die in one of the lord's wars.

Of course, too much freedom breeds anarchy and chaos. To avert that danger, town councils are created, formed of the wealthy and knowledgeable heads of trade and commerce. These worthies levy taxes and tolls and make the laws, which are carried out by the town guard and courts. Town guards are a sturdy lot, for town life has many dangers. After all, the wealth of merchants only invites thieves.

Low taverns cater to men of low natures, and drink brings out sin in all men. Though the walls of towns keep their inhabitants free from armies, monsters, and barbarian hordes, they simultaneously hem those folk in. In the great and crowded rise of houses and shops, the moon and stars are forever lost, and evil deeds are committed in the shelter of darkness. And, once kindled, flame leaps from house to shop like a devouring beast. If not quickly controlled by vigilant guards, fire can burn a whole city to ashes. Yet for all these dangers, townsfolk are rich in power, pride, and mortal goods.

## Guilds

Trade and commerce are the lifeblood of towns. Guilds govern these important enterprises. There are merchant guilds, which govern the behavior of traveling merchants, and serve a mutual aid association to help offset the dangers of the road. Most townsfolk are more familiar with their own craft guilds. Craftsmen in every town, from humble cobblers to wealthy goldsmiths, have their guilds. These guilds insure all members produce work of adequate quality for fair and uniform prices.

None can work longer hours, employ more apprentices, or advertise their wares to the detriment of any other guild member. After all, competition breeds dissent, and dissent breeds poverty for all. Guilds also insure that members have aid in times of sickness, and that families have help with funeral expenses and support when a member dies.

The system provided by the guilds is generally fair and good. When you are young you apprentice to a master, and spend the years necessary to learn the craft working for room, board, and education. After the craft has been learned, and the term of the apprenticeship is up, you become a journeyman. Journeymen must still work for a master, but they are now paid for their labors.

After you have spent enough years to fully master the craft, you may petition the guild council for full membership. To do so, you must create a "masterpiece" to demonstrate your skill, and present it to the guild. This final step is fraught with danger, for guildsmen can be bribed and masterpieces can be created through fraud or even magic.

For a truly inspired journeyman, reputation comes early, and jealous thieves may wait and plan to steal a masterpiece. But, if all is passed well and safely, and the work is judged acceptable, the journeyman becomes a master, with the right to sit on the guild council, work for whomever he will, and to take on apprentices. In this way the guild assures all masters are fully conversant with their chosen craft.

## List of Guilds

All towns of any size and substance have within them most, or all of the following guilds:

**Wool Trades:** Tapiters (makers of tapestry), Weavers, Dyers

**Leather Trades:** Tanners, Curriers

**Building Trades:** Carpenters, Ironmongers, Painters, Glaziers (makers of glass & stained glass), Stonemasons

**Food Trades:** Grocers, Cooks, Brewers, Bakers, Saucemakers, Wine-makers, Butchers

**Outfitting Trades:** Tailors, Cobblers, Saddlers, Hatmakers, Spuriers, Lorimers (makers of tack for horses)

**Armor Trades:** Armorers, Smiths, Bowyers, Fletchers (makers of bows and arrows)

**Household Trades:** Potters, Bucklemakers, Linenweavers, Chaundlers (makers of candles and wax images), Coopers (makers of barrels and containers)

**Other Trades:** Goldsmiths, Bookbinders, Parchment makers, Alchemists, Charm and amulet makers, Shipwrights, Writers of texts, Ostlers (Inn-keepers), Barber-Surgeons

In larger cities many other guilds exist as well. The largest cities are rumored to house the secret guilds, those whose crafts have either been banned by all right-thinking folk, or are so subtle in ancient practice that they must be hidden from ignorant and prying eyes. Sometimes a work, or even a masterpiece, of the secret guilds appears — a jeweled bird that turns and sings with the phases of the moon; a stone sphere that hangs suspended in its box without support of any kind; an imperceptible poison that kills by merest touch; a horse trained to figure numbers and read Latin; a mirror in whose silvery depths unreflected fish are swimming.

Not all guild members are men. Cities offer opportunity for all who can work in an honorable profession. Wives and daughters can join the guild of their husbands or fathers, and widows often inherit their husband's business and position. Many guilds admit all women of good character as members, and a few, such as spinning and block printing, employ only women.

## Confines of the Wall

Many who visit a city or town for the first time are surprised at how crowded and closed in the places are. The reason for this is obvious: defense. Just as a castle and its keep are the defenses of a noble lord, the walls of a city are its defenses against bandits, war, or overly ambitious nobles.

It must always be remembered that many towns had to fight for their freedom, and that to this day many nobles are jealous of this freedom, and would like nothing better than to wrest control of a town. The walls breed crowding, filth, theft, darkness, fire, and even pestilence. Yet, lives goes on, for freedom must have its price.

## Roadways

When you journey to one of the proud cities, your journey is probably on one of the major roads which link

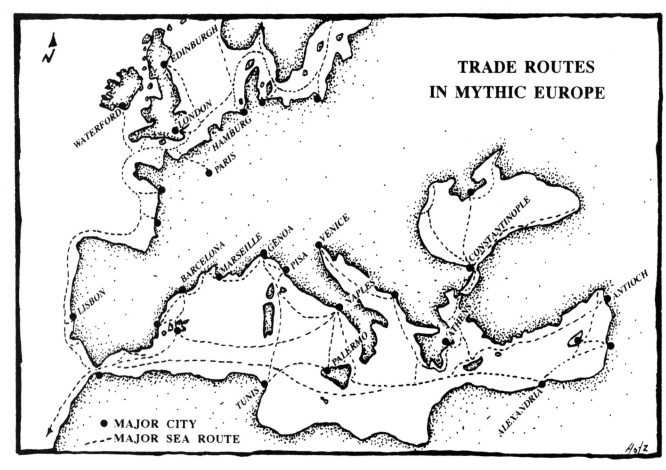

TRADE ROUTES
IN MYTHIC EUROPE

● MAJOR CITY
- - - MAJOR SEA ROUTE

major cities, towns, castles, and monasteries. You travel the same roads that brave merchants and traders travel.

These roads enter a city through large gates which can be closed in times of trouble, and are regularly closed every night after sundown as protection against the people and things that haunt the night. Just outside the gates of the city, along the roads, are the pitiful shacks and decaying hovels of the very poor. Some of these shacks are hospitals for weary and injured travelers, and are run by the clergy. Also outside the walls there are other hospitals, those for wretched lepers and other unfortunates, whom all others avoid.

## City Streets

Once inside the city gates, the picture changes completely. The main roads continue through the city, forming its major streets. These are well maintained roads, with solid cobbles, ditches for the waste to run in, and only a little mud. On these major streets can be found people on foot and on horseback, the carriages of the very wealthy, and wagons for hauling goods. Side streets wind about as they can between the buildings, and are shared by people on foot, geese, dogs, cats, whatever is thrown down

upon them from the windows above, whatever vermin can survive, and a few durable pack mules, hauling those goods too heavy for a man to carry on his back.

To enable more people to live in each great city, many buildings have two, or even three or four, stories. The upper stories are often extended out so that they overhang the lower ones and nearly touch across the street, to give more space inside the house. Light is dim on the backstreets, even on the brightest day.

## Nightfall

While day in a city is a busy and productive time, nights are very different. A city's darkness is beyond the darkness of any peasant village. In this darkness there are dangers greater than stealthy thieves and heartless robbers. The unseemly trades thrive as well. They include usury, selling of stolen goods, gambling, prostitution, and even the horror of diabolism.

Also, let all travelers be warned when visiting the oldest and largest of cities, such as Rome, Paris, or Constantinople, that the dangers of the present can sometimes be outweighed by the dangers of the past. On certain nights terrible ghosts are said to haunt the streets, reenacting the horrors of the many wars, plagues, and riots that have scarred these cities' history.

Even more terrifying are the occasional stories of the ancient tunnels, catacombs, and sewers which lie under many old cities, and which date back to Classical times, or perhaps earlier. In these fell pits are said to live demons and foul undead creatures, which slay all who journey there. It is even said that on particularly Infernal nights, these creatures climb up to the surface. Of course, there are also stories of vast treasures, lost from ancient days, under such cities, but perhaps such treasures are best left where they are. Far better and safer to remain on the surface, to stay home during the night, and to live in a new city, with no dark past to haunt it.

# Markets

Shopping in the city makes for convenient living. Food can be bought, already cooked, at market squares, taverns, and inns. Foodstuffs for cooking at home are also bought at the marker squares. Different kinds of produce are sold on different days. Butter, poultry, meat, milk, fish, and herbs from the countryside brought in for sale. However, some of the craftsmen use their shops as places for making goods, and sell their goods, like cloth and leather, at the markets.

While the markets are busy, the fairs which are held every month or so during the mild months of the year outshine even them. During these fairs, most of which are held on important holidays, the markets, and yes, the city in general truly comes to life. These fairs usually last for eight days. During this time plays and pageants are sponsored and performed by the various guilds for the entertainment and religious instruction of the public. Performers come from far away to put on mimes, puppet shows, and to play music and sing.

---

## York

York is a fairly typical, new English city. It has two market squares, both near the center of the city, where fresh and cooked food is sold, where plays and festivals are performed, and where bards and minstrels display their talents on sunny days. There are cloisters and gardens of monasteries in town, as well as the graveyards of the many churches. Along that line, let it not be said that people of the cities and towns are irreligious. Their faith is as firm as any man's, and it religion gives comfort against the many trials and perils of city life. York has thirty-five churches and eight chapels for its 10,000 inhabitants; there is a place in Church for every citizen.

---

Merchants who have been to places as far away as Paris, Venice, and maybe even Constantinople come to sell their wares, and perhaps tell tales of places few ever see. These fairs are also when hedge wizards come to sell their charms and other wares. The alchemists set up their velvet pavilions as well and sell to the wealthy. Often Magi, in the company of their retainers, come to these fairs to purchase mysterious objects, or simply to enjoy the humble pleasures of the city.

# Work and Play

In most cities, when fairs are not being held, the legal work hours range from just before dawn to sundown. Sunday is, of course, for going to church, and Saturday is a half day. Fairs and other holidays make up eight of the 52 weeks of the year. Visitors are welcome in most cities, although they are expected to be able to care for themselves.

Though cities have only limited space, construction work is still carried out, sometimes to expand the walls, and other times for special or lengthy projects. This is particularly so for cathedrals. Some of the loftiest of these structures take decades to build, like the one in Chartres which took ninety years to complete. Most citizens donate labor or money to help make their cathedral a grand symbol of the worth and holiness of their city. In addition, traveling work gangs often move from town to town, contributing to the construction of cathedrals and other buildings. Because construction can take so long, "traveling" work gangs can become veritable citizens of a city.

# Education

Cities are also centers of learning. Many children, of all social classes, are taught the basics of reading and religion by their parish priest. While books are few, and written by hand, many people of substance own a few. In York there is a school for priests and clerks, which also serves to prepare scholars for university.

This is the age of the university. Most important cities such as Paris, Oxford, Padua, and Orleáns have universities. Students and their masters are part of a guild, much like the craft guilds. Classes may be held in rented buildings or sometimes in rough sheds, but no guild has greater pride than the educated. Students who attend the university of their home town retain their town pride, living together and challenging rivals as a group. As long as they pay their masters' tuition for classes, students are responsible only to the their masters, and masters are responsible only to the Church.

Students often flaunt their unique freedom and mock the nobility by going about armed with daggers and swords. It comes as no surprise that the nobility and students often come to blows. Indeed, the reputation of

## A Parisian of Education

*"So what is it to be a man of Paris at the University? Ah, weep bitter tears that you do not already know. No better life is there, not in this world nor in the next, for it's all for one and one for all, and the Devil take the hindmost. We go where we want, do as we please, and are better men for it. Me, I bow my head to no lord, bend my back to no yoke, and need the prattling of no priest to save my soul. I'll match my sword with the greatest lord in France and laugh at the fools who waste away their lives. The town man is no keener than the cloth he sells, just as the peasant's no better than his goats and pigs. I keep company with Galen and Aristotle, better men than all.*

*The Bishop's preaching against us again. Each day when I wake, I thank the holy Virgin that we of all men do not have to care what the Bishop thinks about anything. They threw us out of our classrooms, so we held classes in the market and on the city green. In my father's time they sent the city guard against us as if we were mere peasants; that the guard regretted loudly on the swords of the men of Paris. The Bishop won't do anything. It's his gall that sets my blood on fire. He seeks to have us called impious — we, who have seen inside the very Temple and touched the veins that carry the living breath of a man through his body, we, who learn at the feet of the Ancients. What right has the Bishop to judge us? If I have not a penny to my name when I have paid my masters for classes, indeed I'll cut a purse. The lord of Coucy has trampled half the harvest, the innkeeper waters his wine. Are they not sinners too? If fathers lock their daughters in when we go out to play, perhaps they fear their wenches' superior taste in men.*

*The people spread tales about us; it is ignorance, or envy. But, I will make one thing clear. They say our beloved Master of Rhetoric, Aristotle, disputed with the Prince of Lies for his position. We do not dispute that, we say only that he won!*

*No one on this earth can dictate to me, save the Masters of the University. Once you have tasted freedom, you will die without it. To be here, I would learn to live without bread. To be a Master is a prize truly worth wagering my soul with Hell."*

students as impoverished, lewd, irreverent, drunken, and rowdy is often well deserved. Many city folk would not be at all surprised if the Devil himself appeared one day and hauled a student off to Hell.

Students generally study for three years, after which they take examinations. Each who passes becomes a *baccalaureus*, who can then assist in teaching. After three more years of study such assistants become masters. Both men and women can be students and masters in most universities. Law, medicine, theology, history, rhetoric, logic, and mathematics are the subjects commonly studied.

# MONEY

The most important thing to remember when using money in **Ars Magica** is that real money, in coins, bills, or any abstract form at all, is a convenience, not a necessity. If all money suddenly vanished off the face of the medieval world, there would be a lot of angry people, but the basics of life could continue as normal. True wealth is measured in solid goods of value, not in money.

The basic unit of wealth is land. Land gives a person food, clothing, and shelter; if you had no land to live on, you would die. But, since land is so important, only crazy or truly desperate people sell it. Grain and livestock are used in barter, but exchanged only when one has a significant surplus. Gold and silver make the ideal money — portable, precious, and useless for anything practical.

Gold and silver money is not modern money, however. When a person uses coins in Mythic Europe, she barters for what she wants. Instead of bartering for what she wants with chickens or bread, she barters with gold or silver.

Coins don't identify their own value. A medieval coin is a piece of precious metal that is printed with the mark of the lord or cleric that had it made. The mark signifies the weight of the coin and the percentage of pure gold or silver in the metal. Whoever has the coin can offer it in barter, and the fact that it is a coin instead of a gold nugget proves it is genuine (an advantage gold and silver have over gems). The minters of coins have them printed with a picture, coat of arms, or image of a cathedral (if the minter is a cleric). The fancy pictures on a coin keep it from being counterfeited, and offer the wealth and fame of the coiner as a guarantee that the coin is good. How many sheep a quarter of an ounce of 80% pure gold is worth depends on what the shepherd wants and is willing to take.

It is always in the best interests of a lord to make his own coins, if people will accept his coin as good. If a lord makes his own coins, he can be sure the coins are good whenever he receives them in payment. However, people are much happier receiving the coins of the King of France than they are those of the Lord of Toulouse.

Many peasants in Mythic Europe live out their lives without ever using a coin. Anyone dealing with poor people may have to barter in goods of lesser value — a meal, a dozen eggs, a yard of cloth, or perhaps a special service from a craftsperson. Establishments which serve travelers regularly have special arrangements and can deal with coins. They often provide a set of goods or services large enough that the total value can be paid in coin — rooms for the night, stable, care and fodder for horses, meals, and ale, for instance. In cities, coins are more common, and every town has merchants whose business involves dealings with them.

Sometimes coin are even cut into halves or quarters, and those smaller coin "shards" are used as change. Half a coin is known as a halfling, and a quarter coin is known as a farthing.

"Paper money" does exist, not as cash, but as checks. A noble can write a letter of indebtedness to a banking house or to another person and sign it, creating easily transported paper money, whose real value in gold or silver can, in theory, be redeemed on demand. The same thing can be done with a deed of ownership of land.

An endorsed check has additional signatures (endorsements) by rich and influential people. In theory, their signatures vouch for the check-writer's honesty. In practice, if the original check-writer doesn't pay up, the money can be collected from the endorser. Obviously, the best checks are the ones endorsed by an archbishop or a king.

One last note on medieval money — it's evil. Any desire for profit beyond what is necessary to stay alive is considered a sin. Loaning money with an interest charge is the sin of usury, though opinion varies on whether any interest is a sin or if only rates above 10, 12.5, or 20% insure a place in Hell. Just to be on the safe side, moneylending and many other merchant enterprises are often left to those damned anyway — Saracens, Jews, and Italian banking families.

## System of Coins

- Florin (Italian, minted in Florence)
- Pound (English)
- Livre (French)
- Franc (French)
- Mark (German)
- Ducat (Italian, minted in Venice)

These are all terms for coins, derived from the value of one pound of silver. Since a one-pound coin is unreasonably heavy, the Italian coins are made of gold of a weight and purity which gives them an equivalent value. There are 240 pennies in one pound. Pennies are made of silver. Everyone's "pounds" and "pennies" are of slightly different purities and values, so, for instance, a franc of Paris might be worth 10% more than a franc of Bordeaux. Eventually, a more standard system came about which added coins of intermediate value:

1 shilling (English) or sous (French) = 12 pennies

1 pound (English) or livre (French) = 20 shillings or sous.

Note: Florins and ducats are the most trusted coins.

## Beginning Wealth

For players who want to keep track of how much wealth their characters possess, a determination system for starting wealth is needed. To calculate starting wealth, refer to the chart below. Make a die roll and multiply the result by the number listed for your character type. That is the number of silver coins you possess. Characters with pertinent Virtues or Flaws have wealth adjusted according to the trait.

**Grog**: simple die x 3

**Companion**: stress die x 5

**Magus**: simple die x 7

## Price List

The following is a price list of items that can be purchased in Provençal (southern France), though the list can easily be adapted to any other local and coinage system. It is provided to help you visualize transactions that might take place in a Saga, and gives you a sense of the relative value of things in Mythic Europe. Of course, prices may vary from time to time; this list is only a general guide. Furthermore, these prices in no way imply that anyone with money can purchase these items. You cannot simply buy a castle or a suit of chain mail, though you can hire stone masons and armorers. Wealth is measured by status and breeding, not by hoards of coins, though this is changing, especially in the larger cities. When the players want to keep track of prices in the Saga, it isn't difficult to extrapolate a complete price system from the items listed here.

When references are made to 1/4 and 1/2 coins, we are speaking of farthings and halflings respectively. Medieval folk used to actually cut their coins in half and in quarters in order to make change, these smaller denominations were actually quite common.

Prices are all given in livres.. They sometimes vary across a range, such as "3-5," depending on the quality of the goods.

### Food

| | |
|---|---|
| Pint of poor wine | 1/4 |
| Pint of good wine | 1/2 |
| Pint of fine wine | 2 |
| Pint of vintage wine | 15 |
| Pint of ale | 1/2 |
| Pint of mead | 1 |
| Pint of brandy | 4 |
| Joint of meat | 1/2 |
| Hunk of cheese | 1/4 |
| Smoked sausages (5) | 2 |

| | |
|---|---|
| Bowl of stew | 1/4 |
| Pint of strawberries | 1/2 |
| Loaf of bread | 1/4 |
| Bushel of carrots | 1 |
| Hearty meal for one | 1 |
| Banquet meal for one | 5 |
| Dram of salt | 1/2 |
| Dram of pepper | 140 |

## Equipment

| | |
|---|---|
| Wooden bowl | 1/2 |
| Pewter bowl | 3 |
| Silver bowl | 87 |
| Iron pan | 2 |
| Iron caldron | 16 |
| 10 feet of rope | 2 |
| Oil lamp | 8 |
| Blank book, 20 pages | 11 |
| Blank book, 50 pages | 18 |
| Illuminated book | 150 |
| Brazier, bronze | 23 |
| Materials for labratory | 800 |
| Silver seal | 75 |
| Gold seal | 320 |
| Splinter from the "True" Cross | 8 |
| Holy relic of local saint | 70 |
| Gold cross | 105 |

## Tools

| | |
|---|---|
| Carpenter's set of tools | 42 |
| Mason's set of tools | 38 |
| Pitchfork | 7 |
| Plow | 12 |
| Scythe | 9 |
| Crowbar | 6 |
| Anvil | 112 |
| Pully 2:1 | 32 |
| Pully 3:1 | 55 |
| Pully 4:1 | 89 |
| Heavy chain, per foot | 22 |
| Sundial | 14 |
| Hourglass | 17 |

## Clothing

| | |
|---|---|
| Hose (stockings) | 1-3 |
| Chemise (shirt) | 1-3 |
| Pellison (gown) | 2-5 |
| Bliaut (tunic) | 2-5 |

| | |
|---|---|
| Mantle (cloak) | 3-9 |
| Wimple (hood) | 1-3 |
| Sandals | 1-2 |
| Clogs | 1-2 |
| Riding boots | 5-9 |
| Belt | 1-3 |

## Services

| | |
|---|---|
| Private room for two at an inn | 2 |
| Bribe for a town guard | 3 |
| Bribe for a magistrate | 18 |
| Servant's services, 1 week | 5 |
| Mercenary's services, 1 week | 8 |
| Harlot's pity | 2 |
| Courtesan's compassion | 8 |
| Pay for the work of a hired serf for 1 year | 10 |
| Pay for the work of a hired knight for 1 day | 20 |
| Pay for the work of a hired archer for 1 day | 5 |
| Cost of renting a cart and two horses for 1 day | 1 |

## Weapons

| | |
|---|---|
| Dagger | 3 |
| Short sword | 38 |
| Broad sword | 98 |
| Bastard sword | 154 |
| Greatsword | 240 |
| Short spear | 2 |
| Long spear | 5 |
| Lance | 30 |
| Throwing axe | 18 |
| Hand axe | 11 |
| Battle axe | 42 |
| Pole axe | 67 |
| Halberd | 144 |
| Quarterstaff | 2 |
| Mace | 20 |
| War maul | 29 |
| Morning star | 39 |
| Military flail | 98 |
| Javelin | 12 |

## Armor

| | |
|---|---|
| Cuirass leather | 7 |
| Cuirass heavy leather | 10 |
| Cuirass ring mail | 23 |
| Cuirass scale mail | 76 |
| Cuirass chain mail | 140 |
| Hauberk leather | 12 |
| Hauberk heavy leather | 17 |
| Hauberk ring mail | 55 |
| Hauberk scale mail | 102 |
| Hauberk chain mail | 205 |
| Full leather | 19 |
| Full heavy leather | 42 |
| Full ring mail | 86 |
| Full scale mail | 155 |
| Full chain mail | 420 |
| Target shield | 8 |
| Round shield | 12 |
| Knight shield | 23 |
| Kite shield | 87 |
| Tower shield | 105 |

## Animals

| | |
|---|---|
| Chicken | 1/2 |
| Ox | 32 |
| Pig | 9 |
| Sheep | 7 |
| Pony | 63 |
| Donkey | 72 |
| Draft horse | 138 |
| Riding horse | 214 |
| Charger | 530 |

## Transportation

| | |
|---|---|
| Passage on ferry | 1/2 |
| Passage on ship | 3-20 |
| Cart | 18 |
| Wagon | 27 |
| Open coach | 54 |
| Closed coach | 98 |
| Rowboat | 54 |
| Longboat | 110 |
| Merchant ship | 3,500 |

## Buildings

| | |
|---|---|
| Forest shack | 80 |
| Peasant cottage | 300 |
| Fortified town house | 4,000 |
| Fortified manor house | 5,000 |
| Small castle | 90,000 |
| Large castle | 125,000 |
| King's castle | 300,000 |

## Income

A year's income
   for a poor knight ............................... 50-60

A year's income
   for a rich knight ................................ 1000-3000

Annual income from
   a grand estate (dukedom) ................. 5000-6000

A year's income
   for a wealthy merchant ..................... 1000

Annual rent on a
   tenant family's acreage ...................... 15-25

## Fines

Traditional fine for
   committing a civil crime ........................ 60

## Bartering

For bartering purposes, eggs, bread, and cheese are the cheapest goods, followed by beer, then wine, meat, cloth and chickens, then cats, then sheep, goats and pigs, then cattle, and finally horses. Decent horses are usually worth more than people.

# Geography

The geography of Europe is uncertain and difficult to master. In places where the barbarian ravages of times past were worst, each lord rules his or her own lands as absolute master, bowing only to neighboring lords powerful enough to defeat the other's knights.

The territories of ancient Greece and Rome are ruled, as they were in ancient times, by their most powerful cities. And in England, there is a strange new means of rule, with a king who is overlord over all lords and masters, not only of vassals and lands, but of a country from sea to sea. As conqueror, Duke William of Normandy claimed all the spoils, and his family rules still.

## Ireland

At the Western edge of the world lies the island of Hibernia, a land too far for even the Romans to conquer. Its people are Celts, hunters and shepherds who speak a barbarian tongue. Curiously, it is this wild land that keeps the greatest monasteries and the finest monks in all Christendom, and the finest Magi of House Verditius.

The Celts are a fierce and proud people who broke the power of the Vikings. They pay homage to no rulers but their own lords. Hibernia is divided into five kingdoms: Ulster, Connacht, Leinster, Meath, and Munster. It is said to be a bitter but green land, and closest of all countries to Arcadia (Faerieland). Arcadian beasts, cattle, horses, dogs, and even monsters are said to sometimes wander onto Hibernian lands, and the Celtic tribes are supposed to fight fiercely for the right to claim the faerie creature.

## British Isles

East of the Hibernian sea lies England, Scotland, and Wales. England is a flat country ruled by a king called John, who is a tyrant and a fool, not much loved either by peasants or by noble lords. The English are descended from Vikings, and are much attached to the taking of land. Their King owns a fief called Aquitaine, encompassing all of the best land in the Southwest of France, and this is a bitter blow indeed to the lords of France. The English King would have Wales and Scotland as well if he could, though God alone knows why.

Much of the country of the English has been tamed for fine farms, and the forests which still linger are the homes of all manner of beasts driven from their ancient lands. Unicorns guard the deepest forests, and do not allow them to be cut. Wales is a poor country, where the people graze for food with the beasts, and burn earth in their fires for heat. They are said to be pagans. Wales is composed of many separate kingdoms, and practically the only thing they can all agree on is that they dislike the English more than they dislike each other.

It is also said that parts of Wales are very magical, and that some of the Welsh kingdoms are led by immortal Magi, or perhaps even faerie nobles. Perhaps this is true, for the English do not seem able to conquer them.

Scotland is a land so forsaken by God that the Romans did not even want it. The Scotsmen know neither English, French, nor Latin, sleep on the bare earth in huts, and eat raw flesh. Their lands are so mountainous that they have neither farms nor folds, and they must hunt and war to live. They are said to be the most terrible warriors in the world, even as the wolf and bull are terrible. The Scotsmen are also said to be pagans who burn strangers alive, and drown their own children in lakes as a sacrifice to their gods. However, Scotsmen are supposed to have their own code of honor, and are fiercely loyal to their own clans. They have no greater nobles, only many petty lords who war constantly with one other. Their Magi are not of the Order of Hermes, and can raise spirits and assume the shapes of horses, wolves, birds, and fish.

### English Channel

Between England and France lies a strait of sea that a clear day may allow sight across. However, the Channel is so plagued with storms that once a knight who once set out upon it was, thirty days after he set out, blown back to the place from which he began.

# France

France is the fairest of lands. In the North is Bretagne, a rocky land that likes England too well, and Normandie, which is another fief of the English King. South of Normandie are the lands of the Duc d'Anjou. East is Blois, ruled by the count of Champagne, then Ile de France, the domain of the King. There, beside the River Seine, lies Paris, which is the greatest city in all the West.

East of the king's lands are Champagne to the North and Burgundy to the South, both ruled by counts rich with the wealth brought by their vineyards. Toulouse lies to the East of the Aquitaine, at the foot of the country. Toulouse, too, would be claimed by the English King, but the lords of France have fought his armies back again and again.

In Toulouse lies the Camargue, where men catch the white horses that come from the sea and train them to carry kings and Magi. The people of this land are rough farmers and herdsmen, very backward in their ways and much mocked for it, but it is said that many of them have a great understanding and power over wild beasts. Indeed, some of these folk claim to have news from far off, heard from the tongues of birds. Others of this folk run in the Festival of the Bulls, garlanding the horns and leaping across the backs of these savage beasts without harm.

In the North of France a tongue is spoken called *langue d'oil*, and in the South the language of the people is called *langue d'oc*. At the border between the lands of France and Iberia live a wild mountain people who speak a tongue unknown to all other men. Some say they are a faerie tribe bound onto this earth. Others say they are Gypsies, or pagans of ancient days. They hide in their mountain valleys, whose entrances only animals know, and have little commerce with the world. They are said to be wizards, skilled in the healing arts; to have power over beasts; to keep wild goats, deer, lynxes, and bears as other men keep cattle and sheep; and to have dealings with faeries. These people are known as the Basques, though none know what they call themselves.

# Spain

South of Toulouse and the Aquitaine lie the kingdoms of Navarre, Aragon, and the lands of the city of Barcelona. Navarre looks to France, and its lord is forever hatching plots to be ruler of that country, but Aragon is a Moorish land, though ruled by a Christian king. Arabic is still spoken there, and Moors and Jews roam freely, mixing with Christians in the city of Saragossa.

Though not so large as other cities, Saragossa is said to be the strangest of towns, where men and near-men from all corners of the world meet, and Moors and Jews practice their bizarre rituals without fear, in the sight of all.

WOC 92

Barcelona lies on the Eastern coast, and carries on great trade with Venice, Florence, and Genoa. It, too, is still Moorish in many ways. The Jews who live in this city are said to hold positions of honor in the King's court, and live in their own walled-off ghettoes within the city.

Across the West to Portugal is the kingdom of Leon and Castille. This land is a bitter enemy of the Moors, and the most Christian kingdom, second in devotions perhaps only to Portugal. Castille and Aragon are enemies indeed, for Aragon hates not the Jew and Moor. It is only the Islamic Moors themselves, who hold all Southern Spain from Castille to the sea, that keep Castille from war with Aragon.

### Cordoba

The Moors call their land in Spain the Caliphate of Cordoba, but Christians call it Andalusia. Its great city on the Southern coast is called Grenada of the thousand wonders. More riches and marvels are to be found here than anywhere else, except perhaps Constantinople.

There is a great University here, where Christian, Moor, and Jew all teach. It has an island reserved solely for the use of falconers, and an institute for training pardals and griffins for use in the hunt. There is a menagerie of creatures from the ends of the earth, and a Palace of Ambassadors, where apartments are fitted in the style of every land. Cordoba's gardens are magical miniatures of each country and clime, and its hall of white marble, created entirely for the entertainment and instruction of demons, is where students are instructed in philosophy and theology.

## Flanders

Beyond France, to the East, lies Flanders on the Northern coast. Though small and visited by most terrible winters, it is the richest land in Christendom, for here is made the cloth that adorns lords and ladies from Grenada to Constantinople. It is said the master craftsmen of Flanders can make anything, from the miniature lands of the gardens of Cordoba to musical instruments that play by themselves.

# Holy Roman Empire

Beyond Flanders is the Holy Roman Empire. Empire it is in name only, being the most impossible collusion of petty lords' lands, free cities, fiefs of Pope and crown, and knights of easy virtue to be found beneath the eyes of God.

From Bohemia, south to Venice, the Germans war with French lords for the lands called Hungary and Styria, wild countries that are witch-haunted and full of monstrous forests. Horses are found here which can fly in the wind, but they are said to be untameable, and of either Infernal or Faerie stock.

## *Teutonic Knights*

In the North the knights of the Teutonic Order hunt pagans and heretics with hounds, and pillage whatever they desire, for German knights know not chivalry. They enter into the great kingdom of Poland to the East, but to the South the kingdom of Bohemia keeps them at bay. It is said that the most powerful of Covenants resides here, in the ancient city of Prague. It is from Prague, as well, that letters from the council of Jewish wizards come, and some say that the Bohemian King has made common cause with both against foreign invaders.

Beyond Poland and Bohemia lie forests too deep for a man on horseback to pass through. The wood is reputedly inhabited by pagans and fairies, wild men riding horses with wings, and witches with huts that walk. Even the most common sorts of beasts found here are magical, faerie, or in league with the Devil. A rooster with a tail of fire is more likely to be met than a dragon, and the peasants know no difference between magic and a natural thing.

# Merchant City States

Where the Holy Roman Empire ends at the southern Alps, there begin the fabulously rich cities of the merchant princes. Genoa, with her face to the West, and Venice, with her face to the East, are the greatest, and between them Milan, Florence, Pisa, and Siena. Each city vies with its neighbor to be the most splendid, the most rich, the farthest traveling, the most powerful, and the most corrupt. Here can be found all the wonders of East and West. Men and goods from every corner of the world come here, to add to all the confusion that a lordless land can suffer.

# The Papal States

Order is restored by the Pope within the territories of Rome. Between Venice and Naples lie the fiefs of the Pope, in which the word of Innocent III is law, and the way of Christ is the only way; the use of all magic is strictly prohibited. Innocent III is suzerain over Sicily, Aragon, Portugal, England, and Poland as well, though only here of his worldly territories is his sovereignty undisputed.

South of the Papal lands chaos resumes, in which the city of Naples is dominant. In the cities of the merchant princes there is a curious inversion of the ordinary way of things. Fairies exist and live in the hearts of cities, and dress in monk's clothes. Diabolism reigns more powerfully than it does anywhere else. Peasants rule. And, in certain places, objects are said to fall upward.

# The Atlantic

Beyond all of these lands are others, less well known. Beyond Hibernia lie the Isles of the West, unnumbered islands scattered on the unforgiving sea. The greatest of these islands is the Isle of Man, where druids are still found and faerie ways are the ways of mortals as well. Some islands are unrooted and move about like beasts, first to one place, then another, so they may not be charted. Sail West past the faerie Isle of Man and you may come to the wild vinyards of Arcadia. Sail too far North and you will come to a place where the sun never sets and the sea turns to jelly, too thick for a ship to pass.

# Scandinavia

Beyond Flanders lie the lands of Scandinavia, some Christian, some pagan, and populated with Viking hordes and God alone knows what else. Here live the Magi of the Order of Odin, and beyond them, strange magics even they fear. In those far lands are men who are not men, men who ride the wind, and men who do not know the hearts or shapes of animals. In the Viking lands live a great number of dragons, especially of a sort without legs or wings, like poisonous black worms.

# Russia

Somewhere to the far North lies the great Christian kingdom of Russia, whose scholars write letters in Greek and whose Magi follow the Order of Hermes. Russia has two great cities, known as golden Kiev and Lord Novgorod the Great. From their traders come furs of unknown creatures, of bears as big as bulls, and bulls as big as elephants. The winter in Russia never ends, for the land is under the spell of the Witch-Queen of the Snows, and none know how to break her rule.

# The Far South

Beyond Spain lie the lands of the Moors, whose kings are magicians who hunt lions and live in palaces without walls. Their knights breed all manner of wild animals for the greater glory of their king and god, and the whole land is under the rule of the Sun.

It is said that beyond the Moors is a Christian kingdom whose ruler is a king without sin. This King is known as Prester John and his lands are the finest in the world, with rivers running with rubies and hyacinths, and gigantic ants mining gold from the earth. The King of this land, and its hermits who live in towers of stone, know the location of Paradise, but it is guarded by angels and may not be entered. Around Paradise there are said to grow trees whose fruit cures all sickness, madness, and despair, no matter the cause; this wondrous fruit may even heal those ailments thought to be otherwise incurable.

## Constantinople

Beyond Venice lies Constantinople, city of the Greeks. Constantinople is the largest city in the world. It is called the city of wonders, the city of jewels, and the city of freaks. It is said that the city's great cathedral is made entirely of hammered gold, and the avenue into the city paved with rubies. Some say, however, that blood is sacrificed at high Mass. It is also said that travelers that go there never return. And yet, we know stories of Constantinople, and of the cedar trees, the courtyards, the hidden palace where all dreams come true, and of the golden apples of the sun.

## Palestine

Beyond Constantinople is Outremer, the kingdoms of Antioch, Tripoli, and Jerusalem. These islands of Christendon lie in the sea of the lands of the Moor King Saladin. They are held by Crusader knights and lords, some pious, some magical, and some worshippers of demons or Moorish gods—all strange to their cousins on European shores.

Beyond the lands of Saladin is Ethiopia, where Prester John, the great Christian King, holds court, as has already been described. Ethiopia is an enormous land, populated by countless tribes of men, some without heads, who have faces in their bellies, some with but one foot, some with one eye, and some with the head of a dog, who are covered in fur and bay at the moon like wolves. Many creatures are spawned here: the cameleopard, the ferocious Ethiopian unicorn, the asps and javelin serpents, the leucrotta, and the griffin. Many of the tribes of men are cannibals or shapeshifters.

The Greeks said the world is a sphere, and few doubt their wisdom. But, of what lies beyond the lands of Ethiopia and Russia, before the world comes round again upon itself, no one can say.

# MYTHIC PLACES

Mythic places are areas where supernatural power is unusually strong. This power can have any Aura — Magical, Faerie, Divine or Infernal — but the Aura of any one place is constant and cannot be altered.

## Celtic Sites

These mythic places are sacred to pagan Celts, and are usually venerated even by Christian peasants. Some are associated with the Druids; almost all have Faerie Aura.

• **Stonehenge:** A large stone circle on the Salisbury Plain in Southern England. It's not associated with the Druids, but with elder powers. On certain holidays at the height of its power, it has a Magical (sun, stars, sky, time) and Faerie (gateway into Arcadia ) Aura +9.

• **The White Horse of Uffington:** The outline of a gigantic horse, cut into the ground in Western England. Faerie Aura +6. Communication with animals, taming of untamable animals, and finding of Familiars are said to occur here.

• **The Cerne Giant:** A human figure with a club, similar to and near the White Horse. Faerie Aura +5. Possible magical Aura for Creo magic only. Fertility magic practiced here has double effect. The giant is said to come to life once every thirteen years.

• **Silbury Hill:** A large earthen mound in Southern England, connected with Stonehenge by a ley line (Faerie path). Faerie Aura +7. A ghostly king in golden armor on a white horse is said to be found here.

• **Isle of Man:** Between England and Ireland. The whole island is said to be near Arcadia, and to be the last retreat of the Druids. There are no areas of Divine or Infernal Aura on the island. Plants and animals are said to be intelligent and aware here, and the human inhabitants are pagan Celts. Faerie Aura +8.

• **New Grange:** In Eastern Ireland there are many tombs along the River Boyne, of which this is the greatest. It is an earthen mound surrounded by a large stone circle. A stone carved with mystic ornaments is set into one side. Four times each year at midnight, the stone is said to roll aside, revealing a passage leading into the mound. Inside, it is said, are three times fifty sons of kings from the old pagan days, and beyond them, an entrance to Faerieland. Faerie Aura +6.

• **Carnac:** In Bretagne, on the Western coast. Mile after mile of standing stones, as many of ten thousand of them, stand in rows and rows of straight lines. They are said to move about at night, protecting herds and killing intruders. Some people, especially nobles and priests, apparently cannot see them at all. Faerie aura +7.

• **Le Temple Rouge:** In Northern France. This is a pagan temple complex, in the middle of a faerie wood. The center temple is a square stone building, guarded by two- and three-headed stone idols on pillars. Horrific stories of demons, monstrous faeries, and human sacrifice are told about the place. The local people do not go near it and may deny its existence. Faerie Aura +8, Infernal Aura (demons, blood sacrifice) +4. The Faerie Aura is "sleeping" and must be brought out to replace the Infernal Aura by appropriate rituals, persons, or objects. Otherwise, the Infernal Aura automatically affects all who enter the temple site.

## Mediterranean Sites

Many of these sites are associated with ghosts, pagan holy sites of forgotten religions, or Classical Greek and Roman magical areas.

• **The Island of Malta:** This island is riddled with underground tombs and shrines, made of rock slabs engraved with mystic signs. No one knows how many there are; probably dozens. Each is an underground labyrinth. The largest has thirty-three rooms and contains the bones of 7,000 people, but many are small and contain mysterious objects and no human remains. The island is controlled by the Knights Templar. Rumors state that they use these places for anything from Christian worship, to magical rituals, to summoning demons. Magical Aura +7.

• **The Camargue:** This is the great land of marshes and beaches in southernmost France. White horses and black bulls run wild here, and the local people venerate them, catching and taming the horses or putting garlands on the horns of the bulls in special rituals. Many odd faerie creatures are said to live in the area, and ancient statues are sometimes thrown up by the sea. Magical Aura +4.

• **Delphi:** This is the most sacred of the Ancient Greek oracles and holy sites. Surrounded by an olive grove, on a mountainside within sight of the sea, Delphi contains Greek ruins and a natural fissure in the earth that sometimes emits strange noises and steam. Magical Aura +7 (divination).

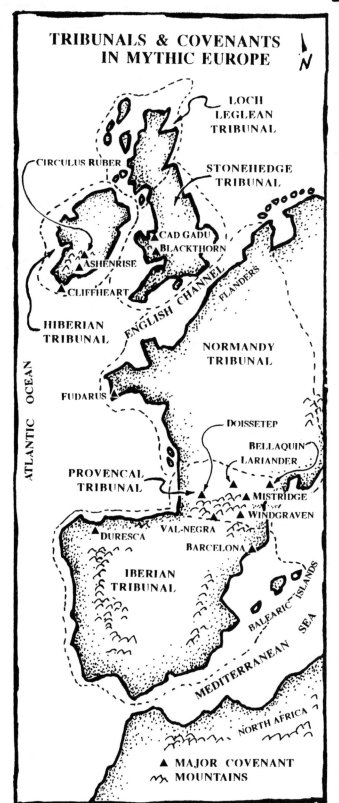

TRIBUNALS & COVENANTS IN MYTHIC EUROPE

N

LOCH LEGLEAN TRIBUNAL

CIRCULUS RUBER

STONEHEDGE TRIBUNAL

CAD GADU
BLACKTHORN

ASHENRISE

CLIFFHEART

HIBERIAN TRIBUNAL

ATLANTIC OCEAN

ENGLISH CHANNEL

FLANDERS

NORMANDY TRIBUNAL

FUDARUS

DOISSETEP

BELLAQUIN
LARIANDER

PROVENCAL TRIBUNAL

MISTRIDGE

WINDGRAVEN

VAL-NEGRA

DURESCA

BARCELONA

IBERIAN TRIBUNAL

BALEARIC ISLANDS

MEDITERRANEAN SEA

NORTH AFRICA

▲ MAJOR COVENANT
ᨆ MOUNTAINS

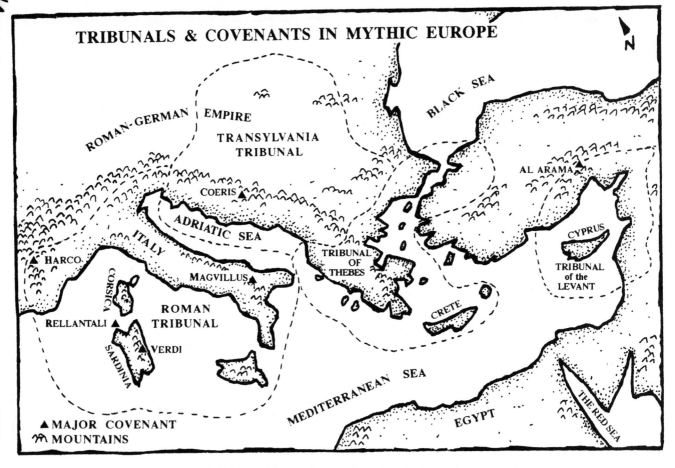

TRIBUNALS & COVENANTS IN MYTHIC EUROPE

N

ROMAN-GERMAN EMPIRE

TRANSYLVANIA TRIBUNAL

BLACK SEA

AL ARAMA ▲

COERIS ▲

ADRIATIC SEA

ITALY

▲ HARCO.

MAGVILLUS ▲

TRIBUNAL OF THEBES

CYPRUS

TRIBUNAL of the LEVANT

CORSICA

ROMAN TRIBUNAL

RELLANTALI ▲

▲ VERDI

CRETE

SARDINIA

MEDITERRANEAN SEA

EGYPT

THE RED SEA

▲ MAJOR COVENANT
ᙢ MOUNTAINS

• **Epidaurus:** In Greece, near Delphi. Epidaurus is a huge outdoor theatre, with a circular performing area and horseshoe-shaped banks of marble seats. People who enter the center circle are said to become either inspired or mad, and ghosts can be seen from the seats on certain nights. Magical Aura +7 (Muto magic, ghosts, possession).

• **Rome:** The entire city has a Dominion Aura +7. Incredibly enough, within the city, many pockets of Infernal, Reason, Magical, and Faerie Aura exist as well. Notable among those small Auras are: The Coliseum, a marble stadium used by the ancient Romans for blood sports. A series of tunnels run beneath. Adepts in diabolism are said to summon demons and ghosts there. Infernal Aura +4. The Vatican, a city within the city that's used by the Pope and his cardinals. The Vatican has a Divine Aura of +7. Certain secluded areas within the Vatican have an Infernal Aura of up to +7, but this Aura must be invoked by a trained diabolist in order for it to overcome the Divine Aura. The Catacombs, a maze of underground passages under the outskirts of the city, used for early Christian bones and mummified bodies. Divine Aura +6, Magical Aura +6.

## Northern Lands

Northern sites are usually either homes of powerful wilderness faeries, ancient pagan sites, or powerful areas of the Order of Odin.

• **The Externsteine:** A complex of partially carved sandstone outcrops in the Teutorburg Forest of Germany. The rocks contain carved cells and natural caves, used as homes by hermit Magi of the mysterious Order of Odin. The rocks guard a vast image of the pagan's god, hanging from a tree shaped into one of the stones, a magical calendar, and a huge stone tree atop the tallest rock. Christian knights have repeatedly tried to take the Externsteine, without success. One legend states that if the Externsteine is taken from the pagans, the Order of Odin will fall. Magical Aura +9.

• **The Bialoweza Forest:** In the kingdom of Poland, this great forest is populated with huge beasts found nowhere else, as well as pagan spirits and powerful faeries. Parts of the forest are the personal reserve of the Polish King. Other areas are abandoned to the wilderness, and populated only by the wild beasts and the King's foresters, who rumored to be a race apart from humanity, capable of assuming the shapes of wild animals. Magical Aura +4, Faerie Aura +4.

• **Sacrificial Bogs:** These are peat bogs which were used by pagans for sacrifices. They are inhabited by ghosts or malevolent faeries. Most bogs claim human and animal victims if they can, and many bogs have spirits with powers of divination. The best known bogs are in Flanders and North Germany, scattered about cold, marshy, forest areas. Magical Aura or Faerie Aura up to +6.

# The Order of Hermes

All Hermetic Magi belong to the Order of Hermes. This order was founded in A.D. 767 by the great Magus and philosopher Bonisagus. Bonisagus codified the laws of magic which allow all possible magical spells to be created using the ten Forms and five Techniques. It is his discovery which made the sharing of magic, and thus the Order, possible.

Bonisagus created the Order of Hermes out of the remains of the Roman cult of Mercury, a magical organization in Classical times. After the collapse of Rome and the cult of Mercury, based as it was on ritual magics requiring hundreds of participants, Bonisagus worked with the Maga Trianoma to unify all of the Magi of Europe. A handful of Magi, from both Celtic and Classical backgrounds, joined with Bonisagus in becoming the founders of the Order of Hermes. They were then joined by Bjornaer, a Maga from a Germanic tradition.

These twelve Magi formed the twelve Houses of the Order, each named after its founder: House Bjornaer, House Bonisagus, House Criamon, House Diedne, House Flambeau, House Jerbiton, House Mercere, House Merinita, House Quaesitoris, House Tremere, House Tytalus, and House Veriditius.

In the early Ninth Century A.D., the Maga Pralix, a student of Tytalus, founded the thirteenth and final House, Ex Miscellanea, which exists primarily to bring non-Hermetically trained Magi into the Order. In the early Eleventh Century war broke out in the Order, and all members of House Diedne were killed or driven into hiding, and the House was disbanded. There are now twelve Houses in the Order of Hermes

# HOUSES OF HERMES

Understanding the twelve Hermetic Houses still in existence is fundamental to understanding the Order. Each House has its own traditions, organizations structure, and breed of Magus. Not all the Magi of a particular House get along, but they usually get along better with one another than they do with anyone else, save for their Covenant brethren.

After spending fifteen years with an exacting master, learning magic, you are likely to have picked up some of your master's ideals, specialties, deficiencies, philosophies, and prejudices. Your master, in turn, has picked these things up from her master, and so on back to the founder of the House. All those who can trace their "lineage" back to the same founder are members of the same House. Some apprentices, however, break tradition and seek membership in a House other than their master's.

Listed below are short descriptions of the Houses, they are described in more detail in the **Order of Hermes** supplement.

• **House Bonisagus:** Bonisagus invented the Hermetic theory of magic, and his student Trianoma masterminded the formation of the Order, so this House has always enjoyed a great deal of respect from other Magi. Bonisagus Magi continue both the theoretical and political traditions, some refining and expanding Hermetic theory, others overseeing the continued political development of the Order.

Most members of this House believe themselves to be of a privileged, gifted elite. However they have a strong tradition for using their knowledge and power for the benefit of the Order. Selfishness is strongly discouraged.

• **House Tytalus:** In their never ending search for conflict, the leaders of House Tytalus went too far in the Tenth Century, and were corrupted by demons. In their arrogance they believed they could master the dark forces, but even those masters of intrigue could not outwit the Hell-spawn. They were executed for the crime of diabolism, and House Tytalus has been distrusted and in disgrace ever since.

The philosophy of Tytalus Magi is to master all forms of conflict, and they promote innovation in many different forms of contest, especially *Certámen*. They do not feel themselves alive unless they are in a constant state of struggle. Those of this House are constantly testing the strengths and weaknesses of others.

• **House Jerbiton:** House Jerbiton is interested in the mundane world and assumes the duty of keeping the Order on good terms with the Church and nobility. This tendency can be assumed to stem from the noble background of every Magus in the House, for their apprentices are often taken from the aristocracy, and ties are often maintained afterward. Other Houses believe Jerbiton Magi are too closely tied to the mundane powers to be trusted, and have little respect for them. In the last century scholars from this House have translated many Arabic versions of Greek texts into Latin.

Those of this House believe that Magi have distanced themselves too much from mundane reality, risking a bloody battle with the mortal powers, and the loss of their own humanity. They try energetically to heal this rift, and pursue the aesthetic arts and Classical knowledge with passion.

• **House Criamon:** This highly secretive House is known for its obscure philosophy, its disdain for simple power, and the habit of its members for marking their faces and bodies with arcane symbols. They are an enigmatic and otherworldly group of Magi, and have little interest in the politics of the Order.

Those of this House seek the experience of the "Enigma," which seems to be some sort of mystical experience.

• **House Bjornaer:** These wizards have been only partially accepted into the Order because their founder was from a Germanic rather than Roman tradition. Their fascination with beasts and the animal side of human nature makes many Magi uneasy. Bjornaer Magi value and appreciate the animal side of their true nature, as well as the human. All Bjornaer Magi learn to take the shape of an animal at will, called a "Heart-Beast," which in some way reflects the inner self of the Magus. (Note: Take this aptitude as a Hermetic Virtue entitled *Heart-Beast* if you play a character from this House).

• **House Verditius:** The Magi of this House depend on magical devices in order to cast their magic. They can only cast Formulaic and Ritual spells through Spell Foci (see *Spell Foci* in the Magic Chapter; Verditius Magi gain no bonuses for using Foci as other Magi do). They cast Spontaneous spells normally. Verditius Magi have achieved significant power by making themselves invaluable to other Magi, creating enchanted items for others. Though Verditius Magi like to pretend they are of lesser power than other Magi, they possess considerable power.

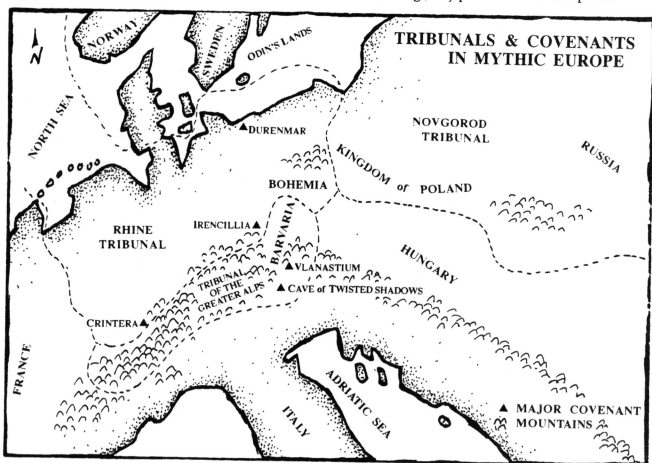

**TRIBUNALS & COVENANTS IN MYTHIC EUROPE**

NORWAY

SWEDEN

ODIN'S LANDS

NOVGOROD TRIBUNAL

RUSSIA

NORTH SEA

▲ DURENMAR

KINGDOM of POLAND

BOHEMIA

RHINE TRIBUNAL

IRENCILLIA ▲

BAVARIA

▲ VLANASTIUM

HUNGARY

TRIBUNAL OF THE GREATER ALPS

▲ CAVE of TWISTED SHADOWS

CRINTERA ▲

FRANCE

ADRIATIC SEA

ITALY

▲ MAJOR COVENANT
MOUNTAINS ⌃⌃

• **House Flambeau:** These aggressive and ferocious Magi often cause trouble in the Order and are known for getting mundanes angry at the Order on a regular basis. Their fearlessness and love for destructive spells make them invaluable on Wizards' Marches and other major military operations. Those of this House believe that the world is full of people and things who cause trouble, and that the only solution is to burn them. While most of them specialize in Ignem, some Flambeau Magi have taken up Perdo as a more "subtle" alternative.

• **House Merinita:** This House is focused on the world of faeries, and its members tend to be just as enigmatic as the creatures they study. They have little to do with other Houses, except when they must defend Arcadia from other Magi. Those of this House eschew the merely mortal, and seek the solution of the Enigma within the mysterious world of the faerie.

• **House Quaesitoris:** This small House investigates wrongdoing and often passes judgement on those who break the Hermetic Code. The Quaesitoris have gained great influence over the years as they have expanded and refined the Peripheral Code of Hermes. They believe the Order will collapse through internal conflict without their fierce preservation of the Code.

One of the highest honors in the Order is to belong to another House and be invited to become Quaesitoris (judges) by the elders of this House, though such judges remain in their own Houses.

• **House Ex Miscellanea:** Though originally founded as a rival order by a renegade from the Order of Hermes, this organization was eventually accepted into the Order as a House of its own. It accepts wizards of all kinds, many of them only nominally Hermetic. Their magic comes from many disparate, non-Hermetic traditions. Most of its members, in fact, originally come from the peasant class. They are a large, diverse, and highly disorganized House. They are called "hedge wizards" by their many detractors in the Order.

• **House Tremere:** This has proven to be a sensible and well organized House, providing strength and courage when it's needed, and holding back when peace is the better alternative. Its members emphasize the importance of judgement, strategy, and detailed planning. They believe in the respect of superiors and in asserting oneself over minions. Dignity is of utmost concern to them.

• **House Mercere:** The founder of this House lost his magical powers but remained involved in the Order. He assumed a non-magical role valuable to other Magi, carrying messages. His followers have become the Redcaps, Hermetic wizards who are officially considered Magi of the Order, even if many of them cannot cast a simple spell. Those of this House know the secrets of many Magi, but use their information only to protect themselves.

They hold Hermetic politics in disdain, and remove themselves from it as much as possible. The few real Magi in this House often travel as Redcaps at least part of the time, collecting information but never revealing that they are spell casters.

# THE CODE OF HERMES

The Order of Hermes is bound together both by its teaching and its code of conduct, which all Magi of the order must swear to obey. The basic code, as written and first spoken by Bonisagus, is as follows:

*"I Bonisagus, hereby swear my everlasting loyalty to the Order of Hermes and its members.*

*I will not deprive nor attempt to deprive any member of the Order of his magical power. I will not slay nor attempt to slay any member of the Order, except in justly executed and formally declared Wizards' War. I hereby understand that Wizards' War is an open conflict between two Magi who may slay each other without breaking this oath, and that should I be slain in a Wizards' War, no retribution shall fall on he who slays me.*

*I will abide by the decisions made by fair vote at Tribunal. I will have one vote at Tribunal, and I will use it prudently. I will respect as equal the votes of all others at Tribunal.*

*I will not endanger the Order through my actions. Nor will I interfere with the affairs of mundanes and thereby bring ruin on my sodalis. I will not deal with devils, lest I imperil my soul and the souls of my sodalis as well. I will not molest the Faeries, lest their vengeance catch my sodalis also.*

*I will not use magic to scry upon members of the Order of Hermes, nor shall I use it to peer into their affairs.*

*I will train apprentices who will swear to this Code, and should any of them turn against the Order and my sodalis, I shall be the first to strike them down and bring them to justice. No apprentice of mine shall be called a Magus until he first swears to uphold this Code.*

*I request that should I break this oath, I be cast out of the Order. If I am cast out of the Order, I ask my sodalis to find me and slay me that my life not continue in degradation and infamy.*

*The enemies of the Order are my enemies. The friends of the Order are my friends. The allies of the Order are my allies. Let us work together as one and grow hale and strong.*

*This oath I hereby swear on the third day of Pisces, in the nine hundred and fifth year of Aries. Woe to they who try to tempt me to break this oath, and woe to me if I succumb to the temptation."*

Other provisions have been added to this code since Bonisagus wrote it, the most important being that no Magus can serve a mundane, even a noble, so no Hermetic Magus can ever be a hireling, or a court wizard. Also, in theory, all Magi who refuse to swear allegiance to the

Order of Hermes should be killed. However, in practice, low-power, peaceful, or other non-dangerous non-Hermetic Magi are most often ignored by the Order.

The only official judgement the Order has for those who break the Code is a Wizards' March. When a Wizards' March is called against a Magus, that individual is declared outcast and is no longer protected by the Code. Any who wish to attack, kill, maim, or rob the offender may do so with impunity and with the full support of the Order. Groups of Magi are encouraged to seek outcasts and put an end to them. The Order does not tolerate wizards who exist beyond its bounds. Older, extremely powerful Magi sometimes take it upon themselves to enforce the Code and uphold the Order by personally leading a Wizards' March.

Often a Wizards' March is threatened unless a Magus "voluntarily" accepts a lesser punishment. Most usually accept, and such punishments range from a fine (in vis) to banishment.

Depending on the political structure in the Tribunal where the crime occurs, a Wizards' March might be a formal thing, including a trial, or it might be a general agreement among several Magi that a certain Magus has gone too far. Those who call a Wizards' March without due cause, however, may be subject to one being called against them. A Wizards' March is no trivial matter.

# TRIBUNALS

A Tribunal is a gathering of Magi to discuss matters of import. The extended Code of the Order defines a Tribunal as minimally consisting of twelve Magi from at least four Covenants. There are thirteen localized Tribunals which have jurisdiction over all of the Covenants in Christendom. These Tribunals meet every seven years, or more often if there are pressing problems.

All Magi who live within the area of a local Tribunal are eligible to attend, participate in the debate, and cast their one vote. Magi vote by using their personal sigils, and if a Magus can't attend a Tribunal, she can appoint another Magus to act as a proxy, giving him her sigil with which he can cast her vote.

Every thirty-three years the Grand Tribunal of the Order of Hermes meets at Durenmar, the *Domus Magnus* of House Bonisagus (which is located in the Black Forest in Germany). The decisions of the Grand Tribunal have power over the whole of the Order. In this century the Grand Tribunal will meet in 1228, 1261, and 1294. Before the Grand Tribunal each of the thirteen Tribunals selects three members to attend the Grand Tribunal, who then carry the sigils of all the Magi who wish them to act as a proxy for them. Also, the heads of every House in the

Order attend, even if they are not selected by their Tribunal to attend.

## Wizards' War

Occasionally, a conflict between two Magi becomes so vicious that only a battle to the death can settle it. The Code makes a provision for these feuds: Wizards' War. This is a tradition of formal conflict in which two or more Magi temporarily step outside the bounds of the Code and are permitted to harm and even kill one another without fear of a Wizards' March.

One Magus initiates the Wizards' War by sending a declaration of war to the other. The message must arrive on the next night of the full moon. The Wizards' War then begins on the rise of the next full moon, and lasts until the following full moon. Injury or destruction of bystanders and other Magi's belongings is expressly forbidden.

Some Magi simply hide when a Wizards' War is called against them, some fortify themselves in their sanctum, and others come out and fight. Wizards' War is epitomized by sabotage; traps and trickery are often employed by those involved. Raids on laboratories and sources of vis are very common. Unjust or constant use of the Wizards' War by a Magus is considered by many just cause for a Wizards' March.

## The Thirteen Tribunals

As mentioned earlier, the whole of Christendom is divided into thirteen Tribunals by the Order of Hermes. The Magi of each Tribunal meet regularly (often once every three years), in order to coordinate their activities and pass judgment on wrongdoers. Provided below are the thirteen Tribunals, listed West to East, and North to South.

• **The Hibernian Tribunal**, which consists of Hibernia (Ireland) and some nearby islands, is a small Tribunal on the western edge of Christendom. It contains seven Covenants with a total of forty-one Magi. Hibernia is a most magical place, with much wild land. Most of its Magi live in isolation from the surrounding population.

• **The Loch Leglean Tribunal** covers Scotland and the northern islands. It contains fourteen Covenants, with a total of one hundred Magi. In addition to being a highly mystical place, the local populace is unusually accepting of Magi. In fact, two of the Covenants are actually clans of Scots, most of whom have no Gift at all.

• **The Stonehenge Tribunal** covers England and Wales. In it are eleven Covenants, containing forty-five Magi. The *Domus Magnus* of House Ex Miscellanea (Cad Gadu) is located in this Tribunal. This is a very disorganized Tribunal, and the rapid clearing of land in England, combined with its burgeoning population, has convinced many Magi that the Order will soon have no place in England.

• **The Iberian Tribunal** covers all of the Iberian peninsula (Spain and Portugal), including territory still held by the Moors. There are ten Covenants with seventy-three Magi in this Tribunal. Magi of the Order, and this Tribunal in particular, are involved on both sides of the ongoing *Reconquista* of Spain from the Moors. The Tribunal is officially neutral concerning the "Moorish problem," but heated debates are common. Pro-Moorish Covenants argue that the Tribunal has largely given in to crusading Flambeau Magi, and have repeatedly threatened to secede. Some Covenants here have vast stores of both mundane and occult knowledge gained from raiding conquered Moslem libraries, or from trading with Moorish scholars.

• **The Normandy Tribunal** covers France, including Burgundy and the Low Countries. It contains twelve Covenants, including Fudarus, the *Domus Magnus* of House Tytalus, with a total of fifty Magi. This is one of the most populated areas in Europe, and the Covenants here hide from mortal society, a task which becomes more difficult every year.

• **The Provençal Tribunal** covers Languedoc, including Gascony and the Pyrenees. It contains eleven Covenants, including Val-Negra, the *Domus Magnus* of House Flambeau, with a total of eighty-four Magi. In many ways this is the cultural and political center of the Order. House Jerbiton is strong here, so relations between the Order and the rest of society are generally quite good.

• **The Rhine Tribunal** consists of the area of the Holy Roman Empire, (Germany and the Rhine Valley, north of the Alps). This was the original heartland of the Order. There are nine Covenants, with ninety Magi. The three most important Covenants in this Tribunal are: Durenmar, *Domus Magnus* of House Bonisagus, and official center of the Order; Crintera, *Domus Magnus* of House Bjornaer; and Irencilla, *Domus Magnus* of House Merinita. In recent years increased settlement has lessened the magical power of this area.

• **The Tribunal of the Greater Alps** consists of the region around the Alps, including Bavaria. There are seven Covenants, including Valnastium, *Domus Magnus* of House Jerbiton, and the Cave of Twisting Shadows, *Domus Magnus* of House Criamon, with a total of one hundred Magi. All Covenants here are quite old, and allow no new Covenants to be formed. Most of these Covenants are located high in the mountains, isolated from the rest of world.

• **The Roman Tribunal** consists of the southernmost part of the Holy Roman empire, the Papal States, the Kingdom of Naples (covering all of Italy), Sicily, Sardinia, Corsica, and one Covenant in North Africa. There are eight Covenants here, including Harco, *Domus Magnus* of House Mercere, Magvillus, *Domus Magnus* of House Quaesitoris, and Verdi, *Domus Magnus* of House Verditius. This is the Tribunal where Magi are most involved in the world, and given the involvement of Magi here in both mortal and Order politics, many Magi here live secret lives, so any estimate of the number of Magi present is futile. The Tribunal is a mass of Byzantine political machinations. Most Covenants maintain lavish townhouses in various large cities, as do many individual Magi. Venice is the center of the Tribunal and is theoretically neutral territory, where all the Covenants have townhouses.

• **The Tribunal of Thebes** consists of the Byzantine Empire (Greece, Asia Minor and the Greek Isles). There are eight Covenants with sixty Magi. One Covenant here actually resides within the walls of the mighty city of Constantinople, while several others reside in Greece, which is much less pressured by the growth of populations and kingdoms than is the rest of Europe.

• **The Transylvanian Tribunal** consists of the Kingdoms of Bulgaria and Hungary. There are five Covenants here, including Coeris, *Domus Magnus* of House Tremere, and a total of forty Magi reside in this Tribunal. This Tribunal consists of some of the most magical land in all of Christendom; the Dominion is extremely weak here, but other powers can be very strong. It is the fastest growing Tribunal in the Order, but for now, it is also firmly controlled by House Tremere.

• **The Tribunal of the Levant** consists of the Christian Kingdom of Outremer, as well as a few Covenants scattered throughout Egypt, Asia Minor, and Syria. There are sixteen Covenants here, with a total of fifty Magi. Many of the Covenants here seek the magical knowledge of the many ancient civilizations who once reigned here, while others have established friendly relations with Muslim sorcerers, and are sharing their knowledge.

• **The Novgorod Tribunal** is the farthest eastern Tribunal in all of Christendom. It consists of the Kingdom of Poland and the Russian Principalities, as well as the Nordic and Slavic lands to the North. There are six Covenants here, with forty Magi. The Mongols, pagan wizards, and hostile Nordic wizards are just a few of the problems involved in living in this harsh and isolated land. However, there are also huge amounts of unsettled land,

and many Bjornaer and Merinita Magi come here to experience life in a true wilderness.

# COVENANT INTERACTION

Covenants are the basic social units of Magi interaction. While some Magi live solitary and isolated lives, most will live the vast majority of their long, active lives in a Covenant. Loyalty to one's own Covenant is generally the strongest loyalty a Magus feels, except perhaps for the bond between apprentice and master (and often apprentice and master belong to the same Covenant).

Many Magi rarely leave their Covenant, and are mostly ignorant of the world beyond its walls. Covenants are the primary way in which Magi from different Houses work together and learn from each other. However, nearly one third of all Covenants are composed only of members of one House.

In general, Covenants are quite isolated, both from each other and from surrounding towns, castles, and monasteries. While Magi from different Covenants may frequently interact, either in person or through magic, Magi are much more inclined to share secrets with, or even work with members of their own Covenant.

Competition and conflict between Covenants is kept in check by the Code, and the restrictions on declaring a Wizards' War. In general rival Covenants are much more likely to try to outdo each other in magic, or to work against each other in Tribunal politics, than to engage in open, violent conflict. One of the most frequent problems between neighboring Covenants is the limited availability of *vis* and other magically important commodities. Conflicts between individual Magi over ownership of magical ingredients are most often solved through *Certámen*, and if they continue, they might be brought to the attention of the local Tribunal.

# WIZARDS AND SOCIETY

The restriction on Magi being hirelings or vassals provides a great deal of protection for the members of the Order. Any noble who wishes to have a court wizard realizes that, even if a Magus is available to buy, blackmail, convince, or coerce into becoming a hireling, the act will result in the other members of the Order intervening to remove the hired Magus. The prospect of such intervention is generally enough to stop even the most power-hungry lord or bishop. Even with this problem largely solved there still remains the question of how Magi may interact with the four other sectors of mundane life: peasants, clergy, nobles, and townspeople.

• **Peasant Relations:** The relations between Magi and peasants are generally quite simple. Most peasants fear Magi, and all things magical, and thus go within shouting distance of a Covenant only if a dire emergency occurs and they have no one else to turn to.

Many Magi find such fear useful, because it keeps peasants from interfering with their work. However, such an attitude of fear and dread can be very problematic. First of all, if the locals live in dread of you, Grogs are hard to find, except perhaps for a few escaped convicts and other undesirables, who figure the locals will never pursue them to the Covenant. Also, food is hard to come by. If the Covenant has its own lands, there must be peasants willing to work them. If the Covenant does not have land, there must be peasants willing to sell the Covenant food. Finally, if peasants fear Magi enough they may blame Magi for every misfortune, and might even ask the local clergy or their lord for aid in wiping out this threat to their existence.

Most Magi, however, feel somewhat protective toward peasants, especially if their Grogs, and perhaps their *consortis*, as well as their food, come from the peasants. In some areas, particularly where Covenants have existed for the longest times, peasants may be comfortable with a Covenant.

While almost all peasants are wary and very respectful of anyone from a Covenant, they may feel they can call on the Covenant for aid in times of trouble, and a few of their children may aspire to be Grogs, or *consortis*. There can be substantial benefits to Magi from such a relationship. No one knows an area like the peasantry. If anything strange or suspicious occurs in the vicinity of a Covenant, there are few better watchdogs than an alert and helpful peasantry.

Peasants who are outcasts from their own society have nothing to lose from interacting with the Covenant. Deformed or unfortunate peasants may help in hopes of some magical reward. Peasants fascinated by magic may seek out the Covenant as a place to live near. A whole group of peasants may even offer to work the Covenant's fields, in perpetuity, in exchange for rights and privileges beyond what peasants usually receive from their lords. In such places, the towns and lands adjoining a Covenant may be populated by the lame, the blind, and the outcast, or a social order entirely different from the medieval norm may prevail. Ordinary peasants may avoid such lands altogether, believing that the Magi of the Covenant have magically twisted the lands.

• **Church Relations:** The clergy are a different matter altogether. The specifics of this interaction are even more complex and variable. Many of the clergy think of the biblical prohibition, "Thou shall not suffer a witch to live," when they meet a Magus, and act accordingly.

However, there are also many clergy who have been educated in the cities, and exposed to the study of the natural world. Such clergy realize there is nothing demonic in the magic of the Order, any more than putting an amethyst under one's tongue to prevent drunkenness is demonic. They are learning to distinguish between the realms. Under such conditions, differences are often forgotten; educated clergy and Magi can be friends and intellectual companions, who hold long discussions on issues most people can never comprehend.

Moreover, some Magi are Christians. The solace of Confession and the joy of Mass are as important to them as to the humblest peasant. In one sense Magi and clergy are natural allies against darkness and ignorance.

Unfortunately, most Magi and clerics are not so tolerant. For such clerics, Magic can only come from God or from Satan. Magi who are obviously not holy, or even particularly acceptable Christians, are considered in league with the Devil. As there are few Magi who follow the Church, much of the Order is considered satanic. Moreover, some clergy worry that the attraction and power of magic will sway people away from the quest for salvation, toward worldly and damning pursuits. On this issue clergy are divided, and it seems unlikely that the Pope will make a decision on the matter soon. To be fair, many Magi (particularly those of House Flambeau) are as intolerant toward the 'mundanes' as any cleric is toward the Order of Hermes.

The Church is much concerned with mundane affairs, the reconquest of Iberia, the Crusades, the Albigensian Heresy in France, and other pressing problems. In theory, supporting Christendom does not break the Hermetic prohibition against working for mundanes, but most Magi would rather sit in their Covenants, and let the world take care of itself, than follow religion. However, members of the clergy can take a very dim view of such disregard for issues important to all good Christians. Of course, some Magi have gone and fought in the Crusades, and the reconquest, much to the delight of the clergy. As long as some of Magi continue to assist the Church in such ways, the Church will probably continue to ignore those Magi who do not come to its aid.

The only major point of religious contention facing the Order now involves the reconquest of Iberia (Spain). Two Covenants actively support the Moors, and consider them to be the true inheritors of Classical civilization. These two Covenants have actively fought on the side of the Moors in several battles, and have threatened to break away form the Order, and join a Muslim magical order if they are forbidden to aid the Moors. These facts have been kept well away from Church's ears, thus far at least. Currently, there is a temporary truce on the issue. Both the pro- and anti-Muslim factions in the Order have agreed to use only magics which "cannot be detected by mortals," (possibly making this the first 'cold war' in history) avoiding any immediate declaration of war by an angered Church.

• **Noble Relations:** The nobility want one thing from Magi: their magical aid in their wars and intrigues. Often canny nobles cultivate the friendship of one or more local Magi in order to obtain "favors." The practice of giving favors does not directly violate the Code, but can bring displeasure on the Magi involved, from both the Order, and from the rivals of the noble they aid.

Jerbiton Magi of noble descent still feel loyalty to their families, friendship to their traditional allies, and may even feel bound by oaths of fealty, even if the Order claims such ties are less important than ties to the Order. These Magi are the ones who most often go on Crusades, or who aid kings and nobles in their conquests.

Many Jerbiton Magi who are of noble birth attempt to maintain their life as a noble as well as their life as a Magus. For all who attempt to do this there arise problems, which are made all the worse by Magi who feel the Order should be as isolated from the mortal world as possible.

Many Covenants are located near the lands of some nobles. Amicable relations are much to be desired, since the wrath of a noble can be a threat even to a powerful Covenant, and direct retaliation can quickly escalate into open warfare. A policy of mutual aid in times of trouble is one of the more common solutions to this problem. However, in some cases this is not possible, both the noble and the Covenant adopting a policy of politely ignoring each other.

• **City Relations:** In the past few centuries another important type of interaction has developed. Now Magi have to deal with cities and towns. Not only are cities and towns places of both trade and great learning, where Magi can find both objects and knowledge they seek, but life in cities and towns is often much more exciting and stimulating than life in some isolated stronghold of fifty people.

Quite a number of Magi in the Roman Tribunal have abandoned Covenant life, and now live happily in various cities in Italy. In addition, there is even a small Covenant which exists secretly in the city of Barcelona. While the Order prohibits Magi from working for powerful merchants, or from setting up a booth in the market where spells are cast for money, many cities recognize the usefulness of having a resident Magus. If the city is threatened, a Magus is perfectly justified in using magic to protect her home, which can result in the protection of the city as a whole. However, Magi often live secretly in a city, and are assumed by the townspeople to be another odd scholar. There are even stories of a number of Magi teaching at universities.

amount of *vis* actually invested in the item. The type of spell invested is also taken into account by these rules:

• Commoners may only buy magic items which have no more than one *vis* point's worth of spells invested in them (after the opening enchantment). In addition, commoners may only buy magic items whose magic affects the item itself or anyone directly touching the item, except in the case of Intéllego spells.

• Minor nobles, bishops, and recently, merchant princes, may buy magic items invested with no more than two *vis* points worth of spells, with the type of spell being subject to the same restrictions as above.

• High nobles and archbishops may purchase magic items invested with no more than three *vis* points worth of spells. The magic of these spells is limited to those spells which work on the item itself, on those touching the item, or on a single distant target. Once again, Intéllego spells are exempt from these limitations.

• Kings and cardinals may purchase items which have no more than four *vis* points of spells invested in them. In addition, no magic item which can directly harm large masses of people at once may be sold to any non-Magus.

## Other Wizards

While most members of the Order of Hermes like to think they are the only true practitioners of magic within Christendom, this is not true. In every large market or fair there are alchemists, amulet-makers, and fortune-tellers. Alchemists even have their own guilds in most cities. However, none of these practitioners can rival even a newly-made Hermetic Magus in power. Many are, in fact, charlatans.

There are, however, others who can equal the Magi of Hermes. The most obvious are diabolists, who get their power from dealing with devils and making dark pacts with Satan. None except the most power-mad and unscrupulous deal in any fashion with such minions of evil. When such are discovered, the nobility, the Church, and the Magi all unite to exterminate that person.

However, not all such rival wizards are so easy to classify. There are a number of limited wizards, who have learned magic from non-Hermetic traditions, but are not tainted with diabolism. Most such wizards are specialists who can command only one element, but this does not mean they cannot be formidable. Such wizards are not bound by the Order, and so are free to work for nobles, towns, or even peasant villages.

These warlocks are often people of low birth, moderate power, and limited ambition, who may help the crops grow in their village, or who may be a weather-witch on board a merchant vessel, or perhaps the protector of a

## Selling Magic

One important point of interaction between the Order and the rest of society involves the selling of magical devices. This is an especially important issue for House Verditius, but it affects all Magi. Earlier in the history of the Order there was an era of unrestrained selling of magical devices to any mortal who could pay the price. However, in 1061 the Quaesitor Iernilus helped negotiate a treaty which regulated the sale of magical devices to mortals. The treaty states that no Magus may take money or goods as payment for any arcane services, except from *consortis*. Of course, this means that *consortis* can sell magical items and devices for Magi. Moreover, the treaty demands that the device be of a type which will eventually wear out, its magic lost.

The rules governing the types of magic items which may be sold are based on both the rank of the person who is the buyer and the power of the item, based on the small farming hamlet or fishing village. Such wizards are generally never noticed by the Order, and if they are, they are often ignored as "hedge wizards," more for their behavior than their actual level of power.

Still, there are some hedge wizards who have higher ambitions. Such people often become, or attempt to become, the court wizards of the highest ranking noble they can impress.

As long as hedge wizards confine their actions to spying, entertainment, and perhaps some discreet assassination, the Order usually leaves them alone. The exception is applied to court wizards who regularly blast rival armies on the field of battle, or claim to be Hermetic Magi. They are quickly "invited" to join the Order and abandon their demeaning occupation. Rejection of the offer means death. As many who have traveled widely know, there is much more magic around than most people suspect. The true number of practitioners of minor magic — shapeshifters, witches, shamans, and even Druids and other Celtic mystics — who live within Christendom would surprise most members of the Order.

chapter ten

agic is the supernatural power on which **Ars Magica** is based, but it is not the only power in the world of Mythic Europe. This Chapter details the powers, or realms, of the world and how they relate to each other.

The main realms of power are Magic, Divine, Infernal, Faerie, and Reason (there is also the realm of the Mundane, but it is not supernaturally empowered). Each of these realms of power is somewhat at odds with the others, though to different degrees. The lines between realms are not drawn simply, with some on one side and others representing a united opposition. Rather, each realm of power stands alone against the others, each with some power over the others.

Each realm also has its own unique inhabitants, whose natures are attuned to the realms in which they exist. These inhabitants include huge winged serpents, monstrous giants, mischievous faeries, deceptive demons, and elusive shapechangers. As these denizens are attuned to their realms, they are often influenced by and often at the mercy of other powers when outside their realms.

The inhuman inhabitants of the realms usually have little to do with common folk, but everyone knows of these creatures, and all but the foolish fear them. Common folk recognize and respect the dangers of the world that lie in waiting. Magi, however, often seek out the denizens of the realms, to meet them and sometimes slay them. This Chapter aids in the creation and use of these creatures, and provides examples of realm creatures.

# Realm Power and Domain

The five main realms exist and interact in various ways. Each has some parts of the world where its powers are strongest and the powers of the other realms are diminished. The effect that one realm has on another depends on how opposed they are.

The Storyguide assigns every place the characters visit both a type of area (Magical, Divine, Infernal, Faerie, or Reason) and a rating (from 1 to 10). This type and rating, collectively called an Aura, combine to determine how each of the other four main powers is aided or reduced in that place. Consult the *Realm Interaction Chart* for details. Some areas far from human settlement are neutral, having no ties to any supernatural realm and no effect on powers used there. Such regions belong to the Mundane realm, which is discussed below.

Sometimes two realms have influence over the same place, but only the stronger holds sway at any one time. A change in the relative strengths of the two realms can cause an area to switch from the influence of one realm to another. For example, a serf village might be built on the site of an old faerie ring. The serfs are loyal followers of the Church, so the Dominion (Divine realm) usually holds power, being the stronger of the two realms at work. However, at night (when the Dominion decreases) and on special days of the year (ancient holidays when the faerie power increases), the Faerie Aura becomes stronger than the Divine, and holds sway. It's then that the faeries emerge from their underground burrows, and from inside old oaks, to frolic and celebrate. Sometimes it's only a small area, like the cellar of a tavern, that feels the touch of a power different from that of its surroundings.

# Realm Interaction

As a Magus, you belong to the Magical realm. If your Covenant is not located in an area with a Magic Aura, you are attuned to the realm of Magic by virtue of your art. As you belong to a realm, other beings belong to the other realms, so they are as affected by different realms as you are. When you enter an area possessed by a realm, the

## Creature Descriptions

Throughout this Chapter creatures from the different realms are described. The format of creature profiles varies slightly depending on what statistics and capabilities a creature has. Most stats (like Characteristics and combat scores) are described elsewhere, but some stats need explanation here.

**Cunning:** The animal equivalent of Intelligence. A creature with a Cunning score might be very clever and wily, but it cannot use reason, or understand speech (unless trained to specific commands).

**Body Levels:** Listed by the penalties associated with them. If a creature has more than one of a given Body Level, the penalty is listed an appropriate number of times, and the numbers are separated by slashes (e.g., two "Light Wound" Levels are listed as "-1/-1").

**Abilities:** Listed as totals, already combined with their most appropriate Characteristics.

**Powers:** Listed with the Technique, Form and Level equivalents, and with any Mystic Point costs for using the powers.

It's also important to know something about the way creature statistics are determined in this Chapter, and in supplements that follow for **Ars Magica.** Under the heading "Vital Statistics" are listed the Size and Characteristics of a creature. Those stats reflect the individual abilities or inabilities, such as speed, of the creature in question. However, traits, like combat traits, that are normally based on Characteristics are actually based on far more than those simple scores. Combat traits like First Strike take into account the creature's Quickness, but go beyond that, including the natural adaptations and other abilities of the creature. Thus, combat and other traits cannot be calculated based on the various scores a creature has. Combat traits and others like them are generated subjectively, not mathematically. So, the scores of a creature you create should be what seems right to you, not what a +2 Dexterity and +3 Strength add to.

## Realm Interaction Chart

**Power Used:**

| Aura Type: | Magic | Divine | Infernal | Faerie |
|---|---|---|---|---|
| Magical Area | + | — | 0 | 1/2+ |
| Dominion | — | + | 3— | 2— |
| Infernal Place | — | 2— | + | 2— |
| Faerie Area | 1/2+ | 2— | — | + |
| Reason | — | — | 0 | 3— |

**Key:**

0 The score of the Aura is ignored.

+Add the Aura's rating to the action

—Subtract the Aura's rating from the action

If a number precedes a sign (e.g., 1/2+, or 3—), that number is multiplied by the Aura's rating to determine the Aura's modifier.

Reason is not included among the *Powers Used* because it is the antithesis of the supernatural. Those attuned to Reason do not believe in the supernatural, so have no "magic" to use in areas of other realms. However, beings attuned to other realms may certainly visit places with an Aura of Reason.

strength of the Aura there influences your spells and powers. The Aura's type also influences you, for different realms have different effects upon one another. For example, in a Divine Aura your magical powers are diminished because your spells defy the beliefs and codes of the Church. However, if you enter a place with a Magical Aura, your magical powers are strengthened because the Aura's nature is akin to the powers you wield.

An Aura affects everything about you that is supernatural. Its rating has a direct bearing on the supernatural actions you perform, and may accentuate or interfere with them. The following is a list of how Aura rating affects different supernatural activities:

• Modifies spellcasting rolls. For Spontaneous spells, the Aura modifier is applied before division.

• Modifies Lab totals (when the lab activity states Aura is a factor).

• Modifies Natural Resistance and Magic Resistance rolls.

• Modifies Ability rolls related to the supernatural (i.e., those of some Exceptional Talents, like Entrancement and Sense Holiness & Unholiness, but not Knowledges).

• Modifies the rating of your source when studying *vis.*

## Designing a Creature

Designing a creature is a challenge, as is any aspect of being a Storyguide. With practice, though, creating creatures becomes relatively easy. What you have to begin with is a concept of what creature the story needs, and what purpose the creature serves. When you have your creature concept, the difficult part is over. All you need now are the creature's abilities and combat stats to make the game run smoothly. Keep an open mind, try different things, change what doesn't work, and you will learn to make interesting monsters that challenge the characters on a variety of levels.

Here is a method for conceptualizing a creature and turning it into a set of numbers for play. Answer the following questions step by step, but move back and rethink things when you need to.

**Purpose:** Why are you creating this creature? For fear, humor, roleplaying, pity, awe or combat? How does it fit into the story and what should it do for the story?

**Image:** What does it look like? Sound like? Smell like? How does it move? Does it have distinguishing features that set it apart from others of its kind?

**Behavior:** What does it do, and why? How intelligent is it? What are its goals and motivations? What are the different ways it responds to the characters, depending on what they do? Is it inherently evil?

**Basic Stats:** Stats for Size, Might, combat, and Abilities. Use the *Size Chart* (p. 109) and the monsters described in this Chapter as standards for stats. Be willing to change these in the midst of a battle if you've made the creature too weak or powerful. Don't forget Passions and Personality Traits.

**Powers and Weaknesses:** What are its mystical abilities, including Level equivalents for spell-like powers? Does it have a special weakness or bane? Are the characters able to know or find out about these powers and weaknesses? Does the creature's corpse have raw *vis* in it?

• Modifies the Level of powers that operate automatically or at will (like a faerie's powers or the powers of some enchanted items). This means the Level of the power is increased or decreased by the Aura rating, gaining new effects (as chosen by the Storyguide) that suit the new Level. If power Level is reduced to 0, the power cannot function.

• Modifies the magical First Strike, Attack, Parry, and Damage scores of a weapon or shield (i.e., those scores that are already magically enhanced or cursed).

• Modifies the Protection score of enchanted armor.

The *Realm Interaction Chart* indicates the degrees to which realms influence each other. The modifiers shown apply to the effect an Aura rating has on you, based on the nature of any supernatural act you perform in the Aura. For example, if you cast an Infernal spell in an area of Divine Aura, your spell roll suffers a penalty of 3 times the Aura's rating.

Auras also affect the number of Botch rolls made when you perform a supernatural act in a foreign realm. For each point in an Aura, roll an extra Botch die. Of course, these extra rolls are not made when you are in an Aura of the same type you're attuned to (i.e., Magi don't make extra Botch rolls when in a Magical Aura, but do when in any other type of Aura). The extra Botch rolls made are based on the original rating of an Aura, not the rating after being halved or multiplied by some factor, if the *Realm Interaction Chart* calls for such a modification.

# The Magic Realm

Magic is commonly described as a subtle, intangible fluid that flows through the world; Hermetic Magi call it

## Creating Creatures

The Storyguide has the responsibility of creating creatures for stories. Your goal is to use supernatural beings to bring more excitement, challenge, mystery, fear, and wonder to the story. This can be accomplished by many means. If you overuse the same creatures, though, they become commonplace and dull. Creatures play an essential role in the narrative, and the characters' encounters with them should serve the ends of the story you are telling.

You can use the creatures provided in this Chapter in your stories, but it's better to invent your own creatures, using those provided here as guides. Do not take the design of a creature lightly. Careful thought can turn what might be just another battle into an encounter of wonder and fear. The characters live in an inherently magical and dangerous world — without mystery and awe, however, all the charm is lost.

### The Creature's Prerogative

If you see creatures as elements of the story, not mere combat opponents, you are fully justified in giving them the "creature's prerogative." That is, until the characters know what a creature can and cannot do, you are free to let it do anything. If the developing story calls for it, give the creature a new power in the midst of the game. If you are subtle and imaginative about making up powers on the spot — and if you do it to enhance the story, not just smash the characters — the players won't object.

If you want an encounter with a beast to be a straight contest between the monster's abilities and the characters', do not exercise the "creature's prerogative;" do put more time and care into designing the creature.

*vis*. Just as one can use water to turn a mill, one can learn to harness *vis* to perform all manner of wonders. Hermetic Magi are the most versatile manipulators of *vis*, but there are other wizards who use it, and countless creatures and beasts live on and use it. As powerful as it may be, *vis* is an earthly element, and as such can have no effect on things beyond the earthly realm (Hell belongs to the earthly realm). Only Divine power can alter such things as life and death and the eternal fate of an immortal soul.

It's important to note the difference between *vis* and raw *vis*. The power of magic, called *vis*, is an energy that flows through the world. Its power may be called upon almost anywhere to work magic. In places where magical energy is high, Magical Auras form. Raw *vis* is the physical manifestation of "fluid" *vis*. Raw *vis* can be harvested to aid in the use of magic. "Fluid" *vis* cannot be harvested; it is simply a presence. Thus, you have to go out and find raw *vis*, but fluid *vis* can be manipulated almost anywhere, producing magical effects such as spells.

# MAGICAL AREAS

These are places where magical energy naturally concentrates; they have a Magical Aura. Sometimes places acquire an Aura after powerful magic is used there, or a powerful creature dies there. Most of the time no one knows why a certain place is magical. Most Magical areas have an Aura rating from 1 to 5. Legendary places are rated around 6. Areas rated up to 10 are almost unheard of. Within a magical area, the Aura is usually uniform throughout. Occasionally, there is some area within a Magical place where energy is more concentrated, granting a higher Aura rating. Sometimes areas possess *regio*, areas of increasingly powerful Aura located on a single spot (see *Regio*, p.336).

Almost all Covenants are located in Magical areas, but usually only in Auras of 1 to 5. More powerful areas are rare and extremely dangerous to live in. If Magi try too often to use magic in a powerful area, they may find themselves being used by the magic instead. Because of this threat, only the most powerful Covenants in Hermetic history have based themselves in areas of strong Magical Aura. And because of this power, these Covenants have not been able to retain apprentices, who have always been too weak to withstand the seductive power of the Magic Aura. Very strange things tend to happen in such Covenants.

Magical areas are intense. Here colors are more striking, sounds more piercing, the day brighter, and the night deeper.

Mundane people who live in magical areas tend to get "weird;" their bodies and personalities warp. Insidiously, the magic penetrates their very core and permanently transforms them.

# DRAGONS AND THEIR KIND

The most powerful and noble of all mortal creatures are dragons. They are so mighty and rare that slaying one

## Creatures and Action Combat

In the Action Combat System, Defense and Soak totals are determined by adding 6 to the Defense and Soak modifiers a character has. When creatures are fought, that same 6 is added to their Defense and Soak scores. Thus, if a creature is listed as having a Defense of +12 and a Soak of +8, the final scores for the Action Combat System are 18 and 14, respectively.

is the stuff of legends, a task worthy of a hero or arch-mage. Dragons are highly intelligent, physically domineering, and often magically potent. Some are so powerful that they are beyond the statistics of **Ars Magica**, and cannot be harmed by normal means.

Related to dragons, but not as powerful as they, are worms, drakes and serpents (listed in descending order of power). They share some abilities of dragons, but lack others.

Worms are mighty creatures, usually lacking limbs, though some have wings. They often have the minds of beasts, but some are intelligent.

Drakes have the general form of the typical dragon (four legs, serpentine neck, bat wings), but are much smaller and more likely to be misshapen. They are not typically bright, but are more likely to be intelligent than worms. Drakes are often mistaken for dragons, and most legends about dragon-slaying knights refer to drakes.

Serpents are glorified snakes, usually with greater size and special powers. They are cunning and often speak, showing more intelligence than the bestial worms or drakes. Some are the size of normal snakes.

# Sigusen, the Dragon of the Tome

**Magic Might**: 65

**Vital Statistics**: Size +6, Intelligence +6, Perception +5, Strength +10, Stamina +9, Presence 0, Communication +3, Dexterity 0, Quickness -1

**Personality Traits**: Curious +6, Cruel +2

**Combat Scores**:

Bite: First Strike +6, Attack +11, Damage +36

Breath: First Strike +12, Attack +8*, Damage +40/+80**

Fatigue n/a, Defense 0 (6), Soak +40 (46)

Body Levels: OK, 0/0/0, -1/-1/-1, -3/-3, -5/-5, Incapacitated

*Can be dodged but not parried.

**Fire damage, see p.162.

**Powers**:

*Fiery Breath, CrIg 50, 5 points* — Causes +40 damage to each target if directed at a large area (a circle 10 paces across) or +80 if directed at a single person.

*Dampen Magic, PeVi 95 , 0 points* — His +65 Magic Resistance protects all things within his cave. Casting any spell, even on oneself, is difficult. This dampening does not affect the magic of Sigusen or his drakes.

Some say that, like his drakes, Sigusen can take human form. He certainly has many other smaller powers too numerous to delineate.

**Description**:

Sigusen is a thin, snake-like dragon with short legs, but dextrous forepaws. He is forty feet from snout to tail. He has wings folded on his back, but no one has ever seen him use them since he spends all his time in his cave, which is atop a mountain in the Pyrenees.

Sigusen is writing a great tome in an ancient language, and is collecting knowledge of all kinds to support his views on the nature of the universe. To further his ends, he collects sagas as well. He has several intelligent drakes living with him (perhaps his children) who can take human form. In human form they seek out scholars and kidnap them, bringing them back to Sigusen, who interrogates them and eats them if they don't provide anything interesting. Some of the drakes are quite well known as vibrant poets, rakes and scholars in the towns which they frequent.

Scholars can come to Sigusen to get answers to their questions, but they are eaten if they don't provide interesting information in return.

Sigusen's heart is worth 60 Ignem *vis*.

**Story**:

A scholar character is kidnapped by Sigusen's drakes, and the other characters must find them to get the victim back. Perhaps the characters must face the great Sigusen himself, to bargain or to fight.

## The Worm of Abbinton

**Magic Might:** 42

**Vital Statistics:** Size +4, Cunning 0, Perception -2, Strength +9, Stamina +9, Presence n/a, Communication n/a, Dexterity -2, Quickness -3

**Personality Traits:** Passive +3

**Combat Scores:**

Bite: First Strike +4, Attack +5, Damage +23

Breath: First Strike +8, Attack spec., Damage spec.

Fatigue +8, Defense 0 (6), Soak +32 (38)

Body Levels: 0/0, -1/-1/-1, -3/-3, -5, Incapacitated

**Powers:**

*Tiny Breath, CrAu 20, 1 point* — A cloud of black smoke envelopes one person, coating the target with black residue. Each Round (including the first) the victim must make a Stamina stress roll of 9+ or lose a Body Level. If the roll is Botched, two Levels are lost. Immersion in spring water cleanses one of the poison.

*Great Breath, CrAu 30, 12 points* — The worm sprays its smoke all around itself, coating everyone within four yards with the poison. This tactic weakens the worm, so it loses a Short-Term Fatigue Level and cannot attack in the following Round.

**Description:**

This worm is a fifty-foot, black, slimy creature that lives in an isolated lake in the mountains, occasionally devouring fishermen and their boats. It has a long head, a cavernous mouth (filled with teeth), and three rows of fins run down its back. The worm sometimes lumbers ashore for unknown reasons, and would wreak havoc should it find its way to a village. On land it moves very slowly, except when moving downhill.

Its teeth are worth 12 pawns of Perdo *vis*, and the poison of its breath is valuable for certain magical experiments (the Storyguide may choose the experiments).

**Story:**

The Magi need the worm's poison, but probably aren't powerful enough to kill it. A valid strategy is to provoke it to breathe on one of the characters, and then drive it away or flee themselves. The characters then need to rinse the poison from the victim and collect it for work in the lab. Who volunteers to be the sponge for the poison?

## Ruklin, the Two-Headed Drake

**Magic Might:** 20

**Vital Statistics:** Size +3, Intelligence +1, Perception +2, Strength +8, Stamina +5, Presence -1, Communication 0, Dexterity -1, Quickness -2

**Personality Traits:** Rapacious +5

**Combat Scores:**

Breath: First Strike +10*, Attack +10**, Damage +20***

Bite: First Strike +6*, Attack +8, Damage +18

Claw: First Strike +6*, Attack +6, Damage +15

Fatigue +6, Defense 0 (6), Soak +24 (30)****

Body Levels: 0/0, -1/-1, -3/-3, -5/-5, Incapacitated

* Can use all attacks each Round; make one First Strike roll and add +10 for breath and +6 for bite and claw.

** Can only be dodged, not parried.

*** Fire damage, see p.162

**** Immune to damage from fire.

**Power:**

*Fiery Breath, CrIg 20, 2 points* — See combat stats.

*Invisibility, PeIm 25, 4 points* — She can become invisible as long as no one is looking at her at the time.

## Description:

This drake is long and sinuous, and she sports two lizard-like heads on the ends of serpentine necks. Ruklin has a pair of golden bat wings, but it takes some effort to fly; usually she leaps from a high place to make getting off the ground easier. Her entire body is covered with copper scales (worth 14 Ignem *vis*).

In combat, Ruklin typically bites with one head and exhales flames from the other. In addition, she can claw once per Round.

## Story:

Ruklin has information the characters need. They can cause her to surrender if they kill one of her heads (each of her Body Levels are divided between her heads), but if they kill the body (cause enough damage to the body to reduce all Body Levels) both heads die and the information is lost — and what if they kill the head that has the information?

# Shashali, the Venomous Riddler

**Magic Might:** 12

**Vital Statistics:** Size -1, Intelligence +2, Perception +2, Strength 0, Stamina +3, Presence +3, Communication +4, Dexterity -2, Quickness +5

**Personality Traits:** Discerning +4, Gullible +1

**Combat Scores:**

Sting: First Strike +7, Attack +5, Damage +5*

Fatigue 0, Defense +8 (14), Soak +4(10)

Body Levels: OK, -1, -3, -5, Incapacitated

* Plus poison. Stamina stress roll of 9+ or lose 3 Body Levels, otherwise 1 is still lost, Botch is death; +1 on roll for each time after the first Shashali has struck that day.

## Description:

Shashali is a ten-foot long, drab-colored serpent about as thick as a human thigh. Its head has brightly-colored scales that form a fascinating pattern. At the end of its tail is a sharp barb filled with poison. Shashali's favorite tactic is to speak to its target in a soft voice while its tail slowly creeps up from the side or rear. It then stings the distracted target and flees. Shashali often has to return to the target to sting it again, as its poison is not strong enough to kill in a single blow.

If engaged in a challenging riddle contest, Shashali forgets its murderous intent.

Its barb is worth 9 pawns of Perdo *vis*.

## Story:

Shashali has trapped the characters in some way, but they've been forewarned of its nature. Can they distract it with riddles and guard themselves long enough to find a way out?

# FANTASTIC BEASTS, BANES OF THE WILDERNESS

Fantastic beasts include powerful creatures with limited magical ability, but incredible physical prowess. Dragonkind could fall under this category, but they warrant treatment of their own.

Be careful when you design fell beasts that their reliance on physical strength does not make them easy prey for Magi. Give these creatures a healthy Magic Might or they will succumb to the first spell cast upon them.

When modelling beasts after those of legend, consider how true you want to be to the original story. For example, the Minotaur of Greek myth was a unique creature, a being capable of challenging a hero's might. Do you want your minotaur to be something similar, an awe-inspiring creature lurking somewhere in a maze, something worth telling stories about? Or, your minotaurs may be a race — stronger than humans and with a nasty disposition for human flesh — but nothing truly exceptional.

# Griffin

**Magic Might:** 30*

**Vital Statistics:** Size +4, Cunning 0, Perception +6, Strength +7, Stamina +9, Presence n/a, Communication n/a, Dexterity +2, Quickness +2

**Personality Traits:** Brave +6

**Combat Scores:**

Claw: First Strike +6, Attack +7, Damage +28

Fatigue n/a, Defense +2(8), Soak +26(32)

Body Levels: OK, 0/0, -1/-1, -3/-3, -5/-5, Incapacitated

* Double Magic Resistance against spells that counter strength, bravery and hunting prowess.

## Description:

The griffin has a lion's body in the back and an eagle's body in the front. It attacks with its talons, reserving its beak for tearing the flesh off its prey and for emergency use. Although ferocious when threatened or hungry, the griffin is not entirely malicious.

The griffin embodies the virtues of bravery and hunting prowess. This nature makes it resistant to spells that would cripple or calm it. Its heart is worth 18 Anímal *vis*.

## Story:

Living atop a rocky crag high in the Pyrenees is a flock of griffins. Dwelling with them is an old hermit who has forgotten how old he is (though he only speaks Classical Latin and says he's the Emperor's Messenger). He leads the griffins though he never leaves the nest.

# GIANTS, THE RACES OF CAIN

Cain fathered a brood of monstrous children by a demoness, and over the years these creatures have bred and spread across the face of Mythic Europe; some are as tall as trees, while others are human-sized but stronger than bulls. A few have exotic abilities, such as the power to shapeshift, to resist normal types of damage, or to use spell-like abilities. They have come to be known as giants and ogres. Regardless of name they all share brute strength, often great size, and usually a hatred and envy for their more beautiful human cousins.

If a particular giant is of enormous size, you may have to change the game's mechanics to suit it. For instance, a shield that stands up fine against axes is not able to stop a tree trunk swung by a giant. A giant can knock down and injure even those who parry its blows.

## Hierbent, Giant of the Frozen Wastes

**Magic Might:** 35

**Vital Statistics:** Size +3, Intelligence -2, Perception -2, Strength +10, Stamina +9, Presence +3, Communication 0, Dexterity -3, Quickness -3

**Personality Traits:** Belligerent +4

**Combat Scores:**

Axe: First Strike +10, Attack +9, Damage +25

Fatigue +3, Defense +2(8), Soak +30(36)*

Body Levels: OK, 0/0/0, -1/-1, -3, -5, Incapacitated

* Fire does +25% damage, but Hierbent is immune to damage from cold.

**Powers:**

*Cloak of Snows, CrAu 40, 0 points*—Hierbent is almost always surrounded by swirling snow or sleet driven by mighty winds, even when he is in lowland regions. This makes fighting him difficult (-2 to offensive and defensive scores, and one extra Botch roll). The power only works where the temperature is near or below freezing.

**Description:**

Hierbent is a sullen giant who roams the snowy, wind-swept peaks of the Pyrenees. He has a huge, frost-covered beard and carries a mighty axe, which was forged for him by dwarfs. He is eager to exchange boasts with his opponents before engaging in battle. Over the years he has slain seven knights. Hierbent has several treasures hidden under massive rocks on various mountaintops. When the winter is hard he strides down into the valleys and farmlands to vent his rage. He is always accompanied by a severe storm on these trips into the lowlands.

His body contains 16 pawns of Córporem vis; his axe is worth 7 Terram vis.

Story:

An early thaw catches Hierbent farther from his mountains than he is comfortable with. As a result he's stranded on a mountaintop near the Covenant, unable to cross the warm valleys below. The characters can hunt the giant down to kill him, or they can help him back home in exchange for some of his treasure.

# SHAPESHIFTERS, THOSE WHO WALK AS BEASTS

Peasants fear wolves and other vicious beasts of the wilds, but even more frightening are those that walk as beasts at night, but live as normal humans during the day. Mortals in beast form are more cunning, bloodthirsty and magical, and less predictable than the beasts whose shape they take. The most common form adopted by shapeshifters is that of the wolf, but other forms are possible.

Shapeshifters have many different origins. Some are inherently magical beings. Some are people who have made pacts with the Prince of Darkness, selling their souls in return for the shapeshifting gift. Some are of faerie blood and are thus changeable like their kin. Others learn magical ceremonies that transform them. And some are the victims of curses; they hate their affliction and have little or no control over it. Such curses are often heredi-tary, or pass to victims who they bite. The origin of a shapeshifter's power determines the power he is aligned with, whether Magical, Infernal or Faerie. In the entry below, a Magical shapeshifter is presented.

Use the stats for normal animals (see below) as guidelines for those of shapeshifters, but feel free to spice them up. A few supernatural abilities, such as the lycanthrope's immunity to weapons other than those of silver, might add a fun touch.

For more rules on shapeshifters, see the **Ars Magica** supplement **The Medieval Bestiary**.

## Suzaria, the White Werewolf

**Magic Might:** 16 (8 while in human form)

**Vital Statistics:** Size 0, Intelligence +2, Perception +3, Strength +3, Stamina +4, Presence +5, Communication 0, Dexterity +1, Quickness +2

**Personality Traits:** Cautious +4, Daring +1

**Combat Scores:**

Bite: First Strike +4, Attack +6, Damage +13

Fatigue +5, Defense +8(14), Soak +6(12)*

Body Levels: 0, -1, -3, -5, Incapacitated

\* Non-silver weapons do half rolled damage; wooden weapons do one-fourth rolled damage.

**Abilities:** Alertness (hunters) 8, Scan (prey) 5, Stealth (stalking) 6

**Powers:**

*Stunning Beauty, ReMe 15, 0 points* — In wolf form Suzaria is even more beautiful than in human form, and anyone intending to attack her must make a Stamina roll of 12+ or hold back at the last moment. Men suffer -3 on the roll. Those that Suzaria is attacking can strike normally. The Storyguide can call for rolls whenever anyone intends to do something that would cause Suzaria harm, such as sounding the alarm when she is spotted, or pointing out to pursuers where she has fled.

**Description:**

Suzaria is an intelligent, strong-spirited woman who learned from her mother how to take the form of a wolf. She rubs a magical jelly over her naked body under the moon atop a magical rock in the woods. As long as the moon is in the night sky, she lives as an exceptionally large and beautiful white wolf. At first she roamed the forest and brought down occasional game, but as she has grown older her hunger has become more ravenous. She has

BOC
92

begun killing her human enemies one by one, and soon will have degenerated so far that she will attack anyone who crosses her path. Local legends about her grow; she is known as the shadow killer.

Though she was once a normal woman, use of the shapeshifting salve has imbued her long white hair with one pawn of Muto vis.

**Story:**

Suzaria-as-wolf approaches the characters when they are camped in the woods, then flees. One of the characters may become obsessed with the beautiful animal, perhaps a Magus who wants it as his Familiar. The obsession is emotional, but be sure the character has a practical reason for wanting the wolf. Eventually that character must choose between destroying the wolf, or allowing her to continue her killing spree as her hunger grows insatiable.

# UNDEAD, STALKERS OF THE NIGHT

The boundary between life and death is hazy, and in the grey area between dwell the undead, those whose deaths have led to a horrid non-life instead of peaceful rest. An undead being is missing some aspect of human life, such as the body in the case of a ghost, or the mind in the case of a zombie. In some ways this weakens them, but in other cases it makes them stronger. Ghosts, for example, cannot be struck by physical weapons, and zombies cannot be demoralized. The undead are driven by inhuman desires to kill and terrify.

Due to their magical nature, undead have many powers. Typical ones include: resistance to thrusting damage (because weapons that pierce do most damage to internal organs, which are superfluous to the undead), immunity to mind-affecting spells (this does not include all ghosts and spirits), immunity to Fatigue, causing fear, and entrancement. Some undead can take the shape of bats, fleas, wolves, or clouds of vapor. The undead can also be vulnerable to fire, and sometimes their own stupidity can defeat them.

Undead can be aligned with Magical or Infernal powers. Magi are able to create simple undead, while more powerful ones tend to controlled by the demonic. The origin of an undead being determines the realm to which it belongs, and determines the nature of its Might score, either Magical or Infernal. The undead shown below belong to the Magic realm.

## Skeletons

**Magic Might:** 5*

**Vital Statistics:** Size 0, Cunning -4, Perception -2, Strength 0, Stamina +3, Presence n/a, Communication n/a, Dexterity 0, Quickness 0

**Combat Scores:**

Attack: By weapon type

Fatigue n/a, Defense by weapon (weapon skill 0), Soak (w/out armor) +8(14)**

Body Levels: OK, Destroyed

* Immune to mind-affecting spells.

** +5 bonus on Soak vs. puncture damage

**Story:**

A Magus from a rival Covenant has been creating skeletons in the caves under her Covenant, and may be under demonic influence. One of the characters discovers this and may investigate.

## Zombies

**Magic Might:** 5*

**Vital Statistics:** Size 0, Cunning -4, Perception -4, Strength +5, Stamina +8, Presence n/a, Communication n/a, Dexterity -3, Quickness -3

**Combat Scores:**

Attack: By weapon type

Fatigue n/a, Defense by weapon (weapon skill 0), Soak (w/out armor) +12(18)**

Body Levels: OK, -3, Immobilized

* Immune to mind-affecting spells

** +5 bonus to Soak vs. puncture damage

**Story:**

Raegle is descended from a long line of grave robbers. When he was young Raegle was content with the meager wealth he gained from his evil robberies, but now he has become a diabolist and has started stealing corpses as well. In his shack in the woods he turns then into zombies and uses them to guard himself against intrusion. The zombies hide up in trees, dropping upon intruders.

# GHOSTS

Ghosts are the spirits of the dead who cannot rest, often tied to the world because of some emotional event. A violent death or lack of proper burial can create a ghost.

Ghosts are interesting beings not because of their combat potential but because of their personalities and magical powers. An enemy ghost can frighten or curse characters, and some ghosts retain the ability to affect the material world in certain ways. The ghosts of miners killed in a cave-in might retain the ability to mine, even though their picks are as insubstantial as they are. They could use this power to affect the material world by causing another cave-in. For more rules on ghosts, see the Ars Magica supplement **The Broken Covenant of Calebais**.

## Harlin, a Fiend of the Night

**Magic Might:** 15*

**Vital Statistics:** Size 0, Intelligence -2, Perception 0, Strength -1, Stamina +3, Presence -2, Communication 0, Dexterity +1, Quickness +3

**Personality Traits:** Impulsive +2, Cautious +1

**Combat Scores:**

Claws: First Strike +3, Attack +6, Damage +12

Fatigue n/a, Defense +6(12), Soak +5(11)**

Body Levels: OK, 0, -1, -3, -5, Incapacitated

* +10 vs. mind spells

** +5 bonus to Soak vs. puncture weapons

**Abilities:** Stealth (around children) 12

**Powers:**

*Suck Breath, PeCo 30, 2 points* — Kills a young child. Harlin must actually inhale the breath of a victim.

**Description:**

Harlin was an evil woman of magical blood who died in childbirth, and now she has returned from the grave to slay children. By day she can take the form of a shrivelled hag, but at night she becomes a horrific corpse-like creature. In this form she sneaks into houses and sucks the breath from the lips of children, leaving them cold and lifeless. She can only enter a house into which she has been invited at least once, so during the day she poses as a woeful traveler to gain admittance to houses where babies live.

Her corpse is worth five pawns of Auram vis.

Against strong opposition she prefers to flee rather than fight, though she fights ferociously if cornered.

**Story:**

The death of a child known to one of the characters involves the Covenant in the mystery of why babies are dying. While they are investigating, the Magi themselves are blamed for the deaths. The best way to stop the killing might be to find Harlin's middle-aged son, whose birth killed his mother, and have him speak with her.

# The Infernal Realm

The Infernal Realm is the realm of evil and decay, physical destruction and moral corruption. Even as the Church works its Divine power to protect the medieval man's soul and buoy it up to Heaven after the body's death, so work the forces of the Devil to steal away the souls of men and drag them into the depths of Hell, there to be tortured and abused by devils until the end of time. Human beings are a damned race, brought low and subject to death due to the sins of our ancestral parents. Adam and Eve tasted of the fruit of the Tree of Knowledge of Good and Evil in the Garden of Eden, and soon after, all the world came under Satan's control.

Fortunately, mankind is capable of salvation because our knowledge of the Divinities is vague at best, and therefore our embrace of evil is equally without full understanding. And beyond this, our fall was not without catalyst. From the beginning, the Great Adversary and his satellites have sought mankind's corruption. Devils are fallen angels; they cannot and will not be Redeemed because of their very natures. So greatly do they comprehend the Divinity's cosmos that they can never be convinced by new arguments or perspectives to seek salvation. Their envy of mankind and the future place of humans in the cosmos is without bounds, as is their capacity for evil as a rejection of all that is Good. It is impossible to force the truth from a demon, or make it act outwardly virtuous, unless such an act serves its future needs. Devils have an eternity to plan and scheme, and a human lifetime is a brief moment in their eyes. For this reason, their plans can seem most opaque.

Ultimately, devils seek to weigh down souls with the baggage of sin, and a love for material things instead of a love for the Divine. Their most potent allies in this cause are diabolists, humans who sell their souls, and worship or seek aid from Hell's inhabitants in return for powers and favors in the material world. Not only do demons win away these souls for their everlasting fires, but they are able to satisfy their lust for chaos, destruction and suffering in the process.

In return for their sacrifice, diabolists are often rewarded with considerable supernatural power. Some can summon demons and use them to their own ends, while others can use powers that are similar to destructive spells.

However, since they are still mortal, diabolists tend not to have plans as subtle or effective as demons. They are also more often moved by personal grievances. For these reasons, diabolists are often found behind plots that are more destructive of the body than of the soul.

When devils are unable to further genuine diabolism, they nurture the next best thing: paganism. Pagans offer the Devil a way to stalemate the forces of Good, because pagan belief imprisons souls in religious devotion that does not direct its energy toward the one true Divinity. And, the most extreme of pagan religions can actually prove useful allies of Hell, especially if they can be manipulated to devote their thoughts and actions to the Infernal way. To most minds of the Church, and therefore mundane man, Magi are pagans, if not diabolists in league with the Devil.

These are only the remote influences of the Infernal realm. The Inferno is not a remote force in the lives of Mythic Europe's people. Demons exist alongside medieval man, ruining his crops, giving him back pains, making the wind howl outside his window at night, and causing him to strike his loved ones in fits of anger. It is proposed by some theologians that it is impossible to drop a needle from the roof of a house without hitting an invisible, malevolent demon in pursuit of a plan of evil.

But if devils are imprisoned in Hell until the end of time, how do they exist alongside man, and how can they be summoned to Earth by foolhardy wizards? Quite simply, they cannot. However, like mortal men, devils have souls, and also have spirits. These spirits rise to the sphere of earth, and in this state are called demons. Hence, a devil is a divine yet warped soul residing in Hell, and a demon is a devil's evil spirit wandering the Earth.

This dichotomy is somewhat simplistic since Hell is home to certain infernal creatures which are not fallen angels, and thus do not possess souls. These beings are not devils, but many Magi argue they are demonic nonetheless. Also, evil spirits can assume physical form on earth, beyond their insubstantial, spiritual essence. Depending on the demon, some must remain predominantly in spiritual form, able to become physical for only short periods of time, while other demons must contend with just the opposite problem.

Regardless of these considerations, demons walk the earth, and they seek man's downfall. When they cannot get people to worship them, or to stop worshipping the Divine, they have other options available to them. The first is destruction: demons are great lovers of killing and violence. Unfortunately, this doesn't serve the long-term interests of the Prince of Darkness, as it tends to send people running to the protection of the Church. A body without a soul is as useless to the Devil as it is to His Divine counterpart.

Violence is, however, an effective strategy against wizards, especially Hermetic Magi who are protected from Infernal powers by their *Parmae Magicae*. Magi are free-spirited individuals, unlikely to run to the Church (because the Dominion interferes with the all-important workings of magic), and yet able to harm demons with spells. Thus, demons tend to bring their more overt powers to bear when confrontations with Magi arise.

However, physical prowess and spell-like powers are not the full extent of the demonic arsenal. Demons seek souls, and damage to a transitory body is a fleeting pleasure in comparison to the eternal reward of a corrupted soul. The act of possession, wherein the demon actually enters the victim's body and takes it over partially or completely, gives the demon the ability to make the subject of possession perform any of a number of "evil" acts. In truth, though, this does not taint the possessed person's soul, regardless of what the neighbors think. A soul can only be corrupted through a human's free will.

As a means to true human corruption, the two most dangerous demonic devices arise: temptation and oppression. The first is self-explanatory. Some moral dilemma is presented, and it is up to the human, with no arm-twisting, to make the right or wrong decision. In making the wrong decision, the mortal taints his soul. Other general situations can provoke emotions that are sinful in nature. For instance, no amount of skill in *Parma Magica* can prevent a Magus from feeling greed upon seeing a rival's collection of *vis*, or envy of the status and influence displayed by a rival. If these feelings cause a Magus to do something malicious, his soul is stained by Hell's evil, putting it into demonic grasp.

Not surprisingly, the Order of Hermes forbids all dealings with demonkind. Any member caught engaging in diabolism is Renounced and made a target of the dreaded Wizards' March. Though the Divine consequences of diabolism on a soul is one reason for the Order's stance, a more practical reason is the danger of

## Areas of Infernal Power

| Area | Aura Rating |
| --- | --- |
| Where Demonic Evil has Happened | 1 |
| Diabolists' Meeting Place | 2 |
| Devil Worship Site | 3 |
| Major Church of the Devil | 5 |
| Infernal Area, Where Demons Meet | 8 |
| Gateway to Hell | 10 |

Areas where the Devil has infected the land are cursed, rated 1 to 4. Where the Devil has an exceptionally strong sway, the rating is 5 to 10. At night the Aura of a cursed place can grow up to double its daytime level.

earning the Church's wrath. Magi and clergy have tenuous relations at present. Diabolism can tilt the scales in favor of all-out war, bringing the Inquisition to bear on the Order.

Oppression is somewhat less personal. Rather than targeting one victim, demons create a general mood that indirectly affects large groups of people. Oppression is a display of "evil" and "unnatural" events that affect the environment and show that demons are ever-vigilant. Basically, oppression is symbolic of the fact that, since the eating of the apple, humanity is damned, and that the world now belongs to the Devil. Everything foul that occurs, from winds that blow away seeds after planting, to snows that cut short the harvest season, arises from demonic oppression. Oppression may be recognized as events that seem intent on breaking the human spirit, without causing direct harm to humanity. The demonic goal is to create an atmosphere in which sour moods and harsh emotions predominate. Thus, evil has the chance to flourish in a man's heart, encouraging him to express his anger through evil acts. The man who sees the world from a spiritual perspective is immune to these oppressions (or rather becomes a martyr to them, thus fortifying his soul).

Yet another form of demonic assault is obsession, which is a direct supernatural attack on a victim. This is not a spell-like power but rather an effect brought about by the actual influence of a demonic spirit's presence. Obsession is distinct from possession because it is perpetrated from without; the demon never enters the human body. Rather, the demon heightens inherent flaws to make the human work against himself. The basic form of obsession arises from the *phantastikos*, an evil idea or image that flashes across the mind, and is usually attributed to the victim's own darker wishes. If the victim of such influence cannot resist his base feelings, his soul is corrupted by his thoughts and actions.

## Demons and Raw Vis

Due to their magical natures, demons often leave behind a physical manifestation of their power. When their corruptive magic touches the earth, raw *vis* can arise. Animál, Ignem, Imágonem and Perdo *vis* are common types. When a demon's powers have no inclination toward one of these Arts, raw *vis* usually manifests itself in the form of Vim *vis*. Such *vis* is usually tainted with evil, but the Storyguide may decide otherwise. When it causes side effects, raw *vis* harvested from a demon's activities can double the number of Botch rolls usually required in an activity. Other twisted, less infrequent side effects can also arise. The existence of this *vis* and its effects are usually determined by your story.

When a demon is defeated or destroyed on earth, the spirit is banished back to Hell. Oftentimes a devil's spirit cannot return to earth for some time as punishment for failed machinations, a lesson taught by the Prince himself. Failure of evil machinations can also result in the Infernal torture of a devil. As many devils operate in the world through spirits, it's rare and exceedingly difficult to defeat a devil and recover its corpse. Such a deed often requires a journey to Hell itself, though the *vis* that may be plundered from the body can justify the attempt. However, some demons have no spirit form (often the case for weak demons), so when they come to earth, they do so in their physical form. However, though some demons can be "killed," their nature is eternal.

Demons destroyed on earth, leaving a corpse behind, can be harvested for *vis*. When a demon is a spirit, banished when defeated, the demon's profile indicates such under Body Levels. When a demon has no spirit form, only a physical form that can be killed on earth, such is also indicated in its profile, under Body Levels.

Harder to produce and harder to resist is the *psychomachia*, or war of virtue. A demon speaks to its victim, as if in the victim's own voice, tempting him to performs acts of evil. In game terms, for any Passion-related or Personality Trait roll a character makes, the demon attacking him may modify the roll (positively or negatively, whichever applies), prompting the character to behave in a sinful or self-indulgent manner. A demon can also demand a personality roll from its victim, even when roleplaying and the situation at hand otherwise make it unnecessary. Demons have scores in *Psychomachia*, the value of which is applied to a character's Passion-related or Personality Trait roll. A *Psychomachia* score of +0 indicates the simple ability to require a personality roll; a demon with a score of 0 isn't powerful enough to modify personality rolls, but can require that they be made. Rolls modified or induced by a demon's *Psychomachia* score are stress rolls, so if the character Botches, he acts in a terribly sinful manner, on his own accord.

In defensive terms, demons and devils are completely immune to fire, spells that detect or force the truth, and spells that make them kind, compassionate, or somehow virtuous.

# INFERNAL AREAS

Most earth-bound demons, and many diabolists, prefer the comfort afforded by areas of Infernal Aura (they both suffer the bonuses and penalties of being in areas of other Auras). Such areas are typical sites for diabolic churches, covens, and the summoning of demons (see the *Areas of Infernal Power Chart* for examples of Auras and their ratings). These regions are among the most vile places in the world: growth of natural plants is stunted and warped, decay and the stench of ill humors abound, and predatory animals living nearby kill, not for survival, but for the pleasure of the suffering they inflict.

Travelers in or near Infernal Auras often find themselves in foul moods, and the activity of outlaws on nearby roads is particularly harsh — the effects of demonic oppression in high concentration. Old wounds, especially those received through malevolence, hurt anew, and old conflicts and personality clashes are remembered again, and possibly reenacted. Of greater concern to Magi, an Infernal Aura acts as a penalty to all uses of magic.

Though they prefer their Infernal homestead, demons often work their evil ways in the mortal world, with no boundary to the mischief, disease and strife they may cause. Not even areas of Infernal Aura are sacred to them. If the loss or destruction of an Infernal Aura causes the corruption of human souls, so be it. However, demons find that souls are more vulnerable to them if mortal men are not constantly reminded of Hell's existence. Restraint in torment is therefore valued, in the hopes that more

souls can be lured from rather than chased to the Church. Indeed, the followers and dupes of the Infernal are spread far and wide throughout the world, even in the Church and Order of Hermes itself, secretly working their dark ways. Thus, thanks to the Dark One and man's own fickle nature, Mythic Europe is a torturous land in which to live.

## Tazzelrik, a Lowly Fiend

**Infernal Might:** 10

**Vital Statistics:** Size 0, Cunning 0, Perception +1, Strength -2, Stamina 0, Presence n/a, Communication -2, Dexterity 0, Quickness +7

**Personality Traits:** Brave -1, Mean +1

**Combat Scores:**

Bite: First Strike +9, Attack +3, Damage +5

Fatigue n/a, Defense +10(16), Soak +6(12)

Body Levels: OK, 0, -1, -3, -5, Destroyed

**Powers:**

*Psychomachia*: Anger +0

**Spirit Form Powers:** None

**Physical Form Powers:**

*The Jump Conjoined, ReCo 15, 2 Points* — When Tazzelrik hops up and down, all who watch him must make a Stamina stress roll of 7+ or begin to hop along with him, allowing no other physical actions. Stress rolls of 8+ may be made each Round to break free. If the first or any other roll Botches, further attempts to stop hopping are made against an Ease Factor of 12. Lasts as long as there are victims, or until Tazzelrik stops jumping.

**Physical Form:**

Tazzelrik is a freakish demon of quite monstrous and ill appearance. Standing as tall as a man, he has a cow's head with green, shaggy hair and hide, and the legs of a large human — but no torso! He walks with a shambling gait, but is well-balanced, and hops around very quickly when trying to avoid mankind.

A piece of corn husk or oat sheaf is found curled between the toes of one of Tazzelrik's feet when destroyed. This crushed and matted plant is worth two pawns of Herbam *vis*.

**Description:**

This bestial fiend is more cowardly than brave, but malice is nonetheless evident in his actions. Tazzelrik lives off the food of the peasants' bad tempers and ill will toward their neighbors. His favorite scheme is to spy on a communal field for a while until he learns of a peasant who must cross another's crop lands to get to his own. Tazzelrik then stomps all over the neighboring peasant's crops in the wake of the more careful passerby. There's bound to be a confrontation between the two peasants, and Tazzelrik's demonic gluttony is temporarily sated.

**Story:**

The Magi (or perhaps this is a Grog-only encounter) come across two peasants arguing in a field, victims of Tazzelrik's mischief. A perceptive group member hears maniacal laughter and sees a green cow's head hopping through the tall wheat. A grand chase through the farmland ensues, ending, perhaps, in a group dance, courtesy of Tazzelrik's malefic power.

# Harkerr, a Senior Pit-Snake Demon

**Infernal Might:** 25*

**Vital Statistics:** Size +2, Intelligence -3, Perception -3, Strength +6, Stamina +5, Presence -3, Communication -1, Dexterity 0, Quickness -2

**Personality Traits:** Impulsive +3, Sadistic +6

**Combat Scores:**

Whip: First Strike +9, Attack +8, Damage Spec., Fatigue n/a, Defense +8(14), Soak +23(29)**

Body Levels: 0, -1/-1, -3/-3, -5, Banished

* double normal Resistance to spells that counter his urge to inflict pain

** only harmed by metal weapons and powerful attacks (such as dragon bites)

**Powers:**

*Psychomachia*: None

**Spirit Form Powers:** None

**Physical Form Powers:** (using whip attacks)

*Death, PeCo 30, 12 Points* — Stamina stress roll of 5+ or die. Even if successful, lose two Body Levels and make a Characteristic loss roll (as for *Aging*, p. 354).

*Burn, CrIg 20, 3 Points* — stress die +18 fire damage.

*Pain, PeCo 15, 1 Point* — Stamina stress roll of 9+ or fall to the ground in pain. Roll again each Round to recover. If any roll Botches, a Body Level is lost with the victim's flailings.

**Physical Form:**

Harkerr appears as a husky man from the waist up, and as a sinewy snake with gray-green scales from the waist down. He is among the class of warrior demons, and as such only appears in physical form; Harkerr cannot revert to spirit form. The lower, snake-like half of his body is worth 12 pawns of Animál *vis*.

**Description:**

A simple-minded demon who has not yet learned to replace his lust for brutality with subtlety and subterfuge, Harkerr is never sent to the mortal world by his devilish master. Instead, he is employed as a taskmaster for the other Pit-Demons, a "torturer of torturers" who must keep his slaves busy tormenting the many souls that his master has seen fit to put under his supervision. Because of his wonderful capacity for inflicting pain and death, Harkerr is a favored subject of diabolic summoning, and for this reason is occasionally brought to the mortal world.

Harkerr carries a whip in his left hand and a shield, bound with human leather, in his right. With his whip, he can use any of the powers listed above, so must strike before his powers can be used. Note that Infernal Might Points are spent before rolling to hit with the whip, so if the whip misses Harkerr is still weakened.

**Story:**

When the characters begin to uncover the plot of some diabolist, Harkerr is summoned in a grand ceremony and sent to destroy them.

# Sainela,
# Negotiator of the Middle Echelons

**Infernal Might:** 64

**Vital Statistics:** Size -1, Intelligence +4 , Perception +4, Strength -3, Stamina -3, Presence +4, Communication +4, Dexterity 0, Quickness +1

**Personality Traits:** Subtle +6, Affable +2

**Combat Scores:**

Hand: First Strike +5, Attack +7, Damage +6

Fatigue n/a, Defense +8(14), Soak +5(11)

Body Levels: OK, 0, -1, -3, Banished

**Powers:**

*Psychomachia*: Pride +4, Curiosity +3, Vanity +1

**Spirit Form Powers:**

*Force Words, CrMe 20, 2 Points* — Sainela can put up to a dozen words into someone's mouth. The target might be surprised to utter these words, but most people are proud enough to defend what they say rather than take the words back. (Have you ever said something you didn't intend to, but pretend to have meant it anyway?)

**Physical Form Powers:**

*Spells (spec.), 1 Point* — Any Mentem spells up to Level 10 and any other spells up to Level 5.

*Create (Creo), 5 Points* — Creates impermanent items, such as weapons, ropes, tents, gold. She uses this power to offer people the things they most desire. These items disappear at the next full moon. Form depends on the item created; equivalent to a Level 10 spell.

**Physical Form:**

Sainela is a stylishly-dressed young woman with a forceful demeanor and a short, red, barbed tail. She disappears in a cloud of sweet-smelling, lavender-hued smoke rather than stay and fight. Her tail is worth 21 pawns of Mentem *vis*.

**Description:**

This devil was an envoy between two powerful Hellish fiefdoms when a subtle diplomatic mission blew up in her face. As a result she lost her position and is now exiled to the mortal world, stripped of most of her usual powers. Rather than brood the centuries away, Sainela has decided to return to work as an ambassador of opposed forces — this time between all of humanity and devilkind. If the resulting efforts earn her the occasional soul along the way, so much the better.

Sainela's specialty is in dealing with people who are not horribly distressed by talking frankly with a demon — Magi, for example. She is reasonable, patient (i.e, subtle), even-tempered and quite sophisticated (with a passion for music, art and philosophy). However, her eventual goal is to corrupt those she deals with, in the cause of "infernal diplomacy."

A common ploy to gain definite moral ground, when her subject is not otherwise moving closer to Hell in word or action, is to offer her victim a chance to speak with the shade of some classical scholar. Lesser demonic spirits usually pretend to be the summoned shade. The victim's agreement to participate in the summoning is a mark in Sainela's favor when the victim's soul is judged, regardless of the reality of the "summoning." After all, the attempt to disturb a resting soul, particularly one in Heaven, is a sin.

**Story:**

Sainela accepts the task of corrupting the Covenant or one of the Magi. She repeatedly offers innocuous aid, posing at first as a young noble lady. She later arranges situations in which the characters need her help. Her goal is to get them used to accepting demons rather than fearing them. As she knows she has centuries to accomplish her mission, she's in no hurry.

# The Faerie Realm

Faeries are the most diverse, enigmatic, and inherently magical beings of all the supernatural powers. The realm of Faerie is as diverse and strange as those spirits and bodies who inhabit it. Faeries are spirits of places, most attuned to the natural world. There are faeries bound to forests, caves, lakes, mountains, and oceans — all places primeval. However, some make their homes in the world of man — mortals rarely know the true origin of mishaps that befall them. There are faeries bound to fields, roads, farms, cities and even churches (though priests hotly deny it). The bond that exists between faeries and their locales is not strictly territorial; the bond manifests itself in the faerie spirit. Faeries therefore share the characteristics of their associated places. Thus, ocean faeries are tempestuous and capricious, house faeries bear semblance to tiny people and domestic animals, road faeries are dark and unrelenting, and faeries of ancient places resemble the peoples and heroes of the legendary past.

The goals of faeries are largely incomprehensible to mortals. They lack any need for food and shelter (indeed, none of them ever die or grow old, they simply exist), so are motivated by a simple desire to amuse themselves, and spend much of their time in games of "let's pretend." Many faeries seem fascinated by humanity and play out elaborate games in the roles of kings, queens, courtiers, jesters, and knights. While playing roles, faeries are ritualistic and rigid in their actions because the games they play often have rules. If faeries pretending to be soldiers are marching down a path, they might consider it against the rules to leave the path, even if staying on it causes harm. Furthermore, they do not use their powers beyond what their roles permit. Mortals can use this lack of flexibility against faerie adversaries.

The strength of most faeries lies in their inherent magical nature, not in their muscle. Some have supernatural strength, but most rely on illusion, deception and other forms of magic to protect themselves. Indeed, with all faerie things appearances can be deceiving. After dawn breaks a pile of gold may prove nothing more than old leaves, and a single oak leaf can hold within it more magical power than the enchanted staff of a mighty Magus.

If it's possible to put faeries in a mortal context, they may be considered the wild opposites of Mythic Europe's mundane folk. They are the restless, endlessly creative, playful, unfathomable, crazed and unleashed side to an otherwise stolid folk. They are the dark, obscure aspect of an honest people who realize, on an intuitive level, that there is much within them that they do not understand and never will. Paradoxia, a follower of Merinita and filia of Jerga, best describes the close relationship between simple folk and faeries:

"The fools in House Jerbiton place humanity above all else, and, more than that, place the nobility as the height of humanity. Humanity has its place, but nobles know nothing except war. Ignore the nobles and the educated when you wish to understand the Fay. Look to the peasants and even the simpletons. They are the mortals closest to nature and truth. Such people know the old stories and truths their "betters" will never understand. When you are intent on exploring a faerie forest, ask the advice of the local peasants. Ignore the nobles and the priests."

# FAERIE AREAS

Since faeries are spirits of places, the places where they reside are by definition distinctive. The presence of faeries imbues a place with supernatural power. Places of Faerie Aura range widely in magnitude and size. The size of an Aura is determined by the physical bounds of the locale, or by the expanse to which the resident faeries journey or extend their power. Thus, a faerie Aura can range from the size of a small rural farmhouse to that of a huge, ancient oak (including regions reached by the tree's roots), to that of a church and its lands, built over a pre-Christian holy site. The magnitude of an Aura's power often reflects upon the might of the faeries that reside there. Auras of limited power tend to be inhabited by faeries that are little more than annoying, or barely more than helpful. These faeries

are almost never capable of killing. On the other hand, Auras of immense power tend to be inhabited by faeries that can will themselves taller than a church spire, and can shake the earth's foundation by word of command. See the *Areas of Faerie Power Chart* for ranges of Aura strength.

Areas of low Faerie power are relatively common, especially in rural and wilderness areas, where mortal man has not spread his influence. If one truth may be applied to all faeriekind, it is their repulsion by the Divine. Faeries cannot bear the presence of the Dominion, and may go into hiding where it holds sway, or may move on to more secluded domains. (They are also offended by iron, even outside weapon form; several different charms known by mortal folk; and fire, which can undermine their illusions and deceptions.) As mortal man carries his beliefs with him, he unwittingly drives faeries before him, so mortal man and Faerie are often incompatible.

However, even if mortals range into and make their homes in Faerie lands, faerie power is not always diminished. Mundanes can be so cautious of faeries, or so vehemently warned by clergy of faerie dangers, that they dare not set foot in dark wood or virgin mountain expanses. Faerie power can also endure the presence of man if relations are established between the two folk. Common

## Areas of Faerie Power

| Area | Faerie Aura |
| --- | --- |
| Outskirts of Faerie Wilderness | 1 |
| Faerie Woods | 2 |
| Important Site in Faerie Woods | 3 |
| Heart of a Faerie Forest | 5 |
| Outskirts of Faerieland | 8 |
| Faerieland | 10 |

men and lowly faeries may even exchange goods or services, but he who cheats or dares raise the ire of the wee folk endangers his life. Oftentimes an exchange of favors may not seem equal to human thought, but may be perfectly equitable or even "a steal" to the faerie mind. Faeries can increase the fertility of crops, animals, and people. They may also befuddle marauding bandits, or simply hold roaringly good parties to liven up the life of a bored farmer (whether he appreciates it or not). In return, faeries may demand wheat (they grow only barley), milk, performances of song and dance, or the repair or loan of household goods. Often, faeries may demand a reward that bears no apparent logic, such as a lock of a child's hair.

Such payment may seem lucrative, until the lock is used in the faeries' magics. . .

Faeries that are amenable to dealings with man are usually from the Seelie Court. The Seelie Court consists of human-like faeries; they are noble, regal, and beautiful (and often elves). The Seelie are also incomparable masters of song and music. Thus, they are the most sociable of faeriekind. Still, there is in each of them a touch of power so great and alien that human life can be seen as irrelevant and annoying, so dealings with even the Seelie are hazardous.

Related to the Seelie Court is the Unseelie Court. This group is comprised of dark, malicious faeries, those who delight in tormenting humans. Generally, these faeries are more brutal and less refined than their brethren. These faeries can be so vicious that their mere approach threatens life and limb. There are dark pools and silent groves, the homes of Unseelie faeries, which the wise know to avoid at all times. And there are Unseelie castles that can only be seen at dusk, where powerful faerie lords reign. You are invited to visit, but cannot pass through the gates again.

Though the Seelie and Unseelie Courts are different in nature, they are not opposed. The Seelie Court may rule a Faerie area during the day, and the Unseelie Court at night. Moreover, while Faerie Courts can rule at different times, the Faerie Realm itself can reign over other Realms on special occasions. On certain nights almost all the wilderness, and even some of the Dominion, falls under Faerie's sway. On these occasions faeries, Seelie and Unseelie, leave their forests and burrows to tread the naked earth. Usually only the most powerful faeries can leave their Faerie homes entirely, but on these special nights Faerie is almost everywhere. At such times it is best that normal folk stay locked up in their homes.

Inciting the wrath of faeries, whether Seelie or Unseelie, is to be avoided at all costs. Being completely wild, there's no rhyme or reason to the pain and torture they can inflict, and being eternal, faeries can hold grudges beyond mortal reckoning. Even Magi are wise to keep the peace with faeries, for not even Hermetic magic is a reliable defense. Indeed, faeries are highly resilient to magic, so the best Magi can do is hold them at bay. Because faeries are so unpredictable, all relations with them are fraught with peril.

Regardless of the dangers posed by Faerie, Magi often risk them in pursuit of magical power. Faerie areas are rich in magic (vis), reason to challenge any peril, particularly for a Magus deprived of magical resources. Raids on Faerie areas can be quite rewarding, but one never knows what to expect, whether the place is of little or immense faerie power.

Sites of powerful Faerie Aura take as many forms as their inconstant inhabitants. Areas of power may stand on ancient pagan lands, may arise on sites favored by faerie queens, or may be erected by faeries intent on protecting valued things, such as an ancient pond. The faeries bound to these sites can be as powerful as the Auras themselves, posing a horrible threat to intruding Magi and overzealous priests. Or, such sites can be the domiciles of innumerable faeries. Though each has little power, their united number gives them strength to be respected and avoided.

Some powerful Faerie sites play a much more alarming and alluring role, though. They are sometimes gateways to Arcadia, Faerieland itself. Such gateways may be small and unassuming, rarely used and little known. Or, they may be massive entranceways, traversed by the greatest of faerie entities. Either way, entrance into Arcadia means certain doom. Mortals do not naturally belong there, and those who enter often fail to return. Even if they do return, they find a day spent in Faerieland is a year, ten years, a hundred years, or only a minute in the mundane world. In some places, monoliths are said to form doorways into Arcadia, with identical monoliths found on the other side. Whether such rumors are true, and whether they originate from a sane teller, is unknown.

In places where the mortal world borders Arcadia, trees and owls may occasionally speak, strange lights may be seen at night, and eyes that peer out at you may not be the eyes of animals. However, such places are still a part of the mortal world. Arcadia is a separate realm altogether. It is a wondrous place, far more beautiful than the mundane realm, and far more bizarre. Sunlight in Faerieland never burns or dazzles, trees are never uneven or sick; everything is naturally perfect. The perfection of Arcadia is not aesthetic or virtuous; perfect evil, perfect hate, and perfect indifference all exist there. The realm is a land untouched by mortal hands; there are no cleared plots, felled trees, or peasant fields. What crops are grown are grown by magic. Furthermore, majestic, mythic and forgotten creatures, as well as deer, wolves, boars, and bears, roam the land's virgin oak forests, protected by powerful animal spirits. While there are few cities in Arcadia, those that stand are inhabited by strange, potent, human-seeming Fay; these cities are large and airy, quite unlike the walled warrens of the mortal world.

Magic, too, is different in Faerieland than it is in the mortal world. Creo and Perdo magics are not reliable there. Most faerie inhabitants can use magic, some of them better than the greatest of Magi, whereas few in mundane existence understand even the simplest magical designs. Like the mortal world, Arcadia is a physical place, but it is also a land of pure enchantment and imagination. Magi of House Merinita all scoff at the idea of making a Map of Arcadia, saying "How can you map the geography of a dream." Being a dream state, Faerieland is often incomprehensible to mortals who go there. Cause and effect do not always follow, and it is easy to become totally disoriented, especially as faeries enjoy leading intruders astray with the glamor of their magic. And yet, some members of House Merinita insist there are laws to Arcadia, that it is not a chaotic place, merely a place with different rules. Whether this is true or not, Arcadia and Faerie itself are best left to faeries, and the foolish among men.

For a complete explanation of faeries and Arcadia, see the **Faeries** supplement for **Ars Magica**.

## Marlossi, Lady of Light

**Faerie Might:** 16

**Vital Statistics:** Size -1, Intelligence +3, Perception +3, Strength -2, Stamina 0, Presence +5, Communication +3 , Dexterity +1, Quickness +1

**Personality Traits:** Regal +4

**Combat Scores:**

Fatigue 0, Defense +3(9), Soak 0(6)*

Body Levels: -1, -3, -5, Incapacitated

*Damage from iron weapons that exceeds her Soak is doubled before Body Level loss is figured.

**Abilities:**

Sing 6 (epic ballads), Play (lyre) 5

**Powers:**

*Disappear, ReCo 20, 1 point* — If grievously threatened, she can suddenly disappear, to where no one knows. If someone is holding her, she cannot disappear, nor can she if bound by iron.

*Heal, CrCo 20, 3 points* — She can permanently heal those she touches, chasing away pain and fear as well. Each use of this power allows for the recovery of a lost Body Level. Certain magical or especially grievous wounds might not be healed by this power. After a person receives Marlossi's healing, all Bravery Personality Trait rolls made in the following day receive a +1 modifier.

**Description:**

Marlossi is a high elf of the Seelie Court. At firsts she seems human, and the only thing that truly sets her apart from a mortal woman is the sense of peace and welcome one feels when looking upon her gentle visage. (Those protected by *Parmae Magicae* do not feel this effect.) She wears a light green gown and simple jewelry. She never leaves the safety of her home in a small Faerie area of the woods. She is most often found in the boisterous company of animal-like faeries, and she relies on them to protect her from physical threats. If struck, she bleeds a liquid that looks like white wine. This "blood" is worth four pawns of Creo *vis*.

**Story:**

The characters are found trespassing on her land, but she graciously accepts them as guests. It becomes apparent, however, that she expects them to perform a dangerous task for her, as "noble people" should for a "regal lady." This task could involve taking back an area controlled by the Unseelie Court, an area once reigned over by Marlossi and the Seelie Court.

# Hybacus, the Feral Musician

**Faerie Might:** 20

**Vital Statistics:** Size +1, Intelligence 0, Perception +2, Strength +4, Stamina +4, Presence +2, Communication +1, Dexterity +1, Quickness +3

**Personality Traits:** Wild +7

**Combat Scores:**

Spear: First Strike +7, Attack +6, Damage +14

Fatigue +8, Defense +4(10), Soak +10(16)*

Body Levels: OK, 0/0, -1, -3, -5, Incapacitated

* Iron does +1 damage

**Powers** (while playing panpipes):

*Enrage, MuMe 20, 2 points* — Hybacus can play wild, violent music. Those hearing it get +2 to Attack, Damage and any rolls that deal with bravery if involved in battle. This works for both sides of a battle, which is fine for satyrs, who love a rousing fight.

*Revelry, MuMe 20, 2 points* — This music makes those at a party feel more riotous and merry (+4 to Reckless, Impulsive and related Passion or Personality Trait rolls).

*Amour, MuMe 20, 2 points* — This music lets those who listen see the beauty in each other and in what is around them, and it raises the desire to possess and please.

**Description:**

Hybacus is a satyr (human body with goat legs and horns) whose greatest joy is to play his panpipes while he and his brothers go on their occasional raids into human villages for women and other booty. When such opportunities do not present themselves, he enjoys playing at drunken parties. Hybacus is not as skilled a warrior as his fellows, but they appreciate the music he provides.

His horns are worth 10 Animál *vis*.

**Story:**

The characters find Hybacus and his rowdy fellows having a party in the woods and are asked to join in. If the characters refuse or are otherwise rude (to satyr sensibilities), they risk being attacked. If they participate in the drinking, wrestling, bragging and singing, the characters make themselves some good (if unpredictable) friends.

## Gizzle, a Goblin of the Mine

**Faerie Might:** 10

**Vital Statistics:** Size -2, Intelligence -2, Perception -1, Strength +3, Stamina +5, Presence -2, Communication 0, Dexterity +4, Quickness +3

**Personality Traits:** Mischievous +4

**Combat Scores:**

Pick: First Strike +6, Attack +4, Damage +11

Fatigue n/a, Defense +5(11), Soak +5(11)*

Body Levels: OK, -1, -5, Incapacitated

* Iron does +1 damage; earth-related attacks do half rolled damage.

**Abilities:** Stealth (tunnels) 8, Alertness (sounds) 6, Athletics (leaping) 4

**Powers:**

*Extinguish Flames, ReIg 10, 2 points* — He can extinguish any flame he sees, up to the size of a torch. Up to three flames may be put out at once, but Gizzle must still spend 2 Faerie Points per flame.

**Description:**

Gizzle and his fellow goblins haunt a mine near the characters' Covenant. Gizzle looks like a four-foot tall, misshapen man with mottled grey skin. He wears crudely woven clothes (but no shoes), and carries a miner's pick with a bronze head. His boisterous laughter can be heard throughout miles of tunnels. Sometimes he amuses himself by causing cave-ins or stealing miners' equipment that he finds lying about, and when in a vile mood he might attack a miner directly.

**Story:**

Gizzle and several other goblins have taken over a valuable section of the mine, killing several miners in the process. The Magi must act decisively to keep the trust of the remaining miners and to keep the mine operating at full potential.

# The Divine Realm

The Divine realm is the manifestation of the supernatural power of the Church and all with faith in the One True Deity. All other powers not of the Church are unholy, and considered aligned with the Devil and the forces of Hell. Of course, those attuned to other powers, like Magi and their Magic realm, perceive the realms in different, often opposing ways. Indeed (as the inserted documents suggest), the Church and the Order of Hermes have two conflicting points of view on the nature of certain supernatural powers. The reality of Mythic Europe lies somewhere in between.

Regardless of varying opinions on the virtue of the Divine and other realms, it cannot be denied that the Divine realm has constant influence over the other realms, including the Magical. A Divine Aura has the effect of limiting Hermetic magic's efficiency and effectiveness. Divine Miracles are also capable of accomplishing feats that Hermetic magic cannot. They can alter the Essential Nature of something, they can reach beyond the Lunar Sphere, and they can pierce the Veil of Death. It goes without saying, then, that the power of the Church and the boundaries it imposes on the Order of Hermes are cause for the contempt many Magi harbor for the Divine. It is very difficult for Magi, who can summon hurricanes and cause earthquakes, to worship a power higher than themselves. There are a few Magi, however, who are professed Christians, and who are pious. There are even a few who have what the Order calls "True Faith," *fides veritas*. It is the Christian Magus who has the most trying life to lead, for he must constantly reconcile two values that defy each other.

At its worst, the Church is a repressive force that treads upon more liberal thought. At its best, the Dominion allows the human soul to express its deepest beauty. So it is that in cathedrals one finds the most delightful music, the most enchanting art, and the most transcendent philosophy. Indeed, The Church is the single greatest outlet for the higher pursuits of civilized people, such as philosophy, art, literature and music.

# DIVINE AREAS

The Dominion (and thus the Church) is an innate part of the mundane world of Mythic Europe. The Church is the only supernatural power that the common folk generally have contact with. The ubiquitous Dominion therefore impacts on Magi and their fellows whenever they enter a village, town, or city where there is, at the least, a physical Church, an ordained priest, and a body of believers. The strength of a Divine Aura reflects on the piety of the believers who participate in it, the size of the populated area, and the faith of the clergy within the area. The Dominion is also focused more strongly in areas and objects that are strongly associated with faith. People, places, and things that have been blessed by an ordained priest can carry extremely fragile Divine Auras, a blessing which vanishes once the person, place, or thing is exposed to sin and the world. Note that Companions and Grogs who have recently attended Mass carry these fragile

blessed Auras with them. Unfortunately, only extremely pious people are able to keep the blessing they receive for long, and in any case a Covenant's Magic Aura probably subsumes the blessing's power.

Entering high levels of a Divine Aura has a definite, but indescribable, sensory experience associated with it. Non-magical people often experience anticipatory nerves and unconscious reverence. If such people are pious they instead feel quiet peace, and if not pious, feel dread and an unnerving guilt. Magi and people with many magical talents instantly sense the presence of a powerful Divine Aura, feeling the Gift within them flicker as a flame exposed to wind. Auras of lesser power might prove a mild irritant to such magical folk, perhaps causing headaches, short tempers and feelings of physical discomfort. People with Faerie or Infernal ties (such as Faerie Blood and Tainted with Evil Virtues and Flaws) immediately feel uncomfortable in Auras of low power, and may find Auras of higher power (e.g., 5+) intolerable. (This intolerance function more on a roleplaying level than a game mechanic level.) Characters with True Faith or Divine ties (e.g., someone with the Guardian Angel Virtue) feel quite comfortable and peaceful, and do not experience the same feelings of nervousness as do normal people.

Though Divine Auras are usually constant in areas inhabited by believers, the strength of Auras can vary. On Sundays and holy days the power of the Dominion increases. At night and on evil days the Dominion's power decreases. Also, Auras carried by the blessed, or Auras somehow carried into another realm, fall victim to the influence of that realm. See the *Areas of Divine Power Chart* for the relative magnitudes of Divine Auras.

# TRUE FAITH AND MIRACLES

Absolute devotion to the Divinities is a means of existence to those who pursue the ultimate faith. Every thought and action is measured in terms of one's piety, and

## Areas of Divine Power

| Area | Divine Power |
| --- | --- |
| Rural Area | 1 |
| Town | 2 |
| Metropolis | 3 |
| Consecrated Ground | 3-5 |
| Small Church | 5 |
| Large Church | 6 |
| Cathedral | 8 |
| Site of a Saint's Martyrdom | 10 |

only those who persist in good thoughts and deeds are able to rise above normal men. People of True Faith (those who have the True Faith Virtue) find inspiration in their faith and are sometimes capable of beseeching Divine favor in the form of Miracles. As Magi must often deal with the Dominion, rules are needed for those with True Faith and for those capable of asking for Miracles.

## True Faith

True Faith is measured in Faith Points, which are in turn a measure of a person's connection to God. Those who give up striving for self-improvement and selflessly dedicate themselves to leading holy lives (as only few in the Church have genuinely done) no longer have Confidence Points, but instead have Faith Points.

There are two ways to gain Faith Points. You may have the True Faith Virtue, which grants you Faith Points from the beginning of the Saga. If you have no Faith Points, and devote your life to the Divine, you may gain 1 point (and thereby lose all your Confidence Points) by spending at least one year in selfless service to God. If your own desire for recognition, esteem, self-respect, or power underlies your actions, you do not get the Faith Point. Once you have 1 Faith Point, you may only gain more through extreme devotion to your faith, such as in spending years in a cave resisting demons who come to tempt you, putting yourself at great risk for your faith's sake, or overcoming habits of thought and behavior that are major stumbling blocks on your spiritual path. (If they are indeed "major stumbling blocks," then overcoming them takes great effort and years of work.) You lose Faith Points if you turn at all from your faith.

A person with 1 Faith Point is rare and somewhat holy, while someone with 5 or more points is exceedingly holy and will most likely be canonized after death. Most of those with high Faith Points attain them only late in life. Some clergy, though certainly not most, and a few reverent lay people have Faith Points.

True Faith protects you from all manner of supernatural powers. Any time you are affected by magic, good or bad, make a stress roll (no Botch). If the result is equal to or lower than your Faith Points, the magic has no effect on you; indeed, no magic affects you during the entire encounter. You may add a relic's Faith Points to your own for this roll. A relic's Faith Points also protect those of piety, even if they lack True Faith. Treat the relic's rating as a score in True Faith. If you are not pious or faithful, however, a relic offers no protection.

Faith Points are used in the game as are Confidence Points (see the Character Chapter, p.57).

*What, then, is the state of these wizards' souls? Should we as Christians revile them, aid them, or pity them? Are they Damned as the followers of Lucifer are Damned? Can they achieve Redemption, Salvation?*

*The Fall of Man was caused by partaking of the Tree of Knowledge of Good and Evil. That knowledge caused man to Fall from his perfect state in the Garden of Eden and forever be cast out of Paradise, for he had turned his back on God. God was then forced to send his only son to provide Redemption and to forge a new covenant so that, through Baptism and Holy Communion, Man might find God once more and achieve Salvation, entering the Kingdom of Heaven.*

*I say to you, then, that these so-called wizards of Hermes have taken a second bite of the Forbidden Fruit. They have learned knowledge which has caused them to further turn their backs on God. Their magical arts have placed them outside His Grace and no longer will the sacraments of the Church be enough to provide them Salvation! They are Lost, and I daresay, easy prey for the Dark One. It is well known that their magical arts cannot influence the Holy Grace of God, that within His Church they cannot hold sway. Truly, only through Satan's auspices may they even utilize their art in a Holy place. To some, the very touch of their feet on consecrated ground is painful. Thus I say let them renounce their art and pray earnestly to God that they might receive his blessing and be welcomed back into His Fold. Let them learn the lesson taught to us by the story of St. Nerius, who was martyred by the kind he forsook! Only by the Will of the Most High will they enter the Kingdom of Heaven!*

*But lo, the dangers of wizardry are not posed to the Hermetic sinners alone. Those who consort with wizards should have a care for their immortal souls as well. Yes, those who dwell with wizards may be exposed to fell Knowledge, and thus turn their backs on God. The same fate will await them all! Already, some of the sinners' companions have become infected with supernatural powers, clearly gifts from the Inferno, and these unfortunate souls have been lost. Our clergy who find themselves on pilgrimage, and passing the vicinity of one of the wizards' so-called covenants, should endeavor to tarry nearby so that those who dwell within and who are not lost should hear Mass and be shriven of their sins.*

*So, we as God's Children should pity the souls of wizards and their allies, and revile them should they turn to the Lord of Lies for their power. And, if they should make a mockery of the sacraments, partaking in Communion without being shriven, let them be Damned for their mortal sin. The Dark One will most certainly seek to use this Hermetic Order as a tool to destroy the Church. We shall then watch this Order and be careful in dealings with it, as a farmer might treat a snake he finds in his garden. And, should the snake rise up to strike, we will smite it.*

*— Bishop Anthony Aurelius, the minutes of a sub-council meeting at the Council of Avignon.*

*I believe that, rather from some extraordinary supernatural source, the Church receives its peculiar aura and powers from its followers' extreme belief in their God. Once Hermetic Magic pierces the Lunar Sphere, we will be better able to understand how their belief fuels the power of the Divine aura. It is well known that for a Divine aura to arise, the power of faith must be inherent to that spot. In the mundane world, the Divine aura arises from a body of worshippers, led by an ordained priest consecrated by the sacrament, worshipping in a church built on consecrated ground. Perhaps the innate power of the common folk's belief, combined with the focusing abilities of the priest, helps to propagate the Divine aura. However, since the Peripheral Code virtually forbids research on the subject, we will most certainly never discover the truth. I daresay it is possible all the various realms are, in one manner or another, simply extensions of our belief — however disturbing the thought might be to our brethren in House Bonisagus.*

*True Faith is another phenomenon I have had the pleasure (and, at times, displeasure) to encounter. True Faith in this age is highly Christian in nature, although records exist of ancient Magi running afoul of priests and priestesses of the Old Gods who shared the same characteristics. True Faith is a power that magic cannot stand against. Once again, we are nearly forbidden from researching such matters, but my theory is that True Faith arises from the powers of belief in a deity, who protects one with some sort of meta-confidence which defies description. True Faith is elusive and extremely hard to codify. It is not normally possessed by clergy (it is clear that the Church does not provide fertile ground for the blossoming of True Faith amongst its clergy), but by hermits, wise women, monks and nuns in far-off cloisters, and by other holy people, most of them outside the hierarchy of the Church. Their faith brings them protection from Hermetic magic and the Divine seems to flow through them in the form of what they call Miracles. Sainted people are said to possess this power, and this perhaps is why certain nonextraordinary persons can call forth miracles in the name of Saints.*

*— excerpt from the diary of Garius, Arch-Mage of House Criamon.*

## Miracles

Miracles are everyday events in the lives of Saints, but to everyone else they are incredibly rare happenings. Miracles are strictly the will of the Divine made manifest in the world. It is impossible to bargain with the Divine for a Miracle — either the Divine sends one or doesn't, and there's very little you can do to convince the Divine one way or another. The occurrence of a Miracle is based on several considerations. If you are very pious, perhaps one with True Faith (although Miracles are sometimes granted to someone in order to convert that individual); if you are in accordance with and aiding the cause of the Divine; if you pray earnestly and selflessly for aid; and if it seems right in the context of the story, then a Miracle may occur.

Generally the Divine has one of three responses to a request for aid. The first is that no Miracle is granted — "Sorry, you're on your own." This usually happens when the aspirant (the person praying for the Miracle) is not sincere, or has caused the trouble for which she is asking help. Sometimes help is denied to test the aspirant's faith.

The second response is that a Miracle is granted but in a subtle or unobtrusive way — *"As I was settling down to my evening prayers I felt the compulsion to go out riding on patrol this evening… good thing, too, or those griffins would have eaten you all."*

The third response is that a Miracle is granted in a grandiose way — *"The clouds part and a flight of angels descends from Heaven to buoy you up out of danger's way!"*

Miracles come from a power above the earth, so no force on earth or from Hell can stop them. There is no Magic Resistance roll against Miracles. And, though a Miracle may not occur because its request is exploitative or self-fulfilling, it may still receive a response. A demon who hears the petition might show up to grant the desire as part of "a deal" (see Botches, under the Miracle rules, below).

Refer to the *Miracles Chart* for help in determining when to implement miraculous events.

Divine creatures are very rare, but often have many beneficial and protective aspects that make them highly sought-after either for help or blessing. Woe to him who pursues a Divine beast out of malice or intent to harm. The unearthly beauty of Divine beasts is often matched by their tremendous ferocity when confronted by enemies of the Divine.

## Alsatia, *Unicornis Dominus*, a Divine Unicorn

**Divine Might**: 65

**Vital Statistics**: Size +1, Cunning +3, Perception +3, Strength +2, Stamina +3, Presence +4, Communication +1, Quickness +4, Dexterity +3

**Passions**: Honor (among Unicorns) +7, Vengeance (those who harm women) +8

**Combat Scores**:

Horn: First Strike +12, Attack +16, Damage +10

Fatigue +7, Defense +12(18), Soak +10(16)

Body Levels: OK, OK, -1, -3, -5, Incapacitated (but see below)

**Abilities**: Tracking (Evil) 3, Sense Holiness/Unholiness (intruders to her forest) 5, Sense Magic 3 (Magical Auras), Chirurgy 5 (maidens)

# Miracles Chart

## How to use this chart:

First, determine the probability that a Miracle of any kind will be granted by adding up the Miracle Ease Factor modifiers (discussed below). Then make a Miracle roll, altered by any modifier from the second half of the chart that applies.

If the Miracle roll exceeds the Ease Factor of the request, the Miracle is granted, and the Storyguide must decide whether the Miracle is of the subtle or grandiose sort. The type is determined based on the Storyguide's needs in the story. If it occurs at the climax of a dramatic tale, a grandiose Miracle of Divine intervention is appropriate. However, if a Miracle is granted for mundane purposes, like the painless passage of a soul from a dying body, a subtle Miracle may be assumed. Ultimately, the type of Miracle granted is based on the Storyguide's needs in the story. Keep in mind that long gone are the days when a request results in the parting of a sea or the scribing of words on a mountainside.

If the Miracle roll does not exceed the Ease Factor of the request, the request goes unanswered. A Botch signifies that a demon is alerted to your needs and may appear to tempt you.

## Miracle Ease Factor modifiers

**Base Ease Factor:** 20

| | |
|---|---:|
| Previous unfulfilled prayer in this area in the past month: | -2 |
| Previous unfulfilled prayer in this area in the past year: | -1 |
| Miracle granted in the area in the past year: | +3 |
| Miracle granted in the area in the past month: | +5 |
| Divine Aura 10: | -5 |
| Divine Aura 6 to 9: | -1 |
| Divine Aura 5 or lower: | 0 |
| Infernal Aura 5 or lower: | +1 |
| Infernal Aura 6 or higher: | +5 |
| High Holy Day (Easter, Christmas): | -2 |
| Saint's Day: | -1 |

## Miracle Roll modifiers (modifiers to the stress roll)

**-20:** supplicant has Infernal or Faerie ties (e.g., Virtues and Flaws like Tainted with Evil, Diabolic Upbringing, Faerie Upbringing, Faerie Blood)

**-10:** supplicant is non-Christian (e.g., Magus, pagan, infidel)

**-5:** supplicant has a sinful Passion (e.g., Lust, Hatred, Vengeance, Pride) or Personality Trait (e.g., Violent, Bitter, Selfish)

**-1:** supplicant is unshriven

**+1:** supplicant has been shriven and received communion in the past hour

**+0:** supplicant has been shriven and received communion in the past month

**+1** per week the supplicant spends in prayerful mediation, doing nothing else (including eating, but not including drinking water and trips to the privy)

**+1:** supplicant is praying within the confines of a shrine to a saint affiliated with the request (e.g., St. Jude for lost causes)

**+2:** supplicant has a totally selfless (and maybe self-sacrificing) request

**+1** per Faith Point the supplicant has

**+1** per point of Meditation Ability the supplicant has

**+3:** innocent believers require justice, repentant believers seek mercy, or helpless believers need strength

**+3:** an entire congregation is praying with you (including the priest!)

**+1:** supplicant is on a Holy Quest

**+1** per point of Divine Aura in a saint's relic the supplicant possesses

**+5:** supplicant is under direct attack by the Infernal

**Note:** It is impossible for a prideful or selfish miracle to occur.

## Powers:

*The Graceful Speech, CrMe 20, 1 point per hour* — Enables Alsatia to speak with all beings, regardless of whether she knows their language or not.

*Flame of God's Wrath, PeIg 20, 2 points* — This causes +25 damage to any creature of Infernal origin or alliance that the horn strikes. Curiously, this flame does not harm or endanger faeries.

*Touch of the Divine Horn, CrCo, CrAn, CrAq 45, 10 points* — A single touch of Alsatia's horn purifies spoiled or poisoned people, animals, or food and drink. Additionally, the same touch instantly heals one Body Level of a wounded person or animal, even if Incapacitated.

*The Crusader's Gallop, ReCo 45, 30 points* — Enables Alsatia to gallop through the veil of reality so that she travels at tremendous speed and arrives at her destination unerringly, no matter how far distant, in the twinkling of an eye.

# The Realm of Reason

The setting of **Ars Magica** is a land inhabited by only a meager number of minds and mindsets, a land largely devoid of inspirational and advanced thought. In fact, the folk of Mythic Europe are bound by the limited thinking of tradition and custom, not by the potential freedom offered by innovation. The ageless Church is the greatest influence upon intellectual activity, imposing its own ideals, dictates and demands on nearly all. Indeed, the common man's life is ruled by mental boundaries imposed by the Church; to contemplate sin and oppose those boundaries is to insure a torturous existence in the Hereafter.

Even the supposedly inspired minds of the Order of Hermes are actually devoid of new and innovative thought; their potential is limited by what has gone in the past, not by what is offered by the future. Many Magi agree, though would never admit, that truly inspirational inventions of magic are long lost in yesteryear. Modern magic, they might whisper, is only a shade of what was once per-

### Description:

Immortal, graceful, and extremely beautiful, Alsatia is one of only a small herd of Divine Unicorns. She travels the world in search of evil, finding it and destroying it wherever she can. Scholars of beasts have determined that the *Unicornis Dominus* is actually a unicorn that has somehow received God's Grace. All Divine Unicorns vigorously defend any woman, maiden or no, and vow to hunt down rapists and molesters with impunity. To the Infernal, the Divine Unicorn appears as a dread beast of vengeance, with a shimmering white flame curling off its horn, and intensely glowing red eyes.

### Story:

A rapist fleeing from the wrath of Alsatia insinuates himself within the Covenant. A Grog patrol is confronted by an enraged Alsatia who can smell the rapist's scent on their bodies. Unless the patrol uses the utmost tact they may find themselves skewered by a flaming horn! If the Grogs negotiate with the creature and offer to bring her to the Covenant, the rapist tries to make a hostage of one of the female covenfolk in order to buy safe passage out. Magi are then forced to decide whether to allow the rapist to leave, in order to catch him and save their friend themselves, or to work with the Unicorn to secure the female's release. Alsatia administers swift justice if she get the chance, even against those who stand in her way.

## True Reason

There are those who completely transcend conventional medieval thought, and even that of their fellow scientific scholars. They look to truth in life and existence beyond any religious or traditional boundary of thought. Not even the Classics are of sufficient revolutionary thought for these minds; these folk look for more absolute and self-evident truths.

These people achieve a state of True Reason. True Reason is a Virtue (p.78) that must be purchased during character creation, or may be achieved by forsaking all previous religious and magical teachings in favor of complete rationality and logic. Such a transition requires that you isolate yourself from society, usually in a university or library of Classical or rational tomes, for one year. After this period you have abandoned your old ways and have 1 Reason Point. More points can be earned by performing great feats of logic. For example, if you discover a scientific explanation for the Plague, and teach people how to preserve themselves from death by means of your science, you gain a Reason Point. If you ever digress from pure logic, deferring to the Divinities or other supernatural powers, you lose Reason Points, maybe all of them.

True Reason is rated in terms of points, like Confidence, but replaces Confidence as True Faith does. True Reason points may be used as Confidence Points are, but bolster your will in terms of how you may explain or understand the phenomena you encounter. For example, you may invest a Reason Point to reroll an attempt to understand a strange language or to acquire a book. They may also be used to get a scene bonus through Passions, if your Passions are related to your pursuit of higher knowledge and understanding, or derive from that pursuit.

True Reason protects you from all manner of supernatural powers, including the Infernal. Any time you are affected by magic, good or bad, make a stress roll (no Botch). If the result is equal to or lower than your Reason Points, the magic has no effect on you; indeed, no magic affects you during the entire encounter.

There is a bad, and even dangerous side to being of True Reason. As you have forsaken the Church, you run the risk of being branded a heretic, or worse, a diabolist. Be careful in how you present yourself to common people, particularly the clergy. Furthermore, you have no social niche in medieval society, and, being ahead of your time, won't have one anywhere until at least the 14th Century. You therefore suffer a penalty equal to your True Reason score in all social interaction rolls (including those involving Magi, though not those involving others attuned to the realm of Reason).

Magi and clergy cannot have True Reason since it precludes magical ability and faith. Characters with faerie backgrounds are also incapable of having True Reason; their spirit is too untamed to allow such structured thought. Grogs are also unlikely to have it, being uneducated and earthy in nature. Thus, Companions are most likely to have True Reason, but those Companions must have an educated background and must have had exposure to the Classics, or Muslim or university teachings.

formed, the old ways having been forgotten or weakened with centuries of dilution. Proof of a fear of innovation thought even lies in the Order's unspoken precepts. Many Magi are aware of magic's slow and methodical demise, and desire to seek out new means of sorcery, but are curtailed by their brethren. The conservative Hermetic mind demands that staid ways remain the same for the sake of order and peace. Devise new magics, they say, and the Order itself shall collapse, for traditional magics will be undone and chaos will be bred again, as in the days before Bonisagus's wisdom. And, thus, the Order of Hermes navigates toward its inevitable death, to disappear into the past, just as all things immutable must.

However, there is in Mythic Europe a spark that fires hope for thought and invention in the future. A few bright new minds are investigating new means by which to look at and understand the world, beyond unthinking ecclesiastical belief and staunch Hermetic restriction. There is dawning an age of reason and rationality where experimentation, induction and deduction are primal. It is an age of thinking that will set the stage for the world to come, and it is a form of thinking that is slowly manifesting itself into the physical world, becoming a realm like that of Magic, Divinity, Faerie and the Infernal.

The realm of Reason derives entirely from new and innovative ways in which to perceive the world. Its followers, pursuers of research and understanding, forge new technologies and sciences that defy the conventions of Mythic Europe and the past. Reason is the very foundation of this way of thought, and Reason challenges

## Areas of Rational Power

| Area | Rational Power |
| --- | --- |
| Library Containing Books of Reason | 1 |
| School of Rational Thought | 2 |
| Library Containing Arabic Tomes, Lab of Rational Experimentation | 3 |
| University, Library Containing Classical Tomes | 4 |

all that rely on belief and hope to survive. Thus, with the coming of Reason, almost all realms are endangered, for if one does not believe in their power, those realms have no bearing on reality. The realm of Reason therefore fits into the medieval paradigm as does no other realm. Those who follow its tenets gain power from it, and power over other realms.

Much of Reason's inspiration comes from rare rediscovered writings of Classical thinkers, such as Aristotle. They bring back previously lost, enlightened forms of thought that make rationality possible. Even rediscovered Classical traditions provide man insight into logic. The traditions of Roman Law, for example, set down new means of perceiving truth. Through these new perceptions and their rationality, laws can be imposed upon life as a whole, thereby imposing the laws of reason on the way the world functions; a rational realm is created. This insight into rationality is the manner of thought that will bring about the Renaissance in centuries to come. For now, though, the movement and its realm is small and isolated, for it is only the Thirteenth Century.

# RATIONAL AREAS

Areas with a Rational Aura arise at sites of rational thought. With the rise of cities and universities, and their wealth of eager minds freed of oppressive rural living, Rational Auras are usually located in urban locales. Indeed, areas of powerful Rational Aura (relatively speaking given the realm's infancy) are concentrated at universities and libraries where the truths of reality are doggedly pursued. This means fact and reason prevail where induction and deduction are most intense and most vaunted. Such places include the University of Pavia, and numerous schools in cities like Rome, Ravenna, Orléans and Bologna.

Auras of Rationality also arise in the workplaces of those who pursue rational philosophy. Such places become "pockets" of logic and reason, thus defying the influence of the other realms. For an indication of the areas of Reason and their potence, see the *Areas of Rational Power Chart*.

The power Reason holds over other realms, though limited now, has the potential to be staggering. As logic disputes the possibility of magic and the existence of faeries, and redefines former conventions of the Divine, it overcomes their power. Thus, the use of magic, faerie power and miracles is severely curtailed in areas of rational power. It's important to note, though, that many rational thinkers still believe in the Divine, but perceive it in different ways — scientific ways — from the Church. That difference in perspective diminishes Divine actions in an Aura of Reason, but not as severely as it can Faerie and Magical actions.

The influence that Reason can have over other realms is so revolutionary that Reason may intrude upon, and exist within, other realms and their areas of power. For example, a city may have a strong religious following, and therefore a strong Divine Aura. However, in various places of advanced thought and learning, such as universities and experimental laboratories, a rational Aura may persist, untainted by the realm that surrounds it. (It should be noted, though, that Hermetic laboratories and libraries do not have Auras of Reason. They are centers of magi*c*al, experimental thought, whereas Auras of Reason arise from *mundane*, experimental thought.)

Even when other supernatural powers have their effect in the Rational realm, those effects may be explained by the followers of Reason by some scientific means, often in a way others cannot begin to comprehend. Indeed, even when beyond their own realms, those who pursue Reason often seek to explain Magical, Faerie, Divine or Infernal spectacles in terms of their own understanding. They announce broad scientific methods that, to their minds, account for what would otherwise seem unaccountable; the reasonable mind is virtually unshakeable, even if one of its number must ponder an event for years in an effort to understand it. However, the modest among the rea-

soned may admit a misunderstanding of strange events simply by acknowledging a lack of knowledge in related scientific fact. That is to say, they allow scientific ignorance to account for weird phenomena.

As reasonable folk may travel to places of other realms, and not be daunted in their rational thought, their actions also suffer no penalties in those realms. As rational folk have no direct effect upon the world, as Magi do with their spells, faeries do with their powers, and the Divine do with their miracles, rational folk behave normally in other realms. Of course, spells, powers and miracles may still affect them normally, but, as previously discussed, they rationalize those effects in logical terms. As reasoned minds suffer no ill effects in other realms, behaving essentially as mundane folk, the realm of Reason is not listed as a "Power Affected" on the *Realm Interaction Chart* (p.308).

The only supernatural power to largely escape the dampening influence of the Rational realm is the Infernal power. The demons of Hell almost always work their ways by deceit and confusion. Thus, their influence is often invisible to the mortal eye, and may easily be overlooked. By keeping their practices secretive, demons retain power in Rational Auras because the logical mind is not provoked into studying or experimenting on Infernal power. Thus, if those of any realm are vulnerable to the Infernal, it is those of the realm of Reason — they don't know they are being corrupted. When a logical person finally perishes to the sin and evil of corruption, it's assumed by his peers that the person has simply strayed from logic, and may become the object of experimentation by those peers.

If a rational Aura may be jeopardized in any other way, it is through the loss of rational thinkers, or the change of the rational mind. The Aura only manifests itself as long as reason prevails. If its followers permanently leave the area, or turn their minds to other subjects, the Aura collapses. The only way an Aura of Rationality may escape this "death" is if the tomes and instruments of logical learning, stored at that place, remain there to embody Reason and all it represents.

# The Mundane Realm

The Mundane realm is the embodiment of all that is normal and mortal. It consists of ordinary people and places which bear no Magical, Faerie, Divine, Infernal or Rational powers or inclinations. Generally speaking,

areas not occupied by another realm are considered Mundane. The Mundane realm has no Aura or rating. In fact, it is the absence of an Aura, so powers used there function without hindrance.

It's important to understand that there's a difference between what's called mundane man and the Mundane realm. Mundane man is the common man of Mythic Europe, including ordinary peasants, townsfolk, and nobility. Clergy are not considered mundane man for they are aligned with the Dominion, nor are Magi and covenfolk (the allies of Magi) considered mundane man for they are aligned with the Magical realm. Superficially, mundane man would appear to belong to the Mundane realm, being non-supernatural. However, mundane man is often a believer in the Church, and exists in a Divine realm, like a city or village. Only common people who dwell outside Divine realms, and who lack faith, are truly part of the Mundane realm.

As other realms have beasts that are aligned to them (except the realm of Reason, for how can a beast think with rationality?), the Mundane does as well. Unlike the beasts of other realms, though, those of the Mundane are ordinary and everyday. However, they are ordinary and everyday by medieval standards, not modern standards, making wild beasts deadly and others strange to our eyes.

## Cat

**Vital Statistics:** Size -3, Cunning +1, Perception +5, Strength -3, Stamina 0, Presence n/a, Communication n/a, Dexterity +3, Quickness +3

**Personality Traits:** Curious +4

**Combat Scores:**

Bite and Claws: First Strike +5, Attack +5, Damage -3

Fatigue 0, Defense +7(13), Soak -2(4)

Body Levels: OK, -3, Incapacitated

**Abilities:** Stealth (hunting) 6, Perfect Balance (narrow perches) 3

## Dog

**Vital Statistics:** Size -2, Cunning 0, Perception +4, Strength 0, Stamina +1, Presence n/a, Communication n/a, Dexterity 0, Quickness 0

**Personality Traits:** Loyal +6

**Combat Scores:**

Bite: First Strike +3, Attack +3, Damage +3

Fatigue +1, Defense +3(9), Soak -1(5)

Body Levels: OK, -1, -5, Incapacitated

### Mule

**Vital Statistics:** Size +2, Cunning -4, Perception -1, Strength +4, Stamina +9, Presence n/a, Communication n/a, Dexterity -4, Quickness -4

**Personality Traits:** Stubborn +6

**Combat Scores:**

Kick: First Strike +6, Attack +5, Damage +8

Fatigue +9, Defense 0(6), Soak +12(18)

Body Levels: OK, 0/0, -1/-1, -3, -5, Incapacitated

### Horse

**Vital Statistics:** Size +2, Cunning -2, Perception 0, Strength +3, Stamina +4, Presence n/a, Communication n/a, Dexterity 0, Quickness 0

**Personality Traits:** Spirited +3

**Combat Scores:**

Hooves: First Strike +4, Attack +4, Damage +7

Fatigue +4, Defense 0(6), Soak +7(13)

Body Levels: OK, 0/0, -1/-1, -3, -5, Incapacitated

### Bird of Prey

**Vital Statistics:** Size -3, Cunning -2, Perception +8, Strength -2, Stamina 0, Presence n/a, Communication n/a, Dexterity +2, Quickness +3

**Personality Traits:** Fierce +5

**Combat Scores:**

Talons: First Strike +7, Attack +6, Damage +4

Fatigue 0, Defense -1(5), Soak +9(15)

Body Levels: OK, -3, Incapacitated

### Wolf

**Vital Statistics:** Size -1, Cunning +3, Perception +4, Strength +1, Stamina +4, Presence n/a, Communication n/a, Dexterity +1, Quickness 0

**Personality Traits:** Brave +5, Cowardly (when spotted) +4

**Combat Scores:**

Bite: First Strike +3, Attack +5, Damage +6

Tackle: First Strike +3, Attack +4, Damage +5

Fatigue +4, Defense +5(11), Soak +5(11)

Body Levels: OK, -1, -3, -5, Incapacitated

### Boar

**Vital Statistics:** Size -1, Cunning -2, Perception -1, Strength +4, Stamina +5, Presence n/a, Communication n/a, Dexterity 0, Quickness 0

**Personality Traits:** Gluttonous +2, Stubborn +3

**Combat Scores:**

Gore: First Strike +4, Attack +8, Damage +18

Fatigue +2, Defense 0(6), Soak +15(21)

Body Levels: OK, 0/0, -1, -3, -5, Incapacitated

### Brown Bear

**Vital Statistics:** Size +2, Cunning +1, Perception +3, Strength +4, Stamina +8, Presence n/a, Communication n/a, Dexterity 0, Quickness 0

**Personality Traits:** Ferocious +3

**Combat Scores:**

Maul: First Strike +6, Attack +12, Damage +16

Tackle: First Strike +6, Attack +6, Damage +14

Fatigue +7, Defense +3(9), Soak +25(31)

Body Levels: Ok, 0/0, -1/-1, -3, -5, Incapacitated

### Great White Stag

**Vital Statistics:** Size +3, Cunning -2, Perception +2, Stamina +8, Presence n/a, Communication n/a, Dexterity +3, Quickness +5

**Personality Traits:** Brave +5

**Combat Scores:**

Antlers: First Strike +8*, Attack +7, Damage +24

Hooves: First Strike +8*, Attack +5, Damage +12

Fatigue +12, Defense 0(6), Soak +16(22)

Body Levels: OK, 0/0, -1/-1, -3/-3, -5, Incapacitated

* Make one roll for both

# Regio and the Realms

Occasionally, within very special supernatural areas, special types of Auras arise. These Auras may exist as part of larger Auras, or may exist as complete supernatural areas in themselves, and may arise within any most type of Aura (Magical, Faerie, Divine or Infernal, but not Reason or Mundane). These special types of Auras are called *regio*. Like normal Auras they have levels of power rated 1 to 10, and are attached to the mundane world. Unlike normal Auras, regio transcend the mundane world, entering into worlds unique to the realm that the Aura is aligned with. (For a complete description of *regio* and the realities into which they enter, see the **Ars Magica** supplement **Faeries**, or the two **Mythic Places** books.)

Regio consist of several levels of Aura, layered one on top of another in order of increasing power. The Aura of lowest power is connected to the mundane world, while higher level Auras are situated on top of it. To picture this phenomenon, imagine the contour lines of a map. The lowest elevations are at the bottom of a hill and highest elevations are at the top. Each contour line from the bottom to the top is representative of a level of Aura within a *regio*; each is a level of reality. Beneath the lowest level is the mundane world itself; imagine that flat land surrounding the hill. And, where the contour lines of a hill become smaller in diameter toward the top of the hill, *regio* levels of higher Aura tend to be spatially smaller than those beneath them.

Regio are also similar to contour lines because the levels of *regio* occupy the same space as contour lines do on a map. In reality, a hill occupies vertical space, but has no vertical dimension on a map. *Regio* levels are like this in that each level is a different supernatural dimension, and all coexist on the same spot on the mundane world. That is, they do not actually stack on another, forming a pyramid. The *regio* diagram demonstrates the spatiality of *regio* pictorially.

There's nothing about *regio* that makes them distinct from other Auras, until one realizes that other levels of reality exist on the same spot. As each higher level of a *regio* is slightly more attuned to a realm (i.e., has a higher Aura strength), each *regio* level looks different from the rest. Lower levels only slightly change in appearance from the mundane world, while higher levels tend to acquire many of the characteristics of their native realms. For instance, at low Aura strength (1-3), an Infernal *regio* level might be slightly warmer in temperature than the lower mundane level. Levels with moderate Aura strength (4-6) might be of higher temperature, might show evidence of burns, and might contain hidden demons. Levels of Infernal *regio* with high Aura strength (7+) might literally be on fire, with demons prancing about.

# Exempli Gratia:

## A Faerie Regio

By way of clarifying what *regio* are, let us look at a supernatural Faerie spring. Using the standard Aura rules, the spring has an Aura of strength 3 to 5, depending on its importance to its locale. Characters can wander about and find this spring if they search long and hard enough. And while faeries might hide the spring with illusions or mislead humans' senses, the spring's actual physical nature does not change; it's still a physical part of the mundane world.

The same spring is physically different when thought of as a regio. The spring now exists on several interconnected but separate levels of differing Aura strength that *occupy the same space*. Each level is physically real by itself, though somewhat different from the rest. The highest level is farthest removed from the mundane world and has the highest Aura. There, the spring could be as the faeries made it: perhaps with a low, engraved marble wall surrounding it, and a fountain located in its middle. A lower *regio* level finds the Aura reduced and the spring less noticeably Faerie in origin, with the engraving faded and the wall looking more like a jumbled pile of rocks. Beneath the lowest level of the *regio* is the mundane world, with no Aura, and the spring is just a plain spring with a few rocks strewn about its edges.

EXAMPLE REGIO
MUNDANE LEVEL
REGIO LEVEL 3
THE BANDITS' TRAIL
REGIO LEVEL 5
TO KÖLN
SPRING
ROCKY SLOPE
TO WEISSWALD
STONE BRIDGE
SIGN POST

# ENTERING AND LEAVING *REGIO*

Traveling in the mundane world, people can enter *regio* just as they can enter Auras of any realm. You physically cross the boundary of the lowest *regio* level, and if you penetrate the magical wards of the *regio*, you disappear from the physical world, entering the supernatural world. As you continue to travel and reach the boundary (or "contour line") of the next level, you may cross it as well, moving deeper into a supernatural realm. To gain entry to a specific *regio* level, one must pass through all levels lower than it. If supernatural forces confound your efforts to find or cross the boundary to the next level, you can be stranded in the level you currently occupy. That level may be the mundane world itself if you fail to penetrate the first level of the *regio*. If you are left in the mundane world, as in the example insert for example, you never find the crumbled faerie wall (located on the lowest supernatural level). Rather, you simply find the mundane spring, and may never be aware of the faeries in other realities around you.

The base chance to enter any *regio* level is two times the Aura score of the level being entered, plus 6. For example, you need an 8+ to enter a *regio* level of Aura 1 (2 x 1 + 6), and a 26+ to enter a level of Aura 10 (2 x 10 + 6).

Leaving *regio* is based on the same roll, but is made using the Aura rating of the level you are trying to leave. For each failed attempt, the Ease Factor of the next attempt goes up by one point. If you fail an attempt to leave, you become lost and wander around the *regio* level.

These Ease Factors are rolled against on a stress die. If you Botch entry into a level, you may never cross its boundary. If you Botch exiting a level, you may never leave that level. The Storyguide may be more lenient, imposing a time limit during which you may not enter or leave, after which you may eventually try again.

Several modifiers may apply to entry and exit rolls, based on the person entering a *regio* level, the realm of the *regio*, and the circumstances of entry. For example, if you have the Faerie Blood Virtue, are entering a Faerie *regio*, and are doing so on Midsummer's Eve, the Storyguide may impose bonuses to your roll, making entry of *regio* levels easier. Alternatively, if you have a Diabolic Upbringing and are trying to enter a level of a Divine *regio*, the Storyguide may impose a penalty to your rolls.

You can enter and leave a *regio* level, or several levels, accidentally or intentionally. If passing through accidentally, you may not notice you've moved into a new reality until physical features around you change dramatically, or you make a Perception + Area Lore (or Faerie Lore, Church Lore, Occult Lore, Hermes Lore, Sense Holiness or Unholiness, or whatever is most applicable) roll of 10+. The Aura rating of the *regio* level is added to this roll, making perception easier. This is also a stress roll. If Botched, you may never realize you're in a different reality.

# MAGIC IN *REGIO*

Supernatural powers or spells used in a *regio* level suffer effects as determined by the *Realm Interaction Chart* (p.308). The Aura of the level occupied is the score used to modify spell and other supernatural rolls.

Use of *vis* in *regio*, of a realm other than the one to which you are aligned, is particularly dangerous. For each pawn of *vis* used, make twice the normal number of Botch rolls. Botches can attract *regio* inhabitants to the spell caster, or can trap you for some time in the *regio* level. And, yes, there are inhabitants of *regio*, just as there are inhabitants of other areas of supernatural Aura. They tend to reside on one *regio* level at a time, though they can cross level boundaries freely. The higher you travel in the *regio*, the stranger, and more supernaturally aligned, regio inhabitants become.

---

# SPECIAL CREATURE TRAITS

Beasts from the different realms tend to have powers bestowed upon them by their realms. These powers require special rules and new terms to account for them in game terms.

### Might Scores

Supernatural creatures have Supernatural Might scores that represent their overall mystical power. The overall Might score remains constant, or changes only as the creature matures. It can only be lowered temporarily, as a creature uses its powers (see below). Might score is used for several purposes:

1) Measure of Power — The Might score gives you a general idea of how powerful a creature is.

2) Regulate Mystic Powers — Some creatures have powers that drain their mystical energy, limiting how often they can use their powers. Such a creature has a number of points equal to its Might, and expends these points by using its powers. If a creature does not have enough points left to pay for a power's use, it can't use that power. All points return within 24 hours.

3) Magic Resistance and Penetration — Except under special circumstances, a creature gets its Might score as a bonus on its Magic Resistance and magic Penetration rolls. If points are being spent on powers, a creature's full Might score is still used for Magic Resistance and Penetration, no matter how many points have been spent on powers.

4) **Determine Effectiveness of Spells** — Many General Level spells only work if their Level is equal to or greater than the Might score of the creature to be affected. A weakened ghost, therefore, is easier to control than one at full Might.

5) **Indicate Source of Power** — Might and points are referred to by their type, depending on the realm from which the creature originates. Thus, there is Faerie Might and Faerie points, and Infernal Might and Infernal points. Supernatural creatures receive bonuses and penalties on their power or magic-related rolls, depending on the type of area they are in (i.e., in an area of Faerie or Infernal Aura). For the ratings of these bonuses and penalties, see the *Realm Interaction Chart*, p. 308.

### Special Powers

These are some suggestions for special powers that you can give your monstrous creations. Specific powers vary from creature to creature in strength and other details.

For powers that are like spells determine a Technique, Form and Level. Even though the creature does not cast spells like a Magus, a power's Technique and Form determine what Arts a Magus can use to resist or counter the power.

#### Emotions

**Fear** — The creature instills fear in others, either through its horrible visage or through a spell-like power. **Emotion Aura** — Others share the emotion felt by the creature, such as satyrs that cause those around them to feel wild. **Entrancement** —binding or controlling people by staring into their eyes.

#### Special Attacks

**Constriction** — squeezing people to death, causing damage that increases from Round to Round. **Fiery Breath**, **Poisonous Bite or Breath** — can cause death, paralysis, insanity or loss of will. **Spiked Tails** — and other natural weapons.

#### Defenses

**Immunities** — completely protect the creature from certain types of spells or damage, such as a fire drake's immunity to fire damage. **Resistance** — gives the creature a bonus on Magic Resistance or Soak against certain types of attacks. **Metal Scales** — protect against weapons and possibly fire or other forms of attack.

### Magic Use

**Spells** — specific spells that the creature can cast, as a Magus can. **Spontaneous Spells** — the casting of any spell up to a certain Level, which can vary by Technique and Form, such as "any Ignem spells up to Level 15 and any other spells up to Level 5." Decide whether either form of spellcasting causes Fatigue for the creature.

### Miscellaneous

**Animal Control** — controlling animals, perhaps only of a similar type. **Shapechange** — turning into humans, trees, rocks, beasts. **Special Senses** — for seeing in the dark, or for detecting lies or magic. **Illusions** — the power of changing appearance, and maybe that of surroundings.

### Weaknesses

Weaknesses can be as interesting a part of your creatures as their powers are. Weaknesses also let you throw powerful creatures at the characters without killing them, as long as they can exploit the creature's weakness. Like powers, weaknesses should make sense and arise from a creature's nature. Weaknesses are not simply to be tacked on.

Finding out what weaknesses a creature has can be part of a story, an important part if the monster is formidable.

Weaknesses include such things as the vampire's fear of garlic, the unicorn's compulsion to lay its head in a virgin's lap, the profound stupidity of an ogre, or the missing scale in a dragon's armor.

### Raw Vis in Creatures

Many supernatural beasts have *vis* in their bodies, *vis* that makes them valuable to Magi. Generally, the more magical and powerful a creature is, the more *vis* it has. This *vis* is always related to a variety of Art; use your imagination. Many beasts simply have Animál *vis*, but poisonous ones might have Perdo *vis*, shapechangers might have Muto *vis*, and creatures related to earth might have Terram *vis*. The kind of *vis* inherent to a creature is not always obvious, however, and not always immediately logical.

# chapter eleven

his Chapter is designed to help you in the creation and maintenance of a Saga, a series of related stories based on the same Covenant and undoubtedly the same characters. Organizing a Saga may initially seem like an enormous task, and it indeed involves considerable work and imagination, but given time, experience, and use of some of the advice presented here, you should have little trouble creating a Saga filled with exciting locales, dastardly villains, and demonic corruption — an **Ars Magica** Saga.

**Ars Magica** is, more than anything else, a game oriented towards the Saga. It is most fulfilling when played over long periods of time, allowing tales of epic scope to come to life. The most intense roleplaying, most spectacular storytelling effects, and deepest emotional attachments occur only after a Saga is evolving. A Saga should go through stages just as Covenants go through Seasons, and once you reach Autumn you may realize just what storytelling is all about.

Good luck in your venture.

## Saga and Drama

The many adventures that players and Storyguides alike participate in are collectively called Sagas. Saga is our word for the ongoing, continually evolving story of the Covenant and its residents, the chronicle of the passage of time and the significant events in the life of the Covenant. In other games the word used is "campaign," but we think Saga is a more evocative and accurate name.

When you say the word Saga many things come to mind. Some ancient Sagas detail the rise and fall of powerful civilizations, while others focus on the emergence of new beliefs and practices that forever change the world as we know it. In **Ars Magica** a Saga portrays the life of the Covenant, from its Spring to Winter Season, and possibly rebirth into a new Spring. Thus, the chief elements that compose a Saga are drama, for if nothing else roleplaying is dramatic.

All Sagas have something in common: there is always something vitally important at stake. Having something worth fighting for is the inspiration for all drama. In a true

Saga, there must be something the characters pursue or defend, something that gives them and their Covenant identity. The item at stake can be something as grandiose as the pursuit of absolute knowledge — the meaning of life. Or, the Covenant may be devoted to using its magical powers to preserve a mysterious, enchanted forest. Indeed, the importance of the item at stake is purely subjective, but there must be enough at risk involved to insure the world suffers or is permanently marked by the item's preservation or loss. The drama must be powerful enough that the players care about what is going on. The more they care, the more drama there is.

# PASSAGE OF TIME

In a Saga, the passage of time first has its effects on the characters, for they are the foci of your stories. It's only through the dimension of time that we can come to see a story in all its glory, and come to understand the characters that inhabit it. Change must occur not only to the Covenant, but to the characters.

The buck-toothed, freckled-faced tomboy, once spurned by all the young boys and incapable of igniting the merest magical spark, matures into an exquisite young woman of immense magical power. The once worrisome, puny page is now the majestic knight in shining armor.

The once timid child-warrior becomes the stalwart guardian of the Covenant.

Time in a Saga not only has its effect on the characters, but on their world and everyone in it. With time's passage, people and places change and great events occur which forever mark the world. For example, a famine may sweep the land, depopulating cities and leaving plague in its wake.

There are other people who live in the world outside the Covenant, and some of them have a tremendous impact on the ongoing Saga. Although the players' characters are without a doubt the main characters of your Saga, it is important to realize that, contrary to popular belief, the world does not revolve solely around their actions. Time has its influence everywhere, and changes people and places, even when the characters are not there to witness that change.

Time therefore determines the rate at which the world, the characters and the Covenant change, just as time determines the rate at which characters and Covenant grow, mature, age and die.

# CHARACTER DEVELOPMENT

Nothing is more important to roleplaying than character development. Most players intuitively understand this, but are sometimes incapable of putting a finger on its significance. It's easy to maintain a low intensity of roleplaying if you don't pursue character development. If you invest little imagination in your character, that character never amounts to anything more than a bunch of numbers. If your character isn't an inspiration, how can your roleplaying be?

However, if you slowly develop your character over the course of the Saga, your alter ego becomes alive with personality and vigor, as does your roleplaying. As all the players add more and more complexity to their characters, the Saga becomes alive with drama and pathos.

Don't worry about accounting for every aspect of a character's identity from the very start; rely on the events of the Saga to flesh out the bare bones. Much of a personality manifests itself during the story as new and unanticipated threats or challenges arise. Thus, fascinating characters often emerge from a Saga totally different from they way they were upon entry. After all, we aren't the same people throughout our lives, so why should our characters be? If you stick too strongly with your character's initial concept, you may never discover the most interesting aspects of that unique persona.

It's easy to say that character development is fundamental to an enjoyable Saga, but how do you perform that development? When creating your character you should decide on some goals to pursue, passions to reveal, and dreams to fulfill. Also ask some basic questions about character identity: Why do you crave to travel to the far reaches of Europe? Why do you aspire to become the best swordsman in the kingdom? Why does the approval of a certain young man mean so much to you? These questions help develop a strong sense of who your character is and where she is going. Answering these questions contributes to the development of the Saga; when you grow, the Saga matures and grows with your contribution. In fact, the Saga may progress in a completely unanticipated direction, as your character may. The surprise of such plot reverses is part of the fun of storytelling. Thus, character development comes naturally, as you decide how your character responds to the world.

# Creating a Saga

A typical Saga lasts for many years (real time) and for scores of game sessions. It is possible for a single Saga to span hundreds of years (game time). Therefore, it is incumbent upon you, the Storyguide, to begin on the right foot, to start with the seeds of a Saga.

You need to begin designing the Saga at the same time the Troupe creates characters. Everyone should throw in their ideas of where to put the Saga, and what to base it on. The Troupe needs to come to some sort of consensus on what the Saga should be like. If no one can agree you need to select someone as the "Supervision Storyguide," and put that person in charge of creating the Saga.

You have a number of decisions to make as you design your Saga. First, you need to decide on a setting. If you are using Mythic Europe, what region are you in or near? You also need to determine the challenges the characters face, and the dangers they must deal with. The primary antagonists of the Covenant need to be delineated.

There are six elements of a Saga which you should concentrate on, in order to create an epic worthy of you. These elements are:

- Name
- Setting
- Supporting Cast
- Antagonists
- Atmosphere
- Motif

And remember, one of the most important aspects of creating a Saga is detailed in the Covenants Chapter, where Covenant creation is explained. After all, the Covenant is the heart of your Saga. Thus, when we discuss Saga creation we refer to the elements of the Saga not described under Covenant creation, elements which need to be dealt with in some fashion.

## Name

Sometime before the Saga begins you need to name it. The name can be fairly important, for it sets the tone of everything else that follows. Most Sagas are named after their Covenants, as is the Mistridge Saga. The name should be suggestive of the theme and potential of the Saga, without giving away any of its secrets.

## Setting

In order to create a Saga worthy of your talents, you need a world that the players can believe in. With each story you run, define the world a little more. Add details of geography, custom, and language. Evoke the world in everything you do. Create an aura about it that makes the players hold their breath when they hear its name. Build it brick by brick, at whatever pace you choose. Indeed, your world is your own, and it increasingly acquires its own unique identity the more you play. No matter how closely or loosely you base your world on historical Europe, your world is ultimately a fantasy world, a product of imagination, a product of *your* imagination. Make of it what you will; it is yours to create.

As a beginning setting you should choose some specific locale in Mythic Europe (or in your own fantasy world). Northern Spain or southern France are good Mythic European choices. The Christians there have beaten back the Moors, Barcelona is growing, troubadours are inventing the modern ideals of love, heresy is widespread, and the forbidding Pyrenees provide refuge for those beasts and wizards who want to distance themselves from civilization. This is the setting of the Mistridge Saga, and is the place in which many **Ars Magica** supplements are set (though you can easily adapt them to any setting). For a wealth of information on this setting, see the **Mistridge** sourcebook for **Ars Magica**.

As for time, the "official" starting date for **Ars Magica** Sagas is A.D.1197. You can set your stories at other times, but, once again, upcoming supplements are set at this date.

## The Supporting Cast

Creating the many people who inhabit your world is one of the most enjoyable jobs a Storyguide has. Your characters should be just as alive as those of the players, and to have them fall short of this criterion cheats everyone of a good story. The more detailed your characters are the more realistically you are able to play them. By no means are we suggesting that you create a separate character sheet for every person in Mythic Europe. Rather, if there's a person that the players' characters meet on a regular basis it's a good idea to write that individual up.

This is especially true of the inhabitants of the Covenant. The use of generic stats is a good idea for the masses. Use those generic stats as a building block for returning characters.

Just as returning figures should be given a few unique stats, figures that are intrinsic to your Saga should be as detailed as the players' characters. These figures include patrons, mentors, and allied wizards. Not only does fully developing an important figure give you a better idea of how the character functions, it eliminates inconsistencies in how you portray the figure. Players often remember things about your characters that you only mention in passing, and as a result forget. If significant figures are fully developed, you retain a record of their natures, and can even drop hints about what they're like.

# Antagonists

No good Saga is complete without the constant intervention of those who visit harm upon the characters. Were it not for the man in black there would be no story to tell. In every classic tale there are protagonists and antagonists. Were it not for the constant threat of evil, good would be a blur, and would inspire only dull stories. Good and evil cannot exist without the each other. Armed with this knowledge one can be sure that as long as there are forces of benevolence, there are also forces of malevolence.

Simply because one is the antagonist does not mean one is unpopular. It's not difficult to recall at least one villain who is as, or more, entertaining than the hero. The villain is often liked because he caters to his base desires — hunger, hatred, and havoc — unlike the hero, who aspires to be more righteous. The villain is often closer to the root of humanity than we care to admit, and we therefore admire his honesty. Sometimes, because he is so vile and audacious, a villain may even steal the show. Those who serve as adversaries to characters should be works of art. Create villains your players love to hate.

Persistence should always be one of the villain's major attributes. Lets face it, historically speaking, the villain doesn't boast the best track record for success. This is partially due to the fact that he possesses a flaw in his otherwise impenetrable defense. It comes as no surprise, really. Everyone has a flaw or two, but, as a rule, the villain has a flaw on a monumental scale. Such a flaw is what causes the villain's downfall. It this good? Of course it is. Heroes tend to have significant flaws as well, making villains and heroes suitable opponents, and satisfying foils for each other's nature.

As the hero and villain become familiar with one another their flaws become more and more apparent, particularly to each other. These flaws are then used against one another to bring about a prescribed response.

Typically, when players become this familiar with a villain, the villain may be dubbed an "Arch-Villain." Unlike the typical villain, the Arch-Villain seems to have nine lives. Surviving by the hair of his proverbial chinny chin-chin, he is always around to inflict harm upon the characters. And why shouldn't he survive? Don't the characters — heroes — make desperate escapes and miraculous rescues? Unlike other villains, you should routinely assign the Arch-Villain Experience Points (he is just as capable of self-improvement as the characters). And, all-important in Arch-Villain creation is the sense of purpose. Why does the villain feel compelled to do evil? This consideration is important. Vile goals are what bring about villain-hero confrontations.

## Villains' Flaws

Through no fault of her own, the heroine has been bested by the villain. Peering up the villain's blood-soaked runesword, the heroine realizes she is about to die. Raising the tainted weapon for the final blow, the villain stays his hand, suddenly inspired. Rather than kill his opponent in one blow — a far too painless fate — the villain elects to throw the heroine into his dungeon, to be publicly executed the next day. Miraculously, the heroine finds a sliding plate in her cell, and makes good her escape, only to face the villain again in another story. Countless villains fall prey to this flaw in judgement. It is just one that they can have. Here are some more:

• **Megalomania:** The villain is so full of herself that she believes it impossible for anyone to be more than a minor threat. Therefore, everyone is insignificant. This belief is so overpowering that she often deals with her problems head on, expecting victory. Sometimes this approach is successful. Most of the time, however, the villain meets someone who is more than her match. Due to her arrogance, the villain never acknowledges the hero's equality, which can lead to her final destruction.

• **Psychosis:** The villain is not in complete control of his mental faculties in any way, shape or form. Driven by insanity to commit acts of evil, this villain is often a tragic product of extreme misfortune. Truly, he is not fully aware of the harm he inflicts. This villain is often extremely intelligent and proves to be a worthy opponent. One obvious drawback is if the hero discovers the source of the villain's derangement. That knowledge can be used against the villain.

• **Incompetent Help:** Good help is always hard to find. The villain has to rely on those who submit to her inhuman leadership. As a result the villain recruits those who collectively share the intelligence of well water. The heroes often outsmart these toadies and escape unscathed. The villain spends half her time punishing his own troops, consequently getting little done.

• **Overwhelming Weakness:** The most fearsome of all villains have equally great weaknesses. It's also common for the villain to be totally oblivious to his weakness. Those who are aware of their weakness are extremely paranoid. The exploitation of this weakness could mean either death or great loss for the villain. Weaknesses can range from a missing scale amidst an otherwise impenetrable hide, to a possessive infatuation with a beautiful princess. Heroes must be ever-vigilant for this type of villain, because this villain is the deadliest of all.

The point is that villains are not true villains without inherent flaws. No one is absolutely perfect. Thus, to create a villain with no flaws is not only unfair, it's not true to humanity. You don't have to have a gigantic neon sign that points out the villain's weakness. Just the mere presence of it is enough.

## Atmosphere

Paramount to creating your Saga is overall atmosphere. Atmosphere is the air of your Saga, one that players should be able to describe with simple buzzwords. Examples of such words include "gloomy", "poetic", "metaphorical", and "chaotic." Buzzwords befitting Sagas set in Mythic Europe might include "desperate" and "fateful." Each and every atmosphere is viable for roleplay. Of course, some work better than others. Although **Ars Magica** is primarily a dark depiction of medieval life, that's not how your Saga must be played. The following are some examples of different atmospheres. Choose one you think is best suited for your Troupe.

• **Humorous:** Lighthearted fantasy is common to many popular novels.

*Conventions:* Most monsters are capable of speech and are sociable. They are prone to ranting and raving about the trials and tribulations of being evil, especially when about to eat you. Wizards are frequently gibbering idiots, and are often "over the hill." Puns are taken literally, turning such things as "babbling brooks" into rivers that don't shut up.

*Suggestions:* Although funny moments arise in any atmosphere, you have to be careful that this atmosphere doesn't become tedious or boring. Try to vary the humor you use to keep players on their toes. Also remember that players expect everything to come out of your mouth to be funny. It's bad enough you have to control everything else in the world, but now you have to be a comedian too.

• **Sword & Sorcery:** This is an atmosphere of extremely high fantasy with a liberal amount of magic and swordplay.

*Conventions:* The enemy is usually evil as well as legion. Heroes, as well as villains, are extremists. Wizards are extremely powerful, and varied in that power. Epic battles are everpresent and determine much in the ongoing Saga. Many different races litter the world and often do not get along with one another. The world picture ranges from near-perfection to absolute chaos.

*Suggestions:* A very nice setting for a Saga. There's plenty of room for experimentation. Those persons not used to Mythic Europe may find this particular atmosphere attractive.

• **Dark Fantasy:** This atmosphere involves horrific settings, and demonic and angelic forces in direct confrontation.

*Conventions:* Enemies are extremely realistic. Grisly acts are common, and death often visits the unwary. There are some fates that are worse than death in this type of atmosphere. Wizards are usually grim reflections of their environment and are dangerous to say the least. Monsters are often legends in their own environment and are not to be taken lightly. What is good and what is evil is a subject of much debate.

*Suggestions:* An excellent atmosphere for **Ars Magica**. Mythic Europe is not a place for the meek. Play up the characters' surroundings, as well as the vileness of the adversaries they face.

## Motif

A motif is a recurring subject, theme, or idea that comes up again and again in an artistic work, and in some subtle way unites every aspect of that work. For your Saga to truly possess scope and depth it must have a motif. You need to invent some sort of recurring feature to provide continuity and meaning to what you are doing.

Ask yourself what should be the dominating feature of the Saga? What issues are the Covenant most concerned with? What issues galvanize and motivate every story? What is the subject of the Saga and who presents it?

A motif can be anything from an ongoing rivalry with a local monastery, to a solemn dedication to save a faerie glade from eradication. A motif can even be an esoteric theme, such as the gradual extinction of magic, and the Covenant's role in that theme. Sometimes even an object, such as a magical statue, can provide a motif for a Saga.

Whatever unique motif you give the Saga, you need to make sure it always plays a role in the Saga's stories. The Troupe should never forget what the focus of the Saga is. Recurring features go far in adding a mood and sense of significance to your Saga. Invent a motif appropriate and unique to your Troupe and weave that motif into your stories.

# The Saga In Play

Some Sagas cover a wide period of time, spanning from one generation to the next. Others can be as short as a few years. Whatever the time span of your Saga, your first order of business is to bring the players' characters together.

Examine how each of the characters knows the others. Why do they trust one another with their very lives? There should be a very strong bond between members of the group. Let's face it, it would be idiotic to travel with people you don't trust. This is why it makes no sense for a group of adventurers to simply be together. Instead, have the players determine how their characters are acquainted. Although mere Covenant membership is a viable cause for teamwork, encourage more compelling character interrelations. Below are some common bonds that characters can share:

**Childhood Buddies:** Perhaps the characters have known one another since they were young, and have forged a bond stronger than that of blood.

**Relatives:** Players frequently choose to have characters that are related to one another. These relations often take the form of Magus/Companion or Magus/Magus combinations. Such combinations are often very effective, as relations often make up for individual weaknesses.

**Rivals:** This option may have good or bad consequences. Each character is in constant competition with the others, and they live together as a means to keep an eye on rivals' successes. Fast friendships can result from such rivalry, but so can the most bitter of hatreds.

**Twist of Fate:** Oftentimes the characters are joined by chance. They may have a shared fate and thus can empathize with one another. Or, maybe a Magus is charmed by the boy-thief who thought he could steal the "old woman's" money.

**Common Goal:** Even though characters may go about tasks differently, they all strive for the same thing. Sometimes characters may not enjoy one another's company, but they respect each other's usefulness. Perhaps they all become friends by the end of the Saga.

However you start your Saga, the Saga's first session should be an interesting one. The players are just starting to get used to their new roles in the Saga. Use this time to form bonds between their characters. The characters shall be together for some time and might as well learn to depend on each other now.

# ENEMIES, FRIENDS, AND BYSTANDERS

While characters have a lot of fun interacting with each other, equal excitement can be found in interacting with other people and with various non-human beings. Remember, the characters are not always out to destroy things. A great deal of fun can be had by simply talking with interesting people, and a little politics and intrigue never hurts either. Use the Character, Saga, and Realms Chapters for guidelines on creating the various entities that populate the world and interact with the characters. If you intend enemies to pose a serious threat to the characters, give them some way to withstand the effects of magic; most people have no defenses against magic.

## TRAVEL

Travel time between important scenes is generally played through quickly. After all, if little of interest happens on the road, you don't want to go through every excruciating moment of the journey. Thus, rules are given for quickly resolving travel. These rules determine how long it takes for characters to get somewhere, and indicate how tired they are afterwards (through Fatigue).

You must rate the difficulty of travel, based primarily on terrain and weather. Once you've determined difficulty, find the category, below, that best suits your determination. Travel time at that difficulty rating is gauged by the slowest member of the party, and is measured in days.

**Easy:** The best of circumstances, such as travel on a straight, level Roman road with a cool, gentle breeze at the characters' backs. (A rather rare condition.)

**Light:** Can be looked upon as the best weather travelers can hope for. Travel along a good road (by medieval standards).

**Medium:** The typical conditions for road travel. On a standard road, with holes, rocks, and ruts caused by rain and heavy wagons. Could also be used as travel on a better road with hostile weather conditions, such as heat or snow. Another good example is travel through a moderately dense forest with a competent guide.

**Hard:** Travel on a typical road with less than favorable weather. Or, travel through the wilderness.

**Very Hard:** Unbearable weather, such as a blizzard or hurricane, or horrible terrain, such as a sloping rock field.

**Terrible:** Same as *Very Hard* except weather and terrain hazards are combined. One does not usually travel under such conditions as fatalities can result.

# REWARDS

Whether as the object of a quest or as the benefit of a dangerous encounter, treasure is a tangible way of showing the characters they have succeeded. Some treasures, such as books and spells, are valuable only to Magi, while others, such as jewelry or other magical devices, can make Companions and Grogs feel like they, as well as Magi, benefit from putting their lives on the line. Give the characters enough treasure to keep the Saga moving, but exercise moderation to keep the players wanting more.

Finding the right balance for your Saga is paramount to your players' satisfaction.

## Raw Vis

Raw *vis* is universally valuable: Magi apply it to a variety of uses, and it often has magical properties of value to other characters. To design raw *vis*, decide first upon its physical characteristics, the Art to which it is attuned, and the amount of *vis* points in it. Raw *vis* is often found within the bodies of supernatural beings. Some *vis* is replenished every year if derived from magical plants or other renewable sources, but if too much is harvested at one time, a source may lose its power, or may wither away. As a matter of fact, doomsayers predict that someday (soon?) supplies of *vis* will die. If this is indeed the case, there may well be dark times ahead for the Order of Hermes.

Since the readiness of raw *vis* largely determines how rapidly Magi grow in power, letting characters find too little or too much causes severe problems in the Saga. At the beginning of the Saga, the Covenant should possess enough raw *vis* to satisfy Magi's needs — five points per Magus, per story (as an average), is about right. Escalate from there as you see fit, but remember that a modicum of frugality is essential. Too much or too little *vis* can destroy a Saga. If some of your Storyguides are too generous in

| Travel Chart | | | |
| --- | --- | --- | --- |
| Difficulty | Foot | Horse | Wagon |
| Easy | 25/1 | 30/1 | 15 |
| Light | 20/2 | 25/1 | 10 |
| Medium | 15/2 | 20/1 | 8 |
| Hard | 10/3 | 12/2 | 3 |
| Very Hard | 5/3 | 3/2 | - |
| Terrible | 2/3 | 1/2 | - |

The first number is miles traveled in one day. The second is the number of Long-Term Fatigue Levels lost every day due to travel conditions. A Fatigue roll of 6+ allows a character to suffer one less Level than indicated. (Yes, if only one Level is called for, a successful roll eliminates it.)

how they reward characters, assign one player to check all rewards given to make sure they do not unbalance the Saga. This player is not the Storyguide, so has no real power.

## Treasure

Sometimes Covenants or characters need money in order to survive or to fund special projects, in which case mundane treasure can act as a source. More often, however, getting money is secondary in a mission. Concentrate, therefore, on the aesthetic qualities of treasure. Allow characters to discover interesting things: hoards of gleaming gold covered in cobwebs, jewelry boxes inlaid with gems (polished gems, but never faceted), scintillating necklaces, thick bracelets of precious metals, and perhaps even a royal crown. Impress the characters visually and they will covet their treasures instead of rushing to the nearest jeweler for quick cash. Mundane rewards like these can make Companions and Grogs feel as if they're gaining something for their efforts.

Let us also remember that the most beautiful treasures in the kingdom can sometimes be cursed, blessed, or haunted.

## Exempli Gratia:

### Tomes

**Quadlarius's Treatise on the Art of Healing:** Medicine 5. A large, leather-bound book written in Latin by an Eighth Century physician. It details his knowledge of medicine, including treatment of those afflicted with magical curses.

**The Grimoire of Halosk of Milsogne:** Intéllego 16, Córporem 12, *Tracing the Trail of Death's Stench* (InCo 30), *Trail* (InCo 30). This Latin book is part of a departed Magus's magical library. In addition to expounding on theories behind detection and magical manipulation of the human body, it has two of Halosk's spells. One of them, *Tracing the Trail of Death's Stench*, has become generally known in the Order of Hermes, but the other, *Trail*, is unique. *Trail* allows the caster to unerringly follow a certain subject, with whom the caster must possess an Arcane Connection, specifically the subject's hair. The spell lasts until the caster physically touches the subject. The description of the spell omits the need for the subject's hair as the Arcane Connection, which Halosk took for granted. When the new owner of the spell learns it does not work, a Magic Theory roll of 13+ allows the Magus to figure out what's missing.

**A Scroll of Thoth:** This papyrus scroll comes from ancient Egypt and is written in hieroglyphics, so one needs magic or secret knowledge to read it. Though the scroll's magic is not Hermetic, it details a powerful Ritual spell that a Magus can learn. The spell, *Ra's Mighty Gaze*, causes the sun to beat mercilessly upon a town for a year so that the ground dries up and cracks. A Hermetic spell that does the same would be Level 60, but this Ritual is only Level 30 because the magic used is suited to the spell's purpose. Casting the spell, however, is always stress, with twice the normal Botch rolls due to the magic's non-Hermetic concepts.

## Tomes

Magical and scholarly tomes can help a literate character learn Knowledges, spells, magical Arts, and the techniques of creating magical items. Tomes are therefore extremely valuable, and prized by Magi over nearly anything else.

Really play up the mystery and romance of books. Make them something to be desired, a magic item of far greater significance than the mightiest enchanted sword.

## Magical Artifacts

Magi often find magic devices during their expeditions, some constructed by fellow Magi, some created by dwarfs, gnomes, elves, demons, faeries or other mystical beings. Give non-Hermetic devices whatever power you see fit; leave the rules for creating invested items to the players.

Keep in mind that magic items do not go away. They can accumulate over the course of the Saga, causing the characters to become a force to be reckoned with. Some of us can remember times when we possessed so many magic items we started forgetting them. In legends, magical items are things of great beauty, and are awe-inspiring to say the least. They are powerful things, not gadgets. Peppering your Saga with miscellaneous magic items only cheapens the grandeur of these awesome creations.

One way to keep magic items from accumulating is to give characters one-use items, such as potions or powders, and to strictly limit the number of unlimited magic items found as treasures. Justification for magic items left behind are few and far between. How many times have the characters just discarded a magic item? If this occurrence is a rarity, why should others in the world act differently? A well-designed magic item makes a character more interesting (especially a Grog or Companion). A poorly-designed magic item overshadows a character and becomes a major character in itself. And, don't be too tightfisted; try to put artifacts into your story for Grogs and Companions. It gives them something to work for and it gives them, as characters, a certain interest.

Once a character finds a magic item, she has to learn how to use it. Some powers are obvious, such as a cape that makes the wearer invisible. Others are more obscure; discovery of their powers requires intense research in the laboratory. An effective combination involves some powers that are obvious and others that are hidden. Also, investing simple items with fantastic power is a good idea. A character might wear a humble wooden ring for years before discovering the magical powers hidden within. The Holy Grail was not all that magnificent in appearance, but it was unparalleled in power.

# Exempli Gratia: Magic Items

Each of the magic items below has a number in parentheses after its description. This number indicates the target number for the investigation of its powers by Magi seeking to discover the magical properties of an item.

### RING OF LIFEKEEPING

Upon donning this ring the wearer automatically loses four Body Levels. If the character is already wounded, donning the ring can kill. The only way to recover Levels lost to the ring is with bed rest (see the Wound *Recovery Chart* in the Combat Chapter to determine recovery time). If, during recovery time, the ring is removed it causes no more damage. It also causes no harm if put on again, but does not bestow its powers upon the wearer. If the wearer keeps the ring throughout his recovery period, the ring's powers are revealed when he is next endangered. The ring absorbs one Body Level of damage that the wearer would normally suffer. One Level can be so absorbed per day. The Level absorbed is the first the wearer would normally lose with each new day.

In addition, the wearer may "lay hands" on another and heal a lost Body Level. However, the wearer cannot heal his own lost Levels, and healing another costs the wearer that day's Body Level of protection. Thus, if the ring has already absorbed a Body Level of damage that the wearer would normally have suffered, another person's wounds cannot be healed until the following day.

This ring was taken from the finger of the martyred Saint Lemar of Bologna. The ring possesses the saint's Divine power and continues to spread his healing ways. The ring's Divine origins explain why those of Infernal background, or even those with the *Tainted With Evil* Flaw, cannot touch the ring without automatically suffering two Body Levels of damage. The ring's powers do not function for such folk. Furthermore, the item's powers are beyond the investigative detections of Magi.

### SALVE OF THE STONE'S STRENGTH

When rubbed over one's naked body (you can wear clothes once it's on), this salve grants strength and resistance to damage. Add +3 to effective Strength and +6 to Soak till the next full moon. In water the wearer also sinks like a stone, but the dwarfs who made the salve don't know this. The characters undoubtedly learn this by accident. After the salve wears off, the user is insatiably hungry and drops two Long-Term Levels. This salve was created by dwarfs for occasional trade with Magi and other mortals. (20)

(continued on next page)

# Exempli Gratia:

### SHIELD OF THE RED LION

This wooden shield has a red lion's face painted on it and was crafted by faeries. The lion is alive, but only interacts with those who impress it. If a character behaves bravely while using the shield, the lion speaks to the character later, during a quiet time, preferably when others are not around. It says, in words only the chosen character can hear, "*Greetings, valiant warrior. I am Andriste, and I am your loyal companion. Call on me and I will put forth a roar to put fear in the hearts of others. Call on me and I will watch over you while you sleep. Call on me one time, and one time only, and I will step out of this shield, and we will fight your enemies side by side. I am Andriste. Call on me in your need.*" From that point on, the character (only) can see the lion's eyes move, but Andriste does not talk any more. No one else can befriend the lion until it rejects the current bearer of the shield (see below).

The bearer of the shield gets +3 on all Brave rolls after having spoken with the lion. Once per day he can call on Andriste to roar, and all who hear it who are not on the chosen warrior's side must make a Brave roll of 6+ or become afraid. At night the character can ask Andriste to keep watch. It roars if it detects a danger to its owner (it has an Alertness score of 10). This roar is separate from the roar that causes fear. The owner may also call Andriste out of the shield, in which case the lion fights to the death alongside the shield's wielder. When killed, or the enemy defeated, the lion bids its companion farewell and departs forever, leaving the character with only a blank shield with which to remember his ally. The lion never returns to the shield, no matter who holds it.

Andriste's combat stats: Faerie Might 22, Intelligence 0, Perception +2, Strength +6, Stamina +5, Presence +3, Communication 0, Dexterity +2, Quickness +4, First Strike +7, Attack +9, Damage +18, Fatigue n/a, Defense +5, Soak +15, Body Levels: OK, 0/0/0, -1, -3, -5.

If the owner of the shield ever acts cowardly while using the shield, the eyes no longer appear to move, the lion never again responds to the character, and the +3 Brave bonus is lost. At this point another bearer of the shield can befriend Andriste.

(A Magus who rolls 25+ while investigating the shield in the lab makes contact with Andriste, who explains something of himself, but not necessarily all. More than anything, he's upset by having been disturbed by someone who is not a warrior.)

# ENDING YOUR SAGA WITH A BANG

Your Saga does not have to end with the death of all its characters. Likewise, your Saga should not end with everyone living happily ever after. The best Sagas make us laugh as well as cry. What separates great Sagas from mediocre ones is the careful balance of joy and trauma. If your Sagas usually end with everyone becoming ruler of all they survey, try something new. Maybe the characters are faced with the dilemma of sacrificing the life of a loved one to save all the lives of a kingdom. Such an option makes for a bittersweet conclusion to a Saga.

Even though some characters die in the course of the Saga, that doesn't mean they're forgotten. Be dramatic about the end of a Saga. This is the last time players have a chance to play their characters, so they should feel satisfied with the closing curtain, and should feel a sense of closure. Make the finale worthwhile. Irony helps to achieve this end. If there was a rainstorm at the beginning of the Saga, describe a lifting storm in the Saga's final scene. The passing storm is a reflection of the Saga's passing, and suggests a change from the start, indicating that the characters' lives have had some effect on the world.

Once a Saga is complete, take the time to thank everyone for their participation. The fantastic stories you've told have been a group effort. You, as Storyguide, painted the scenery, but heroic deeds are for the players to boast of.

# EXPERIENCE

We have established that your character's identity and outlook may change with the progression of the Saga. These changes manifest themselves in the way you understand and roleplay your character, but also have an impact on the game itself. The growth and maturation your character undergoes may be measured in terms of game mechanics. Specifically, your growing worldliness manifests itself in the form of Experience Points, a palpable measure of how much you change. Experience Points are not a mere tally of how many creatures you have killed. They reflect your increasing competence in matters of society, magic, labor and combat. They are gained through the significant encounters of your life, not only in battle, but through interactions with the social, magical and toiling world. Furthermore, Experience Points need not arise solely from the stories of your Saga, but can derive from practice and research you perform between stories.

# GAINING EXPERIENCE POINTS

After you complete a story, the Storyguide determines how successful you are, and how true to the nature of your character you are. She rewards successful characters, and those that are roleplayed well, with Experience Points. There's no rule on the number of points you must receive after each story. It's a very subjective matter, based on how quickly the Storyguide wants your character to advance, and on the relative success of your character's actions in the story (there may have been things to do in the story that you forgot or overlooked, resulting in reduced Experience). The magnitude of the story also influences the number of Experience awarded to the characters. If you save the Order of Hermes from diabolists, you get several Experience Points. If the story only involves a turb's journey to town and the tavern therein, very few Experience Points are gained.

Essentially, the Storyguide takes stock of each character's actions in the story, considers the dangers faced, and ponders the results of failed actions. These factors determine how much Experience is awarded to each character. For a story of average danger and consequence, and in which a character is adequately roleplayed, 2 to 3 Experience Points may be awarded. More or fewer points may be given out if exceptional or poor roleplaying is demonstrated, or if the dangers of the story are tremendous or nonexistent. Listed below are factors the Storyguide may consider in delegating Experience Points. But remember, the number of points awarded is left to you, the Storyguide. If you want the characters to advance slowly, you must limit the number of Experience they gain in a story (1 to 2 points). If you want the characters to quickly become powerful, you may increase the number of points awarded (3 to 5).

## Story Magnitude

This is a measure of how perilous or sweeping the story is. Grand, epic tales usually involve saving large groups of people or lands; the larger the group or territory, the greater the Experience award should be. Though a story may only involve a small group of characters, it may still have an epic flavor. If those characters have to overcome overwhelming odds just to save themselves, or to persevere against personal fears, high Experience is appropriate. Also keep in mind that story magnitude adds to characters' Experience if they succeed in the story, but if they fail in some way, magnitude represents a penalty to Experience.

• **Trifling:** The story is a bit of a lark with no real dangers involved or no substantial knowledge gained — low Experience.

• **Personal:** The characters seek to clear their own names or establish their own reputations, but no dire consequence is involved. The characters experience extreme discomfort unless the problem they face is rectified. The characters must save themselves from death or worse, but no one else is harmed — low to moderate Experience.

• **A Circle:** A small circle of people is affected by the story. They may be friends, the Covenant's Grogs, or a town council. The circle may only be slighted, harmed or killed by the dangers of the story — low to moderate Experience.

• **Covenant:** The characters' Covenant is threatened in the story. This threat may only involve cut supply lines; conversely, it may mean the loss of important magical artifacts and tomes, or even the destruction of the Covenant — low to high Experience.

• **Town/City:** The fate of a large number of people, living in close confines, hangs in the balance of the story. Success or failure at this level could mean the discomfort, harm, or death of 250 to 1000 people — moderate to high Experience.

• **Kingdom:** A great number of lives are in jeopardy. The story might involve diplomatic intrigue, the compromise of a kingdom's secrets, or all-out war. Success or failure on this level is always of consequence — moderate to very high Experience (5 points)

• **All of Europe:** The characters' actions have repercussions felt all over the known world. If you succeed here you're assured lots of Experience (5+), but failure is also heavy (no Experience at all, from any source). In a story of this magnitude, loss of Experience for a failed effort may be the least of your worries.

## Roleplaying

On the average, a decent roleplayer receives one Experience Point for his efforts in a story. Remember that good roleplaying does not always mean congenial roleplaying. If a character is nasty or obstinate, she's not being played well if she always complies with other characters' wishes. Indeed, such behavior calls for a roleplaying *penalty*. No Experience may be awarded for a story in which poor roleplaying is demonstrated, but this penalty does not deny points via other means. A player who doesn't act much, but repeatedly sacrifices his character for the salvation of others may still get Experience for his sacrifices. More than one Experience may be awarded

for a story in which exceptional roleplaying is demonstrated. Two points is fair.

## Personal Sacrifice

If a character gives up something personal in order to further the greater good, she should see some reward from the Storyguide. Personal sacrifice can mean anything from giving up a lucky charm, to forfeiting an enchanted item, to sacrificing one's life — moderate to high Experience.

A "sacrifice" in which you offer up your Familiar is worth no rewards, and may result in an Experience penalty, for you are actually sacrificing the life of another, even if that life is tied inextricably with your own.

## Annual Experience Awards

Note: The following Experience Point awards are for Grog, Companion, and Magus characters. However, as Magi are often occupied by magical pursuits, they have less time to study more mundane abilities, so improve their practical skills at a slower rate than others.

Though Grogs, Companions, and Magi gain Experience Points while adventuring, they are not restricted from learning and training at other times. At the beginning of each year players may announce what their characters intend to study or practice in the coming year, when not preoccupied by foreign troubles and journeys. The focus announced can be an Ability, Passion, or any other trait that can normally be improved through Experience (excluding magical Arts). However, you cannot train in restricted Abilities like Exceptional Talents, Arcane Knowledges, or Formal Knowledges unless you already have one or more of those Abilities, or unless you have a Virtue that grants access to one or more of those Abilities. When the year is complete, Experience Points are awarded to the trait trained. The number of points gained depends on the intensity of study or training, the skill level of any teacher or source, and on the amount of free time you actually get during the year.

One Experience Point is awarded for light study or training, and is applied to the trait chosen for concentration. Two Experience Points are awarded for moderate study or practice. Three points are awarded for intense concentration. Obviously, most players devote their characters to intense concentration, hoping for three Experience. However, the number of stories you're involved in throughout the year reduces the annual award you receive. For every story you're involved in over one, you lose an annual Experience Point. Thus, if you train intensely, but go on three expeditions in the year, you only gain one annual Experience Point.

Magi get fewer annual Experience Points based on the number of Seasons they spend in magical study. For every Season spent studying magic, one less annual Experience Point is gained. Training in arcane Abilities like *Certámen* and *Parma Magica* does not count against annual Experience gained. Indeed, annual Experience may be spent on such endeavors. However, any Season spent to improve the Magic Theory Knowledge counts against any annual Experience gained. The same stands true for Seasons spent learning or inventing spells, and for Seasons spent inventing enchanted items.

You can also lose or even gain annual Experience Points based on your Personality Traits. If you've dedicated yourself to intensive training for the year (three points), but have a Personality Trait of Lazy +2, the Storyguide may require that you make a simple roll to remain true to your intentions. In this case an Ease Factor of 6 is applied. A Lazy roll of 6+ means you lose an Experience Point, your natural inclinations ruining your plans. A lower roll allows you to study normally.

On the other hand, if you have a Personality Trait of Diligent +2, the Storyguide may allow you a roll to get bonus annual points. If the roll is 6+, you apply yourself to your training at every free moment, with the reward of an additional Experience Point. It's advised that annual Experience awards not rise higher than three or four.

Ultimately, you always gain at least one annual Experience Point, as you must get some time to yourself in the year, and Magi must have some chance to improve their less esoteric traits. You can also decide that you train throughout the year to the exclusion of expeditions and magical study, taking no part in stories. If that's the case, you get the full number of annual Experience appropriate for your devotion to training. One reason you might avoid journeys is to study a trait you cannot otherwise get on the road. However, you are far more likely to gain more *overall* Experience on the road than you are at home.

Training to the exclusion of expeditions (stories) is also a good way to account for characters when their players can't make one or more game sessions, depending on how much game time passes during missed sessions. These characters may be designated as training at the Covenant or elsewhere, explaining why they don't participate in adventures. Such training also provides these characters with some advancement, insuring they don't fall too far behind the others when the missing players return.

Finally, to train for a year in a trait requires that you already possess it, or that education in it be available to you. If you're acquiring a new trait, the Experience Points gained are applied as if your current score in the trait is zero. If you want to learn how to sing, you may have to make frequent trips to the local town as everyone at the Covenant is tone-deaf. If a tutor in the desired trait cannot be found, you cannot train in it. Alternately, the tutor may be far enough away to exclude you from Covenant activities, imposing the studying devotion rules, above. A clever Storyguide can also use your annual study as the means for a story. Maybe on a trip to your singing teacher you are ambushed by brigands. A truly nasty Storyguide counts such stories against your studying efforts, reducing the number of Experience you gain for the year.

If you're improving or learning a trait from a teacher or source (like a book), your trait score cannot be raised higher than the score of your teacher or source. Thus, if a book has an Occult Knowledge score of 3, your score in that Ability cannot rise higher than 3 through that source. To study from a book also requires that you have a Scribe score of 3 in the language of the book. The language of most books is Latin, unless a book is from a distant land.

# SPENDING EXPERIENCE POINTS

It's nice to have all these Experience Points, but what can you do with them? Experience Points are used to increase your Ability and Art scores, as well as those of Passion Virtues, if you have any of those. You accumulate Experience Points in each trait until those accumulated points exceed your current trait score by one. At that point your trait score increases by one and your accumulated Experience Point score returns to zero. You can raise the trait score again when you accumulate enough Experience points to exceed that new, higher trait score.

You can also use Experience to Master spells (see the Magic Chapter, p.184). You must accumulate one Experience Point for each 5 Levels of a spell to Master it (you do not have to exceed the Level of the spell, as you do the current score of a trait).

Experience earned after a story can only be spent on Abilities, Passions or Arts you use during the story. To use one of these traits you do not have to make a roll involving it. For instance, if you are leading your allies through a forest, you can apply Experience Points to your Survival Ability, or to other Forester Skills. If the pertinent trait involves a roll in the story, it doesn't matter whether the roll is a success or failure. You can apply Experience to the trait whatever the result of the roll. (Yes, if you want to train in a trait that you don't think you will otherwise use in a story, you may go out of your way to use it. In the story, that action is explained by your desire to experiment with your trait.) To spend Experience on a spell you wish to Master, you have to cast that spell during the story, or at least use it as a Similar spell (see the Magic Chapter, p.175).

You can invest no more than one Experience Point toward a single trait after a story. Points are put on separate traits. The exception to this rule is with annual Experience Points. Since you train in a single trait for a full year, you can invest more than one Experience Point in the trait after the year is up.

It's even possible, though rare, to gain additional Experience Points in a story if you use a trait in a new, imaginative, or demanding way. For example, if you manage to talk an ogre out of eating you by feigning a severe illness, the Storyguide may allow you to immediately take a point toward your Pretend Ability, in the middle of the story. This point is free, and is not counted toward the Experience you earn after the story. Such free points should be awarded only occasionally, to make them valuable and to insure that characters don't rise in power too quickly.

## Experience

After his journey to Mercille, Grimgroth gets two Experience Points. (He lost a third point for forgetting his promise to bury the ghost's remains — remember?) During the story he entered *Certámen*, and devotes one Experience Point to his *Certámen* skill. His score in it is currently 3, and he has thus far accumulated three Experience Points under *Certámen*, so his score now increases by one (this last point makes his accumulated Experience total one point in excess of his current skill score). Thus, his new accumulated Experience score in the Ability is zero. He also used the spell *Broom of the Winds* in the story. He invests an Experience Point toward Mastering it, hoping to rely on it in the future. Since the spell is Level 15, and Grimgroth has accumulated no Experience toward it, he needs two more points before the spell is Mastered.

# AGING

Age is the great equalizer, leading eventually to death. Magi can brew elixirs to slow this process, but even they cannot delay the inevitable. Aging is a destructive process that mounts upon itself — the effects of age only accumulate. The Aging rules presented here reflect that accumulation of suffering, and can be cruel, as they inexorably drain away the vitality of your character. You may decide to retire a character from active play before age takes too heavy a toll. Better to be remembered as a stout warrior or able chirurgeon than an enfeebled husk or doddering fool.

You begin to age once your character turns thirty-five. No Aging rolls need be made until you are thirty-five. That year, however, and every year thereafter, in the Winter Season (a particularly harsh time in the Middle Ages), you must roll on the *Aging Chart*, below.

Make a simple roll, adding one to your roll for every Decrepitude Point your character possesses, and add another one to your roll for every decade of your age. Thus, when you make your first Aging roll at thirty-five,

## Aging Chart

| | |
|---|---|
| 1 | No effect |
| 2 | No effect |
| 3 | No effect |
| 4 | No effect |
| 5 | No effect |
| 6 | Quickness |
| 7 | Perception |
| 8 | Strength |
| 9 | Stamina |
| 10 | Dexterity |
| 11 | Presence |
| 12 | Communication |
| 13 | Intelligence |
| 14 | Gain one Decrepitude |
| 15 | Death |

results in "Gain one Decrepitude," add one Decrepitude Point to your character's total.

If the roll on the *Chart* results in "Death," you must make a Stamina simple roll. A result of 10+ is required to avoid dying of old age. Even if you succeed at this roll, a Decrepitude Point is gained. In the interests of storytelling, death by old age can be considered to occur any time over the next year. However, keep in mind that most people die over the harsh winter, due to poor heating and lack of fresh, wholesome food. Dramatic roleplaying is possible, and a virtual necessity, at the deathbed of a dying character.

Note that this system describes aging in a medieval environment. The aging process takes a very different (and slower) course today. You may notice that it is not possible to die from aging until you are 50 years old or so (unless you possess a great deal of Decrepitude). This is not to say that you cannot die of natural causes before this time, just that you cannot die of old age before this time. Few characters make it to this age, though. Mythic Europe is a dangerous, cruel place which takes its toll on characters. If one of your characters does die of old age treat it as a victory, in that you have managed to survive all the

add 3 to your roll. Compare the rolled result to the *Chart*. The higher you roll the worse are the effects of Aging, so the above modifiers are not beneficial.

If the roll results in a Characteristic, you must make another roll to see you lose a point in that trait. You must get a result of 7+ on a simple roll plus your current Characteristic score to resist the Characteristic point loss. Thus, if you have a zero in Perception and fail your roll, your Perception falls to -1. If your roll on the *Aging Chart*

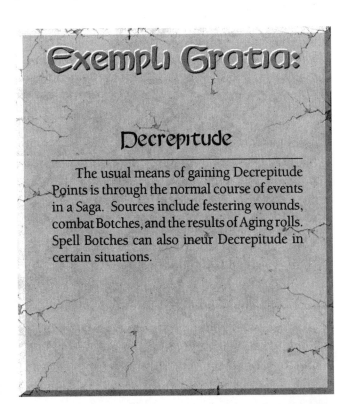

# Exempli Gratia:

## Decrepitude

The usual means of gaining Decrepitude Points is through the normal course of events in a Saga. Sources include festering wounds, combat Botches, and the results of Aging rolls. Spell Botches can also incur Decrepitude in certain situations.

DM/BRIDGES

perils you have faced. Of course, many individuals hate the thought of dying in bed.

## Longevity Potions

Magi, never ones to let themselves fall to the same fate as mundane mortals, are able to brew potions for themselves that slow the aging process. For more information on these elixirs, see the Laboratory Chapter, p. 250.

# WIZARD'S TWILIGHT

*"Learn magic, for it is the only truth of this reality. Become magic, and you will become the essence of truth. Fear not what others call the Twilight, for that realm of dim illumination is not dusk, but is, in fact, dawn."*

— Criamon

For Magi, death is not certain, so perhaps they have some right to call others "mortals" as if they themselves are not. What is certain is that all Magi leave this life, but while all others on the face of the world are pursued by Death, Magi are also pursued by Wizard's Twilight.

Many Magi, especially those who attempt magics too powerful or unpredictable for them to fully control, are overcome by the vis they attempt to direct, and are sometimes sent spinning away from the mortal world by the force of their inundation. Those who have passed on because of Wizard's Twilight cannot be summoned as ghosts, so Hermetic Theory generally holds that departed Magi are not dead in the normal sense.

Magi generally go through a number of Twilights in their lifetime. A period of Twilight might last minutes or days, as uncontrolled magic courses through an afflicted Magus. Though some Magi manage to remain conscious throughout Twilight, and even have limited control of their bodies, most are unconscious, in spasms and fits, or both.

These survivable Twilights can give Magi new insights into their arts, but they can also leave physical deformities and mental aberrations. As the years pass and Magi experience more and more Twilights, they become more vulnerable to final Twilight, when they escape death by leaving the worldly realm through a back door.

## Twilight Points

Each Magus at some point begins collecting Twilight Points. Like Decrepitude, they may not be removed by any known means. Any Magus who gains a total of twenty-four Twilight Points passes into final Twilight and departs from this realm, in spirit if not in form. There are various ways to gain Twilight Points, as discussed below.

Magi do not gain Twilight Points until they begin using a longevity potion. At that point, the lives of Magi begin to rely on magic, and magic begins to hold sway over

them. In the first year of taking a longevity potion, a Magus gains one Twilight Point, with another gained every twenty years thereafter—one on the twentieth year, yet another on the fortieth, and so on.

Twilight Points also come from studying the Art of Vim. Each time a Magus's score increases to a multiple of 5 (5, 10, 15, 20, and so on) a Magus gains one Twilight Point.

Storyguides can assign more points as the result of Botches with spells, or other dramatic, magical effects in the course of a story. Generally, one Twilight Point and an appropriate side effect are plenty. Additionally, Magi may accumulate Twilight Points from some other powerful, continuing exposure to magic, such as using a spell to keep oneself stronger than normal over an extended period of time.

Many points can be gained by going through temporary Twilight, as explained below.

## Temporary Twilight

When a Magus with Twilight Points encounters a powerful, uncontrollable magical force, the Storyguide can elect to have the player roll to see if her character falls into temporary Twilight. As a rule of thumb, the Storyguide may require this roll for double Botches (or worse) with spells and when studying with raw vis in the lab. However, any exposure to powerful, wild magic can precipitate Twilight. Follow these three steps to see whether a Magus suffers Twilight, and to determine what happens if you do:

**1) Roll for Twilight.** Make a stress roll and add your character's Twilight Points. If the total is 24+ you enter temporary Twilight. If not, you avoid Twilight and there is no unusual effect. (You may still suffer the effects of a normal Botch, though, if a Botch is what made you roll for Twilight in the first place.) Confidence rerolls may not be used to affect this roll, though Passions might be applied to modify rolls in your favor (i.e., to reduce roll results). You must justify the application of a Passion in terms of the story and your character's attitudes before the Passion can apply.

**2) Roll for Twilight Points Gained.** When you enter temporary Twilight, make a simple roll and add the result to your character's Twilight Points. If the result is 24+, the character enters final Twilight. Roleplay out the end of the Magus's mortal existence with all appropriate flash and pathos. Your character may hang on for hours or even days, but you are definitely beyond the scope of human knowledge and wisdom, no longer a human being as we understand the term. If you have fewer than twenty-four Twilight Points, you may recover from this Twilight; continue with step three.

**3) Roll for Control.** Make a stress roll + Intelligence. You may add +3 if you are *Strong-Willed*, and you may use

Confidence points to make rerolls, or to apply Passions. The Storyguide rolls a stress die + the Aura strength of the supernatural power that dominates the area (if any) to represent the intensity of the Twilight. The Storyguide may add other bonuses to this roll if the Twilight should be more intense than usual (e.g., it's the result of a quadruple Botch). If you roll higher than the Storyguide, you have enough control over the experience to avoid dangers and to learn something: roll on the *Good Effects Chart*. If your roll is equal to or less than the Storyguide's, the Twilight is too powerful for you to assimilate: roll on the *Bad Effects Chart*. If you Botch your roll against the Storyguide, roll on the *Bad Effects Chart* and suffer an especially damaging version of the affliction indicated. These rolls can also be used as guidelines for deciding how long the Twilight lasts (longer for higher intensities), and for how much control you retain over your body (more if your roll is considerably higher than the intensity). There is, however, no strict correlation between internal (psychic) and external (bodily) control, and your actions during the Twilight should be roleplayed out to fit the character and the story.

## Good Effects

**Increased Understanding:** Normally a Magus can only write a book that describes an Art up to half his own score. If you get this effect, you understand your highest

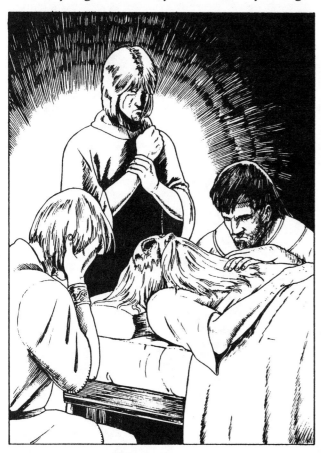

### Good Effects Chart

| | |
|---|---|
| 1-3 | Increased Understanding |
| 4-5 | Experience Points in Affinity |
| 6 | Increase in Art |
| 7 | Experience Points in Magic Theory |
| 8 | Experience Points in Arcane Ability |
| 9 | Special |
| 10 | Roll Twice: One effect on this chart; for the second effect, roll normally to determine if it's Good or Bad. If a second roll on this chart results in a "10," ignore the result and reroll. |

### Bad Effects Chart

| | |
|---|---|
| 1-2 | Blatant Gift |
| 3-4 | Deficiency |
| 5 | Wild Magic |
| 6 | Mental Defect |
| 7 | Physical Defect |
| 8 | Automatic Magic |
| 9 | Special |
| 10 | Roll Twice: One effect on this chart; for the other effect, roll normally to see if it's Good or Bad. If a second roll on this chart results in a "10," ignore the result and reroll. |

Note: Passions cannot be applied to rolls on either chart.

Art more clearly and can write a tome that describes the Art (and only that Art) up to two-thirds of your score. For example, Caecus, with a Perdo score of 22, can write a tome that describes Perdo up to level 14, two-thirds of 22.

Each successive time you get this effect, the fraction goes one step closer to 100% (i.e., 3/4, 4/5, 5/6, 1). The great magical tomes of the Order have almost all been written by Magi who have undergone Twilight and have brought back insights to share with the rest of the Order.

**Experience Points in Affinity:** Roll a simple die and add the result in Experience Points to an Affinity (as per the *Magical Affinity* Virtue) you have. If you have no Affinity, or your Affinity is opposed to the circumstances of the Twilight, you may gain a new Affinity. In that case, divide the simple roll by two, the result being the number of purchase points used to determine your score in the new Affinity.

# Exempli Gratia:

## Personal Twilight

Each Magus has a unique experience in Twilight, which is determined by the kind of magic the Magus uses. Grimgroth has led a political life and has not avidly pursued powerful magics as many Magi do, so he has suffered only two Twilights in his long years. The first time was when peasants, under the influence of a demon, attacked him and his small group as they were traveling to Doissetep for Tribunal. He attempted a powerful Spontaneous spell and failed utterly. He fell on the ground, screaming and writhing, while his companions, without the Magus to help them, had to resort to violence to fend off the peasants.

Grimgroth apparently recovered and continued to the Tribunal, but was markedly changed: short-tempered, babbling from time to time, and prone to wandering away from the Tribunal. Finally, after the last vote, Grimgroth fell into a deep sleep and had to be carried home to Mistridge. When he awoke, he remembered only snatches of the Tribunal.

A fellow Magus, Consuelia, has since told him that he was most likely in Twilight throughout the Tribunal, and that only his strong will and sense of purpose let him use even a portion of his faculties during that time. Most of his actions, however, including his votes, were probably beyond his direct control.

Since that Twilight, Grimgroth has shown a greater understanding of political affairs within the Order, but one after-effect of the Twilight is that he is likely to fly into an unreasonable rage when certain topics related to the Tribunal are mentioned.

Grimgroth suffered another Twilight, resulting from a Muto Mentem Certámen with a Criamon Magus. This time he fell into uncontrollable fits of laughter. His ally, Clavius, was about to use a spell to calm him, but Samantha, Grimgroth's familiar at the time, stopped him and stood guard over Grimgroth's body. Grimgroth laughed for over an hour, recovered, showed signs of disorientation for a week, and has been "normal" ever since. Some, however, have noted that he is much more sullen now than he had been.

For example, Caecus goes through Twilight while attempting to heal a Companion of a dread disease (Creo Córporem), and receives this effect. Experience in his Perdo Affinity doesn't make sense because he's using Creo Magic, so he gets a new Affinity. The player and Storyguide agree the Affinity can't be with Córporem because Caecus has a *Deficiency* Flaw with that Art, and it cannot be with Creo because that doesn't fit the style of a Perdo Magus. The Storyguide gives him an Affinity with healing, and his player rolls a six on the simple die. That means three purchase points for a new Affinity, which becomes a score of two (according to advanced character creation rules).

**Experience Points in Arcane Ability:** Make a simple roll and apply that many Experience Points to an Arcane Ability. It could be Faerie Lore if you enter Twilight in a faerie forest, or *Certámen* if your Twilight results from *Certámen*.

**Experience Points in Magic Theory:** Make a simple roll and add that many Experience Points to Magic Theory.

**Increase in Art:** Roll a simple die and multiply the result by three. Treat the result as if it is the score of a book that you study for a Season (see p.238 of the Laboratory Chapter). The Art raised depends on the circumstances of the Twilight, or it could be that of your personal specialty. Your Art score increases by one point in any event.

## Ghosts and Twilight

A Magus lost to the world through Twilight does not leave a ghost behind. No Hermetic magic can contact a Magus lost to Twilight. In fact, Magi that die and return as ghosts still have Twilight points, and the process of summoning or controlling them can cause them to go through Twilight. For this reason, the ghosts of Magi from centuries before are quite rare; most have left the world by Twilight, either before or after death.

**Special:** Whatever effect the Storyguide deems appropriate. You might gain a minor magical ability, or improve one you already have. Anything relevant to the circumstances can happen.

## Bad Effects

Note: Like Twilight Points, these effects cannot be removed by any earthly means.

**Blatant Gift:** From now on your magical aura is stronger, always close to the surface of your being. You gain the *Blatant Gift* Flaw. If you already have it, roll again. If you have the *Gentle Gift* Virtue, you lose it, but do not gain the *Blatant Gift*.

**Deficiency:** You suffer the *Minor Magic Deficiency* Flaw with one Art, probably one that is opposed to your best Art. If you already have a M*inor Magic Deficiency* in that Art, you now have a *Major* one. If you already have a *Major Magic Deficiency* in the Art, you get a *Major Deficiency* in another Art.

**Wild Magic:** You gain the Flaw *Wild Magic*. If you already have it, roll again.

**Mental Defect:** The surge of magic has warped your mind. If you have a mental Flaw, such as an *Obsession* or *Fear*, it might be exaggerated. Otherwise, a quirk might grow worse and become an actual Flaw, or you may pick up some defect related to the circumstances of the Twilight.

**Physical Defect:** The power of magic coursing through you has permanently injured your body. You might gain a Decrepitude Point, lose some hearing, become lame, or simply be disfigured. (Use Flaws as guidelines.)

**Automatic Magic:** Your magic oozes out of you of its own accord. Your very presence causes small magical effects of some type appropriate to your magic or to the Twilight itself. For example, Caecus might cause things near him to crack, decay, age, or become weaker because he has a strong Perdo score. These effects are limited in strength and distance and can never be directed by will. They may come and go or vary greatly in power from day to day.

**Special:** Anything that, in the judgement of the Storyguide, suits your unique magical bent or the Twilight, such as a *Susceptibility* Flaw to the supernatural realm dominating the area where the Twilight occurs (if other than Magic).

## Story and Character Considerations for Twilight

Wizard's Twilight is a highly variable and personal event for every Magus, and as such can add much to a story or character. The rules here are designed to cover the basics so that players who suffer from Twilight feel they suffer from bad luck, not a cruel Storyguide. Likewise, those whose characters benefit do not feel that the Storyguide has given them special favor; the dice determine it. On the other hand, the more that you, as Storyguide or player, are willing to determine about a given Twilight, the more appropriate you can make it to the story and character involved. That is, the rules are made to be set aside if your own imagination is more powerful.

One simple question of staging Twilight is timing. If a Magus undergoes Twilight during a battle, it is best to tell

the player that the afflicted character falls into fits, and leave it at that. Let the rest of the players enjoy the fight without slowing everything down for the character in Twilight. If, however, a Magus experiences Twilight while the other characters are free to interact, you may wish to detail the event and draw it out for full dramatic effect. The affected character can fight for control while the others try to ease their fellow through the experience.

The immediate effects of Twilight are up to the Storyguide. Sometimes a Magus is simply knocked unconscious or paralyzed, but other Twilights send Magi into violent fits. The uncontrolled magic often leaks out of a Magus in Twilight, causing strange magical effects. A Magus in Twilight because of a Muto spell might change forms randomly, or suffer bizarre, shifting distortions of the body. These effects can even spread to the Magus's vicinity, causing minor transformations of surrounding rocks, animals, and people. Storyguides can also determine the nature of a given Twilight to suit the dramatic needs of the story and the general tone of the Saga (e.g., high fantasy versus dark, medieval flavor).

Feel free to alter the effects that the dice indicate, or make up your own. The random charts provide a default system to use when player and Storyguide cannot agree on what should happen to a character. In addition, most Twilights leave some kind of mark on the character, called the "Touch of Magic." This touch can be a physical discoloration, a quirk, a tic, or any other minor interesting detail. An example is Grimgroth's tendency to become enraged at the mention of topics debated at the Tribunal where he was in Twilight.

## Other Uses for Twilight

Wizard's Twilight does not always occur entirely by chance. It can be more common under certain rare conditions. For example, you may want to include in your Saga some of the following things:

**A powerful magical item that often causes Twilight** — This potent device relies on the user's ability to control magic, so it can only be used by wizards. The powers of the item are so strong, however, that any Botch made while using it causes the Magus to roll for Twilight.

**A magical trap** — A Magus writes a "spell" into a tome that actually sends the caster into Twilight. It is a trap for those who steal the book and use the "spell."

**Supernatural encounters** — Demons and faeries can precipitate Twilight because the potent magic they use does not mesh perfectly with Hermetic magic. Magi who are trying to discover the secrets of faerie magic may find themselves going through Twilight as a result.

# Wizard's Twilight

Caecus has gained Twilight Points from the following sources:

| | |
|---|---|
| Vim score of 12 | (2) |
| Longevity potions for 20+ years | (2) |
| Peering into his master's crystal when he was an apprentice | (4) |
| Total Twilight Points | (8) |

Caecus faces a demon that has pursued him from Hibernia, and is trying to kill the Magus to keep him from sharing what he has learned about Hell with Magi in Languedoc. Grabbing a handful of magical powder (raw vis), Caecus foregoes finesse and lets fly with a Spontaneous Perdo Vim spell. He rolls a zero, and with his seven points of raw vis, must make eight Botch rolls. Two of them come up zeroes, and the Storyguide tells Caecus to roll for Twilight.

He rolls a one, picks up the die and gets a ten, doubled is 20, +8 is 28. As this total is over 24, Caecus goes into Twilight. Privately, the Storyguide decides that Caecus has accidentally made a supernatural connection with the demon, something few minds can survive without damage. The Storyguide says, *"Both Caecus and the demon fall to the ground, writhing, spitting, and screaming."*

The Storyguide then decides that the longer it takes Caecus's allies to kill the demon, the more intense the Twilight becomes, so he does not let Caecus roll for control yet. Caecus also has to roll to see how many Twilight Points he gains: 2, for a new total of 10.

Some of Caecus's allies try to aid him, though he shows no response. One, a favored Grog, tries to talk him out of it, and the Storyguide decides this can either help Caecus control the Twilight, or distract him from the effort. The Grog makes a Communication roll and adds +3 for the strong friendship between the Grog and

Caecus, but the total is still only seven. The Storyguide decides that a moderate result has no effect either way. The other characters dispatch the helpless demon, but it takes them long enough that the Storyguide decides to add +1 to intensity roll of the Twilight, to be made against Caecus's control roll.

Caecus rolls 8 + 3 (Intelligence) = 11 for control, while the Storyguide rolls 6 + 3 (Magic Aura) + 1 (demon's contact) = 10 for intensity. Caecus may roll on the *Good Effects Chart*. Since this is Caecus's first Twilight, he has no firm idea whether he will suffer or benefit from the experience (even if the player can make a good guess). The Storyguide also rules that, with the demon dead, Caecus can stop throwing a fit, but he remains incoherent and helpless for hours. When the characters get Caecus to Val-Negra, the other Magi examine him to determine if he is all right. Caecus rolls a die to determine the result of the Twilight, and the player and Storyguide talk over the result.

The die come up four: Experience Points in Affinity. It would be logical to give Caecus Experience with his Perdo Affinity, since he was attempting a Perdo spell, but that does not take into account the unique contact with the demon. An Affinity with destroying demons makes sense, but also overlaps with the Perdo Affinity Caecus already has. The Storyguide finally lets Caecus decide between a +2 bonus for destroying demons (which would be on top of his Perdo Affinity) and Experience in Occult Lore. Caecus's player decides that he would have spent more time focused on his abilities than the demon, so picks the demon-slaying bonus.

As for the "Touch of Magic," Caecus suggests that he gives off a faint whiff of brimstone when working magic, and the Storyguide agrees.

Caecus regains his strength at Val-Negra and comes through the experience stronger, but one step closer to that eventual, final, Twilight.

# Storytelling

## chapter twelve

aving arrived at this Chapter, you have now reached the end of your education. Your basic understanding of the art of magic is now complete. However, you may be far from mastering the vagaries of storytelling. Such proficiency only comes from much training and experience, and from the insight and wisdom that the passage of time accords. This is something only you can give yourself; there is little we can do to help you. However we can illuminate the path ahead, and that is the purpose of what follows.

This Chapter contains rules and advice for creating and playing your own stories, and for inventing and maintaining a Saga. Both can be very difficult tasks, full of complications and uncertainty. However, the process of storytelling provides an outlet for your imagination, and inspires a certain amount of pride when you exercise your imagination.

This Chapter offers guidance on how to get the most out of **Ars Magica**, not only for yourself, but for all the players. Learn what you can from that which makes sense to you, and ignore all the rest. Not all of our thoughts on roleplaying are for everyone.

## The Storyteller

In the modern age the job of storyteller has fallen into the hands of the movie director and the TV producer. Exorbitant budgets are spent to recreate that which, long ago, required but a village elder to relate. People don't tell stories any more; we are given stories, spoon-fed them since before we can speak.

Of course, we could tell stories to each other if we wanted to, but we've been spoiled. Unfortunately, it's no longer enough that one has a good story to tell. If it's not accompanied by startling feats of electronic wizardry, a story is deemed second-rate, or just plain boring. Stories flicker across our eyes, and no longer live in our imaginations.

In the Dark Ages there were no VCRs or cinemas. To know someone who could weave tales to touch the heart or chill the soul was a blessing indeed. No wide-angle shots or telephoto lenses were needed, just the vivid imagination of the listener, who created a world more vibrant and colorful than any Steven Spielberg ever could. This ability to imagine is an ability most of us have, tragically, lost.

Our ancestors had few means through which to teach their young about the mistakes of elders, and about the guiding myths of culture. They had even fewer outlets of entertainment. However, one of the few outlets they had was storytelling. Storytelling on a personal, everyday level was a part of life. It enabled people to keep going. It made them wise with the passage of years. Remember, the legends of King Arthur survived many hundreds of lifetimes before they were ever committed to parchment. Imagine what those legends meant to people, people for whom legends were more than just words, but truth.

Imagine what we have lost.

Roleplaying, however, may give the power of imagination back to us. Storytelling games such as Ars Magica provide us the opportunity to exercise our creative minds, to tell our own stories, and to create our own myths. The power behind these games, the thing which makes them so popular, is that they let us have our own thoughts, and create our own truths. It is a power we grow to savor, and are loath to do without.

# WHAT IS A STORYGUIDE ANYWAY?

The role of a Storyguide would, at first glance, seem to involve nothing more than simply catering to the desires of players. It's easy to believe your job is to "entertain the guests." This can't be farther from the truth, though. The Storyguide's job is to inform as well as to entertain, to enliven as well as to engage. Where the role of storyteller is a complex one, that of Storyguide is even more complex, combining as it does the problems of a game as well as a story. In order to understand just what being a Storyguide encompasses, you must first understand a Storyguide's responsibilities.

The Storyguide is unlike the Gamemaster of most other roleplaying games. The Gamemaster's job often revolves around enforcement of rules and regulations, in order to keep a game moving smoothly. This is not what a storyteller's job should involve, and is not what the Storyguide's job involves. In Ars Magica, it's the Storyguide's duty to weave an epic story, a story in which the players might, through their characters, perform heroic acts and epic deeds that are the stuff of legend and myth. The Storyguide enacts the world in which these myths are created, and in so doing perpetuates the stories that a storyteller narrates. Rules are of secondary importance to the storytelling event.

## Character Roles

The role of Storyguide calls for a great deal of character acting. This is perhaps one of the most demanding tasks of storytelling, but is also the most fun. On the many journeys the players' characters undertake, they are likely to run into a variety of villains, heroes and, of course, damsels in distress. You have to enact all of these people. It's not so much switching roles that's difficult, but being convincing in them.

Being convincing in a role is accomplished by practice, and by accepting the fact that you sometimes look foolish. Sure, sometimes you get to act as though you're the valorous knight, who rides into the sunset astride a pale horse. However, you also get your share of playing Emo, the village idiot. Don't shortchange your players by making all the characters they meet shallow and one-dimensional. This only induces your players to refrain from social interaction. If they don't see you hamming it up, they may feel peculiar doing it themselves.

Indeed, the energy and vigor you put into your characters is often absorbed by the players. If you are listless and insipid in your roleplaying, they may be too. But, if your excitement comes through in your characters, the whole story picks up. Your control over the tempo and pace of the story is directly related to how you play your characters. Your role is one of the most direct and immediate ways to affect the energy and emotional intensity of the game, so try to master roleplaying as quickly as you can.

## Creating Roles

The best way to develop most character roles is by observation. When trying to emulate a particular dialect or frame of mind, watch movies or television shows (documentaries work well) in order to get a better grasp of what you are trying to create. (Yes, TV can have a role in your stories, but as a tool, not a storyteller.) Each character you create should have something unique about him, something that makes him different from all the other characters you play. Such things as a "rustic accent" or a "gravelly voice" can evoke much in a character. If you aren't comfortable using accents and different vocal qualities, think about wearing different hats or coats. Regardless of what you do, make it clear to the players who it is you are playing at any particular time, but do so without actually stating who you are.

Your roleplaying often serves as a cue to the players, stating, "Yes, we're roleplaying now so stop acting like yourself and get into character." Thus, you need to concentrate on what you're doing to be sure the players receive your signals. Such cues can involve anything from "get ready for a fight," to "let's get serious here," to "this is a time of sadness, we should not be laughing." Once the

players recognize your cues, they will begin to intuitively understand when roleplaying is necessary. Before long, you won't need to say a word and your group will be acting like a completely different bunch of people.

Below are some examples of popular entertainment roles you can draw from to help in your search for good character models. Don't just copy everything about a model you like, and never tell the players when you're drawing from a model. All they'll do is draw from that source too, and before long your whole group will be behaving like a single caricature. If the players figure out who you're emulating with your acting style, your role may not be subtle enough.

The characters above are just a few possible role models that can influence your creation of a role. The different roles you, as Storyguide, play become a part of you and, if developed carefully, acquire their own goals and outlooks on life. Given time these roles become your prized possessions in the stories you tell, and should never be trivialized.

There is even a way to determine whether you're performing well, with the unknowing assistance of your players. When they talk amongst themselves, in or out of character, the good Storyteller's players refer to his different characters as separate entities. If you reach a point where your characters are completely dissociated from your identity, you can perform the vilest of deeds through evil characters, and the players will never blame you for their ill fortune.

# BEING A STORYGUIDE

There is very little one can say with assurance about being a Storyguide, little you can say that someone else won't oppose. There really is no right or wrong way to be a Storyguide. Basically, if you can keep the players enthusiastic about the game, you're doing a good job. However, being a better Storyguide should always be foremost on your list. The following are some suggestions on being a better Storyguide. Take these as you will and apply them only if you see their merit.

## Things to Do

• Let the players control their characters — Restricting the players' freedom of expression is one of the things you should never do. Players have little say in how the world functions, save through their characters' actions and statements. If this freedom is restricted, the players may as well stay home. Besides, with all the characters you have to enact in a story, influencing the characters' actions only adds to your burden.

| Character Traits | Character/Production |
|---|---|
| Overbearing | Darth Vader, *Star Wars* |
| Silly and Rural | Gomer Pyle |
| Evil | Darkness, *Legend* |
| Cunning | Hans Gruber, *Die Hard* |
| Wise | Yoda, *Star Wars* |
| Dense/Macho | Jack Burton, *Big Trouble in Little China* |
| Horrid | Freddie, *Nightmare on Elm Street* |
| Mysterious | Batman, *Batman* |
| Psychotic | Dr. Hannibal Lecter, *Silence of the Lambs* |
| Intellectual | Spock, *Star Trek* |
| Charming | James Bond, *You Only Live Twice* |
| Chivalrous | King Arthur, *Excalibur* |
| Vengeful | Captain Hook, *Peter Pan* |
| Precocious | Calvin, *Calvin and Hobbes* |

• Describe things in detail — The more lavishly you describe things the more your players can envision them. Get your Troupe to close their eyes while you describe things and people. Imagination is a very potent tool; use it to your advantage.

• Reward roleplaying — Just like children, we want rewards for a job well done, even if it's just verbal praise. So, if a member of your Troupe plays above and beyond the accepted norm, don't let her efforts go unrewarded. Publicly award her the Emmy for the evening, the prize being a bonus Experience or Confidence Point. With luck, the award inspires dramatic competition in the next game session.

• Ask your players' opinions on rules — Because rules of play have a profound effect on character actions, let your Troupe decide on what's best. After all, the players pay attention to the rules too — if the combat rules favor missile weapons, don't your players run out and buy bows? Although you're the Storyguide, no one likes a dictator. Be firm on some rules and flexible on others.

• Come prepared — Nothing ruins the moment like an unprepared participant. Your disorganization can break the mood of an otherwise engrossing scene. This doesn't mean you have to spend every waking hour preparing for your session, insuring everyone has full-color maps of their sanctums. It's simply a good idea to give the needs of your story some thought before sitting down to the table. That way the story runs a lot smoother and everyone has a good time.

• Go beyond the rules — The rules are for keeping characters in line. If your imagination constantly reaches beyond the bounds of the rules, forget the rules. In fact, letting your imagination loose is true to some elements of a story, more so than respecting the rules. How enigmatic are faeries whose powers can all be looked up in the tables?

## Things Not to Do

• Don't play favorites — It's no fun to watch a Storyguide and his star player enjoying themselves while you just sit there. Stealing the show is an experience that all members of the Troupe should enjoy. Everyone should have his moment in the sun, but no one should be allowed to constantly bask in the light. Your job as storyteller is to keep the spotlight moving from player to player, giving everyone a turn. Provide something for everyone to do, Magi and Grogs alike.

• Don't forget characters' special abilities — There's nothing worse than having to replay the beginning of an ambush because you forget a Companion's Premonitions Ability. Look over the character sheets before a session begins and take a few notes. You need to know the players' characters as well as you know the plot.

• Don't give your players everything — Too many characters are showered with gifts from the Storyguide. A casual stroll down Main Street is not reason enough to provide them with a runesword, nor is a night on the town enough to yield a queen of raw vis. There's no sense of accomplishment to be found if you hand out all sorts of goodies. Instead, reward the characters for a job well done, but make them earn it.

• Don't persecute — Many Storyguides seem to get a kick out of destroying players' characters. When a player comes up with an idea for a character, it's her private creation, and should be treated as something valuable. Constantly "killing off" characters solicits two responses. First, players become less concerned with character well-being, and simply play for lack of anything better to do. Second, after making up a fifth character in two weeks, players create less inspired characters, which weakens the fabric of your game and stories.

• Don't haphazardly break the rules — Even though the rules are simply there to discourage disputes between players, you shouldn't overlook them indiscriminately. If you're going to change a rule, even for a single scene, the players should understand why the change is implemented, and the change should make sense. If the rules seem to change without rhyme or reason, the logic of your world collapses. And, if you're going to change rules, remember the change you make or your stories lose consistency. Repeated, unjustified rule deviations may simply inspire accusations of unfairness. After all, why must the players abide by the rules if you never do?

### Multiple Storyguides

Since players may switch characters from story to story, it's an easy transition to switch Storyguides as well. Doing so keeps the world wondrous and unpredictable, and somehow makes it more realistic, rather than a pale representation born of a single mind. The product of shared creativity is inevitably more brilliant than that of a single imagination.

In **Ars Magica** it's suggested that you switch Storyguides on a regular basis, sharing the world as well as the Covenant. Though this may be a radical concept, trust us in that it's not only workable, but an exceptional style of play. When you share the Storyguide's chair the vitality of the game is preserved, and an infusion of new ideas abounds. Furthermore, while you may describe one area of Mythic Europe, another Storyguide may develop another. Thus, multiple Storyguides actually diminish the work one must perform.

The one true danger of multiple Storyguides lies in the infringement of one on the creations of another. To keep another Storyguide from ruining your plans, reserve areas of the world for your sole control. If you say, "I get Duke Pere and his lands," then you can create that background without the other players' interference. Moreover, by dividing up realms of influence in the game, you can concentrate on the type of play you enjoy, such as politicking with nobility. If you don't care to create stories that involve them, you can leave faerie forests, Hermetic intrigue, and city adventures to other Storyguides.

If another Storyguide does do something that upsets the stability or progress of the Saga, there are a variety of solutions. Other Storyguides can repair the damage when it's their turn to run, either by decree — "that didn't happen" — or by running a story that reverses the effects of the previous story. If one Storyguide consistently warps the Saga in ways unacceptable to the others, it may be wise to invite him to act as a full-time player.

# STORYTELLING IDEAS

Much of your time between game sessions is probably spent in contemplation of new story ideas. Inspiration can come from an assortment of mediums. Books and movies are reliable sources. Although books and films are viable sources for stories, however, it's important to go beyond them. If you get a majority of your ideas from a particular film, what happens if everyone in your Troupe sees it as well? Try to make your stories an amalgamation of good ideas. Therefore, when someone thinks she knows where the story is headed, she is pleasantly (or unpleasantly) surprised.

In **Ars Magica** there are some basic plots that occur at least once in a Covenant's lifetime. Although these story ideas are not unique by any means, it's up to you to make them so, tailoring them to the needs of your Troupe. Use these plots as a springboard for your own original stories.

**VIS HUNT:** Worth more than simple gold, raw vis is the commodity Magi value most highly. Rumors of vis sightings motivate Magi to travel to the far reaches of Mythic Europe in order to obtain even scant quantities of this precious substance. Used to make items of power, or to enable Magi to perform rituals, nothing gets a Magus's attention like a rook of vis. However, Companions and Grogs need more than a rumor to get them interested. Vis can still be a treasure for them, for it sometimes grants magical protection or even powers, but Companions and Grogs often need further motivation to go on such a hunt. Vis can sometimes be used by folk as a bargaining chip with Magi.

Vis should never be so plentiful that it becomes passe. If vis was always present in the Covenant there would be no reason for Magi to venture forth from their sanctums. The search for raw vis also gives Magi the opportunity to deal with the more mundane aspects of life; it gets them out there. Some Covenants even require that Magi contribute to the supply of raw vis. This may not be because the Covenant needs the vis, but because the Covenant doesn't want its members becoming recluses.

## Beginning and Endings

The time immediately before and immediately after a story is important for keeping track of character and Covenant progress. Here are some suggestions for how to use this time.

**BEFORE:** Determine Experience for time that has passed, and roleplay a council meeting of Magi to share ideas. These meetings establish events that have occurred between stories, and set the scene for the story about to begin. In Winter, roll for Aging (see the Saga Chapter).

**AFTER:** Assign Experience and Confidence Points, and make appropriate adjustments to Personality Traits and Reputations. You must also account for what's acquired during the story; divide treasure, recover from wounds, and make relevant notes for the Covenant library. You might also plan something for the Covenant's future, based on events of the story.

*Story:* A spring has been found in a strange forest. The spring renews life to the bones of fish that are thrown into it. This magical nature is the means of nourishment for a camp of mundanes that now lives at the spring. The Magi discover the spring and discover it bears tremendous amounts of Aquam *vis* . However, if the Magi take any of the raw *vis* the spring loses its power and the villagers starve (not to mention persecute the Magi).

**EXPLORATION:** A roleplaying favorite is the exploration of new areas. This gives the Troupe an opportunity to broaden their horizons, or perhaps an opportunity to boost their reputations. Exploration is a time to introduce new characters to your Saga, for new lands mean new acquaintances. Unexplored lands can take any form from enchanted glades to dark and fetid catacombs. The rewards from such adventure can range from riches to a wealth of knowledge.

Rumors are usually what get characters interested in the journey they must undergo. Sometimes, after an extended period in their laboratories, Magi feel the need to explore the unknown. Who knows what they find? Use the exploration story to introduce characters to new customs and fresh ideas. They might encounter some people that they know little about, or might stumble upon ancient legends just now coming true.

*Story:* A dying Redcap from an allied Covenant arrives at the characters' door with tales of strange goings on within his Covenant. Upon arriving at the Covenant, the characters find the Covenant is completely dominated by the Infernal realm. Once good friends are now minions of the damned. Can the characters find the source of evil, and save their friends before the forces of evil steal their souls?

**TRIBUNAL:** Magi, usually no more than three, must travel to a Tribunal to represent their Covenant. Give everyone who is not playing a character from the Covenant a Magus from another Covenant. Thus, all players take part in the Tribunal, and may talk, conspire, befriend, or double-cross to their hearts' content. Make room where you play for people to walk around and talk in private. Emphasize roleplaying and diplomacy over dice rolling and physical violence. Be sure to present some conflict, though, so characters have something to struggle over (though probably not physically).

Tribunal stories are perfect for a large group. You might even invite people to participate who don't normally play, to make the story even more complicated, and to initiate new players to the game.

*Story:* In addition to normal squabbles over land and alleged wrongs perpetrated by various Magi, the Tribunal addresses the problem of a baron who is hostile to the Order, who is gathering power, and who is "secretly" preparing to attack local Covenants. The Tribunal is divided on what to do, so the characters' words, actions, and votes count. The Covenant most likely to be attacked first by the baron is an unpopular one, perhaps that of the characters.

**MYSTERY:** A classic story inspiration is the timeless mystery. In Hermetic mysteries, unlike conventional mysteries, those skilled in the art of magic make for difficult apprehension. Plot twists abound and are necessary to keep the players off balance. Remember, when all evidence points to a single person, she is usually innocent.

Supernatural barriers are bound to hamper characters' progress in a mystery. If the perpetrator takes refuge in a church, the characters' magical powers are largely thwarted, and other means must be used to catch the culprit. Magic used by the culprit can also make his implication virtually impossible. These barriers become all the more daunting as the characters uncover more and more of the truth. And, grisly scenes of death always serve to make characters apprehensive about facing the guilty party.

Essential to a mystery is the chase scene. After the offender is singled out, he undoubtedly makes a break for it. You must understand that, when the villain resorts to this type of defense, he surely does anything to escape persecution. Killing, maybe again if murder was the original crime, may be a possibility. Make all chase scenes fast-paced, giving players quick descriptions and allowing them little time to react to events.

*Story*: One of the Covenant's leading Magi is murdered. When all the evidence uncovered leads everyone to think he was secretly a diabolist, another murder occurs. As time progresses the characters discover that the dead Magus's apprentice, Bebo, a sweet little boy, is actually a demon incognito!

**TROUBLE ON THE HOME FRONT:** Sometimes a story comes home to the characters. Making characters move through their home, trying to solve a problem or capture an intruder, gives them a better sense of the place in which they live. It also keeps them from sleeping so easily in their beds at night.

*Story*: Dark faeries have cursed the food brought to the Covenant, and those who eat it start running around the Covenant pursuing obscure aims (give characters a temporary score of 5 in any one Personality Trait or Passion). Convince the players to roleplay these obsessions. Some involve breaking things or attacking people, while others require screaming and carrying on. Characters who recover their sanity must use brawn, magic, and diplomacy to restore order.

**FAERIES:** A story involving faeries is a story in which your imagination should run wild. Anytime faeries enter the scene, it should be a scene to remember. Faeries are fun-loving creatures with little to no respect for the "silly" traditions that humans live by. Established norms like mortality take on a whole new meaning when faeries are involved — either they don't understand it or they offer you ageless life. Take time spent with faeries as a kind of vacation.

Normal rules of reality do not apply while in the Faerie realm. Characters may find they can fly when they think about wonderful things. They might even float when they giggle. Things in the Faerie realm might even assume a literal approach to the world. Blueberries might make you sad, and spear grass might pierce your feet. Try to boggle the characters'/players' minds when dealing with faerie lands. No one understands these creatures, because they almost never make sense.

Keep in mind that faerie lands are not always cheery and bright, either. Most of the time a faerie land mimics the lands that surround it, often in an effort not to be recognized. So, if war and pestilence are in the general vicinity of a faerie area, don't count on the faeries being glad you came.

*Story*: One of the characters falls ill with a magical ailment. While looking through tomes in the library, a Magus discovers a cure. The kicker is that the flower needed for the cure only grows at the center of a powerful faerie area. After locating the area, the characters learn the faeries are more than happy to share the flower, but the characters must first pass the test of faeriehood.

**THE CITY STREETS:** The characters may travel into the heart of mundane society, the city. A truly wide variety of stories can be told within the confines of the city walls. Despite their amazing intellects, many Magi are ignorant when it comes to street smarts. Elsewhere, Magi are the group leaders, but in the city their effective leadership becomes a point of contention. Companions and Grogs find their time to shine in the city, taking the lead role in the story.

The unfortunate downfall of the city as a story environment is the ever-present Dominion. Magical actions are severely curtailed here. That might be a good thing, though, as a city is full of people who might unite against strangers who throw spells around. Indeed, the city proves one of the clergy's greatest weapons against Magi of the Order, since here, in front of countless witnesses, the Church can condemn wizards and gain the greatest possible support. For these reasons Magi are used to going incognito in populated centers.

*Story*: A small boy is being persecuted by a vicious group of priests because he has displayed an ability to manipulate things at a distance. Occasionally, he even has glimpses of the future. The boy, Tibit, is cold, tired and dirty. Crying, and on the lam from his persecutors, he looks to the characters for shelter. Tibit is a very intelligent child who will someday become a Magus of great power.

The characters must devise some means of getting Tibit out of town.

# ADVANCED STORYTELLING

There are a number of things that you can try once you've mastered the basics of being a Storyguide. These are techniques and special effects that can add greater depth to a story, but if used improperly can weaken a story. Thus, you should have some experience as a Storyguide and player before attempting any of these feats. Some of the things we describe are difficult even for an experienced actor to attempt, and must be carefully planned and executed in order to work effectively. If you can pull these stunts off, however, you may create scenes the players never forget.

• **FLASHBACKS:** Flashbacks are a way to roleplay out scenes in a character's past, as a way of putting new emphasis and focus on the story. The flashback is a second story which is told alongside the main story. You can either personally tell the second story, or have the player take her character into it and play it out. You can even specifically design the flashback story so it can be played alternately with the primary story, as a sort of interlude between the main acts. The two stories can be disconnected by time or space, but must be connected in theme, mood or subject. The secondary story must relate to the primary story, must reflect upon it, and must make the primary more complete.

Many flashbacks concern a character's childhood. The player of that character could play herself, another player her best friend, and another her sister. Yes, all the players can get involved in one character's flashback. Flashbacks are a good technique to use when characters are in a faerie forest. The second story can be explained as the waking dream of a character who has eaten faerie food.

• **PARALLEL STORY:** A parallel story, much like a flashback, is played out as a second story alongside the first. However, the second story takes place at the same time as the first. It can be expected that at some point the two stories intersect and the characters from each meet. You probably don't want to conclude the parallel story until near the end of the primary one. It's essential that you time things carefully.

• **SYMBOLISM:** Having something in a story actually represent something else is an ancient literary technique, and symbolism can add a great deal of depth and intensity to a story. By judiciously referring to and emphasizing the symbols inherent in a story, you can add power to your themes, and make a point or two along the way. There are many symbols contained in **Ars Magica**, and though we cannot describe them all, we can detail some of them for you.

Magic is symbolic of the unseen forces which are always around us, but which we do not fully understand. Depending on your world view, magic can be anything from the tide of history, to the power of myth, to the mystery of synchronicity. Magic is what we cannot understand, but what we attempt to use.

The Church is symbolic of orthodoxy and conservatism, including the good and bad sides of each. The Church protects but the Church also represses. The comforting reality of quiet places is contained in the Dominion.

Faeries are symbolic of the primal self that exists within all of us, of the id which longs to be free. Faeries are what we would be like if we didn't repress so many of our urges and desires.

The Infernal forces are symbolic of that which we fear, of that which is hidden most deeply within ourselves. Demons are most often invisible spirits who attempt to twist and warp everything they touch, and in that they are like the destructive spirit which all of us possess.

---

### Story Timing

How much time passes in between stories? This is no idle question. Every Season that passes is another Season of study for the Magi, and every year that passes is another year closer to death for all characters. Therefore, you need to regulate the amount of time that slips by. If stories occur in rapid succession, Magi do not progress far in their arts and spells, and age may never get a chance to affect those who begin the Saga when young. On the other hand, the more time that passes, the faster Magi progress, and the faster Companions and Grogs deteriorate. A delicate balance lies in between, when stories punctuate characters' lives, but also allow them to grow in between.

One way to decide on the passage of time between stories is to set a standard, such as one story per year. You could also use a simple die roll to determine the number of Seasons that pass. A more complex system involves resolving a string of connected stories quickly, one after another, after which there is a lull of several Seasons or even years.

If you have no standard, each Storyguide can decide on how much time passes before the next story is played. Remember that few characters make their living by adventuring. Adventures are the exceptional activities that, thankfully, happen only once in a long while. So, characters must live out something of a normal life between stories if they are going to support themselves.

---

Reason is the veneer which some try to impose upon the chaos and terror of the world in order to make life bearable. Reason is also a means by which to justify that which we do, usually unethical – to make our faults seem virtues. Reason is therefore symbolic of lies we tell ourselves, and occasionally see through to perceive the anarchy beyond.

Grogs are symbolic of all the oppressed people of the Middle Ages, of everyone on the bottom of the heap. In the very baseness of their personality, Grogs convey the flavor of medieval squalor.

Companions are symbolic of freedom and liberty, and are heralds of a new age in which the medieval standards of feudalism no longer exist. Companions are like modern man transported to the medieval world.

Covenants are symbolic of hearth and home. The Covenant is a little bit of our world placed in a medieval setting. Being magic, the Covenant has what approaches "modern conveniences," and the egalitarianism of its Magi makes the Covenant's social structure substantially different from that of the feudal world.

Magi are symbolic of the ancient archetype of the wise man or woman, who is ostracized from society and forced to live on the outskirts of the village, but to whom everyone comes for advice and remedies for ills, both physical and emotional. There is also something of the

scholar in the Magus, and it is in the juxtaposition of these two symbols that this character gains most of its symbolic potential.

# MOODS

The moods you create in a story dramatically influence how your players react to the story. To create any sort of emotional ambience is extremely taxing, but always pays off in the end. The basic technique of doing so is fairly simple. Players often reflect the attitude and emotions of the Storyguide. They look for cues from the Storyguide, and when they get them, they use them. So, if you're acting silly, don't expect your players to act differently. Stick to your guns when creating a mood, and only break the

## Roleplaying Emotions

There are some different roleplaying techniques you can use to express the emotions you are trying to evoke. Techniques for expressing some of the most dramatic and common emotions are described below:

• **HATRED:** Make your speech pompous and overbearing. Insult and belittle the characters. Look down your nose at them. Sneer and suck your teeth. Act as though the characters reek with odor. A sure way of creating a powerful mood of hatred involves restraining characters from attacking the object of their hatred. This restraint can be anything from physical to moral.

• **LUST:** Slowly exaggerate pronunciations with your tongue as often as you can. Allow words to tumble out of your mouth. Groan and moan when appropriate. Always ask questions. As long as you do, you control the conversation. Look intently at your players though half-open eyes. Lick your lips at the sound of a good plan. Work on the real world atmosphere; the room should be dimly lit, with appropriate music.

• **HORROR:** You should change your speech patterns abruptly, and often speak in deep monotones. Describe characters met as somehow unnatural. Allow yourself to be interrupted only if absolutely necessary. Inspire fear by luring characters into unrecognizable places. Raise your voice at peak times, or when immediate action must be taken.

Facial features need precise control during scenes of horror. Wrinkle your brow and widen your eyes when you describe unrecognizable things. Explode with emotion when the object of fear is finally upon the characters. In terms of real world atmosphere, darkness is essential. If there are candles available, use them. Turning out the lights has a nice effect as well. Try to make the room cold if you can.

mood if absolutely necessary.

To correctly go about creating a mood, you, as the Storyguide, must decide beforehand what your target emotion is: horror, pity, disgust, or maybe lust. After choosing the target emotion, the rest is relatively simple. You can be reasonably sure that the same thing that causes horror or lust in you does the same for others. After thinking about the mood you want (this usually takes no longer than a few minutes with practice), put on your blinders and pursue the mood with reckless abandon. Accept no foreign moods in your scene; they are simply nonexistent. If you want to evoke horror, don't let anyone joke around. Everything you say and do must reflect the mood you're trying to establish. Use the examples below as insights into ways to express moods.

### The Sounds of Battle

Most stories end after the meeting of the two main powers involved, and they settle their differences in combat. This is often the most exciting scene of a story, but to simply toss the opportunity away with a mere die roll is extremely anticlimactic. The battles of your stories should be fast-paced, engrossing, and should leave the players drained.

When we play a roleplaying game we attempt to create epic stories worthy of many retellings. Given this general

truth, it is disheartening to see combat reduced to a simple die roll. A die roll only serves one purpose in the scheme of battle: the representation of luck. Granted, every once in a while someone gets lucky and lands a good shot. Lady Luck cannot be ignored, but it is more rewarding in the storytelling event to evoke the drama of battle by means other than die rolls.

This drama can be achieved through the efforts of the Storyguide. First, you must exquisitely describe battle scenes. Let the players know what surrounds them and what they perceive with all five of their senses. If the players know what's around, they will make use of those surroundings rather than make simple die rolls. But, if you do a haphazard job of describing the area, it undoubtedly leads to confusion.

For example, suppose you describe an inn where the characters decide to rest. You explain, "Ok *you have come to a somewhat sleazy inn, its name is oh. . . The Slaughtered Lamb. You reserve three rooms, and go to bed.*" Later that evening the characters are set upon by bandits and have to fight for their lives at the inn. Without knowing the situation of the inn, players are inclined to simply swing their swords and roll the dice. Also, a skimpy area description creates confusion. One player assumes the inn is more than one story high, and tells you he runs to the stairs. Another character might have done the same had her player known about the stairs, but now that character is incapacitated because of your faulty scene description. A complete scene description insures that story monotony and breakdowns do not occur.

Here's an example of how you can make scene descriptions part of a battle's narrative: "*After your exhausting week-long trek, you stumble into a rather old-looking inn called The Slaughtered Lamb. In the reception area there is a bar that has sundry metal mugs surrounding it. Behind the bar, standing directly in front of you, is a man who appears to be the innkeeper, a rather plump old fellow with shifty eyes and a toothless grin. After taking your money, he shows each of you to your rooms. Walking down a dark hallway, you smell the mildew that has festered here over the years. All rooms seem to be on the ground level and, though from outside you guessed there is more than one level, there are no stairs to be seen.*" No one expects you to describe everything in detail, but when there is bound to be combat the characters should be aware of their surroundings. With a description like this, the characters know what they're dealing with and may try to use that environment inventively, making die rolls more exotic and entertaining. Thus, battle is made vital and fun.

Not only must the surroundings of battle be described in detail, so must the actions of battle. Most battles tend to involve a trading of blows from one combatant to another, once again flirting with boredom. To avoid this trap, you should describe what happens after an exchange of blows. And, your description of events should be enthusiastic, to get players involved in the description. For example, after a swing that misses, you might announce, *"Your blow glances off his shield, but crashes through the bannister beside him. If you're lucky, you may push him off the stairs in your next attack."* These kinds of statements fire player imagination, just as involved battlefield descriptions do. Given this enthusiasm, die rolls assume much less significance, and imagination takes control.

## R.I.P.

The above letters have become something of an enigma in roleplaying. The only rule a Storyguide should obey is the dead rule: once someone dies, let her rest in peace! The cliché of the character who miraculously survives death is tired and boring. If you absolutely have to use it, use it with a terribly fun villain. And, unless a player makes a terrible fuss, don't revive players' characters.

The reasons are quite simple, really:

• If you allow characters to rise from the dead, the once-sacred gift of life is trivialized.

• There is no spell in the Order of Hermes that covers resurrection, so rebirth cannot be accounted for by the magical means available to the characters.

• Death is as absolute as it gets. To belittle the event means imminent danger becomes trifling, and players won't respect the drama of your stories.

• When you die your soul goes to Heaven, Hell, or remains trapped on earth. Once you go to your reward or damnation, your soul is irretrievably lost to the folks in Mythic Europe, so you cannot be reborn. Only if your soul wanders the earth can you be resurrected, and even then your soul may reject its former body.

All in all, death is final. That's the way of the world.

# THE PLAYER AND STORYTELLING

Though your role as player has limited application to the creation of stories you partake in, your role is still vital to the evolution of the story. The Storyguide creates the premise for the tale and has an idea of what can happen in it. You, however, decide what happens in the story by determining your character's actions and statements. The storytelling event is therefore a reconciliation of both Storyguide and player input. This being the case, players may need advice on how to contribute to the story, just as the Storyguide may need advice on how to create the story. The material that follows is advice for the player.

## How to be a Good Player

As a player in **Ars Magica** you have the responsibility of deciding the actions and words of your character(s), and of participating productively in the story. Do not underestimate the influence, good or bad, your playing style can have on the story. If someone roleplays well, and with intensity, it's all the more easy for others in the Troupe to do the same; expressive roleplaying is contagious.

Most players fall into two categories: proactive and reactive. The best roleplayers are neither.

A proactive player is extremely motivated. She often goes off on her own and creates her own stories. Proactive players have a fierce imagination, and set afire everything they touch, giving light and life to the Saga. This behavior keeps the Storyguide on his toes and leads to many exciting story ideas. However, when overdone, the proactive player seeks to be in the limelight constantly, overshadowing everyone else, including the Storyguide. The proactive player sometimes even struggles with the Storyguide on which way the story should progress, demanding changes in the Storyguide's most basic story plans. Although enthusiasm is welcome, it's important to remember who's in charge of the story. You always have a right to play your character as you envision her, but don't ruin everyone else's fun in the process. You have power over the story as a character. As a player you should be part of the team.

Reactive players are the opposite of proactive players. They seek only to solve immediate problems and have no goals of character development. After a story is complete, the characters of reactive players simply lie around and wait until the next time they're "activated." Thus, reactive players only act when goaded by the other players. In the

extreme, reactive players don't say anything and follow the other characters from scene to scene, attacking what they are allowed to. Reactive players have no motivation. Other members of your Troupe undoubtedly wonder why these people bother to show up. Sadly, reactive players are often novice roleplayers who have not fully grasped the ideas behind the game.

Obviously, the picture painted here is none too good. Perhaps you yourself are not a proactive or reactive player, but odds are you know at least one. No one is perfect, and just because someone in your Troupe is one doesn't mean he's hopeless. Not everyone can become a master player within the span of a few hours. In truth, it takes the majority of roleplayers years to become well-versed in the esoterics of the art. Everyone has to start somewhere, and everyone matures at different rates. Concentrate on your own maturing skills, not the deficiencies of others, and you will be well served by your wisdom.

## Things to Do

There are several guidelines you can follow as a player that improve the quality of the game for both you and everyone else. You will undoubtedly cultivate even more ideas on your own, but here are some to begin with.

• Respect your Storyguide — Nothing delays a scene like an unnecessary argument with the Storyguide. You obviously feel an injustice has been done or you wouldn't protest. However, this doesn't give you permission to ruin everyone else's evening. Remember, you're roleplaying to have fun, not to argue. Save all the disagreements for after the session.

• Play out your abilities — The numbers on your character sheet are not simply there to fill the page. They're there to serve as a guide, so you can play your character more realistically. If your Dexterity is -3, don't spend your time juggling knives, unless you want to be injured. Just because you don't have abilities that are superhuman doesn't make you any less a hero.

• Keep notes — When you least expect it you need to know the name of the crazy crone who slapped you three weeks ago. Notes are important in a game; you can't always rely on your memory.

• Try to fit in — The people you travel with are your friends. Even more than that, you entrust them with your very life. Intraparty disputes can ruin a good story. Sometimes arguments arise, and can make for a realistic story, but they usually disturb the unity of the Troupe. Just remember that the enemy is not within your Troupe… usually.

• Participate fully — This can never be stated enough. Everyone is there to have a good time. So are you. Don't sit there like a bump on a log, participate! You get out of a session exactly what you put into it.

• Try to make sense out of the story — The degree to which you "get into the story" is up to you, and is often related to how much you respect the Storyguide. If the Storyguide says something occurs, it's up to you to make sense of it in your imagination. Don't argue with the Storyguide, just become all the more creative in your imagination. If you don't let the world become real in your mind, it cannot become real in terms of the game.

## Things Not to Do

• Don't be Disruptive — The Storyguide is going out of her way to provide you with an entertaining story. The least that you can do is respect her work and not be disruptive. Creating dramatic scenes is hard work, and when you're being disruptive, it makes the task all the harder.

• Don't let your egotism get in the way of the story — Play characters who get along with the other characters, and don't screw everything up for the others. Don't hog all the attention. Make sure everyone else has a chance to do things as well as you.

• Don't be late — It's no secret, everyone is busy doing something. However, other people are depending on you

to make it to the game on time. Try to avoid being late, and if you can't avoid it, call ahead so the others don't become frustrated.

• Don't come unprepared — As a player you really don't have that much to remember: dice, rulebooks, pens/pencils, paper, and your character sheet. Yes, some people actually forget their characters! As a precaution, give your Storyguide a copy of your character, just in case you're in a hurry.

• Don't pick on new players — Some experienced players actually get their jollies from tormenting those who have less knowledge than they —*"Oh yeah, all dragons like to be tickled!"* Causing new characters to die or become severely injured is not a means of entertainment. Think of how you'd feel if that's how you were introduced to roleplaying. If you persist in picking on someone, don't be surprised if they don't return.

P.S. The do's and don'ts of being a player are really about consideration, and understanding the group nature of the Troupe. Everyone is there to have a good time, not just you, so show a bit of respect to those who adventure with you.

# CHARACTER ROLES

Remember that every character plays an equal role in your stories, even if they aren't exactly equal in power. Imagine each story as being an episode in a soap opera, in which the central plot revolves around the same group of individuals, but with about four or five subplots occurring simultaneously. The story (or subplot) of each character is equal in importance and interest, whether the character is a Grog or Magus, and the sum of these stories creates the plot of the "adventure." When you roleplay, attempt to appreciate the stories of the other characters at least as much as your appreciate your own. Add something to their stories as well as your own, and do things to make those stories real and evocative. Different conflicts are often important to different characters. Does the Magus manage to retrieve the staff of Askataunggasay? Does the Companion manage to overcome her hatred of the old Baron? Does the young Grog manage to prove his bravery and win the respect of the sergeant? These subplots can make your entire roleplaying experience a great deal more satisfying. And, if other players watch closely when you roleplay, you are provided with an appreciative audience when important things occur in your character's life.

# CHOOSING WHO TO PLAY

Character conception is a very rewarding process. If you consider all the steps carefully, you end up with a character that keeps you entertained for years to come. There's no proper way to construct a character. As long as you come up with a persona that satisfies you, you've done a good job.

Knowing the personality you play is important, but you must also decide on the role you play in **Ars Magica**. Is it the hard-working Grog, the carefree Companion, or the all-powerful Magus? Even though there are three primary character roles, you can create an infinite variety of characters (for examples see the *Vocations* in the Character Creation Chapter).

Also remember that, with Troupe-style play, you can change identities with each story. In our Troupe we hold a council meeting of the Magi (and some of the Companions) at the beginning of each story. This tradition results in some truly remarkable roleplaying and provides a strong sense of continuity throughout the Saga. It also gives all the players a chance to roleplay their Magus characters every story, at least for a while, allowing for steady character development. Best of all, it provides a chance for the players to decide who goes on the latest mission, and who remains at home.

## Playing a Magus

The Magus is the most demanding character type to play. For one thing, you must be familiar with the magic rules to make fast decisions about using spells. The difference between well-used and poorly-used spells is enormous, so if you try to play a Magus when you're not familiar with your capacities, you might jeopardize the mission and the lives of every party member. Remember, you are the one ultimately responsible for the success or failure of the mission.

As a Magus you are also one of the primary foci of the story. The goals of the mission are primarily yours, and your fellows usually accompany you in order to aid you in your task. You have authority over the Grogs, and you command respect (one hopes) among the Companions. While the thrill of leadership can be enticing, it is a great responsibility. It can therefore be more relaxing to play a character without that responsibility.

If you do play a Magus, don't force your leadership on the other characters, particularly if that spoils the fun for the other players. Certainly, do not force "cooperation" with your magical powers; disgruntled Grogs may find it tempting to slit the throat of a Magus while he sleeps.

Flaunting your power by punishing those who travel with you is going too far, even if it makes sense in the story. Remember that even if an action is "in character," you, the player, bear full responsibility for the effects it has on the other players, because you created your character in the first place.

Also, be sure not to make any of the other players feel left out or useless — you are the leader of the Troupe as well as the mission party. Avoid leaving the rest of the group sitting around while you're out having fun, such as by turning into a bird to scout around, or by conversing with a tree for a week. However, in some Troupes, when the Magus is thus occupied, the other characters use the time to pursue old rivalries, blossoming friendships, and ongoing jokes. There's always a way to roleplay, even when the Storyguide isn't available.

## Playing a Companion

Companions are perhaps the easiest type of character to play for they are so much like characters from other fantasy roleplaying games. They do not hold the legendary powers of Magi, but nor are they under the direct command of superiors as are Grogs. Companions have enough virtues and abilities to make them extremely interesting characters to play. Indeed, some Troupes play a more traditional style of Saga using Companions alone.

As a Companion, you must decide what your relationship with the Covenant is based on, and must do the same with Magi who lead an expedition. Are you good natured and obedient, or are you free-spirited and irresponsible? We understand the temptation is to be free-spirited. After all, we play games to get away from being told what to do. But, if no one listens to the leader, nothing gets done.

Besides, when your turn comes to play a Magus, you may appreciate helpful Companions, so it's a good idea to be one yourself. Having a superior doesn't mean losing all your free will, it merely involves a different role from that of an equal.

Companions have the important role of guiding Magi through a world they do not understand — the mundane world. Most Magi are products of the laboratory and a rarified intellectual existence. They are babes in the woods when in comes to mortal society. Companions must mediate between Magi and 'normal folk' (sometimes even Grogs).

## Playing a Grog

Grogs demand something unique from a player: obedience and loyalty. Covenants do not retain Grogs who are disloyal or insubordinate, so to play your character right you must generally follow orders. Roleplaying a complete and interesting character without being powerful can be difficult, especially for less experienced roleplayers. The role is a rewarding one, though. Think of Grogs as the Marine grunts of the Saga, the characters who dig the trenches and rush the enemy lines — the heroes of innumerable war movies. In movies these characters are especially vivid. In roleplaying they can be as well.

One way to play Grogs is to play up their quirks. If your Companion is insufferably stubborn, or severely hampered by low Perception, constantly roleplaying that character can become boring. But you can play out a Grog's obstinacy or spiteful temper with boundless enthusiasm, knowing that you aren't stuck with that role for long (i.e., you can always play another of the Covenant's Grogs next time). Thus, Grogs can be useful and fun for providing you with a change and diversion from your more "mainstay" characters. By acting as a foil, Grogs can become the most well-defined and infamous characters in your Saga.

Since Grogs are less demanding to play than Companions or Magi, it's common to play more than one Grog, or to play a Grog along with a Magus or Companion. Grogs are often brought along on a journey and played by whoever has the energy or time to give them personality. It's important that Grogs not be played as nameless henchmen. They play an important role in a Saga, and should not be ignored.

# INDEX LISTING

## (s) denotes a spell

# ChARACTER

Name_____ Age_____ Gender_____

Player_____ Year Born_____ Size_____

Covenant_____ Current Year_____ Confidence_____

Saga_____ Decrepitude_____ Current Cnf_____

## Characteristics

Intelligence [_____]
Perception [_____]

Strength [_____]
Stamina [_____]

Presence [_____]
Communication [_____]

Dexterity [_____]
Quickness [_____]

Specialty

## Abilities

|  | Scr | Exp |
|---|---|---|
| [_____] |  |  |
| [_____] |  |  |
| [_____] |  |  |
| [_____] |  |  |
| [_____] |  |  |
| [_____] |  |  |
| [_____] |  |  |
| [_____] |  |  |
| [_____] |  |  |
| [_____] |  |  |
| [_____] |  |  |
| [_____] |  |  |
| [_____] |  |  |
| [_____] |  |  |
| [_____] |  |  |
| [_____] |  |  |
| [_____] |  |  |
| [_____] |  |  |
| [_____] |  |  |
| [_____] |  |  |
| [_____] |  |  |
| [_____] |  |  |
| [_____] |  |  |
| [_____] |  |  |

Specialty

## Combat

| Weapon | 1st Rate | Atk | Dam |
|---|---|---|---|
|  |  |  |  |
|  |  |  |  |
|  |  |  |  |
|  |  |  |  |
|  |  |  |  |

1st = Speed + Skill + Quick – Enc.
Atk = Attack Bonus + Skill + Dex.
Dam = Damage Bonus + Skill + Str

Soak = Protection + Stm + Size (+ 6 Action)
Fatigue = Stm – Enc

## Armor

Type _____

Protection [___] Load [___]

| Defense | Action | Dueling |
|---|---|---|
| Parry w/ |  |  |
| Parry w/ |  |  |
| Dodge |  |  |

Parry = Skill + Parry Bonus – Size (+6 Action)
Dodge = Skill + Quick – Enc – Size (+6 Action)

## Body Levels

| | Dueling Soak Total | | Action Soak Total |
|---|---|---|---|

## Fatigue Levels

| | Fatigue Total |
|---|---|

| Body Levels | Dueling | Action | | Fatigue Levels |
|---|---|---|---|---|
| Unhurt | ✗ | | ✗ | Fresh |
| hurt | 0 | 0 | | Winded |
| Light Wounds | –1 | –1 | | Weary |
| Medium Wounds | –3 | –3 | | Tired |
| heavy Wounds | –5 | –5 | | Dazed |
| Incapacitated | | | | Unconscious |

## Virtues & Flaws

## Personality Traits

## Reputation

_____ _____ ____

_____ ____ ____

Specialty

## Equipment

| Item | Load | | Item | Load |
|------|------|---|------|------|
| | | | | |
| | | | | |
| | | | | |
| | | | | |
| | | | | |
| | | | | |
| | | | | |
| | | | | |

Total Load [      ] – Str [   + ] = [      ] Encumbrance

If Strength is 0 or negative, then total load = Enc.

## Troupe Roster

| Character | Player | Notes |
|-----------|--------|-------|
| | | |
| | | |
| | | |
| | | |
| | | |
| | | |

## Notes

# hERMETIC TRAITS

## Magic Arts

### Techniques

Creo ☐

Intèllego ☐

Muto ☐

Perdo ☐

Rego ☐

### Forms

Animàl ☐

Aquam ☐

Auram ☐

Còrporem ☐

herbam ☐

Ignem ☐

Imàgonem ☐

Mentem ☐

Terram ☐

Vim ☐

## Bond Score

☐

## Cord Strengths

Gold ☐

Silver ☐

Bronze ☐

## Familiar _____

Intelligence ____    Strength ____    Presence ____    Dexterity ____

Perception ____    Stamina ____    Communication ____    Quickness ____

## Familiar Bond Qualities

☐ _____

☐ _____

☐ _____

☐ _____

☐ _____

## Magus Bond Qualities

☐ _____

☐ _____

☐ _____

☐ _____

☐ _____

## Spell Casting Speed

☐

Quickness + Finesse – Encumbrance

### Formulaic

Technique + Form + Stamina – Encumbrance

### Ritual Magic

Formulaic + Meditation

### Spontaneous Magic

Technique + Form + Intelligence – Encumbrance

### Basic Lab Total

Technique + Form + Intelligence + Magic Theory

## Wizard's Sigil

_____

_____

## Twilight Points ☐

## Effects of Twilight

_____

_____

_____

_____

_____

_____

_____

_____

_____

_____

# MAGUS GRIMOIRE

| Spell Title | Level | Tech & Form | Total Bonus | Mastery |
|---|---|---|---|---|
| | | | | |

Foci & Notes:

| | | | | |
|---|---|---|---|---|

Foci & Notes:

| | | | | |
|---|---|---|---|---|

Foci & Notes:

| | | | | |
|---|---|---|---|---|

Foci & Notes:

| | | | | |
|---|---|---|---|---|

Foci & Notes:

| | | | | |
|---|---|---|---|---|

Foci & Notes:

| | | | | |
|---|---|---|---|---|

Foci & Notes:

| | | | | |
|---|---|---|---|---|

Foci & Notes:

| | | | | |
|---|---|---|---|---|

Foci & Notes:

| | | | | |
|---|---|---|---|---|

Foci & Notes:

| | | | | |
|---|---|---|---|---|

Foci & Notes:

# Parting Words

Though this book may be the first you've ever seen of **Ars Magica**, the game has been around for years. This is actually the third edition of the rules, and also the last. Much of what you see in this book is inspired by or extracted from the first and second editions. This being the case, we owe a great deal of thanks to Jonathan Tweet, one of the game's creators, who, though not directly involved in the third edition, is essentially responsible for its existence and content. Thanks is also owed to Lisa Stevens, for her extensive contributions to the game as a whole.

We also have to thank all the enthusiasts of previous editions who have risked their money on this one. We hope you're satisfied with the book, and are content with the rule and theme changes we've implemented. It's difficult to change a game, making it more clear, concise, and approachable, without offending some of its die-hard followers.

You may even be wondering why we've bothered with a third edition of **Ars Magica**. Certainly many people felt the second edition was perfectly useful. True, previous editions had their strengths, but they also had many weaknesses. Some rules were rather quirky and not all-together useful or understandable. Some major omissions, such as a Covenants chapter from the second

edition, also plagued our previous attempts. Such omissions left editions incomplete; you couldn't really play the game in its entirety based on what was written. And, to be honest, our presentation skills were somewhat lacking with previous editions. This edition therefore applies the production skills and experience we've acquired over the years, hopefully creating a book that's not only a game, but a piece of art.

Ultimately, this game is for you, and we sincerely hope it meets your high standards. If you have any questions or comments about this book, address them to:

**Ars Magica** Developer
c/o White Wolf
4598B Stonegate Industrial Boulevard
Stone Mountain, GA 30083
Other Products

Several supplements are available for **Ars Magica** second edition, and are still fully compatible with the third edition. The following books are available at a game or book store near you, or directly from White Wolf:

**The Order of Hermes**, **Covenants**, **Medieval Bestiary**, **Broken Covenant of Calebais**, **The Tempest**, **Faeries: the Complete Handbook of the Seelie**, **Pact of Pasaquine**, **A Winter's Tale**, **Black Death**, **Mythic Places**, and **More Mythic Places**.

391

Of course, many releases are also planned for **Ars Magica** third edition. Some include:

**Mistridge:** The Covenant of Mistridge is described in full detail, offering you a setting in which to begin your first Saga, or a unique setting for your characters to visit.

*Parma Fabula:* The Story Shield. This heavy, card stock Storyguide screen puts all the game's charts and tables at your disposal, and offers a wealth of reference material for your needs.

**Deadly Legacy:** In this full-length story, young characters forging out on their own must travel Mythic Europe in search of the legendary and possibly monstrous ancestor of a mundane noble. Who knows what power may be garnered from the legends, and who knows what other forces pursue them?

**Mythic Europe:** The long-awaited source reference that details the official setting of the game. This book offers all you need to know about locales, legends, dangers, and secrets of the lands — everything you need to tell stories in Mythic Europe.

**A Midsummer Night's Dream:** Part one of the Four Seasons Tetralogy. In this campaign supplement, characters from a Spring Covenant must deal with the angered powers of forest faeries and Celtic gods. Before the tale is told, your Covenant may mature to its Summer, if you survive.

**Maleficium:** A full-fledged sourcebook devoted to the realm of the Infernal. Finally the deceptions, secrets and society of the Underworld are yours to command, and torment your Troupe.

**Pax Dei:** The companion to the **Maleficium**, this sourcebook introduces you to the full might and glory of the Dominion. The Church has tremendous influence over mundane man. Though Magi may scoff at their power, no spell may defy the will of the Divinities.

**Non-Hermetic Wizards — Shamans:** The first in a series of non-Hermetic wizard books, this supplement introduces new rules, background information, and ideas for roleplaying wizards from beyond the Order of Hermes, the Shamans. This supplement is useful for players and Storyguides alike.